Antony C. Sutton

The Wall Street Trilogy

OmniaVeritas

Antony C. Sutton
(1925-2002)

Wall Street & the Bolshevik Revolution
1974
Wall Street and FDR
1975
Wall Street and the rise of Hitler
1976

Published by
Omnia Veritas Ltd

OmniaVeritas

www.omnia-veritas.com

WALL STREET AND THE BOLSHEVIK REVOLUTION 15
PREFACE 18
CHAPTER I 19

    THE ACTORS ON THE REVOLUTIONARY STAGE 19

CHAPTER II 23

    TROTSKY LEAVES NEW YORK TO COMPLETE THE REVOLUTION 23

        Woodrow Wilson and a passport for Trotsky 26
        Canadian Government documents on Trotsky's release 28
        Canadian military intelligence views Trotsky 32
        Trotsky's intentions and objectives 35

CHAPTER III 38

    LENIN AND GERMAN ASSISTANCE FOR THE BOLSHEVIK REVOLUTION 38

        The Sisson documents 41
        The tug-of-war in Washington 43

CHAPTER IV 46

    WALL STREET AND WORLD REVOLUTION 46

        American bankers and tsarist loans 49
        Olof Aschberg in New York, 1916 53
        Olof Aschberg in the Bolshevik Revolution 54
        NYA Banken and Guaranty Trust join Ruskombank 56
        Guaranty Trust and German espionage in the United States, 1914- 1917 ... 59
        The Garanty Trust - Minotto - Caillaux threads 62

CHAPTER V 65

    THE AMERICAN RED CROSS MISSION IN RUSSIA — 1917 65

American Red Cross mission to Russia, 1917 .... *66*
The 1917 American Red Cross mission to Russia *68*
American Red Cross mission to Rumania *72*
Thompson in Kerensky's Russia *74*
Thompson gives the Bolsheviks $1 Million *75*
Socialist mining promoter Raymond Robins *76*
The International Red Cross and Revolution *78*

CHAPTER VI 80

CONSOLIDATION AND EXPORT OF THE REVOLUTION 80

A consultation with Lloyd George *82*
Thompson's intentions and objectives *85*
Thompson returns to the United States *87*
The unofficial ambassadors: Robins, Lockhart, and Sadoul *89*
Exporting the Revolution: Jacob H. Rubin *93*
Exporting the Revolution: Robert Minor *94*

CHAPTER VII 101

THE BOLSHEVIKS RETURN TO NEW YORK 101

A raid on the Soviet bureau in New York *102*
Corporate allies for the Soviet bureau *106*
European bankers aid the Bolsheviks *108*

CHAPTER VIII 111

120 BROADWAY, NEW YORK CITY 111

American International Corporation *113*
The influence of American International on the Revolution *117*
The Federal Reserve Bank of New York *120*
American-Russia Industrial Syndicate Inc. *121*
John Reed: Establishment Revolutionary *122*
John Reed and the Metropolitan Magazine *123*

CHAPTER IX 128

GUARANTY TRUST GOES TO RUSSIA 128

Wall Street comes to the aid of Professor Lomonossoff 129
The stage is for commercial exploitation of Russia 136
Germany and the United States struggle for Russian business 138
Soviet gold and American banks 140
Max May of Guaranty Trust becomes Director of Ruskombank 142

CHAPTER X 144

J.P. MORGAN GIVES A LITTLE HELP TO THE OTHER SIDE 144

United Americans formed to fight Communism 144
United Americans reveals "Startling disclosures" on Reds 145
Conclusions concerning United Americans 146
Morgan and Rockefeller aid Kolchak 147

CHAPTER XI 150

THE ALLIANCE OF BANKERS AND REVOLUTION 150

The evidence presented: a synopsis 150
The explanation for the unholy alliance 153
The Marburg Plan 154

APPENDIX I 159

DIRECTORS OF MAJOR BANKS, FIRM, AND INSTITUTIONS MENTIONED IN THIS BOOK (AS IN 1917-1918) 159

APPENDIX II 163

THE JEWISH-CONSPIRACY THEORY OF THE BOLSHEVIK REVOLUTION 163

APPENDIX III 168

SELECTED DOCUMENTS FROM GOVERNMENT FILES OF THE UNITED STATES AND GREAT BRITAIN................... 168

    Document n°1 168
    Document n°2 169
    Document n°3 170
    Document n°4 173
    Document n°5 175
    Document n°7 178
    Document n°8 178
    Document n°9 182
    Document n°10 183

WALL STREET AND FDR 185
ABOUT PROFESSOR SUTTON 187
CHAPTER 1 189

    ROOSEVELTS AND DELANOS 189

        The Delano family and Wall Street 194
        The Roosevelt family and Wall Street 198

CHAPTER 2 203

    POLITICS IN THE BONDING BUSINESS 203

        Politicians as bond writers 204
        Political influence and contract awards 207
        The pay-off for Fidelity & Deposit Company 211

CHAPTER 3 213

    FDR: INTERNATIONAL SPECULATOR 213

        The German hyperinflation of 1922-23 213
        The background of William Schall 216
        United European Investors, LTD. 217
        Investigation of United European Investors, LTD. 220

Chancellor Wilhelm Cuno and HAPAG..*223*
The International Germanic Trust Company..*224*

CHAPTER 4..227

FDR: CORPORATE PROMOTER...227

American Investigation Corporation...*227*
Politics, patents, and landing rights...*232*
FDR in the vending machine business..*238*
Georgia Warm Springs Foundation..*239*

CHAPTER 5..243

THE GENESIS OF CORPORATE SOCIALISM..243

The origins of Corporate Socialism...*244*
Making Society work for the Few..*245*
The Corporate Socialists argue their case..*247*

CHAPTER 6..256

PRELUDE TO THE NEW DEAL..256

Assemblyman Clinton Roosevelt's NRA — 1841..*257*
Bernard Baruch's wartime dictatorship..*259*
Paul Warburg and creation of the Federal Reserve system..................................*263*
The International Acceptance Bank, Inc...*267*

CHAPTER 7..270

ROOSEVELT, HOOVER, AND THE TRADE COUNCILS..270

A Medieval New Deal...*270*
The American Construction Council...*271*

CHAPTER 8..277

WALL STREET BUYS THE NEW DEAL..277

 Bernard Baruch's influence on FDR..*278*
 Wall Street finances the 1928 presidential campaign..........................*280*
 Herbert Hoover's election funds...*284*
 Wall Street backs FDR for Governor of New York................................*286*
 Wall Street elects FDR in 1932..*288*

CHAPTER 9..290

FDR AND THE CORPORATE SOCIALISTS...290

 The Swope Plan...*290*
 The Swope family..*290*
 Socialist planners of the 1930s..*294*
 Socialists greet the Swope Plan..*296*
 The Tree Musketeers of NRA...*298*
 The oppression of small business..*299*

CHAPTER 10..306

FDR, MAN ON THE WHITE HORSE...306

 Grayson M-P. Murphy Company, 52 Broadway....................................*307*
 Ackson Martindell, 14 Wall Street..*311*
 Gerald C. Macguire's testimony..*313*
 Suppression of Wall Street involvement..*315*
 An assessment of the Butler affair..*322*

CHAPTER 11..323

THE CORPORATE SOCIALISTS AT 120 BROADWAY, NEW YORK CITY.....................323

 The Bolshevik Revolution and 120 Broadway......................................*323*
 The Federal Reserve Bank of New York and 120 Broadway..................*324*
 American International Corporation and 120 Broadway......................*326*
 The Butler affair and 120 Broadway..*327*

Franklin D. Roosevelt and 120 Broadway *329*
Conclusions about 120 Broadway *330*

CHAPTER 12 332

FDR AND THE CORPORATE SOCIALISTS 332

APPENDIX A 339

THE SWOPE PLAN 339

APPENDIX B 346

Sponsors of Plans Presented for Economic Planning in the United States at April 1932 346

SELECTED BIBLIOGRAPHY 347
WALL STREET AND THE RISE OF HITLER 351
PREFACE 355
INTRODUCTION 356

UNEXPLORED FACETS OF NAZIISM 356

Hjalmar Horace Greeley Schacht *360*

CHAPTER ONE 362

WALL STREET PAVES THE WAY FOR HITLER 362

1924: The Dawes Plan *364*
1928: The Young Plan *366*
B.I.S. — The Apex of Control *367*
Building the German Cartels *369*

CHAPTER TWO 373

THE EMPIRE OF I.G. FARBEN 373

The Economic Power of I. G. Farben	*374*
Polishing I. G. Farben's Public Image	*382*
The American I.G. Farben	*384*

CHAPTER THREE 388

GENERAL ELECTRIC FUNDS HITLER 388

General Electric in Weimar Germany	*389*
General Electric and the Financing of Hitler	*393*
Technical Cooperation with Krupp	*396*

CHAPTER FOUR 401

STANDARD OIL FUELS WORLD WAR II 401

Ethyl Lead for the Wehrmacht	*406*
Standard Oil of New Jersey and Synthetic Rubber	*408*
The Deutsche-Amerikanische Petroleum A.G. (DAPAG)	*409*

CHAPTER FIVE 410

I.T.T. WORKS BOTH SIDES OF THE WAR 410

Baron Kurt von Schroder and the I.T.T.	*412*
Westrick, Texaco, and I.T.T.	*414*
I.T.T. in Wartime Germany	*415*

CHAPTER SIX 419

HENRY FORD AND THE NAZIS 419

Henry Ford: Hitler's First Foreign Backer	*420*
Henry Ford Receives a Nazi Medal	*422*
Ford Motor Company Assists the German War Effort	*423*

CHAPTER SEVEN 427

Who Financed Adolf Hitler? 427

Some Early Hitler Backers 427
Fritz Thyssen and W.A. Harriman Company of New York 430
Financing Hitler in the March 1933 General Election 435
The 1933 Political Contributions 438

CHAPTER EIGHT 442

Putzi: Friend of Hitler and Roosevelt 442

Putzi's Role in the Reichstag Fire 445
Roosevelt's New Deal and Hitler's New Order 447

CHAPTER NINE 450

Wall Street and the Nazi Inner Circle 450

The S.S. Circle of Friends 452
I.G. Farben and the Keppler Circle 453
Wall Street in the S.S. Circle 454

CHAPTER TEN 459

The Myth of "Sidney Warburg" 459

Who Was "Sidney Warburg"? 459
A Synopsis of the Suppressed "Sidney Warburg" Book 462
James Paul Warburg's Affidavit 466
Does James Warburg intend to mislead? 470

CHAPTER ELEVEN 473

Wall Street-Nazi Collaboration in World War II 473

American I.G. in World War II 476
Were American Industrialists and Financiers Guilty of War Crimes? 480

CHAPTER TWELVE 483

CONCLUSIONS 483

The Pervasive Influence of International Bankers *485*
Is the United States Ruled by a Dictatorial Elite? *487*
The New York Elite as a Subversive Force *489*
The Slowly Emerging Revisionist Truth *492*

APPENDIX A 496

PROGRAM OF THE NATIONAL SOCIALIST GERMAN WORKERS PARTY 496

THE PROGRAM 496

APPENDIX B 499

AFFIDAVIT OF HJALMAR SCHACHT 499

APPENDIX C 501

Entries in the "National Trusteeship" Account Found in the Files of the Delbruck, Schickler Co. Bank *501*

APPENDIX D 504

LETTER FROM U.S. WAR DEPARTMENT TO ETHYL CORPORATION 504

APPENDIX E 506

EXTRACT FROM MORGENTHAU DIARY (GERMANY) REGARDING SOSTHENES BEHN OF I.T.T. 506

SELECTED BIBLIOGRAPHY 509

WALL STREET AND
THE BOLSHEVIK REVOLUTION

Antony C. Sutton

To those unknown Russian libertarians, also known as Greens, who in 1919 fought both the Reds and the Whites in their attempt to gain a free and voluntary Russia.

Preface

Since the early 1920s, numerous pamphlets and articles, even a few books, have sought to forge a link between "international bankers" and "Bolshevik revolutionaries." Rarely have these attempts been supported by hard evidence, and never have such attempts been argued within the framework of a scientific methodology. Indeed, some of the "evidence" used in these efforts has been fraudulent, some has been irrelevant, much cannot be checked. Examination of the topic by academic writers has been studiously avoided; probably because the hypothesis offends the neat dichotomy of capitalists versus Communists (and everyone knows, of course, that these are bitter enemies). Moreover, because a great deal that has been written borders on the absurd, a sound academic reputation could easily be wrecked on the shoals of ridicule. Reason enough to avoid the topic.

Fortunately, the State Department Decimal File, particularly the 861.00 section, contains extensive documentation on the hypothesized link. When the evidence in these official papers is merged with nonofficial evidence from biographies, personal papers, and conventional histories, a truly fascinating story emerges.

We find there was a link between *some* New York international bankers and *many* revolutionaries, including Bolsheviks. These banking gentlemen — who are here identified — had a financial stake in, and were rooting for, the success of the Bolshevik Revolution.

Who, why — and for how much — is the story in this book.

March 1974
Antony C. Sutton

CHAPTER I

THE ACTORS ON THE REVOLUTIONARY STAGE

Dear Mr. President: I am in sympathy with the Soviet form of government as that best suited for the Russian people...
Letter to President Woodrow Wilson (October 17, 1918) from William Lawrence Saunders, chairman, Ingersoll-Rand Corp.; director, American International Corp.; and deputy chairman, Federal Reserve Bank of New York.

The frontispiece in this book was drawn by cartoonist Robert Minor in 1911 for the *St. Louis Post-Dispatch*. Minor was a talented artist and writer who doubled as a Bolshevik revolutionary, got himself arrested in Russia in 1915 for alleged subversion, and was later bank-rolled by prominent Wall Street financiers. Minor's cartoon portrays a bearded, beaming Karl Marx standing in Wall Street with *Socialism* tucked under his arm and accepting the congratulations of financial luminaries J.P. Morgan, Morgan partner George W. Perkins, a smug John D. Rockefeller, John D. Ryan of National City Bank, and Teddy Roosevelt — prominently identified by his famous teeth — in the background. Wall Street is decorated by Red flags. The cheering crowd and the airborne hats suggest that Karl Marx must have been a fairly popular sort of fellow in the New York financial district.

Was Robert Minor dreaming? On the contrary, we shall see that Minor was on firm ground in depicting an enthusiastic alliance of Wall Street and Marxist socialism. The characters in Minor's cartoon — Karl Marx (symbolizing the future revolutionaries Lenin and Trotsky), J. P. Morgan, John D. Rockefeller — and indeed Robert Minor himself, are also prominent characters in this book.

The contradictions suggested by Minor's cartoon have been brushed under the rug of history because they do not fit the accepted conceptual spectrum of political left and political right. Bolsheviks are at the left end of the political spectrum and Wall Street financiers are at the right end; *therefore,* we implicitly reason, the two groups have nothing in common and any alliance between the two is absurd. Factors contrary to this neat conceptual arrangement are usually rejected as bizarre observations or unfortunate errors. Modern history possesses such a built-in duality and certainly if too many uncomfortable facts have been rejected and brushed under the rug, it is an inaccurate history.

On the other hand, it may be observed that both the extreme right and the extreme left of the conventional political spectrum are absolutely collectivist. The national socialist (for example, the fascist) and the international socialist (for example, the Communist) both recommend totalitarian politico-economic systems based on naked, unfettered political power and individual coercion. Both systems require monopoly control of society. While monopoly control of industries was once the objective of J. P. Morgan and J. D. Rockefeller, by the late nineteenth century the inner sanctums of Wall Street understood that the most efficient way to gain an unchallenged monopoly was to "go political" and make society go to work for the monopolists — under the name of the public good and the public interest. This strategy was detailed in 1906 by Frederick C. Howe in his *Confessions of a Monopolist.*[1] Howe, by the way, is also a figure in the story of the Bolshevik Revolution.

Therefore, an alternative conceptual packaging of political ideas and politico-economic systems would be that of ranking the degree of individual freedom versus the degree of centralized political control. Under such an ordering the corporate welfare state and socialism are at the same end of the spectrum. Hence we see that attempts at monopoly control of society can have different labels while owning common features.

Consequently, one barrier to mature understanding of recent history is the notion that all capitalists are the bitter and unswerving enemies of all Marxists and socialists. This erroneous idea originated with Karl Marx and was undoubtedly useful to his purposes. In fact, the idea is nonsense. There has been a continuing, albeit concealed, alliance between international political capitalists and international revolutionary socialists — to their mutual benefit. This alliance has gone unobserved largely because historians — with a few notable exceptions — have an unconscious Marxian bias and are thus locked into the impossibility of any such alliance existing. The open-minded reader should bear two clues in mind: monopoly capitalists are the bitter enemies of laissez-faire entrepreneurs; and, given the weaknesses of socialist central planning, the totalitarian socialist state is a perfect captive market for monopoly capitalists, if an alliance can be made with the socialist powerbrokers. Suppose — and it is only hypothesis at this point — that American monopoly capitalists were able to reduce a planned socialist Russia to the status of a captive technical colony? Would not this be the logical twentieth-century internationalist extension of the Morgan railroad monopolies and the Rockefeller petroleum trust of the late nineteenth century?

Apart from Gabriel Kolko, Murray Rothbard, and the revisionists, historians have not been alert for such a combination of events. Historical reporting, with rare exceptions, has

---

[1] "These are the rules of big business. They have superseded the teachings of our parents and are reducible to a simple maxim: Get a monopoly; let Society work for you: and remember that the best of all business is politics, for a legislative grant, franchise, subsidy or tax exemption is worth more than a Kimberly or Comstock lode, since it does not require any labor, either mental or physical, lot its exploitation" (Chicago: Public Publishing, 1906), p. 157.

been forced into a dichotomy of capitalists versus socialists. George Kennan's monumental and readable study of the Russian Revolution consistently maintains this fiction of a Wall Street-Bolshevik dichotomy[2]. *Russia Leaves the War* has a single incidental reference to the J.P. Morgan firm and no reference at all to Guaranty Trust Company. Yet both organizations are prominently mentioned in the State Department files, to which frequent reference is made in this book, and both are part of the core of the evidence presented here. Neither self-admitted "Bolshevik banker" Olof Aschberg nor Nya Banken in Stockholm is mentioned in Kennan yet both were central to Bolshevik funding. Moreover, in minor yet crucial circumstances, at least crucial for *our* argument, Kennan is factually in error. For example, Kennan cites Federal Reserve Bank director William Boyce Thompson as leaving Russia on November 27, 1917. This departure date would make it physically impossible for Thompson to be in Petrograd on December 2, 1917, to transmit a cable request for $1 million to Morgan in New York. Thompson in fact left Petrograd on December 4, 1918, two days after sending the cable to New York. Then again, Kennan states that on November 30, 1917, Trotsky delivered a speech before the Petrograd Soviet in which he observed, "Today I had here in the Smolny Institute two Americans closely connected with American Capitalist elements "According to Kennan, it "is difficult to imagine" who these two Americans "could have been, if not Robins and Gumberg." But in [act Alexander Gumberg was Russian, not American. Further, as Thompson was still in Russia on November 30, 1917, then the two Americans who visited Trotsky were more than likely Raymond Robins, a mining promoter turned do-gooder, and Thompson, of the Federal Reserve Bank of New York.

The Bolshevization of Wall Street was known among well informed circles as early as 1919. The financial journalist Barron recorded a conversation with oil magnate E. H. Doheny in 1919 and specifically named three prominent financiers, William Boyce Thompson, Thomas Lamont and Charles R. Crane:

> Aboard S.S. Aquitania, Friday Evening, February 1, 1919.
> Spent the evening with the Dohenys in their suite. Mr. Doheny said: If you believe in democracy you cannot believe in Socialism. Socialism is the poison that destroys democracy. Democracy means opportunity for all. Socialism holds out the hope that a man can quit work and be better off. Bolshevism is the true fruit of socialism and if you will read the interesting testimony before the Senate Committee about the middle of January that showed up all these pacifists and peace-makers as German sympathizers, Socialists, and Bolsheviks, you will see that a majority of the college professors in the United States are teaching socialism and Bolshevism and that fifty-two college professors were on so-called peace

---

[2] George F. Kennan, *Russia Leaves the War* (New York: Atheneum, 1967); and *Decision to Intervene, Soviet-American Relations, 1917-1920* (Princeton, N.J.: Princeton University Press, 1958).

committees in 1914. President Eliot of Harvard is teaching Bolshevism. The worst Bolshevists in the United States are not only college professors, of whom President Wilson is one, but capitalists and the wives of capitalists and neither seem to know what they are talking about. William Boyce Thompson is teaching Bolshevism and he may yet convert Lamont of J.P. Morgan & Company. Vanderlip is a Bolshevist, so is Charles R. Crane. Many women are joining the movement and neither they, nor their husbands, know what it is, or what it leads to. Henry Ford is another and so are most of those one hundred historians Wilson took abroad with him in the foolish idea that history can teach youth proper demarcations of races, peoples, and nations geographically.[3]

In brief, this is a story of the Bolshevik Revolution and its aftermath, but a story that departs from the usual conceptual straitjacket approach of capitalists versus Communists. Our story postulates a partnership between international monopoly capitalism and international revolutionary socialism for their mutual benefit. The final human cost of this alliance has fallen upon the shoulders of the individual Russian and the individual American. Entrepreneurship has been brought into disrepute and the world has been propelled toward inefficient socialist planning as a result of these monopoly maneuverings in the world of politics and revolution.

This is also a story reflecting the betrayal of the Russian Revolution. The tsars and their corrupt political system were ejected only to be replaced by the new powerbrokers of another corrupt political system. Where the United States could have exerted its dominant influence to bring about a free Russia it truckled to the ambitions of a few Wall Street financiers who, for their own purposes, could accept a centralized tsarist Russia or a centralized Marxist Russia but not a decentralized free Russia. And the reasons for these assertions will unfold as we develop the underlying and, so far, untold history of the Russian Revolution and its aftermath.[4]

---

[3] Arthur Pound and Samuel Taylor Moore, *They Told Barron* (New York: Harper & Brothers, 1930), pp. 13-14.

[4] There is a parallel, and also unknown, history with respect to the Makhanovite movement that fought both the "Whites" and the "Reds" in the Civil War of 1919-20 (see Voline, *The Unknown Revolution* [New York: Libertarian Book Club, 1953]). There was also the "Green" movement, which fought both Whites and Reds. The author has never seen even one isolated mention of the Greens4 in any history of the Bolshevik Revolution. Yet the Green Army was at least 700,000 strong!

Chapter II

Trotsky Leaves New York to Complete the Revolution

You will have a revolution, a terrible revolution. What course it takes will depend much on what Mr. Rockefeller tells Mr. Hague to do. Mr. Rockefeller is a symbol of the American ruling class and Mr. Hague is a symbol of its political tools.
                    Leon Trotsky, in New York Times, December 13, 1938.
                                (Hague was a New Jersey politician)

In 1916, the year preceding the Russian Revolution, internationalist Leon Trotsky was expelled from France, officially because of his participation in the Zimmerwald conference but also no doubt because of inflammatory articles written for *Nashe Slovo*, a Russian-language newspaper printed in Paris. In September 1916 Trotsky was politely escorted across the Spanish border by French police. A few days later Madrid police arrested the internationalist and lodged him in a "first-class cell" at a charge of one-and-one-half pesetas per day. Subsequently Trotsky was taken to Cadiz, then to Barcelona finally to be placed on board the Spanish Transatlantic Company steamer *Monserrat*. Trotsky and family crossed the Atlantic Ocean and landed in New York on January 13, 1917.

Other Trotskyites also made their way westward across the Atlantic. Indeed, one Trotskyite group acquired sufficient immediate influence in Mexico to write the Constitution of Querétaro for the revolutionary 1917 Carranza government, giving Mexico the dubious distinction of being the first government in the world to adopt a Soviet-type constitution.

How did Trotsky, who knew only German and Russian, survive in capitalist America? According to his autobiography, *My Life*, "My only profession in New York was that of a revolutionary socialist." In other words, Trotsky wrote occasional articles for *Novy Mir*, the New York Russian socialist journal. Yet we know that the Trotsky family apartment in New York had a refrigerator and a telephone, and, according to Trotsky, that the family occasionally traveled in a chauffeured limousine. This mode of living puzzled the two young Trotsky boys. When they went into a tearoom, the boys would anxiously demand of their mother, "Why doesn't the chauffeur come in?"[5] The stylish living standard is also at odds with Trotsky's reported income. The only funds that Trotsky admits receiving in 1916 and 1917 are $310, and, said Trotsky, "I distributed the $310 among five emigrants who were returning to Russia." Yet Trotsky had paid for a first-class cell in Spain, the Trotsky family had traveled across Europe to the United States, they had acquired an excellent apartment in New York — paying rent three months in advance — and they had use of a chauffeured limousine. All this on the earnings of an impoverished revolutionary for a few articles for the low-circulation Russian-language newspaper *Nashe* Slovo in Paris and *Novy Mir* in New York!

Joseph Nedava estimates Trotsky's 1917 income at $12.00 per week, "supplemented by some lecture fees."[6] Trotsky was in New York in 1917 for three months, from January to March, so that makes $144.00 in income from *Novy Mir* and, say, another $100.00 in lecture fees, for a total of $244.00. Of this $244.00 Trotsky was able to give away $310.00 to his friends, pay for the New York apartment, provide for his family — and find the $10,000 that was taken from him in April 1917 by Canadian authorities in Halifax. Trotsky claims that those who said he had other sources of income are "slanderers" spreading "stupid calumnies" and "lies," but unless Trotsky was playing the horses at the Jamaica racetrack, it can't be done. Obviously Trotsky had an unreported source of income.

What was that source? In *The Road to Safety,* author Arthur Willert says Trotsky earned a living by working as an electrician for Fox Film Studios. Other writers have cited other occupations, but there is no evidence that Trotsky occupied himself for remuneration otherwise than by writing and speaking.

Most investigation has centered on the verifiable fact that when Trotsky left New York in 1917 for Petrograd, to organize the Bolshevik phase of the revolution, he left with $10,000. In 1919 the U.S. Senate Overman Committee investigated Bolshevik propaganda and German money in the United States and incidentally touched on the source of Trotsky's $10,000. Examination of Colonel Hurban, Washington attaché to the Czech legation, by the Overman Committee yielded the following:

> COL. HURBAN: Trotsky, perhaps, took money from Germany, but Trotsky will deny it. Lenin would not deny it. Miliukov proved that he got $10,000 from some Germans while he was in America. Miliukov had the proof, but he denied it. Trotsky did, although Miliukov had the proof.
> SENATOR OVERMAN: It was charged that Trotsky got $10,000 here.

---

[5] Leon Trotsky, *My Life* (New York: Scribner's, 1930), chap. 22.
[6] Joseph Nedava, *Trotsky and the Jews* (Philadelphia: Jewish Publication Society of America, 1972), p. 163.

COL. HURBAN: I do not remember how much it was, but I know it was a question between him and Miliukov.
SENATOR OVERMAN: Miliukov proved it, did he?
COL. HURBAN: Yes, sir.
SENATOR OVERMAN: Do you know where he got it from?
COL. HURBAN: I remember it was $10,000; but it is no matter. I will speak about their propaganda. The German Government knew Russia better than anybody, and they knew that with the help of those people they could destroy the Russian army.
(At 5:45 o'clock p.m. the subcommittee adjourned until tomorrow, Wednesday, February 19, at 10:30 o'clock a.m.)[7]

It is quite remarkable that the committee adjourned abruptly before the *source* of Trotsky's funds could be placed into the Senate record. When questioning resumed the next day, Trotsky and his $10,000 were no longer of interest to the Overman Committee. We shall later develop evidence concerning the financing of German and revolutionary activities in the United States by New York financial houses; the origins of Trotsky's $10,000 will then come into focus.

An amount of $10,000 of German origin is also mentioned in the official British telegram to Canadian naval authorities in Halifax, who requested that Trotsky and party en route to the revolution be taken off the S.S. *Kristianiafjord* (see page 28). We also learn from a British Directorate of Intelligence report[8] that Gregory Weinstein, who in 1919 was to become a prominent member of the Soviet Bureau in New York, collected funds for Trotsky in New York. These funds originated in Germany and were channeled through the *Volkszeitung*, a German daily newspaper in New York and subsidized by the German government.

While Trotsky's funds are officially reported as German, Trotsky was actively engaged in American politics immediately prior to leaving New York for Russia and the revolution. On March 5, 1917, American newspapers headlined the increasing possibility of war with Germany; the same evening Trotsky proposed a resolution at the meeting of the New York County Socialist Party "pledging Socialists to encourage strikes and resist recruiting in the event of war with Germany."[9] Leon Trotsky was called by the *New York Times* "an exiled Russian revolutionist." Louis C. Fraina, who cosponsored the Trotsky resolution, later — under an alias — wrote an uncritical book on the Morgan financial empire entitled *House*

---

[7] United States, Senate, *Brewing and Liquor Interests and German and Bolshevik Propaganda* (Subcommittee on the Judiciary), 65th Cong., 1919.
[8] Special Report No. 5, *The Russian Soviet Bureau in the United States,* July 14, 1919, Scotland House, London S.W.I. Copy in U.S. State Dept. Decimal File, 316-23-1145.
[9] *New York Times,* March 5, 1917.

of Morgan.[10] The Trotsky-Fraina proposal was opposed by the Morris Hillquit faction, and the Socialist Party subsequently voted opposition to the resolution.[11]

More than a week later, on March 16, at the time of the deposition of the tsar, Leon Trotsky was interviewed in the offices of *Novy Mir.* The interview contained a prophetic statement on the Russian revolution:

> "... the committee which has taken the place of the deposed Ministry in Russia did not represent the interests or the aims of the revolutionists, that it would probably be shortlived and step down in favor of men who would be more sure to carry forward the democratization of Russia."[12]

The "men who would be more sure to carry forward the democratization of Russia," that is, the Mensheviks and the Bolsheviks, were then in exile abroad and needed first to return to Russia. The temporary "committee" was therefore dubbed the Provisional Government, a title, it should be noted, that was used from the start of the revolution in March and not applied ex post facto by historians.

WOODROW WILSON AND A PASSPORT FOR TROTSKY

President Woodrow Wilson was the fairy godmother who provided Trotsky with a passport to return to Russia to "carry forward" the revolution. This American passport was accompanied by a Russian entry permit and a British transit visa. Jennings C. Wise, in *Woodrow Wilson: Disciple of Revolution,* makes the pertinent comment, "Historians must never forget that Woodrow Wilson, despite the efforts of the British police, made it possible for Leon Trotsky to enter Russia with an American passport."

President Wilson facilitated Trotsky's passage to Russia at the same time careful State Department bureaucrats, concerned about such revolutionaries entering Russia, were unilaterally attempting to tighten up passport procedures. The Stockholm legation cabled the State Department on June 13, 1917, just *after* Trotsky crossed the Finnish-Russian border, "Legation confidentially informed Russian, English and French passport offices at Russian

---

[10] Lewis Corey, House of Morgan: A Social Biography of the Masters of Money (New York: G. W. Watt, 1930).

[11] Morris Hillquit. (formerly Hillkowitz) had been defense attorney for Johann Most, alter the assassination of President McKinley, and in 1917 was a leader of the New York Socialist Party. In the 1920s Hillquit established himself in the New York banking world by becoming a director of, and attorney for, the International Union Bank. Under President Franklin D. Roosevelt, Hillquit helped draw up the NRA codes for the garment industry.

[12] *New York Times,* March 16, 1917.

frontier, Tornea, considerably worried by passage of suspicious persons bearing American passports."[13]

To this cable the State Department replied, on the same day, "Department is exercising special care in issuance of passports for Russia"; the department also authorized expenditures by the legation to establish a passport-control office in Stockholm and to hire an "absolutely dependable American citizen" for employment on control work.[14] But the bird had flown the coop. Menshevik Trotsky with Lenin's Bolsheviks were already in Russia preparing to "carry forward" the revolution. The passport net erected caught only more legitimate birds. For example, on June 26, 1917, Herman Bernstein, a reputable New York newspaperman on his way to Petrograd to represent the *New York Herald*, was held at the border and refused entry to Russia. Somewhat tardily, in mid-August 1917 the Russian embassy in Washington requested the State Department (and State agreed) to "prevent the entry into Russia of criminals and anarchists... numbers of whom have already gone to Russia."[15]

Consequently, by virtue of preferential treatment for Trotsky, when the S.S. *Kristianiafjord* left New York on March 26, 1917, Trotsky was aboard and holding a U.S. passport — and in company with other Trotskyite revolutionaries, Wall Street financiers, American Communists, and other interesting persons, few of whom had embarked for legitimate business. This mixed bag of passengers has been described by Lincoln Steffens, the American Communist:

> The passenger list was long and mysterious. Trotsky was in the steerage with a group of revolutionaries; there was a Japanese revolutionist in my cabin. There were a lot of Dutch hurrying home from Java, the only innocent people aboard. The rest were war messengers, two from Wall Street to Germany.[16]

Notably, Lincoln Steffens was on board en route to Russia at the specific invitation of Charles Richard Crane, a backer and a former chairman of the Democratic Party's finance committee. Charles Crane, vice president of the Crane Company, had organized the Westinghouse Company in Russia, was a member of the Root mission to Russia, and had made no fewer than twenty-three visits to Russia between 1890 and 1930. Richard Crane, his son, was confidential assistant to then Secretary of State Robert Lansing. According to the former ambassador to Germany William Dodd, Crane "did much to bring on the Kerensky

---

[13] U.S. State Dept. Decimal File, 316-85-1002.
[14] Ibid.
[15] Ibid., 861.111/315.
[16] Lincoln Steffens, *Autobiography* (New York: Harcourt, Brace, 1931), p. 764. Steffens was the "go-between" for Crane and Woodrow Wilson.

revolution which gave way to Communism."[17] And so Steffens' comments in his diary about conversations aboard the S.S. *Kristianiafjord* are highly pertinent:"... all agree that the revolution is in its first phase only, that it must grow. Crane and Russian radicals on the ship think we shall be in Petrograd for the re-revolution.[18]

Crane returned to the United States when the Bolshevik Revolution (that is, "the re-revolution") had been completed and, although a private citizen, was given firsthand reports of the progress of the Bolshevik Revolution as cables were received at the State Department. For example, one memorandum, dated December 11, 1917, is entitled "Copy of report on Maximalist uprising for Mr Crane." It originated with Maddin Summers, U.S. consul general in Moscow, and the covering letter from Summers reads in part:

> I have the honor to enclose herewith a copy of same [above report] with the request that it be sent for the confidential information of Mr. Charles R. Crane. It is assumed that the Department will have no objection to Mr. Crane seeing the report.[19]

In brief, the unlikely and puzzling picture that emerges is that Charles Crane, a friend and backer of Woodrow Wilson and a prominent financier and politician, had a known role in the "first" revolution and traveled to Russia in mid-1917 in company with the American Communist Lincoln Steffens, who was in touch with both Woodrow Wilson and Trotsky. The latter in turn was carrying a passport issued at the orders of Wilson and $10,000 from supposed German sources. On his return to the U.S. after the "re-revolution," Crane was granted access to official documents concerning consolidation of the Bolshevik regime: This is a pattern of interlocking — if puzzling — events that warrants further investigation and suggests, though without at this point providing evidence, some link between the financier Crane and the revolutionary Trotsky.

CANADIAN GOVERNMENT DOCUMENTS ON TROTSKY'S RELEASE[20]

Documents on Trotsky's brief stay in Canadian custody are now de-classified and available from the Canadian government archives. According to these archives, Trotsky was removed by Canadian and British naval personnel from the S.S. *Kristianiafjord* at Halifax, Nova Scotia, on April 3, 1917, listed as a German prisoner of war, and interned at the Amherst, Nova Scotia, internment station for German prisoners. Mrs. Trotsky, the two Trotsky boys, and

---

[17] William Edward Dodd, *Ambassador Dodd's Diary, 1933-1938* (New York: Harcourt, Brace, 1941), pp. 42-43.
[18] Lincoln Steffens, *The Letters of Lincoln Steffens* (New York: Harcourt, Brace, 1941), p. 396.
[19] U.S. State Dept. Decimal File, 861.00/1026.
[20] This section is based on Canadian government records.

five other men described as "Russian Socialists" were also taken off and interned. Their names are recorded by the Canadian files as: Nickita Muchin, Leiba Fisheleff, Konstantin Romanchanco, Gregor Teheodnovski, Gerchon Melintchansky and Leon Bronstein Trotsky (all spellings from original Canadian documents).

Canadian Army form LB-I, under serial number 1098 (including thumb prints), was completed for Trotsky, with a description as follows: "37 years old, a political exile, occupation journalist, born in Gromskty, Chuson, Russia, Russian citizen." The form was signed by Leon Trotsky and his full name given as Leon Bromstein *(sic)* Trotsky.

The Trotsky party was removed from the S.S. *Kristianiafjord* under official instructions received by cablegram of March 29, 1917, London, presumably originating in the Admiralty with the naval control officer, Halifax. The cablegram reported that the Trotsky party was on the *"Christianiafjord" (sic)* and should be "taken off and retained pending instructions." The reason given to the naval control officer at Halifax was that "these are Russian Socialists leaving for purposes of starting revolution against present Russian government for which Trotsky is reported to have 10,000 dollars subscribed by Socialists and Germans."

On April 1, 1917, the naval control officer, Captain O. M. Makins, sent a confidential memorandum to the general officer commanding at Halifax, to the effect that he had "examined all Russian passengers" aboard the S.S. *Kristianiafjord* and found six men in the second-class section: "They are all avowed Socialists, and though professing a desire to help the new Russian Govt., might well be in league with German Socialists in America, and quite likely to be a great hindrance to the Govt. in Russia just at present." Captain Makins added that he was going to remove the group, as well as Trotsky's wife and two sons, in order to intern them at Halifax. A copy of this report was forwarded from Halifax to the chief of the General Staff in Ottawa on April 2, 1917.

The next document in the Canadian files is dated April 7, from the chief of the General Staff, Ottawa, to the director of internment operations, and acknowledges a previous letter (not in the files) about the internment of Russian socialists at Amherst, Nova Scotia: "... in this connection, have to inform you of the receipt of a long telegram yesterday from the Russian Consul General, MONTREAL, protesting against the arrest of these men as they were in possession of passports issued by the Russian Consul General, NEW YORK, U.S.A."

The reply to this Montreal telegram was to the effect that the men were interned "on suspicion of being German," and would be released only upon definite proof of their nationality and loyalty to the Allies. No telegrams from the Russian consul general in New York are in the Canadian files, and it is known that this office was reluctant to issue Russian passports to Russian political exiles. However, there *is* a telegram in the files from a New York attorney, N. Aleinikoff, to R. M. Coulter, then deputy postmaster general of Canada. The postmaster general's office in Canada had no connection with either internment of prisoners of war or military activities. Accordingly, this telegram was in the nature of a personal, nonofficial intervention. It reads:

> DR. R. M. COULTER, Postmaster Genl. OTTAWA Russian political exiles returning to Russia detained Halifax interned Amherst camp. Kindly investigate and advise cause of the detention and names of all detained. Trust as champion of freedom you will intercede on their behalf. Please wire collect. NICHOLAS ALEINIKOFF

On April 11, Coulter wired Aleinikoff, "Telegram received. Writing you this afternoon. You should receive it tomorrow evening. R. M. Coulter." This telegram was sent by the Canadian Pacific Railway Telegraph but charged to the Canadian Post Office Department. Normally a private business telegram would be charged to the recipient and this was not official business. The follow-up Coulter letter to Aleinikoff is interesting because, after confirming that the Trotsky party was held at Amherst, it states that they were suspected of propaganda against the present Russian government and "are supposed to be agents of Germany." Coulter then adds,"... they are not what they represent themselves to be"; the Trotsky group is "...not detained by Canada, but by the Imperial authorities." After assuring Aleinikoff that the detainees would be made comfortable, Coulter adds that any information "in their favour" would be transmitted to the military authorities. The general impression of the letter is that while Coulter is sympathetic and fully aware of Trotsky's pro-German links, he is unwilling to get involved. On April 11 Arthur Wolf of 134 East Broadway, New York, sent a telegram to Coulter. Though sent from New York, this telegram, after being acknowledged, was also charged to the Canadian Post Office Department.

Coulter's reactions, however, reflect more than the detached sympathy evident in his letter to Aleinikoff. They must be considered in the light of the fact that these letters in behalf of Trotsky came from two American residents of New York City and involved a Canadian or Imperial military matter of international importance. Further, Coulter, as deputy postmaster general, was a Canadian government official of some standing. Ponder, for a moment, what would happen to someone who similarly intervened in United States affairs! In the Trotsky affair we have two American residents corresponding with a Canadian deputy postmaster general in order to intervene in behalf of an interned Russian revolutionary.

Coulter's subsequent action also suggests something more than casual intervention. After Coulter acknowledged the Aleinikoff and Wolf telegrams, he wrote to Major General Willoughby Gwatkin of the Department of Militia and Defense in Ottawa — a man of significant influence in the Canadian military — and attached copies of the Aleinikoff and Wolf telegrams:

These men have been hostile to Russia because of the way the Jews have been treated, and are now strongly in favor of the present Administration, so far as I know. Both are responsible men. Both are reputable men, and I am sending their telegrams to you for what they may be worth, and so that you may represent them to the English authorities if you deem it wise.

Obviously Coulter knows — or intimates that he knows — a great deal about Aleinikoff and Wolf. His letter was in effect a character reference, and aimed at the root of the internment problem — London. Gwatkin was well known in London, and in fact was on loan to Canada from the War Office in London.[21]

Aleinikoff then sent a letter to Coulter to thank him

> most heartily for the interest you have taken in the fate of the Russian Political Exiles... You know me, esteemed Dr. Coulter, and you also know my devotion to the cause of Russian freedom... Happily I know Mr. Trotsky, Mr. Melnichahnsky, and Mr. Chudnowsky... intimately.

It might be noted as an aside that if Aleinikoff knew Trotsky "intimately," then he would also probably be aware that Trotsky had declared his intention to return to Russia to overthrow the Provisional Government and institute the "re-revolution." On receipt of Aleinikoff's letter, Coulter immediately (April 16) forwarded it to Major General Gwatkin, adding that he became acquainted with Aleinikoff "in connection with Departmental action on United States papers in the Russian language" and that Aleinikoff was working "on the same lines as Mr. Wolf... who was an escaped prisoner from Siberia."

Previously, on April 14, Gwatkin sent a memorandum to his naval counterpart on the Canadian Military Interdepartmental Committee repeating that the internees were Russian socialists with *"10,000* dollars subscribed by socialists and Germans." The concluding paragraph stated: *"On* the other hand there are those who declare that an act of high-handed injustice has been done." Then on April 16, Vice Admiral C. E. Kingsmill, director of the Naval Service, took Gwatkin's intervention at face value. In a letter to Captain Makins, the naval control officer at Halifax, he stated, "The Militia authorities request that a decision as to their (that is, the six Russians) disposal may be hastened." A copy of this instruction was relayed to Gwatkin who in turn informed Deputy Postmaster General Coulter. Three days later Gwatkin applied pressure. In a memorandum of April 20 to the naval secretary,

---

[21] Gwatkin's memoramada in the Canadian government files are not signed, but initialed with a cryptic mark or symbol. The mark has been identified as Gwatkin's because one Gwatkin letter (that of April 21) with that cryptic mark was acknowledged.

he wrote, "Can you say, please, whether or not the Naval Control Office has given a decision?"

On the same day (April 20) Captain Makins wrote Admiral Kingsmill explaining his reasons for removing Trotsky; he refused to be pressured into making a decision, stating, "I will cable to the Admiralty informing them that the Militia authorities are requesting an early decision as to their disposal." However, the next day, April 21, Gwatkin wrote Coulter: "Our friends the Russian socialists are to be released; and arrangements are being made for their passage to Europe." The order to Makins for Trotsky's release originated in the Admiralty, London. Coulter acknowledged the information, "which will please our New York correspondents immensely."

While we can, on the one hand, conclude that Coulter and Gwatkin were intensely interested in the release of Trotsky, we do not, on the other hand, know why. There was little in the career of either Deputy Postmaster General Coulter or Major General Gwatkin that would explain an urge to release the Menshevik Leon Trotsky.

Dr. Robert Miller Coulter was a medical doctor of Scottish and Irish parents, a liberal, a Freemason, and an Odd Fellow. He was appointed deputy postmaster general of Canada in 1897. His sole claim to fame derived from being a delegate to the Universal Postal Union Convention in 1906 and a delegate to New Zealand and Australia in 1908 for the "All Red" project. All Red had nothing to do with Red revolutionaries; it was only a plan for all-red or all-British fast steamships between Great Britain, Canada, and Australia.

Major General Willoughby Gwatkin stemmed from a long British military tradition (Cambridge and then Staff College). A specialist in mobilization, he served in Canada from 1905 to 1918. Given only the documents in the Canadian files, we can but conclude that their intervention in behalf of Trotsky is a mystery.

CANADIAN MILITARY INTELLIGENCE VIEWS TROTSKY

We can approach the Trotsky release case from another angle: Canadian intelligence. Lieutenant Colonel John Bayne MacLean, a prominent Canadian publisher and businessman, founder and president of MacLean Publishing Company, Toronto, operated numerous Canadian trade journals, including the *Financial Post*. MacLean also had a long-time association with Canadian Army Intelligence.[22]

In 1918 Colonel MacLean wrote for his own *MacLean's* magazine an article entitled "Why Did We Let Trotsky Go? How Canada Lost an Opportunity to Shorten the War."[23] The

---

[22] H.J. Morgan, Canadian Men and Women of the Times, 1912, 2 vols. (Toronto: W. Briggs, 1898-1912).
[23] June 1919, pp. 66a-666. Toronto Public Library has a copy; the issue of *MacLean's* in which Colonel MacLean's article appeared is not easy to find and a frill summary is provided below.

article contained detailed and unusual information about Leon Trotsky, although the last half of the piece wanders off into space remarking about barely related matters. We have two clues to the authenticity of the information. First, Colonel MacLean was a man of integrity with excellent connections in Canadian government intelligence. Second, government records since released by Canada, Great Britain, and the United States confirm MacLean's statement to a significant degree. Some MacLean statements remain to be confirmed, but information available in the early 1970s is not necessarily inconsistent with Colonel MacLean's article.

MacLean's opening argument is that "some Canadian politicians or officials were chiefly responsible for the prolongation of the war [World War I], for the great loss of life, the wounds and sufferings of the winter of 1917 and the great drives of 1918."

Further, states MacLean, these persons were (in 1919) doing everything possible to prevent Parliament and the Canadian people from getting the related facts. Official reports, including those of Sir Douglas Haig, demonstrate that but for the Russian break in 1917 the war would have been over a year earlier, and that "the man chiefly responsible for the defection of Russia was Trotsky... acting under German instructions."

Who was Trotsky? According to MacLean, Trotsky was not Russian, but German. Odd as this assertion may appear it does coincide with other scraps of intelligence information: to wit, that Trotsky spoke better German than Russian, and that he was the Russian executive of the German "Black Bond." According to MacLean, Trotsky in August 1914 had been "ostentatiously" expelled from Berlin[24]; he finally arrived in the United States where he organized Russian revolutionaries, as well as revolutionaries in Western Canada, who "were largely Germans and Austrians traveling as Russians." MacLean continues:

> Originally the British found through Russian associates that Kerensky,[25] Lenin and some lesser leaders were practically in German pay as early as 1915 and they uncovered in 1916 the connections with Trotsky then living in New York. From that time he was closely watched by... the Bomb Squad. In the early part of 1916 a German official sailed for New York. British Intelligence officials accompanied him. He was held up at Halifax; but on their instruction he was passed on with profuse apologies for the necessary delay. After much manoeuvering he arrived in a dirty little newspaper office in the slums and there found Trotsky, to whom he bore important instructions. From June 1916, until they passed him

---

[24] See also Trotsky, *My Life*, p. 236.
[25] See Appendix 3.

on [to] the British, the N.Y. Bomb Squad never lost touch with Trotsky. They discovered that his real name was Braunstein and that he was a German, not a Russian.[26]

Such German activity in neutral countries is confirmed in a State Department report (316-9-764-9) describing organization of Russian refugees for revolutionary purposes.

Continuing, MacLean states that Trotsky and four associates sailed on the "S.S. *Christiania*" (sic), and on April 3 reported to "Captain Making" (sic) and were taken off the ship at Halifax under the direction of Lieutenant Jones. (Actually a party of nine, including six men, were taken off the S.S. *Kristianiafjord*. The name of the naval control officer at Halifax was Captain O. M. Makins, R.N. The name of the officer who removed the Trotsky party from the ship is not in the Canadian government documents; Trotsky said it was "Machen.") Again, according to MacLean, Trotsky's money came "from German sources in New York." Also:

> generally the explanation given is that the release was done at the request of Kerensky but months before this British officers and one Canadian serving in Russia, who could speak the Russian language, reported to London and Washington that Kerensky was in German service.[27]

Trotsky was released "at the request of the British Embassy at Washington... [which] acted on the request of the U.S. State Department, who were acting for someone else." Canadian officials "were instructed to inform the press that Trotsky was an American citizen travelling on an American passport; that his release was specially demanded by the Washington State Department." Moreover, writes MacLean, in Ottawa "Trotsky had, and continues to have, strong underground influence. There his power was so great that orders were issued that he must be given every consideration."

The theme of MacLean's reporting is, quite evidently, that Trotsky had intimate relations with, and probably worked for, the German General Staff. While such relations have been established regarding Lenin — to the extent that Lenin was subsidized and his return to Russia facilitated by the Germans — it appears certain that Trotsky was similarly aided. The $10,000 Trotsky fund in New York was from German sources, and a recently declassified document in the U.S. State Department files reads as follows:

---

[26] According to his own account, Trotsky did not arrive in the U.S. until January 1917. Trotsky's real name was Bronstein; he invented the name "Trotsky." "Bronstein" is German and "Trotsky" is Polish rather than Russian. His first name is usually given as "Leon"; however, Trotsky's first book, which was published in Geneva, has the initial "N," not "L."

[27] See Appendix 3; this document was obtained in 1971 from the British Foreign Office but apparently was known to MacLean.

March 9, 1918 to: American Consul, Vladivostok from Polk, Acting Secretary of State, Washington D.C.
For your confidential information and prompt attention: Following is substance of message of January twelfth from Von Schanz of German Imperial Bank to Trotsky, quote Consent imperial bank to appropriation from credit general staff of five million roubles for sending assistant chief naval commissioner Kudrisheff to Far East.

This message suggests some liaison between Trotsky and the Germans in January 1918, a time when Trotsky was proposing an alliance with the West. The State Department does not give the provenance of the telegram, only that it originated with the War College Staff. The State Department did treat the message as authentic and acted on the basis of assumed authenticity. It is consistent with the general theme of Colonel MacLean's article.

TROTSKY'S INTENTIONS AND OBJECTIVES

Consequently, we can derive the following sequence of events: Trotsky traveled from New York to Petrograd on a passport supplied by the intervention of Woodrow Wilson, and with the declared intention to "carry forward" the revolution. The British government was the immediate source of Trotsky's release from Canadian custody in April 1917, but there may well have been "pressures." Lincoln Steffens, an American Communist, acted as a link between Wilson and Charles R. Crane and between Crane and Trotsky. Further, while Crane had no official position, his son Richard was confidential assistant to Secretary of State Robert Lansing, and Crane senior was provided with prompt and detailed reports on the progress of the Bolshevik Revolution. Moreover, Ambassador William Dodd (U.S. ambassador to Germany in the Hitler era) said that Crane had an active role in the Kerensky phase of the revolution; the Steffens letters confirm that Crane saw the Kerensky phase as only one step in a continuing revolution.

The interesting point, however, is not so much the communication among dissimilar persons like Crane, Steffens, Trotsky, and Woodrow Wilson as the existence of at least a measure of agreement on the procedure to be followed — that is, the Provisional Government was seen as "provisional," and the "re-revolution" was to follow.

On the other side of the coin, interpretation of Trotsky's intentions should be cautious: he was adept at double games. Official documentation clearly demonstrates contradictory actions. For example, the Division of Far Eastern Affairs in the U.S. State Department received on March 23, 1918, two reports stemming from Trotsky; one is inconsistent with the other. One report, dated March 20 and from Moscow, originated in the Russian newspaper *Russkoe*

Slovo. The report cited an interview with Trotsky in which he stated that any alliance with the United States was impossible:

> The Russia of the Soviet cannot align itself... with capitalistic America for this would be a betrayal It is possible that Americans seek such an rapprochement with us, driven by its antagonism towards Japan, but in any case there can be no question of an alliance by us of any nature with a bourgeoisie nation.[28]

The other report, also originating in Moscow, is a message dated March 17, 1918, three days earlier, and from Ambassador Francis: "Trotsky requests five American officers as inspectors of army being organized for defense also requests railroad operating men and equipment."[29]

This request to the U.S. is of course inconsistent with rejection of an "alliance."

Before we leave Trotsky some mention should be made of the Stalinist show trials of the 1930s and, in particular, the 1938 accusations and trial of the "Anti-Soviet bloc of rightists and Trotskyites." These forced parodies of the judicial process, almost unanimously rejected in the West, may throw light on Trotsky's intentions.

The crux of the Stalinist accusation was that Trotskyites were paid agents of international capitalism. K. G. Rakovsky, one of the 1938 defendants, said, or was induced to say, "We were the vanguard of foreign aggression, of international fascism, and not only in the USSR but also in Spain, China, throughout the world." The summation of the "court" contains the statement, "There is not a single man in the world who brought so much sorrow and misfortune to people as Trotsky. He is the vilest agent of fascism... "[30]

Now while this may be no more than verbal insults routinely traded among the international Communists of the 1930s and 40s, it is also notable that the threads behind the self-accusation are consistent with the evidence in this chapter. And further, as we shall see later, Trotsky was able to generate support among international capitalists, who, incidentally, were also supporters of Mussolini and Hitler.[31]

So long as we see all international revolutionaries and all international capitalists as implacable enemies of one another, then we miss a crucial point — that there has indeed been some operational cooperation between international capitalists, including fascists. And there is no a priori reason why we should reject Trotsky as a part of this alliance.

---

[28] U.S. State Dept. Decimal File, 861.00/1351.
[29] U.S. State Dept. Decimal File, 861.00/1341.
[30] *Report of Court Proceedings in the Case of the Anti-Soviet "Bloc of Rightists and Trotskyites"* Heard Before the Military Collegium of the Supreme Court of the USSR (Moscow: People's Commissariat of Justice of the USSR, 1938), p. 293.
[31] See: Thomas Lamont of the Morgans was an early supporter of Mussolini.

This tentative, limited reassessment will be brought into sharp focus when we review the story of Michael Gruzenberg, the chief Bolshevik agent in Scandinavia who under the alias of Alexander Gumberg was also a confidential adviser to the Chase National Bank in New York and later to Floyd Odium of Atlas Corporation. This dual role was known to and accepted by both the Soviets and his American employers. The Gruzenberg story is a case history of international revolution allied with international capitalism.

Colonel MacLean's observations that Trotsky had "strong underground influence" and that his "power was so great that orders were issued that he must be given every consideration" are not at all inconsistent with the Coulter-Gwatkin intervention in Trotsky's behalf; or, for that matter, with those later occurrences, the Stalinist accusations in the Trotskyite show trials of the 1930s. Nor are they inconsistent with the Gruzenberg case. On the other hand, the only known direct link between Trotsky and international banking is through his cousin Abram Givatovzo, who was a private banker in Kiev before the Russian Revolution and in Stockholm after the revolution. While Givatovzo professed antibolshevism, he was in fact acting in behalf of the Soviets in 1918 in currency transactions.

Is it possible an international web (:an be spun from these events? First there's Trotsky, a Russian internationalist revolutionary with German connections who sparks assistance from two supposed supporters of Prince Lvov's government in Russia (Aleinikoff and Wolf, Russians resident in New York). These two ignite the action of a liberal Canadian deputy postmaster general, who in turn intercedes with a prominent British Army major general on the Canadian military staff. These are all verifiable links.

In brief, allegiances may not always be what they are called, or appear. We can, however, *surmise* that Trotsky, Aleinikoff, Wolf, Coulter, and Gwatkin in acting for a common limited objective also had some common higher goal than national allegiance or political label. To emphasize, there is no absolute proof that this is so. It is, at the moment, only a logical supposition from the facts. A loyalty higher than that forged by a common immediate goal need have been no more than that of friendship, although that strains the imagination when we ponder such a polyglot combination. It may also have been promoted by other motives. The picture is yet incomplete.

Chapter III

Lenin and German assistance for the Bolshevik Revolution

It was not until the Bolsheviks had received from us a steady flow of funds through various channels and under varying labels that they were in a position to be able to build up their main organ Pravda, to conduct energetic propaganda and appreciably to extend the originally narrow base of their party.
Von Kühlmann, minister of foreign affairs, to the kaiser, December 3, 1917

In April 1917 Lenin and a party of 32 Russian revolutionaries, mostly Bolsheviks, journeyed by train from Switzerland across Germany through Sweden to Petrograd, Russia. They were on their way to join Leon Trotsky to "complete the revolution." Their trans-Germany transit was approved, facilitated, and financed by the German General Staff. Lenin's transit to Russia was part of a plan approved by the German Supreme Command, apparently not immediately known to the kaiser, to aid in the disintegration of the Russian army and so eliminate Russia from World War I. The possibility that the Bolsheviks might be turned against Germany and Europe did not occur to the German General Staff. Major General Hoffman has written, *"We* neither knew nor foresaw the danger to humanity from the consequences of this journey of the Bolsheviks to Russia."[32]

At the highest level the German political officer who approved Lenin's journey to Russia was Chancellor Theobald von Bethmann-Hollweg, a descendant of the Frankfurt banking family Bethmann, which achieved great prosperity in the nineteenth century. Bethmann-Hollweg was appointed chancellor in 1909 and in November 1913 became the subject of the first vote of censure ever passed by the German Reichstag on a chancellor. It was Bethmann-Hollweg who in 1914 told the world that the German guarantee to Belgium was a mere "scrap of paper." Yet on other war matters — such as the use of unrestricted submarine warfare — Bethmann-Hollweg was ambivalent; in January 1917 he told the kaiser, "I can give Your Majesty neither my assent to the unrestricted submarine warfare nor my refusal." By 1917 Bethmann-Hollweg had lost the Reichstag's support and resigned

---
[32] Max Hoffman, War Diaries and Other Papers (London: M. Secker, 1929), 2:177.

— but not before approving transit of Bolshevik revolutionaries to Russia. The transit instructions from Bethmann-Hollweg went through the state secretary Arthur Zimmermann — who was immediately under Bethmann-Hollweg and who handled day-to-day operational details with the German ministers in both Bern and Copenhagen — to the German minister to Bern in early April 1917. The kaiser himself was not aware of the revolutionary movement until after Lenin had passed into Russia.

While Lenin himself did not know the precise source of the assistance, he certainly knew that the German government was providing some funding. There were, however, intermediate links between the German foreign ministry and Lenin, as the following shows:

```
LENIN'S TRANSFER TO RUSSIA IN APRIL 1917
Final decision    BETHMANN-HOLLWEG
                  (Chancellor)
Intermediary I    ARTHUR ZIMMERMANN
                  (State Secretary)
Intermediary II   BROCKDORFF-RANTZAU
                  (German Minister in Copenhagen)
Intermediary III  ALEXANDER ISRAEL
                  HELPHAND
                  (alias PARVUS)
Intermediary IV   JACOB FURSTENBERG
                  (alias GANETSKY)
                  LENIN, in Switzerland
```

From Berlin Zimmermann and Bethmann-Hollweg communicated with the German minister in Copenhagen, Brockdorff-Rantzau. In turn, Brockdorff-Rantzau was in touch with Alexander Israel Helphand (more commonly known by his alias, Parvus), who was located in Copenhagen.[33] Parvus was the connection to Jacob Furstenberg, a Pole descended from a wealthy family but better known by his alias, Ganetsky. And Jacob Furstenberg was the immediate link to Lenin.

Although Chancellor Bethmann-Hollweg was the final authority for Lenin's transfer, and although Lenin was probably aware of the German origins of the assistance, Lenin cannot be termed a German agent. The German Foreign Ministry assessed Lenin's probable actions in Russia as being consistent with their own objectives in the dissolution of the existing power structure in Russia. Yet both parties also had hidden objectives: Germany wanted

---

[33] Z. A. B. Zeman and W. B. Scharlau, *The Merchant of Revolution... The Life of Alexander Israel Helphand* (Parvus), 1867-1924 (New York: Oxford University Press, 1965).

priority access to the postwar markets in Russia, and Lenin intended to establish a Marxist dictatorship.

The idea of using Russian revolutionaries in this way can be traced back to 1915. On August 14 of that year, Brockdorff-Rantzau wrote the German state undersecretary about a conversation with Helphand (Parvus), and made a strong recommendation to employ Helphand, *"an* extraordinarily important man whose unusual powers I feel we *must* employ for duration of the war... "[34] Included in the report was a warning: *"It might perhaps be risky to want to use the powers ranged behind Helphand, but it would certainly be an admission of our own weakness if we were to refuse their services out of fear of not being able to direct them."*[35]

Brockdorff-Rantzau's ideas of directing or controlling the revolutionaries parallel, as we shall see, those of the Wall Street financiers. It was J.P. Morgan and the American International Corporation that attempted to control both domestic and foreign revolutionaries in the United States for their own purposes.

A subsequent document[36] outlined the terms demanded by Lenin, of which the most interesting was point number seven, which allowed "Russian troops to move into India"; this suggested that Lenin intended to continue the tsarist expansionist program. Zeman also records the role of Max Warburg in establishing a Russian publishing house and adverts to an agreement dated August 12, 1916, in which the German industrialist Stinnes agreed to contribute two million rubles for financing a publishing house in Russia.[37]

Consequently, on April 16, 1917, a trainload of thirty-two, including Lenin, his wife Nadezhda Krupskaya, Grigori Zinoviev, Sokolnikov, and Karl Radek, left the Central Station in Bern en route to Stockholm. When the party reached the Russian frontier only Fritz Plattan and Radek were denied entrance into Russia. The remainder of the party was allowed to enter. Several months later they were followed by almost 200 Mensheviks, including Martov and Axelrod.

It is worth noting that Trotsky, at that time in New York, also had funds traceable to German sources. Further, Von Kuhlmann alludes to Lenin's inability to broaden the base of his Bolshevik party until the Germans supplied funds. Trotsky was a Menshevik who turned Bolshevik only in 1917. This suggests that German funds were perhaps related to Trotsky's change of party label.

---

[34] Z. A. B. Zeman, Germany and the Revolution in Russia, 1915-1918. Documents from the Archives of the German Foreign Ministry (London: Oxford University Press, 1958).
[35] Ibid.
[36] Ibid., p. 6, doc. 6, reporting a conversation with the Fstonian intermediary Keskula.
[37] Ibid., p. 92, n. 3.

THE SISSON DOCUMENTS

In early 1918 Edgar Sisson, the Petrograd representative of the U.S. Committee on Public Information, bought a batch of Russian documents purporting to prove that Trotsky, Lenin, and the other Bolshevik revolutionaries were not only in the pay of, but also agents of, the German government.

These documents, later dubbed the "Sisson Documents," were shipped to the United States in great haste and secrecy. In Washington, D.C. they were submitted to the National Board for Historical Service for authentication. Two prominent historians, J. Franklin Jameson and Samuel N. Harper, testified to their genuineness. These historians divided the Sisson papers into three groups. Regarding Group I, they concluded:

> We have subjected them with great care to all the applicable tests to which historical students are accustomed and... upon the basis of these investigations, we have no hesitation in declaring that we see no reason to doubt the genuineness or authenticity of these fifty-three documents.[38]

The historians were less confident about material in Group II. This group was not rejected as outright forgeries, but it was suggested that they were copies of original documents. Although the historians made "no confident declaration" on Group III, they were not prepared to reject the documents as outright forgeries.

The Sisson Documents were published by the Committee on Public Information, whose chairman was George Creel, a former contributor to the pro-Bolshevik *Masses*. The American press in general accepted the documents as authentic. The notable exception was the *New York Evening Post*, at that time owned by Thomas W. Lamont, a partner in the Morgan firm. When only a few installments had been published, the *Post* challenged the authenticity of all the documents.[39]

We now know that the Sisson Documents were almost all forgeries: only one or two of the minor German circulars were genuine. Even casual examination of the German letterhead suggests that the forgers were unusually careless forgers perhaps working for the gullible American market. The German text was strewn with terms verging on the ridiculous: for example, *Bureau* instead of the German word *Büro;* *Central* for the German *Zentral;* etc.

---

[38] U.S., Committee on Public Information, *The German-Bolshevik Conspiracy*, War Information Series, no. 20, October 1918.
[39] *New York Evening Post*, September 16-18, 21; October 4, 1918. It is also interesting, but not conclusive of anything, that the Bolsheviks also stoutly questioned the authenticity of the documents.

That the documents are forgeries is the conclusion of an exhaustive study by George Kennan[40] and of studies made in the 1920s by the British government. Some documents were based on authentic information and, as Kennan observes, those who forged them certainly had access to some unusually good information. For example, Documents 1, 54, 61, and 67 mention that the Nya Banken in Stockholm served as the conduit for Bolshevik funds from Germany. This conduit has been confirmed in more reliable sources. Documents 54, 63, and 64 mention Furstenberg as the banker-intermediary between the Germans and the Bolshevists; Furstenberg's name appears elsewhere in authentic documents. Sisson's Document 54 mentions Olof Aschberg, and Olof Aschberg by his own statements was the "Bolshevik Banker." Aschberg in 1917 was the director of Nya Banken. Other documents in the Sisson series list names and institutions, such as the German Naptha-Industrial Bank, the Disconto Gesellschaft, and Max Warburg, the Hamburg banker, but hard supportive evidence is more elusive. In general, the Sisson Documents, while themselves outright forgeries, are nonetheless based partly on generally authentic information.

One puzzling aspect in the light of the story in this book is that the documents came to Edgar Sisson from Alexander Gumberg (alias Berg, real name Michael Gruzenberg), the Bolshevik agent in Scandinavia and later a confidential assistant to Chase National Bank and Floyd Odium of Atlas Corporation. The Bolshevists, on the other hand, stridently repudiated the Sisson material. So did John Reed, the American representative on the executive of the Third International and whose paycheck came from *Metropolitan* magazine, which was owned by J.P. Morgan interests.[41] So did Thomas Lamont, the Morgan partner who owned the *New York Evening Post*. There are several possible explanations. Probably the connections between the Morgan interests in New York and such agents as John Reed and Alexander Gumberg were highly flexible. This *could* have been a Gumberg maneuver to discredit Sisson and Creel by planting forged documents; or perhaps Gumberg was working in his own interest.

The Sisson Documents "prove" exclusive German involvement with the Bolsheviks. They also have been used to "prove" a Jewish-Bolshevik conspiracy theory along the lines of that of the Protocols of Zion. In 1918 the U.S. government wanted to unite American opinion behind an unpopular war with Germany, and the Sisson Documents dramatically "proved" the exclusive complicity of Germany with the Bolshevists. The documents also provided a smoke screen against public knowledge of the events to be described in this book.

---

[40] George F. Kennan, "The Sisson Documents," *Journal of Modern History* 27-28 (1955-56): 130-154.
[41] John Reed, *The Sisson Documents* (New York: Liberator Publishing, n.d.).

THE TUG-OF-WAR IN WASHINGTON[42]

A review of documents in the State Department Decimal File suggests that the State Department and Ambassador Francis in Petrograd were quite well informed about the intentions and progress of the Bolshevik movement. In the summer of 1917, for example, the State Department wanted to stop the departure from the U.S. of "injurious persons" (that is, returning Russian revolutionaries) but was unable to do so because they were using new Russian and American passports. The preparations for the Bolshevik Revolution itself were well known at least six weeks before it came about. One report in the State Department files states, in regard to the Kerensky forces, that it was "doubtful whether government... [can] suppress outbreak." Disintegration of the Kerensky government was reported throughout September and October as were Bolshevik preparations for a coup. The British government warned British residents in Russia to leave at least six weeks before the Bolshevik phase of the revolution.

The first full report of the events of early November reached Washington on December 9, 1917. This report described the low-key nature of the revolution itself, mentioned that General William V. Judson had made an unauthorized visit to Trotsky, and pointed out the presence of Germans in Smolny — the Soviet headquarters.

On November 28, 1917, President Woodrow Wilson ordered no interference with the Bolshevik Revolution. This instruction was apparently in response to a request by Ambassador Francis for an Allied conference, to which Britain had already agreed. The State Department argued that such a conference was impractical. There were discussions in Paris between the Allies and Colonel Edward M. House, who reported these to Woodrow Wilson as "long and frequent discussions on Russia." Regarding such a conference, House stated that England was "passively willing," France "*in*differently against," and Italy "actively so." Woodrow Wilson, shortly thereafter, approved a cable authored by Secretary of State Robert Lansing, which provided financial assistance for the Kaledin movement (December 12, 1917). There were also rumors filtering into Washington that "monarchists working with the Bolsheviks and same supported by various occurrences and circumstances"; that the Smolny government was absolutely under control of the German General Staff; and rumors elsewhere that "many or most of them [that is, Bolshevists] are from America."

In December, General Judson again visited Trotsky; this was looked upon as a step towards recognition by the U.S., although a report dated February 5, 1918, from Ambassador Francis to Washington, recommended against recognition. A memorandum originating with

---

[42] This part is based on section 861.00 of the U.S. State Dept. Decimal File, also available as National Archives rolls 10 and 11 of microcopy 316.

Basil Miles in Washington argued that "we should deal with all authorities in Russia including Bolsheviks." And on February 15, 1918, the State Department cabled Ambassador Francis in Petrograd, stating that the "department desires you gradually to keep in somewhat closer and informal touch with the Bolshevik authorities using such channels as will avoid any official recognition."

The next day Secretary of State Lansing conveyed the following to the French ambassador J. J. Jusserand in Washington: "*It* is considered inadvisable to take any action which will antagonize at this time any of the various elements of the people which now control the power in Russia..."[43]

On February 20, Ambassador Francis cabled Washington to report the approaching end of the Bolshevik government. Two weeks later, on March 7, 1918, Arthur Bullard reported to Colonel House that German money was subsidizing the Bolsheviks and that this subsidy was more substantial than previously thought. Arthur Bullard (of the U.S. Committee on Public Information) argued: *"we* ought to be ready to help any honest national government. But men or money or equipment sent to the present rulers of Russia will be used against Russians at least as much as against Germans."[44]

This was followed by another message from Bullard to Colonel House: "I strongly advise against giving material help to the present Russian government. Sinister elements in Soviets seem to be gaining control."

But there were influential counterforces at work. As early as November 28, 1917, Colonel House cabled President Woodrow Wilson from Paris that it was "exceedingly important" that U.S. newspaper comments advocating that "Russia should be treated as an enemy" be "suppressed." Then next month William Franklin Sands, executive secretary of the Morgan-controlled American International Corporation and a friend of the previously mentioned Basil Miles, submitted a memorandum that described Lenin and Trotsky as appealing to the masses and that urged the U.S. to recognize Russia. Even American socialist Walling complained to the Department of State about the pro-Soviet attitude of George Creel (of the U.S. Committee on Public Information), Herbert Swope, and William Boyce Thompson (of the Federal Reserve Bank of New York).

On December 17, 1917, there appeared in a Moscow newspaper an attack on Red Cross colonel Raymond Robins and Thompson, alleging a link between the Russian Revolution and American bankers:

---

[43] U.S. State Dept. Decimal File, 861.00/1117a. The same message was conveyed to the Italian ambassador.
[44] See Arthur Bullard papers at Princeton University.

> Why are they so interested in enlightenment? Why was the money given the socialist revolutionaries and not to the constitutional democrats? One would suppose the latter nearer and dearer to hearts of bankers.

The article goes on to argue that this was because American capital viewed Russia as a future market and thus wanted to get a firm foothold. The money was given to the revolutionaries because

> the backward working men and peasants trust the social revolutionaries. At the time when the money was passed the social revolutionaries were in power and it was supposed they would remain in control in Russia for some time.

Another report, dated December 12, 1917, and relating to Raymond Robins, details "negotiation with a group of American bankers of the American Red Cross Mission"; the "negotiation" related to a payment of two million dollars. On January 22, 1918, Robert L Owen, chairman of the U.S. Senate Committee on Banking and Currency and linked to Wall Street interests, sent a letter to Woodrow Wilson recommending de facto recognition of Russia, permission for a shipload of goods urgently needed in Russia, the appointment of representatives to Russia to offset German influence, and the establishment of a career-service group in Russia.

This approach was consistently aided by Raymond Robins in Russia. For example, on February 15, 1918, a cable from Robins in Petrograd to Davison in the Red Cross in Washington (and to be forwarded to William Boyce Thompson) argued that support be given to the Bolshevik authority for as long as possible, and that the new revolutionary Russia will turn to the United States as it has "broken with the German imperialism." According to Robins, the Bolsheviks wanted United States assistance and cooperation together with railroad reorganization, because "by generous assistance and technical advice in reorganizing commerce and industry America may entirely exclude German commerce during balance of war."

In brief, the tug-of-war in Washington reflected a struggle between, on one side, old-line diplomats (such as Ambassador Francis) and lower-level departmental officials, and, on the other, financiers like Robins, Thompson, and Sands with allies such as Lansing and Miles in the State Department and Senator Owen in the Congress.

CHAPTER IV

WALL STREET AND WORLD REVOLUTION

What you Radicals and we who hold opposing views differ about, is not so much the end as the means, not so much what should be brought about as how it should, and can, be brought about...
Otto H. Kahn, director, American International Corp., and partner, Kuhn, Loeb & Co., speaking to the League/or Industrial Democracy, New York, December 30, 1924

Before World War I, the financial and business structure of the United States was dominated by two conglomerates: Standard Oil, or the Rockefeller enterprise, and the Morgan complex of industries — finance and transportation companies. Rockefeller and Morgan trust alliances dominated not only Wall Street but, through interlocking directorships, almost the entire economic fabric of the United States.[45] Rockefeller interests monopolized the petroleum and allied industries, and controlled the copper trust, the smelters trust, and the gigantic tobacco trust, in addition to having influence in some Morgan properties such as the U.S. Steel Corporation as well as in hundreds of smaller industrial trusts, public service operations, railroads, and banking institutions. National City Bank was the largest of the banks influenced by Standard Oil-Rockefeller, but financial control extended to the United States Trust Company and Hanover National Bank as well as to major life insurance companies — Equitable Life and Mutual of New York.

The great Morgan enterprises were in steel, shipping, and the electrical industry; they included General Electric, the rubber trust, and railroads. Like Rockefeller, Morgan controlled financial corporations — the National Bank of Commerce and the Chase National Bank, New York Life Insurance, and the Guaranty Trust Company. The names J.P. Morgan and Guaranty Trust Company occur repeatedly throughout this book. In the early part of the twentieth century the Guaranty Trust Company was dominated by the Harriman interests. When the elder Harriman (Edward Henry) died in 1909, Morgan and associates bought into Guaranty Trust as well as into Mutual Life and New York Life. In 1919 Morgan also bought control of Equitable Life, and the Guaranty Trust Company absorbed an additional six lesser trust companies. Therefore, at the end of World War I the Guaranty Trust and Bankers

---

[45] John Moody, *The Truth about the Trusts* (New York: Moody Publishing, 1904).

Trust were, respectively, the first and second largest trust companies in the United States, both dominated by Morgan interests.[46]

American financiers associated with these groups were involved in financing revolution even before 1917. Intervention by the Wall Street law firm of Sullivan & Cromwell into the Panama Canal controversy is recorded in 1913 congressional hearings. The episode is summarized by Congressman Rainey:

> It is my contention that the representatives of this Government [United States] made possible the revolution on the isthmus of Panama. That had it not been for the interference of this Government a successful revolution could not possibly have occurred, and I contend that this Government violated the treaty of 1846. I will be able to produce evidence to show that the declaration of independence which was promulgated in Panama on the 3rd day of November, 1903, was prepared right here in New York City and carried down there — prepared in the office of Wilson (sic) Nelson Cromwell[47].

Congressman Rainey went on to state that only ten or twelve of the top Panamanian revolutionists plus "the officers of the Panama Railroad & Steamship Co., who were under the control of William Nelson Cromwell, of New York and the State Department officials in Washington," knew about the impending revolution.[48] The purpose of the revolution was to deprive Colombia, of which Panama was then a part, of $40 million and to acquire control of the Panama Canal.

The best-documented example of Wall Street intervention in revolution is the operation of a New York syndicate in the Chinese revolution of 1912, which was led by Sun Yat-sen. Although the final gains of the syndicate remain unclear, the intention and role of the New York financing group are fully documented down to amounts of money, information on affiliated Chinese secret societies, and shipping lists of armaments to be purchased. The New York bankers syndicate for the Sun Yat-sen revolution included Charles B. Hill, an attorney with the law firm of Hunt, Hill & Betts. In 1912 the firm was located at 165 Broadway, New York, but in 1917 it moved to 120 Broadway (see chapter eight for the significance of this address). Charles B. Hill was director of several Westinghouse subsidiaries, including Bryant Electric, Perkins Electric Switch, and Westinghouse Lamp — all affiliated with Westinghouse Electric whose New York office was also located at 120 Broadway. Charles R.

---

[46] The J. P. Morgan Company was originally founded in London as George Peabody and Co. in 1838. It was not incorporated until March 21, 1940. The company ceased to exist in April 1954 when it merged with the Guaranty Trust Company, then its most important commercial bank subsidiary, and is today known as the Morgan Guarantee Trust Company of New York.
[47] United States, House, Committee on Foreign Affairs, *The Story of Panama*, Hearings on the Rainey Resolution, 1913. p. 53.
[48] Ibid., p. 60.

Crane, organizer of Westinghouse subsidiaries in Russia, had a known role in the first and second phases of the Bolshevik Revolution (see page 26).

The work of the 1910 Hill syndicate in China is recorded in the Laurence Boothe Papers at the Hoover Institution.[49] These papers contain over 110 related items, including letters of Sun Yat-sen to and from his American backers. In return for financial support, Sun Yat-sen promised the Hill syndicate railroad, banking, and commercial concessions in the new revolutionary China.

Another case of revolution supported by New York financial institutions concerned that of Mexico in 1915-16. Von Rintelen, a German espionage agent in the United States[50], was accused during his May 1917 trial in New York City of attempting to "embroil" the U.S. with Mexico and Japan in order to divert ammunition then flowing to the Allies in Europe.[51] Payment for the ammunition that was shipped from the United States to the Mexican revolutionary Pancho Villa, was made through Guaranty Trust Company. Von Rintelen's adviser, Sommerfeld, paid $380,000 via Guaranty Trust and Mississippi Valley Trust Company to the Western Cartridge Company of Alton, Illinois, for ammunition shipped to El Paso, for forwarding to Villa. This was in mid-1915. On January 10, 1916, Villa murdered seventeen American miners at Santa Isabel and on March 9, 1916, Villa raided Columbus, New Mexico, and killed eighteen more Americans.

Wall Street involvement in these Mexican border raids was the subject of a letter (October 6, 1916) from Lincoln Steffens, an American Communist, to Colonel House, an aide' to Woodrow Wilson:

> My dear Colonel House:
> Just before I left New York last Monday, I was told convincingly that "Wall Street" had completed arrangements for one more raid of Mexican bandits into the United States: to be so timed and so atrocious that it would settle the election.[52]

Once in power in Mexico, the Carranza government purchased additional arms in the United States. The American Gun Company contracted to ship 5,000 Mausers and a shipment license was issued by the War Trade Board for 15,000 guns and 15,000,000 rounds of ammunition. The American ambassador to Mexico, Fletcher, "flatly refused to recommend or sanction the shipment of any munitions, rifles, etc., to Carranza."[53] However, intervention by Secretary of State Robert Lansing reduced the barrier to one of a temporary delay, and

---

[49] Stanford, Calif. See also the Los Angeles Times, October 13, 1966.
[50] Later codirector with Hjalmar Schacht (Hitler's banker) and Emil Wittenberg, of the Nationalbank für Deutschland.
[51] United States, Senate, Committee on Foreign Relations, *Investigation of Mexican Affairs*, 1920.
[52] Lincoln Steffens, *The Letters of Lincoln Steffens* (New York: Harcourt, Brace, 1941, P. 386)
[53] U.S., Senate, Committee on Foreign Relations, *Investigation of Mexican Affairs*, 1920, pts. 2, 18, p. 681.

"in a short while... [the American Gun Company] would be permitted to make the shipment and deliver."[54]

The raids upon the U.S. by the Villa and the Carranza forces were reported in the *New York Times* as the "Texas Revolution" (a kind of dry run for the Bolshevik Revolution) and were undertaken jointly by Germans and Bolsheviks. The testimony of John A. Walls, district attorney of Brownsville, Texas, before the 1919 Fall Committee yielded documentary evidence of the link between Bolshevik interests in the United States, German activity, and the Carranza forces in Mexico.[55] Consequently, the Carranza government, the first in the world with a Soviet-type constitution (which was written by Trotskyites), was a government with support on Wall Street. The Carranza revolution probably could not have succeeded without American munitions and Carranza would not have remained in power as long as he did without American help.[56]

Similar intervention in the 1917 Bolshevik Revolution in Russia revolves around Swedish banker and intermediary Olof Aschberg. Logically the story begins with prerevolutionary tsarist loans by Wall Street bank syndicates.

AMERICAN BANKERS AND TSARIST LOANS

In August 1914 Europe went to war. Under international law neutral countries (and the United States was neutral until April 1917) could not raise loans for belligerent countries. This was a question of law as well as morality.

When the Morgan house floated war loans for Britain and France in 1915, J.P. Morgan argued that these were not war loans at all but merely a means of facilitating international trade. Such a distinction had indeed been elaborately made by President Wilson in October 1914; he explained that the sale of bonds in the U.S. for foreign governments was in effect a loan of savings to belligerent governments and did not finance a war. On the other hand, acceptance of Treasury notes or other evidence of debt in payment for articles was only a means of facilitating trade and not of financing a war effort.[57]

Documents in the State Department files demonstrate that the National City Bank, controlled by Stillman and Rockefeller interests, and the Guaranty Trust, controlled by Morgan interests, jointly raised substantial loans for the belligerent Russia before U.S. entry into the war, and that these loans were raised *after* the State Department pointed out to these firms

---

[54] Ibid.
[55] *New York Times*, January 23, 1919.
[56] U.S., Senate, Committee on Foreign Relations, op. cit., pp. 795-96.
[57] U.S., Senate, Hearings Before the Special Committee Investigating the Munitions Industry, 73-74th Cong., 1934-37, pt. 25, p. 76-66.

that they were contrary to international law. Further, negotiations for the loans were undertaken through official U.S. government communications facilities under cover of the top-level "Green Cipher" of the State Department. Below are extracts from State Department cables that will make the case.

On May 94, 1916, Ambassador Francis in Petrograd sent the following cable to the State Department in Washington for forwardin to Frank Arthur Vanderlip, then chairman of the National City Bank in New York. The cable was sent in Green Cipher and was enciphered and deciphered by U.S. State Department officers in Petrograd and Washington at the taxpayers' expense (file 861.51/110).

> 563, May 94, 1 p.m.
> For Vanderlip National City Bank New York. Five. Our previous opinions credit strengthened. We endorse plan cabled as safe investment plus very attractive speculation in roubles. In view of guarantee of exchange rate have placed rate somewhat above present market. Owing unfavorable opinion created by long delay have on own responsibility offered take twenty-five million dollars. We think large portion of all should be retained by bank and allied institutions. With clause respect customs bonds become practical lien on more than one hundred and fifty million dollars per annum customs making absolute security and secures market even if *defect*. We consider three [years?] option on bonds very valuable and for that reason amount of rouble credit should be enlarged by group or by distribution to close friends. American International should take block and we would inform Government. Think group should be formed at once to take and issue of bonds... should secure full cooperation guaranty. Suggest you see Jack personally, use every endeavor to get them really work otherwise cooperate guarantee form new group. Opportunities here during the next ten years very great along state and industrial financiering and if this transaction consummated doubtless should be established. In answering bear in mind situation regarding cable.
>
> MacRoberts Rich.

FRANCIS, AMERICAN AMBASSADOR[58]

There are several points to note about the above cable to understand the story that follows. First, note the reference to American International Corporation, a Morgan firm, and a name that turns up again and again in this story. Second, "guarantee" refers to Guaranty Trust Company. Third, *"MacRoberts"* was Samuel MacRoberts, a vice president and the executive manager of National City Bank.

---

[58] U.S. State Dept. Decimal File, 861.51/110 (316-116-682).

On May 24, 1916, Ambassador Francis cabled a message from Rolph Marsh of Guaranty Trust in Petrograd to Guaranty Trust in New York, again in the special Green Cipher and again using the facilities of the State Department. This cable reads as follows:

> 565, May 24, 6 p.m.
> for Guaranty Trust Company New York: Three.
> Olof and self consider the new proposition takes care Olof and will help rather than harm your prestige. Situation such cooperation necessary if big things are to be accomplished here. Strongly urge your arranging with City to consider and act jointly in all big propositions here. Decided advantages for both and prevents playing one against other. City representatives here desire (hand written) such co-operation. Proposition being considered eliminates our credit in name also option but we both consider the rouble credit with the bond option in propositions. Second paragraph offers wonderful profitable opportunity, strongly urge your acceptance. Please cable me full authority to act in connection with City. Consider our entertaining proposition satisfactory situation for us and permits doing big things. Again strongly urge your taking twenty-five million of rouble credit. No possibility loss and decided speculative advantages. Again urge having Vice President upon the ground. Effect here will be decidedly good. Resident Attorney does not carry same prestige and weight. This goes through Embassy by code answer same way. See cable on possibilities.
> ROLPH MARSH. FRANCIS, AMERICAN AMBASSADOR

Note:—Entire Message in Green Cipher. TELEGRAPH ROOM[59]

"Olof" in the cable was Olof Aschberg, Swedish banker and head of the Nya Banken in Stockholm. Aschberg had been in New York in 1915 conferring with the Morgan firm on these Russian loans. Now, in 1916, he was in Petrograd with Rolph Marsh of Guaranty Trust and Samuel MacRoberts and Rich of National City Bank ("City" in cable) arranging loans for a Morgan-Rockefeller consortium. The following year, Aschberg, as we shall see later, would be known as the "Bolshevik Banker," and his own memoirs reproduce evidence of his right to the title.

The State Department files also contain a series of cables between Ambassador Francis, Acting Secretary Frank Polk, and Secretary of State Robert Lansing concerning the legality and propriety of transmitting National City Bank and Guaranty Trust cables at public expense. On May 25, 1916, Ambassador Francis cabled Washington as follows and referred to the two previous cables:

> 569, May 25, one p.m.

---

[59] U.S. State Dept. Decimal File, 861.51/112.

My telegram 563 and 565 May twenty-fourth are sent for local representatives of institutions addressed in the hope of consummating loan which would largely increase international trade and greatly benefit [diplomatic relations?]. Prospect for success promising. Petrograd representatives consider terms submitted very satisfactory but fear such representations to their institutions would prevent consummation loan if Government here acquainted these proposals.

FRANCIS, AMERICAN AMBASSADOR.[60]

The basic reason cited by Francis for facilitating the cables is "the hope of consummating loan which would largely increase international trade." Transmission of commercial messages using State Department facilities had been prohibited, and on June 1, 1916, Polk cabled Francis:

842

In view of Department's regulation contained in its circular telegraphic instruction of March fifteenth, (discontinuance of forwarding Commercial messages)[61] 1915, please explain why messages in your 563, 565 and 575, should be communicated.
Hereafter please follow closely Department's instructions.
Acting. Polk
861.51/112/110

Then on June 8, 1916, Secretary of State Lansing expanded the prohibition and clearly stated that the proposed loans were illegal:

860 Your 563, 565, May 24, g: 569 May 25.1 pm Before delivering messages to Vanderlip and Guaranty Trust Company, I must inquire whether they refer to Russian Government loans of any description. If they do, I regret that the Department can not be a party to their transmission, as such action would submit it to justifiable criticism because of participation by this Government in loan transaction by a belligerent for the purpose of carrying on its hostile operations. Such participation is contrary to the accepted rule of international law that neutral Governments should not lend their assistance to the raising of war loans by belligerents.

The last line of the Lansing cable as written, was not transmitted to Petrograd. The line read: "Cannot arrangements be made to send these messages through Russian channels?"
How can we assess these cables and the parties involved?

---

[60] U.S. State Dept. Decimal File, 861.51/111.
[61] Handwritten in parentheses.

Clearly the Morgan-Rockefeller interests were not interested in abiding by international law. There is obvious intent in these cables to supply loans to belligerents. There was no hesitation on the part of these firms to use State Department facilities for the negotiations. Further, in spite of protests, the State Department allowed the messages to go through. Finally, and most interesting for subsequent events, Olof Aschberg, the Swedish banker, was a prominent participant and intermediary in the negotiations on behalf of Guaranty Trust. Let us therefore take a closer look at Olof Aschberg.

OLOF ASCHBERG IN NEW YORK, 1916

Olof Aschberg, the "Bolshevik Banker" (or "Bankier der Weltrevolution," as he has been called in the German press), was owner of the Nya Banken, founded 1912 in Stockholm. His codirectors included prominent members of Swedish cooperatives and Swedish socialists, including G. W. Dahl, K. G. Rosling, and C. Gerhard Magnusson.[62] In 1918 Nya Banken was placed on the Allied black-list for its financial operations in behalf of Germany. In response to the blacklisting, Nya Banken changed its name to Svensk Ekonomiebolaget. The bank remained under the control of Aschberg, and was mainly owned by him. The bank's London agent was the British Bank of North Commerce, whose chairman was Earl Grey, former associate of Cecil Rhodes. Others in Aschberg's interesting circle of business associates included Krassin, who was until the Bolshevik Revolution (when he changed color to emerge as a leading Bolshevik) Russian manager of Siemens-Schukert in Petrograd; Carl Furstenberg, minister of finance in the first Bolshevik government; and Max May, vice president in charge of foreign operations for Guaranty Trust of New York. Olof Aschberg thought so highly of Max May that a photograph of May is included in Aschberg's book.[63]

In the summer of 1916 Olof Aschberg was in New York representing both Nya Banken and Pierre Bark, the tsarist minister of finance. Aschberg's prime business in New York, according to the *New York Times* (August 4, 1916), was to negotiate a $50 million loan for Russia with an American banking syndicate headed by Stillman's National City Bank. This business was concluded on June 5, 1916; the results were a Russian credit of $50 million in New York at a bank charge of 7 1/2 percent per annum, and a corresponding 150-million-ruble credit for the NCB syndicate in Russia. The New York syndicate then turned around and issued 6 1/2 percent certificates in its own name in the U.S. market to the amount of $50 million. Thus, the NCB syndicate made a profit on the $50 million loan to

---

[62] Olof Aschberg, *En Vandrande Jude Från Glasbruksgatan* (Stockholm: Albert Bonniers Förlag, n.d.), pp. 98-99, which is included in *Memoarer* (Stockholm: Albert Bonniers Förlag, 1946). See also Gästboken (Stockholm: Tidens Förlag, 1955) for further material on Aschberg.
[63] Aschberg, p. 123.

Russia, floated it on the American market for another profit, and obtained a 150- million-ruble credit in Russia.

During his New York visit on behalf of the tsarist Russian government, Aschberg made some prophetic comments concerning the future for America in Russia:

> The opening for American capital and American initiative, with the awakening brought by the war, will be country-wide when the struggle is over. There are now many Americans in Petrograd, representatives of business firms, keeping in touch with the situation, and as soon as the change comes a huge American trade with Russia should spring up.[64]

OLOF ASCHBERG IN THE BOLSHEVIK REVOLUTION

While this tsarist loan operation was being floated in New York, Nya Banken and Olof Aschberg were funneling funds from the German government to Russian revolutionaries, who would eventually bring down the "Kerensky committee" and establish the Bolshevik regime.

The evidence for Olof Aschberg's intimate connection with financing the Bolshevik Revolution comes from several sources, some of greater value than others. The Nya Banken and Olof Aschberg are prominently cited in the Sisson papers (see chapter three); however, George Kennan has systematically analyzed these papers and shown them to be forged, although they are probably based in part on authentic material. Other evidence originates with Colonel B. V. Nikitine, in charge of counterintelligence in the Kerensky government, and consists of twenty-nine telegrams transmitted from Stockholm to Petrograd, and vice versa, regarding financing of the Bolsheviks. Three of these telegrams refer to banks — telegrams 10 and 11 refer to Nya Banken, and telegram 14 refers to the Russo-Asiatic Bank in Petrograd. Telegram 10 reads as follows:

> Gisa Furstenberg Saltsjobaden. Funds very low cannot assist if really urgent give 500 as last payment pencils huge loss original hopeless instruct Nya Banken cable further 100 thousand Sumenson.

Telegram 11 reads:

> Kozlovsky Sergievskaya 81. First letters received Nya Banken telegraphed cable who Soloman offering local telegraphic agency refers to Bronck Savelievich Avilov.

---

[64] *New York Times*, August 4, 1916.

Fürstenberg was the intermediary between Parvus (Alexander I. Helphand) and the German government. About these transfers, Michael Futrell concludes:

> It was discovered that during the last few months she [Evegeniya Sumenson] had received nearly a million rubles from Furstenberg through the Nya Banken in Stockholm, and that this money came from German sources.[65]

Telegram 14 of the Nikitine series reads: "Furstenberg Saltsjöbaden. Number 90 period hundred thousand into Russo-Asiatic Sumenson." The U.S. representative for Russo-Asiatic was MacGregor Grant Company at 120 Broadway, New York City, and the bank was financed by Guaranty Trust in the U.S. and Nya Banken in Sweden.

Another mention of the Nya Banken is in the material "The Charges Against the Bolsheviks," which was published in the Kerensky period. Particularly noteworthy in that material is a document signed by Gregory Alexinsky, a former member of the Second State Duma, in reference to monetary transfers to the Bolsheviks. The document, in part, reads as follows:

> In accordance with the information just received these trusted persons in Stockholm were: the Bolshevik Jacob Furstenberg, better known under the name of "Hanecki" (Ganetskii), and Parvus (Dr. Helfand); in Petrograd: the Bolshevik attorney, M. U. Kozlovsky, a woman relative of Hanecki — Sumenson, engaged in speculation together with Hanecki, and others. Kozlovsky is the chief receiver of German money, which is transferred from Berlin through the "Disconto-Gesellschaft" to the Stockholm "Via Bank," and thence to the Siberian Bank in Petrograd, where his account at present has a balance of over 2,000,000 rubles. The military censorship has unearthed an uninterrupted exchange of telegrams of a political and financial nature between the German agents and Bolshevik leaders [Stockholm-Petrograd].[66]

Further, there is in the State Dept. files a Green Cipher message from the U.S. embassy in Christiania (named Oslo, 1925), Norway, dated February 21, 1918, that reads: "Am informed that Bolshevik funds are deposited in Nya Banken, Stockholm, Legation Stockholm advised. Schmedeman."[67]

Finally, Michael Furtell, who interviewed Olof Aschberg just before his death, concludes that Bolshevik funds were indeed transferred from Germany through Nya Banken and Jacob Furstenberg in the guise of payment for goods shipped. According to Futrell, Aschberg

---

[65] Michael Futrell, *Northern Underground* (London: Faber and Faber, 1963), p. 162.
[66] See Robert Paul Browder and Alexander F. Kerensky, *The Russian Provisional government, 1917* (Stanford, Calif.: Stanford University Perss, 1961), 3: 1365. "Via Bank" is obviously Nya Banken.
[67] U.S. State Dept. Decimal File, 861.00/1130.

confirmed to him that Furstenberg had a commercial business with Nya Banken and that Furstenberg had also sent funds to Petrograd. These statements are authenticated in Aschberg's memoirs (see page 70). In sum, Aschberg, through his Nya Banken, was undoubtedly a channel for funds used in the Bolshevik Revolution, and Guaranty Trust was indirectly linked through its association with Aschberg and its interest in MacGregor Grant Co., New York, agent of the Russo-Asiatic Bank, another transfer vehicle.

NYA BANKEN AND GUARANTY TRUST JOIN RUSKOMBANK

Several years later, in the fall of 1922, the Soviets formed their first international bank. It was based on a syndicate that involved the former Russian private bankers and some new investment from German, Swedish, American, and British bankers. Known as the Ruskombank (Foreign Commercial Bank or the Bank of Foreign Commerce), it was headed by Olof Aschberg; its board consisted of tsarist private bankers, representatives of German, Swedish, and American banks, and, of course, representatives of the Soviet Union. The U.S. Stockholm legation reported to Washington on this question and noted, in a reference to Aschberg, that "his reputation is poor. He was referred to in Document 54 of the Sisson documents and Dispatch No. 138 of January 4, 1921 from a legation in Copenhagen."[68]

The foreign banking consortium involved in the Ruskombank represented mainly British capital. It included Russo-Asiatic Consolidated Limited, which was one of the largest private creditors of Russia, and which was granted £3 million by the Soviets to compensate for damage to its properties in the Soviet Union by nationalization. The British government itself had already purchased substantial interests in the Russian private banks; according to a State Department report, "The British Government is heavily invested in the consortium in question."[69]

The consortium was granted extensive concessions in Russia and the bank had a share capital of ten million gold rubles. A report in the Danish newspaper *National Titende* stated that "possibilities have been created for cooperation with the Soviet government where this,

---

[68] U.S. State Dept. Decimal File, 861.516/129, August 28, 1922. A State Dept. report from Stockholm, dated October 9, 1922 (861.516/137), states in regard to Aschberg, "I met Mr. Aschberg some weeks ago and in the conversation with him he substantially stated all that appeared in this report. He also asked me to inquire whether he could visit the United States and gave as references some of the prominent banks. In connection with this, however, I desire to call the department's attention to Document 54 of the Sisson Documents, and also to many other dispatches which this legation wrote concerning this man during the war, whose reputation and standing is not good. He is undoubtedly working closely in connection with the Soviets, and during the entire war he was in close cooperation with the Germans" (U.S. State Dept. Decimal File, 861.516/137, Stockholm, October 9, 1922. The report was signed by Ira N. Morris).

[69] Ibid. 861.516/130, September 13, 1922.

by political negotiations, would have been impossible."[70] In other words, as the newspaper goes on to say, the politicians had failed to achieve cooperation with the Soviets, but "it may be taken for granted that the capitalistic exploitation of Russia is beginning to assume more definite forms."[71]

In early October 1922 Olof Aschberg met in Berlin with Emil Wittenberg, director of the Nationalbank fur Deutschland, and Scheinmann, head of the Russian State Bank. After discussions concerning German involvement in the Ruskombank, the three bankers went to Stockholm and there met with Max May, vice president of the Guaranty Trust Company. Max May was then designated director of the Foreign Division of the Ruskombank, in addition to Schlesinger, former head of the Moscow Merchant Bank; Kalaschkin, former head of the Junker Bank; and Ternoffsky, former head of the Siberian Bank. The last bank had been partly purchased by the British government in 1918. Professor Gustav Cassell of Sweden agreed to act as adviser to Ruskombank. Cassell was quoted in a Swedish newspaper *(Svenskadagbladet* of October 17, 1922) as follows:

> That a bank has now been started in Russia to take care of purely banking matters is a great step forward, and it seems to me that this bank was established in order to do something to create a new economic life in Russia. What Russia needs is a bank to create internal and external commerce. If there is to be any business between Russia and other countries there must be a bank to handle it. This step forward should be supported in every way by other countries, and when I was asked my advice I stated that I was prepared to give it. I am not in favor of a negative policy and believe that every opportunity should be seized to help in a positive reconstruction. The great question is how to bring the Russian exchange back to normal. It is a complicated question and will necessitate thorough investigation. To solve this problem I am naturally more than willing to take part in the work. To leave Russia to her own resources and her own fate is folly.[72]

The former Siberian Bank building in Petrograd was used as the head office of the Ruskombank, whose objectives were to raise short-term loans in foreign countries, to introduce foreign capital into the Soviet Union, and generally to facilitate Russian overseas trade. It opened on December 1, 1922, in Moscow and employed about 300 persons.

In Sweden Ruskombank was represented by the Svenska Ekonomibolaget of Stockholm, Olof Aschberg's Nya Banken under a new name, and in Germany by the Garantie und

---

[70] Ibid.
[71] Ibid.
[72] Ibid., 861.516/140, Stockholm, October 23, 1922.

Creditbank fur Den Osten of Berlin. In the United States the bank was represented by the Guaranty Trust Company of New York. On opening the bank, Olof Aschberg commented:

> The new bank will look after the purchasing of machinery and raw material from England and the United States and it will give guarantees for the completion of contracts. The question of purchases in Sweden has not yet arisen, but it is hoped that such will be the case later on.[73]

On joining Ruskombank, Max May of Guaranty Trust made a similar statement:

> The United States, being a rich country with well developed industries, does not need to import anything from foreign countries, but... it is greatly interested in exporting its products to other countries and considers Russia the most suitable market for that purpose, taking into consideration the vast requirements of Russia in all lines of its economic life.[74]

May stated that the Russian Commercial Bank was "very important" and that it would "largely finance all lines of Russian industries."

From the very beginning the operations of the Ruskombank were restricted by the Soviet foreign- trade monopoly. The bank had difficulties in obtaining advances on Russian goods deposited abroad. Because they were transmitted in the name of Soviet trade delegations, a great deal of Ruskombank funds were locked up in deposits with the Russian State Bank. Finally, in early 1924 the Russian Commercial Bank was fused with the Soviet foreign-trade commissariat, and Olof Aschberg was dismissed from his position at the bank because, it was claimed in Moscow, he had misused bank funds. His original connection with the bank was because of his friendship with Maxim Litvinov. Through this association, so runs a State Department report, Olof Aschberg had access to large sums of money for the purpose of meeting payments on goods ordered by Soviets in Europe:

> These sums apparently were placed in the Ekonomibolaget, a private banking company, owned by Mr. Aschberg. It is now alledged [sic] that a large portion of these funds were employed by Mr. Aschberg for making investments for his personal account and that he is now endeavoring to maintain his position in the bank through his possession of this money. According to my informant Mr. Aschberg has not been the sole one to profit by his

---

[73] Ibid., 861.516/147, December 8, 1922.
[74] Ibid., 861.516/144, November 18, 1922.

operations with the Soviet funds, but has divided the gains with those who are responsible for his appointment in the Russian Commerce Bank, among them being Litvinoff.[75]

Ruskombank then became Vneshtorg, by which it is known today.

We now have to retrace our steps and look at the activities of Aschberg's New York associate, Guaranty Trust Company, during World War I, to lay the foundation for examination of its role in the revolutionary era in Russia.

GUARANTY TRUST AND GERMAN ESPIONAGE IN THE UNITED STATES, 1914-1917[76]

During World War I Germany raised considerable funds in New York for espionage and covert operations in North America and South America. It is important to record the flow of these funds because it runs from the same firms — Guaranty Trust and American International Corporation — that were involved in the Bolshevik Revolution and its aftermath. Not to mention the fact (outlined in chapter three) that the German government also financed Lenin's revolutionary activities.

A summary of the loans granted by American banks to German interests in World War I was given to the 1919 Overman Committee of the United States Senate by U.S. Military Intelligence. The summary was based on the deposition of Karl Heynen, who came to the United States in April 1915 to assist Dr. Albert with the commercial and financial affairs of the German government. Heynen's official work was the transportation of goods from the United States to Germany by way of Sweden, Switzerland, and Holland. In fact, he was up to his ears in covert operations.

The major German loans raised in the United States between 1915 and 1918, according to Heynen, were as follows: The first loan, of $400,000, was made about September 1914 by the investment bankers Kuhn, Loeb & Co. Collateral of 25 million marks was deposited with Max M. Warburg in Hamburg, the German affiliate of Kuhn, Loeb & Co. Captain George B. Lester of U.S. Military Intelligence told the Senate that Heynen's reply to the question "Why did you go to Kuhn, Loeb & Co?" was, "Kuhn, Loeb & Co. we considered the natural bankers of the German government and the Reichsbank."

---

[75] Ibid., 861.316/197, Stockholm, March 7, 1924.
[76] This section is based on the Overman Committee hearings, U.S., Senate, *Brewing and Liquor Interests and German and Bolshevik Propaganda*, Hearings before the Subcommittee on the Judiciary, 65th Cong., 1919, 2:2154-74.

The second loan, of $1.3 million, did not come directly from the United States but was negotiated by John Simon, an agent of the Suedeutsche Disconto-Gesellschaft, to secure funds for making shipments to Germany.

The third loan was from the Chase National Bank (in the Morgan group) in the amount of three million dollars. The fourth loan was from the Mechanics and Metals National Bank in the amount of one million dollars. These loans financed German espionage activities in the United States and Mexico. Some funds were traced to Sommerfeld, who was an adviser to Von Rintelen (another German espionage agent) and who was later associated with Hjalmar Schacht and Emil Wittenberg. Sommerfeld was to purchase ammunition for use in Mexico. He had an account with the Guaranty Trust Company and from this payments were made to Western Cartridge Co. of Alton, Illinois, for ammunition that was shipped to El Paso for use in Mexico by Pancho Villa's bandits. About $400,000 was expended on ammunition, Mexican propaganda, and similar activities.

The then German ambassador Count Von Bernstorff has recounted his friendship with Adolph von Pavenstedt, a senior partner of Amsinck & Co., which was controlled and in November 1917 owned by American International Corporation. American International figures prominently in later chapters; its board of directors contained the key names on Wall Street: Rockefeller, Kahn, Stillman, du Pont, Winthrop, etc. According to Von Bernstorff, Von Pavenstedt was "intimately acquainted with all the members of the Embassy."[77] Von Bernstorff himself regarded Von Pavenstedt as one of the most respected, "if not *the* most respected imperial German in New York."[78] Indeed, Von Pavenstedt was "for many years a Chief pay master of the German spy system in this country."[79] In other words, there is no question that Armsinck & Co., controlled by American International Corporation, was intimately associated with the funding of German wartime espionage in the United States. To clinch Von Bernstorff's last statement, there exists a photograph of a check in favor of Amsinck & Co., dated December 8, 1917 — just four weeks after the start of the Bolshevik Revolution in Russia — signed Von Papen (another German espionage operator), and having a counterfoil bearing the notation "travelling expenses on Von W [i.e., Von Wedell]." French Strothers,[80] who published the photograph, has stated that this check is evidence that Von Papen "became an accessory after the fact to a crime against American laws"; it also makes Amsinck & Co. subject to a similar charge.

Paul Bolo-Pasha, yet another German espionage agent, and a prominent French financier formerly in the service of the Egyptian government, arrived in New York in March 1916

---

[77] Count Von Bernstorff, *My Three Years in America* (New York: Scribner's, 1920), p. 261.
[78] Ibid.
[79] Ibid.
[80] French Strothers, *Fighting Germany's Spies* (Garden City, N.Y.: Doubleday, Page, 1918), p. 152.

with a letter of introduction to Von Pavenstedt. Through the latter, Bolo-Pasha met Hugo Schmidt, director of the Deutsche Bank in Berlin and its representative in the United States. One of Bolo-Pasha's projects was to purchase foreign newspapers so as to slant their editorials in favor of Germany. Funds for this program were arranged in Berlin in the form of credit with Guaranty Trust Company, with the credit subsequently made available to Amsinck & Co. Adolph von Pavenstedt, of Amsinck, in turn made the funds available to Bolo-Pasha.

In other words, both Guaranty Trust Company and Amsinck & Co., a subsidiary of American International Corporation, were directly involved in the implementation of German espionage and other activities in the United States. Some links can be established from these firms to each of the major German operators in the U.S. — Dr. Albert, Karl Heynen, Von Rintelen, Von Papan, Count Jacques Minotto (see below), and Paul Bolo-Pasha.

In 1919 the Senate Overman Committee also established that Guaranty Trust had an active role in financing German World War I efforts in an "unneutral" manner. The testimony of the U.S. intelligence officer Becker makes this clear:

> In this mission Hugo Schmidt [of Deutsche Bank] was very largely assisted by certain American banking institutions. It was while we were neutral, but they acted to the detriment of the British interests, and I have considerable data on the activity of the Guaranty Trust Co. in that respect, and would like to know whether the committee wishes me to go into it.
> SENATOR NELSON: That is a branch of the City Bank, is it not?
> MR. BECKER: No.
> SENATOR OVERMAN: If it was inimical to British interests it was unneutral, and I think you had better let it come out.
> SENATOR KING: Was it an ordinary banking transaction?
> MR. BECKER: That would be a matter of opinion. It has to do with camouflaging exchange so as to make it appear to be neutral exchange, when it was really German exchange on London. As a result of those operations in which the Guaranty Trust Co. mainly participated between August 1, 1914, and the time America entered the war, the Deutsche Banke in its branches in South America succeeded in negotiating £4,670,000 of London exchange in war time.
> SENATOR OVERMAN: I think that is competent.[81]

What is really important is not so much that financial assistance was given to Germany, which was only illegal, as that directors of Guaranty Trust were financially assisting the

---

[81] U.S., Senate, Overman Committee, 2:2009.

Allies at the same time. In other words, Guaranty Trust was financing both sides of The conflict. This raises the question of morality.

THE GARANTY TRUST - MINOTTO - CAILLAUX THREADS[82]

Count Jacques Minotto is a most unlikely but verifiable and persistent thread that links the Bolshevik Revolution in Russia with German banks, German World War I espionage in the United States, the Guaranty Trust Company in New York, the abortive French Bolshevik revolution, and the related Caillaux-Malvy espionage trials in France.

Jacques Minotto was born February 17, 1891, in Berlin, the son of an Austrian father descended from Italian nobility, and a German mother. Young Minotto was educated in Berlin and then entered employment with the Deutsche Bank in Berlin in 1912. Almost immediately Minotto was sent to the United States as assistant to Hugo Schmidt, deputy director of the Deutsche Bank and its New York representative. After a year in New York, Minotto was sent by the Deutsche Bank to London, where he circulated in prominent political and diplomatic circles. At the outbreak of World War I, Minotto returned to the United States and immediately met with the German ambassador Count Von Bernstorff, after which he entered the employ of Guaranty Trust Company in New York. At Guaranty Trust, Minotto was under the direct orders of Max May, director of its foreign department and an associate of Swedish banker Olof Aschberg. Minotto was no minor bank official. The interrogatories of the Caillaux trials in Paris in 1919 established that Minotto worked directly under Max May. On October 25, 1914, Guaranty Trust sent Jacques Minotto to South America to make a report on the political, financial, and commercial situation. As he did in London, Washington, and New York, so Minotto moved in the highest diplomatic and political circles here. One purpose of Minotto's mission in Latin America was to establish the mechanism by which Guaranty Trust could be used as an intermediary for the previously mentioned German fund raising on the London money market, which was then denied to Germany because of World War I. Minotto returned to the United States, renewed his association with Count Von Bernstorff and Count Luxberg, and subsequently, in 1916, attempted to obtain a position with U.S. Naval Intelligence.

---

[82] This section is based on the following sources (as well as those cited elsewhere): Jean Bardanne, *Le Colonel Nicolai: espion de genie* (Paris: Editions Sibonney, n.d.); Cours de Justice, *Affaire Caillaux, Loustalot et Comby: Procedure Generale Interrogatoires* (Paris, 1919), pp. 349-50, 937-46; Paul Vergnet, *L'Affaire Caillaux* (Paris 1918), especially the chapter titled "Marx de Mannheim"; Henri Guernut, Emile Kahn, and Camille M. Lemercier, *Etudes documentaires sur L'Affaire Caillaux* (Paris, n.d.), pp. 1012-15; and George Adam, *Treason and Tragedy: An Account of French War Trials* (London: Jonathan Cape, 1929).

After this he was arrested on charges of pro-German activities. When arrested Minotto was working at the Chicago plant of his father-in-law Louis Swift, of Swift & Co., meatpackers. Swift put up the security for the $50,000 bond required to free Minotto, who was represented by Henry Veeder, the Swift & Co. attorney. Louis Swift was himself arrested for pro-German activities at a later date. As an interesting and not unimportant coincidence, "Major" Harold H. Swift, brother of Louis Swift, was a member of the William Boyce Thompson 1917 Red Cross Mission to Petrograd — that is, one of the group of Wall Street lawyers and businessmen whose intimate connections with the Russian Revolution are to be described later. Helen Swift Neilson, sister of Louis and Harold Swift, was later connected with the pro-Communist Abraham Lincoln Center "Unity." This established a minor link between German banks, American. banks, German espionage, and, as we shall see later, the Bolshevik Revolution.[83]

Joseph Caillaux was a famous (sometimes called notorious) French politician. He was also associated with Count Minotto in the latter's Latin America operations for Guaranty Trust, and was later implicated in the famous French espionage cases of 1919, which had Bolshevik connections. In 1911, Caillaux became minister of finance and later in the same year became premier of France. John Louis Malvy became undersecretary of state in the Caillaux government. Several years later Madame Caillaux murdered Gaston Calmette, editor of the prominent Paris newspaper *Figaro*. The prosecution charged that Madame Caillaux murdered Calmette to prevent publication of certain compromising documents. This affair resulted in the departure of Caillaux and his wife from France. The couple went to Latin America and there met with Count Minotto, the agent of the Guaranty Trust Company who was in Latin America to establish intermediaries for German finance. Count Minotto was socially connected with the Caillaux couple in Rio de Janeiro and Sao Paulo, Brazil, in Montevideo, Uruguay, and in Buenos Aires, Argentina. In other words, Count Minotto was a constant companion of the Caillaux couple while they were in Latin America.[84] On returning to France, Caillaux and his wife stayed at Biarritz as guests of Paul Bolo-Pasha, who was, as we have seen, also a German espionage operator in the United States and France.[85] Later, in July 1915, Count Minotto arrived in France from Italy, met with the Caillaux couple; the same year the Caillaux couple also visited Bolo-Pasha again in Biarritz. In other words, in 1915 and 1916 Caillaux established a continuing social relationship with Count Minotto and Bolo-Pasha, both of whom were German espionage agents in the United States.

Bolo-Pasha's work in France was to gain influence for Germany in the Paris newspapers *Le Temps* and *Figaro*. Bolo-Pasha then went to New York, arriving February 24, 1916. Here

---

[83] This Interrelationship is dealt with extensively in the three-volume Overman Committee report of 1919. See bibliography.
[84] See Rudolph Binion, *Defeated Leaders* (New York: Columbia University Press, 1960).
[85] George Adam, Treason and Tragedy: An Account of French War Trials (London: Jonathan Cape, 1929).

he was to negotiate a loan of $2 million — and here he was associated with Von Pavenstedt, the prominent German agent with Amsinck & Co.[86] Severance Johnson, in *The Enemy Within*, has connected Caillaux and Malvy to the 1918 abortive French Bolshevik revolution, and states that if the revolution had succeeded, "Malvy would have been the Trotsky of France had Caillaux been its Lenin."[87] Caillaux and Malvy formed a radical socialist party in France using German funds and were brought to trial for these subversive efforts. The court interrogatories in the 1919 French espionage trials introduce testimony concerning New York bankers and their relationship with these German espionage operators. They also set forth the links between Count Minotto and Caillaux, as well as the relationship of the Guaranty Trust Company to the Deutsche Bank and the cooperation between Hugo Schmidt of Deutsche Bank and Max May of Guaranty Trust Company. The French interrogatory (page 940) has the following extract from the New York deposition of Count Minotto (page 10, and retranslated from the French):

> QUESTION: Under whose orders were you at Guaranty Trust? REPLY: Under the orders of Mr. Max May.
> QUESTION: He was a Vice President?
> ANSWER: He was Vice President and Director of the Foreign Department.

Later, in 1922, Max May became a director of the Soviet Ruskom-bank and represented the interests of Guaranty Trust in that bank. The French interrogatory establishes that Count Minotto, a German espionage agent, was in the employ of Guaranty Trust Company; that Max May was his superior officer; and that Max May was also closely associated with Bolshevik banker Olof Aschberg. In brief: Max May of Guaranty Trust was linked to illegal fund raising and German espionage in the United States during World War I; he was linked indirectly to the Bolshevik Revolution and directly to the establishment of Ruskombank, the first international bank in the Soviet Union.

It is too early to attempt an explanation for this seemingly inconsistent, illegal, and sometimes immoral international activity. In general, there are two plausible explanations: the first, a relentless search for profits; the second — which agrees with the words of Otto Kahn of Kuhn, Loeb & Co. and of American International Corporation in the epigraph to this chapter — the realization of socialist aims, aims which "should, and can, be brought about" by nonsocialist means.

---

[86] Ibid.
[87] *The Enemy Within* (London: George Allen & Unwin, 1920).

Chapter V

The American Red Cross Mission in Russia — 1917

> *Poor Mr. Billings believed he was in charge of a scientific mission for the relief of Russia... He was in reality nothing but a mask — the Red Cross complexion of the mission was nothing but a mask.*
>
> Cornelius Kelleher, assistant to William Boyce Thompson
> (in George F. Kennan, Russia Leaves the War)

The Wall Street project in Russia in 1917 used the Red Cross Mission as its operational vehicle. Both Guaranty Trust and National City Bank had representatives in Russia at the time of the revolution. Frederick M. Corse of the National City Bank branch in Petrograd was attached to the American Red Cross Mission, of which a great deal will be said later. Guaranty Trust was represented by Henry Crosby Emery. Emery was temporarily held by the Germans in 1918 and then moved on to represent Guaranty Trust 'in China.

Up to about 1915 the most influential person in the American Red Cross National Headquarters in Washington, D.C. was Miss Mabel Boardman. An active and energetic promoter, Miss Boardman had been the moving force behind the Red Cross enterprise, although its endowment came from wealthy and prominent persons including J. P. Morgan, Mrs. E. H. Harriman, Cleveland H. Dodge, and Mrs. Russell Sage. The 1910 fund-raising campaign for $2 million, for example, was successful only because it was supported by these wealthy residents of New York City. In fact, most of the money came from New York City. J.P. Morgan himself contributed $100,000 and seven other contributors in New York City amassed $300,000. Only one person outside New York City contributed over $10,000 and that was William J. Boardman, Miss Boardman's father. Henry P. Davison was chairman of the 1910 New York Fund-Raising Committee and later became chairman of the War Council of the American Red Cross. In other words, in World War I the Red Cross depended heavily on Wall Street, and specifically on the Morgan firm.

The Red Cross was unable to cope with the demands of World War I and in effect was taken over by these New York bankers. According to John Foster Dulles, these businessmen "viewed the American Red Cross as a virtual arm of government, they envisaged making an incalculable contribution to the winning of the war."[88] In so doing they made a mockery of the Red Cross motto: "Neutrality and Humanity."

In exchange for raising funds, Wall Street asked for the Red Cross War Council; and on the recommendation of Cleveland H. Dodge, one of Woodrow Wilson's financial backers, Henry P. Davison, a partner in J.P. Morgan Company, became chairman. The list of administrators of the Red Cross then began to take on the appearance of the New York Directory of Directors: John D. Ryan, president of Anaconda Copper Company (see frontispiece); George W. Hill, president of the American Tobacco Company; Grayson M.P. Murphy, vice president of the Guaranty Trust Company; and Ivy Lee, public relations expert for the Rockefellers. Harry Hopkins, later to achieve fame under President Roosevelt, became assistant to the general manager of the Red Cross in Washington, D.C.

The question of a Red Cross Mission to Russia came before the third meeting of this reconstructed War Council, which was held in the Red Cross Building, Washington, D.C., on Friday, May 29, 1917, at 11:00 A.M. Chairman Davison was deputed to explore the idea with Alexander Legge of the International Harvester Company. Subsequently International Harvester, which had considerable interests in Russia, provided $200,000 to assist financing the Russian mission. At a later meeting it was made known that William Boyce Thompson, director of the Federal Reserve Bank of New York, had "offered to pay the entire expense of the commission"; this offer was accepted in a telegram: "Your desire to pay expenses of commission to Russia is very much appreciated and from our point of view very important."[89]

The members of the mission received no pay. All expenses were paid by William Boyce Thompson and the $200,000 from International Harvester was apparently used in Russia for political subsidies. We know from the files of the U.S. embassy in Petrograd that the U.S. Red Cross gave 4,000 rubles to Prince Lvoff, president of the Council of Ministers, for "relief of revolutionists" and 10,000 rubles in two payments to Kerensky for "relief of political refugees."

AMERICAN RED CROSS MISSION TO RUSSIA, 1917

In August 1917 the American Red Cross Mission to Russia had only a nominal relationship with the American Red Cross, and must truly have been the most unusual Red Cross Mission in history. All expenses, including those of the uniforms — the members were all colonels,

---

[88] John Foster Dulles, *American Red Cross* (New York: Harper, 1950).
[89] Minutes of the War Council of the American National Red Cross (Washington, D.C., May 1917)

majors, captains, or lieutenants — were paid out of the pocket of William Boyce Thompson. One contemporary observer dubbed the all-officer group an "Haytian Army":

> The American Red Cross delegation, about forty Colonels, Majors, Captains and Lieutenants, arrived yesterday. It is headed by Colonel (Doctor) Billings of Chicago, and includes Colonel William B. Thompson and many doctors and civilians, all with military titles; we dubbed the outfit the "Haytian Army" because there were no privates. They have come to fill no clearly defined mission, as far as I can find out, in fact Gov. Francis told me some time ago that he had urged they not be allowed to come, as there were already too many missions from the various allies in Russia. Apparently, this Commission imagined there was urgent call for doctors and nurses in Russia; as a matter of fact there is at present a surplus of medical talent and nurses, native and foreign in the country and many haft-empty hospitals in the large cities.[90]

The mission actually comprised only twenty-four (not forty), having military rank from lieutenant colonel down to lieutenant, and was supplemented by three orderlies, two motion-picture photographers, and two interpreters, without rank. Only five (out of twenty-four) were doctors; in addition, there were two medical researchers. The mission arrived by train in Petrograd via Siberia in August 1917. The five doctors and orderlies stayed one month, returning to the United States on September 11. Dr. Frank Billings, nominal head of the mission and professor of medicine at the University of Chicago, was reported to be disgusted with the overtly political activities of the majority of the mission. The other medical men were William S. Thayer, professor of medicine at Johns Hopkins University; D. J. McCarthy, Fellow of Phipps Institute for Study and Prevention of Tuberculosis, at Philadelphia; Henry C. Sherman, professor of food chemistry at Columbia University; C. E. A. Winslow, professor of bacteriology and hygiene at Yale Medical School; Wilbur E. Post, professor of medicine at Rush Medical College; Dr. Malcolm Grow, of the Medical Officers Reserve Corps of the U.S. Army; and Orrin Wightman, professor of clinical medicine, New York Polyclinic Hospital. George C. Whipple was listed as professor of sanitary engineering at Harvard University but in fact was partner of the New York firm of Hazen, Whipple & Fuller, engineering consultants. This is significant because Malcolm Pirnie — of whom more later — was listed as an assistant sanitary engineer and employed as an engineer by Hazen, Whipple & Fuller.

The majority of the mission, as seen from the table, was made up of lawyers, financiers, and their assistants, from the New York financial district. The mission was financed by William B. Thompson, described in the official Red Cross circular as "Commissioner and Business Manager; Director United States Federal Bank of New York." Thompson brought

---

[90] Gibbs Diary, August 9, 1917. State Historical Society of Wisconsin.

along Cornelius Kelleher, described as an attache to the mission but actually secretary to Thompson and with the same address — 14 Wall Street, New York City. Publicity for the mission was handled by Henry S. Brown, of the same address. Thomas Day Thacher was an attorney with Simpson, Thacher & Bartlett, a firm founded by his father, Thomas Thacher, in 1884 and prominently involved in railroad reorganization and mergers. Thomas as junior first worked for the family firm, became assistant U.S. attorney under Henry L. Stimson, and returned to the family firm in 1909. The young Thacher was a close friend of Felix Frankfurter and later became assistant to Raymond Robins, also on the Red Cross Mission. In 1925 he was appointed district judge under President Coolidge, became solicitor general under Herbert Hoover, and was a director of the William Boyce Thompson Institute.

THE 1917 AMERICAN RED CROSS MISSION TO RUSSIA

Members from Wall Street financial community and their affiliations	Medical doctors	Orderlies, interpreters, etc.
Andrews (Liggett & Myers Tobacco)	Billings (doctor)	Brooks (orderly)
Barr (Chase National Bank)	Grow (doctor)	Clark (orderly)
Brown (c/o William B. Thompson)	McCarthy (medical research; doctor)	Rocchia (orderly)
Cochran (McCann Co.)	Post (doctor)	
Kelleher (c/o William B. Thompson)	Sherman (food chemistry)	Travis (movies)
Nicholson (Swirl & Co.)	Thayer (doctor)	Wyckoff (movies)
Pirnie (Hazen, Whipple & Fuller)		
Redfield (Stetson, Jennings & Russell)	Wightman (medicine)	Hardy (justice)
Robins (mining promoter)	Winslow (hygiene)	Horn (transportation)
Swift (Swift & Co.)		
Thacher (Simpson, Thacher & Bartlett)		
Thompson (Federal Reserve Bank of N.Y.)		
Wardwell (Stetson, Jennings & Russell)		
Whipple (Hazen, Whipple & Fuller)		
Corse (National City Bank)		
Magnuson (recommended by confidential agent of Colonel Thompson)		

Alan Wardwell, also a deputy commissioner and secretary to the chairman, was a lawyer with the law firm of Stetson, Jennings & Russell of 15 Broad Street, New York City, and H. B. Redfield was law secretary to Wardwell. Major Wardwell was the son of William Thomas Wardwell, long-time treasurer of Standard Oil of New Jersey and Standard Oil of New York. The elder Wardwell was one of the signers of the famous Standard Oil trust agreement, a member of the committee to organize Red Cross activities in the Spanish American War, and a director of the Greenwich Savings Bank. His son Alan was a director not only of Greenwich Savings, but also of Bank of New York and Trust Co. and the Georgian Manganese Company (along with W. Averell Harriman, a director of Guaranty Trust). In 1917 Alan Wardwell was affiliated with Stetson, Jennings 8c Russell and later joined Davis, Polk, Wardwell, Gardner & Read (Frank L. Polk was acting secretary of state during the Bolshevik Revolution period). The Senate Overman Committee noted that Wardwell was favorable to the Soviet regime although Poole, the State Department official on the spot, noted that "Major Wardwell has of all Americans the widest personal knowledge of the terror" (316-23-1449). In the 1920s Wardwell became active with the Russian-American Chamber of Commerce in promoting Soviet trade objectives.

The treasurer of the mission was James W. Andrews, auditor of Liggett & Myers Tobacco Company of St. Louis. Robert I. Barr, another member, was listed as a deputy commissioner; he was a vice president of Chase Securities Company (120 Broadway) and of the Chase National Bank. Listed as being in charge of advertising was William Cochran of 61 Broadway, New York City. Raymond Robins, a mining promoter, was included as a deputy commissioner and described as "a social economist." Finally, the mission included two members of Swift & Company of Union Stockyards, Chicago. The Swifts have been previously mentioned as being connected with German espionage in the United States during World War I. Harold H. Swift, deputy commissioner, was assistant to the vice president of Swift & Company; William G. Nicholson was also with Swift & Company, Union Stockyards.

Two persons were unofficially added to the mission after it arrived in Petrograd: Frederick M. Corse, representative of the National City Bank in Petrograd; and Herbert A. Magnuson, who was "very highly recommended by John W. Finch, the confidential agent in China of Colonel William B. Thompson."[91]

The Pirnie papers, deposited at the Hoover Institution, contain primary material on the mission. Malcolm Pirnie was an engineer employed by the firm of Hazen, Whipple & Fuller, consulting engineers, of 42 Street, New York City. Pirnie was a member of the mission, listed on a manifest as an assistant sanitary engineer. George C. Whipple, a partner in the firm, was also included in the group. The Pirnie papers include an original telegram from

---

[91] Billings report to Henry P. Davison, October 22, 1917, American Red Cross Archives.

William B. Thompson, inviting assistant sanitary engineer Pirnie to meet with him and Henry P. Davison, chairman of the Red Cross War Council and partner in the J.P. Morgan firm, before leaving for Russia. The telegram reads as follows:

> WESTERN UNION TELEGRAM New York, June 21, 1917
> To Malcolm Pirnie
> I should very much like to have you dine with me at the Metropolitan Club, Sixteenth Street and Fifth Avenue New York City at eight o'clock tomorrow Friday evening to meet Mr. H. P. Davison.
> W. B. Thompson, 14 Wall Street

The files do not elucidate why Morgan partner Davison and Thompson, director of the Federal Reserve Bank — two of the most prominent financial men in New York — wished to have dinner with an assistant sanitary engineer about to leave for Russia. Neither do the files explain why Davison was subsequently unable to meet Dr. Billings and the commission itself, nor why it was necessary to advise Pirnie of his inability to do so. But we may surmise that the official cover of the mission — Red Cross activities — was of significantly less interest than the Thompson-Pirnie activities, whatever they may have been. We do know that Davison wrote to Dr. Billings on June 25, 1917:

> Dear Doctor Billings:
> It is a disappointment to me and to my associates on the War Council not have been able to meet in a body the members of your Commission...

A copy of this letter was also mailed to assistant sanitary engineer Pirnie with a personal letter from Morgan banker Henry P. Davison, which read:

> My dear Mr. Pirnie:
> You will, I am sure, entirely understand the reason for the letter to Dr. Billings, copy of which is enclosed, and accept it in the spirit in which it is sent...

The purpose of Davison's letter to Dr. Billings was to apologize to the commission and Billings for being unable to meet with them. We may then be justified in supposing that some deeper arrangements were made by Davison and Pirnie concerning the activities of the mission in Russia and that these arrangements were known to Thompson. The probable nature of these activities will be described later.[92]

The American Red Cross Mission (or perhaps we should call it the Wall Street Mission to Russia) also employed three Russian-English interpreters: Captain Ilovaisky, a Russian Bolshevik; Boris Reinstein, a Russian-American, later secretary to Lenin, and the head of Karl Radek's Bureau of International Revolutionary Propaganda, which also employed John Reed and Albert Rhys Williams; and Alexander Gumberg (alias Berg, real name Michael Gruzenberg), who was a brother of Zorin, a Bolshevik minister. Gumberg was also the chief Bolshevik agent in Scandinavia. He later became a confidential assistant to Floyd Odlum of Atlas Corporation in the United States as well as an adviser to Reeve Schley, a vice president of the Chase Bank.

It should be asked in passing: How useful were the translations supplied by these interpreters? On September 13, 1918, H. A. Doolittle, American vice consul at Stockholm, reported to the secretary of state on a conversation with Captain Ilovaisky (who was a "close personal friend" of Colonel Robins of the Red Cross Mission) concerning a meeting of the Murman Soviet and the Allies. The question of inviting the Allies to land at Murman was under discussion at the Soviet, with Major Thacher of the Red Cross Mission acting for the Allies. Ilovaisky interpreted Thacher's views for the Soviet. "Ilovaisky spoke at some length in Russian, supposedly translating for Thacher, but in reality for Trotsky... "to the effect that "the United States would never permit such a landing to occur and urging the speedy recognition of the Soviets and their politics."[93] Apparently Thacher suspected he was being mistranslated and expressed his indignation. However, "Ilovaisky immediately telegraphed the substance to Bolshevik headquarters and through their press bureau had it appear in all the papers as emanating from the remarks of Major Thacher and as the general opinion of all truly accredited American representatives."[94]

Ilovaisky recounted to Maddin Summers, U.S. consul general in Moscow, several instances where he (Ilovaisky) and Raymond Robins of the Red Cross Mission had manipulated the Bolshevik press, especially "in regard to the recall of the Ambassador, Mr. Francis." He admitted that they had not been scrupulous, "but had acted according to their ideas of right, regardless of how they might have conflicted with the politics of the accredited American representatives."[95]

---

[92] The Pirnie papers also enable us to fix exactly the dates that members of the mission left Russia. In the case of William B. Thompson, this date is critical to the argument of this book: Thompson left Petrograd for London on December 4, 1917. George F. Kennan states Thompson left Petrograd on November 27, 1917 *(Russia Leaves the War,* p. 1140).
[93] U.S. State Dept. Decimal File, 861.00/3644.
[94] Ibid.
[95] Ibid.

This then was the American Red Cross Mission to Russia in 1917.

AMERICAN RED CROSS MISSION TO RUMANIA

In 1917 the American Red Cross also sent a medical assistance mission to Rumania, then fighting the Central Powers as an ally of Russia. A comparison of the American Red Cross Mission to Russia with that sent to Rumania suggests that the Red Cross Mission based in Petrograd had very little official connection with the Red Cross and even less connection with medical assistance. Whereas the Red Cross Mission to Rumania valiantly upheld the Red Cross twin principles of "humanity" and "neutrality," the Red Cross Mission in Petrograd flagrantly abused both.

The American Red Cross Mission to Rumania left the United States in July 1917 and located itself at Jassy. The mission consisted of thirty persons under Chairman Henry W. Anderson, a lawyer from Virginia. Of the thirty, sixteen were either doctors or surgeons. By comparison, out of twenty-nine individuals with the Red Cross Mission to Russia, only three were doctors, although another four members were from universities and specialized in medically related fields. At the most, seven could be classified as doctors with the mission to Russia compared with sixteen with the mission to Rumania. There was about the same number of orderlies and nurses with both missions. The significant comparison, however, is that the Rumanian mission had only two lawyers, one treasurer, and one engineer. The Russian mission had fifteen lawyers and businessmen. None of the Rumanian mission lawyers or doctors came from anywhere near the New York area but all, except one (an "observer" from the Department of Justice in Washington, D.C.), of the lawyers and businessmen with the Russian mission came from that area. Which is to say that more than half the total of the Russian mission came from the New York financial district. In other words, the relative composition of these missions confirms that the mission to Rumania had a legitimate purpose — to practice medicine — while the Russian mission had a non-medical and strictly political objective. From its personnel, it could be classified as a commercial or financial mission, but from its actions it was a subversive political action group.

Personnel with the American Red Cross missions to Russia and Rumania, 1917

Personnel	AMERICAN RED CROSS MISSION TO	
	Russia	Rumania
Medical (doctors and surgeons)	7	16
Orderlies, nurses	7	10
Lawyers and businessmen	15	4
TOTAL	29	30

SOURCES: American Red Cross, Washington, D.C.
U.S. Department of State, Petrograd embassy, Red Cross file, 1917.

The Red Cross Mission to Rumania remained at its post in Jassy for the remainder of 1917 and into 1918. The medical staff of the American Red Cross Mission in Russia — the seven doctors — quit in disgust in August 1917, protested the political activities of Colonel Thompson, and returned to the United States. Consequently, in September 1917, when the Rumanian mission appealed to Petrograd for American doctors and nurses to help out in the near crisis conditions in Jassy, there were no American doctors or nurses in Russia available to go to Rumania.

Whereas the bulk of the mission in Russia occupied its time in internal political maneuvering, the mission in Rumania threw itself into relief work as soon as it arrived. On September 17, 1917, a confidential cable from Henry W. Anderson, chairman of the Rumania mission, to the American ambassador Francis in Petrograd requested immediate and urgent help in the form of $5 million to meet an impending catastrophe in Rumania. Then followed a series of letters, cables, and communications from Anderson to Francis appealing, unsuccessfully, for help.

On September 28, 1917, Vopicka, American minister in Rumania, cabled Francis at length, for relay to Washington, and repeated Anderson's analysis of the Rumanian crisis and the danger of epidemics — and worse — as winter closed in:

> Considerable money and heroic measures required prevent far reaching disaster... Useless try handle situation without someone with authority and access to government... With proper organization to look after transport receive and distribute supplies.

The hands of Vopicka and Anderson were tied as all Rumanian supplies and financial transactions were handled by the Red Cross Mission in Petrograd — and Thompson and his staff of fifteen Wall Street lawyers and businessmen apparently had matters of greater concern that Rumanian Red Cross affairs. There is no indication in the Petrograd embassy files at the U.S. State Department that Thompson, Robins, or Thacher concerned himself at any time in 1917 or 1918 with the urgent situation in Rumania. Communications from Rumania went to Ambassador Francis or to one of his embassy staff, and occasionally through the consulate in Moscow.

By October 1917 the Rumanian situation reached the crisis point. Vopicka cabled Davison in New York (via Petrograd) on October 5:

> Most urgent problem here... Disastrous effect feared... Could you possibly arrange special shipment... Must rush or too late.

Then on November 5 Anderson cabled the Petrograd embassy saying that delays in sending help had already "cost several thousand lives." On November 13 Anderson cabled Ambassador Francis concerning Thompson's lack of interest in Rumanian conditions:

> Requested Thompson furnish details all shipments as received but have not obtained same... Also requested him keep me posted as to transport conditions but received very little information.

Anderson then requested that Ambassador Francis intercede on his behalf in order to have funds for the Rumanian Red Cross handled in a separate account in London, directly under Anderson and removed from the control of Thompson's mission.

THOMPSON IN KERENSKY'S RUSSIA

What then was the Red Cross Mission doing? Thompson certainly acquired a reputation for opulent living in Petrograd, but apparently he undertook only two major projects in Kerensky's Russia: support for an American propaganda program and support for the Russian Liberty Loan. Soon after arriving in Russia Thompson met with Madame Breshko-Breshkovskaya and David Soskice, Kerensky's secretary, and agreed to contribute $2 million to a committee of popular education so that it could "have its own press and... engage a staff of lecturers, with cinematograph illustrations" (861.00/ 1032); this was for the propaganda purpose of urging Russia to continue in the war against Germany. According to Soskice, "a packet of 50,000 rubles" was given to Breshko-Breshkovskaya with the statement, "This is for you to expend according to your best judgment." A further 2,100,000 rubles was deposited into a current bank account. A letter from J. P. Morgan to the State Department (861.51/190) confirms that Morgan cabled 425,000 rubles to Thompson at his request for the Russian Liberty Loan; J. P. also conveyed the interest of the Morgan firm regarding "the wisdom of making an individual subscription through Mr. Thompson" to the

Russian Liberty Loan. These sums were transmitted through the National City Bank branch in Petrograd.

THOMPSON GIVES THE BOLSHEVIKS $1 MILLION

Of greater historical significance, however, was the assistance given to the Bolsheviks first by Thompson, then, after December 4, 1917, by Raymond Robins.

Thompson's contribution to the Bolshevik cause was recorded in the contemporary American press. The *Washington Post* of February 2, 1918, carried the following paragraphs:

> GIVES BOLSHEVIKI A MILLION
> W. B. Thompson, Red Cross Donor, Believes Party Misrepresented. New York, Feb. 2 (1918). William B. Thompson, who was in Petrograd from July until November last, has made a personal contribution of $1,000,000 to the Bolsheviki for the purpose of spreading their doctrine in Germany and Austria.
> Mr. Thompson had an opportunity to study Russian conditions as head of the American Red Cross Mission, expenses of which also were largely defrayed by his personal contributions. He believes that the Bolsheviki constitute the greatest power against Pro-Germanism in Russia and that their propaganda has been undermining the militarist regimes of the General Empires.
> Mr. Thompson deprecates American criticism of the Bolsheviki. He believes they have been misrepresented and has made the financial contribution to the cause in the belief that it will be money well spent for the future of Russia as well as for the Allied cause.

Hermann Hagedorn's biography *The Magnate: William Boyce Thompson and His Time (1869-1930)* reproduces a photograph of a cablegram from J.P. Morgan in New York to W. B. Thompson, "Care American Red Cross, Hotel Europe, Petrograd." The cable is date-stamped, showing it was received at Petrograd "8-Dek 1917" (8 December 1917), and reads:

> New York Y757/5 24W5 Nil — Your cable second received. We have paid National City Bank one million dollars as instructed — Morgan.

The National City Bank branch in Petrograd had been exempted from the Bolshevik nationalization decree — the only foreign or domestic Russian bank to have been so exempted. Hagedorn says that this million dollars paid into Thompson's NCB account was used for "political purposes."

SOCIALIST MINING PROMOTER RAYMOND ROBINS[96]

William B. Thompson left Russia in early December 1917 to return home. He traveled via London, where, in company with Thomas Lamont of the J.P. Morgan firm, he visited Prime Minister Lloyd George, an episode we pick up in the next chapter. His deputy, Raymond Robins, was left in charge of the Red Cross Mission to Russia. The general impression that Colonel Robins presented in the subsequent months was not overlooked by the press. In the words of the Russian newspaper *Russkoe Slovo,* Robins "on the one hand represents American labor and on the other hand American capital, which is endeavoring through the Soviets to gain their Russian markets."[97]

Raymond Robins started life as the manager of a Florida phosphate company commissary. From this base he developed a kaolin deposit, then prospected Texas and the Indian territories in the late nineteenth century. Moving north to Alaska, Robins made a fortune in the Klondike gold rush. Then, for no observable reason, he switched to socialism and the reform movement. By 1912 he was an active member of Roosevelt's Progressive Party. He joined the 1917 American Red Cross Mission to Russia as a "social economist."

There is considerable evidence, including Robins' own statements, that his reformist social-good appeals were little more than covers for the acquisition of further power and wealth, reminiscent of Frederick Howe's suggestions in *Confessions of a Monopolist.* For example, in February 1918 Arthur Bullard was in Petrograd with the U.S. Committee on Public Information and engaged in writing a long memorandum for Colonel Edward House. This memorandum was given to Robins by Bullard for comments and criticism before transmission to House in Washington, D.C. Robins' very unsocialistic and imperialistic comments were to the effect that the manuscript was "uncommonly discriminating, far-seeing and well done," but that he had one or two reservations — in particular, that recognition of the Bolsheviks was long overdue, that it should have been effected immediately, and that had the U.S. so recognized the Bolsheviks, "I believe that we would now be in control of the surplus resources of Russia and have control officers at all points on the frontier."[98]

This desire to gain "control of the surplus resources of Russia" was also obvious to Russians. Does this sound like a social reformer in the American Red Cross or a Wall Street mining promoter engaged in the practical exercise of imperialism?

---

[96] Robins is the correct spelling. The name is consistently spelled "Robbins" in the Stale Department files.
[97] U.S. State Dept. Decimal File, 316-11-1265, March 19, 1918.
[98] Bullard ms., U.S. State Dept. Decimal File, 316-11-1265.

In any event, Robins made no bones about his support for the Bolshevists.[99] Barely three weeks after the Bolshevik phase of the Revolution started, Robins cabled Henry Davison at Red Cross headquarters: "Please urge upon the President the necessity of our continued intercourse with the Bolshevik Government." Interestingly, this cable was in reply to a cable instructing Robins that the "President desires the withholding of direct communications by representatives of the United States with the Bolshevik Government."[100] Several State Department reports complained about the partisan nature of Robins' activities. For example, on March 27, 1919, Harris, the American consul at Vladivostok, commented on a long conversation he had had with Robins and protested gross inaccuracies in the latter's reporting. Harris wrote, "Robins stated to me that no German and Austrian prisoners of war had joined the Bolshevik army up to May 1918. Robbins knew this statement was absolutely false." Harris then proceeded to provide the details of evidence available to Robins.[101]

Harris concluded, "Robbins deliberately misstated facts concerning Russia at that time and he has been doing it ever since."

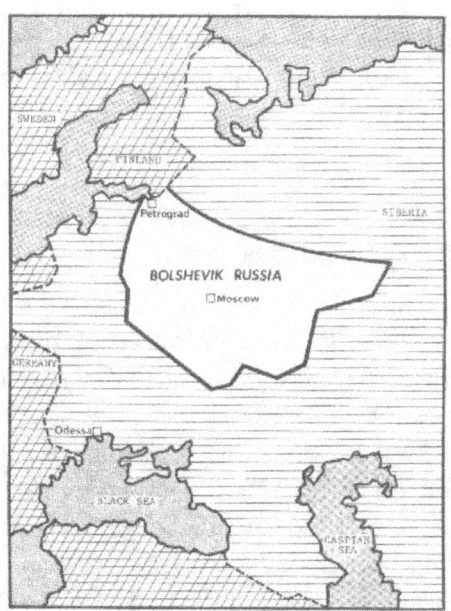

---

[99] The *New World Review* (fall 1967, p. 40) comments on Robins, noting that he was "in sympathy with the aims of the Revolution, although a capitalist."
[100] Petrograd embassy, Red Cross file.
[101] U.S. State Dept. Decimal File, 861.00/4168.

Limit of Area Controlled by Bolsheviks, January 1918

On returning to the United States in 1918, Robins continued his efforts in behalf of the Bolsheviks. When the files of the Soviet Bureau were seized by the Lusk Committee, it was found that Robins had had "considerable correspondence" with Ludwig Martens and other members of the bureau. One of the more interesting documents seized was a letter from Santeri Nuorteva (alias Alexander Nyberg), the first Soviet representative in the U.S., to "Comrade Cahan," editor of the *New York Daily Forward*. The letter called on the party faithful to prepare the way for Raymond Robins:

> (To Daily) FORWARD July 6, 1918
> Dear Comrade Cahan:
> It is of the utmost importance that the Socialist press set up a clamor immediately that Col. Raymond Robins, who has just returned from Russia at the head of the Red Cross Mission, should be heard from in a public report to the American people. The armed intervention danger has greatly increased. The reactionists are using the Czecho-Slovak adventure to bring about invasion. Robins has all the facts about this and about the situation in Russia generally. He takes our point of view.
> I am enclosing copy of Call editorial which shows a general line of argument, also some facts about Czecho-Slovaks.
> Fraternally,
> PS&AU Santeri Nuorteva

THE INTERNATIONAL RED CROSS AND REVOLUTION

Unknown to its administrators, the Red Cross has been used from time to time as a vehicle or cover for revolutionary activities. The use of Red Cross markings for unauthorized purposes is not uncommon. When Tsar Nicholas was moved from Petrograd to Tobolsk allegedly for his safety (although this direction was towards danger rather than safety), the train carried Japanese Red Cross placards. The State Department files contain examples of revolutionary activity under cover of Red Cross activities. For example, a Russian Red Cross official (Chelgajnov) was arrested in Holland in 1919 for revolutionary acts (316-21-107). During the Hungarian Bolshevik revolution in 1918, led by Bela Kun, Russian members of the Red Cross (or revolutionaries operating as members of the Russian Red Cross) were found in Vienna and Budapest. In 1919 the U.S. ambassador in London cabled Washington startling news; through the British government he had learned that "several Americans who had arrived in this country in the uniform of the Red Cross and who stated that they were Bolsheviks... were proceeding through France to Switzerland to spread Bolshevik propaganda."

The ambassador noted that about 400 American Red Cross people had arrived in London in November and December 1918; of that number one quarter returned to the United States and "the remainder insisted on proceeding to France." There was a later report on January 15, 1918, to the effect that an editor of a labor newspaper in London had been approached on three different occasions by three different American Red Cross officials who offered to take commissions to Bolsheviks in Germany. The editor had suggested to the U.S. embassy that it watch American Red Cross personnel. The U.S. State Department took these reports seriously and Polk cabled for names, stating, "If true, I consider it of the greatest importance" (861.00/3602 and /3627).

To summarize: the picture we form of the 1917 American Red Cross Mission to Russia is remote from one of neutral humanitarianism. The mission was in fact a mission of Wall Street financiers to influence and pave the way for control, through either Kerensky or the Bolshevik revolutionaries, of the Russian market and resources. No other explanation will explain the actions of the mission. However, neither Thompson nor Robins was a Bolshevik. Nor was either even a consistent socialist. The writer is inclined to the interpretation that the socialist appeals of each man were covers for more prosaic objectives. Each man was intent upon the commercial; that is, each sought to use the political process in Russia for personal financial ends. Whether the Russian people wanted the Bolsheviks was of no concern. Whether the Bolshevik regime would act against the United States — as it consistently did later — was of no concern. The single overwhelming objective was to gain political and economic influence with the new regime, whatever its ideology. If William Boyce Thompson had acted alone, then his directorship of the Federal Reserve Bank would be inconsequential. However, the fact that his mission was dominated by representatives of Wall Street institutions raises a serious question — in effect, whether the mission was a planned, premeditated operation by a Wall Street syndicate. This the reader will have to judge for himself, as the rest of the story unfolds.

CHAPTER VI

CONSOLIDATION AND EXPORT OF THE REVOLUTION

> *Marx's great book Das Kapital is at once a monument of reasoning and a storehouse of facts.*
>
> Lord Milner, member of the British War Cabinet, 1917, and director of the London Joint Stock Bank.

William Boyce Thompson is an unknown name in twentieth-century history, yet Thompson played a crucial role in the Bolshevik Revolution.[102] Indeed, if Thompson had not been in Russia in 1917, subsequent history might have followed a quite different course. Without the financial and, more important, the diplomatic and propaganda assistance given to Trotsky and Lenin by Thompson, Robins, and their New York associates, the Bolsheviks may well have withered away and Russia evolved into a socialist but constitutional society.

Who was William Boyce Thompson? Thompson was a promoter of mining stocks, one of the best in a high-risk business. Before World War I he handled stock-market operations for the Guggenheim copper interests. When the Guggenheims needed quick capital for a stock-market struggle with John D. Rockefeller, it was Thompson who promoted Yukon Consolidated Goldfields before an unsuspecting public to raise a $3.5 million war chest. Thompson was manager of the Kennecott syndicate, another Guggenheim operation, valued at $200 million. It was Guggenheim Exploration, on the other hand, that took up Thompson's options on the rich Nevada Consolidated Copper Company. About three quarters of the original Guggenheim Exploration Company was controlled by the Guggenheim family, the Whitney family (who owned *Metropolitan* magazine, which employed the Bolshevik John Reed), and John Ryan. In 1916 the Guggenheim interests reorganized into Guggenheim Brothers and brought in William C. Potter, who was formerly with Guggenheim's American Smelting and Refining Company but who was in 1916 first' vice president of Guaranty Trust.

Extraordinary skill in raising capital for risky mining promotions earned Thompson a personal fortune and directorships in Inspiration Consolidated Copper Company, Nevada

---

[102] For a biography see Hermann Hagedorn, *The Magnate: William Boyce Thompson and His Time (1869-1930)* (New York: Reynal & Hitchcock, 1935).

Consolidated Copper Company, and Utah Copper Company — all major domestic copper producers. Copper is, of course, a major material in the manufacture of munitions. Thompson was also director of the Chicago Rock Island & Pacific Railroad, the Magma Arizona Railroad and the Metropolitan Life Insurance Company. And of particular interest for this book, Thompson was "one of the heaviest stockholders in the Chase National Bank." It was Albert H. Wiggin, president of the Chase Bank, who pushed Thompson for a post in the Federal Reserve System; and in 1914 Thompson became the first full-term director of the Federal Reserve Bank of New York — the most important bank in the Federal Reserve System.

By 1917, then, William Boyce Thompson was a financial operator of substantial means, demonstrated ability, with a flair for promotion and implementation of capitalist projects, and with ready access to the centers of political and financial power. This was the same man who first supported Aleksandr Kerensky, and who then became an ardent supporter of the Bolsheviks, bequeathing a surviving symbol of this support — a laudatory pamphlet in Russian, "Pravda o Rossii i Bol'shevikakh."[103]

Before leaving Russia in early December 1917 Thompson handed over the American Red Cross Mission to his deputy Raymond Robins. Robins then organized Russian revolutionaries to implement the Thompson plan for spreading Bolshevik propaganda in Europe (see Appendix 3). A French government document confirms this: "It appeared that Colonel Robins... was able to send a subversive mission of Russian bolsheviks to Germany to start a revolution there."[104] This mission led to the abortive German Spartacist revolt of 1918. The overall plan also included schemes for dropping Bolshevik literature by airplane or for smuggling it across German lines.

Thompson made preparations in late 1917 to leave Petrograd and sell the Bolshevik Revolution to governments in Europe and to the U.S. With this in mind, Thompson cabled Thomas W. Lamont, a partner in the Morgan firm who was then in Paris with Colonel E. M. House. Lamont recorded the receipt of this cablegram in his biography:

> Just as the House Mission was completing its discussions in Paris in December 1917, I received an arresting cable from my old school and business friend, William Boyce Thompson, who was then in Petrograd in charge of the American Red Cross Mission there.[105]

---

[103] Polkovnik' Villiam' Boic' Thompson', "Pravda o Rossii i Bol'shevikakh" (New York: Russian-American Publication Society, 1918).

[104] John Bradley, *Allied Intervention in Russia* (London: Weidenfeld and Nicolson, 1968).

[105] Thomas W. Lamont, *Across World Frontiers* (New York: Harcourt, Brace, 1959), p. 85. See also pp. 94-97 for massive breast-beating over the failure of President Wilson to act promptly to befriend the Soviet regime. Corliss Lamont, his son, became a [font-line domestic leftist in the U.S.

Lamont journeyed to London and met with Thompson, who had left Petrograd on December 5, traveled via Bergen, Norway, and arrived in London on December 10. The most important achievement of Thompson and Lamont in London was to convince the British War Cabinet — then decidedly anti-Bolshevik — that the Bolshevik regime had come to stay, and that British policy should cease to be anti-Bolshevik, should accept the new realities, and should support Lenin and Trotsky. Thompson and Lamont left London on December 18 and arrived in New York on December 25, 1917. They attempted the same process of conversion in the United States.

A CONSULTATION WITH LLOYD GEORGE

The secret British War Cabinet papers are now available and record the argument used by Thompson to sell the British government on a pro-Bolshevik policy. The prime minister of Great Britain was David Lloyd George. Lloyd George's private and political machinations rivaled those of a Tammany Hall politician — yet in his lifetime and for decades after, biographers were unable, or unwilling, to come to grips with them. In 1970 Donald McCormick's *The Mask of Merlin* lifted the veil of secrecy. McCormick shows that by 1917 David Lloyd George had bogged *"too* deeply in the mesh of international armaments intrigues to be a free agent" and was beholden to Sir Basil Zaharoff, an international armaments dealer, whose considerable fortune was made by selling arms to both sides in several wars.[106] Zaharoff wielded enormous behind-the-scenes power and, according to McCormick, was consulted on war policies by the Allied leaders. On more than one occasion, reports McCormick, Woodrow Wilson, Lloyd George, and Georges Clemenceau met in Zaharoff's Paris home. McCormick notes that "Allied statesmen and leaders were obliged to consult him before planning any great attack." British intelligence, according to McCormick, "discovered documents which incriminated servants of the Crown as secret agents of Sir Basil Zaharoff *with the knowledge of Lloyd George.*"[107] In 1917 Zaharoff was linked to the Bolsheviks; he sought to divert munitions away from anti-Bolsheviks and had already intervened in behalf of the Bolshevik regime in both London and Paris.

In late 1917, then — at the time Lamont and Thompson arrived in London — Prime Minister Lloyd George was indebted to powerful international armaments interests that were allied to the Bolsheviks and providing assistance to extend Bolshevik power in Russia. The British prime minister who met with William Thompson in 1917 was not then a free agent;

---

[106] Donald McCormick, *The Mask of Merlin* (London: MacDonald, 1963; New York: Holt, Rinehart and Winston, 1964), p. 208. Lloyd George's personal life would certainly leave him open to blackmail.
[107] Ibid. McCormick's italics.

Lord Milner was the power behind the scenes and, as the epigraph to this chapter suggests, favorably inclined towards socialism and Karl Marx.

The "secret" War Cabinet papers give the "Prime Minister's account of a conversation with Mr. Thompson, an American returned from Russia,"[108] and the report made by the prime minister to the War Cabinet after meeting with Thompson.[109] The cabinet paper reads as follows:

> The Prime Minister reported a conversation he had had with a Mr. Thompson — an American traveller and a man of considerable means — who had just returned from Russia, and who had given a somewhat different impression of affairs in that country from what was generally believed. The gist of his remarks was to the effect that the Revolution had come to stay; that the Allies had not shown themselves sufficiently sympathetic with the Revolution; and that MM. Trotzki and Lenin were not in German pay, the latter being a fairly distinguished Professor. Mr. Thompson had added that he considered the Allies should conduct in Russia an active propaganda, carried out by some form of Allied Council composed o[men especially selected [or the purpose; further, that on the whole, he considered, having regard to the character of the de facto Russian Government, the several Allied Governments were not suitably represented in Petrograd. In Mr. Thompson's opinion, it was necessary for the Allies to realise that the Russian army and people *were* out of the war, and that the Allies would have to choose between Russia as the friendly or a hostile neutral. The question was discussed as to whether the Allies ought not to change their policy in regard to the de facto Russian Government, the Bolsheviks being stated by Mr. Thompson to be and-German. In this connection Lord Robert Cecil drew attention to the conditions of the armistice between the German and Russian armies, which provided, inter alia, for trading between the two countries, and for the establishment of a Purchasing Commission in Odessa, the whole arrangement being obviously dictated by the Germans. Lord Robert Cecil expressed the view that the Germans would endeavour to continue the armistice until the Russian army had melted away.
>
> Sir Edward Carson read a communication, signed by M. Trotzki, which had been sent to him by a British subject, the manager of the Russian branch of the Vauxhall Motor Company, who had just returned from Russia [Paper G.T. — 3040]. This report indicated that M. Trotzki's policy was, ostensibly at any rate, one of hostility to the organisation of civilised society rather than pro-German. On the other hand, it was suggested that an assumed attitude of this kind was by no means inconsistent with Trotzki's being a German agent,

---

[108] British War Cabinet papers, no. 302, sec. 2 (Public Records Office, London).
[109] The written memorandum that Thompson submitted to Lloyd George and that became the basis for the War Cabinet statement is available from U.S. archival sources and is printed in full in Appendix 3.

whose object was to ruin Russia in order that Germany might do what she desired in that country.

After hearing Lloyd George's report and supporting arguments, the War Cabinet decided to go along with Thompson and the Bolsheviks. Milner had a former British consul in Russia — Bruce Lockhart — ready and waiting in the wings. Lockhart was briefed and sent to Russia with instructions to work informally with the Soviets.

The thoroughness of Thompson's work in London and the pressure he was able to bring to bear on the situation are suggested by subsequent reports coming into the hands of the War Cabinet, from authentic sources. The reports provide a quite different view of Trotsky and the Bolsheviks from that presented by Thompson, and yet they were ignored by the cabinet. In April 1918 General Jan Smuts reported to the War Cabinet his talk with General Nieffel, the head of the French Military Mission who had just returned from Russia:

> Trotski (sic)... was a consummate scoundrel who may not be pro-German, but is thoroughly pro-Trotski and pro-revolutionary and cannot in any way be trusted. His influence is shown by the way he has come to dominate Lockhart, Robins and the French representative. He [Nieffel] counsels great prudence in dealing with Trotski, who he admits is the only really able man in Russia.[110]

Several months later Thomas D. Thacher, Wall Street lawyer and another member of the American Red CrAss Mission to Russia, was in London. On April 13, 1918, Thacher wrote to the American ambassador in London to the effect that he had received a request from H. P. Davison, a Morgan partner, *"to* confer with Lord Northcliffe" concerning the situation in Russia and then to go on to Paris "for other conferences." Lord Northcliffe was ill and Thacher left with yet another Morgan partner, Dwight W. Morrow, a memorandum to be submitted to Northcliffe on his return to London.[111] This memorandum not only made explicit suggestions about Russian policy that supported Thompson's position but even stated that "the fullest assistance should be given to the Soviet government in its efforts to organize a volunteer revolutionary army." The four main proposals in this Thacher report are:

> First of all... the Allies should discourage Japanese intervention in Siberia.
> In the second place, the fullest assistance should be given to the Soviet Government in its efforts to organize a volunteer revolutionary army.

---

[110] Complete memorandum is in U.S. State Dept. Decimal File, 316-13-698.
[111] War Cabinet papers, 24/49/7197 (G.T. 4322) Secret, April 24, 1918.

Thirdly, the Allied Governments should give their moral support to the Russian people in their efforts to work out their own political systems free from the domination of any foreign power...

Fourthly, until the time when open conflict shall result between the German Government and the Soviet Government of Russia there will be opportunity for peaceful commercial penetration by German agencies in Russia. So long as there is no open break, it will probably be impossible to entirely prevent such commerce. Steps should, therefore, be taken to impede, so far as possible, the transport of grain and raw materials to Germany from Russia.[112]

THOMPSON'S INTENTIONS AND OBJECTIVES

Why would a prominent Wall Street financier, and director of the Federal Reserve Bank, want to organize and assist Bolshevik revolutionaries? Why would not one but several Morgan partners working in concert want to encourage the formation of a Soviet "volunteer revolutionary army" — an army supposedly dedicated to the overthrow of Wall Street, including Thompson, Thomas Lamont, Dwight Morrow, the Morgan firm, and all their associates?

Thompson at least was straightforward about his objectives in Russia: he wanted to keep Russia at war with Germany (yet he argued before the British War Cabinet that Russia was out of the war anyway) and to retain Russia as a market for postwar American enterprise. The December 1917 Thompson memorandum to Lloyd George describes these aims.[113] The memorandum begins, "The Russian situation is lost and Russia lies entirely open to unopposed German exploitation..." and concludes, "I believe that intelligent and courageous work will still prevent Germany from occupying the field to itself and thus exploiting Russia at the expense of the Allies." Consequently, it was German commercial and industrial exploitation of Russia that Thompson feared (this is also reflected in the Thacher memorandum) and that brought Thompson and his New York friends into an alliance with the Bolsheviks. Moreover, this interpretation is reflected in a quasi-jocular statement made by Raymond Robins, Thompson's deputy, to Bruce Lockhart, the British agent:

> You will hear it said that I am the representative of Wall Street; that I am the servant of William B. Thompson to get Altai copper for him; that I have already got 500,000 acres of the best timber land in Russia for myself; that I have already copped off the Trans-

---

[112] Letter reproduced in full in Appendix 3. It should be noted that we have identified Thomas Lamont, Dwight Morrow, and H. P. Davison as being closely involved in developing policy towards the Bolsheviks. All were partners in the J.P. Morgan firm. Thacher was with the law firm Simpson, Thacher & Bartlett and was a close friend of Felix Frankfurter.
[113] See Appendix 3.

Siberian Railway; that they have given me a monopoly of the platinum of Russia; that this explains my working for the soviet... You will hear that talk. Now, I do not think it is true, Commissioner, but let us assume it is true. Let us assume that I am here to capture Russia for Wall Street and American business men. Let us assume that you are a British wolf and I am an American wolf, and that when this war is over we are going to eat each other up for the Russian market; let us do so in perfectly frank, man fashion, but let us assume at the same time that we are fairly intelligent wolves, and that we know that if we do not hunt together in this hour the German wolf will eat us both up, and then let us go to work.[114]

With this in mind let us take a look at Thompson's personal motivations. Thompson was a financier, a promoter, and, although without previous interest in Russia, had personally financed the Red Cross Mission to Russia and used the mission as a vehicle for political maneuvering. From the total picture we can deduce that Thompson's motives were primarily financial and commercial. Specifically, Thompson was interested in the Russian market, and how this market could be influenced, diverted; and captured for postwar exploitation by a Wall Street syndicate, or syndicates. Certainly Thompson viewed Germany as an enemy, but less a political enemy than an economic or a commercial enemy. German industry and German banking were the real enemy. To outwit Germany, Thompson was willing to place seed money on any political power vehicle that would achieve his objective. In other words, Thompson was an American imperialist fighting against German imperialism, and this struggle was shrewdly recognized and exploited by Lenin and Trotsky.

The evidence supports this apolitical approach. In early August 1917, William Boyce Thompson lunched at the U.S. Petrograd embassy with Kerensky, Terestchenko, and the American ambassador Francis. Over lunch Thompson showed his Russian guests a cable he had just sent to the New York office of J.P. Morgan requesting transfer of 425,000 rubles to cover a personal subscription to the new Russian Liberty Loan. Thompson also asked Morgan to "inform my friends I recommend these bonds as the best war investment I know. Will be glad to look after their purchasing here without compensation"; he then offered personally to take up twenty percent of a New York syndicate buying five million rubles of the Russian loan. Not unexpectedly, Kerensky and Terestchenko indicated "great gratification" at support from Wall Street. And Ambassador Francis by cable promptly informed the State Department that the Red Cross commission was "working harmoniously with me," and that it would have an "excellent effect."[115] Other writers have recounted how Thompson attempted to convince the Russian peasants to support Kerensky by investing $1 million of his own

---

[114] U.S., Senate, *Bolshevik Propaganda*, Hearings before a Subcommittee of the Committee on the Judiciary, 65th Cong., 1919, p. 802.
[115] U.S. State Dept. Decimal File, 861.51/184.

money and U.S. government funds on the same order of magnitude in propaganda activities. Subsequently, the Committee on Civic Education in Free Russia, headed by the revolutionary "Grandmother" Breshkovskaya, with David Soskice (Kerensky's private secretary) as executive, established newspapers, news bureaus, printing plants, and speakers bureaus to promote the appeal — "Fight the kaiser and save the revolution." It is noteworthy that the Thompson-funded Kerensky campaign had the same appeal — "Keep Russia in the war" — as had his financial support of the Bolsheviks. The common link between Thompson's support of Kerensky and his support of Trotsky and Lenin was — "continue the war against Germany" and keep Germany out of Russia.

In brief, behind and below the military, diplomatic, and political aspects of World War I, there was another battle raging, namely, a maneuvering for postwar world economic power by international operators with significant muscle and influence. Thompson was not a Bolshevik; he was not even pro-Bolshevik. Neither was he pro-Kerensky. Nor was he even pro-American. *The overriding motivation was the capturing of the postwar Russian market.* This was a commercial, not an ideological, objective. Ideology could sway revolutionary operators like Kerensky, Trotsky, Lenin et al., but not financiers.

The Lloyd George memorandum demonstrates Thompson's partiality for neither Kerensky nor the Bolsheviks: "After the overthrow of the last Kerensky government we materially aided the dissemination of the Bolshevik literature, distributing it through agents and by aeroplanes to the Germany army."[116] This was written in mid-December 1917, only five weeks after the start of the Bolshevik Revolution, and less than four months after Thompson expressed his support of Kerensky over lunch in the American embassy.

THOMPSON RETURNS TO THE UNITED STATES

Thompson then returned and toured the United States with a public plea for recognition of the Soviets. In a speech to the Rocky Mountain Club of New York in January 1918, Thompson called for assistance for the emerging Bolshevik government and, appealing to an audience composed largely of Westerners, evoked the spirit of the American pioneers:

> These men would not have hesitated very long about extending recognition and giving the fullest help and sympathy to the workingman's government of Russia, because in 1819 and the years following we had out there bolsheviki governments... and mighty good governments too.[117]

---

[116] See Appendix 3.
[117] Inserted by Senator Calder into the *Congressional Record,* January 31, 1918, p. 1409.

It strains the imagination to compare the pioneer experience of our Western frontier to the ruthless extermination of political opposition then under way in Russia. To Thompson, promoting this was no doubt looked upon as akin to his promotion of mining stocks in days gone by. As for those in Thompson's audience, we know not what they thought; however, no one raised a challenge. The speaker was a respected director of the Federal Reserve Bank of New York, a self-made millionaire (and that counts for much). And after all, had he not just returned from Russia? But all was not rosy. Thompson's biographer Hermann Hagedorn has written that Wall Street was "stunned" that his friends were "shocked" and "said he had lost his head, had turned Bolshevist himself."[118]

While Wall Street wondered whether he had indeed "turned Bolshevik," Thompson found sympathy among fellow directors on the board of the Federal Reserve Bank of New York. Codirector W. L. Saunders, chairman of Ingersoll-Rand Corporation and a director of the FRB, wrote President Wilson on October 17, 1918, stating that he was "in sympathy with the Soviet form of Government"; at the same time he disclaimed any ulterior motive such as "preparing now to get the trade of the world after the war.[119]

Most interesting of Thompson's fellow directors was George Foster Peabody, deputy chairman of the Federal Reserve Bank of New York and a close friend of socialist Henry George. Peabody had made a fortune in railroad manipulation, as Thompson had made his fortune in the manipulation of copper stocks. Peabody then became active in behalf of government ownership of railroads, and openly adopted socialization.[120] How did Peabody reconcile his private-enterprise success with promotion of government ownership? According to his biographer Louis Ware, "His reasoning told him that it was important for this form of transport to be operated as a public service rather than for the advantage of private interests." This high-sounding do-good reasoning hardly rings true. It would be more accurate to argue that given the dominant political influence of Peabody and his fellow financiers in Washington, they could by government control of railroads more easily avoid the rigors of competition. Through political influence they could manipulate the police power of the state to achieve what they had been unable, or what was too costly, to achieve under private enterprise. In other words, the police power of the state was a means of maintaining a private monopoly. This was exactly as Frederick C. Howe had proposed. The idea of a centrally planned socialist Russia must have appealed to Peabody. Think of it — one

---

[118] Hagedorn, op. tit., p. 263.
[119] U.S. State Dept. Decimal File, 861.00/3005.
[120] Louis Ware, *George Foster Peabody* (Athens: University of Georgia Press, 1951).

gigantic state monopoly! And Thompson, his friend and fellow director, had the inside track with the boys running the operation![121]

THE UNOFFICIAL AMBASSADORS: ROBINS, LOCKHART, AND SADOUL

The Bolsheviks for their part correctly assessed a lack of sympathy among the Petrograd representatives of the three major Western powers: the United States, Britain and France. The United States was represented by Ambassador Francis, undisguisedly out of sympathy with the revolution. Great Britain was represented by Sir James Buchanan, who had strong ties to the tsarist monarchy and was suspected of having helped along the Kerensky phase of the revolution. France was represented by Ambassador Paleologue, overtly anti-Bolshevik. In early 1918 three additional personages made their appearance; they became *de facto* representatives of these Western countries and edged out the officially recognized representatives.

Raymond Robins took over the Red Cross Mission from W. B. Thompson in early December 1917 but concerned himself more with economic and political matters than obtaining relief and assistance for poverty-stricken Russia. On December 26, 1917, Robins cabled Morgan partner Henry Davison, temporarily the director general of the American Red Cross: "Please urge upon the President the necessity of our continued intercourse with the Bolshevik Government."[122] On January 23, 1918, Robins cabled Thompson, then in New York:

> Soviet Government stronger today than ever before. Its authority and power greatly consolidated by dissolution of Constituent Assembly... Cannot urge too strongly importance of prompt recognition of Bolshevik authority... Sisson approves this text and requests you to show this cable to Creel. Thacher and Wardwell concur.[123]

Later in 1918, on his return to the United States, Robins submitted a report to Secretary of State Robert Lansing containing this opening paragraph: "American economic cooperation with Russia; Russia will welcome American assistance in economic reconstruction."[124]

Robins' persistent efforts in behalf of the Bolshevik cause gave him a certain prestige in the Bolshevik camp, and perhaps even some political influence. The U.S. embassy in

---

[121] If this argument seems too farfetched, the reader should see Gabriel Kolko, *Railroads and Regulation 1877-1916* (New York: W. W. Norton, 1965), which describes how pressures for government control and formation of the Interstate Commerce Commission came from the railroad *owners*, not from farmers and users of railroad services.
[122] C. K. Cumming and Waller W. Pettit, *Russian-American Relations, Documents and Papers* (New York: Harcourt, Brace & Howe, 1920), doc. 44.
[123] Ibid., doc. 54.
[124] Ibid., doc. 92.

London claimed in November 1918 that "Salkind owe[s] his appointment, as Bolshevik Ambassador to Switzerland, to an American... no other than Mr. Raymond Robins."[125] About this time reports began filtering into Washington that Robins was himself a Bolshevik; for example, the following from Copenhagen, dated December 3, 1918:

> Confidential. According to a statement made by Radek to George de Patpourrie, late Austria Hungarian Consul General at Moscow, Colonel Robbins [*sic*], formerly thief of the American Red Cross Mission to Russia, is at present in Moscow negotiating with the Soviet Government and arts as the intermediary between the Bolsheviki and their friends in the United States. The impression seems to be in some quarters that Colonel Robbins is himself a Bolsheviki while others maintain that he is not but that his activities in Russia have been contrary to the interest of Associated Governments.[126]

Materials in the files of the Soviet Bureau in New York, and seized by the Lusk Committee in 1919, confirm that both Robins and his wife were closely associated with Bolshevik activities in the United States and with the formation of the Soviet Bureau in New York.[127]

The British government established unofficial relations with the Bolshevik regime by sending to Russia a young Russian-speaking agent, Bruce Lockhart. Lockhart was, in effect, Robins' opposite number; but unlike Robins, Lockhart had direct channels to his Foreign Office. Lockhart was not selected by the foreign secretary or the Foreign Office; both were dismayed at the appointment. According to Richard Ullman, Lockhart was "selected for his mission by Milner and Lloyd George themselves... "Maxim Litvinov, acting as unofficial Soviet representative in Great Britain, wrote for Lockhart a letter of introduction to Trotsky; in it he called the British agent "a thoroughly honest man who understands our position and sympathizes with us.[128]

We have already noted the pressures on Lloyd George to take a pro-Bolshevik position, especially those from William B. Thompson, and those indirectly from Sir Basil Zaharoff and Lord Milner. Milner was, as the epigraph to this chapter suggests, exceedingly prosocialist. Edward Crankshaw has succinctly outlined Milner's duality.

> Some of the passages [in Milner] on industry and society... are passages which any Socialist would be proud to have written. But they were not written by a Socialist. They were written by "the man who made the Boer War." Some of the passages on Imperialism and the

---

[125] U.S. State Dept. Decimal File, 861.00/3449. But see Kennan, *Russia Leaves the War*, pp. 401-5.
[126] Ibid., 861.00 3333.
[127] See chapter seven.
[128] Richard H. Ullman, *Intervention and the War* (Princeton, N.J.: Princeton University Press, 1961), t). 61.

white man's burden might have been written by a Tory diehard. They were written by the student of Karl Marx.[129]

According to Lockhart, the socialist bank director Milner was a man who inspired in him "the greatest affection and hero-worship."[130] Lockhart recounts how Milner personally sponsored his Russian appointment, pushed it to cabinet level, and after his appointment talked "almost daily" with Lockhart. While opening the way for recognition of the Bolsheviks, Milner also promoted financial support for their opponents in South Russia and elsewhere, as did Morgan in New York. This dual policy is consistent with the thesis that the *modus operandi* of the politicized internationalists — such as Milner and Thompson — was to place state money on any revolutionary or counterrevolutionary horse that looked a possible winner. The internationalists, of course, claimed any subsequent benefits. The clue is perhaps in Bruce Lockhart's observation that Milner was a man who "believed in the highly organized state."[131]

The French government appointed an even more openly Bolshevik sympathizer, Jacques Sadoul, an old friend of Trotsky.[132]

In sum, the Allied governments neutralized their own diplomatic representatives in Petrograd and replaced them with unofficial agents more or less sympathetic to the Bolshevists.

The reports of these unofficial ambassadors were in direct contrast to pleas for help addressed to the West from inside Russia. Maxim Gorky protested the betrayal of revolutionary ideals by the Lenin- Trotsky group, which had imposed the iron grip of a police state in Russia:

> We Russians make up a people that has never yet worked in freedom, that has never yet had a chance to develop all its powers and its talents. And when I think that the revolution gives us the possibility of free work, of a many-sided joy in creating, my heart is tilled with great hope and joy, even in these cursed days that are besmirched with blood and alcohol.
> There is where begins the line of my decided and irreconcilable separation [tom the insane actions of the People's Commissaries. I consider Maximalism in ideas very useful for the boundless Russian soul; its task is to develop in this soul great and bold needs, to call forth the so necessary fighting spirit and activity, to promote initiative in this indolent soul and to give it shape and life in general.

---

[129] Edward Crankshaw, *The Forsaken Idea: A Study of Viscount Milner* (London: Longmans Green, 1952), p. 269.
[130] Robert Hamilton Bruce Lockhart, *British Agent* (New York: Putnam's, 1933), p. 119.
[131] Ibid., p. 204.
[132] See Jacques Sadoul, *Notes sur la révolution bolchevique* (Paris: Éditions de la sirène, 1919).

> But the practical Maximalism of the Anarcho-Communists and visionaries from the Smolny is ruinous for Russia and, above all, for the Russian working class. The People's Commissaries handle Russia like material for an experiment. The Russian people is for them what the Horse is for learned bacteriologists who inoculate the horse with typhus so that the anti-typhus lymph may develop in its blood. Now the Commissaries are trying such a predestined-to-failure experiment upon the Russian people without thinking that the tormented, half-starved horse may die.
>
> The reformers from the Smolny do not worry about Russia. They are cold-bloodedly sacrificing Russia in the name of their dream of the worldwide and European revolution. And just as long as I can, I shall impress this upon the Russian proletarian: "Thou art being led to destruction} Thou art being used as material for an inhuman experiment!"

Also in contrast to the reports of the sympathetic unofficial ambassadors were the reports from the old-line diplomatic representatives. Typical of many messages flowing into Washington in early 1918 — particularly after Woodrow Wilson's expression of support for the Bolshevik governments — was the following cable from the U.S. legation in Bern, Switzerland:

> For Polk. President's message to Consul Moscow not understood here and people are asking why the President expresses support of Bolsheviki, in view of rapine, murder and anarchy of these bands.[133]

Continued support by the Wilson administration for the Bolsheviks led to the resignation of De Witt C. Poole, the capable American charge d'affaires in Archangel (Russia):

> It is my duty to explain frankly to the department the perplexity into which I have been thrown by the statement of Russian policy adopted by the Peace Conference, January 22, on the motion of the President. The announcement very happily recognizes the revolution and confirms again that entire absence of sympathy for any form of counter revolution which has always been a key note of American policy in Russia, but it contains not one [word] of condemnation for the other enemy of the revolution — the Bolshevik Government.[134]

Thus even in the early days of 1918 the betrayal of the libertarian revolution had been noted by such acute observers as Maxim Gorky and De Witt C. Poole. Poole's resignation shook the State Department, which requested the "utmost reticence regarding your desire to resign" and stated that "it will be necessary to replace you in a natural and normal

---

[133] U.S. State Dept. Decimal File, 861.00/1305, March 15, 1918.
[134] Ibid., 861.00/3804.

manner in order to prevent grave and perhaps disastrous effect upon the morale of American troops in the Archangel district which might lead to loss of American lives."[135]

So not only did Allied governments neutralize their own government representatives but the U.S. ignored pleas from within and without Russia to cease support of the Bolsheviks. Influential support of the Soviets came heavily from the New York financial area (little effective support emanated from domestic U.S. revolutionaries). In particular, it came from American International Corporation, a Morgan-controlled firm.

EXPORTING THE REVOLUTION: JACOB H. RUBIN

We are now in a position to compare two cases — not by any means the only such cases — in which American citizens Jacob Rubin and Robert Minor assisted in exporting the revolution to Europe and other parts of Russia.

Jacob H. Rubin was a banker who, in his own words, "helped to form the Soviet Government of Odessa."[136] Rubin was president, treasurer, and secretary of Rubin Brothers of 19 West 34 Street, New York City. In 1917 he was associated with the Union Bank of Milwaukee and the Provident Loan Society of New York. The trustees of the Provident Loan Society included persons mentioned elsewhere as having connection with the Bolshevik Revolution: P. A. Rockefeller, Mortimer L. Schiff, and James Speyer.

By some process — only vaguely recounted in his book *I Live to Tell*[137] — Rubin was in Odessa in February 1920 and became the subject of a message from Admiral McCully to the State Department (dated February 13, 1920, 861.00/6349). The message was to the effect that Jacob H. Rubin of Union Bank, Milwaukee, was in Odessa and desired to remain with the Bolshevists — "Rubin does not wish to leave, has offered his services to Bolsheviks and apparently sympathizes with them." Rubin later found his way back to the U.S. and gave testimony before the House Committee on Foreign Affairs in 1921:

> I had been with the American Red Cross people at Odessa. I was there when the Red Army took possession of Odessa. At that time I was favorably inclined toward the Soviet Government, because I was a socialist and had been a member of that party for 20 years. I must admit that to a certain extent I helped to form the Soviet Government of Odessa.[138]

---

[135] Ibid.
[136] U.S., House, Committee on Foreign Affairs, *Conditions in Russia*, 66th Cong., 3d sess., 1921.
[137] Jacob H. Rubin, I Live to Tell: The Russian Adventures of an American Socialist (Indianapolis: Bobbs-Merrill, 1934).
[138] U.S., House, Committee on Foreign Affairs, op. cit.

While adding that he had been arrested as a spy by the Denikin government of South Russia, we learn little more about Rubin. We do, however, know a great deal more about Robert Minor, who was caught in the act and released by a mechanism reminiscent of Trotsky's release from a Halifax prisoner-of-war camp.

EXPORTING THE REVOLUTION: ROBERT MINOR

Bolshevik propaganda work in Germany,[139] financed and organized by William Boyce Thompson and Raymond Robins, was implemented in the field by American citizens, under the supervision of Trotsky's People's Commissariat for Foreign Affairs:

> One of Trotsky's earliest innovations in the Foreign Office had been to institute a Press Bureau under Karl Radek and a Bureau of International Revolutionary Propaganda under Boris Reinstein, among whose assistants were John Reed and Albert Rhys Williams, and the full blast of these power-houses was turned against the Germany army.
> A German newspaper, Die Fackel (The Torch), was printed in editions of half a million a day and sent by special train to Central Army Committees in Minsk, Kiev, and other cities, which in turn distributed them to other points along the front.[140]

Robert Minor was an operative in Reinstein's propaganda bureau. Minor's ancestors were prominent in early American history. General Sam Houston, first president of the Republic of Texas, was related to Minor's mother, Routez Houston. Other relatives were Mildred Washington, aunt of George Washington, and General John Minor, campaign manager for Thomas Jefferson. Minor's father was a Virginia lawyer who migrated to Texas. After hard years with few clients, he became a San Antonio judge.

Robert Minor was a talented cartoonist and a socialist. He left Texas to come East. Some of his contributions appeared in *Masses,* a pro-Bolshevik journal. In 1918 Minor was a cartoonist on the staff of the *Philadelphia Public Ledger.* Minor left New York in March 1918 to report the Bolshevik Revolution. While in Russia Minor joined Reinstein's Bureau of International Revolutionary Propaganda (see diagram), along with Philip Price, correspondent of the *Daily Herald* and *Manchester Guardian,* and Jacques Sadoul, the unofficial French ambassador and friend of Trotsky.

Excellent data on the activities of Price, Minor, and Sadoul have survived in the form of a Scotland Yard (London) Secret Special Report, No. 4, entitled, "The Case of Philip Price

---

[139] See George G. Bruntz, *Allied Propaganda and the Collapse of the German Empire in 1918* (Stanford, Calif.: Stanford University Press, 1938), pp. 144-55; see also herein p. 82.
[140] John W. Wheeler-Bennett, *The Forgotten Peace* (New York: William Morrow, 1939).

and Robert Minor," as well as in reports in the files of the State Department, Washington, D.C.[141] According to this Scotland Yard report, Philip Price was in Moscow in mid-1917, before the Bolshevik Revolution, and admitted, "I am up to my neck in the Revolutionary movement." Between the revolution and about the fall of 1918, Price worked with Robert Minor in the Commissariat for Foreign Affairs.

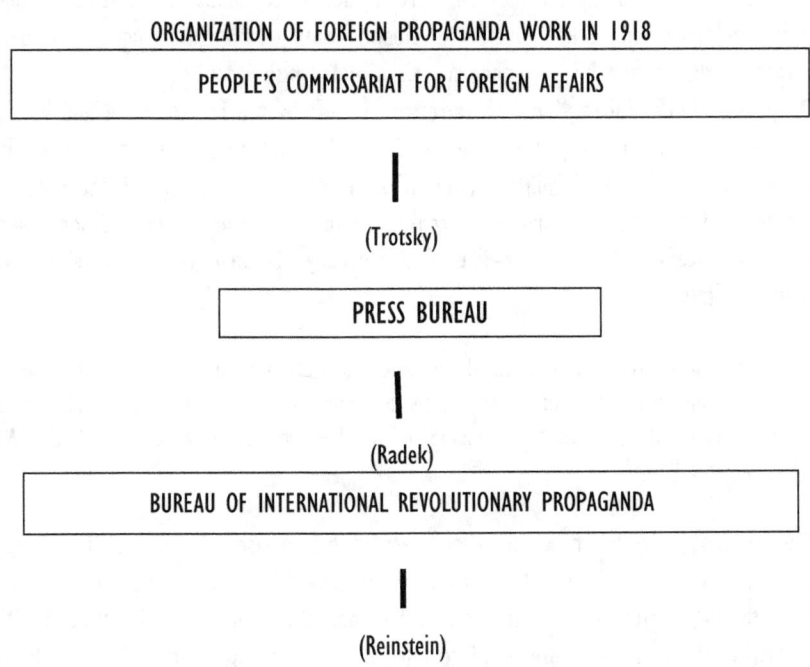

ORGANIZATION OF FOREIGN PROPAGANDA WORK IN 1918

PEOPLE'S COMMISSARIAT FOR FOREIGN AFFAIRS

(Trotsky)

PRESS BUREAU

(Radek)

BUREAU OF INTERNATIONAL REVOLUTIONARY PROPAGANDA

(Reinstein)
Field Operatives
John Reed Louis Bryant Albert Rhys Williams
Robert Minor Philip Price Jacques Sadoul

In November 1918 Minor and Price left Russia and went to Germany.[142] Their propaganda products were first used on the Russian Murman front; leaflets were dropped by Bolshevik airplanes amongst British, French, and American troops — according to William Thompson's program.[143] The decision to send Sadoul, Price, and Minor to Germany was made by the Central Executive Committee of the Communist Party. In Germany their activities came to the notice of British, French, and American intelligence. On February 15, 1919, Lieutenant J. Habas of the U.S. Army was sent to Düsseldorf, then under control of a Spartacist

---

[141] There is a copy of this Scotland Yard report in U.S. Start' Dept. Decimal File, 316-23-1184 9.
[142] Joseph North, *Robert Minor: Artist and Crusader* (New York: International Publishers, 1956).
[143] Samples of Minor's propaganda tracts are still in the U.S. State Dept. files. See p. 197-200 on Thompson.

revolutionary group; he posed as a deserter from the American army and offered his services to the Spartacists. Habas got to know Philip Price and Robert Minor and suggested that some pamphlets be printed for distribution amongst American troops. The Scotland Yard report relates that Price and Minor had already written several pamphlets for British and American troops, that Price had translated some of Wilhelm Liebknecht's works into English, and that both were working on additional propaganda tracts. Habas reported that Minor and Price said they had worked together in Siberia printing an English-language Bolshevik newspaper for distribution by air among American and British troops.[144]

On June 8, 1919, Robert Minor was arrested in Paris by the French police and handed over to the American military authorities in Coblenz. Simultaneously, German Spartacists were arrested by the British military authorities in the Cologne area. Subsequently, the Spartacists were convicted on charges of conspiracy to cause mutiny and sedition among Allied forces. Price was arrested but, like Minor, speedily liberated. This hasty release was noted in the State Department:

> Robert Minor has now been released, for reasons that are not quite clear, since the evidence against him appears to have been ample to secure conviction. The release will have an unfortunate effect, for Minor is believed to have been intimately connected with the IWW in America.[145]

The mechanism by which Robert Minor secured his release is recorded in the State Department files. The first relevant document, dated June 12, 1919, is from the U.S. Paris embassy to the secretary of state in Washington, D.C., and marked URGENT AND CONFIDENTIAL.[146] The French Foreign Office informed the embassy that on June 8, Robert Minor, "an American correspondent," had been arrested in Paris and turned over to the general headquarters of the Third American Army in Coblenz. Papers found on Minor appear "to confirm the reports furnished on his activities. It would therefore seem to be established that Minor has entered into relations in Paris with the avowed partisans of Bolshevism." The embassy regarded Minor as a "particularly dangerous man." Inquiries were being made of the American military authorities; the embassy believed this to be a matter within the jurisdiction of the military alone, so that it contemplated no action although instructions would be welcome.

---

[144] See Appendix 3.
[145] U.S. State Dept. Decimal File, 316-23-1184.
[146] Ibid., 861.00/4680 (316-22-0774).

On June 14, Judge R. B. Minor in San Antonio, Texas, telegraphed Frank L. Polk in the State Department:

> Press reports detention my son Robert Minor in Paris for unknown reasons. Please do all possible to protect him I refer to Senators from Texas. [sgd.] R. P. Minor, District Judge, San Antonio, Texas.[147]

Polk telegraphed Judge Minor that neither the State Department nor the War Department had information on the detention of Robert Minor, and that the case was now before the military authorities at Coblenz. Late on June 13 the State Department received a "strictly confidential urgent" message from Paris reporting a statement made by the Office of Military Intelligence (Coblenz) in regard to the detention of Robert Minor: "Minor was arrested in Paris by French authorities upon request of British Military Intelligence and immediately turned over to American headquarters at Coblenz."[148] He was charged with writing and disseminating Bolshevik revolutionary literature, which had been printed in Dusseldorf, amongst British and American troops in the areas they occupied. The military authorities intended to examine the charges against Minor, and if substantiated, to try him by court-martial. If the charges were not substantiated, it was their intention to turn Minor over to the British authorities, "who originally requested that the French hand him over to them."[149] Judge Minor in Texas independently contacted Morris Sheppard, U.S. senator from Texas, and Sheppard contacted Colonel House in Paris. On June 17, 1919, Colonel House sent the following to Senator Sheppard:

> Both the American Ambassador and I are following Robert Minor's case. Am informed that he is detained by American Military authorities at Cologne on serious charges, the exact nature of which it is difficult to discover. Nevertheless, we will take every possible step to insure just consideration for him.[150]

Both Senator Sheppard and Congressman Carlos Bee (14th District, Texas) made their interest known to the State Department. On June 27, 1919, Congressman Bee requested facilities so that Judge Minor could send his son $350 and a message. On July 3 Senator Sheppard wrote Frank Polk, stating that he was "very much interested" in the Robert Minor case, and wondering whether State could ascertain its status, and whether Minor was properly under the jurisdiction of the military authorities. Then on July 8 the Paris embassy cabled

---

[147] Ibid., 861.00/4685 (/783).
[148] U.S. State Dept. Decimal File, 861.00/4688 (/788).
[149] Ibid.
[150] Ibid., 316-33-0824.

Washington: "Confidential. Minor released by American authorities... returning to the United States on the first available boat." This sudden release intrigued the State Department, and on August 3 Secretary of State Lansing cabled Paris: "Secret. Referring to previous, am very anxious to obtain reasons for Minor's release by Military authorities."

Originally, U.S. Army authorities had wanted the British to try Robert Minor as "they feared politics might intervene in the United States to prevent a conviction if the prisoner was tried by American court-martial." However, the British government argued that Minor was a United States citizen, that the evidence showed he prepared propaganda against American troops in the first instance, and that, consequently — so the British Chief of Staff suggested — Minor should be tried before an American court. The British Chief of Staff did "consider it of the greatest importance to obtain a conviction if possible."[151]

Documents in the office of the Chief of Staff of the Third Army relate to the internal details of Minor's release.[152] A telegram of June 23, 1919, from Major General Harbord, Chief of Staff of the Third Army (later chairman of the Board of International General Electric, whose executive center, coincidentally, was also at 120 Broadway), to the commanding general, Third Army, stated that Commander in Chief John J. Pershing "directs that you suspend action in the case against Minor pending further orders." There is also a memorandum signed by Brigadier General W. A. Bethel in the office of the judge advocate, dated June 28, 1919, marked "Secret and Confidential," and entitled "Robert Minor, Awaiting Trial by a Military Commission at Headquarters, 3rd Army." The memo reviews the legal case against Minor. Among the points made by Bethel is that the British were obviously reluctant to handle the Minor case because "they fear American opinion in the event of trial by them of an American for a war offense in Europe," even though tire offense with which Minor is charged is as serious "as a man can commit." This is a significant statement; Minor, Price, and Sadoul were implementing a program designed by Federal Reserve Bank director Thompson, a fact confirmed by Thompson's own memorandum (see Appendix 3). Was not therefore Thompson (and Robins), to some degree, subject to the same charges?

After interviewing Siegfried, the witness against Minor, and reviewing the evidence, Bethel commented:

> I thoroughly believe Minor to be guilty, but if I was sitting in court, I would not put guilty on the evidence now available — the testimony of one man only and that man acting in the character of a detective and informer.

---

[151] U.S. State Dept. Decimal File, 861.00/4874.
[152] Office of Chief of Staff, U.S. Army, National Archives, Washington, D.C.

Bethel goes on to state that it would be known within a week or ten days whether substantial corroboration of Siegfried's testimony was available. If available, "I think Minor should be tried," but "if corroboration cannot be had, I think it would be better to dismiss the case."

This statement by Bethel was relayed in a different form by General Harbord in a telegram of July 5 to General Malin Craig (Chief of Staff, Third Army, Coblenz):

> With reference to the case against Minor, unless other witnesses than Siegfried have been located by this time C in C directs the case be dropped and Minor liberated. Please acknowledge and state action.

The reply from Craig to General Harbord (July 5) records that Minor was liberated in Paris and adds, "This is in accordance with his own wishes and suits our purposes." Craig also adds that other witnesses *had* been obtained.

This exchange of telegrams suggests a degree of haste in dropping the charges against Robert Minor, and haste suggests pressure. There was no significant attempt made to develop evidence. Intervention by Colonel House and General Pershing at the highest levels in Paris and the cablegram from Colonel House to Senator Morris Sheppard give weight to American newspaper reports that both House and President Wilson were responsible for Minor's hasty release without trial.[153]

Minor returned to the United States and, like Thompson and Robins before him, toured the U.S. promoting the wonders of Bolshevik Russia.

By way of summary, we find that Federal Reserve Bank director William Thompson was active in promoting Bolshevik interests in several ways — production of a pamphlet in Russian, financing Bolshevik operations, speeches, organizing (with Robins) a Bolshevik revolutionary mission to Germany (and perhaps France), and with Morgan partner Lamont influencing Lloyd George and the British War Cabinet to effect a change in British policy. Further, Raymond Robins was cited by the French government for organizing Russian Bolsheviks for the German revolution. We know that Robins was undisguisedly working for Soviet interests in Russia and the United States. Finally, we find that Robert Minor, one of the revolutionary propagandists used in Thompson's program, was released under circumstances suggesting intervention from the highest levels of the U.S. government.

---

[153] U.S., Senate, *Congressional Record,* October 1919, pp. 6430, 6664-66, 7353-54; and *New York Times,* October It, 1919. See also *Sacramento Bee,* July 17, 1919.

Obviously, this is but a fraction of a much wider picture. These are hardly accidental or random events. They constitute a coherent, continuing pattern over several years. They suggest powerful influence at the summit levels of several governments.

CHAPTER VII

THE BOLSHEVIKS RETURN TO NEW YORK

Martens is very much in the limelight. There appears to be no doubt about his connection with the Guarantee [sic] Trust Company. Though it is surprising that so large and influential an enterprise should have dealings with a Bolshevik concern.
                                        Scotland Yard Intelligence Report, London, 1919[154]

Following on the initial successes of the revolution, the Soviets wasted little time in attempting through former U.S. residents to establish diplomatic relations with and propaganda outlets in the United States. In June 1918 the American consul in Harbin cabled Washington:

> Albert R. Williams, bearer Department passport 52,913 May 15, 1917 proceeding United States to establish information bureau for Soviet Government for which he has written authority. Shall I visa?[155]

Washington denied the visa and so Williams was unsuccessful in his attempt to establish an information bureau here. Williams was followed by Alexander Nyberg (alias Santeri Nuorteva), a former Finnish immigrant to the United States in January 1912, who became the first operative Soviet representative in the United States. Nyberg was an activtive propagandist. In fact, in 1919 be was, according to J. Edgar Hoover (in a letter to the U.S. Committee on Foreign Affairs), "the forerunner of LCAK Martens anti with Gregory Weinstein the most active individual of official Bolshevik propaganda in the United States."[156]

Nyberg was none too successful as a diplomatic representative or, ultimately, as a propagandist. The State Departmment files record an interview with Nyberg by the counselors' office, dated January 29, 1919. Nyberg was accompanied by H. Kellogg, described as "an American citizen, graduate of Harvard," and, more surprisingly, by a Mr. McFarland, an attorney for the Hearst organization. The State Department records show that Nyberg made

---

[154] Copy in U.S. State Dept. Decimal File, 316-22-656.
[155] Ibid., 861.00/1970.
[156] U.S., House, Committee on Foreign Affairs, *Conditions in Russia*, 66th Cong., 3d sess., 1921, p. 78.

"many misstatements in regard to the attitude to the Bolshevik Government" and claimed that Peters, the Lett terrorist police chief in Petrograd, was merely a "kind-hearted poet." Nyberg requested the department to cable Lenin, "on the theory that it might be helpful in bringing about the conference proposed by the Allies at Paris."[157] The proposed message, a rambling appeal to Lenin to gain international acceptance appearing at the Paris Conference, was not sent.[158]

A RAID ON THE SOVIET BUREAU IN NEW YORK

Alexander Nyberg (Nuorteva) was then let go and replaced by the Soviet Bureau, which was established in early 1919 in the World Tower Building, 110 West 40 Street, New York City. The bureau was headed by a German citizen, Ludwig C. A. K. Martens, who is usually billed as the first ambassador of the Soviet Union in the United States, and who, up to that time, had been vice president of Weinberg & Posner, an engineering firm located at 120 Broadway, New York City. Why the "ambassador" and his offices were located in New York rather than in Washington, D.C. was not explained; it does suggest that trade rather than diplomacy was its primary objective. In any event, the bureau promptly issued a call lot Russian trade with the United States. Industry had collapsed and Russia direly needed machinery, railway goods, clothing, chemicals, drugs — indeed, everything utilized by a modern civilization. In exchange the Soviets offered gold and raw materials. The Soviet Bureau then proceeded to arrange contracts with American firms, ignoring the facts of the embargo and nonrecognition. At the same time it was providing financial support for the emerging Communist Party U.S.A.[159]

On May 7, 1919, the State Department slapped down business intervention in behalf of the bureau (noted elsewhere), and repudiated Ludwig Martens, the Soviet Bureau, and the Bolshevik government of Russia. This official rebuttal did not deter the eager order-hunters in American industry. When the Soviet Bureau offices were raided on June 12, 1919, by representatives of the Lusk Committee of the state of New York, files of letters to and from American businessmen, representing almost a thousand firms, were unearthed. The British Home Office Directorate of Intelligence "Special Report No. 5 (Secret)," issued from Scotland Yard, London, July 14, 1919, and written by Basil H. Thompson, was based on this seized material; the report noted:

---

[157] U.S. State Dept. Decimal File, 316-19-1120.
[158] Ibid.
[159] See Benjamin Gitlow, U.S., House, *Un-American Propaganda Activities* (Washington, 1939), vols. 7-8, p. 4539.

... Every effort was made from the first by Martens and his associates to arouse the interest of American capitalists and there are grounds tot believing that the Bureau has received financial support from some Russian export firms, as well as from the Guarantee [*sic*] Trust Company, although this firm has denied the allegation that it is financing Martens' organisation.[160]

It was noted by Thompson that the monthly rent of the Soviet Bureau offices was $300 and the office salaries came to about $4,000. Martens' funds to pay these bills came partly from Soviet couriers — such as John Reed and Michael Gruzenberg — who brought diamonds from Russia for sale in the U.S., and partly from American business firms, including the Guaranty Trust Company of New York. The British reports summarized the files seized by the Lusk investigators from the bureau offices, and this summary is worth quoting in full:

(1) There was an intrigue afoot about the time the President first went to France to get the Administration to use Nuorteva as an intermediary with the Russian Soviet Government, with a view to bring about its recognition by America. Endeavour was made to bring Colonel House into it, and there is a long and interesting letter to Frederick C. Howe, on whose support and sympathy Nuorteva appeared to rely. There are other records connecting Howe with Martens and Nuorteva.

(2) There is a file of correspondence with Eugene Debs.

(3) A letter from Amos Pinchot to William Kent of the U.S. Tariff Commission in an envelope addressed to Senator Lenroot, introduces Evans Clark "now in the Bureau of the Russian Soviet Republic." "He wants to talk to you about the recognition of Kolchak and the raising of the blockade, etc."

(4) A report to Felix Frankfurter, dated 27th May, 1919 speaks of the virulent campaign vilifying the Russian Government.

(5) There is considerable correspondence between a Colonel and Mrs. Raymond Robbins [*sic*] and Nuorteva, both in 1918 and 1919. In July 1918 Mrs. Robbins asked Nuorteva for articles for "Life and Labour," the organ of the National Women's Trade League. In February and March, 1919, Nuorteva tried, through Robbins, to get invited to give evidence before the Overman Committee. He also wanted Robbins to denounce the Sisson documents.

(6) In a letter from the Jansen Cloth Products Company, New York, to Nuorteva, dated March 30th, 1918, E. Werner Knudsen says that he understands that Nuorteva intends to make arrangements for the export of food-stuffs through Finland and he offers his services.

---

[160] Copy in [U.S. State Dept. Decimal File, 316-22-656. Confirmation of Guaranty Trust involvement tomes in later intelligence reports.

We have a file on Knudsen, who passed information to and from Germany by way of Mexico with regard to British shipping.[161]

Ludwig Martens, the intelligence report continued, was in touch with all the leaders of "the left" in the United States, including John Reed, Ludwig Lore, and Harry J. Boland, the Irish rebel. A vigorous campaign against Aleksandr Kolchak in Siberia had been organized by Martens. The report concludes:

> [Martens'] organization is a powerful weapon for supporting the Bolshevik cause in the United States and... he is in close touch with the promoters of political unrest throughout the whole American continent.

The Scotland Yard list of personnel employed by the Soviet Bureau in New York coincides quite closely with a similar list in the Lusk Committee files in Albany, New York, which are today open for public inspection.[162] There is one essential difference between the two lists: the British analysis included the name "Julius Hammer" whereas Hammer was omitted from the Lusk Committee report.[163] The British report characterizes Julius Hammer as follows:

> In Julius Hammer, Martens has a real Bolshevik and ardent Left Wing adherent, who came not long ago from Russia. He was one of the organizers of the Left Wing movement in New York, and speaks at meetings on the same platform with such Left Wing leaders as Reed, Hourwich, Lore and Larkin.

There also exists other evidence of Hammer's work in behalf of the Soviets. A letter from National City Bank, New York, to the U.S. Treasury Department stated that documents received by the bank from Martens were "witnessed by a Dr. Julius Hammer for the Acting Director of the Financial Department" of the Soviet Bureau.[164]

The Hammer family has had close ties with Russia and the Soviet regime from 1917 to the present. Armand Hammer is today able to acquire the most lucrative of Soviet contracts. Jacob, grandfather of Armand Hammer, and Julius were born in Russia. Armand, Harry, and

---

[161] On Frederick C. Howe see pp. 16, 177, for an early statement of the manner in which financiers use society and its problems for their own ends; on Felix Frankfurter, later Supreme Court justice, see Appendix 3 for an early Frankfurter letter to Nuorteva; on Raymond Robins see p. 100.

[162] The Lusk Committee list of personnel in the Soviet Bureau is printed in Appendix 3. The list includes Kenneth Durant, aide to Colonel House; Dudley Field Malone, appointed by President Wilson as collector of customs for the Port of New York; and Morris Hillquit, the financial intermediary between New York banker Eugene Boissevain on the one hand, and John Reed and Soviet agent Michael Gruzenberg on the other.

[163] Julius Hammer was the father of Armand Hammer, who today is chairman of the Occidental Petroleum Corp. of Los Angeles.

[164] See Appendix 3.

Victor, sons of Julius, were born in the United States and are U.S. citizens. Victor was a well-known artist; his son — also named Armand — and granddaughter are Soviet citizens and reside in the Soviet Union. Armand Hammer is chairman of Occidental Petroleum Corporation and has a son, Julian, who is director of advertising and publications for Occidental Petroleum.

Julius Hammer was a prominent member and financier of the left wing of the Socialist Party. At its 1919 convention Hammer served with Bertram D. Wolfe and Benjamin Gitlow on the steering committee that gave birth to the Communist Party of the U.S.

In 1920 Julius Hammer was given a sentence of three-and-one-half to fifteen years in Sing Sing for criminal abortion. Lenin suggested — with justification — that Julius was "imprisoned on the charge of practicing illegal abortions but in fact because of communism."[165] Other U.S. Communist Party members were sentenced to jail for sedition or deported to the Soviet Union. Soviet representatives in the United States made strenuous but unsuccessful efforts to have Julius and his fellow party members released.

Another prominent member of the Soviet Bureau was the assistant secretary, Kenneth Durant, a former aide to Colonel House. In 1920 Durant was identified as a Soviet courier. Appendix 3 reproduces a letter to Kenneth Durant that was seized by the U.S. Department of Justice in 1920 and that describes Durant's close relationship with the Soviet hierarchy. It was inserted into the record of a House committee's hearings in 1920, with the following commentary:

> MR. NEWTON: It is a mailer of interest to this committee to know what was the nature of that letter, and I have a copy of the letter that I Want inserted in the record in connection with the witness' testimony. MR. Mason: That letter has never been shown to the witness. He said that he never saw the letter, and had asked to see it, and that the department had refused to show it to him. We would not put any witness on the stand and ask him to testify to a letter without seeing it.
> MR. NEWTON: The witness testified that he has such a letter, and he testified that they found it in his coat in the trunk, I believe. That letter was addressed to a Mr. Kenneth Durant, and that letter had within it another envelope which was likewise sealed. They were opened by the Government officials and a photostatic copy made. The letter, I may say, is signed by a man by the name of *"Bill."* It refers specifically to soviet moneys on deposit in Christiania, Norway, a portion of which they waist turned over here to officials of the soviet government in this country.[166]

---

[165] V. I. Lenin, *Polnoe Sobranie Sochinenii*, 5th ed. (Moscow, 1958), 53:267.
[166] U.S., House, Committee. on Foreign Affairs, *Conditions in Russia*, 66th Cong., 3d sess., 1921, p. 75. "Bill" was William Bobroff, Soviet agent.

Kenneth Durant, who acted as Soviet courier in the transfer of funds, was treasurer lot the Soviet Bureau and press secretary and publisher of *Soviet Russia,* the official organ of the Soviet Bureau. Durant came from a well-to-do Philadelphia family. He spent most of his life in the service of the Soviets, first in charge of publicity work at the Soviet Bureau then from 1923 to 1944 as manager of the Soviet *Tass* bureau in the United States. J. Edgar Hoover described Durant as "at all times... particularly active in the interests of Martens and of the Soviet government."[167]

Felix Frankfurter — later justice of the Supreme Courts — was also prominent in the Soviet Bureau files. A letter from Frankfurter to Soviet agent Nuorteva is reproduced in Appendix 3 and suggests that Frankfurter had some influence with the bureau.

In brief, the Soviet Bureau could not have been established without influential assistance from within the United States. Part of this assistance came from specific influential appointments to the Soviet Bureau staff and part came from business firms outside the bureau, firms that were reluctant to make their support publicly known.

CORPORATE ALLIES FOR THE SOVIET BUREAU

On February 1, 1920, the front page of the *New York Times* carried a boxed notation stating that Martens was to be arrested and deported to Russia. At the same time Martens was being sought as a witness to appear before a subcommittee of the Senate Foreign Relations Committee investigating Soviet activity in the United States. After lying low for a few days Martens appeared before the committee, claimed diplomatic privilege, and refused to give up "official" papers in his possession. Then after a flurry of publicity, Martens "relented," handed over his papers, and admitted to revolutionary activities in the United States with the ultimate aim of overthrowing the capitalist system.

Martens boasted to the news media and Congress that big corporations, the Chicago packers among them, were aiding the Soviets:

> Affording to Martens, instead of farthing on propaganda among the radicals and the proletariat he has addressed most of his efforts to winning to the side of Russia the big business and manufacturing interests of this country, the packers, the United States Steel Corporation, the Standard Oil Company and other big concerns engaged in international trade. Martens asserted that most of the big business houses of the country were aiding him in his effort to get the government to recognize the Soviet government.[168]

---

[167] Ibid., p. 78.
[168] *New York Times,* November 17, 1919.

This claim was expanded by A. A. Heller, commercial attache at the Soviet Bureau:

> "Among the people helping us to get recognition from the State Department are the big Chicago packers, Armour, Swift, Nelson Morris and Cudahy.... Among the other firms are... the American Steel Export Company, the Lehigh Machine Company, the Adrian Knitting Company, the International Harvester Company, the Aluminum Goods Manufacturing Company, the Aluminum Company of America, the American Car and Foundry Export Company, M.C.D. Borden & Sons."[169]

The *New York Times* followed up these claims and reported comments of the firms named. "I have never heard of this man [Martens] before in my life," declared G. F. Swift, Jr., in charge of the export department of Swift & Co. "Most certainly I am sure that we have never had any dealings with him of any kind."[170] The *Times* added that O. H. Swift, the only other member of the firm that could be contacted, "also denied any knowledge whatever of Martens or his bureau in New York." The Swift statement was evasive at best. When the Lusk Committee investigators seized the Soviet Bureau files, they found correspondence between the bureau and almost all the firms named by Martens and Heller. The "list of firms that offered to do business with Russian Soviet Bureau," compiled from these files, included an entry (page 16), "Swift and Company, Union Stock Yards, Chicago, Ill." In other words, Swift *had* been in communication with Martens despite its denial to the *New York Times*.

The *New York Times* contacted United States Steel and reported, "Judge Elbert H. Gary said last night that there was no foundation for the statement with the Soviet representative here had had any dealings with the United States Steel Corporation." This is technically correct. The United States Steel Corporation is not listed in the Soviet files, but the list *does* contain (page 16) an affiliate, "United States Steel Products Co., 30 Church Street, New York City."

The Lusk Committee list records the following about other firms mentioned by Martens and Heller: Standard Oil — not listed. Armour 8c Co., meatpackers — listed as "Armour Leather" and "Armour & Co. Union Stock Yards, Chicago." Morris Go., meatpackers, is listed on page 13. Cudahy — listed on page 6. American Steel Export Co. — listed on page 2 as located at the Woolworth Building; it had offered to trade with the USSR. Lehigh Machine Co. — not listed. Adrian Knitting Co. — listed on page 1. International Harvester Co. — listed on page 11. Aluminum Goods Manufacturing Co. — listed on page 1. Aluminum Company of America — not listed. American Car and Foundry Export — the closest listing

---

[169] Ibid.
[170] Ibid.

is "American Car Co. — Philadelphia." M.C.D. Borden & Sons — listed as located at 90 Worth Street, on page 4.

Then on Saturday, June *21,* 1919, Santeri Nuorteva (Alexander Nyberg) confirmed in a press interview the role of International Harvester:

Q: [by *New York Times* reporter]: What is your business?
A: Purchasing director tot Soviet Russia.
Q: What did you do to accomplish this?
A: Addressed myself to American manufacturers.
Q: Name them.
A: International Harvester Corporation is among them.
Q: Whom did you see?
A: Mr. Koenig.
Q: Did you go to see him?
A: Yes.
Q: Give more names.
A: I went to see so many, about 500 people and I can't remember all the names. We have files in the office disclosing them.[171]

In brief, the claims by Heller and Martens relating to their widespread contacts among certain U.S. firms were substantiated by the office files of the Soviet Bureau. On the other hand, for their own good reasons, these firms appeared unwilling to confirm their activities.

EUROPEAN BANKERS AID THE BOLSHEVIKS

In addition to Guaranty Trust and the private banker Boissevain in New York, some European bankers gave direct help to maintain and expand the Bolshevik hold on Russia. A 1918 State Department report from our Stockholm embassy details these financial transfers. The department commended its author, stating that his *"reports on conditions in Russia, the spread of Bolshevism in Europe, and financial questions... have proved most helpful to the Department. Department is much gratified by your capable handling of the legation's business."*[172] According to this report, one of these "Bolshevik bankers" acting in behalf of the emerging Soviet regime was Dmitri Rubenstein, of the former Russo-French bank in Petrograd. Rubenstein, an associate of the notorious Grigori Rasputin, had been jailed in prerevolutionary Petrograd in connection with the sale of the Second Russian Life Insurance

---

[171] *New York Times,* June 21, 1919.
[172] U.S. State Dept. Decimal File, 861.51/411, November 23, 1918.

Company. The American manager and director of the Second Russian Life Insurance Company was John MacGregor Grant, who was located at 120 Broadway, New York City. Grant was also the New York representative of Putiloff's Banque Russo-Asiatique. In August 1918 Grant was (for unknown reasons) listed on the Military Intelligence Bureau "suspect list."[173] This may have occurred because Olof Aschberg in early 1918 reported opening a foreign credit in Petrograd "with the John MacGregor Grant Co., export concern, which it [Aschberg] finances in Sweden and which is financed in America by the Guarantee [sic] Trust Co."[174] After the revolution Dmitri Rubenstein moved to Stockholm and became financial agent for the Bolsheviks. The State Department noted that while Rubenstein was "not a Bolshevik, he has been unscrupulous in moneT' making, and it is suspected that he may be making the contemplated visit to America in Bolshevik interest and for Bolshevik pay.[175]

Another Stockholm "Bolshevik banker" was Abram Givatovzo, brother-in-law of Trotsky and Lev Kamenev. The State Department report asserted that while Givatovzo pretended to be "very anti- Bolshevik," he had in fact received "large sums" of moneT' from the Bolsheviks by courier for financing revolutionary operations. Givatovzo was part of a syndicate that included Denisoff of the former Siberian bank, Kamenka of the Asoff Don Bank, and Davidoff of the Bank of Foreign Commerce. This syndicate sold the assets of the former Siberian Bank to the British government.

Yet another tsarist private banker, Gregory Lessine, handled Bolshevik business through the firm of Dardel and Hagborg. Other "Bolshevik bankers" named in the report are stirrer and Jakob Berline, who previously controlled, through his wife, the Petrograd Nelkens Bank. Isidor Kon was used by these bankers as an agent.

The most interesting of these Europe-based bankers operating in behalf of the Bolsheviks was Gregory Benenson, formerly chairman in Petrograd of the Russian and English Bank — a bank which included on its board of directors Lord Balfour (secretary of state for foreign affairs in England) and Sir I. M. H. Amory, as well as S. H. Cripps and H. Guedalla. Benenson traveled to Petrograd after the revolution, then on to Stockholm. He came. said one State Department official, "bringing to my knowledge ten million rubles with him as he offered them to me at a high price for the use of our Embassy Archangel." Benenson had an arrangement with the Bolsheviks to exchange sixty million rubles for £1.5 million sterling.

In January 1919 the private bankers in Copenhagen that were associated with Bolshevik institutions became alarmed by rumors that the Danish political police had marked the Soviet legation and those persons in contact with the Bolsheviks for expulsion from Denmark. These bankers and the legation hastily attempted to remove their funds from Danish banks

---

[173] Ibid., 316-125-1212.
[174] U.S., Department of State, Foreign Relations of the United States: 1918, Russia, 1:373.
[175] U.S. State Dept. Decimal File, 861.00/4878, July,' 21, 1919.

— in particular, seven million rubles from the Revisionsbanken.[176] Also, confidential documents were hidden in the offices of the Martin Larsen Insurance Company.

Consequently, we can identify a pattern of assistance by capitalist bankers for the Soviet Union. Some of these were American bankers, some were tsarist bankers who were exiled and living in Europe, and some were European bankers. Their common objective was profit, not ideology.

The questionable aspects of the work of these "Bolshevik bankers," as they were called, arises from the framework of contemporary events in Russia. In 1919 French, British, and American troops were fighting Soviet troops in the Archangel region. In one clash in April 1919, for example, American casualties were one officer, .five men killed, and nine missing.[177] Indeed, at one point in 1919 General Tasker H. Bliss, the U.S. commander in Archangel, affirmed the British statement that "Allied troops in the Murmansk and Archangel districts were in danger of extermination unless they were speedily reinforced."[178] Reinforcements were then on the way under the command of Brigadier General W. P. Richardson.

In brief, while Guaranty Trust and first-rank American firms were assisting the formation of the Soviet Bureau in New York, American troops were in conflict with Soviet troops in North Russia. Moreover, these conflicts were daily reported in the *New York Times,* presumably read by these bankers and businessmen. Further, as we shall see in chapter ten, the financial circles that were supporting the Soviet Bureau in New York also formed in New York the "United Americans" — a virulently anti-Communist organization predicting bloody revolution, mass starvation, and panic in the streets of New York.

---

[176] Ibid., 316-21-115/21.
[177] *New York Times,* April 5, 1919.
[178] Ibid.

Chapter VIII

120 Broadway, New York City

William B. Thompson, who was in Petrograd from July until November last, has made a personal contribution of $1,000,000 to the Bolsheviki for the purpose of spreading their doctrine in Germany and Austria...

Washington Post, February 2, 1918

While collecting material for this book a single location and address in the Wall Street area came to the fore — 120 Broadway, New York City. Conceivably, this book could have been written incorporating only persons, firms, and organizations located at 120 Broadway in the year 1917. Although this research method would have been forced and unnatural, it would have excluded only a relatively small segment of the story.

The original building at 120 Broadway was destroyed by fire before World War I. Subsequently the site was sold to the Equitable Office Building Corporation, organized by General T. Coleman du Pont, president of du Pont de Nemours Powder Company.[179] A new building was completed in 1915 and the Equitable Life Assurance Company moved back to its old site. In passing we should note an interesting interlock in Equitable history. In 1916 the cashier of the Berlin Equitable Life office was William Schacht, the father of Hjalmar Horace Greeley Schacht — later to become Hitler's banker, and financial genie. William Schacht was an American citizen, worked thirty years for Equitable in Germany, and owned a Berlin house known as "Equitable Villa." Before joining Hitler, young Hjalmar Schacht served as a member of the Workers and Soldiers Council (a soviet) of Zehlendoff; this he left in 1918 to join the board of the Nationalbank fur Deutschland. His codirector at DONAT was Emil Wittenberg, who, with Max May of Guaranty Trust Company of New York, was a director of the first Soviet international bank, Ruskombank.

In any event, the building at 120 Broadway was in 1917 known as the Equitable Life Building. A large building, although by no means the largest office building in New York

---

[179] By a quirk the papers of incorporation for the Equitable Office Building were drawn up by Dwight W. Morrow, later a Morgan partner, but then a member of the law firm of Simpson, Thacher & Bartlett. The Thacher firm contributed two members to the 1917 American Red Cross Mission to Russia (see chapter five).

City, it occupies a one-block area at Broadway and Pine, and has thirty-four floors. The Bankers Club was located on the thirty-fourth floor. The tenant list in 1917 in effect reflected American involvement in the Bolshevik Revolution and its aftermath. For example, the headquarters of the No. 2 District of the Federal Reserve System — the New York area — by far the most important of the Federal Reserve districts, was located at 120 Broadway. The offices of several individual directors of the Federal Reserve Bank of New York and, most important, the American International Corporation were also at 120 Broadway. By way of contrast, Ludwig Martens, appointed by the Soviets as the first Bolshevik "ambassador" to the United States and head of the Soviet Bureau, was in 1917 the vice president of Weinberg & Posner — and also had offices at 120 Broadway.[180]

Is this concentration an accident? Does the geographical contiguity have any significance? Before attempting to suggest an answer, we have to switch our frame of reference and abandon the left- right spectrum of political analysis.

With an almost unanimous lack of perception the academic world has described and analyzed international political relations in the context of an unrelenting conflict between capitalism and communism, and rigid adherence to this Marxian formula has distorted modern history. Tossed out from time to time are odd remarks to the effect that the polarity is indeed spurious, but these are quickly dispatched to limbo. For example, Carroll Quigley, professor of international relations at Georgetown University, made the following comment on the House of Morgan:

> More than fifty years ago the Morgan firm decided to infiltrate the Left-wing political movements in the United States. This was relatively easy to do, since these groups were starved for funds and eager for a voice to reach the people. Wall Street supplied both. The purpose was not to destroy, dominate or take over...[181]

Professor Quigley's comment, apparently based on confidential documentation, has all the ingredients of an historical bombshell if it can be supported. We suggest that the Morgan firm infiltrated not only the domestic left, as noted by Quigley, but also the foreign left — that is, the Bolshevik movement and the Third International. Even further, through friends in the U.S. State Department, Morgan and allied financial interests, particularly the Rockefeller family, have exerted a powerful influence on U.S.-Russian relations from World War I to the present. The evidence presented in this chapter will suggest that two of the

---

[180] The John MacGregor Grant Co., agent for the Russo-Asiatic Bank (involved in financing the Bolsheviks), was at 120 Broadway — and financed by Guaranty Trust Company.

[181] Carroll Quigley, *Tragedy and Hope* (New York: Macmillan, 1966), p. 938. Quigley was writing in 1965, so this places the start of the infiltration at about 1915, a date consistent with the evidence here presented.

operational vehicles for infiltrating or influencing foreign revolutionary movements were located at 120 Broadway: the first, the Federal Reserve Bank of New York, heavily laced with Morgan appointees; the second, the Morgan- controlled American International Corporation. Further, there was an important interlock between the Federal Reserve Bank of New York and the American International Corporation — C. A. Stone, the president of American International, was also a director of the Federal Reserve Bank.

The tentative hypothesis then is that this unusual concentration at a single address was a reflection of purposeful actions by specific firms and persons and that these actions and events cannot be analyzed within the usual spectrum of left-right political antagonism.

AMERICAN INTERNATIONAL CORPORATION

The American International Corporation (AIC) was organized in New York on November 22, 1915, by the J.P. Morgan interests, with major participation by Stillman's National City Bank and the Rockefeller interests. The general office of AIC was at 120 Broadway. The company's charter authorized it to engage in any kind of business, except banking and public utilities, in any country in the world. The stated purpose of the corporation was to develop domestic and foreign enterprises, to extend American activities abroad, and to promote the interests of American and foreign bankers, business and engineering.

Frank A. Vanderlip has described in his memoirs how American International was formed and the excitement created on Wall Street over its business potential.[182] The original idea was generated by a discussion between Stone & Webster — the international railroad contractors who "were convinced there was not much more railroad building to be done in the United States" — and Jim Perkins and Frank A. Vanderlip of National City Bank (NCB).[183] The original capital authorization was $50 million and the board of directors represented the leading lights of the New York financial world. Vanderlip records that he wrote as follows to NCB president Stillman, enthusing over the enormous potential for American International Corporation:

> James A. Farrell and Albert Wiggin have been invited [to be on the board] but had to consult their committees before accepting. I also have in mind asking Henry Walters and Myron T. Herrick. Mr. Herrick is objected to by Mr. Rockefeller quite strongly but Mr. Stone wants him and I feel strongly that he would be particularly desirable in France. The whole thing has gone along with a smoothness that has been gratifying and the reception of it

---

[182] Frank A. Vanderlip, *From Farm Boy to Financier* (New York: A. Appleton-Century, 1935).
[183] Ibid., p. 267.

has been marked by an enthusiasm which has been surprising to me even though I was so strongly convinced we were on the right track.

I saw James J. Hill today, for example. He said at first that he could not possibly think of extending his responsibilities, but after I had finished telling him what we expected to do, he said he would be glad to go on the board, would take a large amount of stock and particularly wanted a substantial interest in the City Bank and commissioned me to buy him the stock at the market.

I talked with Ogden Armour about the matter today for the first time. He sat in perfect silence while I went through the story, and, without asking a single question, he said he would go on the board and wanted $500,000 stock.

Mr. Coffin [of General Electric] is another man who is retiring from everything, but has 'become so enthusiastic over this that he was willing to go on the board, and offers the most active cooperation.

I felt very good over getting Sabin. The Guaranty Trust is altogether the most active competitor we have in the field and it is of great value to get them into the fold in this way. They have been particularly enthusiastic at Kuhn, Loeb's. They want to take up to $2,500,000. There was really quite a little competition to see who should get on the board, but as I had happened to talk with Kahn and had invited him first, it was decided he should go on. He is perhaps the most enthusiastic of any one. They want half a million stock for Sir Ernest Castle[184] to whom they have cabled the plan and they have back from him approval of it.

I explained the whole matter to the Board [of the City Bank] Tuesday and got nothing but favorable comments.[185]

Everybody coveted the AIC stock. Joe Grace (of W. R. Grace & Co.) wanted $600,000 in addition to his interest in National City Bank. Ambrose Monell wanted $500,000. George Baker wanted $250,000. And "William Rockefeller tried, vainly, to get me to put him down for $5,000,000 of the common."[186]

By 1916 AIC investments overseas amounted to more than $23 million and in 1917 to more than $27 million. The company established representation in London, Paris, Buenos Aires, and Peking as well as in Petrograd, Russia. Less than two years after its formation AIC was operating on a substantial scale in Australia, Argentina, Uruguay, Paraguay, Colombia, Brazil, Chile, China, Japan, India, Ceylon, Italy, Switzerland, France, Spain, Cuba, Mexico, and other countries in Central America.

---

[184] Sir Ernest Cassel, prominent British financier.
[185] Ibid., pp. 268-69. It should be noted that several names mentioned by Vanderlip turn up elsewhere in this book: Rockefeller, Armour, Guaranty Trust, and (Otto) Kahn all had some connection more or less with the Bolshevik Revolution and its aftermath.
[186] Ibid., p. 269.

American International owned several subsidiary companies outright, had substantial interests in yet other companies, and operated still other firms in the United States and abroad. The Allied Machinery Company of America was founded in February 1916 and the entire share capital taken up by American International Corporation. The vice president of American International Corporation was Frederick Holbrook, an engineer and formerly head of the Holbrook Cabot & Rollins Corporation. In January 1917 the Grace Russian Company was formed, the joint owners being W. R. Grace & Co. and the San Galli Trading Company of Petrograd. American International Corporation had a substantial investment in the Grace Russian Company and through Holbrook an interlocking directorship.

AIC also invested in United Fruit Company, which was involved in Central American revolutions in the 1920s. The American International Shipbuilding Corporation was wholly owned by AIC and signed substantial contracts for war vessels with the Emergency Fleet Corporation: one contract called for fifty vessels, followed by another contract for forty vessels, followed by yet another contract for sixty cargo vessels. American International Shipbuilding was the largest single recipient of contracts awarded by the U.S. government Emergency Fleet Corporation. Another company operated by AIC was G. Amsinck & Co., Inc. of New York; control of the company was acquired in November 1917. Amsinck was the source of financing for German espionage in the United States (see page 66). In November 1917 the American International Corporation formed and wholly owned the Symington Forge Corporation, a major government contractor for shell forgings. Consequently, American International Corporation had significant interest in war contracts within the United States and overseas. It had, in a word, a vested interest in the continuance of World War I.

The directors of American International and some of their associations were (in 1917):

J. OGDEN ARMOUR Meatpacker, of Armour & Company, Chicago; director of the National City Bank of New York; and mentioned by A. A. Heller in connection with the Soviet Bureau.
GEORGE JOHNSON BALDWIN Of Stone & Webster, 120 Broadway. During World War I Baldwin was chairman of the board of American International Shipbuilding, senior vice president of American International Corporation, director of G. Amsinck (Von Pavenstedt of Amsinck was a German espionage paymaster in the U.S., see page 65), and a trustee of the Carnegie Foundation, which financed the Marburg Plan for international socialism to be controlled behind the scenes by world finance (see page 174-6).
C. A. COFFIN Chairman of General Electric (executive office: 120 Broadway), chairman of cooperation committee of the American Red Cross.
W. E. COREY (14 Wall Street) Director of American Bank Note Company, Mechanics and Metals Bank, Midvale Steel and Ordnance, and International Nickel Company; later director of National City Bank.

ROBERT DOLLAR San Francisco shipping magnate, who attempted in behalf of the Soviets to import tsarist gold rubles into U.S. in 1920, in contravention of U.S. regulations.
PIERRE S. DU PONT Of the du Pont family.
PHILIP A. S. FRANKLIN Director of National City Bank.
J.P. GRACE Director of National City Bank.
R. F. HERRICK Director, New York Life Insurance; former president of the American Bankers Association; trustee of Carnegie Foundation.
OTTO H. KAHN Partner in Kuhn, Loeb. Kahn's father came to America in 1948, "having taken part in the unsuccessful German revolution of that year." According to J. H. Thomas (British socialist, financed by the Soviets), "Otto Kahn's face is towards the light."
H. W. PRITCHETT Trustee of Carnegie Foundation.
PERCY A. ROCKEFELLER Son of John D. Rockefeller; married to Isabel, daughter of J. A. Stillman of National City Bank.
JOHN D. RYAN Director of copper-mining companies, National City Bank, and Mechanics and Metals Bank. (See frontispiece to this book.)
W. L. SAUNDERS Director the Federal Reserve Bank of New York, 120 Broadway, and chairman of Ingersoll-Rand. According to the *National Cyclopaedia* (26:81): "Throughout the war he was one of the President's most trusted advisers." See page 15 for his views on the Soviets.
J. A. STILLMAN President of National City Bank, after his father (J. Stillman, chairman of NCB) died in March 1918.
C. A. STONE Director (1920-22) of Federal Reserve Bank of New York, 120 Broadway; chairman of Stone & Webster, 120 Broadway; president (1916-23) of American International Corporation, 120 Broadway.
T. N. VAIL President of National City Bank of Troy, New York
F. A. VANDERLIP President of National City Bank.
E. S. WEBSTER Of Stone & Webster, 120 Broadway.
A. H. WIGGIN Director of Federal Reserve Bank of New York in the early 1930s.
BECKMAN WINTHROPE Director of National City Bank.
WILLIAM WOODWARD Director of Federal Reserve Bank of New York, 120 Broadway, and Hanover National Bank.

The interlock of the twenty-two directors of American International Corporation with other institutions is significant. The National City Bank had no fewer than ten directors on the board of AIC; Stillman of NCB was at that time an intermediary between the Rockefeller and Morgan interests, and both the Morgan and the Rockefeller interests were represented directly on AIC. Kuhn, Loeb and the du Ponts each had one director. Stone & Webster had three directors. No fewer than four directors of AIC (Saunders, Stone, Wiggin, Woodward) either were directors of or were later to join the Federal Reserve Bank of New York. We have noted in an earlier chapter that William Boyce Thompson, who contributed funds and his considerable prestige to the Bolshevik Revolution, was also a director of the Federal Reserve Bank of New York — the directorate of the FRB of New York comprised only nine members.

THE INFLUENCE OF AMERICAN INTERNATIONAL ON THE REVOLUTION

Having identified the directors of AIC we now have to identify their revolutionary influence.

As the Bolshevik Revolution took hold in central Russia, Secretary of State Robert Lansing requested the views of American International Corporation on the policy to be pursued towards the Soviet regime. On January 16, 1918 — barely two months after the takeover in Petrograd and Moscow, and before a fraction of Russia had come under Bolshevik control — William Franklin Sands, executive secretary of American International Corporation, submitted the requested memorandum on the Russian political situation to Secretary Lansing. Sands covering letter, headed 120 Broadway, began:

> To the Honourable January 16, 1918 Secretary of State
> Washington D.C.
> Sir
> I have the honor to enclose herewith the memorandum which you requested me to make for you on my view of the political situation in Russia.
> I have separated it into three parts; an explanation of the historical causes of the Revolution, told as briefly as possible; a suggestion as to policy and a recital of the various branches of American activity at work now in Russia.[187]

Although the Bolsheviks had only precarious control in Russia — and indeed were to come near to losing even this in the spring of 1918 — Sands wrote that already (January 1918) the United States had delayed too long in recognizing "Trotzky." He added, "Whatever ground may have been lost, should be regained now, even at the cost of a slight personal triumph for Trotzky."[188]

> Firms located at, or near, 120 Broadway:
> American International Corp 120 Broadway
> National City Bank 55 Wall Street
> Bankers Trust Co Bldg 14 Wall Street
> New York Stock Exchange 13 Wall Street/12 Broad

---

[187] U.S. State Dept. Decimal File, 861.00/961.
[188] Sands memorandum to Lansing, p. 9.

Morgan Building corner Wall & Broad
Federal Reserve Bank of NY 120 Broadway
Equitable Building 120 Broadway
Bankers Club 120 Broadway
Simpson, Thather & Bartlett 62 Cedar St
William Boyce Thompson 14 Wall Street
Hazen, Whipple & Fuller 42nd Street Building
Chase National Bank 57 Broadway
McCann Co 61 Broadway
Stetson, Jennings & Russell 15 Broad Street
Guggenheim Exploration 120 Broadway
Weinberg & Posner 120 Broadway
Soviet Bureau 110 West 40th Street
John MacGregor Grant Co 120 Broadway
Stone & Webster 120 Broadway
General Electric Co 120 Broadway
Morris Plan of NY 120 Broadway
Sinclair Gulf Corp 120 Broadway
Guaranty Securities 120 Broadway
Guaranty Trust 140 Broadway

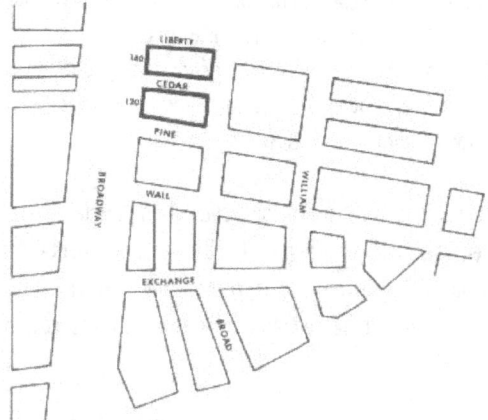

Map of Wall Street Area Showing Office Locations

Sands then elaborates the manner in which the U.S. could make up for lost time, parallels the Bolshevik Revolution to "our own revolution," and concludes: "I have every reason to believe that the Administration plans for Russia will receive all possible support from Congress, and the hearty endorsement of public opinion in the United States."

In brief, Sands, as executive secretary of a corporation whose directors were the most prestigious on Wall Street, provided an emphatic endorsement of the Bolsheviks and the Bolshevik Revolution, and within a matter of weeks after the revolution started. And as a director of the Federal Reserve Bank of New York, Sands had just contributed $1 million to the Bolsheviks — such endorsement of the Bolsheviks by banking interests is at least consistent.

Moreover, William Sands of American International was a man with truly uncommon connections and influence in the State Department.

Sands' career had alternated between the State Department and Wall Street, In the late nineteenth and early twentieth century he held various U.S. diplomatic posts. In 1910 he left the department to join the banking firm of James Speyer to negotiate an Ecuadorian loan, and for the next two years represented the Central Aguirre Sugar Company in Puerto Rico. In 1916 he was in Russia on "Red Cross work" — actually a two-man "Special Mission" with Basil Miles — and returned to join the American International Corporation in New York.[189]

In early 1918 Sands became the known and intended recipient of certain Russian "secret treaties." If the State Department files are to be believed, it appears that Sands was also a courier, and that he had some prior access to official documents — prior, that is, to U.S. government officials. On January 14, 1918, just two days before Sands wrote his memo on policy towards the Bolsheviks, Secretary Lansing caused the following cable to be sent in Green Cipher to the American legation in Stockholm: "Important official papers for Sands to bring here were left at Legation. Have you forwarded them? Lansing." The reply of January 16 from Morris in Stockholm reads: "Your 460 January 14, 5 pm. Said documents forwarded Department in pouch number 34 on December 28th." To these documents is attached another memo, signed "BM" (Basil Miles, an associate of Sands): "Mr. Phillips. They failed to give Sands 1st installment of secret treaties wh. [which] he brought from Petrograd to Stockholm."[190]

Putting aside the question why a private citizen would be carrying Russian secret treaties and the question of the content of such secret treaties (probably an early version of the so-called Sisson Documents), we can at least deduce that the AIC executive secretary traveled

---

[189] William Franklin Sands wrote several books, including *Undiplomatic Memoirs* (New York: McGraw-Hill, 1930), a biography covering the years to 1904. Later he wrote *Our Jungle Diplomacy* (Chapel Hill: University of North Carolina Press, 1941), an unremarkable treatise on imperialism in Latin America. The latter work is notable only for a minor point on page 102: the willingness to blame a particularly unsavory imperialistic adventure on Adolf Stahl, a New York banker, while pointing oust quite unnecessarily that Stahl was of "German-Jewish origin." In August 1918 he published an article, "Salvaging Russia," in *Asia, to* explain support of the Bolshevik regime.

[190] All the above in U.S. State Dept. Decimal File, 861.00/969.

from Petrograd to Stockholm in late 1917 and must indeed have been a privileged and influential citizen to have access to secret treaties.[191]

A few months later, on July 1, 1918, Sands wrote to Treasury Secretary McAdoo suggesting a commission for "economic assistance to Russia." He urged that since it would be difficult for a government commission to "provide the machinery" for any such assistance, "it seems, therefore, necessary to call in the financial, commercial and manufacturing interest of the United States to provide such machinery under the control of the Chief Commissioner or whatever official is selected by the President for this purpose."[192] In other words, Sands obviously intended that any commercial exploitation of Bolshevik Russia was going to include 120 Broadway.

THE FEDERAL RESERVE BANK OF NEW YORK

The certification of incorporation of the Federal Reserve Bank of New York was filed May 18, 1914. It provided for three Class A directors representing member banks in the district, three Class B directors representing commerce, agriculture, and industry, and three Class C directors representing the Federal Reserve Board. The original directors were elected in 1914; they proceeded to generate an energetic program. In the first year of organization the Federal Reserve Bank of New York held no fewer than 50 meetings.

From our viewpoint what is interesting is the association between, on the one hand, the directors of the Federal Reserve Bank (in the New York district) and of American International Corporation, and, on the other, the emerging Soviet Russia.

In 1917 the three Class A directors were Franklin D. Locke, William Woodward, and Robert H. Treman. William Woodward was a director of American International Corporation (120 Broadway) and of the Rockefeller-controlled Hanover National Bank. Neither Locke nor Treman enters our story. The three Class B directors in 1917 were William Boyce Thompson, Henry R. Towne, and Leslie R. Palmer. We have already noted William B. Thompson's substantial cash contribution to the Bolshevik cause. Henry R. Towne was chairman of the board of directors of the Morris Plan of New York, located at 120 Broadway; his seat was later taken by Charles A. Stone of American International Corporation (120 Broadway) and of Stone & Webster (120 Broadway). Leslie R. Palmer does not come into our story. The three Class C directors were Pierre Jay, W. L. Saunders, and George Foster Peabody. Nothing is known about Pierre Jay, except that his office was at 120 Broadway and he appeared to be significant only as the owner of Brearley School, Ltd. William Lawrence Saunders was

---

[191] The author cannot forbear comparing the treatment of academic researchers. In 1973, for example, the writer was still denied access to some State Department files *dated 1919.*
[192] U.S. State Dept. Decimal File, 861.51/333.

also a director of American International Corporation; he openly avowed, as we have seen, pro-Bolshevik sympathies, disclosing them in a letter to President Woodrow Wilson (see page 15). George Foster Peabody was an active socialist (see page 99-100).

In brief, of the nine directors of the Federal Reserve Bank of New York, four were physically located at 120 Broadway and two were then connected with American International Corporation. And at least four members of AIC's board were at one time or another directors of the FRB of New York. We could term all of this significant, but regard it not necessarily as a dominant interest.

AMERICAN-RUSSIA INDUSTRIAL SYNDICATE INC.

William Franklin Sands' proposal for an economic commission to Russia was not adopted. Instead, a private vehicle was put together to exploit Russian markets and the earlier support given the Bolsheviks. A group of industrialists from 120 Broadway formed the American-Russian Industrial Syndicate Inc. to develop and foster these opportunities. The financial backing for the new firm came from the Guggenheim Brothers, 120 Broadway, previously associated with William Boyce Thompson (Guggenheim controlled American Smelting and Refining, and the Kennecott and Utah copper companies); from Harry F. Sinclair, president of Sinclair Gulf Corp., also 120 Broadway; and from James G. White of J. G. White Engineering Corp. of 43 Exchange Place — the address of the American-Russian Industrial Syndicate.

In the fall of 1919 the U.S. embassy in London cabled Washington about Messrs. Lubovitch and Rossi "representing American-Russian Industrial Syndicate Incorporated What is the reputation and the attitude of the Department toward the syndicate and the individuals?"[193]

To this cable State Department officer Basil Miles, a former associate of Sands, replied:

> ... Gentlemen mentioned together with their corporation are of good standing being backed financially by the White, Sinclair and Guggenheim interests for the purpose of opening up business relations with Russia.[194]

So we may conclude that Wall Street interests had quite definite ideas of the manner in which the new Russian market was to be exploited. The assistance and advice proffered

---

[193] U.S. State Dept. Decimal File, 861.516 84, September 2, 1919.
[194] Ibid.

in behalf of the Bolsheviks by interested parties in Washington and elsewhere were not to remain unrewarded.

JOHN REED: ESTABLISHMENT REVOLUTIONARY

Quite apart from American International's influence in the State Department is its intimate relationship — which AIC itself called "control" — with a known Bolshevik: John Reed. Reed was a prolific, widely read author of the World War I era who contributed to the Bolshevik-oriented *Masses*,[195] and to the Morgan-controlled journal *Metropolitan*. Reed's book on the Bolshevik Revolution, *Ten Days That Shook the World*, sports an introduction by Nikolai Lenin, and became Reed's best-known and most widely read literary effort. Today the book reads like a superficial commentary on current events, is interspersed with Bolshevik proclamations and decrees, and is permeated with that mystic fervor the Bolsheviks know will arouse foreign sympathizers. After the revolution Reed became an American member of the executive committee of the Third International. He died of typhus in Russia in 1920.

The crucial issue that presents itself here is not Reed's known pro-Bolshevik tenor and activities, but how Reed who had the entire confidence of Lenin ("Here is a book I should like to see published in millions of copies and translated into all languages," commented Lenin in *Ten Days*), who was a member of the Third International, and who possessed a Military Revolutionary Committee pass (No. 955, issued November 16, 1917) giving him entry into the Smolny Institute (the revolutionary headquarters) at any time as the representative of the "American Socialist press," was also — despite these things — a puppet under the "control" of the Morgan financial interests through the American International Corporation. Documentary evidence exists for this seeming conflict (see below and Appendix 3).

Let's fill in the background. Articles for the *Metropolitan* and the *Masses* gave John Reed a wide audience for reporting the Mexican and the Russian Bolshevik revolutions. Reed's biographer Granville Hicks has suggested, in *John Reed*, that "he was... the spokesman of the Bolsheviks in the United States." On the other hand, Reed's financial support from 1913 to 1918 came heavily from the *Metropolitan* — owned by Harry Payne Whitney, a director of the Guaranty Trust, an institution cited in every chapter of this book — and also' from the New York private banker and merchant Eugene Boissevain, who channeled funds to Reed both directly and through the pro-Bolshevik *Masses*. In other words, John Reed's financial support came from two supposedly competing elements in the political spectrum. These funds

---

[195] Other contributors to the *Masses* mentioned in this book were journalist Robert Minor, chairman of the, U.S. Public Info, marion Committee; George Creel; Carl Sandburg, poet- historian; and Boardman Robinson, an artist.

were for writing and may be classified as: payments from *Metropolitan* from 1913 onwards for articles; payments from *Masses* from 1913 onwards, which income at least in part originated with Eugene Boissevain. A third category should be mentioned: Reed received some minor and apparently unconnected payments from Red Cross commissioner Raymond Robins in Petrograd. Presumably he also received smaller sums for articles written for other journals, and book royalties; but no evidence has been found giving the amounts of such payments.

JOHN REED AND THE *METROPOLITAN* MAGAZINE

The *Metropolitan* supported contemporary establishment causes including, for example, war preparedness. The magazine was owned by Harry Payne Whitney (1872-1930), who founded the Navy League and was partner in the J.P. Morgan firm. In the late 1890s Whitney became a director of American Smelting and Refining and of Guggenheim Exploration. Upon his father's death in 1908, he became a director of numerous other companies, including Guaranty Trust Company. Reed began writing for Whitney's *Metropolitan* in July 1913 and contributed a half-dozen articles on the Mexican revolutions: "With Villa in Mexico," "The Causes Behind/Mexico's Revolution," "If We Enter Mexico," "With Villa on the March," etc. Reed's sympathies were with revolutionist Pancho Villa. You will recall the link (see page 65) between Guaranty Trust and Villa's ammunition supplies.

In any event, *Metropolitan* was Reed's main source of income. In the words of biographer Granville Hicks, "Money meant primarily work for the *Metropolitan* and incidentally articles and stories for other paying magazines." But employment by *Metropolitan* did not inhibit Reed from writing articles critical of the Morgan and Rockefeller interests. One such piece, *"At* the Throat of the Republic" *(Masses,* July 1916), traced the relationship between munitions industries, the national security-preparedness lobby, the interlocking directorates of the Morgan-Rockefeller interest, "and showed that they dominated both the preparedness societies and the newly formed American International Corporation, organized for the exploitation of backward countries."[196]

In 1915 John Reed was arrested in Russia by tsarist authorities, and the *Metropolitan* intervened with the State Department in Reed's behalf. On June 21, 1915, H. J. Whigham wrote Secretary of State Robert Lansing informing him that John Reed and Boardman Robinson (also arrested and also a contributor to the *Masses)* were in Russia "with commission from the *Metropolitan* magazine to write articles and to make illustrations in the Eastern field of the War." Whigham pointed out that neither had "any desire or

---

[196] Granville Hicks, *John Reed, 1887-1920* (New York: Macmillan, 1936), p. 215.

authority from us to interfere with the operations of any belligerent powers that be." Whigham's letter continues:

> If Mr. Reed carried letters of introduction from Bucharest to people in Galicia of an anti-Russian frame of mind I am sure that it was done innocently with the simple intention of meeting as many people as possible...

Whigham points out to Secretary Lansing that John Reed was known at the White House and had given "some assistance" to the administration on Mexican affairs; he concludes: "*We* have the highest regard for Reed's great qualities as a writer and thinker and we are very anxious as regards his safety."[197] The Whigham letter is not, let it be noted, from an establishment journal in support of a Bolshevik writer; it is from an establishment journal in support of a Bolshevik writer for the *Masses* and similar revolutionary sheets, a writer who was also the author of trenchant attacks ("The Involuntary Ethics of Big Business: A Fable for Pessimists," for example) on the same Morgan interests that owned *Metropolitan*.

The evidence of finance by the private banker Boissevain is incontrovertible. On February 23, 1918, the American legation at Christiania, Norway, sent a cable to Washington in behalf of John Reed for delivery to Socialist Party leader Morris Hillquit. The cable stated in part: "Tell Boissevain must draw on him but carefully." A cryptic note by Basil Miles in the State Department files, dated April 3, 1918, states, "If Reed is coming home he might as well have money. I understand alternatives are ejection by Norway or polite return. If this so latter seems preferable." This protective note is followed by a cable dated April 1, 1918, and again from the American legation at Christiania: "John Reed urgently request Eugene Boissevain, 29 Williams Street, New York, telegraph care legation $300.00."[198] This cable was relayed to Eugene Boissevain by the State Department on April 3, 1918.

Reed apparently received his funds and arrived safely back in the United States. The next document in the State Department files is a letter to William Franklin Sands from John Reed, dated June 4, 1918, and written from Crotonon-Hudson, New York. In the letter Reed asserts that he has drawn up a memorandum for the State Department, and appeals to Sands to use his influence to get release of the boxes of papers brought back from Russia. Reed concludes, "Forgive me for bothering you, but I don't know where else to turn, and I can't afford another trip to Washington." Subsequently, Frank Polk, acting secretary of state, received a letter from Sands regarding the release of John Reed's papers. Sands' letter,

---

[197] U.S. State Dept. Decimal File, 860d.1121 R 25/4.
[198] Ibid., 360d.1121/R25/18. According to Granville Hicks in *John Reed*, "*Masses* could not pay his [Reed's] expenses. Finally, friends of the magazine, notably Eugene Boissevain, raised the money" (p. 249).

dated June 5, 1918, from 120 Broadway, is here reproduced in full; it makes quite explicit statements about control of Reed:

120 BROADWAY NEW YORK
June fifth, 1918
My dear Mr. Polk:
I take the liberty of enclosing to you an appeal from John ("Jack") Reed to help him, if possible, to secure the release of the papers which he brought into the country with him from Russia.
I had a conversation with Mr. Reed when he first arrived, in which he sketched certain attempts by the Soviet Government to initiate constructive development, and expressed the desire to place whatever observations he had made or information he had obtained through his connection with Leon Trotzky, at the disposal of our Government. I suggested that he write a memorandum on this subject for you, and promised to telephone to Washington to ask you to give him an interview for this purpose. He brought home with him a mass of papers which were taken from him for examination, and on this subject also he wished to speak to someone in authority, in order to voluntarily offer an>, information they might contain to the Government, and to ask for the release of those which he needed for his newspaper and magazine work.
I do not believe that Mr. Reed is either a "Bolshevik" or a "dangerous anarchist," as I have heard him described. He is a sensational journalist, without doubt, but that is all. He is not trying to embarrass our Government, and for this reason refused the "protection" which I understand was offered to him by Trotzky, when he returned to New York to face the indictment against him in the "Masses" trial. He is liked by the Petrograd Bolsheviki, however, and, therefore, anything which our police may do which looks like "persecution" will be resented in Petrograd, which I believe to be undesirable because unnecessary. *He can be handled and controlled much better by other means than through the police.*
I have not seen the memorandum he gave to Mr. Bullitt — *I wanted him to let me see it first and perhaps to edit it,* but he had not the opportunity to do so.
I hope that you will not consider me to be intrusive in this matter or meddling with matters which do not concern me. I believe it to be wise not to offend the Bolshevik leaders *unless and until it may become necessary to do so — if it should become necessary — and* it is unwise to look on every one as a suspicious or even dangerous character, who has had friendly relations with the Bolsheviki in Russia. *I think it better policy to attempt to use such people for our own purposes in developing our policy toward Russia, if it is possible to do so.* The lecture which Reed was prevented by the police from delivering in Philadelphia (he lost his head, came into conflict with the police and was arrested) is the only lecture on Russia which I would have paid to hear, if I had not already seen his notes on the subject. It covered a subject which we might quite possibly find to be a point of contact with the Soviet Government, from which to begin constructive work!

Can we not use him, instead of embittering him and making him an enemy? He is not well balanced, but he is, unless I am very much mistaken, *susceptible to discreet guidance and might be quite useful.*
Sincerely yours, William Franklin Sands
The Honourable Frank Lyon Polk
Counselor for the Department of State Washington, D.C.
WFS:AO Enclosure[199]

The significance of this document is the hard revelation of direct intervention by an officer (executive secretary) of American International Corporation in behalf of a known Bolshevik. Ponder a few of Sands' statements about Reed: "He can be handled and controlled much better by other means than through the police"; and, "Can we not use him, instead of embittering him and making him an enemy?... he is, unless I am very much mistaken, susceptible to discreet guidance and might be quite useful." Quite obviously, the American International Corporation viewed John Reed as an agent or a potential agent who could be, and probably had already been, brought under its control. The fact that Sands was in a position to request editing a memorandum by Reed (for Bullitt) suggests some degree of control had already been established.

Then note Sands' potentially hostile attitude towards — and barely veiled intent to provoke — the Bolsheviks: "I believe it to be wise not to offend the Bolshevik leaders unless and *until it may become necessary to do so* — if it should become necessary . . ." (italics added).

This is an extraordinary letter in behalf of a Soviet agent from a private U.S. citizen whose counsel the State Department had sought, and continued to seek.

A later memorandum, March 19, 1920, in the State files reported the arrest of John Reed by the Finnish authorities at Abo, and Reed's possession of English, American and German passports. Reed, traveling under the alias of Casgormlich, carried diamonds, a large sum of money, Soviet propaganda literature, and film. On April 21, 1920, the American legation at Helsingfors cabled the State Department:

> Am forwarding by the next pouch certified copies of letters from Emma Goldman, Trotsky, Lenin and Sirola found in Reed's possession. Foreign Office has promised to furnish complete record of the Court proceedings.

---

[199] U.S. State Dept. Decimal File, 360. D. 1121.R/20/221/2, /R25 (John Reed). The letter was transferred by Mr. Polk to the State Department archives on May 2, 1935. All italics added.

Once again Sands intervened: "I knew Mr. Reed personaly."²⁰⁰ And, as in 1915, *Metropolitan* magazine also came to Reed's aid. H. J. Whigham wrote on April 15, 1920, to Bainbridge Colby in the State Department: "Have heard John Reed in danger of being executed in Finland. Hope the State Dept. can take immediate steps to see that he gets proper trial. Urgently request prompt action."²⁰¹ This was in addition to an April 13, 1920 telegram from Harry Hopkins, who was destined for fame under President Roosevelt:

> Understand State Dept. has information Jack Reed arrested Finland, will be executed. As one of his friends and yours and on his wife's behalf urge you take prompt action prevent execution and secure release. Feel sure can rely your immediate and effective intervention.²⁰²

John Reed was subsequently released by the Finnish authorities.

This paradoxical account on intervention in behalf of a Soviet agent can have several explanations. One hypothesis that fits other evidence concerning Wall Street and the Bolshevik Revolution is that John Reed was in effect an agent of the Morgan interests — perhaps only half aware of his double role — that his anticapitalist writing maintained the valuable myth that *all* capitalists are in perpetual warfare with all socialist revolutionaries. Carroll Quigley, as we have already noted, reported that the Morgan interests financially supported domestic revolutionary organizations and anticapitalist writings.²⁰³ And we have presented in this chapter irrefutable documentary evidence that the Morgan interests were also effecting control of a Soviet agent, interceding on his behalf and, more important, generally intervening in behalf of Soviet interests with the U.S. government. These activities centered at a single address: 120 Broadway, New York City.

---

[200] Ibid., 360d.1121 R 25/72.
[201] Ibid.
[202] This was addressed to Bainbridge Colby, ibid., 360d.1121 R 25/30. Another letter, dated April 14, 1920, and addressed to the secretary of state from 100 Broadway, New York, was from W. Bourke Cochrane; it also pleaded for the release of John Reed.
[203] Quigley, op. cit.

Chapter IX

Guaranty Trust Goes to Russia

Soviet Government desire Guarantee [sic] Trust Company to become fiscal agent in United States for all Soviet operations and contemplates American purchase Eestibank with a view to complete linking of Soviet fortunes with American financial interests.
William H. Coombs, reporting to the U.S. embassy in London, June 1, 1920 (U.S. State Dept. Decimal File, 861.51/752). ("Eestibank" was an Estonian bank)

In 1918 the Soviets faced a bewildering array of internal and external problems. They occupied a mere fraction of Russia. To subdue the remainder, they needed foreign arms, imported food, outside financial support, diplomatic recognition, and — above all — foreign trade. To gain diplomatic recognition and foreign trade, the Soviets first needed representation abroad, and representation in turn required financing through gold or foreign currencies. As we have already seen, the first step was to establish the Soviet Bureau in New York under Ludwig Martens. At the same time, efforts were made to transfer funds to the United States and Europe for purchases of needed goods. Then influence was exerted in the U.S. to gain recognition or to obtain the export licenses needed to ship goods to Russia.

New York bankers and lawyers provided significant — in some cases, critical — assistance for each of these tasks. When Professor George V. Lomonossoff, the Russian technical expert in the Soviet Bureau, needed to transfer funds from the chief Soviet agent in Scandinavia, a prominent Wall Street attorney came to his assistance — using official State Department channels and the acting secretary of state as an intermediary. When gold had to be transferred to the United States, it was American International Corporation, Kuhn, Loeb & Co., and Guaranty Trust that requested the facilities and used their influence in Washington to smooth the way. And when it came to recognition, we find American firms pleading .with Congress and with the public to endorse the Soviet regime.

Lest the reader should deduce — too hastily — from these assertions that Wall Street was indeed tinged with Red, or that Red flags were flying in the street (see frontispiece), we also in a later chapter present evidence that the J.P. Morgan firm financed Admiral Kolchak in Siberia. Aleksandr Kolchak was fighting the Bolsheviks, to install his own brand of authoritarian rule. The firm also contributed to the anti-Communist United Americans organization.

WALL STREET COMES TO THE AID OF PROFESSOR LOMONOSSOFF

The case of Professor Lomonossoff is a detailed case history of Wall Street assistance to the early Soviet regime. In late 1918 George V. Lomonossoff, member of the Soviet Bureau in New York and later first Soviet commissar of railroads, found himself stranded in the United States without funds. At this time Bolshevik funds were denied entry into the United States; indeed, there was no official recognition of the regime at all. Lomonossoff was the subject of a letter of October 24, 1918, from the U.S. Department of Justice to the Department of State.[204] The letter referred to Lomonossoff's Bolshevik attributes and pro-Bolshevik speeches. The investigator concluded, "Prof. Lomonossoff is not a Bolshevik although his speeches constitute unequivocal support for the Bolshevik cause." Yet Lomonossoff was able to pull strings at the highest levels of the administration to have $25,000 transferred from the Soviet Union through a Soviet espionage agent in Scandinavia (who was himself later to become confidential assistant to Reeve Schley, a vice president of Chase Bank). All this with the assistance of a member of a prominent Wall Street firm of attorneys![205]

The evidence is presented in detail because the details themselves point up the close relationship between certain interests that up to now have been thought of as bitter enemies. The first indication of Lornonossoff's problem is a letter dated January 7, 1919, from Thomas L. Chadbourne of Chadbourne, Babbitt 8e Wall of 14 Wall Street (same Address as William Boyce Thompson's) to Frank Polk, acting secretary of state. Note the friendly salutation and casual reference to Michael Gruzenberg, alias Alexander Gumberg, chief Soviet agent in Scandinavia and later Lomonossoff's assistant:

> Dear Frank: You were kind enough to say that if I could inform you of the status of the $25,000 item of personal funds belonging to Mr. & Mrs. Lomonossoff you would set in motion the machinery necessary to obtain it here for them.
> I have communicated with Mr. Lomonossoff with respect to it, and he tells me that Mr. Michael Gruzenberg, who went to Russia for Mr. Lomonossoff prior to the difficulties between Ambassador Bakhmeteff and Mr. Lomonossoff, transmitted the information to him respecting this money through three Russians who recently arrived from Sweden, and Mr. Lomonossoff

---
[204] U.S. State Dept. Decimal File, 861.00/3094.
[205] This section is from U.S., Senate, *Russian Propaganda*, hearings before a subcommittee of the Committee on Foreign Relations, 66th Cong., 2d sess., 1920.

believes that the money is held at the Russian embassy in Stockholm, Milmskilnad Gaten 37. If inquiry from the State Department should develop this to be not the place where the money is on deposit, then the Russian embassy in Stockholm can give the exact address of Mr. Gruzenberg, who can give the proper information respecting it. Mr. Lomonossoff does not receive letters from Mr. Gruzenberg, although he is informed that they have been written: nor have any of his letters to Mr. Gruzenberg been delivered, he is also informed. For this reason it is impossible to be more definite than I have been, but I hope something can be done to relieve his and his wife's embarrassment for lack of funds, and it only needs a little help to secure this money which belongs to them to aid them on this side of the water.
Thanking you in advance for anything you can do, I beg to remain, as ever,
Yours sincerely, Thomas L. Chadbourne.

In 1919, at the time this letter was written, Chadbourne was a dollar-a-year man in Washington, counsel and director of the U.S. War Trade Board, and a director of the U.S. Russian Bureau Inc., an official front company of the U.S. government. Previously, in 1915, Chadbourne organized Midvale Steel and Ordnance to take advantage of war business. In 1916 he became chairman of the Democratic Finance Committee and later a director of Wright Aeronautical and of Mack Trucks.

The reason Lomonossoff was not receiving letters from Gruzenberg is that they were, in all probability, being intercepted by one of several governments taking a keen interest in the latter's activities.

On January 11, 1919, Frank Polk cabled the American legation in Stockholm:

> Department is in receipt of information that $25,000, personal funds of... Kindly inquire of the Russian Legation informally and personally if such funds are held thus. Ascertain, if not, address of Mr. Michael Gruzenberg, reported to be in possession of information on this subject. Department not concerned officially, merely undertaking inquiries on behalf of a former Russian official in this country.
> Polk, Acting

Polk appears in this letter to be unaware of Lomonossoff's Bolshevik connections, and refers to him as "a former Russian official in this country." Be that as it may, within three days Polk received a reply from Morris at the U.S. Legation in Stockholm:

> January 14, 3 p.m. 3492. Your January 12, 3 p.m., No. 1443.
> Sum of $25,000 of former president of Russian commission of ways of communication in United States not known to Russian legation; neither can address of Mr. Michael Gruzenberg be obtained.

Morris

Apparently Frank Polk then wrote to Chadbourne (the letter is not included in the source) and indicated that State could find neither Lomonossoff nor Michael Gruzenberg. Chadbourne replied on January 21, 1919:

> Dear Frank: Many thanks for your letter of January 17. I understand that there are two Russian legations in Sweden, one being the soviet and the other the Kerensky, and I presume your inquiry was directed to the soviet legation as that was the address I gave you in my letter, namely, Milmskilnad Gaten 37, Stockholm.
> Michael Gruzenberg's address is, Holmenkollen Sanitarium, Christiania, Norway, and I think the soviet legation could find out all about the funds through Gruzenberg if they will communicate with him.
> Thanking you for taking this trouble and assuring you of my deep appreciation, I remain, Sincerely yours, Thomas L. Chadbourne

We should note that a Wall Street lawyer had the address of Gruzenberg, chief Bolshevik agent in Scandinavia, at a time when the acting secretary of state and the U.S. Stockholm legation had no record of the address; nor could the legation track it down. Chadbourne also presumed that the Soviets were the official government of Russia, although that government was not recognized by the United States, and Chadbourne's official government position on the War Trade Board would require him to know that.

Frank Polk then cabled the American legation at Christiania, Norway, with the address of Michael Gruzenberg. It is not known whether Polk knew he was passing on the address of an espionage agent, but his message was as follows:

> To American Legation, Christiania. January 25, 1919. It is reported that Michael Gruzenberg is at Holmenkollen Sanitarium. Is it possible for you to locate him and inquire if he has any knowledge respecting disposition of $25,000 fund belonging to former president of Russian mission of ways of communication in the United States, Professor Lomonossoff.
> Polk, Acting

The U.S. representative (Schmedeman) at Christiania knew Gruzenberg well. Indeed, the name had figured in reports from Schmedeman to Washington concerning Gruzenberg's pro-Soviet activities in Norway. Schmedeman replied:

> January 29, 8 p.m. 1543. Important. Your January 25, telegram No. 650.
> Before departing to-day for Russia, Michael Gruzenberg informed our naval attache that when in Russia some few months ago he had received, at Lomonossoff's request, $25,000

from the Russian Railway Experimental Institute, of which Prof. Lomonossoff was president. Gruzenberg claims that to-day he cabled attorney for Lomonossoff in New York, Morris Hillquitt *[sic]*, that he, Gruzenberg, is in possession of the money, and before forwarding it is awaiting further instructions from the United States, requesting in the cablegram that Lomonossoff be furnished with living expenses for himself and family by Hillquitt pending the receipt of the money.[206]

As Minister Morris was traveling to Stockholm on the same train as Gruzenberg, the latter stated that he would advise further with Morris in reference to this subject.

Schmedeman

The U.S. minister traveled with Gruzenberg to Stockholm where he received the following cable from Polk:

It is reported by legation at Christiania that Michael Gruzenberg, has for Prof. G. Lomonossoff, the... sum of $25,000, received from Russian Railway Experimental Institute. If you can do so without being involved with Bolshevik authorities, department will be glad for you to facilitate transfer of this money to Prof. Lomonossoff in this country. Kindly reply.

Polk, Acting

This cable produced results, for on February 5, 1919, Frank Polk wrote to Chadbourne about a "dangerous bolshevik agitator," Gruzenberg:

My Dear Tom: I have a telegram from Christiania indicating that Michael Gruzenberg has the $25,000 of Prof. Lomonossoff, and received it from the Russian Railway Experimental Institute, and that he had cabled Morris Hillquitt [*sic*], at New York, to furnish Prof. Lomonossoff money for living expenses until the fund in question can be transmitted to him. As Gruzenberg has just been deported from Norway as a dangerous bolshevik agitator, he may have had difficulties in telegraphing from that country. I understand he has now gone to Christiania, and while it is somewhat out of the department's line of action, I shall be glad, if you wish, to see if I can have Mr. Gruzenberg remit the money to Prof. Lomonossoff from Stockholm, and am telegraphing our minister there to find out if that can be done.

Very sincerely, yours, Frank L. Polk

The telegram from Christiania referred to in Polk's letter reads as follows:

---

[206] Morris Hillquit was the intermediary between New York banker Eugene Boissevain and John Reed in Petrograd.

February 3, 6 p.m., 3580. Important. Referring department's january 12, No. 1443, $10,000 has now been deposited in Stockholm to my order to be forwarded to Prof. Lomonossoff by Michael Gruzenberg, one of the former representatives of the bolsheviks in Norway. I informed him before accepting this money that I would communicate with you and inquire if it is your wish that this money be forwarded to Lomonossoff. Therefore I request instructions as to my course of action.
Morris

Subsequently Morris, in Stockholm, requested disposal instructions for a $10,000 draft deposited in a Stockholm bank. His phrase "[this] has been my only connection with the affair" suggests that Morris was aware that the Soviets could, and probably would, claim this as an officially expedited monetary transfer, since this action *implied* approval by the U.S. of such monetary transfers. Up to this time the Soviets had been required to smuggle money into the U.S.

Four p.m. February 12, 3610, Routine.
With reference to my February 3, 6 p.m., No. 3580, and your February 8, 7 p.m., No. 1501. It is not clear to me whether it is your wish for me to transfer through you the $10,000 referred to Prof. Lomonossoff. Being advised by Gruzenberg that he had deposited this money to the order of Lomonossoff in a Stockholm bank and has advised the bank that this draft could be sent to America through me, provided I so ordered, has been my only connection with the affair. Kindly wire instructions.
Morris

Then follows a series of letters on the transfer of the $10,000 from A/B Nordisk Resebureau to Thomas L. Chadbourne at 520 Park Avenue, New York City, through the medium of the State Department. The first letter contains instructions from Polk, on the mechanics of the transfer; the second, from Morris to Polk, contains $10,000; the third, from Morris to A/B Nordisk Resebureau, requesting a draft; the fourth is a reply from the bank with a check; and the fifth is the acknowledgment.

Your February 12, 4 p.m., No. 3610.
Money may be transmitted direct to Thomas L. Chadbourne, 520 Park Avenue, New York City,
Polk, Acting

* * * * *

Dispatch, No. 1600, March 6, 1919:
The Honorable the Secretary of State, Washington

Sir: Referring to my telegram, No. 3610 of February 12, and to the department's reply, No. 1524 of February 19 in regard to the sum of $10,000 for Professor Lomonossoff, I have the honor herewith to inclose a copy of a letter which I addressed on February 25 to A. B. Nordisk Resebureau, the bankers with whom this money was deposited; a copy of the reply of A. B. Nordisk Resebureau, dated February 26; and a copy of my letter to the A. B. Nordisk Resebureau, dated February 27.

It will be seen from this correspondence that the bank was desirous of having this money forwarded to Professor Lomonossoff. I explained to them, however, as will be seen from my letter of February 27, that I had received authorization to forward it directly to Mr. Thomas L. Chadbourne, 520 Park Avenue, New York City. I also inclose herewith an envelope addressed to Mr. Chadbourne, in which are inclosed a letter to him, together with a check on the National City Bank of New York for $10,000.

I have the honor to be, sir, Your obedient servant,
Ira N. Morris

* * * * *

A. B. Nordisk Reserbureau,
No. 4 Vestra Tradgardsgatan, Stockholm.
Gentlemen: Upon receipt of your letter of January 30, stating that you had received $10,000 to be paid out to Prof. G. V. Lomonossoff, upon my request, I immediately telegraphed to my Government asking whether they wished this money forwarded to Prof. Lomonossoff. I am to-day in receipt of a reply authorizing me to forward the money direct to Mr. Thomas L. Chadbourne, payable to Prof. Lomonossoff. I shall be glad to forward it as instructed by my Government.

I am, gentlemen,
Very truly, yours, Ira N. Morris

* * * * *

Mr. I. N. Morris,
American Minister, Stockholm
Deal Sir: We beg to acknowledge the receipt of your favor of yesterday regarding payment of dollars 10,000 — to Professor G. V. Lomonossoff, and we hereby have the pleasure to inclose a check for said amount to the order of Professor G. V. Lomonossoff, which we understand that you are kindly forwarding to this gentleman. We shall be glad to have your receipt for same, arid beg to remain,

Yours, respectfully,
A. B. Nordisk Reserbureau
E. Molin

* * * * *

A. B. Nordisk Resebureau, Stockholm
Gentlemen: I beg to acknowledge receipt of your letter of February 26, inclosing a check for $10,000 payable to Professor G. V. Lomonossoff. As I advised you in my letter of

February 25, I have been authorized to forward this check to Mr. Thomas L. Chadbourne, 520 Park Avenue, New York City, and I shall forward it to this gentleman within the next few days, unless you indicate a wish to the contrary.
Very truly, yours, Ira N. Morris

Then follow an internal State Department memorandum and Chadbourne's acknowledgment:

Mr. Phillips to Mr. Chadbourne, April 3, 1919.
Sir: Referring to previous correspondence regarding a remittance of ten thousand dollars from A. B. Norsdisk Resebureau to Professor G. V. Lomonossoff, which you requested to be transmitted through the American Legation at Stockholm, the department informs you that it is in receipt of a dispatch from the American minister at Stockholm dated March 6, 1919, covering the enclosed letter addressed to you, together with a check for the amount referred to, drawn to the order to Professor Lomonossoff.
I am, sir, your obedient servant
William Phillips, Acting Secretary of State.
Inclosure: Sealed letter addressed Mr. Thomas L. Chadbourne, inclosed with 1,600 from Sweden.

* * * * *

Reply of Mr. Chadbourne, April 5, 1919.
Sir: I beg to acknowledge receipt of your letter of April 3, enclosing letter addressed to me, containing check for $10,000 drawn to the order of Professor Lomonossoff, which check I have to- day delivered.
I beg to remain, with great respect,
Very truly, yours, Thomas L. Chadbourne

Subsequently the Stockholm legation enquired concerning Lomonossoff's address in the U.S. and was informed by the State Department that "as far as the department is aware Professor George V. Lomonossoff can be reached in care of Mr. Thomas L. Chadbourne, 520 Park Avenue, New York City."

It is evident that the State Department, for the reason either of personal friendship between Polk and Chadbourne or of political influence, felt it had to go along and act as bagman for a Bolshevik agent — just ejected from Norway. But why would a prestigious establishment law firm be so intimately interested in the health and welfare of a Bolshevik emissary? Perhaps a contemporary State Department report gives the clue:

Martens, the Bolshevik representative, and Professor Lomonossoff are banking on the fact that Bullitt and his party will make a favorable report to the Mission and the President regarding conditions in Soviet Russia and that on the basis of this report the Government of the United States will favor dealing with the Soviet Government as, proposed by Martens. March 29, 1919.[207]

THE STAGE IS FOR COMMERCIAL EXPLOITATION OF RUSSIA

It was commercial exploitation of Russia that excited Wall Street, and Wall Street had lost no time in preparing its program. On May 1, 1918 — an auspicious date for Red revolutionaries — the American League to Aid and Cooperate with Russia was established, and its program approved in a conference held in the Senate Office Building, Washington, D.C. The officers and executive committee of the league represented some superficially dissimilar factions. Its president was Dr. Frank J. Goodnow, president of Johns Hopkins University. Vice presidents were the ever active William Boyce Thompson, Oscar S. Straus, James Duncan, and Frederick C. Howe, who wrote *Confessions of a Monopolist*, the rule book by which monopolists could control society. The Treasurer was George P. Whalen, vice president of Vacuum Oil Company. Congress was represented by Senator William Edgar Borah and Senator John Sharp Williams, of the Senate Foreign Relations Committee; Senator William N. Calder; and Senator Robert L. Owen, chairman of the Banking and Currency Committee. House members were Henry R. Cooper and Henry D. Flood, chairman of the House Foreign Affairs Committee. American business was represented by Henry Ford; Charles A. Coffin, chairman of the board of General Electric Company; and M. A. Oudin, then foreign manager of General Electric. George P. Whalen represented Vacuum Oil Company, and Daniel Willard was president of the Baltimore & Ohio Railroad. The more overtly revolutionary element was represented by Mrs. Raymond Robins, whose name was later found to be prominent in the Soviet Bureau files and in the Lusk Committee hearings; Henry L. Slobodin, described as a "prominent patriotic socialist"; and Lincoln Steffens, a domestic Communist of note.

In other words, this was a hybrid executive committee; it represented domestic revolutionary elements, the Congress of the United States, and financial interests prominently involved with Russian affairs.

Approved by the executive committee was a program that emphasized the establishment of an official Russian division in the U.S. government "directed by strong men." This division would enlist the aid of universities, scientific organizations, and other institutions to study the "Russian question," would coordinate and unite organizations within the United States "for the safeguarding of Russia," would arrange for a "special intelligence committee for

---

[207] U.S. State Dept. Decimal File, 861.00/4214a.

the investigation of the Russian matter," and, generally, would itself study and investigate what was deemed to be the "Russian question." The executive committee then passed a resolution supporting President Woodrow Wilson's message to the Soviet congress in Moscow and the league affirmed its own support for the new Soviet Russia.

A few weeks later, on May 20, 1918, Frank J. Goodnow and Herbert A. Carpenter, representing the league, called upon Assistant Secretary of State William Phillips and impressed upon him the necessity for establishing an "official Russian Division of the Government to coordinate all Russian matters. They asked me [wrote Phillips] whether they should take this matter up with the President."[208]

Phillips reported this directly to the secretary of state and on the next day wrote Charles R. Crane in New York City requesting his views on the American League to Aid and Cooperate with Russia. Phillips besought Crane, "I really want your advice as to how we should treat the league... We do not want to stir up trouble by refusing to cooperate with them. On the other hand it is a queer committee and I don't quite 'get it.'"[209]

In early June there arrived at the State Department a letter from William Franklin Sands of American International Corporation for Secretary of State Robert Lansing. Sands proposed that the United States appoint an administrator in Russia rather than a commission, and opined that "the suggestion of an allied military force in Russia at the present moment seems to me to be a very dangerous one."[210] Sands emphasized the possibility of trade with Russia and that this possibility could be advanced "by a well chosen administrator enjoying the full confidence of the government"; he indicated that "Mr. Hoover" might fit the role.[211] The letter was passed to Phillips by Basil Miles, a former associate of Sands, with the expression, "I think the Secretary would find it worthwhile to look through."

In early June the War Trade Board, subordinate to the State Department, passed a resolution, and a committee of the board comprising Thomas L. Chadbourne (Professor Lomonossoff's contact), Clarence M. Woolley, and John Foster Dulles submitted a memorandum to the Department of State, urging consideration of ways and means "to bring about closer and more friendly commercial relations between the United States and Russia." The board recommended a mission to Russia and reopened the question whether this should result from an invitation from the Soviet government.

Then on June 10, M. A. Oudin, foreign manager of General Electric Company, expressed his views on Russia and clearly favored a "constructive plan for the economic assistance"

---

[208] Ibid., 861.00/1938.
[209] Ibid.
[210] Ibid., 861.00/2003.
[211] Ibid.

of Russia.[212] In August 1918 Cyrus M. McCormick of International Harvester wrote to Basil Miles at the State Department and praised the President's program for Russia, which McCormick thought would be "a golden opportunity."[213]

Consequently, we find in mid-1918 a concerted effort by a segment of American business — obviously prepared to open up trade — to take advantage of its own preferred position regarding the Soviets.

GERMANY AND THE UNITED STATES STRUGGLE FOR RUSSIAN BUSINESS

In 1918 such assistance to the embryonic Bolshevik regime was justified on the grounds of defeating Germany and inhibiting German exploitation of Russia. This was the argument used by W. B. Thompson and Raymond Robins in sending Bolshevik revolutionaries and propaganda teams into Germany in 1918. The argument was also employed by Thompson in 1917 when conferring with Prime Minister Lloyd George about obtaining British support for the emerging Bolshevik regime. In June 1918 Ambassador Francis and his staff returned from Russia and urged President Wilson "to recognize and aid the Soviet government of Russia."[214] These reports made by the embassy staff to the State Department were leaked to the press and widely printed. Above all, it was claimed that delay in recognizing the Soviet Union would aid Germany "and helps the German plan to foster reaction and counter-revolution."[215] Exaggerated statistics were cited to support the proposal — for example, that the Soviet government represented ninety percent of the Russian people "and the other ten percent is the former propertied and governing class... Naturally they are displeased."[216] A former American official was quoted as saying, "If we do nothing — that is, if we just let things drift — we help weaken the Russian Soviet Government. And that plays Germany's game."[217] So, it was recommended that "a commission armed with credit and good business advice could help much."

Meanwhile, inside Russia the economic situation had become critical and the inevitability of an embrace with capitalism dawned on the Communist Party and its planners. Lenin crystallized this awareness before the Tenth Congress of the Russian Communist Party:

> Without the assistance of capital it will be impossible for us to retain proletarian power in an incredibly ruined country in which the peasantry, also ruined, constitutes the

---

[212] Ibid., 861.00/2002.
[213] Ibid.
[214] Ibid., M 316-18-1306.
[215] Ibid.
[216] Ibid.
[217] Ibid.

overwhelming majority — and, of course, for this assistance capital will squeeze hundreds per cent out of us. This is what we have to understand. Hence, either this type of economic relations or nothing[218]

Then Leon Trotsky was quoted as saying, "What we need here is an organizer like Bernard M. Baruch."[219]

Soviet awareness of its impending economic doom suggests that American and German business was attracted by the opportunity of exploiting the Russian market for needed goods; the Germans, in fact, made an early start in 1918. The first deals made by the Soviet Bureau in New York indicate that earlier American financial and moral support of the Bolsheviks was paying off in the form of contracts.

The largest order in 1919-20 was contracted to Morris & Co., Chicago meatpackers, for fifty million pounds of food products, valued at approximately $10 million. The Morris meatpacking family was related to the Swift family. Helen Swift, later connected with the Abraham Lincoln Center "Unity," was married to Edward Morris (of the meatpacking firm) and was also the brother of Harold H. Swift, a "major" in the 1917 Thompson Red Cross Mission to Russia.

---

[218] V. I. Lenin, Report to the Tenth Congress of the Russian Communist Party, (Bolshevik), March 15, 1921.
[219] William Reswick, *I Dreamt Revolution* (Chicago: Henry Regnery, 1952), p. 78.

CONTRACTS MADE IN 1919 BY THE SOVIET BUREAU WITH U.S. FIRMS			
Date of Contract	Firm	Goods Sold	Value
July 7, 1919	Milwaukee Shaper Co.*	Machinery	$45,071
July 30, 1919	Kempsmith Mfg. Co.*	Machinery	97,470
May 10, 1919	F. Mayer Boot & Shoe*	Boots	1,201,250
August 1919	Steel Sole Shoe & Co.*	Boots	58,750
July 23, 1919	Eline Berlow, N.Y.	Boots	3,000,000
July 24, 1919	Fischmann & Co.	Clothing	3,000,000
September 29, 1919	Weinberg & Posner	Machinery	3,000,000
October 27, 1919	LeHigh Machine Co.	Printing presses	4,500,000
January 22, 1920	Morris & Co. Chicago	50 million pounds of food products	10,000,000

*Later handled through Bobroff Foreign Trade and Engineering Co., Milwaukee.

SOURCE: U.S., Senate, *Russian Propaganda*, hearings before a subcommittee of the Committee on Foreign Relations, 66th Cong., 2d sess., 1920, p. 71.

Ludwig Martens was formerly vice president of Weinberg & Posner, located at 120 Broadway, New York City, and this firm was given a $3 million order.

SOVIET GOLD AND AMERICAN BANKS

Gold was the only practical means by which the Soviet Union could pay for its foreign purchases and the international bankers were quite willing to facilitate Soviet gold shipments. Russian gold exports, primarily imperial gold coins, started in early 1920, to Norway and Sweden. These were transshipped to Holland and Germany for other world destinations, including the United States.

In August 1920, a shipment of Russian gold coins was received at the Den Norske Handelsbank in Norway as a guarantee for payment of 3,000 tons of coal by Niels Juul and Company in the U.S. in behalf of the Soviet government. These coins were transferred to the Norges Bank for safekeeping. The coins were examined and weighed, were found to have been minted before the outbreak of war in 1914, and were therefore genuine imperial Russian coins.[220]

Shortly after this initial episode, the Robert Dollar Company of San Francisco received gold bars, valued at thirty-nine million Swedish kroner, in its Stockholm account; the gold "bore the stamp of the old Czar Government of Russia." The Dollar Company agent in

---

[220] U.S. State Dept. Decimal File, 861.51/815.

Stockholm applied to the American Express Company for facilities to ship the gold to the United States. American Express refused to handle the shipment. Robert Dollar, it should be noted, was a director of American International Company; thus AIC was linked to the first attempt at shipping gold direct to America.[221]

Simultaneously it was reported that three ships had left Reval on the Baltic Sea with Soviet gold destined for the U.S. The S.S. *Gauthod* loaded 216 boxes of gold under the supervision of Professor Lomonossoff — now returning to the United States. The S.S. *Carl Line* loaded 216 boxes of gold under the supervision of three Russian agents. The S.S. *Ruheleva* was laden with 108 boxes of gold. Each box contained three poods of gold valued at sixty thousand gold rubles each. This was followed by a shipment on the S.S. *Wheeling Mold*.

Kuhn, Loeb & Company, apparently acting in behalf of Guaranty Trust Company, then inquired of the State Department concerning the official attitude towards the receipt of Soviet gold. In a report the department expressed concern because if acceptance was refused, then "the gold [would] probably come back on the hands of the War Department, causing thereby direct governmental responsibility and increased embarrassment."[222] The report, written by Merle Smith in conference with Kelley and Gilbert, argues that unless the possessor has definite knowledge as to imperfect title, it would be impossible to refuse acceptance. It was anticipated that the U.S. would be requested to melt the gold in the assay office, and it was thereupon decided to telegraph Kuhn, Loeb & Company that no restrictions would be imposed on the importation of Soviet gold into the United States.

The gold arrived at the New York Assay Office and was deposited not by Kuhn, Loeb & Company — but by Guaranty Trust Company of New York City. Guaranty Trust then inquired of the Federal Reserve Board, which in turn inquired of the U.S. Treasury, concerning acceptance and payment. The superintendent of the New York Assay Office informed the Treasury that the approximately seven million dollars of gold had no identifying marks and that "the bars deposited have already been melted in United States mint bars." The Treasury suggested that the Federal Reserve Board determine whether Guaranty Trust Company had acted "for its own account, or the account of another in presenting the gold," and particularly "whether or not any transfer of credit or exchange transaction has resulted from the importation or deposit of the gold."[223]

On November 10, 1920, A. Breton, a vice president of the Guaranty Trust, wrote to Assistant Secretary Gilbert of the Treasury Department complaining that Guaranty had not received from the assay office the usual immediate advance against deposits of "yellow

---

[221] Ibid., 861.51/836.
[222] Ibid., 861.51,/837, October 4, 1920.
[223] Ibid., 861.51/837, October 24, 1920.

metal left with them for reduction." The letter states that Guaranty Trust had received satisfactory assurances that the bars were the product of melting French and Belgium coins, although it had purchased the metal in Holland. The letter requested that the Treasury expedite payment for the gold. In reply the Treasury argued that it "does not purchase gold tendered to the United States mint or assay offices which is known or suspected to be of Soviet origin," and in view of known Soviet sales of gold in Holland, the gold submitted by Guaranty Trust Company was held to be a "doubtful case, with suggestions of Soviet origin." It suggested that the Guaranty Trust Company could withdraw the gold from the assay office at any time it wished or could "present such further evidence to the Treasury, the Federal Reserve Bank of New York or the Department of State as may be necessary to clear the gold of any suspicion of Soviet origin."[224]

There is no file record concerning final disposition of this case but presumably the Guaranty Trust Company was paid for the shipment. Obviously this gold deposit was to implement the mid-1920 fiscal agreement between Guaranty Trust and the Soviet government under which the company became the Soviet agent in the United States (see epigraph to this chapter).

It was determined at a later date that Soviet gold was also being sent to the Swedish mint. The Swedish mint "melts Russian gold, assays it and affixes the Swedish mint stamp at the request of Swedish banks or other Swedish subjects owing the gold."[225] And at the same time Olof Aschberg, head of Svenska Ekonomie A/B (the Soviet intermediary and affiliate of Guaranty Trust), was offering "unlimited quantities of Russian gold" through Swedish banks.[226]

In brief, we can tie American International Corporation, the influential Professor Lomonossoff, Guaranty Trust, and Olof Aschberg (whom we've previously identified) to the first attempts to import Soviet gold into the United States.

MAX MAY OF GUARANTY TRUST BECOMES DIRECTOR OF RUSKOMBANK

Guaranty Trust's interest in Soviet Russia was renewed in 1920 in the form of a letter from Henry C. Emery, assistant manager of the Foreign Department of Guaranty Trust, to De Witt C. Poole in the State Department. The letter was dated January 21, 1920, just a few weeks before Allen Walker, the manager of the Foreign Department, became active in forming the virulent anti-Soviet organization United Americans (see page 165). Emery posed

---

[224] Ibid., 861.51/853, November 11, 1920.
[225] Ibid., 316-119, 1132.
[226] Ibid., 316-119-785. This report has more data on transfers of Russian gold through other countries and intermediaries. See also 316-119-846.

numerous questions about the legal basis of the Soviet government and banking in Russia and inquired whether the Soviet government was the de facto government in Russia.[227] "Revolt before 1922 planned by Reds," claimed United Americans in 1920, but Guaranty Trust had started negotiations with these same Reds and was acting as the Soviet agent in the U.S. in mid-1920.

In January 1922 Secretary of Commerce Herbert Hoover, interceded with the State Department in behalf of a Guaranty Trust scheme to set up exchange relations with the "New State Bank at Moscow." This scheme, wrote Herbert Hoover, "would not be objectionable if a stipulation were made that all monies coming into their possession should be used for the purchase of civilian commodities in the United States"; and after asserting that such relations appeared to be in line with general policy, Hoover added, "It might be advantageous to have these transactions organized in such a manner that we know what the movement is instead of disintegrated operations now current." Of course, such "disintegrated operations" are consistent with the operations of a free market, but this approach Herbert Hoover rejected in favor of channeling the exchange through specified and controllable sources in New York. Secretary of State Charles E. Hughes expressed dislike of the Hoover-Guaranty Trust scheme, which he thought could be regarded as de facto recognition of the Soviets while the foreign credits acquired might be used to the disadvantage of the United States. A noncommittal reply was sent by State to Guaranty Trust. However, Guaranty went ahead (with Herbert Hoover's support), participated in formation of the first Soviet international bank, and Max May of Guaranty Trust became head of the foreign department of the new Ruskombank.

---

[227] Ibid., 861.516/86.

CHAPTER X

J.P. MORGAN GIVES A LITTLE HELP TO THE OTHER SIDE

I would not sit down to lunch with a Morgan — except possibly to learn something of his motives and attitudes.
           William E. Dodd, Ambassador Dodd's Diary, 1933-1938

So far our story has revolved around a single major financial house — Guaranty Trust Company, the largest trust company in the United States and controlled by the J.P. Morgan firm. Guaranty Trust used Olof Aschberg, the Bolshevik banker, as its intermediary in Russia before and after the revolution. Guaranty was a backer of Ludwig Martens and his Soviet Bureau, the first Soviet representatives in the United States. And in mid-1920 Guaranty was the Soviet fiscal agent in the U.S.; the first shipments of Soviet gold to the United States also traced back to Guaranty Trust.

There is a startling reverse side to this pro-Bolshevik activity — Guaranty Trust was a founder of United Americans, a virulent anti-Soviet organization which noisily threatened Red invasion by 1922, claimed that $20 million of Soviet funds were on the way to fund Red revolution, and forecast panic in the streets and mass starvation in New York City. This duplicity raises, of course, serious questions about the intentions of Guaranty Trust and its directors. Dealing with the Soviets, even backing them, can be explained by apolitical greed or simply profit motive. On the other hand, spreading propaganda designed to create fear and panic while at the same time encouraging the conditions that give rise to the fear and panic is a considerably more serious problem. It suggests utter moral depravity. Let's first look more closely at the anti-Communist United Americans.

UNITED AMERICANS FORMED TO FIGHT COMMUNISM[228]

---

[228] *New York Times*, June 21, 1919.

In 1920 the organization United Americans was founded. It was limited to citizens of the United States and planned for five million members, "whose sole purpose would be to combat the teachings of the socialists, communists, I.W.W., Russian organizations and radical farmers societies."

In other words, United Americans was to fight all those institutions and groups believed to be anticapitalist.

The officer's of the preliminary organization established to build up United Americans were Allen Walker of the Guaranty Trust Company; Daniel Willard, president of the Baltimore 8c Ohio Railroad; H. H. Westinghouse, of Westinghouse Air Brake Company; and Otto H. Kahn, of Kuhn, Loeb 8c Company and American International Corporation. These Wall Streeters were backed up by assorted university presidents arid Newton W. Gilbert (former governor of the Philippines). Obviously, United Americans was, at first glance, exactly the kind of organization that establishment capitalists would be expected to finance and join. Its formation should have brought no great surprise.

On the other hand, as we have already seen, these financiers were also deeply involved in *supporting* the new Soviet regime in Russia — although this support was behind the scenes, recorded only in government files, and not to be made public for 50 years. As part of United Americans, Walker, Willard, Westinghouse, and Kahn were playing a double game. Otto H. Kahn, a founder of the anti-Communist organization, was reported by the British socialist J. H. Thomas as having his "face towards the light." Kahn wrote the preface to Thomas's book. In 1924 Otto Kahn addressed the League for Industrial Democracy and professed common objectives with this activist socialist group (see page 49). The Baltimore & Ohio Railroad (Willard's employer) was active in the development of Russia during the 1920s. Westinghouse in 1920, the year United Americans was founded, was operating a plant in Russia that had been exempted from nationalization. And the role of Guaranty Trust has already been minutely described.

UNITED AMERICANS REVEALS "STARTLING DISCLOSURES" ON REDS

In March 1920 the *New York Times* headlined an extensive, detailed scare story about Red invasion of the United States within two years, an invasion which was to be financed by $20 million of Soviet funds "obtained by the murder and robbery of the Russian nobility."[229]

United Americans had, it was revealed, made a survey of "radical activities" in the United States, and had done so in its role as an organization formed to "preserve the

---

[229] Ibid., March 28, 1920.

Constitution of the United States with the representative form of government and the right of individual possession which the Constitution provides."

Further, the survey, it was proclaimed, had the backing of the executive board, "including Otto H. Kahn, Allen Walker of the Guaranty Trust Company, Daniel Willard," and others. The survey asserted that

> the radical leaders are confident of effecting a revolution within two years, that the start is to be made in New York City with a general strike, that Red leaders have predicted much bloodshed and that the Russian Soviet Government has contributed $20,000,000 to the American radical movement.

The Soviet gold shipments to Guaranty Trust in mid-1920 (540 boxes of three poods each) were worth roughly $15,000,000 (at $20 a troy ounce), and other gold shipments through Robert Dollar and Olof Aschberg brought the total very close to $20 million. The information about Soviet gold for the radical movement was called "thoroughly reliable" and was "being turned over to the Government." The Reds, it was asserted, planned to starve New York into submission within four days:

> Meanwhile the Reds count on a financial panic within the next few weeks to help their cause along. A panic would cause distress among the workingmen and thus render them more susceptible to revolution doctrine.

The United Americans' report grossly overstated the number of radicals in the United States, at first tossing around figures like two or five million and then settling for precisely 3,465,000 members in four radical organizations. The report concluded by emphasizing the possibility of bloodshed and quoted "Skaczewski, President of the International Publishing Association, otherwise the Communist Party, [who] boasted that.the time was coming soon when the Communists would destroy utterly the present form of society."

In brief, United Americans published a report without substantiating evidence, designed to scare the man in the street into panic: The significant point of course is that this is the same group that was responsible for protecting and subsidizing, indeed assisting, the Soviets so they could undertake these same plans.

CONCLUSIONS CONCERNING UNITED AMERICANS

Is this a case of the right hand not knowing what the left hand was doing? Probably not. We are talking about heads of companies, eminently successful companies at that. So

United Americans was probably a ruse to divert public — and official — attention from the subterranean efforts being made to gain entry to the Russian market.

United Americans is the only documented example known to this writer of an organization assisting the Soviet regime and also in the forefront of opposition to the Soviets. This is by no means an inconsistent course of action, and further research should at least focus on the following aspects:

(a) Are there other examples of double-dealing by influential groups generally known as the establishment?

(b) Can these examples be extended into other areas? For example, is there evidence that labor troubles have been instigated by these groups?

(c) What is the ultimate purpose of these pincer tactics? Can they be related to the Marxian axiom: thesis versus antithesis yields synthesis? It is a puzzle why the Marxist movement would attack capitalism head-on if its objective was a Communist world and if it truly accepted the dialectic. If the objective is a Communist world — that is, if communism is the desired synthesis — and capitalism is the thesis, then something apart from capitalism or communism has to be antithesis. Could therefore capitalism be the thesis and communism the antithesis, with the objective of the revolutionary groups and their backers being a synthesizing of these two systems into some world system yet undescribed?

MORGAN AND ROCKEFELLER AID KOLCHAK

Concurrently with these efforts to aid the Soviet Bureau and United Americans, the J.P. Morgan firm, which controlled Guaranty Trust, was providing financial assistance for one of the Bolshevik's primary opponents, Admiral Aleksandr Kolchak in Siberia. On June 23, 1919, Congressman Mason introduced House Resolution 132 instructing the State Department "to make inquiry as to all and singular as to the truth of... press reports" charging that Russian bondholders had used their influence to bring about the "retention of American troops in Russia" in order to ensure continued payment of interest on Russian bonds. According to a file memorandum by Basil Miles, an associate of William F. Sands, Congressman Mason charged that certain banks were attempting to secure recognition of Admiral Kolchak in Siberia to get payment on former Russian bonds.

Then in August 1919 the secretary of state, Robert Lansing, received from the Rockefeller-influenced National City Bank of New York a letter requesting official comment on a proposed loan of $5 million to Admiral Kolchak; and from J.P. Morgan & Co. and other bankers another letter requesting the views of the department concerning an additional proposed £10 million sterling loan to Kolchak by a consortium of British and American bankers.[230]

Secretary Lansing informed the bankers that the U.S. had not recognized Kolchak and, although prepared to render him assistance, "the Department did not feel it could assume the responsibility of encouraging such negotiations but that, nevertheless, there seemed to be no objection to the loan provided the bankers deemed it advisable to make it."[231]

Subsequently, on September 30, Lansing informed the American consul general at Omsk that the "loan has since gone through in regular course"[232] Two fifths was taken up by British banks and three fifths by American banks. Two thirds of the total was to be spent in Britain and the United States and the remaining one third wherever the Kolchak Government wished. The loan was secured by Russian gold (Kolchak's) that was shipped to San Francisco. The timing of the previously described Soviet exports of gold suggests that cooperation with the Soviets on gold sales was determined on the heels of the Kolchak gold-loan agreement.

The Soviet gold sales and the Kolchak loan also suggest that Carroll Quigley's statement that Morgan interests infiltrated the domestic left applied also to overseas revolutionary *and* counterrevolutionary movements. Summer 1919 was a time of Soviet military reverses in the Crimea and the Ukraine and this black picture may have induced British and American bankers to mend their fences with the anti-Bolshevik forces. The obvious rationale would be to have a foot in all camps, and so be in a favorable position to negotiate for concessions and business after the revolution or counterrevolution had succeeded and a new government stabilized. As the outcome of any conflict cannot be seen at the start, the idea is to place sizable bets on all the horses in the revolutionary race. Thus assistance was given on the one hand to the Soviets and on the other to Kolchak — while the British government was supporting Denikin in the Ukraine and the French government went to the aid of the Poles.

In autumn 1919 the Berlin newspaper *Berliner Zeitung am Mittak* (October 8 and 9) accused the Morgan firm of financing the West Russian government and the Russian-German forces in the Baltic fighting the Bolsheviks — both allied to Kolchak. The Morgan firm strenuously denied the charge: "This firm has had no discussion, or meeting, with the West Russian Government or with anyone pretending to represent it, at any time."[233] But if the financing charge was inaccurate there is evidence of collaboration. Documents found by Latvian government intelligence among the papers of Colonel Bermondt, commander of the

---

[230] U.S. State Dept. Decimal File, 861.51/649.
[231] Ibid., 861.51/675
[232] Ibid., 861.51/656
[233] Ibid., 861.51/767 — a letter from J. P. Morgan to Department of State, November 11, 1919. The financing itself was a hoax (see AP report in State Department files following the Morgan letter).

Western Volunteer Army, confirm "the relations claimed existing between Kolchak's London Agent and the German industrial ring which was back of Bermondt."[234]

In other words, we know that J.P. Morgan, London, and New. York bankers financed Kolchak. There is also evidence that connects Kolchak and his army with other anti-Bolshevik armies. And there seems to be little question that German industrial and banking circles were financing the all- Russian anti-Bolshevik army in the Baltic. Obviously bankers' funds have no national flag.

---

[234] Ibid., 861.51/6172 and /6361.

Chapter XI

The Alliance of Bankers and Revolution

> *The name Rockefeller does not connote a revolutionary, and my life situation has fostered a careful and cautious attitude that verges on conservatism. I am not given to errant causes...*
>
> John D. Rockefeller III, The Second American Revolution
> (New York: Harper & Row. 1973)

The Evidence Presented: A Synopsis

Evidence already published by George Katkov, Stefan Possony, and Michael Futrell has established that the return to Russia of Lenin and his party of exiled Bolsheviks, followed a few weeks later by a party of Mensheviks, was financed and organized by the German government.[235] The necessary funds were transferred in part through the Nya Banken in Stockholm, owned by Olof Aschberg, and the dual German objectives were: (a) removal of Russia from the war, and (b) control of the postwar Russian market.[236]

We have now gone beyond this evidence to establish a continuing working relationship between Bolshevik banker Olof Aschberg and the Morgan-controlled Guaranty Trust Company in New York before, during, and after the Russian Revolution. In tsarist times Aschberg was the Morgan agent in Russia and negotiator for Russian loans in the United States; during 1917 Aschberg was financial intermediary for the revolutionaries; and after the revolution Aschberg became head of Ruskombank, the first Soviet international bank, while Max May, a vice president of the Morgan- controlled Guaranty Trust, became director and chief of the Ruskom-bank foreign department. We have presented documentary evidence of a continuing working relationship between the Guaranty Trust Company and the Bolsheviks. The directors of Guaranty Trust in 1917 are listed in Appendix 1.

---

[235] Michael Futrell, *Northern Underground* (London: Faber and Faber, 1963); Stefan Possony, *Lenin: The Compulsive Revolutionary* (London: George Allen & Unwin, 1966); and George Katkov, "German Foreign Office Documents on Financial Support to the Bolsheviks in 1917," *International Affairs* 32 (Royal Institute of International Affairs, 1956).
[236] Ibid., especially Katkov.

Moreover, there is evidence of transfers of funds from Wall Street bankers to international revolutionary activities. For example, there is the statement (substantiated by a cablegram) by William Boyce Thompson — a director of the Federal Reserve Bank of New York, a large stockholder in the Rockefeller-controlled Chase Bank, and a financial associate of the Guggenheims and the Morgans — that he (Thompson) contributed $1 million to the Bolshevik Revolution for propaganda purposes. Another example is John Reed, the American member of the Third International executive committee who was financed and supported by Eugene Boissevain, a private New York banker, and who was employed by Harry Payne Whitney's *Metropolitan* magazine. Whitney was at that time a director of Guaranty Trust. We also established that Ludwig Martens, the first Soviet "ambassador" to the United States, was (according to British Intelligence chief Sir Basil Thompson) backed by funds from Guaranty Trust Company. In tracing Trotsky's funding in the U.S. we arrived at German sources, yet to be identified, in New York. And though we do not know the precise German sources of Trotsky's funds, we *do* know that Von Pavenstedt, the chief German espionage paymaster in the U.S., was also senior partner of Amsinck & Co. Amsinck was owned by the ever-present American International Corporation — also controlled by the J.P. Morgan firm.

Further, Wall Street firms including Guaranty Trust were involved with Carranza's and Villa's wartime revolutionary activities in Mexico. We also identified documentary evidence concerning. a Wall Street syndicate's financing of the 1912 Sun Yat-sen revolution in China, a revolution that is today hailed by the Chinese Communists as the precursor of Mao's revolution in China. Charles B. Hill, New York attorney negotiating with Sun Yat-sen in behalf of this syndicate, was a director of three Westinghouse subsidiaries, and we have found that Charles R. Crane of Westinghouse in Russia was involved in the Russian Revolution.

Quite apart from finance, we identified other, and possibly more significant, evidence of Wall Street involvement in the Bolshevik cause. The American Red Cross Mission to Russia was a private venture of William B. Thompson, who publicly proffered partisan support to the Bolsheviks. British War Cabinet papers now available record that British policy was diverted towards the Lenin- Trotsky regime by the personal intervention of Thompson with Lloyd George in December 1917. We have reproduced statements by director Thompson and deputy chairman William Lawrence Saunders, both of the Federal Reserve Bank of New York, strongly favoring the Bolshevists. John Reed not only was financed from Wall Street, but had consistent support for his activities, even to the extent of intervention with the State Department from William Franklin Sands, executive secretary of American International Corporation. In the sedition case of Robert Minor there are strong indications and some circumstantial evidence that Colonel Edward House intervened to have Minor released. The significance of the Minor case is that William B. Thompson's program for Bolshevik revolution in Germany was the very program Minor was implementing when arrested in Germany.

Some international agents, for example Alexander Gumberg, worked for Wall Street *and* the Bolsheviks. In 1917 Gumberg was the representative of a U.S. firm in Petrograd, worked for Thompson's American Red Cross Mission, became chief Bolshevik agent in Scandinavia until he was deported from Norway, then became confidential assistant to Reeve Schley of Chase Bank in New York and later to Floyd Odium of Atlas Corporation.

This activity in behalf of the Bolsheviks originated in large part from a single address: 120 Broadway, New York City. The evidence for this observation is outlined but no conclusive reason is given for the unusual concentration of activity at a single address, except to state that it appears to be the foreign counterpart of Carroll Quigley's claim that J.P. Morgan infiltrated the domestic left. Morgan also infiltrated the international left.

The Federal Reserve Bank of New York was at 120 Broadway. The vehicle for this pro-Bolshevik activity was American International Corporation — at 120 Broadway. AIC views on the Bolshevik regime were requested by Secretary of State Robert Lansing only a few weeks after the revolution began, and Sands, executive secretary of AIC, could barely restrain his enthusiasm for the Bolshevik cause. Ludwig Martens, the Soviet's first ambassador, had been vice president of Weinberg & Posner, which was also located at 120-Broadway. Guaranty Trust Company was next door at 140 Broadway but Guaranty Securities Co. was at 120 Broadway. In 1917 Hunt, Hill & Betts was at 120 Broadway, and Charles B. Hill of this firm was the negotiator in the Sun Yat-sen dealings. John MacGregor Grant Co., which was financed by Olof Aschberg in Sweden and Guaranty Trust in the United States, and which was on the Military Intelligence black list, was at 120 Broadway. The Guggenheims and the executive heart of General Electric (also interested in American International) were at 120 Broadway. We find it therefore hardly surprising that the Bankers Club was also at 120 Broadway, on the top floor (the thirty-fourth).

It is significant that support for the Bolsheviks did not cease with consolidation of the revolution; therefore, this support cannot be wholly explained in terms of the war with Germany. The American-Russian syndicate formed in 1918 to obtain concessions in Russia was backed by the White, Guggenheim, and Sinclair interests. Directors of companies controlled by these three financiers included Thomas W. Lamont (Guaranty Trust), William Boyce Thompson (Federal Reserve Bank), and John Reed's employer Harry Payne Whitney (Guaranty Trust). This strongly suggests that the syndicate was formed to cash in on earlier support for the Bolshevik cause in the revolutionary period. And then we found that Guaranty Trust financially backed the Soviet Bureau in New York in 1919.

The first really concrete signal that previous political and financial support was paying off came in 1923 when the Soviets formed their first international bank, Ruskombank. Morgan associate Olof Aschberg became nominal head of this Soviet bank; Max May, a vice president of Guaranty Trust, became a director of Ruskom-bank, and the Ruskombank promptly appointed Guaranty Trust Company its U.S. agent.

THE EXPLANATION FOR THE UNHOLY ALLIANCE

What motive explains this coalition of capitalists and Bolsheviks?

Russia was then — and is today — the largest untapped market in the world. Moreover, Russia, then and now, constituted the greatest potential competitive threat to American industrial and financial supremacy. (A glance at a world map is sufficient to spotlight the geographical difference between the vast land mass of Russia and the smaller United States.) Wall Street must have cold shivers when it visualizes Russia as a second super American industrial giant.

But why allow Russia to become a competitor and a challenge to U.S. supremacy? In the late nineteenth century, Morgan/Rockefeller, and Guggenheim had demonstrated their monopolistic proclivities. In *Railroads and Regulation 1877-1916* Gabriel Kolko has demonstrated how the railroad owners, not the farmers, wanted state control of railroads in order to preserve their monopoly and abolish competition. So the simplest explanation of our evidence is that a syndicate of Wall Street financiers enlarged their monopoly ambitions and broadened horizons on a global scale. *The gigantic Russian market was to be converted into a captive market and a technical colony to be exploited by a few high-powered American financiers and the corporations under their control.* What the Interstate Commerce Commission and the Federal Trade Commission under the thumb of American industry could achieve for that industry at home, a planned socialist government could achieve for it abroad — given suitable support and inducements from Wall Street and Washington, D.C.

Finally, lest this explanation seem too radical, remember that it was Trotsky who appointed tsarist generals to consolidate the Red Army; that it was Trotsky who appealed for American officers to control revolutionary Russia and intervene in behalf of the Soviets; that it was Trotsky who squashed first the libertarian element in the Russian Revolution and then the workers and peasants; and that recorded history *totally* ignores the 700,000-man Green Army composed of ex-Bolsheviks, angered at betrayal of the revolution, who fought the Whites *and* the Reds. In other words, we are suggesting that the Bolshevik Revolution was an alliance of statists: statist revolutionaries and statist financiers aligned against the genuine revolutionary libertarian elements in Russia.[237]

---

[237] See also Voline (V.M. Eichenbaum), *Nineteen-Seventeen: The Russian Revolution Betrayed* (New York: Libertarian Book Club, n.d.).

'The question now in the readers' minds must be, were these bankers also secret Bolsheviks? No, of course not. The financiers were without ideology. It would be a gross misinterpretation to assume that assistance for the Bolshevists was ideologically motivated, in any narrow sense. The financiers were *power-motivated* and therefore assisted *any* political vehicle that would give them an entree to power: Trotsky, Lenin, the tsar, Kolchak, Denikin — all received aid, more or less. All, that is, but those who wanted a truly free individualist society.

Neither was aid restricted to statist Bolsheviks and statist counter-Bolsheviks. John P. Diggins, in *Mussolini and Fascism: The View from America*,[238] has noted in regard to Thomas Lamont of Guaranty Trust that of all American business leaders, the one who most vigorously patronized the cause of Fascism was Thomas W. Lamont. Head of the powerful J.P. Morgan banking network, Lamont served as something of a business consultant for the government of Fascist Italy.

Lamont secured a $100 million loan for Mussolini in 1926 at a particularly crucial time for the Italian dictator. We might remember too that the director of Guaranty Trust was the father of Corliss Lamont, a domestic Communist. This evenhanded approach to the twin totalitarian systems, communism and fascism, was not confined to the Lamont family. For example, Otto Kahn, director of American International Corporation and of Kuhn, Leob & Co., felt sure that "American capital invested in Italy will find safety, encouragement, opportunity and reward."[239] This is the same Otto Kahn who lectured the socialist League of Industrial Democracy in 1924 that *its* objectives were *his* objectives. They differed only — according to Otto Kahn — over the means of achieving these objectives.

Ivy Lee, Rockefeller's public relations man, made similar pronouncements, and was responsible for selling the Soviet regime to the gullible American public in the late 1920s. We also have observed that Basil Miles, in charge of the Russian desk at the State Department and a former associate of William Franklin Sands, was decidedly helpful to the businessmen promoting Bolshevik causes; but in 1923 the same Miles authored a profascist article, "Italy's Black Shirts and Business."[240] "Success of the Fascists is an expression of Italy's youth," wrote Miles while glorifying the fascist movement and applauding its esteem for American business.

THE MARBURG PLAN

---

[238] Princeton, N.J.: Princeton University Prss, 1972.
[239] Ibid., p. 149.
[240] Nation's Business, February 1923, pp. 22-23.

The Marburg Plan, financed by Andrew Carnegie's ample heritage, was produced in the early years of the twentieth century. It suggests premeditation for this kind of superficial schizophrenia, which in fact masks an integrated program of power acquisition: "What then if Carnegie and his unlimited wealth, the international financiers and the Socialists could be organized in a movement to compel the formation of a league to enforce peace."[241]

The governments of the world, according to the Marburg Plan, were to be socialized while the ultimate power would remain in the hands of the international financiers "to control its councils and enforce peace [and so] provide a specific for all the political ills of mankind."[242]

This idea was knit with other elements with similar objectives. Lord Milner in England provides the transatlantic example of banking interests recognizing the virtues and possibilities of Marxism. Milner was a banker, influential in British wartime policy, and pro-Marxist.[243] In New York the socialist "X" club was founded in 1903. It counted among its members not only the Communist Lincoln Steffens, the socialist William English Walling, and the Communist banker Morris Hillquit, but also John Dewey, James T. Shotwell, Charles Edward Russell, and Rufus Weeks (vice president of New York Life Insurance Company). The annual meeting of the Economic Club in the Astor Hotel, New York, witnessed socialist speakers. In 1908, when A. Barton Hepburn, president of Chase National Bank, was president of the Economic Club, the main speaker was the aforementioned Morris Hillquit, who "had abundant opportunity to preach socialism to a gathering which represented wealth and financial interests."[244]

From these unlikely seeds grew the modern internationalist movement, which included not only the financiers Carnegie, Paul Warburg, Otto Kahn, Bernard Baruch, and Herbert Hoover, but also the Carnegie Foundation and its progeny *International Conciliation.* The trustees of Carnegie were, as we have seen, prominent on the board of American International Corporation. In 1910 Carnegie donated $10 million to found the Carnegie Endowment for International Peace, and among those on the board of trustees were Elihu Root (Root Mission to Russia, 1917), Cleveland H. Dodge (a financial backer of President Wilson), George W. Perkins (Morgan partner), G. J. Balch (AIC and Amsinck), R. F. Herrick (AIC), H. W. Pritchett (AIC), and other Wall Street luminaries. Woodrow Wilson came under the powerful influence of — and indeed was financially indebted to — this group of internationalists.

---

[241] Jennings C. Wise, *Woodrow Wilson: Disciple of Revolution* (New York: Paisley Press, 1938), p.45.
[242] Ibid., p.46.
[243] See p. 89.
[244] Morris Hillquit, *Loose Leaves from a Busy Life* (New York: Macmillan, 1934), p. 81.

As Jennings C. Wise has written, "Historians must never forget that Woodrow Wilson... made it possible for Leon Trotsky to enter Russia with an American passport."[245]

But Leon Trotsky also declared himself an internationalist. We have remarked with some interest his high-level internationalist connections, or at least friends, in Canada. Trotsky then was not pro- Russian, or pro-Allied, or pro-German, as many have tried to make him out to be. Trotsky was *for* world revolution, *for* world dictatorship; he was, in one word, an internationalist.[246] Bolshevists and bankers have then this significant common ground — internationalism. Revolution and international finance are not at all inconsistent if the result of revolution is to establish more centralized authority. International finance prefers to deal with central governments. The last thing the banking community wants is laissez-faire economy and decentralized power because these would disperse power.

This, therefore, is an explanation that fits the evidence. This handful of bankers and promoters was not Bolshevik, or Communist, or socialist, or Democrat, or even American. Above all else these men wanted markets, preferably captive international markets — and a monopoly of the captive world market as the ultimate goal. They wanted markets that could be exploited monopolistically without fear of competition from Russians, Germans, or anyone else — including American businessmen outside the charmed circle. This closed group was apolitical and amoral. In 1917, it had a single-minded objective — a captive market in Russia, all presented under, and intellectually protected by, the shelter of a league to enforce the peace.

Wall Street did indeed achieve its goal. American firms controlled by this syndicate were later to go on and build the Soviet Union, and today are well on their way to bringing the Soviet military- industrial complex into the age of the computer.

Today the objective is still alive and well. John D. Rockefeller expounds it in his book *The Second American Revolution* — which sports a five-pointed star on the title page.[247] The book contains a naked plea for humanism, that is, a plea that our first priority is to work for others. In other words, a plea for collectivism. Humanism is collectivism. It is notable that the Rockefellers, who have promoted this humanistic idea for a century, have not turned their OWN property over to others... Presumably it is implicit in their recommendation that *we* all work *for* the Rockefellers. Rockefeller's book promotes collectivism under the guises of "cautious conservatism" and "the public good." It is in effect a plea for the continuation of the earlier Morgan-Rockefeller support of collectivist enterprises and mass subversion of individual rights.

---

[245] Wise, op. cit., p. 647
[246] Leon Trotsky, *The Bolsheviki and World Peace* (New York: Boni & Liveright, 1918).
[247] In May 1973 Chase Manhattan Bank (chairman, David Rockefeller) opened it Moscow office at 1 Karl Marx Square, Moscow. The New York office is at 1 Chase Manhattan Plaza.

In brief, the public good has been, and is today, used as a device and an excuse for self- aggrandizement by an elitist circle that pleads for world peace and human decency. But so long as the reader looks at world history in terms of an inexorable Marxian conflict between capitalism and communism, the objectives of such an alliance between international finance and international revolution remain elusive. So will the ludicrousness of promotion of the public good by plunderers. If these alliances still elude the reader, then he should ponder the obvious fact that these same international interests and promoters are always willing to determine what *other* people should do, but are signally unwilling to be first in line to give up their own wealth and power. Their mouths are open, their pockets are closed.

This technique, used by the monopolists to gouge society, was set forth in the early twentieth century by Frederick C. Howe in *The Confessions of a Monopolist.*[248] First, says Howe, politics is a necessary part of business. To control industries it is necessary to control Congress and the regulators and thus make society go to work for you, the monopolist. So, according to Howe, the two principles of a successful monopolist are, "First, let Society work for you; and second, make a business of politics."[249] These, wrote Howe, are the basic "rules of big business."

Is there any evidence that this magnificently sweeping objective was also known to Congress and the academic world? Certainly the possibility was known and known publicly. For example, witness the testimony of Albert Rhys Williams, an astute commentator on the revolution, before the Senate Overman Committee:

> ... it is probably true that under the soviet government industrial life will perhaps be much slower in development than under the usual capitalistic system. But why should a great industrial country like America desire the creation and consequent competition of another great industrial rival? Are not the interests of America in this regard in line with the slow tempo of development which soviet Russia projects for herself?
> SENATOR WOLCOTT: Then your argument is that it would be to the interest of America to have Russia repressed?
> MR. WILLIAMS: Not repressed...
> SENATOR WOLCOTT: You say. Why should America desire Russia to become an industrial competitor with her?
> MR. WILLIAMS: This is speaking from a capitalistic standpoint. The whole interest of America is not, I think, to have another great industrial rival, like Germany, England, France, and Italy, thrown on the market in competition. I think another government over there besides

---

[248] Chicago: Public Publishin, n.d.
[249] Ibid.

the Soviet government would perhaps increase the tempo or rate of development of Russia, and we would have another rival. Of course, this is arguing from a capitalistic standpoint.
SENATOR WOLCOTT: So you are presenting an argument here which you think might appeal to the American people, your point being this, that if we recognize the Soviet government of Russia as it is constituted we will be recognizing a government that can not compete with us in industry for a great many years?
MR. WILLIAMS: That is a fact.
SENATOR WOLCOTT: That is an argument that under the Soviet government Russia is in no position, for a great many years at least, to approach America industrially?
MR. WILLIAMS: Absolutely.[250]

And in that forthright statement by Albert Rhys Williams is the basic clue to the revisionist interpretation of Russian history over the past half century.

Wall Street, or rather the Morgan-Rockefeller complex represented at 120 Broadway and 14 Wall Street, had something very close to Williams' argument in mind. Wall Street went to bat in Washington for the Bolsheviks. It succeeded. The Soviet totalitarian regime survived. In the 1930s foreign firms, mostly of the Morgan-Rockefeller group, built the five-year plans. They have continued to build Russia, economically and militarily.[251] On the other hand, Wall Street presumably did not foresee the Korean War and the Vietnam War — in which 100,000 Americans and countless allies lost their lives to Soviet armaments built with this same imported U.S. technology. What seemed a farsighted, and undoubtedly profitable, policy for a Wall Street syndicate, became a nightmare for millions outside the elitist power circle and the ruling class.

---

[250] U.S., Senate, *Bolshevik Propaganda*, hearings before a subcommittee of the Committee on the Judiciary, 65th Cong., pp. 679-80. See also herein p. 107 for the role of Williams in Radek's Press Bureau.
[251] See Antony C. Sutton, *Western Technology and Soviet Economic Development*, 3 vols. (Stanford, Calif.: Hoover Institution, 1968, 1971, 1973); see also *National Suicide: Military Aid to the Soviet Union* (New York: Arlington House, 1973).

APPENDIX I

DIRECTORS OF MAJOR BANKS, FIRM, AND INSTITUTIONS MENTIONED IN THIS BOOK (AS IN 1917-1918)

AMERICAN INTERNATIONAL CORPORATION (120 Broadway)
J. Ogden Armour
G. J. Baldwin
C. A. Coffin
W. E. Corey
Robert Dollar
Pierre S. du Pont
Philip A. S. Franklin
J. P. Grace
R. F. Herrick
Otto H. Kahn
H. W. Pritchett
Percy A. Rockefeller
John D. Ryan
W.L. Saunders
J.A. Stillman
C.A. Stone
T.N. Vail
F.A. Vanderlip
E.S. Webster
A.H. Wiggin
Beckman Winthrop
William Woodward

CHASE NATIONAL BANK
J. N. Hill
A. B. Hepburn
S. H. Miller
C. M. Schwab
H. Bendicott
Guy E. Tripp
Newcomb Carlton
D.C. Jackling
E.R. Tinker
A.H. Wiggin
John J. Mitchell

EQUITABLE TRUST COMPANY (37-43 Wall Street)
Charles B. Alexander
Albert B. Boardman
Robert.C. Clowry
Howard E. Cole
Henry E. Cooper
Paul D. Cravath Hunter
Franklin Wm. Cutcheon
Henry E. Huntington
Edward T. Jeffrey
Otto H. Kahn
Alvin W. Krech
James W. Lane
S. Marston
Charles G. Meyer

Bertram Cutler
Thomas de Witt Cuyler
Frederick W. Fuller
Robert Goelet
Carl R. Gray
Charles Hayden
Bertram G. Work

George Welwood Murray
Henry H. Pierce
Winslow S. Pierce
Lyman Rhoades
Walter C. Teagle
Henry Rogers Winthrop

FEDERAL ADVISORY COUNCIL (1916)
Daniel G. Wing, Boston, District No. 1
J. P. Morgan, New York, District No. 2
Levi L. Rue, Philadelphia, District No. 3
W. S. Rowe, Cincinnati, District No. 4
J. W. Norwood, Greenville, S.C., District No. 5
C. A. Lyerly, Chattanooga, District No. 6
J. B. Forgan, Chicago, Pres., District No. 7
Frank O. Watts, St. Louis, District No. 8
C. T. Jaffray, Minneapolis, District No. 9
E. F. Swinney, Kansas City, District No. 10
T. J. Record, Paris, District No. 11
Herbert Fleishhacker, San Francisco, District No. 12

FEDERAL RESERVE BANK OF NEW YORK (120 Broadway)
William Woodward (1917)
Robert H. Treman (1918)   Class A
Franklin D. Locke (1919)

Charles A. Stone (1920)
Wm. B. Thompson (1918)   Class B
L. R. Palmer (1919)

Pierre Jay (1917)
George F. Peabody (1919)   Class C
William Lawrence Saunders (1920)

FEDERAL RESERVE BOARD
William G. M'Adoo   Adolph C. Miller (1924)
Charles S. Hamlin (1916)   Frederic A. Delano (1920)
Paul M. Warburg (1918)   W.P.G. Harding (1922)
John Skelton Williams

GUARANTY TRUST COMPANY (140 Broadway)
Alexander J. Hemphill (Chairman)
Charles H. Allen   Edgar L. Marston
A. C. Bedford Grayson   M-P Murphy
Edward J. Berwind   Charles A. Peabody
W. Murray Crane   William C. Potter
T. de Witt Cuyler   John S. Runnells
James B. Duke   Thomas F. Ryan
Caleb C. Dula   Charles H. Sabin
Robert W. Goelet   John W. Spoor
Daniel Guggenheim   Albert Straus
W. Averell Harriman   Harry P. Whitney
Albert H. Harris   Thomas E. Wilson
Walter D. Hines   London Committee:
Augustus D. Julliard   Arthur J. Fraser (Chairman)
Thomas W. Lamont   Cecil F. Parr
William C. Lane   Robert Callander

NATIONAL CITY BANK
P. A. S. Franklin   P.A. Rockefeller
J.P. Grace   James Stillman
G. H. Dodge   W. Rockefeller
H. A. C. Taylor   J. O. Armour
R. S. Lovett   J.W. Sterling
F. A. Vanderlip   J.A. Stillman
G. H. Miniken   M.T. Pyne
E. P. Swenson   E.D. Bapst
Frank Trumbull   J.H. Post
Edgar Palmer   W.C. Procter

NATIONALBANK FÜR DEUTSCHLAND
(As in 1914, Hjalmar Schacht joined board in 1918)
Emil Wittenberg   Hans Winterfeldt
Hjalmar Schacht   Th Marba
Martin Schiff   Paul Koch
Franz Rintelen

SINCLAIR CONSOLIDATED OIL CORPORATION (120 Broadway)
Harry F. Sinclair   James N. Wallace

H. P. Whitney	Edward H. Clark
Wm. E. Corey	Daniel C. Jackling
Wm. B. Thompson	Albert H. Wiggin

J. G. WHITE ENGINEERING CORPORATION

James Brown	C.E. Bailey
Douglas Campbell	J.G. White
G. C. Clark, Jr.	Gano Dunn
Bayard Dominick, Jr.	E.G. Williams
A. G. Hodenpyl	A.S. Crane
T. W. Lamont	H.A. Lardner
Marion McMillan	G.H. Kinniat
J. H. Pardee	A.F. Kountz
G. H. Walbridge	R.B. Marchant
E. N. Chilson	Henry Parsons
A. N. Connett	

APPENDIX II

THE JEWISH-CONSPIRACY THEORY OF THE BOLSHEVIK REVOLUTION

There is an extensive literature in English, French, and German reflecting the argument that the Bolshevik Revolution was the result of a "Jewish conspiracy"; more specifically, a conspiracy by Jewish world bankers. Generally, world control is seen as the ultimate objective; the Bolshevik Revolution was but one phase of a wider program that supposedly reflects an age-old religious struggle between Christianity and the "forces of darkness."

The argument and its variants can be found in the most surprising places and from quite surprising persons. In February 1920 Winston Churchill wrote an article — rarely cited today — for the *London Illustrated Sunday Herald* entitled *"Zionism* Versus Bolshevism." In this' article Churchill concluded that it was "particularly important... that the National Jews in every country who are loyal to the land of their adoption should come forward on every occasion... and take a prominent part in every measure for combatting the Bolshevik conspiracy." Churchill draws a line between "national Jews" and what he calls "international Jews." He argues that the "international and for the most atheistical Jews" certainly had a "very great" role in the creation of Bolshevism and bringing about the Russian Revolution. He asserts (contrary to fact) that with the exception of Lenin, "the majority" of the leading figures in the revolution were Jewish, and adds (also contrary to fact) that in many cases Jewish interests and Jewish places of worship were excepted by the Bolsheviks from their policies of seizure. Churchill calls the international Jews a "sinister confederacy" emergent from the persecuted populations of countries where Jews have been persecuted on account of their race. Winston Churchill traces this movement back to Spartacus-Weishaupt, throws his literary net around Trotsky, Bela Kun, Rosa Luxemburg, and Emma Goldman, and charges: "This world-wide conspiracy for the overthrow of civilisation and for the reconstitution of society on the basis of arrested development, of envious malevolence, and impossible equality, has been steadily growing."

Churchill then argues that this conspiratorial Spartacus-Weishaupt group has been the mainspring of every subversive movement in the nineteenth century. While pointing out that Zionism and Bolshevism are competing for the soul of the Jewish people, Churchill (in 1920) was preoccupied with the role of the Jew in the Bolshevik Revolution and the existence of a worldwide Jewish conspiracy.

Another well-known author in the 1920s, Henry Wickham Steed describes in the second volume of his *Through 30 Years 1892-1922* (p. 302) how he attempted to bring the Jewish-conspiracy concept to the attention of Colonel Edward M. House and President Woodrow Wilson. One day in March 1919 Wickham Steed called Colonel House and found him disturbed over Steed's recent criticism of U.S. recognition of the Bolsheviks. Steed pointed out to House that Wilson would be discredited among the many peoples and nations of Europe and "insisted that, unknown to him, the prime movers were Jacob Schiff, Warburg and other international financiers, who wished above all to bolster up the Jewish Bolshevists in order to secure a field for German and Jewish exploitation of Russia."[252] According to Steed, Colonel House argued for the establishment of economic relations with the Soviet Union.

Probably the most superficially damning collection of documents on the Jewish conspiracy is in the State Department Decimal File (861.00/5339). The central document is one entitled "Bolshevism and Judaism," dated November 13, 1918. The text is in the form of a report, which states that the revolution in Russia was engineered "in February 1916" and "it was found that the following persons and firms were engaged in this destructive work":

(1) Jacob Schiff — Jew
(2) Kuhn, Loeb & Company — Jewish Firm
    Management: Jacob Schiff — Jew
    Felix Warburg — Jew
    Otto H. Kahn — Jew
    Mortimer L. Schiff — Jew
    Jerome J. Hanauer — Jew
(3) Guggenheim — Jew
(4) Max Breitung — Jew
(5) Isaac Seligman — Jew

The report goes on to assert that there can be no doubt that the Russian Revolution was started and engineered by this group and that in April 1917

> Jacob Schiff in fact made a public announcement and it was due to his financial influence that the Russian revolution was successfully accomplished and in the Spring 1917 Jacob Schitf started to finance Trotsky, a Jew, for the purpose of accomplishing a social revolution in Russia.

---

[252] See Appendix 3 for Schiff's actual role.

The report contains other miscellaneous information about Max Warburg's financing of Trotsky, the role of the Rheinish-Westphalian syndicate and Olof Aschberg of the Nya Banken (Stockholm) together with Jivotovsky. The anonymous author (actually employed by the U.S. War Trade Board)[253] states that the links between these organizations and their financing of the Bolshevik Revolution show how "the link between Jewish multi-millionaires and Jewish proletarians was forged." The report goes on to list a large number of Bolsheviks who were also Jews and then describes the actions of Paul Warburg, Judus Magnes, Kuhn, Loeb & Company, and Speyer & Company.

The report ends with a barb at "International Jewry" and places the argument into the context of a Christian-Jewish conflict backed up by quotations from the Protocols of Zion. Accompanying this report is a series of cables between the State Department in Washington and the American embassy in London concerning the steps to be taken with these documents:[254]

> 5399 Great Britain, TEL. 3253 i pm October 16, 1919 In Confidential File Secret for Winslow from Wright. Financial aid to Bolshevism & Bolshevik Revolution in Russia from prominent Am. Jews: Jacob Schiff, Felix Warburg, Otto Kahn, Mendell Schiff, Jerome Hanauer, Max Breitung & one of the Guggenheims. Document re- in possession of Brit. police authorities from French sources. Asks for any facts re-.
>
> * * * * *
>
> Oct. 17 Great Britain TEL. 6084, noon r c-h 5399 Very secret. Wright from Winslow. Financial aid to Bolshevik revolution in Russia from prominent Am. Jews. No proof re- but investigating. Asks to urge Brit. authorities to suspend publication at least until receipt of document by Dept.
>
> * * * * *
>
> Nov. 28 Great Britain TEL. 6223 R 5 pro. 5399
> FOR WRIGHT. Document re financial aid to Bolsheviki by prominent American jews. Reports — identified as French translation of a statement originally prepared in English by Russian citizen in Am. etc. Seem most unwise to give — the distinction of publicity.

It was agreed to suppress this material and the files conclude, "I think we have the whole thing in cold storage."

---

[253] The anonymous author was a Russian employed by the U.S. War Trade Board. One of the three directors of the U.S. War Trade Board at this time was John Foster Dulles.
[254] U.S. State Dept. Decimal File, 861.00/5399.

Another document marked "Most Secret" is included with this batch of material. The provenance of the document is unknown; it is perhaps FBI or military intelligence. It reviews a translation of the Protocols of the Meetings of the Wise Men of Zion, and concludes:

> In this connection a letter was sent to Mr. W. enclosing a memorandum from us with regard to certain information from the American Military Attache to the effect that the British authorities had letters intercepted from various groups of international Jews setting out a scheme for world dominion. Copies of this material will be very useful to us.

This information was apparently developed and a later British intelligence report makes the flat accusation:

> SUMMARY: There is now definite evidence that Bolshevism is an international movement controlled by Jews; communications are passing between the leaders in America, France, Russia and England with a view to concerted action.[255]

However, none of the above statements can be supported with hard empirical evidence. The most significant information is contained in the paragraph to the effect that the British authorities possessed "letters intercepted from various groups of international Jews setting out a scheme for world dominion." If indeed such letters exist, then they would provide support (or nonsupport) for a presently unsubstantiated hypothesis: to wit, that the Bolshevik Revolution and other revolutions are the work of a worldwide Jewish conspiracy.

Moveover, when statements and assertions are not supported by hard evidence and where attempts to unearth hard evidence lead in a circle back to the starting point — particularly when everyone is quoting everyone else — then we must reject the story as spurious. *There is no concrete evidence that Jews were involved in the Bolshevik Revolution because they were Jewish.* There may indeed have been a higher proportion of Jews involved, but given tsarist treatment of Jews, what else would we expect? There were probably many Englishmen or persons of English origin in the American Revolution fighting the redcoats. So what? Does that make the American Revolution an English conspiracy? Winston Churchill's statement that Jews had a "very great role" in the Bolshevik Revolution is supported only by distorted evidence. The list of Jews involved in the Bolshevik Revolution must be weighed against lists of non-Jews involved in the revolution. When this scientific procedure is adopted, the proportion of foreign Jewish Bolsheviks involved falls to less than twenty percent of the

---

[255] Great Britain, Directorate of Intelligence, *A Monthly Review of the Progress of Revolutionary Movements Abroad*, no. 9, July 16, 1913 (861.99/5067).

total number of revolutionaries — and these Jews were mostly deported, murdered, or sent to Siberia in the following years. Modern Russia has in fact maintained tsarist anti-Semitism.

It is significant that documents in the State Department files confirm that the investment banker Jacob Schiff, often cited as a source of funds for the Bolshevik Revolution, was in fact *against* support of the Bolshevik regime.[256] This position, as we shall see, was in direct contrast to the Morgan-Rockefeller promotion of the Bolsheviks.

The persistence with which the Jewish-conspiracy myth has been pushed suggests that it may well be a deliberate device to divert attention from the real issues and the real causes. The evidence provided in this book suggests that the New York bankers who were also Jewish had relatively minor roles in supporting the Bolsheviks, while the New York bankers who were also Gentiles (Morgan, Rockefeller, Thompson) had major roles.

What better way to divert attention from the *real* operators than by the medieval bogeyman of anti-Semitism?

---

[256] See Appendix 3.

Antony C. Sutton

Appendix III

Selected Documents from Government Files of the United States and Great Britain

Note: Some documents comprise several papers that form a related group.

DOCUMENT N°1 Cable from Ambassador Francis in Petrograd to U.S. State Department and related letter from Secretary of State Robert Lansing to President Woodrow Wilson (March 17, 1917)

DOCUMENT N°2 British Foreign Office document (October 1917) claiming Kerensky was in the pay of the German government and aiding the Bolsheviks

DOCUMENT N°3 Jacob Schiff of Kuhn, Loeb & Company and his position on the Kerensky and Bolshevik regimes (November 1918)

DOCUMENT N°4 Memorandum from William Boyce Thompson, director of the Federal Reserve Bank of New York, to the British prime minister David Lloyd George (December 1917)

DOCUMENT N°5 Letter from Felix Frankfurter to Soviet agent Santeri Nuorteva (May 9, 1918)

DOCUMENT N°6 Personnel of the Soviet Bureau, New York, 1920; list from the New York State Lusk Committee files

DOCUMENT N°7 Letter from National City Bank to the U.S. Treasury referring to Ludwig Martens and Dr. Julius Hammer (April 15, 1919)

DOCUMENT N°8 Letter from Soviet agent William (Bill) Bobroff to Kenneth Durant (August 3, 1920)

DOCUMENT N°9 Memo referring to a member of the J. P. Morgan firm and the British director of propaganda Lord Northcliffe (April 13, 1918)

DOCUMENT N°10 State Department Memo (May 29, 1922) regarding General Electric Co.

Document N°1

Cable from Ambassador Francis in Petrograd to the Department of State in Washington, D.C., dated March 14, 1917, and reporting the first stage of the Russian Revolution (861.00/273).

>Petrograd Dated March 14, 1917, Recd. 15th, 2:30 a.m.
>Secretary of State, Washington

1287. Unable to send a cablegram since the eleventh. Revolutionists have absolute control in Petrograd and are making strenuous efforts to preserve order, which successful except in rare instances. No cablegrams since your 1251 of the ninth, received March eleventh. Provisional government organized under the authority of the Douma which refused to obey the Emperor's order of the adjournment. Rodzianko, president of the Douma, issuing orders over his own signature. Ministry reported to have resigned. Ministers found are taken before the Douma, also many Russian officers and other high officials. Most if not all regiments ordered to Petrograd have joined the revolutionists after arrival. American colony safe. No knowledge of any injuries to American citizens.
FRANCIS,
American Ambassador

On receipt of the preceding cable, Robert Lansing, Secretary of State, made its contents available to President Wilson (861.00/273):

PERSONAL AND CONFIDENTIAL
My Dear Mr. President:
I enclose to you a very important cablegram which has just come from Petrograd, and also a clipping from the New York WORLD of this morning, in which a statement is made by Signor Scialoia, Minister without portfolio in the Italian Cabinet, which is significant in view of Mr. Francis' report. My own impression is that the Allies know of this matter and I presume are favorable to the revolutionists since the Court party has been, throughout the war, secretely pro- German.
Faithfully yours, ROBERT LANSING
Enclosure: The President, The White House

COMMENT
The significant phrase in the Lansing-Wilson letter is "My own impression is that the Allies know of this matter and I presume are favorable to the revolutionists since the Court party has been, throughout the war, secretely pro-German." It will be recalled (chapter two) that Ambassador Dodd claimed that Charles R. Crane, of Westinghouse and of Crane Co. in New York and an adviser to President Wilson, was involved in this first revolution.

Document N°2

Memorandum from Great Britain Foreign Office file FO 371/ 2999 (The War — Russia), October 23, 1917, file no. 3743.
DOCUMENT

Personal (and) Secret.

Disquieting rumors have reached us from more than one source that Kerensky is m German pay and that he and his government are doing their utmost to weaken (and) disorganize Russia, so as to arrive at a situation when no other course but a separate peace would be possible. Do you consider that there is any ground for such insinuations, and that the government by refraining from any effective action are purposely allowing the Bolshevist elements to grow stronger?

If it should be a question of bribery we might be able to compete successfully if it were known how and through what agents it could be done, although it is not a pleasant thought.

COMMENT
Refers to information that Kerensky was in German pay.

DOCUMENT N°3

Consists of four parts:
(a) Cable from Ambassador Francis, April 27, 1917, in Petrograd to Washington, D.C., requesting transmission of a message from prominent Russian Jewish bankers to prominent Jewish bankers in New York and requesting their subscription to the Kerensky Liberty Loan (861.51/139).
(b) Reply from Louis Marshall (May 10, 1917) representing American Jews; he declined the invitation while expressing support for the American Liberty Loan (861.51/143).
(c) Letter from Jacob Schiff of Kuhn, Loeb (November 25, 1918) to State Department (Mr. Polk) relaying a message from Russian Jewish banker Kamenka calling for Allied help *against* the Bolsheviks ("because Bolshevist government does not represent Russian People").
(d) Cable from Kamenka relayed by Jacob Schiff.

DOCUMENTS

(a) Secretary of State Washington.
1229, twenty-seventh.
Please deliver following to Jacob Schiff, Judge Brandies [*sic*], Professor Gottheil, Oscar Strauss [*sic*], Rabbi Wise, Louis Marshall and Morgenthau:
"We Russian Jews always believed that liberation of Russia meant also our liberation. Being deeply devoted to country we placed implicit trust temporary Government. We know the unlimited economic power of Russia and her immense natural resources and the emancipation we obtained will enable us to participate development country. We firmly believe that victorious finish of the war owing help our allies and United States is near.

Temporary Government issuing now new public loan of freedom and we feel our national duty support loan high vital for war and freedom. We are sure that Russia has an unshakeable power of public credit and will easily bear a.11 necessary financial burden. We formed special committee of Russian Jews for supporting loan consisting representatives financial, industrial trading circles and leading public men.

We inform you here of and request our brethern beyong [sic] the seas to support freedom of Russian which became now case humanity and world's civilization. We suggest you form there special committee and let us know of steps you may take Jewish committee support success loan of freedom. Boris Kamenka, Chairman, Baron Alexander Gunzburg, Henry Silosberg."

FRANCIS

* * * * *

(b) Dear Mr. Secretary:

After reporting to our associates the result of the interview which you kindly granted to Mr. Morgenthau, Mr. Straus and myself, in regard to the advisability of calling for subscriptions to the Russian Freedom Loan as requested in the cablegram of Baron Gunzburg and Messrs. Kamenka and Silosberg of Petrograd, which you recently communicated to us, we have concluded to act strictly upon your advice. Several days ago we promised our friends at Petrograd an early reply to their call for aid. We would therefore greatly appreciate the forwarding of the following cablegram, provided its terms have your approval:

"Boris Kamenka,

Don Azov Bank, Petrograd.

Our State Department which we have consulted regards any present attempt toward securing public subscriptions here for any foreign loans inadvisable; the concentration of all efforts for the success of American war loans being essential, thereby enabling our Government to supply funds to its allies at lower interest rates than otherwise possible. Our energies to help the Russian cause most effectively must therefore necessarily be directed to encouraging subscriptions to American Liberty Loan. Schiff, Marshall, Straus, Morgenthau, Wise, Gonheil."

You are of course at liberty to make any changes in the phraseology of this suggested cablegram which you may deem desirable and which will indicate that our failure to respond directly to the request that has come to us is due to our anxiety to make our activities most efficient.

May I ask you to send me a copy of the cablegram as forwarded, with a memorandum of the cost so that the Department may be promptly reimbursed.

I am, with great respect, Faithfully yours, [sgd.] Louis Marshall. The Secretary of State Washington, D.C.

* * * * *

(c) Dear Mr. Polk:

Will you permit me to send you copy of a cablegram received this morning and which I think, for regularity's sake, should be brought to the notice of the Secretary of State or your good self, for such consideration as it might be thought well to give this.

Mr. Kamenka, the sender of this cablegram, is one of the leading men in Russia and has, I am informed, been financial advisor both of the Prince Lvoff government and of the Kerensky government. He is President of the Banque de Commerce de l'Azov Don of Petrograd, one of the most important financial institutions of Russia, but had, likely, to leave Russia with the advent of Lenin and his "comrades."

Let me take this opportunity to send sincere greetings to you and Mrs. Polk and to express the hope that you are now in perfect shape again, and that Mrs. Polk and the children are in good health.

Faithfully yours, [sgd.] Jacob H. Schiff
Hon. Frank L. Polk Counsellor of the State Dept. Washington, D.C.
MM-Encl. [Dated November 25, 1918]

* * * * *

(d) Translation:

The complete triumph of liberty and right furnishes me a new opportunity to repeat to you my profound admiration for the noble American nation. Hope to see now quick progress on the part of the Allies to help Russia in reestablishing order. Call your attention also to pressing necessity of replacing in Ukraine enemy troops at the very moment of their retirement in order to avoid Bolshevist devastation. Friendly intervention of Allies would be greeted everywhere with enthusiasm and looked upon as democratic action, because Bolshevist government does not represent Russian people. Wrote you September 19th. Cordial greetings.

[sgd.] Kamenka

COMMENT

This is an important series because it refutes the story of a Jewish bank conspiracy behind the Bolshevik Revolution. Clearly Jacob Schiff of Kuhn, Loeb was not interested in supporting the Kerensky Liberty Loan and Schiff went to the trouble of drawing State Department attention to Kamenka's pleas for Allied intervention against the Bolsheviks. Obviously Schiff and fellow banker Kamenka, unlike J.P. Morgan and John D. Rockefeller, were as unhappy about the Bolsheviks as they had been about the tsars.

DOCUMENT N°4

Description
Memorandum from William Boyce Thompson (director of the Federal Reserve Bank of New York) to Lloyd George (prime minister of Great Britain), December 1917.
DOCUMENT

FIRST
The Russian situation is lost and Russia lies entirely open to unopposed German exploitation unless a radical reversal of policy is at once undertaken by the Allies.

SECOND
Because of their shortsighted diplomacy, the Allies since the Revolution have accomplished nothing beneficial, and have done considerable harm to their own interests.

THIRD
The Allied representatives in Petrograd have been lacking in sympathetic understanding of the desire of the Russian people to attain democracy. Our representatives were first connected officially with the Czar's regime. Naturally they have been influenced by that environment.

FOURTH
Meanwhile, on the other hand, the Germans have conducted propaganda that has undoubtedly aided them materially in destroying the Government, in wrecking the army and in destroying trade and industry. If this continues unopposed it may result in the complete exploitation of the great country by Germany against the Allies.

FIFTH
I base my opinion upon a careful and intimate study of the situation both outside and inside official circles, during my stay in Petrograd between August 7 and November 29, 1917.

SIXTH
"What can be done to improve the situation of the Allies in Russia"?
The diplomatic personnel, both British and American, should be changed to one democratic in spirit and capable of sustaining democratic sympathy.
There should be erected a powerful, unofficial committee, with headquarters in Petrograd, to operate in the background, so to speak, the influence of which in matters of policy should be recognized and accepted by the DIPLOMATIC, CONSULAR and MILITARY officials of the Allies. Such committee should be so composed in personnel as to make it possible to entrust to it wide discretionary powers. It would presumably undertake work in various channels. The nature of which will become obvious as the task progress. es; it. would aim to meet all new conditions as they might arise.

SEVENTH

It is impossible now to define at all completely the scope of this new Allied committee. I can perhaps assist to a better understanding of its possible usefulness and service by making a brief reference to the work which I started and which is now in the hands of Raymond Robins, who is well and favorably known to Col. Buchan — a work which in the future will undoubtedly have to be somewhat altered and added to in order to meet new conditions. My work has been performed chiefly through a Russian "Committee on Civic Education" aided by Madame Breshkovsky, the Grandmother of the Revolution. She was assisted by Dr. David Soskice, the private secretary of the then Prime Minister Kerensky (now of London); Nicholas Basil Tchaikovsky, at one time Chairman of the Peasants Co-operative Society, and by other substantial social revolutionaries constituting the saving element of democracy as between the extreme "Right" of the official and property-owning class, and the extreme "Left" embodying the most radical elements of the socialist parties. The aim of this committee, as stated in a cable message from Madame Breshkovsky to President Wilson, can be gathered from this quotation: "A widespread education is necessary to make Russia an orderly democracy. We plan to bring this education to the soldier in the camp, to the workman in the factory, to the peasant in the village." Those aiding in this work realized that for centuries the masses had been under the heel of Autocracy which had given them not protection but oppression; that a democratic form of government in Russian could be maintained only BY THE DEFEAT OF THE GERMAN ARMY; BY THE OVERTHROW OF GERMAN AUTOCRACY. Could free Russia, unprepared for great governmental responsibilities, uneducated, untrained, be expected long to survive with imperial Germany her next door neighbor? Certainly not. Democratic Russia would become speedily the greatest war prize the world has even known.

The Committee designed to have an educational center in each regiment of the Russian army, in the form of Soldiers' Clubs. These clubs were organized as rapidly as possible, and lecturers were employed to address the soldiers. The lecturers were in reality teachers, and it should be remembered that there is a percentage of 90 among the soldiers of Russia who can neither read nor write. At the time of the Bolshevik outbreak many of these speakers were in the field making a fine impression and obtaining excellent results. There were 250 in the city of Moscow alone. It was contemplated by the Committee to have at least 5000 of these lecturers. We had under publication many newspapers of the "A B C" class, printing matter in the simplest style, and were assisting about 100 more. These papers carried the appeal for patriotism, unity and co-ordination into the homes of the workmen and the peasants.

After the overthrow of the last Kerensky government we materially aided the dissemination of the Bolshevik literature, distributing it through agents and by aeroplanes to the German army. If the suggestion is permissible, it might be well to consider whether it would not be desirable to have this same Bolshevik literature sent into Germany and Austria across the West and Italian fronts.

EIGHTH

The presence of a small number of Allied troops in Petrograd would certainly have done much to prevent the overthrow of the Kerensky government in November. I should like to suggest for your consideration, if present conditions continue, the concentration of all the British and French Government employes in Petrograd, and if the necessity should arise it might be formed into a fairly effective force. It might be advisable even to pay a small sum to a Russian force. There is also a large body of volunteers recruited in Russia, many of them included in the Inteligentzia of "Center" class, and these have done splendid work in the trenches. They might properly be aided.

NINTH

If you ask for a further programme I should say that it is impossible to give it now. I believe that intelligent and courageous work will still prevent Germany from occupying the field to itself and thus exploiting Russia at the expense of the Allies. There will be many ways in which this service can be rendered which will become obvious as the work progresses.

COMMENT

Following this memorandum the British war cabinet changed its policy to one of tepid pro- Bolshevism. Note that Thompson admits to distribution of Bolshevik literature by his agents. The confusion over the date on which Thompson left Russia (he states November 29th in this document) is cleared up by the Pirnie papers at the Hoover Institution. There were several changes of travel plans and Thompson was still in Russia in early December. The memorandum was probably written in Petrograd in late November.

DOCUMENT N°5

DESCRIPTION

Letter dated May 9, 1918, from Felix Frankfurter (then special assistant to the secretary of war) to Santeri Nuorteva (alias for Alexander Nyberg), a Bolshevik agent in the United States. Listed as Document No. 1544 in the Lusk Committee files, New York:

DOCUMENT

WAR DEPARTMENT WASHINGTON May 9, 1918
My dear Mr. Nhorteva [*sic*]:
Thank you very much for your letter of the 4th. I knew you would understand the purely friendly and wholly unofficial character of our talk, and I appreciate the prompt steps you have taken to correct your Sirola* letter. Be wholly assured that nothing has transpired which diminishes my interest in the questions which you present. Quite the contrary. I am much interested in** the considerations you are advancing and for the point of view you

are urging. The issues*** at stake are the interests that mean much for the whole world. To meet them adequately we need all the knowledge and wisdom we can possibly get****.
Cordially yours, Felix Frankfurter
Santeri Nuorteva, Esq.
* Yrjo Sirola was a Bolshevik and commissar in Finland.
** Original text, "continually grateful to you for."
*** Original text, "interests."
**** Original text added "these days."

COMMENT

This letter by Frankfurter was written to Nuorteva/Nyberg, a Bolshevik agent in the United States, at a time when Frankfurter held an official position as special assistant to Secretary of War Baker in the War Department. Apparently Nyberg was willing to change a letter to commissar "Sirola" according to Frankfurter's instructions. The Lusk Committee acquired the original Frankfurter draft including Frankfurter's changes and not the letter received by Nyberg.

THE SOVIET BUREAU IN 1920

Position	Name	Citizenship	Born	Former Employment
Representative of USSR	Ludwig C.A.K. MARTENS	German	Russia	V-P of Weinberg & Posner Engineering (120 Broadway)
Office manager	Gregory WEINSTEIN	Russian	Russia	Journalist
Secretary	Santeri NUORTEVA	Finnish	Russia	Journalist
Assistant secretary	Kenneth DURANT	U.S.	U.S.	(1) U.S. Committee on Public Information (2) Former aide to Colonel House
Private secretary to NUORTEVA	Dorothy KEEN	U.S.	U.S.	High school
Translator	Mary MODELL	Russian	Russia	School in Russia
File clerk	Alexander COLEMAN	U.S.	U.S.	High school
Telephone clerk	Blanche ABUSHEVITZ	Russian	Russia	High school
Office attendant	Nestor KUNTZEVICH	Russian	Russia	—
Military expert	Lt. Col. Boris Tagueeff Roustam BEK	Russian	Russia	Military critic on *Daily Express* (London)
Commercial Department				
Director	A. HELLER	Russian	U.S.	International Oxygen Company
Secretary	Ella TUCH	Russian	U.S.	U.S. firms

Clerk	Rose HOLLAND	U.S.	U.S.	Gary School League
Clerk	Henrietta MEEROWICH	Russian	Russia	Social worker
Clerk	Rose BYERS	Russian	Russia	School
Statistician	Vladimir OLCHOVSKY	Russian	Russia	Russian Army

Information Department

Director	Evans CLARK	U.S.	U.S.	Princeton University
Clerk	Nora G. SMITHMAN	U.S.	U.S.	Ford Peace Expedition
Steno	Etta FOX	U.S.	U.S.	War Trade Board
—	Wilfred R. HUMPHRIES	U.K.	—	American Red Cross

Technical Dept.

Director	Arthur ADAMS	Russian	U.S.	—

Educational Dept.

Director	William MALISSOFF	Russian	U.S.	Columbia University

Medical Dept.

Director	Leo A. HUEBSCH	Russian	U.S.	Medical doctor
	D. H. DUBROWSKY	Russian	U.S.	Medical doctor

Legal Dept.

Director	Morris HILLQUIT	Lithuanian	—	—
	Counsel retained: Charles RECHT			
	Dudley Field MALONE			
	George Cordon BATTLE			

Dept. of Economics & Statistics

Director	Isaac A. HOURWICH	Russian	U.S.	U.S. Bureau of Census
	Eva JOFFE	Russian	U.S.	National Child Labor Commission
Steno	Elizabeth GOLDSTEIN	Russian	U.S.	Student

Editorial Staff of Soviet Russia

Managing editor	Jacob W. HARTMANN	U.S.	U.S.	College of City of New York
Steno	Ray TROTSKY	Russian	Russia	Student
Translator	Theodore BRESLAUER	Russian	Russia	—
Clerk	Vastly IVANOFF	Russian	Russia	—
Clerk	David OLDFIELD	Russian	Russia	—
Translator	J. BLANKSTEIN	Russian	Russia	—

SOURCE: U.S., House, *Conditions in Russia* (Committee on Foreign Affairs), 66th Cong., 3rd sess. (Washington, D.C., 1921). See also British list in U.S. State Department Decimal File, 316-22- 656, which also has the name of Julius Hammer.

DOCUMENT N°7

DESCRIPTION
Letter from National City Bank of New York to the U.S. Treasury, April 15, 1919, with regard to Ludwig Martens and his associate Dr. Julius Hammer (316-118).

DOCUMENT

> The National City Bank of New York
> New York, April 15, 1919
> Honorable Joel Rathbone,
> Assistant Secretary of the Treasury Washington, D.C.
> Dear Mr. Rathbone:
> I beg to hand you herewith photographs of two documents which we have received this morning by registered mail from a Mr. L. Martens who claims to be the representative in the United States of the Russian Socialist Federal Soviet Republic, and witnessed by a Dr. Julius Hammer for the Acting Director of the Financial Department.
> You will see from these documents that there is a demand being made upon us for any and all funds on deposit with us in the name of Mr. Boris Bakhmeteff, alleged Russian Ambassador in the United States, or in the name of any individual, committee, or mission purporting to act in behalf of the Russian Government in subordination to Mr. Bakhmeteff or directly.
> We should be very glad to receive from you whatever advice or instructions you may care to give us in this matter.
> Yours respectfully, [sgd.] J. H. Carter, Vice President.
> JHC:M Enclosure

COMMENTS
The significance of this letter is related to the long-time association (1917-1974) of the Hammer family with the Soviets.

DOCUMENT N°8

DESCRIPTION

Letter dated August 3, 1920, from Soviet courier "Bill" Bobroff to Kenneth Durant, former aide to Colonel House. Taken from Bobroff by U.S. Department of Justice.

DOCUMENT

Department of Justice Bureau of Investigation,
15 Park Row, New York City, N. Y., August 10, 1920
Director Bureau of Investigation
United States Department of Justice, Washington, D.C.

Dear Sir: Confirming telephone conversation with Mr. Ruch today, I am transmitting herewith original documents taken from the effects of B. L. Bobroll, steamship *Frederick VIII.*

The letter addressed Mr. Kenneth Durant, signed by Bill, dated August 3, 1920, together with the translation from "Pravda," July 1, 1920, signed by Trotzki, and copies of cablegrams were found inside the blue envelope addressed Mr. Kenneth Durant, 228 South Nineteenth Street, Philadelphia, Pa. This blue envelope was in turn sealed inside the white envelope attached.

Most of the effects of Mr. Bobroff consisted of machinery catalogues, specifications, correspondence regarding the shipment of various equipment, etc., to Russian ports. Mr. Bobroff was closely questioned by Agent Davis and the customs authorities, and a detailed report of same will be sent to Washington.

Very truly yours,
G. F. Lamb, Division Superintendent

LETTER TO KENNETH DURANT

Dear Kenneth: Thanks for your most welcome letter. I have felt very much cut off and hemmed in, a feeling which has been sharply emphasized by recent experiences. I have felt distressed at inability to force a different attitude toward the bureau and to somehow get funds to you. To cable $5,000 to you, as was done last week, is but a sorry joke. I hope the proposal to sell gold in America, about which we have been cabling recently, will soon be found practicable. Yesterday we cabled asking if you could sell 5,000,000 rubles at a minimum of 45 cents, present market rate being 51.44 cents. That would net at least $2,225,000. L's present need is $2,000,000 to pay Niels Juul & Co., in Christiania, for the first part of the coal shipment from America to Vardoe, Murmansk, and Archangel. The first ship is nearing Vardoe and the second left New York about July 28. Altogether, Niels Juul & Co., or rather the Norges' Bank, of Christiania, on their and our account, hold $11,000,000 gold rubles of ours, which they themselves brought from Reval to Christiania, as security for our coal order and the necessary tonnage, but the offers for purchase of this gold that they have so far been able to get are very poor, the best being $575 per kilo, whereas the rate offered by the American Mint or Treasury Department is now $644.42, and considering the large sum involved it would be a shame to let it go at too heavy a loss.

I hope that ere you get this you will have been able to effect the sale, at the same time thus getting a quarter of a million dollars or more for the bureau. If we can't in some way pay the $2,000,000 in Christiania, that was due four days ago, within a very short time, Niels Juul & Co. will have the right to sell our gold that they now hold at the best price then obtainable, which, as stated above, is quite low.

We don't know yet how the Canadian negotiations are going on. We understand Nuorteva turned over the strings to Shoen when N.'s arrest seemed imminent. We don't at this writing know where Nuorteva is. Our guess is that after his enforced return to England from Esbjerg, Denmark, Sir Basil Thomson had him shipped aboard a steamer for Reval, but we have not yet heard from Reval that he has arrived there, and we certainly would hear from Goukovski or from N. himself. Humphries saw Nuorteva at Esbjerg, and is himself in difficulties with the Danish police because of it. All his connections are being probed for; his passport has been taken away: he has been up twice for examination, and it looks as if he will be lucky if he escapes deportation. It was two weeks ago that Nuorteva arrived at Esbjerg, 300 miles from here, but having no Danish visé, the Danish authorities refused to permit him to land, and he was transferred to a steamer due to sail at 8 o'clock the following morning. By depositing 200 kroner he was allowed shore leave for a couple of hours. Wanting to get Copenhagen on long-distance wire and having practically no more money, he once more pawned that gold watch of his for 25 kroner, therewith getting in touch with Humphries, who within half an hour jumped aboard the night train, slept on the floor, and arrived at Esbjerg at 7:30. Humphries found Nuorteva, got permission from the captain to go aboard, had 20 minutes with N., then had to go ashore and the boat sailed. Humphries was then invited to the police office by two plain-clothes men, who had been observing the proceedings. He was closely questioned, address taken, then released, and that night took train back to Copenhagen. He sent telegrams to Ewer, of Daily Herald, Shoen, and to Kliskho, at 128 New Bond Street, urging them to be sure and meet Nuorteva's boat, so that N. couldn't again be spirited away, but we don't know yet just what happened. The British Government vigorously denied that they had any intention of sending him to Finland. Moscow has threatened reprisals if anything happens to him. Meantime, the investigation of H. has begun. He was called upon at his hotel by the police, requested to go to headquarters (but not arrested), and we understand that his case is now before the minister of justice. Whatever may be the final outcome, Humphries comments upon the reasonable courtesy shown him, contrasting it with the ferocity of the Red raids in America. He found that at detective headquarters they knew of some of his outgoing letters and telegrams.

I was interested in your favorable comment upon the Krassin interview of Tobenken's (you do not mention the Litvinoff one), because I had to fight like a demon with L. to get the opportunities for Tobenken. Through T. arrived with a letter from Nuorteva, as also did Arthur Ruhl, L. brusquely turned down in less than one minute the application T. was making to go into Russia, would hardly take time to hear him, saying it was impossible to allow two correspondents from the same paper to enter Russia. He gave a visé to Ruhl, largely because of a promise made last summer to Ruhl by L. Ruhl then went off to Reval, there to await the permission that L. had cabled asking Moscow to give. Tobenken, a nervous, almost a broken man because of his turn down, stayed here. I realized the mistake that had been made by the snap judgment, and started in on the job of getting it changed. Cutting a long story short, I got him to Reval with a letter to Goukovsky from L. In the meantime Moscow refused Ruhl, notwithstanding L's visé. L. was maddened at affront to his visé, and insisted that it be honored. It was, and Ruhl prepared to leave. Suddenly word came from Moscow to Ruhl revoking the permission and to Litvinoff, saying that information had reached Moscow that Ruhl was in service of State Department. At time of writing, both Tobenken and Ruhl are in Reval, stuck.

I told L. this morning of the boat leaving tomorrow and of the courier B. available, asked him if he had anything to write to Martens, offered to take it in shorthand for him, but no, he said he had nothing to write about that I might perhaps send duplicates of our recent cables to Martens.

Kameneff passed by here on a British destroyer en route to London, and didn't stop off here at all, and Krassin went direct from Stockholm. Of the negotiations, allied and Polish, and of the general situation you know about as much as we do here. L's negotiations with the Italians have finally resulted in establishing of mutual representation. Our representative, Vorovsky, has already gone to Italy and their representative, M. Gravina, is en route to Russia. We have just sent two ship loads of Russian wheat to Italy from Odessa.

Give my regards to the people of your circle that I know. With all good wishes to you.
Sincerely yours, Bill

The batch of letters you sent — 5 Cranbourne Road, Charlton cum Hardy, Manchester, has not yet arrived.

L's recommendation to Moscow, since M. asked to move to Canada, is that M. should be appointed there, and that N., after having some weeks in Moscow acquainting himself first hand, should be appointed representative to America.

L. is sharply critical of the bureau for giving too easily visés and recommendations. He was obviously surprised and incensed when B. reached here with contracts secured in Moscow upon strength of letters given to him by M. The later message from M. evidently didn't reach Moscow. What L. plans to do about it I don't know. I would suggest that M. cable in cipher his recommendation to L. in this matter. L. would have nothing to do with B. here. Awkward situation may be created.

L. instanced also the Rabinoff recommendation.

Two envelopes, Mr. Kenneth Durant, 228 South Nineteenth Street, Philadelphia, Pa., U.S.A.

SOURCE: U.S. State Department Decimal File, 316-119-458/64.

NOTE: IDENTIFICATION OF INDIVIDUALS

William (Bill) L. BOBROFF: Soviet courier and agent. Operated Bobroff Foreign Trading and Engineering Company of Milwaukee. Invented the voting system used in the Wisconsin Legilature.
Kenneth DURANT: Aide to Colonel House; see text.
SHOEN: Employed by International Oxygen Co., owned by Heller, a prominent financier and Communist.
EWER: Soviet agent, reporter for *London Daily Herald.*
KLISHKO: Soviet agent in Scandinavia
NUORTEVA Also known as Alexander Nyberg, first Soviet representative in United States; see text.
Sir Basil THOMPSON: Chief of British Intelligence
"L": LITVINOFF.
"H": Wilfred Humphries, associated with Martens and Litvinoff, member of Red Cross in Russia.
KRASSIN: Bolshevik commissar of trade and labor, former head of Siemens-Schukert in Russia.

COMMENTS
This letter suggests close ties between Bobroff and Durant.

DOCUMENT N°9

DESCRIPTION
Memorandum referring to a request from Davison (Morgan partner) to Thomas Thacher (Wall Street attorney associated with the Morgans) and passed to Dwight Morrow (Morgan partner), April 13, 1918.

DOCUMENT

> The Berkeley Hotel, London
> April 13th, 1918.
> Hon. Walter H. Page,
> American Ambassador to England, London.
> Dear Sir:
> Several days ago I received a request from Mr. H. P. Davison, Chairman of the War Council of the American Red Cross, to confer with Lord Northcliffe regarding the situation in Russia, and then to proceed to Paris for other conferences. Owing to Lord Northcliffe's illness I have not been able to confer with him, but am leaving with Mr. Dwight W. Morrow, who is now staying at the Berkeley Hotel, a memorandum of the situation which Mr. Morrow will submit to Lord Northcliffe on the latter's return to London.

For your information and the information of the Department I enclose to you, herewith, a copy of the memorandum.
Respectfully yours,
[sgd.] Thomas D. Thacher.

COMMENT

Lord Northcliffe had just been appointed director of propaganda. This is interesting in the light of William B. Thompson's subsidizing of Bolshevik propaganda and his connection with the Morgan- Rockefeller interests.

DOCUMENT N° 10

DESCRIPTION

This document is a memorandum from D.C. Poole, Division of Russian Affairs in the Department of State, to the secretary of state concerning a conversation with Mr. M. Oudin of General Electric.

DOCUMENT

> May 29, 1922
> Mr. Secretary:
> Mr. Oudin, of the General Electric Company, informed me this morning that his company feels that the time is possibly approaching to begin conversations with Krassin relative to a resumption of business in Russia. I told him that it is the view of the Department that the course to be pursued in this matter by American firms is a question of business judgment and that the Department would certainly interpose no obstacles to an American firm resuming operations in Russia on any basis which the firm considered practicable.
> He said that negotiations are now in progress between the General Electric Company and the Allgemeine Elektrizitats Gesellschaft for a resumption of the working agreement which they had before the war. He expects that the agreement to be made will include a provision for cooperation of Russia.
> Respectfully, DCP D.C. Poole

COMMENT

This is an important document as it relates to the forthcoming resumption of relations with Russia by an important American company. It illustrates that the initiative came from the company, not from the State Department, and that no consideration was given to the effect of transfer of General Electric technology to a self-declared enemy. This GE agreement was the first step down a road of major technical transfers that led directly to the deaths of 100,000 Americans and countless allies.

Wall Street and FDR

ABOUT PROFESSOR SUTTON

"And if one prevail against him, two shall withstand him; and a threefold cord is not quickly broken" (Ecclesiastes 4:12).

Professor Sutton (1925-2002).

Though he was a prolific author, Professor Sutton will always be remembered by his great trilogy: *Wall St. and the Bolshevik Revolution, Wall St. and the Rise of Hitler,* and *Wall St. and FDR.*

Professor Sutton left rainy, cloudy England for sunny California in 1957. He was a voice crying in the academic wilderness when most of the U. S. colleges had sold their souls for Rockefeller Foundation money.

Of course he came to this country believing that it was the land of the *free* and the home of *brave.*

ANTONY C. SUTTON was born in London in 1925 and educated at the universities of London, Gottingen, and California. A citizen of the United States since 1962, he was a Research Fellow at the Hoover Institution for War, Revolution and Peace at Stanford, California from 1968 to 1973, where he produced the monumental three-volume study, *Western Technology and Soviet Economic Development.*

In 1974, Professor Sutton completed *National Suicide: Military Aid to the Soviet Union*, a best-selling study of Western, primarily American, technological and financial assistance to the U.S.S.R. *Wall Street and the Rise of Hitler* is his fourth book exposing the role of American corporate insiders in financing international socialism. The two other books in this series are *Wall Street and the Bolshevik Revolution* and *Wall Street and FDR.*

Antony C. Sutton

Professor Sutton has contributed articles to Human Events, The Review of the News, Triumph, Ordnance, National Review, and many other journals. He is currently working on a two-part study of the Federal Reserve System and the manipulation of the U.S. economic system. Married and the father of two daughters, he lived in California.

CHAPTER I

ROOSEVELTS AND DELANOS

The real truth of the matter is, as you and I know, that a financial element in the larger centers has owned the Government ever since the days of Andrew Jackson—and I am not wholly excepting the Administration of W.W.[257] The country is going through a repetition of Jackson's fight with the Bank of the United States—only on a far bigger and broader basis.
    President Franklin Delano Roosevelt to Col. Edward Mandell House, November 21, 1933, F.D.R.: His Personal Letters (New York: Duell, Sloan and Pearce 1950), p. 373.

This book[258] portrays Franklin Delano Roosevelt as a Wall Street financier who, during his first term as President of the United States, reflected the objectives of financial elements concentrated in the New York business establishment. Given the long historical association—since the late 18th century—of the Roosevelt and Delano families with New York finance and FDR's own career from 1921 to 1928 as banker and speculator at 120 Broadway and 55 Liberty Street, such a theme should not come as a surprise to the reader. On the other hand, FDR biographers Schlesinger, Davis, Freidel, and otherwise accurate Roosevelt commentators appear to avoid penetrating very far into the recorded and documented links between New York bankers and FDR. We intend to present the facts of the relationship, as recorded in FDR's letter files. These are new facts only in the sense that they have not previously been published; they are readily available in the archives for research, and consideration of this information suggests a reassessment of FDR's role in the history of the 20th century.

Perhaps it always makes good politics to appear before the American electorate as a critic, if not an outright enemy, of the international banking fraternity. Without question Franklin D. Roosevelt, his supporters, and biographers portray FDR as a knight in shining armor wielding the sword of righteous vengeance against the robber barons in the skyscrapers

---

[257] W.W. is Woodrow Wilson—editor's not.
[258] A previous volume, Antony C. Sutton, *Wall Street and the Bolshevik Revolution*, (New Rochelle, N.Y., Arlington House, 1974), hereafter cited as Sutton, *Bolshevik Revolution*, explored the links between Wall Street financiers and the Bolshevik Revolution. In great part, allowing for deaths and new faces, this book focuses on the same segment of the New York financial establishment.

of downtown Manhattan. For instance, the Roosevelt Presidential campaign of 1932 consistently attacked President Herbert Hoover for his alleged association with international bankers and for pandering to the demands of big business. Witness the following FDR blast in the depths of the Great Depression at Hoover's public support for business and individualism, uttered in the campaign address in Columbus, Ohio, August 20, 1932:

> Appraising the situation in the bitter dawn of a cold morning after, what do we find? We find two thirds of American industry concentrated in a few hundred corporations and actually managed by not more than five human individuals.
> We find more than half of the savings of the country invested in corporate stocks and bonds, and made the sport of the American stock market.
> We find fewer than three dozen private banking houses, and stock selling adjuncts of commercial banks, directing the flow of American capital.
> In other words, we find concentrated economic power in a few hands, the precise opposite of the individualism of which the President speaks.[259]

This statement makes Franklin Delano Roosevelt appear as another Andrew Jackson, contesting a bankers' monopoly and their strangle-hold on American industry. But was FDR also an unwilling (or possibly a willing) tool of the Wall Street bankers, as we could infer from his letter to Colonel Edward House, cited in the epigraph to this chapter?

Clearly if, as Roosevelt wrote to House, a "financial element in the larger cities has owned the Government ever since the days of Andrew Jackson," then neither Hoover nor Roosevelt was being intellectually honest in his presentation of the issues to the American public. The gut issues presumably were the identity of this "financial element" and how and by what means it maintained its "ownership" of the U.S. Government.

Putting this intriguing question temporarily to one side, the pervasive historical image of FDR is one of a President fighting on behalf of the little guy, the man in the street, in the midst of unemployment and financial depression brought about by big business speculators allied with Wall Street. We shall find, on the contrary, that this image distorts the truth to the extent that it portrays FDR as an enemy of Wall Street; this is simply because most historians probing into Wall Street misdeeds have been reluctant to apply the same standards of probity to Franklin D. Roosevelt as to other political leaders. What is a sin for Herbert Hoover or even 1928 Democratic Presidential candidate Al Smith is presumed

---

[259] The Public Papers and Addresses of Franklin D. Roosevelt, Volume I (New York: Random House, 1938), p. 679.

a virtue in the case of FDR. Take Ferdinand Lundberg in *The Rich and the Super-Rich*.[260] Lundberg also looks at Presidents and Wall Street and makes the following assertion:

> In 1928 Al Smith had his chief backing, financial and emotional, from fellow- Catholic John J. Raskob, prime minister of the Du Ponts. If Smith had won he would have been far less a Catholic than a Du Pont President.[261]

Now the Du Ponts were indeed heavy, very heavy, contributors to the 1928 Al Smith Democratic Presidential campaign. These contributions are examined in detail in this volume in Chapter 8, "Wall Street Buys the New Deal," and no quarrel can be made with this assertion. Lundberg then moves on to consider Smith's opponent Herbert Hoover and writes:

> Hoover, the Republican, was a J. P. Morgan puppet; Smith his democratic opponent, was in the pocket of the Du Ponts, for whom J. P. Morgan & Company was the banker.

Lundberg omits the financial details, but the Du Ponts and Rockefellers are certainly on record in Congressional investigations as the largest contributors to the 1928 Hoover campaign. But Wall Street withdrew its support of Herbert Hoover in 1932 and switched to FDR. Lundberg omits to mention this critical and pivotal withdrawal. Why did Wall Street switch? Because, as we shall see later, Herbert Hoover would not adopt the Swope Plan created by Gerard Swope, long-time president of General Electric. By contrast, FDR accepted the plan, and it became FDR's National Industrial Recovery Act. So while Hoover was indebted to Wall Street, FDR was much more so. Arthur M. Schlesinger Jr. in *The Crisis of the Old Order*. 1919-1933 comes closer to the point than any establishment historian, but like other Rooseveltophiles fails to carry the facts to their ultimate and logical conclusions. Schlesinger notes that after the 1928 election the Democratic Party had a debt of $1.6 million and "Two of the leading creditors, John J. Raskob and Bernard Baruch, were philanthropic Democratic millionaires, prepared to help carry the party along until 1932".[262] John J. Raskob was vice president of Du Pont and also of General Motors, the largest corporation in the United States. Bernard Baruch was by his own admissions at the very heart of Wall Street speculation. Schlesinger adds that, in return for Wall Street's benevolence, "they naturally expected influence in shaping the party's organization and policy."[263] Unfortunately, Arthur Schlesinger, who (unlike most Rooseveltian biographers) has his finger on the very pulse of the problem, drops the question to continue with a discussion of the superficialities

---

[260] New York: Lyle Stuart, 1968.
[261] Ibid., p. 172.
[262] Boston: Riverside Press, 1957, p. 273.
[263] Ibid.

of politics—conventions, politicians, political give-and-take, and the occasional clashes that mask the underlying realities. Obviously, the hand on the purse ultimately decrees which policies are implemented, when, and by whom.

A similar protective attitude for FDR may be found in the four-volume biography by Frank Freidel, *Franklin D. Roosevelt*.[264] Discussing the shattering failure of the Bank of the United States just before Christmas 1930, Freidel glosses over FDR's negligence while Governor of the State of New York. The Bank of the United States had 450,000 depositors, of which 400,000 accounts held less than $400. In other words, the Bank of the United States was a little man's bank. A report by Senator Robert Moses on the condition of an earlier banking failure—City Trust—had been ignored by Governor F. D. Roosevelt, who appointed another commission that produced milder recommendations for banking reform. Freidel poses the question:

> Why had he [FDR] failed to fight through reform legislation which would have prevented the Bank of the United States debacle? These are sharp questions that critics of Roosevelt asked at the time and later.[265]

Freidel concludes that the answer lies in FDR's "personal confidence in the banking community." Why did FDR have this complete confidence? Because, writes Freidel,

> Herbert Lehman was one of the soundest as well as politically the most liberal of Wall Street bankers; in banking matters Roosevelt seems to have followed Lehman's lead, and that was to cooperate as far as possible with the banking titans.[266]

This is something like saying that, if your banker is a liberal and loses your money, that's OK, because after all he is a liberal and a supporter of FDR. On the other hand, however, if your banker loses your money and happens not to be a liberal or a supporter of FDR, then he is a crook and must pay the price of his sins.

The four-volume Freidel biography has but a single chapter on FDR as "Businessman," the most space given by any major FDR biographer. Even Freidel reduces important ventures to a mere paragraph. For example, while the American Investigation Corporation venture is

---

[264] This series is: Frank Freidel, Franklin D. Roosevelt: The Apprenticeship. (1952), hereafter cited as Freidel, The Apprenticeship; Freidel, Franklin D. Roosevelt: The Ordeal (1954), hereafter cited as Freidel, The Ordeal; Freidel, Franklin D. Roosevelt: The Triumph (1956), hereafter cited as Freidel, The Triumph; Freidel, Franklin D. Roosevelt, Launching The New Deal (1973). All four volumes published in Boston by Little, Brown.
[265] Freidel, The Triumph, op. cit., p. 187.
[266] Ibid., p. 188.

not named, an associated venture, General Air Service, is mentioned, but dismissed with a paragraph:

> In 1923, together with Owen D. Young, Benedict Crowell (who had been Assistant Secretary of War under Wilson), and other notables, he organized the General Air Service to operate helium-filled dirigibles between New York and Chicago.[267]

We shall see that there was a lot more to General Air Service (and more importantly the unmentioned American Investigation Corporation) than this paragraph indicates. In particular, exploration of the Freidel phrase "and other notables" suggests that FDR had entree to and worked in cooperation with some prominent Wall Street elements.

Why do Schlesinger, Freidel, and other lesser FDR biographers avoid the issue and show reluctance to pursue the leads? Simply because, when you probe the facts, Roosevelt was a creation of Wall Street, an integral part of the New York banking fraternity, and had the pecuniary interests of the financial establishment very much at heart.

When the information is laid out in detail, it is absurd to think that Wall Street would hesitate for a second to accept Roosevelt as a welcome candidate for President: he was one of their own, whereas businessman Herbert Hoover had worked abroad for 20 years before being recalled by Woodrow Wilson to take over the Food Administration in World War I.

To be specific, Franklin D. Roosevelt was, at one time or another during the 1920s, a vice president of the Fidelity & Deposit Company (120 Broadway); the president of an industry trade association, the American Construction Council (28 West 44th Street); a partner in Roosevelt & O'Connor (120 Broadway); a partner in Marvin, Hooker & Roosevelt (52 Wall Street); the president of United European Investors, Ltd. (7 Pine Street); a director of International Germanic Trust, Inc. (in the Standard Oil Building at 26 Broadway); a director of Consolidated Automatic Merchandising Corporation, a paper organization; a trustee of Georgia Warm Springs Foundation (120 Broadway); a director of American Investigation Corporation (37-39 Pine Street); a director of Sanitary Postage Service Corporation (285 Madison Avenue); the chairman of the General Trust Company (15 Broad Street); a director of Photomaton (551 Fifth Avenue); a director of Mantacal Oil Corporation (Rock Springs, Wyoming); and an incorporator of the Federal International Investment Trust.

That's a pretty fair list of directorships. It surely earns FDR the title of Wall Streeter *par excellence*. Most who work on "the Street" never achieve, and probably never even dream about achieving, a record of 11 corporate directorships, two law partnerships, and the presidency of a major trade association.

---

[267] Freidel, The Ordeal, op. cit., p. 149.

In probing these directorships and their associated activities, we find that Roosevelt was a banker and a speculator, the two occupations he emphatically denounced in the 1932 Presidential election. Moreover, while banking and speculation have legitimate roles in a free society— indeed, they are essential for a sane monetary system—both can be abused. FDR's correspondence in the files deposited at the FDR Library in Hyde Park yields evidence—and evidence one reads with a heavy heart—that FDR was associated with the more unsavory elements of Wall Street banking and speculation, and one can arrive at no conclusion other than that FDR used the political arena, not the impartial market place, to make his profits.[268]

So we shall find it not surprising that the Wall Street groups that supported Al Smith and Herbert Hoover, both with strong ties to the financial community, also supported Franklin D. Roosevelt. In fact, at the political crossroads in 1932, when the choice was between Herbert Hoover and FDR, Wall Street chose Roosevelt and dropped Hoover.

Given this information, how do we explain FDR's career on Wall Street? And his service to Wall Street in creating, in partnership with Herbert Hoover, the trade associations of the 1920s so earnestly sought by the banking fraternity? Or FDR's friendship with key Wall Street operators John Raskob and Barney Baruch? To place this in perspective we must go back in history and examine the background of the Roosevelt and Delano families, which have been associated with New York banking since the 18th century.

THE DELANO FAMILY AND WALL STREET

The Delano family proudly traces its ancestors back to the Actii, a 600 B.C. Roman family. They are equally proud of Franklin Delano Roosevelt. Indeed, the Delanos claim that the Delano influence was the predominant factor in FDR's life work and accounts for his

---

[268] This raises a legitimate question concerning the scope of this book and the nature of the relevant evidence. The author is interested only in establishing the relationship between Wall Street and FDR and drawing conclusions from that relationship. Therefore, episodes that occurred in 1921, while FDR was on Wall Street, but not associated directly with his financial activities, are omitted. For example, in 1921 the Senate Naval Affairs Committee issued a report with 27 conclusions, almost all critical of FDR, and posing serious moral questions. The first conclusion in the Senate report reads: "That immoral and lewd acts were practiced under instructions or suggestions, by a number of the enlisted personnel of the United States Navy, in and out of uniform, for the purpose of securing evidence against sexual perverts, and authorization for the use of these enlisted men as operators or detectives was given both orally and in writing to Lieut. Hudson by Assistant Secretary Franklin D. Roosevelt, with the knowledge and consent of Josephus Daniels, Secretary of the Navy." The 26 related conclusions and the minority report are contained in United States Senate, Committee on Naval Affairs, 67th Congress, 1st Session, Alleged Immoral Conditions at Newport (R.I.) Naval Training Station (Washington: Government Printing Office, 1921). However, while FDR's conduct in the U.S. Navy may have been inexcusable and may or may not reflect on his moral fiber, such conduct is not pertinent to this book, and these incidents are omitted. It should also be noted that, where FDR's correspondence is of critical import for the argument of this book, it is the practice to quote sections verbatim, without paraphrasing, to allow the reader to make his own interpretations.

extraordinary achievements. Be that as it may, there is no question that the Delano side of the family links FDR to many other rulers and other politicians. According to the Delano family history,[269] "Franklin shared common ancestry with one third of his predecessors in the White House." The Presidents linked to FDR on the Delano side are John Adams, James Madison, John Quincy Adams, William Henry Harrison, Zachary Taylor, Andrew Johnson, Ulysses S. Grant, Benjamin Harrison, and William Howard Taft. On the Roosevelt side of the family, FDR was related to Theodore Roosevelt and Martin Van Buren, who married Mary Aspinwall Roosevelt. The wife of George Washington, Martha Dandridge, was among FDR's ancestors, and it is claimed by Daniel Delano that Winston Churchill and Franklin D. Roosevelt were "eighth cousins, once removed."[270] This almost makes the United States a nation ruled by a royal family, a mini monarchy.

The reader must make his own judgment on Delano's genealogical claims; this author lacks the ability to analyze the confused and complex family relationships involved. More to the point and without question, the Delanos were active in Wall Street in the 1920s and 1930s and long before. The Delanos were prominent in railroad development in the United States and abroad. Lyman Delano (1883-1944) was a prominent railroad executive and maternal grandfather of Franklin D. Roosevelt. Like FDR, Lyman began his career in the insurance business, with the Northwestern Life Insurance of Chicago, followed by two years with Stone & Webster.[271] For most of his business life Lyman Delano served on the board of the Atlantic Coast Line Railroad, as president in 1920 and as chairman of the board from 1931 to 1940. Other important affiliations of Lyman Delano were director (along with W. Averell Harriman) of the Aviation Corporation, Pan American Airways, P & O Steamship Lines, and half a dozen railroad companies.

Another Wall Street Delano was Moreau Delano, a partner in Brown Brothers & Co. (after 1933 it absorbed Harriman & Co. to become Brown Brothers, Harriman) and a director of Cuban Cane Products Co. and the American Bank Note Company.

The really notable Delano on Wall Street was FDR's "favorite uncle" (according to Elliott Roosevelt), Frederic Adrian Delano (1863-1953), who started his career with the Chicago, Burlington and Quincy Railroad and later assumed the presidency of the Wheeling & Lake Erie Railroad, the Wabash Railroad, and in 1913 the Chicago, Indianapolis and Louisville Railway. "Uncle Fred" was consulted in 1921 at a critical point in FDR's infantile paralysis attack, quickly found Dr. Samuel A. Levine for an urgently needed diagnosis, and arranged

---

[269] Daniel W. Delano, Jr., Franklin Roosevelt and the Delano Influence (Pittsburgh, Pa.: Nudi Publications, 1946), p. 53.
[270] Ibid., p. 54.
[271] See Sutton, Bolshevik Revolution, op. cit., pp. 128, 130-3, 136 on Stone & Webster.

for the special private train to transport FDR from Maine to New York as he began the long and arduous road to recovery.[272]

In 1914 Woodrow Wilson appointed Uncle Fred to be a member of the Federal Reserve Board. Intimate Delano connections with the international banking fraternity are exemplified by a confidential letter from central banker Benjamin Strong to Fred Delano requesting confidential FRB data:[273]

> (Personal)
> December 11, 1916
> My Dear Fred: Would it be possible for you to send me in strict confidence the figures obtained by the Comptroller as to holdings of foreign securities by national banks? I would be a good deal influenced in my opinion in regard the present situation if I could get hold of these figures, which would be treated with such confidence as you suggest.
> If the time ever comes when you are able to slip away for a week or so for a bit of a change and rest, why not take a look at Denver and incidentally pay me a visit? There are a thousand things I would like to talk over with you.
> Faithfully yours,
> Benjamin Strong
> Hon. F. A. Delano
> Federal Reserve Board, Washington, D.C.

Following World War I Frederic Delano devoted himself to what is euphemistically known as public service, while continuing his business operations. In 1925 Delano was chairman of the League of Nations International Committee on opium production; in 1927 he was chairman of the Commission on Regional Planning in New York; he then became active in sponsoring the National Park Commission. In 1934 FDR named Uncle Fred Delano as chairman of the National Resources Planning Board. The Industrial Committee of the National Resources Planning Board, which presumably Frederic Delano had some hand in choosing, was a happy little coterie of socialist planners, including Laughlin Currie, Leon Henderson, Isador Lublin (prominent in the transfer of industrial technology to the USSR in the pre-Korean War era), and Mordecai Ezekiel.

The advisor to the Board was Beardsley Ruml.

---

[272] Elliott Roosevelt and James Brough, An Untold Story: The Roosevelts of Hyde Park (New York: Putnam's, 1973), pp. 142, 147-8.
[273] United States Senate, Hearings before the Special Committee Investigating the Munitions Industry, 74th Congress, Second Session, Part 25, "World War Financing and United States Industrial Expansion 1914-1915, J. P. Morgan & Company" (Washington: Government Printing Office, 1937), p. 10174, Exhibit No. 3896.

Then from 1931 to 1936, while involved in socialist planning schemes, Delano was also chairman of the board of the Federal Reserve Bank of Richmond, Virginia. In brief, Frederic Delano was simultaneously both capitalist and planner.

Delano left a few writings from which we can glean some concept of his political ideas. There we find support for the thesis that the greatest proponents of government regulation are the businessmen who are to be regulated, although Delano does warn that government ownership of railroads can be carried too far:

> Government ownership of railroads is a bugaboo which, though often referred to, the public does not demand. If government ownership of railways comes, it will come because the owners of railways prefer it to government regulation, and it will be a sorry day for the republic when regulation is carried to such an extreme that the owners of the railways are unwilling to accept any longer the responsibilities of management.[274]

However, in another book, written about 20 years later, Delano is much more receptive to government planning:

> A big problem in planning is that of educating the people. If the public only realized that there can be social gains from directed effort, and that the time to accomplish most by planning comes before the need of making changes are manifested, the other problems of planning could be more easily solved.[275]

Further:

> The above brief classification of the problem involved in planning serves as a basis for indicating the need for both direct and indirect social control.

Very few people really know the best use of land for their own advantage, to say nothing of planning its use for the common good. Institutions have done a great deal in educating farmers how to plan individual farms, and yet many of the farms in this country are poorly organized.[276]

---

[274] Frederic A. Delano, Are Our Railroads Fairly Treated? Address before the Economic Club of New York, April 29, 1913, p. 11.
[275] Frederic A. Delano, What About the Year 2000? Joint Committee on Bases of Sound Land Policy, n.d., pp. 138-9.
[276] Ibid., p. 141.

In brief, the Delano side of the family has undertaken capitalist enterprises and has Wall Street interests going well back into the 19th century. By the 1930s, however, Frederic Delano had abandoned capitalist initiative for socialist planning.

THE ROOSEVELT FAMILY AND WALL STREET

Franklin Delano Roosevelt was also descended on the Roosevelt side from one of the oldest banking families in the United States. FDR's great-grandfather James Roosevelt founded the Bank of New York in 1784 and was its president from 1786 to 1791. The investment banking firm of Roosevelt & Son of New York City was founded in 1797, and in the 1930s George E. Roosevelt, FDR's cousin, was the fifth member of the family in direct succession to head the firm. So the New York City banking roots of the Roosevelt family extend without interruption back into the late 18th century. In the industrial sphere James Roosevelt built the first American sugar refinery in New York City in the 1740s, and Roosevelts still had connections with Cuban sugar refining in the 1930s. FDR's father, also named James Roosevelt, was born at Hyde Park, New York in 1828 into this old and distinguished family. This James Roosevelt graduated from Harvard Law School in 1851, became a director of the Consolidated Coal Company of Maryland and, like the Delanos in subsequent years was associated with the development of transportation, first as general manager of the Cumberland & Pennsylvania Railroad, and then as president of the Louisville, New Albany & Chicago Railroad, the Susquehanna Railroad Co., Champlain Transportation Co., Lake George Steamboat Co., and New York & Canada Railroad Co. James Roosevelt was also vice president and manager of the Delaware & Hudson Canal Co. and chairman of the Maritime Canal Company of Nicaragua, but most significantly was an organizer of the Southern Railway Security Company, established in 1871 and one of the first of the security holding companies formed to buy up and consolidate railroads. The Southern Railway Security Company was a consolidation or cartelization scheme similar in its monopolistic principle to the trade associations formed by Franklin D. Roosevelt in the 1920s and to the National Recovery Act, another cartelization scheme, of the New Deal. James Roosevelt's second wife was Sara, daughter of Warren Delano, and their son was Franklin Delano Roosevelt, later President of the United States.

Franklin was educated at Groton and Harvard, then went on to Columbia Law School. According to his son Elliott,[277] FDR "never graduated or took a degree, but he was able to pass his New York State bar examination."[278] FDR's first job was with the old established

---

[277] Elliott Roosevelt, An Untold Story, op. cit., p. 43.
[278] Ibid., p. 67.

downtown law firm of Carter, Ledyard and Milburn, whose principal client was J. Pierpont Morgan, and in three years FDR worked his way up from minor legal research posts to the firm's municipal court and admiralty divisions. We should note in passing that, when FDR first went to Washington D.C. in 1916 to become Assistant Secretary of the Navy, it was Thomas W. Lamont—international banker and most influential of the Morgan partners—who leased the FDR home in New York.[279]

There were other Roosevelts on Wall Street. George Emlen Roosevelt (1887-1963) was a cousin of both Franklin and Theodore Roosevelt. In 1908, George Emlen became a member of the family banking firm Roosevelt & Son. In January 1934, after passage of FDR's Banking Act of 1933, the firm was split into three individual units: Roosevelt & Son, with which George Roosevelt remained as a senior partner, Dick & Merle-Smith, and Roosevelt & Weigold. George Emlen Roosevelt was a leading railroad financier, involved in no fewer than 14 railroad reorganizations, as well as directorships in several important companies, including the Morgan-controlled Guaranty Trust Company,[280] the Chemical Bank, and the Bank for Savings in New York. The full list of George Emlen's directorships at 1930 requires six inches of small print in Poor's *Directory of Directors*.

Another Morgan-associated Roosevelt was Theodore Roosevelt, 26th President of the United States and the grandson of Cornelius Roosevelt, one of the founders of the Chemical National Bank. Like Clinton Roosevelt, whom we shall discuss later, Theodore served as a New York State Assemblyman from 1882-1884; he was appointed a member of the U.S. Civil Service Commission in 1889, Police Commissioner of New York City in 1895, and Assistant Secretary of the Navy in 1897; and was elected Vice President in 1900 to become President of the United States upon the assassination of President McKinley in 1901. Theodore Roosevelt was reelected President in 1904, to become founder of the Progressive Party, backed by J. P. Morgan money and influence, and so launched the United States on the road to the welfare state. The longest section of the platform of the Progressive Party was that devoted to "Business" and reads in part:

> We therefore demand a strong national regulation of interstate corporations. The corporation is an essential part of modern business. The concentration of modern business, in some degree, is both inevitable and necessary for national and international business efficiency.

---

[279] See Sutton, Bolshevik Revolution, for numerous citations to Thomas Lamont's connections with the Bolshevik Revolution in 1917, while residing in FDR's leased house in New York.

[280] It is important to note as we develop the story of FDR in Wall Street that Guaranty Trust is prominent in the earlier Sutton, Bolshevik Revolution.

The only really significant difference between this statement backed by Morgan money and the Marxian analysis is that Karl Marx thought of concentration of big business as inevitable rather than "necessary." Yet Roosevelt's Progressive Party plugging for business regulation was financed by Wall Street, including the Morgan-controlled International Harvester Corporation and J. P. Morgan partners. In Kolko's words:

> The party's financial records for 1912 list C. K. McCormick, Mr. and Mrs. Medill McCormick, Mrs. Katherine McCormick, Mrs. A. A. McCormick, Fred S. Oliver, and James H. Pierce. The largest donations for the Progressives, however, came from Munsey, Perkins, the Willard Straights of the Morgan Company, Douglas Robinson, W. E. Roosevelt, and Thomas Plant.[281]

There is, of course, a long Roosevelt political tradition, centered on the State of New York and the Federal government in Washington, that parallels this Wall Street tradition. Nicholas Roosevelt (1658-1742) was in 1700 a member of the New York State Assembly. Isaac Roosevelt (1726-1794) was a member of the New York Provincial Congress. James I. Roosevelt (1795-1875) was a member of the New York State Assembly in 1835 and 1840 and a member of the U.S. House of Representatives between 1841 and 1843. Clinton Roosevelt (1804-1898), the author of an 1841 economic program remarkably similar to Franklin Roosevelt's New Deal (see Chapter 6) was a member of the New York State Assembly in 1835. Robert Barnwell Roosevelt (1829-1906) was a member of the U.S. House of Representatives in 1871-73 and U.S. Minister to Holland 1888-1890. Then, of course, as we have noted, there was President Theodore Roosevelt. Franklin continued the Theodore Roosevelt political tradition as a New York State Senator (1910-1913), Assistant Secretary of the Navy (1913-1920), Governor of the State of New York (1928-1930), and then President (1933-1945).

While FDR was in office, other Roosevelts assumed minor offices. Theodore Roosevelt, Jr. (1887-1944) was a member of the New York State Assembly from 1919 to 1921 and then continued the virtual Roosevelt Navy monopoly as Assistant Secretary of the Navy from 1921 to 1924, Governor of Puerto Rico from 1922 to 1932, and Governor General of the Philippines from 1932 to 1933. Nicolas Roosevelt was Vice Governor of the Philippines in 1930. Other Roosevelts have continued this political tradition since the New Deal era.

An alliance of Wall Street and political office is implicit in this Roosevelt tradition. The policies implemented by the many Roosevelts have tended toward increased state intervention into business, desirable to some business elements, and therefore the Roosevelt search for political office can fairly be viewed as a self-seeking device. The euphemism of "public

---

[281] Gabriel Kolko, The Triumph of Conservatism (London: Free Press, 1963), p. 202.
Willard Straight was owner of The New Republic.

service" is a cover for utilizing the police power of the state for personal ends, a thesis we must investigate. If the Roosevelt tradition had been one of uncompromising *laissez-faire*, of getting the state out of business rather than encouraging intervention into economic activities, then our assessment would necessarily be quite different. However, from at least Clinton Roosevelt in 1841 to Franklin D. Roosevelt, the political power accumulated by the Roosevelt clan has been used on the side of regulating business in the interests of restricting competition, encouraging monopoly, and so bleeding the consumer in the interests of a financial élite. Further, we must consider the observation conveyed by Franklin D. Roosevelt to Edward House and cited in the epigraph to this chapter, that "a financial element in the large centers has owned the government ever since the days of Andrew Jackson." Consequently, it is pertinent to conclude this introductory chapter with the 1943 observations of William Allen White, an honest editor if ever there was one, who made one of the best literary critiques on this financial establishment in the context of World War II; this, it should be noted, was after ten years of FDR and at the peak of Roosevelt's political power:

> One cannot move about Washington without bumping into the fact that we are running two wars—a foreign war and a domestic one.
> The domestic war is in the various war boards. Every great commodity industry in this country is organized nationally and many of them, perhaps most of them are parts of great national organizations, cartels, agreements, which function on both sides of the battle front. Here in Washington every industry is interested in saving its own self. It wants to come out of the war with a whole hide and with its organization unimpaired, legally or illegally. One is surprised to find men representing great commodity trusts or agreements or syndicates planted in the various war boards. It is silly to say New Dealers run this show. It's run largely by absentee owners of amalgamated industrial wealth, men who either directly or through their employers control small minority blocks, closely organized, that manipulate the physical plants of these trusts.
> For the most part these managerial magnates are decent, patriotic Americans. They have great talents. If you touch them in nine relations of life out of ten they are kindly, courteous, Christian gentlemen.
> But in the tenth relation, where it touches their own organization, they are stark mad, ruthless, unchecked by God or man, paranoics, in fact, as evil in their design as Hitler.
> They are determined to come out of this war victorious for their own stockholders—which is not surprising. It is understandable also for Hitler to desire to come out of this war at any cost victorious for the German people.
> But this attitude of the men who control the great commodity industries, and who propose to run them according to their own judgment and their own morals, do not make a pretty picture for the welfare of the common man.

These international combinations of industrial capital are fierce troglodyte animals with tremendous power and no social brains. They hover like an old silurian reptile about our decent more or less Christian civilization—like great dragons in this modern day when dragons are supposed to be dead.[282]

---

[282] Quoted from George Seldes, One Thousand Americans (New York: Boni & Gaer, 1947), pp. 149-150.

CHAPTER 2

POLITICS IN THE BONDING BUSINESS[283]

I am going to take advantage of our old friendship and ask you if you can help me out any [sic] in an effort to get fidelity and contract bonds from the powers that be in Brooklyn.
   Franklin D. Roosevelt to Congressman J. A. Maher, March 2, 1922.

In early 1921 Franklin D. Roosevelt became vice president of the Fidelity & Deposit Company of Maryland and resident director of the company's New York office at 120 Broadway. Fidelity & Deposit of Maryland was an established insurance company specializing in the bonding and surety policies required on government and corporate contracts and a range of individual employments ranging from secretary of a trade union to employees of stock brokerage houses. In fact, a potential for bonding business exists wherever a contractor or employee can violate a fiduciary trust or fail to complete a contract, as in construction projects. In brief, bonding is a specialized field of insurance covering the risk of noncompliance. In 1921 Fidelity & Deposit was the fourth largest such bonding house in the United States, but not to be confused with the Fidelity and Casualty Company of New York, another insurance company, which incidentally had W. Emlen Roosevelt, FDR's cousin, on its board of directors.

Why did Van-Lear Black, owner of The Baltimore Sun and board chairman of Fidelity & Deposit, hire insurance novice Franklin D. Roosevelt as vice president of the important New York office? Almost certainly he hired FDR because the bonding business is unusually dependent upon political influence. Reading through FDR's Fidelity & Deposit letter files from 1921 to 1928, we find that only rarely do price or service appear as competitive elements in bonding. The main competitive weapons are "Whom do you know?" and "What are your politics?" In other words, politics is a substitute for the market place. Politics was FDR's forte and Van-Lear Black knew his bonding world when he acquired FDR. It is important to note the political nature of the bonding business because FDR's biographers have, in some

---

[283] This chapter is based on the FDR papers at Hyde Park, New York: specifically Group 14, file entitled "Fidelity & Deposit Co. of Maryland, Correspondence of FDR as Vice President, 1921-1928."

cases, suggested that FDR, a business novice, was relatively useless to VanLear Black. For example, Frank Freidel writes:

> Whether Van-Lear Black hired him because it was a smart business move or merely to collect a celebrity is impossible to determine. The worst Wall Streeters unfriendly to Roosevelt were able to charge was that the company wasted the twenty-five thousand dollars per year it paid him in salary.[284]

What then were the roles of politics and politicians in the bonding business in New York State in the 1920s?

POLITICIANS AS BOND WRITERS

The pervasive political nature of the bonding business is reflected in a contemporary, but anonymous, news clipping found in the FDR letter files and carefully marked by FDR himself. The clip refers to New York State government officials negotiating state contracts while at the same time acting as members of private bond-issuing firms selling security bonds to state contractors. The newspaper aptly headed the column "All Under One Roof" and reported that Daniel P. O'Connell, a member of the Albany bonding firm O'Connell Brothers & Corning and simultaneously in charge of the public affairs of the city and county of Albany, was endeavoring to exert a statewide influence over the issue of his bonds, to the dismay of competing bond writers:

> Whereas, formerly Daniel P. has been somewhat busy going on the bonds of various and sundry constituents, hereafter he will do his utmost, it is said, to wish his bonds on other persons, especially contractors doing business with the city and county.
> His advent into the bondwriting world has been about as welcome as a snowstorm would be to a blushing bride on a bright and sunny June morning. Local insurance men, Democrats as well as Republicans, it is said, who have been engaged in writing contractors' bonds for many years, resent Daniel P's coming into their field, while perhaps admiring his ambition and display of courage and all that sort of thing; and in state political circles it is said that Royal K. Fuller, state commissioner of the bureau of canals and waterways, is fearful that if Daniel P. succeeds in the local field [it will be] to his (Mr. Fuller's) detriment, or

---

[284] Freidel, The Ordeal, op. cit., p. 138. Freidel is unfair to Roosevelt. No evidence is given of Wall Street criticism of the appointment. Criticism is unlikely—given the political nature of the business, that politics was FDR's strength, and the long Roosevelt tradition on "the Street."

rather to the detriment of the bondwriting firm with which he is connected and for whose benefit, it is said, he uses the influence of his position.

Bond writer cum office holder O'Connell then wrote soliciting letters to all Albany city and county contractors to the effect that he was in the bonding business at the City Savings Bank Building, owned incidentally by Albany Mayor Hackett and which also happened to be the headquarters of the Albany county Democratic organization. O'Connell's letter to State contractors concluded with the appeal:

> I would appreciate it if you will allow this office the opportunity of serving you. A telephone call or letter addressed to me at this office will receive prompt attention.

It is important to note this prevailing and apparently acceptable use of political office and influence to feather one's own nest. In the light of the evidence below, it suggests that FDR was merely following the contemporary mores of his environment. The use of politics to obtain bond business is reflected in the FDR letter files and essentially is the only way he obtained bonding business while vice president of Fidelity & Deposit Company. Of course, his letters soliciting business to the other Wall Street Roosevelts are entirely legitimate. We find for example, a letter to "Dear Cousin Emlen" (W. Emlen Roosevelt of Roosevelt & Son, 30 Pine Street) dated March 10, 1922 to inquire about obtaining the scheduled bond for the Buffalo, Rochester and Pittsburgh Railway Company, a bond then written by the competing National Surety Company. Emlen replied promptly on March 16 that he "was able to speak to the President about the matter." This must have stirred FDR's imagination because on March 16, 1922 he wrote to "Dear George" (George E. Roosevelt), also at Roosevelt & Son, inquiring about the blanket bond taken out by the firm itself for its own protection.

Trade unions were a special FDR target for business; as each union local secretary and treasurer is required to have a bond, this was a lucrative field. On December 13, 1921 general secretary treasurer E. C. Davison of the International Association of Machinists wrote FDR:

> We are now carrying the bulk of our bonding business with your company, which we were influenced to do in a great measure by the fact of your connection with this concern.

Then on January 26, 1922 Joseph F. Valentine, president of the International Molder's Union of North America, wrote to FDR that he was most appreciative of all FDR's efforts for the union while acting as Assistant Secretary of the Navy and

> I have a desire to give the Fidelity and Deposit Company of Maryland as much of our business as possible ... as soon as our existing bonds have lapsed, it will be a personal pleasure to have your Company handle our business in the future.

Union officials in Washington and elsewhere were prompt to request their locals to divert business to their old friend FDR and away from other bonding companies. In turn, local union officials were prompt to report on their diverting actions, information in turn promptly conveyed to FDR. For example, the president of the International Association of Boilermakers wrote to Secretary Berres of the Metal Trades Department, A. F. of L., in Washington, D.C.:

> ... You may rest assured that anything that I can do to be of service to Mr. Roosevelt in his new position will be a pleasure on my part, and I am today writing Mr. Roosevelt.

Naturally FDR exploited his old political friends to the utmost and with a commendable attention to detail. In a sales pitch dated March 2, 1922 addressed to Congressman J. A. Maher, FDR wrote two letters, not one. The first letter read in part:

> Howe [Louis Howe, FDR's right-hand man] told me of his conversation over the telephone with you and I am inclosing a more formal letter for exhibition purposes. This is a little friendly note lest you think I have suddenly grown formal since I have adopted Wall Street as my business address.
> Do come over and see me. I know it will do your soul good to hear the language which Brother Berres and various others connected with the Labor Bureau, are using in regard to the present administration in general and Congressmen in particular. If the Missus happens to be out of hearing when you arrive I will repeat some of the more quotable extracts.

FDR enclosed for Congressman Maher a more formal letter obviously to be shown around to Maher's friends stating precisely what it was he wanted: "fidelity and contracts bonds from the powers that be in Brooklyn:"

> I am going to take advantage of our old friendship and ask you if you can help me out any in an effort to get fidelity and contract bonds from the powers that be in Brooklyn. There are a large number of bonds needed in connection with the city government work, besides the personal bonds which every city official has to give, and I am in hopes that some of my old friends will be willing to remember me. Unfortunately, I cannot take this matter up with them myself at the present time, but as all my friends are your friends I feel that if you have the time and inclination, you can be of real help to me. I assure you the favor will not soon be forgotten.

Later we shall see how successful this approach was for F & D.

POLITICAL INFLUENCE AND CONTRACT AWARDS

FDR's political contacts and influences were of course well known within Fidelity & Deposit, and he was repeatedly called upon by other members of the firm to use his political expertise and personal credit to generate bond business, even outside New York. This may be exemplified by a letter dated August 23, 1928 from F & D director F. A. Price, in charge of the Chicago office, about business from local Chicago politicians. Price wrote "Dear Franklin" with a message that, since the death of Chicago political leader George Brennan, several names had been proposed as leaders of the local Democratic Party machine. Brennan before his death requested that M. L. Igoe be his successor, Price writes FDR:

> You undoubtedly got in touch with him while at Houston and in the event you have a personal acquaintance with him, I would like to have you give me as strong a letter of introduction to him as possible.

Price noted that recently when in Baltimore he had discussions with F & D company president Charles Miller about "the thought of making some deal with the new democratic leader in Illinois. It is with this view in mind that I wish the letter of introduction." As machine politics in Chicago has been notorious for its low ethical standards, it requires little imagination to visualize the kind of deal Price was suggesting and which FDR used his name and influence to further.

That personal friendship alone was insufficient to get bonding business and that some variety of sweetener was used is brought out in a letter on the New York political situation dated September 23, 1925 from John Griffin, in charge of the New York office contract division, to "My Dear Mr. Roosevelt." It discusses the complex interconnections between New York political offices and the bond brokerage business. In part the letter reads:

> The big victory of Walker over Hylan will, of course, make a new set-up in the bond broker situation. Sinnott & Canty, from whom we were able to get some bonds in the early part of the Hylan Administration and in the latter part were not so much favored, will no doubt be out of it and either Charles F. Murphy, Jr., Hyman & McCall, Jim Hoey, or a man named McLaughlin, a brother of the Banking Superintendent, will be the favored one. As I see it, our strongest connection will be through Al Smith into Charlie Murphy or McCall or McLaughlin as Hoey has his own Company—the Columbia Casualty Company.
>
> Perhaps Murphy receives from the National Surety Company, or the Company to whom he gives business now, a larger commission than we might be willing to give for his direct

business, but a word into his ear through you and, of course, through the Governor and possibly Jimmie Walker, would at least put us under the most favored nation clause or [for] any division of these bonds as you know all of them must be divided between two or more companies.

I know all of these people pretty well and favorably, but mere personal friendship will not be sufficient.

A meticulous reading of this internal company letter suggests that kickbacks were the usual way to get bond business from New York government agencies; note the paragraph, "Perhaps Murphy receives from the National Surety Company, or the Company to whom he gives business now, a larger commission than we might be willing to give for his direct business." The concluding sentence, "... mere personal friendship will not be sufficient" has an ominous ring.

Politicization of the surety business, so obvious in Chicago and New York, extended also to the Federal government contract arena in Washington D.C. On May 5, 1926 F & D second vice president F. A. Bach in Baltimore wrote FDR about a $11/4; million Veterans Bureau building projected for construction that spring:

> Dear Franklin,
> Among other projects of the Veterans Bureau this spring is one involving approximately a million and a quarter dollars at Bedford, Mass., and I am secretly hoping that through influence such as knowing Mrs. Rogers, Representative of Massachusetts, that we might have some chance of getting a piece of that business although, of course, the biggest project will be at North Port, Long Island.

Similarly, to a contact in a "firm holding Navy contracts" FDR wrote:

> A casual reference in a letter from one of my old friends in the Navy Department to the award of some 8-inch gun forgings to your company, brought to my mind the very pleasant relations we held during my term as Assistant Secretary of the Navy, and I wondered if you would feel like letting my company write some of the contract bonds that you are obliged to give the government from time to time. I would like very much to have one of our representatives call.

Louis Howe, FDR's right-hand man, also worked at F & D offices, also actively solicited bonds, and was not at all backward about canvassing business. Howe's letter to Homer Ferguson of the Newport News Shipbuilding Company in December 1921 noted that the company had entered bids on construction of the vessel Leviathan and thanked Ferguson for the bond:

If by any chance the fact that this was Mr. Roosevelt's company influenced you in making this award it would cheer Mr. Roosevelt tremendously if you could write him a little line to that effect.

These political methods of doing business are, of course, a long way from the competitive market place of the college textbooks. It would be naïve to think that political preference and personal friendship have no role, or only a minor role, in business relationships. In reviewing FDR's bond business, however, it is difficult to visualize another business in which politics plays such an all-encompassing role as it did in the bonding and surety business in the 1920s. The morality of kickbacks and of the use of political office to generate personal business is questionable, and the legality is definitely doubtful. Much less obvious is the consequent loss of economic efficiency and loss to society as a whole. If purchase and sale of such bonds is determined by price and past performance—and personal acquaintance can be a legitimate factor in judging past performance—then the market place will yield maximum economic benefits and efficiency for society. In a politicized business atmosphere these impartial competitive factors are eliminated, economic efficiency is foregone, and benefits are reduced. We have, in effect, a microcosm of a socialist economy in which all decisions are politicized to the detriment of society as a whole. In brief, FDR's bonding operations were to some degree antisocial.

Yet other letters in the Roosevelt files provide authentic glimpses into the back rooms of 1920 era politics, the wheeling and dealing that has so often degenerated into outright corruption. Witness an FDR letter dated July 11, 1928 to first vice president George L. Radcliffe in Baltimore relating to the manner in which John J. Raskob became Chairman of the Democratic National Committee. Raskob was vice president of Du Pont and of General Motors and consequently as much a member of the Wall Street establishment as could be found anywhere:

> At a meeting last night the Governor [Smith] definitely decided on John J. Raskob as Chairman of the National Committee. He said he wanted an organizer and a man who would bring the Democratic Party into favor with the business interests of the country. My first judgment is that it is a grave mistake as he is a Catholic; secondly, he is even wetter than Smith, seeking the repeal of the Eighteenth Amendment: and third, he is the head of the largest business organization in the world. I fear that it will permanently drive away a host of people in the south and west, and rural east who are not particularly favorable to Smith, but who up to today have been seeping back into the Party.
> I don't know Raskob very well, but expect to have a conference with him within a few days, and will mention among other things the possibility of V. L. B. [Van-Lear Black].

Later in this book we shall record the enormous funds poured into the Democratic Party by Raskob and the quid pro quo for big business: the New Deal and the National Recovery Administration (NRA).

On August 24, 1927 another letter to George Radcliffe outlined the manner in which the bonding industry could get together on behalf of James Beha, then Superintendent of Insurance in the State of New York. This quotation confirms the fact that "regulated" industries are no more than political devices to keep unwelcome competition at bay and that the regulators can be in the pockets and act on behalf of the supposedly regulated industry:

> Vic Cullen[285] and I have just had a talk in regard to Superintendent Beha. Vic says that he thinks there is some move on foot initiated by Joyce, to get Beha into the National in some capacity and Cullen makes what to me seems a most worthwhile suggestion. It is that Beha might become the head of the Surety Association. We all like Beha and trust him; he is a man of courage and independence, and I cannot think of any one better suited for the position. Of course, it would cost a high salary—my thought is $35,000 a year—but this divided up among all of the members, amounts to but a drop in the bucket.
>
> If you think well of this suggestion, Cullen and I both feel that you are the man, rather than either of us, to approach the heads of the American, U. S. F. & G. and one or two others in an informal and confidential way.

On the other hand, there were attempts in New York to eliminate abuses in the bonding business. One such effort was that by State Architect Sullivan W. Jones to eliminate a state requirement for bonds. Governor Al Smith was at first induced to extend his approval to the Jones plan. This brought a swift letter to FDR from R.H. Towner at 160 Broadway to the effect that the Jones Plan would be disastrous and (if) "Governor Smith (has gone) astray some of his friends ought to put him right." FDR's prompt reply to Towner was, "I hope to see the Governor in the next couple of weeks and will then talk to him like a Dutch uncle about Jones' plan." We read no more in the FDR files about abolishing compulsory surety bonds in the State of New York.

That F & D's office was hard nosed about its own interests is reflected even in relatively minor matters: for example, no New York business association was able to win F & D financial support. On August 5, 1926 a request from the Better Business Bureau of New York for a subscription evoked a cold response from F & D. FDR passed the letter to vice president Cullen to prepare a "suitable reply," and Cullen promptly turned down the Better Business Bureau. This turn-down was supported by president Charles R. Miller in Baltimore,

---

[285] Cullen was Manager of the New York production office.

"I am not so keen on making a contribution toward the Better Business Bureau at this time...." Then the Merchants Association of New York wrote FDR on May 23, 1925 about membership of F & D in their association. Again Cullen argued that "the Merchants Association is of absolutely no benefit to us." No law requires membership in better business associations, but these brush-offs make suspect do-gooder social appeals from these nonjoiners.

THE PAY-OFF FOR FIDELITY & DEPOSIT COMPANY

This brief review of Franklin D. Roosevelt's career from 1921 to 1928 as vice president of Fidelity & Deposit Company in New York suggests the philosophical road Roosevelt followed for the next two decades. The bonding business was pervasively political, and FDR in politics was like a duck in water. Political contacts made during his service as Assistant Secretary of the Navy were utilized to the full, new political contacts, encouraged by the Baltimore management of F & D, were made, and FDR had seven years to practice this art of politics in business. The results for F & D were exceptionally good. Business expanded, in some measure perhaps because almost all business expanded in the 1920s, but almost certainly to a major extent because of FDR's political activities. In the period January 1st, 1923 to January 1st, 1924 Fidelity & Deposit showed a gain of $3 million in the year and surged into third place among the bonding companies, a good jump ahead of U.S. Fidelity and Casualty Co., its displaced competitor. The figures read:

Surety Company Bonds in the State of New York

	Jan. 1, 1923	Jan. 1, 1924	Gain/loss
Fidelity & Deposit Co.	$ 7,033,100	$10,184,600	+$3,151,500
National Surety Co.	$14,993,000	$15,677,550	+ 684,550
Fidelity & Casualty Co. Surety Co. of New York	$ 3,211,900	$ 3,215,150	+ 3,250
Aetna Casualty & Surety Co.	$ 5,517,200	4,799,500	– 717,700
U.S. Fidelity & Casualty Co.	$ 8,064,500	$ 6,817,000	– 1,247,500
American Surety Co.	$13,263,125	$12,127,400	– 1,125,725

The Fidelity & Deposit office at 120 Broadway was FDR's base of operations in the 1920s, but the bonding business, successful as it was, was not FDR's only business activity. Other interesting endeavors will be explored in subsequent chapters. These seven years in a politically charged business atmosphere—a microcosm of a socialist society, because socialist societies are also politically run economies—were undoubtedly a determining influence in

FDR's later approaches to solutions of national economic problems. This was FDR's first exposure to the business world. It was not an exposure to the competitive market elements of price and product quality; it was exposure to business on the basis of "Whom do you know?" and "What are your politics?" — ultimately the most inefficient and unprofitable bases possible for business enterprise.

CHAPTER 3

FDR: INTERNATIONAL SPECULATOR

One of the most morale-damaging aspects of the inflation was the "sack of Germany" that occurred at the height of the [1923] inflation. Anyone who possessed dollars or sterling was king in Germany. A few American dollars would allow a man to live like a millionaire. Foreigners swarmed into the country, buying up family treasures, estates, jewelry and art works at unbelievable low prices.
  Marjori Palmer, 1918-1923 German Hyperinflation, (New York: Traders Press, 1967)

Franklin D. Roosevelt was organizer and president of several speculative international financial enterprises linking Germany and the United States, and in particular one enterprise to profit from the ruinous German hyperinflation of 1922-23. In 1922 FDR became president and was one of the organizers of United European Investors, Ltd., with a Canadian charter, but based at 160 Broadway, New York. In 1927 FDR was also organizer of the International Germanic Trust Company, Inc. and the Federal International Investment Trust, which never got off the ground. By far the most important of these speculative enterprises in the world of international finance was United European Investors, Ltd., formed to accumulate German marks deposited in the United States and to reinvest these marks in Germany by purchasing property from destitute Germans. Fully to understand the scope and meaning of United European and to follow the activities of International Germanic Trust Company, we need to make a brief review of German financial conditions in the early 1920s.

THE GERMAN HYPERINFLATION OF 1922-23

Lionel Robbins, the prominent British economist, has described the German inflation of 1922-23:

> It was the most colossal thing of its kind in history: and next probably to the Great War itself, it must bear responsibility for many of the political and economic difficulties of our generation. It destroyed the wealth of the more solid elements of German society: and left

behind a moral and economic disequilibrium, a breeding ground for the disasters which have followed. Hitler is the foster child of the inflation.[286]

The Treaty of Versailles imposed a massive reparations burden upon a defeated Germany, a country already financially weak from fighting World War I with deficit spending and postwar territorial reduction, with consequently reduced natural resources. Reparations have an effect on the balance of payments similar to imports. They require either taxation or deficit spending to offset the drain. If the course of deficit spending is followed, the result will be inflationary, and this was the course followed in Germany.

Germany was obligated by the Allies to make recompense for all damage to private property, except in Russia and to pay all costs of Allied troops on German soil, but no maximum limit was set on the demands. Germany had forthwith to surrender 100 billion gold marks, with payments of one billion gold marks annually after 1921. The final payments plan worked out at the "London Ultimatum" in May 1921 reflected these harsh and impossible terms and so provided a clear incentive to inflate to remove the burden of direct payments.

What is extraordinary about the reparations program is the identity of the so-called experts engaged in making the reparations arrangements, incidentally creating the monetary and social chaos alluded to by Lionel Robbins. The 1923 Reparations Committee had as its U.S. members Brigadier General Charles G. Dawes and Owen D. Young of the General Electric Company.

The 1928 Committee of Experts on the Young Plan comprised, on the American side, Owen D. Young and J.P. Morgan, with Thomas N. Perkins and Thomas W. Lamont as alternates. On the German side the members were Hjalmar Schacht and A. Voegler, with C. Melchior and L. Kastl as alternates.

In brief, the General Electric-Morgan elements prominent in the Bolshevik Revolution, and as we shall see also prominent in the New Deal, were the negotiators of a scheme generally regarded as one of the prime causes of World War II—and incidentally a scheme in which these same financiers, as well as Franklin Delano Roosevelt, were to profit.

It is also worthy of note that businessmen on the German side of the reparations negotiations were associated with the rise of National Socialism in Germany.

Witness Hallgarten in his essay "Adolf Hitler and German Heavy Industry:"

> ... in November 1918 a group of the Reich's most prominent businessmen, comprising Stinnes, Albert Voegler (then director of the Gelsenkirchen Mining Co., Ltd.), Carl Friedrich

---

[286] Constantino Bresciani-Turroni, The Economics of Inflation: a Study of Currency Depreciation in Post War Germany, 1914-1923 (London: Allen & Unwin, 1937), "Foreword," p. 5.

von Siemens, Felix Deutsche (of German General Electric), Director Mankiewitz of the Deutsche Bank, and Director Salomonsohn, of the Diskontogesellschaft, financed the movement of a Hitler forerunner, one Dr. Eduard Stadtler, who demanded the establishment of a German National Socialist state.[287]

The pertinent point is that the Felix Deutsche mentioned was a director of German General Electric and the American reparations representatives included Owen D. Young of General Electric, while the Albert Voegler mentioned by Hallgarten was the German representative in the Young-Plan negotiations.

The depreciation of the German mark into worthless paper currency as a result of this reparations burden imposed by these men is illustrated in the following table:

The German Mark in Terms of[288]

Date	Foreign Exchange (1913=1.00)	German Wholesale Prices
January 1913	1.0	1.0
January 1920	15.4	12.6
January 1921	15.4	14.4
January 1922	45.7	36.7
July 1922	117.0	101.0

The inflation accelerated following the formation of United European Investors, Ltd., with Franklin D. Roosevelt as President and John von Berenberg Gossler as a member of the German advisory board:

January 1923	4,279.0	2,785.0
July 1923	84,150.0	74,787.0
August 1923	1,100,100.0	944,041.0

The inflation went entirely out of control following the dismissal of Chancellor Wilhelm Cuno, who returned as president of HAPAG, and co directors John von Berenberg Gossler and Max Warburg:

September 1923	23,540,000.0	23,949,000.0
October 1923	6,014,300,000.0	7,095,500,000.0
Nobember 1923	1,000,000,000,000.0	750,000,000,000.0

The policies that led to the ruinous German inflation were initiated under Chancellor Wilhelm Cuno, who was, immediately prior to becoming Chancellor, the president of Hamburg-America Line (HAPAG). Two of Cuno's co directors at HAPAG were Max Warburg,

---

[287] George W. F. Hallgarten, "Adolf Hitler and German Heavy Industry" in Journal of Economic History, Summer 1952, p. 224.
[288] Source: Statistisches Jahrbuch für das Deutsche Reich.

Hamburg banker and brother of Paul Warburg, member of the Federal Reserve System Advisory Board in the United States, and John von Berenberg Gossler, a member of the German advisory board of Franklin D. Roosevelt's United European Investors, Ltd.

Cuno was dismissed as German Chancellor in August 1923, but it will be noted from the table that inflation was already out of hand, and in November of that year the mark had depreciated to zero. The point to be made is that Wilhelm Cuno was Chancellor in 1922-23, when the mark was rapidly depreciating, and that Cuno came from a business circle that was able and willing to take pecuniary and personal advantage of the German inflation.

This terrifying monetary inflation and the ultimate collapse of the German mark in 1923 ruined the German middle class and benefited three groups: a few German big businessmen, a few foreign businessmen who were in a position to gain advantage from the inflation, and the rising Hitler movement. As president of United European Investors, Ltd., Franklin D. Roosevelt was among those foreign businessmen who took advantage of Germany's misery for their own gain.

THE BACKGROUND OF WILLIAM SCHALL

Unfortunately, there is a deeper perspective to this question of what could be called an élitist group preying on the world's misfortune. In the previous volume in this series, *Wall Street and the Bolshevik Revolution*, we identified personal links between Wall Street financiers and Bolshevik revolutionaries. Some of these same personal links can be extended to FDR and United European Investors. The precisely established links previously implicated the then German Ambassador to the United States, Count von Bernstorff, and his friend Adolph von Pavenstedt, senior partner in Amsinck & Co., who was "for many years a chief paymaster of the German spy system in this country."[289] Amsinck & Co. was controlled by the J. P. Morgan, John D. Rockefeller, and other New York financial interests through American International Corporation. With Guaranty Trust Company, the American International Corporation constituted the central points for financing German and Bolshevik espionage in the United States and North America during World War I. Adolph von Pavenstedt and Edmund Pavenstedt, the two Amsinck partners, were also members of another financial house, Müller, Schall & Company. And it is at Müller, Schall that in 1922 we find Franklin D. Roosevelt and his United European Investors, Ltd.

---

[289] See Sutton, Bolshevik Revolution, op. cit., pp. 64-67, and Johann-Heinrich von Bernstorff, My Three Years in America (New York: Scribner's, 1920), p. 261.

After the public disclosures in 1918 of the connection between Amsinck & Co. and German espionage, the German interests in Müller, Schall & Co. were represented by Edmund S. Payne, a New York attorney. Müller, Schall & Co. was formally liquidated, and a "new" firm—William Schall & Co.—took its place at the same address, 45 William Street, New York City. The new firm, formed in January 1918, included the two original partners, William Schall and Carl Müller, who were now joined by John Hanway of Harris, Forbes & Co., Frank M. Welty, vice president of the American Colonial Bank of Puerto Rico, and attorney Edmund S. Payne, a partner in the law firm of Rounds, Hatch, Dillingham & Debevoise, who represented the German interests of the former Müller, Schall & Co.

The Pavenstedts were also "heavily interested in Puerto Rican sugar properties and owned and controlled the Central Los Canos."[290] William Schall was president of the Colonial Bank of Puerto Rico and president of the South Puerto Rico Sugar Company. Similarly, the Roosevelt family had interests in the Caribbean sugar industry going back to the late 18th century, and George Emlen Roosevelt was in 1918 a director of Cuban Cane Products Co. in New York. It is therefore conceivable that through this common interest in Caribbean sugar the Pavenstedts and Roosevelts became known to each other. In any event, it was the Schall-Pavenstedt group, previously part of the German espionage operation in the United States, that in 1921-22 merged with Franklin D. Roosevelt and several dubious financial entrepreneurs to form United European Investors, Ltd. to profit from the crushing burden of German inflation.

UNITED EUROPEAN INVESTORS, LTD.

The original organizing group for United European Investors, Ltd. comprised the aforementioned William Schall and Franklin D. Roosevelt, joined by A. R. Roberts, Charles L. Gould, and Harvey Fisk & Sons. The 60,000 preferred shares issued were held by Harvey Fisk & Sons ($25,000), Franklin D. Roosevelt ($10,000) and Schall, Roberts, and Gould ($5,000 each). In brief, FDR was the largest individual preferred shareholder of the incorporating group.

United European Investors, Ltd. was granted an unusual Canadian charter that provided the company with unique powers, including the right to promote trade and commerce between Canada and any other country; to acquire title to property; underwrite or otherwise deal in bonds, stocks, and shares; act as brokers and agents; undertake all kinds of functions in regard to purchase, exchange, and transfer of stocks and shares; lend money; carry on any business, "manufacturing or otherwise;" and buy and sell property. In fact, on reading

---

[290] Paul Haber, The House of Roosevelt (New York: Authors Publishing Co., 1936), p. 71.

the charter, it is difficult to visualize any activity that could not be carried out under its numerous clauses.[291]

The capital stock was divided into two segments: Canadian $60,000 divided into 60,000 preference shares and 60,000 ordinary shares, denominated in 10,000 German marks. The objective of the company as noted in the contemporary press was to invest the many billions of German marks then held in the United States and Canada in German real property:

Once marks are invested in property in Germany, the funds should begin to earn money immediately and the funds cannot disappear, since they are represented by the ownership of tangible property, and the advantage may still be taken of a possible rise in exchange value. Compared with this, the holding of mark currency or drafts is a most hazardous operation and the funds are either idle or earning very little. Besides if the exchange quotation should approach the vanishing point, there would be nothing tangible left for the holders of marks or drafts. The capital of the company will be invested in improved real estate, mortgages, financing of goods in transit and participation in profitable industrial and commercial enterprises.[292]

Reference to the preceding table recording depreciation of the German mark (page 39) confirms the remarkable timeliness of United European Investors, Ltd. In July 1922 the mark, with 1913 as a base of 100, was at 117 in foreign exchange. This reflects a heavy rate of inflation of the mark, but nothing to distinguish it from inflation in many other countries. Yet the U.E.I. brochure specifically mentions the possibility of the mark's "approaching the vanishing point," which it did achieve a year later in November 1923.

The actual investment of U.E.I. was carried out in Germany by a German advisory board that occupied an office in Hamburg headed by Senator August Lattman, formerly a partner in G. Amsinck & Company of New York (see page 41). The second member of this German board was Senator John von Berenberg Gossler, head of the Hamburg banking firm Berenberg, Gossler & Co. Berenberg, Gossler was also a member of the management board of the Hamburg-America Line (HAPAG); other members were Wilhelm Cuno, at that time Chancellor of Germany and responsible for his country's economic policy, and Max Warburg, brother of Paul Warburg, member of the Federal Reserve Board in the United States.

In a letter dated November 11, 1922 to U.E.I., the German Advisory Board recorded its initial investments: "All the investments so far made are of first class industrial shares." However, the prospectus issued in the U.S. emphasized investment in real estate, and on this point the German board wrote:

---

[291] The copy of the U.E.I. charter in FDR's files carries an amendment by A. B. Copp, Canadian Secretary of State, that prohibits building of railways and issue of paper money.

[292] This is taken from a press release marked "From Hon. Franklin D. Roosevelt" in the FDR files.

As to investing in mortgages we understand your point of view but shall eventually come back to the question in case we shall be able to offer you mortgages with a gold clause which might be possible, and would exclude any additional risk in case the mark should further decline.

There is no mention anywhere in the United European Investors file of the purchase of real property or any other of the tangibles mentioned in the company charter and the public announcements.

The investments made by the board during the next few years were stocks of German companies. Further, the investment prices were cited in an unusual manner, not in German marks or absolute figures of any kind, but as a percentage increase, presumably from a 1913 base, which enabled the German Board to write to New York, "the shares which you so far bought have risen considerably with the depreciation of the mark."

These shares and the percentage increase cited included, for example:

Deutsche Maschinen A.G.	bought at 1350% now quoted 1805%
Allgemeine Elektricitäts Gesellschaft	bought at 740% now quoted 5000%
Nobel Dynamit	bought at 1119% now quoted 3975%

The German Board did not mention the fact that the depreciation of the mark in terms of the U.S. dollar had been greater than the advance in the prices of the shares they bought as quoted in German marks. In effect, the claims of rising share prices made were illusory. One earlier writer has described it this way: "untrue and pure bunco steering, evidently intended to gull other holders of German marks to invest them with a company that could perform such miracles."[293]

This was not, however, of concern to the New York board of directors. At the regular meeting of the board held January 15, 1923 Franklin D. Roosevelt called the meeting to order, and George W. Muller acted as secretary. It was then recorded that the mark value of the German stock investments so far made by the company was more or less 73 million marks, and this investment was currently quoted at 420 million marks.

There is an interesting letter in FDR's files from Professor Homer B. Vanderblue, Professor of Business Economics at Harvard University, asking for explanations about the U.E.I. investment program. The letter was addressed to FDR, as president of the company, but replied to by Edmund S. Paine, who stated that the original idea of investing in tangible property, such as real estate, had proven impracticable as it "would entail a very heavy overhead owing to the necessity of supervision and operation," and so it was decided to

---

[293] Haber, The House of Roosevelt, op. cit., pp. 81-2.

invest only in German stocks "representing the indirect ownership in tangible assets." Paine added that the theory justified itself to a "remarkable degree:"

> Taking as a test the first Mks 60,000,000 invested by the company, we find that the appreciation in price of the securities has somewhat exceeded the depreciation in the exchange value of the mark. In other words, the securities purchased could probably be sold today for a price in marks which would bring somewhat more in dollars than could have been secured by the holders of marks had they sold them at the time of the investment in spite of the fact that the value of their marks has gone down tremendously.

However, Paine to the contrary, a "Statement of Conditions as of January 31st 1923" located in FDR's files records that the book value per share of common stock at that time was $2.62 per share, while the average book value at the time of investment was $2.64—in other words, a slight decline.

At the directors meeting of September 19, 1923 it was confirmed that the total dollar value of investment was about $120,000, and in May 1925 this was still approximately the amount recorded in the treasury. However, in the intervening years following stabilization of the mark, conditions improved and a statement dated May 12, 1926 shows a net worth of $147,098.07, with 17,275 shares outstanding, and then equal to $8.50 per share. On May 21st, 1926 the company offered to buy all stock offered within 90 days at $7.50 a share. In May 1926 FDR resigned as president and accepted the offer of $7.50 per unit for his 1005 common stock shares.

Did the American holders of German marks who invested in United European investors gain or lose on their investment? If we suppose they held their stock to 1926 and accepted the company offer at $7.50 per common share unit, then buying at the issue price of 10,000 German marks in September 1922 (the date offered) they would have lost considerably. In September 1922 the dollar-mark exchange rate was $1.00 to 764 German marks. Thus a 10,000 mark share would be equivalent to $13.00 per share, and a share held from 1922 to 1926 would have realized a loss of approximately $5.50 per share; on the other hand, a shareholder would have avoided total depreciation and a loss of all his funds from holding on.

INVESTIGATION OF UNITED EUROPEAN INVESTORS, LTD.

The Roberts-Gould element that joined FDR and Schall on the Board of U.E.I. had a poor reputation on "the Street". In fact, Roberts and Gould were under investigation for suspected criminal activities. In July 1922, when United European was in the early stages of incorporation, a Mr. Crary, an old-time investigator for Proudfoot's Mercantile Agency—the top ranking investigation agency used by prestigious Wall Street firms—approached FDR's secretary, Miss Le Hand. Crary conveyed to "Missy" information about what he termed a "band of crooks with offices at 7 Pine Street" and with a nameplate on the door inscribed "United European Investors, Ltd." Missy Le Hand carried the information to FDR's right-hand man Louis Howe, who in turn raised the problem with Schall's earlier partner Müller. From Müller and other sources, Howe learned that Roberts and Gould were a part of this alleged "band of crooks" who, according to Crary, were "engaged in all manner of disreputable promoting and ... he is certain that they have as a member of their force an ex-convict under an assumed name with a most unsavory reputation."[294] When the name United European Investors, Ltd. was posted on their office door at 7 Pine Street, investigator Crary, who had been routinely watching the office for a year, began quietly probing Roberts and Gould. Although Roberts was never in the 7 Pine Street office, Crary found that Gould "had been in the habit of using that office for at least a year, and was considered one of their (i.e., the crooks') tried and true friends." Gould's association with "the crooks" made Crary suspicious because, while the Proudfoot Agency had previously given Gould "a clean enough record," it had also put him in "the professional promoter class."

Crary's investigation was undertaken on behalf of the owners of the building at 7 Pine Street, "who intend to dispossess the whole bunch in a short time." It was during the investigation that the Proudfoot Agency came upon a circular listing the name of Franklin D. Roosevelt as president of United European Investors, Ltd. and William Schall as its banker. The evidence unearthed by the Proudfoot Agency was substantiated to Louis Howe by a Mr. Hanway, a member of the stock brokerage firm of Harris, Forbes. Hanway said he had "been familiar with Mr.

Gould's activities for a number of years, and that he so thoroughly distrusted him as to lead him to make every effort to prevent from meeting Schall originally."

Even further, the Proudfoot Agency suspected that Gould had attempted to acquire confidential information from them and that Gould was acting as "a spy for the crooks to find out what knowledge Proudfoot & Company had of their crooked deals."

All this information was duly reported by Howe in a letter ("Dear Boss") to FDR (July 29, 1922). Probably most businessmen faced with this caliber of partner would abandon any proposed operation such as United European Investors, but Howe's memorandum to FDR recommends nothing of the kind. It reads in part:

> My recommendations are as follows: That Gould and Roberts be directed to immediately find new offices, preferably in a church or some other respectable place. That we get rid

---

[294] Information taken from letter Howe-FDR, June 29, 1922 in United European Investors, Ltd. files.

of Roberts, who is a wild man on publicity anyway, and who has no important function in this game, and that closest watch be kept of Gould. If Mr. Crary actually turns up the circular I would tear off the roof over it and make sure that its use is stopped until we are ready to make a formal announcement. I think it would be wise to insist that during the summer I be made a member of the Board of Directors, particularly as both Jenks and Rogers will be away most of the time and some one wants to watch every action taken.

In other words, Howe suggests that precautions against double-dealing will be sufficient and that the best way to do this is to put Louis Howe on the board of directors.

In any event, the enterprise went forward as planned; Roberts became Secretary of the U.E.I., and Gould, alleged spy for the crooks, retained his role as active promoter and continued to report periodically to FDR by letter on the progress of their fund-raising efforts. On July 20, before Howe reported to FDR the substance of the Proudfoot investigation, Gould had written FDR from the Southern Hotel, Baltimore about his talks with Edward Clark & Co., the Baltimore bankers, whose partner Herbert Clark had known FDR from their Harvard days. Then on August 13, 1923 Gould wrote FDR from the Canadian Club of New York to relay telegrams received from William Schall in Europe and concluded:

> I was sorry to hear you were again under the weather. Probably too much overdoing, one must not try to go to (sic) fast after such an illness. In any case I hope to have the pleasure of seeing you before I return to Europe in early September.

There is no clue that FDR communicated in any way with Gould, and the next letter in the files is from Gould to FDR, dated September 14, 1923 and also written from the Canadian Club of New York. This letter criticized the "jealous bankers whose scheme we hurt, and whose plans were upset. Had we not issued today we would have failed."

Gould then concludes, "Thank you for the great & noble way you have stood behind us, and I personally feel it was your strong attitude which is making our project a complete success," adding that when he (Gould) called on the large banks and trust companies to present "their proposal" he found "On every hand your name [FDR] was applauded as being the master mind in securing the proper operation to aid the unfortunate American investor," and that if FDR could have heard these comments from "the largest financial houses" it would have given him "great satisfaction."

On the basis of these letters, we must conclude that FDR knowingly entered a business arrangement with persons whose reputation was, to say the least, dubious, and that this business arrangement was continued after evidence of impropriety was brought to FDR's attention by Missy Le Hand and Louis Howe.

There is only superficial evidence that the whole United European Investors operation was designed by Roosevelt. When Gould tells FDR that his "name was applauded as being the master mind," it is reasonable to assume that Gould was flattering Roosevelt for his own purposes. There is really no evidence either way in the files or elsewhere that Roosevelt's background and financial knowledge were sufficient to originate a plan as ingenious as U.E.I.

Chancellor Wilhelm Cuno and HAPAG

The disastrous depreciation of the German mark that was the raison d'être of United European Investors was concentrated in the period mid-1922 to November 1923. The table indicates how inflation got completely out of hand after mid-1922. The German Chancellor between mid-1922 and August 1923 was Wilhelm Cuno (1876-1933). Cuno was originally a civil servant, always active in politics, and in November 1917 was elected a director of the Hamburg-America Line (HAPAG).

When Ballin, the president of HAPAG, committed suicide in 1918, Cuno became its president. After May 10, 1921 Karl Wirth was German Chancellor, and Walter Rathenau, the president of German General Electric (A.E.G.), was Minister for Reparations. Then followed a series of dramatic events. The German Minister of Finance Matthias Erzberger was assassinated August 26, 1921. In January 1922 Rathenau became Foreign Minister and on June 24, 1922 was also assassinated. In October of 1922 Friedrich Ebert was Reich Chancellor and Wilhelm Cuno of HAPAG was appointed German Chancellor. The depreciation of the mark occurred under Cuno and culminated in the financial crisis and his dismissal in August 1923. Cuno returned to the presidency of the Hamburg-America Line. We might note in passing the prevalence of corporate presidents in contemporary politics: e.g., German General Electric's Rathenau and HAPAG's Cuno. Owen D. Young of General Electric in the U.S. was also creator of the Young Plan for German Reparations, and German General Electric (A.E.G.) president Rathenau was German Reparations Minister in 1922. These appointments are usually explained on the basis of "the best man for the job" but, given the evidence presented in the last chapter on politics in the bonding business, we can justifiably express skepticism about this explanation. It is much more likely that the Youngs, Cunos, Rathenaus—and the Roosevelts—were mixing business and politics for their own pecuniary gain. Unfortunately, while we must leave unanswered the key question of how far these elitist groups used the state apparatus for their own ends, it is clear that, when we probe the background of Wilhelm Cuno, we arrive back at Franklin D. Roosevelt and the formation of United European Investors, Ltd. Cuno, under whose auspices the great German inflation raged, was a director of the Hamburg-America Line; John von Berenberg Gossler, the United European Investors adviser in Germany, was also a member of the board of that company.

In sum, Cuno and Gossler were on the same board of directors at HAPAG. Cuno's policies were essentially responsible for the German inflation of 1922-23 while his co director Gossler, in cooperation with Franklin D. Roosevelt, was making profit out of the very same inflation policies. It makes one ponder.

THE INTERNATIONAL GERMANIC TRUST COMPANY

The International Germanic Trust Company, founded in 1927, was prompted, according to its promoters, by a demand for American banking institutions in central Europe. Among the organizers of the trust as approved by the Banking Department of the State of New York were Franklin D. Roosevelt; Herman A. Metz, a director of I. G. Farben; James A. Beha, Superintendent of Insurance for the State of New York; and E. Roland Harriman of the international banking firm of W. A. Harriman & Co. The president of the associated International Germanic Company and chairman of the executive committee of the trust company was Harold G. Aron, who had had more than his share of law suits involving stock promotion. The main offices of the International Germanic Trust were on the ground floor of 26 Broadway, the Standard Oil Building in New York. The authorized capital consisted of 30,000 shares to provide a capital of $3 million and a surplus of $2 million. In its application to the banking department the company was represented by Senator Robert F. Wagner; although not listed among the organizers, FDR's old friend, James A. Beha, Superintendent of Insurance for the State of New York, became a member of the board of directors.

The objectives of the company as stated by its president, Harold G. Aron, were:

> There appears to be a real need for an institution of sufficient size and backing, to take the place of those institutions which existed before the war and were primarily concerned in financing commercial intercourse between America and the Central European business world. Through its incorporators the trust company will have and develop relations both with Americans of German descent throughout this country and with business and banking institutions in Germany. It is the intention of the company to stress particularly the development of its foreign and trust departments, and to provide an effective fiscal agency in the expected liquidation of German properties and trusts still in Government custody.
>
> The company will, from the outset, be assured the support of important organizations and societies in this country, and the small depositor both in and outside of New York City will be welcome. It will aim to distribute its shares widely and in comparatively small amounts. There will be no voting trust nor individual or group control.

Roosevelt was involved in the flotation of the proposed company. A telegram dated April 7, 1927 from Julian Gerrard, president of the trust company, to FDR requested him to telegraph Frank Warder, Superintendent of Banks in the State of New York, to the effect that he (Roosevelt) was interested in the trust company. It was anticipated that this intervention would clear the delay in granting the charter. Board meetings were held in the Standard Oil Building, in FDR's office, and in the Bankers Club, the latter both located at 120 Broadway. The first meeting of the organization committee was held at the Bankers Club Friday May 27, 1927; although FDR was unable to attend, he wrote Julian M. Gerrard, "What is the news of the trust company?" Again on August 15, 1927 FDR asked Gerrard, "How is the organization work proceeding and what is being done in regard to the stock subscriptions?"

A considerable part of the FDR letter files of this promotion consists of requests for employment, stock in the proposed company, or related favors. For example, the National Park Bank of New York wrote FDR July 26, 1927 that it was interested in the creation of the International Germanic Trust Company and would be pleased to "have one of our officers address that body, going into detail regarding our facilities." In other words, the National Park Bank was looking for deposit business. FDR promised to take up the matter with the organization committee of the new trust company. Then on August 12, 1927 Roosevelt's partner Basil O'Connor dropped him a note: "Dear Franklin, On the Germanic Bank, see if you can get me 100 shares." The stock issue itself was heavily oversubscribed. It was planned to issue 30,000 shares, but total requests by September 12 were in excess of 109,000 shares, and by September 20 applications exceeded 200,000 shares from approximately 1900 individuals. The trust notified FDR on October 3, 1927 that his allotment was 120 shares at $170 per share and must be taken up by October 5. The telegram added that the issue was heavily oversubscribed and quoted at 187 bid, 192 asked, which would give FDR a profit on an immediate resale. This telegram from Howe added, "Would like ten of your shares for Grace if you are willing."

FDR was duly elected a member of the board of directors and notified on November 4, 1927 that the first meeting of the board would be held Friday, November 11 at the Bankers Club at 120 Broadway. However, Basil O'Connor, Roosevelt's law partner, apparently had cold feet or received adverse information on the promotion because he wrote FDR on November 14:

> I don't know what our position now is in this matter but if it is as when I parted I feel very badly about it. The proposition has not helped us any (with) other banking connections on which I have been working on a year and frankly it has all the earmarks that Gerrard (sic) thinks he can "kid you."

O'Connor suggested that FDR should resign from the board because "heretofore I have been able to say we have no banking affiliations, that was wrong. I can't say that now." Apparently, FDR did not immediately take this advice, because on January 19, 1928 he was notified of reelection as director for the coming year, but in a letter dated January 27, 1928 FDR wrote Gerrard as follows:

> Dear Julian,
> The more I consider my directorship and the trust company and the International Germanic Company, the more I am inclined to feel that it is somewhat futile. I have already told you of my partner's and my feelings in regard to extraneous connections on the part of either of us which involve merely attending occasional meetings and nothing more. It is somewhat difficult of course for me to go to the meetings at 26 Broadway in view of the steps but, frankly, I feel that in retaining my directorship I am accomplishing little either for myself or for the Trust Company or the International Germanic Company.

Whereupon FDR offered his resignation. It is notable that the reasons for resigning were "I am accomplishing little either for myself or for the trust company." In view of the rather unsavory reputation of the promoters, this explanation is a little weak.

Chapter 4

FDR: Corporate Promoter

The meshes of our banking laws have been woven so loosely as to permit the escape of those meanest of all criminals who squander the funds of hundreds of small depositors in reckless speculation for private gain. The entire Banking Law is in need of revision and the Banking Department needs immediately far more adequate inspection facilities.
Franklin Delano Roosevelt, Annual Message to New York State Legislature,
January 1, 1930.

Quite apart from floating speculative enterprises in the field of international finance, FDR was intimately involved in domestic flotations, at least one of which was of some substance. The most important of these ventures was organized by a prominent group including Owen D. Young of General Electric (the ever-present Young of the Young Plan for German reparations described in the last chapter) and S. Bertron of Bertron Griscom, investment bankers in New York. This syndicate created the American Investigation Corporation in 1921. In 1927 followed Photomaton, Inc. and in 1928 the Sanitary Postage Service Corporation. Then Roosevelt became a director of CAMCO, Consolidated Automatic Merchandising Corporation, but only briefly, resigning upon his election as Governor of the State of New York. As we read in the above epigraph, by 1930 FDR has had second thoughts about playing with other peoples' money.

American Investigation Corporation

German scientists and engineers made an early and successful start in the use of lighter-than-air vehicles or airships for passenger and freight transportation. As early as 1910 Germany operated scheduled airship passenger services. Patents for airships were seized in World War I by the U.S. Government under the 1917 Trading with the Enemy Act, and after the war Germany was forbidden by the Reparations Commission to construct airships. This left the field open to American enterprise. The opportunities presented by German work and development restrictions in Germany were observed by a group of Wall Street financiers: S.R. Bertron of Bertron, Griscom & Co. (40 Wall Street) and not surprisingly, since he was intimately involved in German reparations, by Owen D. Young of General Electric (120 Broadway). This group was particularly interested in the profitable opportunities for development of airship transportation in the United States. On January 10, 1921, as FDR was unpacking his bags in the offices of the Fidelity & Deposit Company at 120 Broadway, he received a letter from Bertron which read in part:

> My dear Mr. Roosevelt:
> Representing the small group of prominent men here who are becoming greatly interested in the question of air transportation, I had a long conference with Army officials in Washington last week in regard to it. I am advised that you, as Assistant Secretary of the Navy, are very familiar with this subject and I should like immensely to discuss it with you....

FDR and Bertron met to discuss air transportation over lunch at the Down Town Association. We can surmise that Bertron filled in Roosevelt on technical developments up to that time. We know from the files that there was also a meeting between Owen D. Young, S.R. Bertron, and engineer-attorney Fred S. Hardesty, representing the German patent holders, who had good connections in Washington where the seized patents were in the custody of the Alien Property Custodian and had yet to be released.

This second meeting yielded a preliminary compact dated January 19, 1921 known as the Hardesty-Owen-Bertron agreement that planned the road to development of commercial airship operations in the U.S. A syndicate was subsequently formed by Owen-Bertron to "investigate all phases of aerial navigation, legislation required and methods of fund raising." Hardesty and his associates turned over to the syndicate all their data and rights in exchange for a refund of their out-of-pocket expenses of $20,000 incurred to that date and an interest in the syndicate. FDR's role was that of fund raiser, using his numerous political contacts throughout the United States. On May 17, 1921 Bertron wrote FDR that he had been trying to raise funds from people in St. Louis, Cincinnati, and Chicago, while Stanley Fahnestock, a partner in his firm, had been making the rounds in California and Chicago. Lewis Stevenson, another syndicate member, was at work among his contacts in the mid-West. So Bertron appealed to FDR for a set of personal introductions to potential contributors:

> Stevenson is very anxious for you to give him a line to Edward Hurley, E. F. Carey and Charles Piez, all of whom you know. He would like a letter also to Edward Hines, R.P. Lamont, and H.C. Chatfield-Taylor. I am afraid this is a large order. Won't you do your best?

FDR acknowledged Bertron's request, to the effect that he was sending letters to Stevenson "introducing him to Edward Hurley and to Charles Piez and E.F. Carey. I am afraid I don't know the others." Charles Piez, president of Link-Belt Company in Chicago, excused himself from participation on the ground that "... I am practicing the most rigid economy, bending a deaf ear to the most inviting and alluring prospects," and citing the "deplorable shape" of the industry. (This plea of poverty was supported by Piez's letter to FDR, on old stock stationary, with the new address printed over the old one—hardly becoming a president of a major corporation such as Link-Belt Company). Edward N. Hurley wrote that he was "not very active in business," but when next in New York "I am going to make it a point to call on you and check up the past."

On June 1st, Lewis Stevenson reported to Roosevelt on his fundraising progress in the mid-West. He confirmed the fact that Piez was short of funds and that Hurley wanted to talk later, but that Carey might have some interest:

> Charles Swift, Thomas Wilson, both packers, are now considering the proposition, as are Potter Palmer, Chauncey McCormick and a dozen others. Since securing Marshall Field I have added to our list C. Bai Lehme, a zinc smelter of very large means; Mr. Wrigley, junior member of the great chewing-gum firm; John D. Black, of Winston, Strawn & Shaw; B.M. Winston and Hampton Winston, of Winston & Company, and Lawrence Whiting, president of the new Boulevard Bridge Bank. Gradually I am getting together a desirable group but I must confess it is discouragingly slow and hard work. My experience has been I can convince an individual of the feasibility of this scheme but as soon as he discusses it with his friends, who know nothing whatever of the proposition, they develop a serious doubt in his mind which I have to combat all over again. As a result of my observation abroad I am firm in my belief it can be made a success.

Stevenson concluded by requesting a letter of introduction to prominent Chicago attorney Levy Meyer. It is clear that by the end of June 1921 Stevenson had induced a number of prominent Chicago citizens, including Marshall Field, Philip N. Wrigley, and Chauncey McCormick, to sign on the dotted line.

So far as FDR is concerned, his sales letters on this project would do credit to a professional salesman. Witness his letter to Colonel Robert R. McCormick, of the Chicago newspaper empire:

> Dear Bert:
> As you happen to be a progressively minded person I am asking Mr. Lewis G. Stevenson to have a talk with you about something which at first blush may seem a perfectly wild idea. However, it is really something very different and all I can tell you is that a good many

of us here, such as Young of the General Electric Company, Bertron of Bertron Griscom & Co, and a number of other perfectly respectable citizens have shown enough interest to look into the question further. All of this relates to the establishment of commercial dirigible lines in the United States...

Similar letters went to Chauncey McCormick, Frank S. Peabody of Peabody Coal, and Julius Rosenwald of Sears, Roebuck. These initiatives were followed up with personal dinners. For example, on April 21, 1921 FDR wrote to Frank Peabody:

... is there any possibility you may be able to dine with Mr. Bertron, Mr. Snowden Fahnestock and several others of us at the Union Club next Monday evening at 7:30? Bertron is just back from the other side and has some very interesting data in regard to these commercial dirigibles, which have proved successful in Germany.

FDR added that the group "will promise not to hold you up against your will." To which a reluctant Peabody telegraphed, "Impossible to be there, would not be at all afraid of being held up would have enjoyed visit with you immensely."

To Edsel B. Ford FDR wrote, "I am sending this note by Mr. G. Hall Roosevelt, my brother-in-law, who is familiar with the whole matter." G. Hall Roosevelt, who happened to work for General Electric as a division manager, proved himself to be an alert negotiator, but not sufficiently so to win Ford during the early stages.

However, by February 18, 1922 the American Investigation Corporation had compiled a very healthy list of subscribers, as the following partial list confirms[295]:

---

[295] List dated Feb. 18, 1922 in FDR files.

Name	Affiliation	Location
W.E. Boeing	President, Boeing Airplane Co.	Seattle
Edward H. Clark	President, Homestake Mining Co.	New York
Benedict Crowell	Crowell & Little Construction Co.	Cleveland
Arthur V. Davis	President, Aluminum Co. of America	Pittsburgh
L.L. Dunham	Equitable Building Association	New York
Snowden A. Fahnestock	Bertron, Griscom & Co.	New York
Marshall Field, III	Capitalist	Chicago
E.M. Herr	President, Westinghouse Electric & Mfg. Co.	Pittsburg
J.R. Lovejoy	Vice President, General Electric Company	New York
John R. McCune	President, Union National Bank	Pittsburgh
Samuel McRoberts	Capitalist	New York
R.B. Mellon	President, Mellon National Bank	Pittsburgh
W.L. Mellon	President, Gulf Oil Co.	Pittsburgh
Theodore Pratt	Standard Oil Company	New York
Franklin D. Roosevelt	Vice President, Fidelity & Deposit Co.	New York
Philip N. Wrigley	Vice President, Wm. Wrigley Co.	Chicago
Owen D. Young	Vice President, General Electric Co.	New York

The initial board of directors included National City Bank vice president Samuel McRoberts[296], William B. Joyce, president of National Surety Company—one of FDR's competitors in the bonding and surety business—and Benedict Crowell, former Assistant Secretary of War and chairman of the board of the Cleveland construction company Crowell & Little Construction. Snowden A. Fahnestock of Bertron, Griscom was the son of New York financier Gibson Fahnestock and a partner in the stock brokerage firm of Fahnestock & Company. Gibson's brother William Fahnestock, a partner in the same firm, was director of several major corporations including Western Union and, with Allen Dulles, of Gold Dust Corporation. David Goodrich, another subscriber, was chairman of the board of B.F. Goodrich Company and a director of American Metals Company of New Mexico.

It should be noted with care that this enterprise was a private venture where the risk and the rewards were taken by experienced and clear-sighted capitalists. No criticism can be made of the financing of this venture; the criticism lies in the manner in which it acquired its main asset, the German patents.

The president's report for the year 1922, issued on January 8, 1923, summarizes the A. I. C. achievements to that date.

The German Reparations Commission refused to allow construction of large airships in Germany, and there was a delay in the completion and test of the new apparatus designed by the U.S. Bureau of Mines for the economical manufacture of helium gas, but it was

---

[296] Samuel McRoberts figures prominently in Sutton, Bolshevik Revolution, op. cit.

considered that A.I.C. was within a few months of the time to appeal to the public for financial support. According to this report, the first stage of the work had been brought to a close by signing a contract on March 11, 1922 between the American Investigation Corporation and the Schuette-Lanz Company whereby the American Investigation Corporation secured the world patent rights on the Schuette designs and methods of construction for rigid airships. The contract provided for installment payments and included an agreement with Schuette-Lanz either to construct an airship or to provide the services of the experts to undertake construction in the U.S.

The company had "definitely determined through the Department of State that the Reparations Commission and Council of Ambassadors would not consent to the construction in Germany of the full sized ship considered by the American Investigation Corporation," and so Dr. Schuette was requested to visit the U.S. to reach a final agreement. The ultimate object, continues the report, is the establishment of the airship industry in the U.S. and "is never lost sight of; nevertheless obtaining the first ship from Germany at less cost and built by the best experts is highly desirable."

The importance of ensuring a supply of helium gas for airships was highlighted by the destruction of the British R. 38 and the Italian *Roma* airships. After consultation with the Helium Board and the chief chemist of the Bureau of Mines, a decision on the helium question was deferred until completion of the improved apparatus the Bureau was designing for the production of commercial helium. Under the terms of the agreement between the American Investigation Corporation and Washington engineer Hardesty and his associates, in addition to the $20,000 provided to cover their work before the formation of the American Investigation Corporation, certain actual out-of-pocket expenses were to be repaid for assistance in organizing the corporation. The final agreement was, however, conditional upon the signing of a contract regarding the share which Mr. Hardesty and his associates were to receive in the American Investigation Corporation and any of its subsidiary companies in return for their promotion work: above all, it required that the German patents held on behalf of the American public by the Alien Property Custodian be released to the A.I.C.

POLITICS, PATENTS, AND LANDING RIGHTS

Consequently, the A.I.C. syndicate had a major hurdle to overcome before work could begin on commercial development of airships in the U.S. This political hurdle—to acquire the rights to the Schuette-Lanz airship construction patents—required the astute political assistance of FDR. These rights were German, but under the control of the U.S. Government. By U.S. law, seized alien property can be disposed of only by auction sale and competitive bidding. However, we find in the report of the president of A.I.C. dated May 26, 1922 that

A.I.C. was then "the owner of the present Schuette-Lanz patents" and listed 24 patents and 6 patent applications originating in Germany, 6 applications originating in England, and 13 patents and 6 applications originating in the United States. The report continued: "In the U.S. 7 patents are subject to return by the Alien Property Custodian. Through filing assignments all new U.S. patents are being issued directly in care of A.I.C." How, then, did the A.I.C. syndicate obtain the German patents held in trust by the U.S.? This is particularly important because no record exists of auctions or competitive bidding. The A.I.C. report notes only:

> The interests of A.I.C. were protected by the collaboration in drawing the contracts and assignments of Mr. J. Pickens Neagle (Solicitor of the Navy Department) Franklin Roosevelt, Mr. Howe and Blackwood Brothers.

This certainly raises the question of the propriety of a U.S. Navy Department solicitor acting on behalf of a private syndicate. The German patents were sprung loose from the U.S. Government for A.I.C. by the personal intervention of Franklin D. Roosevelt. Let's see how he went about the job.

Franklin D. Roosevelt was former Assistant Secretary of the Navy, one of a series of Roosevelts to hold the job, and consequently had good political contacts in the Navy Department. In mid-1921 FDR began to probe among his old Navy friends on two questions: (1) the position of the Schuette patents and (2) the possibility of acquiring private use for the A.I.C. syndicate of the Lakehurst naval base for A.I.C. airships. On May 4, 1921 Admiral R.R. Byrd in the Office of Naval Operations acknowledged an invitation to visit FDR's estate at Campobello. Nine months later, on May 23, 1922, Commander E.S. Land, of the Navy Bureau of Aeronautics, also acknowledged an invitation to visit FDR when next in New York. Land added that there "appears to be little likelihood of my going to New York during the next three or four weeks. If you could advise me relative to the nature of your inquiries, I might be able to give you some information along the lines desired."

FDR replied to Commander Land in a letter marked *Personal*, but sent to the Navy Department, to the effect that his inquiry could not be made by telephone or letter. FDR then briefly reviewed the position of A.I.C. and stated that the company "is about to go ahead with the actual construction and operation of dirigibles," but needed to know more about the U.S. government's program for such craft: "I am not looking for any confidential information but merely such facts as I feel sure I could obtain without much difficulty were I able to go to Washington myself."

This information is, wrote FDR to Land, "for the good of the cause generally," and he then offered to defray Commander Land's expenses if he would visit New York. This apparently had little success because on June 1 FDR again requested the information and pushed even further: "Incidentally would there be any objection to our getting a copy of the Zeppelin contract? Theoretically they are all public documents."

In the final analysis, it was Pickens Neagle of the Judge Advocate Generals Office in the Navy who was the prime mover in obtaining the required German patents for A.I.C.; Neagle was obviously making himself useful to FDR in other areas, as well. On May 15, 1922 FDR wrote Neagle about Hardesty, the engineer-attorney handling the patent negotiations in Washington:

> Both Mr. Fahnestock and I passed without question the very modest sum that Hardesty put in for you, [Neagle] and I feel sure that the Directors will approve of this when they meet, which will not be long now.

Navy Solicitor Neagle replied to this on June 16 to give FDR information about possible bonding business:

> I am ashamed to mention so small a thing as the bond that would accompany a contract for $29,000 but things are very dull in the Government contracting line just now. The Midvale Steel and Ordnance Company just received an award of contract for 8" gun forgings totaling a trifle under $29,000. The bond will be for an amount equal to something like 15 to 20 percent of the amount of the contract.

Again, on August 9, 1922 Neagle wrote to Louis Howe and referred to FDR's Navy papers, which were apparently undergoing the customary examination within the department before release to FDR. FDR's problem was to stop the papers "going through the hands of file clerks or inquisitive people with little sense of responsibility or meddlesome novices." The Navy Department would not release the papers without proper examination, even after Neagles' personal intervention. Writes Neagle to FDR:

> I didn't see any way in which I could induce Mr. Curtis to change his view on the subject so I left it in that condition with the mental reservation however that you will be down here soon yourself and perhaps shake him loose.

The file to this point suggests that Pickens Neagle, Solicitor in the office of the Judge Advocate General of the Navy was working more on behalf of FDR than the taxpayer and the Navy Department. The contents of this file then shift to the attempt to acquire use of the German patents for A.I.C.; these letters are no longer on navy stationery, but on plain paper, without a printed address but signed by Neagle. On February 16, 1922 a letter to Howe from Neagle relates that

> our office this aft. (sic) returned to Aeronautics Bureau that suggested form of contract with endorsement saying the station might be leased to the A.I.C. and [Navy] employees furloughed for the corporation to employ.

Neagle added that, although navy officers could not direct and supervise A.I.C. employees, they could be detailed into private industry to learn the business of building airships. This private information is followed by a formal letter to Fahnestock of A.I.C. from Neagle (now wearing his official hat as Solicitor in the U.S. Navy) to confirm the fact that the navy was willing to lease the station and plant at Cape May, a permission revocable without notice. Another dated January 6, 1923 reports that Hardesty has signed a contract that "ought to be acceptable to the Corporation."

It is clear that the Schuette patents were transferred without public auction and competitive bidding, but by private agreement between the U.S. government and attorneys acting on behalf of a private company. This was a violation of the Trading with the Enemy Act.

The files also record another Navy Department employee rushing to the aid of FDR. A letter dated March 31, 1923 from M.N. McIntyre, head of the Navy News Bureau, to Louis Howe suggested that A.I.C. get hold of the "German airship being built for the Navy," as well as access to the naval base at Lakehurst. McIntyre is refreshingly open about his proposed political assistance: "If you will let me know where you stand on the Lakehurst proposition there may be something I can do to help 'grease' the ways. The same applies to the other suggestion."

We can establish from the files that FDR and his syndicate were able to call on sources of information and assistance within the Navy Department. Precisely how then did A.I.C. get control of the Schuette-Lanz patents? These were supposedly public property to be disposed of by competitive bidding. The Hardesty report of February 1921 explains the legal status of the patents and throws more light on their transfer.

The patents had been seized by the Alien Property Custodian and up to that time licensed only to the War and Navy Departments. An application was submitted January 10, 1921 by Fred Hardesty, submitting the information that a corporation (presumably A.I.C.) was to be formed that needed the patents, but Hardesty denied "that the patents themselves are of great intrinsic value." In other words, Hardesty walked a tightrope. The A.I.C. had absolute need of the patents to protect themselves from outsiders. At the same time, argues Hardesty, the patents really had no great value. They are required, he wrote to the Alien

Property Custodian, "to form a moral bulwark for us against aggression of outside parties." Hardesty argued that the public interest was vitally involved and that he would be "pleased to receive information as to the value that has been set on the patents, if their value has been appraised, and as to the terms of and conditions on which they might be sold to us."

Attached to this letter in the FDR files is a "Memorandum for Mr. Hardesty" on the Johann Schuette patents that appears to have originated in the Alien Property Custodian's Office. The memorandum confirms the fact that the patents were held under the Trading with the Enemy Act of 1917, that the only right remaining to the German holder was the right to claim release, and that such claims must be settled as directed by Congress. It is unlikely, states the memorandum, that the patents would be sold by the Alien Property Custodian but, if the patents were offered for sale, "there would be little or no competition, as there are probably very few companies in existence or proposed that contemplate using them, and that therefore the prices offered would not be very high." The memorandum then gets to the crux of the problem facing A.I.C.:

> The A.P.C. makes sales of patents, other than sales to the Government, only to American citizens at public sale to the highest bidder after public advertisement unless the President shall otherwise determine. Purchasing property from the A.P.C. for an undisclosed principal or for re-sale to a person not a citizen of the United States, or for the benefit of a person not a citizen of the United States is forbidden under severe penalty.

This leaves open the possibility that the Secretary of War or the Secretary of the Navy might recommend immediate sale to the President "as a matter of sound business policy in the public interest."

The syndicate then attempted to go the Presidential route, apparently with success. On February 4, 1921 FDR in New York wrote Hardesty in Washington, D.C., "I agree with you that we should do something immediately in regard to the Schuette patents, and at least make the try before the present administration goes out."

Then a memorandum of services rendered in the files records that on both February 9 and 17, 1921 FDR went to Washington and at least met with the Alien Property Custodian. Subsequently, Schuette granted power of attorney to Hardesty, and the patents were released by the Alien Property Custodian, although not immediately. The FDR files do not contain original signed documents on the release, only drafts of documents, but as the patents were ultimately released to A.I.C. it can be assumed that these working drafts are reasonably close to the final signed document. One document signed by both the Alien Property Custodian and German patentee Johann Schuette reads as follows:

It is hereby further understood and agreed by and between the parties hereto that the price or prices at which the above enumerated patents of Johann Schuette may be sold to the American Investigation Corporation by the Alien Property Custodian are and shall be considered only a nominal value of said patents fixed and agreed on by and between the parties hereto and the actual value thereof; and that the said agent shall give, execute, and deliver to the Alien Property Custodian an unqualified release by and on the part of the said Johann Schuette and his said agent and their and each of their heirs and assigns and legal representatives of all claims, demands, etc.

It is clear from this document (1) that the Alien Property Custodian sold the patents to A.I. C., (2) that it charged A.I.C. only a "nominal price," (3) that there was no competitive bidding for the patents, and (4) that the former German holder Schuette was granted an interest either directly or indirectly. All four actions appear to be contrary to the requirements of the Trading with the Enemy Act of 1917 (see p. 000), even if there was Presidential authority for procedures (1) and (2).

Subsequently, on May 9, 1922 a contract was drawn between American Investigation Corporation and Johann Schuette. This paid Schuette $30,000 in cash, with a further $220,000 payable in monthly installments, with the last payment due not later than July 1, 1923. In the event of failure to pay by A.I.C., all rights in the patents would be turned over to Schuette. A stock allowance was granted Schuette, who in turn was to provide cooperation and technical assistance to A.I.C. There is also in the FDR files an internal memorandum that appears to be written on the typewriter normally used for FDR's letters; therefore, it is possibly a memo drawn up either by FDR or more probably by Louis Howe. This memorandum summarized the A.I.C. strategy. It lists "What we have to sell" and answers this question as follows:

1. The Schuette-Lanz patents, described as fundamental and needed by Ford's engineers also working on airship construction.

2. "A tentative contract to the Navy whereby over a million dollars in construction of a plant and building hangar are saved. This is our property as contract proposed is in exchange for license to use the Schuette patents by the Navy." In other words, A.I.C. not only was able to acquire the patents without public bidding in behind-the-scenes political maneuvers, but also acquired the right to sell them back to the Navy. This is the kind of deal most poor taxpayers don't even dream about, although they foot the bills in the end.

3. All the data, designs, and tests of the Schuette-Lanz patents.

4. An arrangement for production of helium.

5. "A list of stockholders comprised of men of public spirit and considerable means."

6. This wasn't enough, because the next section is headed "What we Need" and lists (1) funds and (2) work. The memo then proposes an amalgamation of A.I.C. work with that of Ford engineers.

We can summarize the FDR's American Investigation Corporation deal as follows:

First, the A.I.C. was able through the personal intervention of Franklin D. Roosevelt to obtain seized patents as a gift or at a nominal price. The law required that such seized patents be offered for public bidding and not for the advantage of the former German owner. In practice, they were released behind closed doors as a result of private understanding between FDR and the Alien Property Custodian, possibly with Presidential intervention, although no trace of such assistance can be found. These patents, previously described as of no value, then became the subject of a contract involving payment of $250,000 to German citizen Schuette and the main asset of a company to promote airship construction in the U.S. On the face of the documents in the files, there is a prima facie violation of the law both by FDR and the Alien Property Custodian.

Second, these patents appear to have been released for the indirect benefit of a foreign party, a procedure subject to severe penalties under the law.

Third, the A.I.C. was able to obtain use of navy facilities valued at $1 million and official information from within the Navy Department.

Fourth, the only risk taken by the Wall Street operators was to put the enterprise together. The patents were obtained nominally, the funds came from outside New York City, and the expertise was German or that of the Ford Motor Company. Franklin Delano Roosevelt provided the political leverage to put together a deal that was on the face of it illegal and certainly a long way from the "public trust" FDR and his associates were fond of promoting in their writings and speeches.

FDR IN THE VENDING MACHINE BUSINESS

Automatic postage stamp machine sales started in 1911, but were not really efficient outlets until development of the Shermack machine in the 1920s. In 1927 the Sanitary Postage Stamp Corporation was formed to market Shermack machines for the automatic dispensing of postage stamps, previously sold in stores in loose form that exposed the user, according to the firm's sales literature, to transmission of disease. The firm's board of directors consisted of the inventor Joseph J. Shermack, Edward S. Steinam, J.A. de Camp (120 Broadway), banker George W. Naumburg, A.J. Sach, Nathan S. Smyth, and Franklin D. Roosevelt.

By April 1927 the company was selling about 450 machine installations a week. According to a letter written by FDR to A.J. Sach, vice president of the company, there were major problems with collections; in fact, ten stamp locations had not been heard from in over six months, and cash was short. FDR made the eminently sensible suggestion that salesmen should stop selling for a week and spend the released time on cash collections. Apart from such occasional suggestions, FDR's role in Sanitary Postage Stamp was nominal. Henry Morgenthau, Jr. got him into it originally and even paid the original subscription of $812.50 for FDR's initial 100 shares: "You can send me a check for the same at your leisure." FDR mailed his check the same day. The sponsors issued FDR 3000 shares of common stock "in consideration of the services you have rendered," obviously for use of his name as a bait for investors.

FDR resigned in late 1928 upon his election as Governor of New York.

FDR also was director of CAMCO (Consolidated Automatic Merchandising Corporation), but never took an active part in its flotation. CAMCO was a holding company designed to take over 70 per cent of the outstanding capital stock of a number of companies, including Sanitary Postage Stamp Corporation, and is notable because the board of directors included, not only FDR, but Saunders Norwell, who from 1926 to 1933 was president of the Remington Arms Company. In 1933 Remington Arms was sold to the Du Pont Company. In Chapter 10 we will probe the Butler Affair, an abortive attempt to install a dictatorship in the White House. Both Remington Arms and Du Pont are named in the suppressed testimony of the Congressional investigation committee. Yet in 1928 we find FDR and Saunders Norvell as co directors in CAMCO.

GEORGIA WARM SPRINGS FOUNDATION

FDR's personal and highly commendable struggle to regain use of his legs after a 1921 polio attack led him to the mineral waters of Georgia Warm Springs. Regaining some strength, FDR decided to convert the springs, derelict and almost unused, into a business proposition to aid other polio victims.

Unfortunately, the precise source of the major funds used to develop Georgia Warm Springs cannot be determined from the FDR files as they exist today. The FDR folder on Georgia Warm Springs is relatively skimpy, and it is exceedingly unlikely that it contains all the papers relating to development of the project. The folder gives the appearance of having been screened before release to the Hyde Park archives. There is no public record of the funding for Georgia Warm Springs. Given FDR's tight personal finances during the 1920s, it is unlikely that the funds came from his personal resources. We do have some evidence for three sources of funds. First, it is more than likely that his mother, Mrs. James Roosevelt, was one. In fact, Eleanor Roosevelt wrote FDR, "Don't let yourself in for too much money and don't make Mama put in much, for if she lost she'd never get over it!"[297] Second, Edsel B. Ford is reported to have contributed funds to build the enclosure of the swimming pool, but was not a trustee of the foundation. Third, and most important, the original property was owned by corporate socialist, George Foster Peabody. According to FDR's son, Elliott Roosevelt, there was a sizeable personal note on the property itself, and this note was probably held by Peabody:

> On April 29, 1926, he acquired the derelict property, where Loyless was running ever deeper into debt. At the peak of his obligations as the new proprietor, Father had precisely $201,667.83 invested in the place in the form of a demand note, which was not completely paid off until after his death, and then only from a life insurance policy he had taken out in Warm Springs' favor. The $200,000-plus represented more than two thirds of everything he owned. It was the only time he took such a monumental risk. Mother was terrified that if this went the way of so many of his business ventures, none of us boys could go to college, a fate which I, for one, was more than ready to face.[298]

It is significant that Elliott Roosevelt reports the existence of a $200,000 demand note that was not paid off until FDR's death. It is a reasonable supposition, moreover, that the funds were put up by some or all of the trustees. This places FDR in the same position as Woodrow Wilson, beholden to his Wall Street creditors. As these trustees were among the most powerful men in Wall Street, the charge that FDR was "in the grip of the bankers" is at least plausible.

It is therefore reasonable to suppose that the funds for Georgia Warm Springs were put up, or were under the control of, the trustees of the Georgia Warm Springs Foundation and the associated Meriweather Reserve. The trustees of the foundation in 1934 and their main business affiliations are listed below:

---

[297] Elliott Roosevelt, The Untold Story, op. cit., p. 232.
[298] Ibid.

Georgia Warm Springs Foundation: Trustees in 1934[299]

Name of Trustee[300]	Chief Affiliations
Franklin D. Roosevelt	President of the United States of America
Basil O'Connor	Attorney, 120 Broadway, former law partner of FDR
Jeremiah Milbank	Director, Chase National Bank of N.Y.
James A. Moffett	Vice President & director, Standard Oil of New Jersey
George Foster Peabody	Original owner of the property and holder of the note on Georgia Warm Springs
Leighton McCarthy	Director of Aluminum, Ltd (Canadian subsidiary of ALCOA)
Eugene S. Wilson	President, American Telephone & Telegraph (195 Broadway)
William H. Woodin	Secretary of the Treasury under FDR
Henry Pope	Director of Link-Belt Company
Cason J. Callaway	President of Callaway Mills, Inc. of New York

The trustees of Georgia Warm Springs obviously tie FDR to Wall Street. The most prominent of these were Eugene Smith Wilson (1879-1973), a vice president of American Telephone and Telegraph of 195 Broadway, New York City. Wilson also held directorships in numerous other telephone companies, including Northwestern and Southwestern Bell and the Wisconsin Telephone Company. In 1919 he was attorney for Western Electric, then became counsel for A. T. & T. before appointment as vice president in 1920. Wilson had a long association with the campaign against polio, became associated with Franklin D. Roosevelt, and in the mid-1930s was a member of the investment committee of the Georgia Warm Springs Foundation. His fellow directors on A. T. & T. included John W. Davis, who turns up in the Butler Affair (see Chapter 10).

Another of the Georgia Warm Springs trustees was James A. Moffett, a vice president of Standard Oil of New Jersey. Walter Teagle of the same company was one of the key administrators of NRA.

Trustee Jeremiah Milbank was director of the Rockfeller-controlled Chase National Bank and the Equitable Trust Company.

Trustee William H. Woodin was a director of the Federal Reserve Bank of New York from 1926 to 1931 and was appointed Secretary of the Treasury by Franklin D. Roosevelt after strongly supporting FDR's 1932 election bid. Woodin resigned within six months, but because of ill health, not for any lack of interest in holding the Treasury position.

---

[299] Taken from letter dated March 5, 1932 from Fred Botts, Business Manager at Warm Springs, to FDR at The White House.

[300] Trustees also included Frank C. Root, of Greenwich, Conn., Keith Morgan of New York City, and resident trustee Arthur Carpenter.

Trustee George Peabody has been identified in the previous volume[301] and was prominently associated with the 1917 Bolshevik Revolution in Russia and the Federal Reserve Bank of New York.

---

[301] Sutton, Bolshevik Revolution, op. cit.

Chapter 5

The Genesis of Corporate Socialism

While society is struggling toward liberty, these famous men who put themselves at its head are filled with the spirit of the seventeenth and eighteenth centuries. They think only of subjecting mankind to the philanthropic tyranny of their own social inventions.
Frederic Bastiat, The Law, (New York: Foundation for Economic Education, 1972), p. 52

We have described Franklin D. Roosevelt's seven-year career on "the Street" that ended with his election as Governor of New York in 1928. This description was taken from FDR's own letter files. To avoid possible misinterpretation, portions of these letters were reproduced verbatim and at length. On the basis of these letters, there is no question that FDR used political influence almost exclusively to gain bonding business while vice president of Fidelity & Deposit Co.; that significant and questionable international financial and political links surface in the case of United European Investors and International Germanic Trust; and that his intimate associates ranged from Owen D. Young, president of General Electric, a member of the élitist financial establishment, to men described by an agent of the Proudfoot Agency as a "band of crooks."

There is one persistent theme running through FDR's method of doing business: he used the political route to an extraordinary degree. In other words, FDR employed for personal gain the police power of the state as implemented by regulatory agencies, by government regulation, and by government officials through his intercession, for example, with the Alien Property Custodian, the U.S. Navy, the Federal Reserve System, and the Insurance Superintendent of the State of New York. All these political contacts made while in public service gave FDR his competitive edge in business. These are political devices, not devices born of the market place. They are devices reflecting political coercion, not voluntary exchange in the free market.

The next four chapters comprising Part Two of this book expand upon this theme of politicization of business enterprise. First, we cast a wider net to formulate the thesis of corporate socialism and identify some prominent corporate socialists, mostly associated with FDR. Then we move back in time to the 1840's to one of FDR's ancestors, Assemblyman Clinton Roosevelt of New York and his early version of NRA. This scheme is compared to Baruch's War Industries Board in 1917, the operation of the Federal Reserve System, and the Roosevelt-Hoover American Construction Council of the 1920s. Finally, in the last chapter of this part we detail the financial investment of Wall Street in the New Deal.

THE ORIGINS OF CORPORATE SOCIALISM

Old John D. Rockefeller and his 19th century fellow-capitalists were convinced of one absolute truth: that no great monetary wealth could be accumulated under the impartial rules of a competitive laissez faire society. The only sure road to the acquisition of massive wealth was monopoly: drive out your competitors, reduce competition, eliminate laissez-faire, and above all get state protection for your industry through compliant politicians and government regulation. This last avenue yields a legal monopoly, and a legal monopoly always leads to wealth.

This robber baron schema is also, under different labels, the socialist plan. The difference between a corporate state monopoly and a socialist state monopoly is essentially only the identity of the group controlling the power structure. The essence of socialism is monopoly control by the state using hired planners and academic sponges. On the other hand, Rockefeller, Morgan, and their corporate friends aimed to acquire and control their monopoly and to maximize its profits through influence in the state political apparatus; this, while it still needs hired planners and academic sponges, is a discreet and far more subtle process than outright state ownership under socialism. Success for the Rockefeller gambit has depended particularly upon focusing public attention upon largely irrelevant and superficial historical creations, such as the myth of a struggle between capitalists and communists, and careful cultivation of political forces by big business. We call this phenomenon of corporate legal monopoly—market control acquired by using political influence—by the name of corporate socialism.

The most lucid and frank description of corporate socialism and its mores and objectives is to be found in a 1906 booklet by Frederick Clemson Howe, *Confessions of a Monopolist*.[302]

Frederick Howe's role in the 1917 Bolshevik Revolution and its aftermath was described in *Wall Street and the Bolshevik Revolution*.[303] Howe also emerges in Roosevelt's New Deal

---

[302] Frederic C. Howe, Confessions of a Monopolist (Chicago: Public Publishing Co. 1906). The sponsor of Howe's book was the same publisher who in 1973 put out a collectivist dirge by John D. Rockefeller III entitled The Second American Revolution.

[303] Sutton, Bolshevik Revolution, op. cit.

as consumer counsel in the Agricultural Adjustment Administration. So Howe's interest in society and its problems spans the early 20th century, from his association with Newton D. Baker, later Secretary of War, to communist Lincoln Steffens. As a special U.S. Commissioner, Howe made studies of municipal ownership of public utilities in England and in 1914 was appointed by President Wilson as U.S. Commissioner of Immigration.

What is the secret of making great wealth? Howe answers the question as follows: "Mr. Rockefeller may think he made his hundreds of millions by economy, by saving on his gas bills, but he didn't. He managed to get the people of the globe to work for him...."[304]

In brief, corporate socialism is intimately related to making society work for the few.

MAKING SOCIETY WORK FOR THE FEW

This is the significant theme in Howe's book, expressed time and time again, with detailed examples of the "let others work for you" system at work. How did Mr. Rockefeller and his fellow monopolists get the globe to work for them? It went like this, according to Howe:

> This is the story of something for nothing—of making the other fellow pay. This making the other fellow pay, of getting something for nothing, explains the lust for franchises, mining rights, tariff privileges, railway control, tax evasions. All these things mean monopoly, and all monopoly is bottomed on legislation.
> And monopoly laws are born in corruption. The commercialism of the press, or education, even of sweet charity, is part of the price we pay for the special privileges created by law. The desire of something for nothing, of making the other fellow pay, of monopoly in some form or other, is the cause of corruption. Monopoly and corruption are cause and effect.
> Together, they work in Congress, in our Commonwealths, in our municipalities. It is always so. It always has been so. Privilege gives birth to corruption, just as the poisonous sewer breeds disease. Equal chance, a fair field and no favors, the "square deal" are never corrupt. They do not appear in legislative halls nor in Council Chambers. For these things mean labor for labor, value for value, something for something. This is why the little business man, the retail and wholesale dealer, the jobber, and the manufacturer are not the business men whose business corrupts politics.[305]

Howe's opposite to this system of corrupt monopoly is described as "labor for labor, value for value, something for something." But these values are also the essential hall marks

---

[304] Howe, op. cit., p. 145.
[305] Howe, op. cit., pp. V-VI.

of a market system, that is, a purely competitive system, where market clearing prices are established by impartial interaction of supply and demand in the market place. Such an impartial system cannot, of course, be influenced or corrupted by politics. The monopoly economic system based on corruption and privilege described by Howe is a politically run economy. It is at the same time also a system of disguised forced labor, called by Ludwig von Mises the *Zwangswirtschaft* system, a system of compulsion. It is this element of compulsion that is common to all politically run economies: Hitler's New Order, Mussolini's corporate state, Kennedy's New Frontier, Johnson's Great Society, and Nixon's Creative Federalism. Compulsion was also an element in Herbert Hoover's reaction to the depression and much more obviously in Franklin D. Roosevelt's New Deal and the National Recovery Administration.

It is this element of compulsion that enables a few—those who hold and gain from the legal monopoly—to live in society at the expense of the many. Those who control or benefit from the legislative franchises and regulation and who influence the government bureaucracies at the same time are determining the rules and regulations to protect their present wealth, prey on the wealth of others, and keep out new entrants from their business. For example, to make the point clear, the Interstate Commerce Commission, created in 1880, exists to restrict competition in the transportation industry, not to get the best deal possible for shippers. Similarly, the Civil Aeronautics Board exists to protect the domestic aviation industry, not the airline traveler. For a current example, among hundreds, witness the CAB seizure in July 1974 of a Philippines Air Lines (PAL) DC-10 at San Francisco airport. What sin had PAL committed? The airline merely substituted a DC-10 plane, for which equipment CAB had not granted permission, for a DC-8. Who gained? The domestic U.S. airlines, because of less competition. Who lost? The traveler denied seats and a choice of equipment. Any doubts about whose side the CAB might be on were dispelled by an article a few weeks later in *The Wall Street Journal* (August 13, 1974) entitled "CAB Is an Enthusiastic Backer of Moves to Trim Airline Service, Increase Fares." This piece contained a gem by CAB vice chairman Whitney Gillilland: "We've had too much emphasis on passenger convenience in the past." Gillilland added that the CAB must be more tolerant of capacity-packed planes, "even if it may mean somebody has to wait a day to get a flight."

In brief, regulatory agencies are devices to use the police power of the state to shield favored industries from competition, to protect their inefficiencies, and to guarantee their profits. And, of course, these devices are vehemently defended by their wards: the regulated businessmen or, as we term them, "the corporate socialists."

This system of legal compulsion is the modern expression of Frederic Bastiat's dictum that socialism is a system where everyone attempts to live at the expense of everyone else.

Consequently, corporate socialism is a system where those few who hold the legal monopolies of financial and industrial control profit at the expense of all others in society.

In modern America the most significant illustration of society as a whole working for the few is the 1913 Federal Reserve Act. The Federal Reserve System is, in effect, a private banking monopoly, not answerable to Congress or the public, but with legal monopoly control over money supply without let or hindrance or even audit by the General Accounting Office.[306] It was irresponsible manipulation of money supply by this Federal Reserve System that brought about the inflation of the 1920s, the 1929 Depression, and so the presumed requirement for a Roosevelt New Deal. In the next chapter we shall examine more closely the Federal Reserve System and its originators. For the moment, let's look more closely at the arguments made by the Wall Street financier-philosophers to justify their "making society work for the few" credo.

THE CORPORATE SOCIALISTS ARGUE THEIR CASE

One can trace a literary path by which prominent financiers have pushed for national planning and control for their own benefit and that ultimately evolved into the Roosevelt New Deal.

In the years following the 1906 publication of Howe's *Confessions of a Monopolist*, Wall Street financiers made book-length literary contributions, none quite as specific as Howe, but all pushing for the legal institutions that would grant the desired monopoly and the control that flows from this monopoly. From these books, we can trace New Deal ideas and the theoretical base upon which corporate socialism later came to be justified. Two themes are common in these Wall Street literary efforts. First, that individualism, individual effort, and individual initiative are out of date and that "destructive" competition, usually termed "blind competition" or "dog-eat-dog competition" is outmoded, unwanted, and destructive of human ideals. Second, we can identify a theme that follows from this attack on individualism and competition to the effect that great advantages accrue from cooperation, that cooperation advances technology, and that cooperation prevents the "wastes of competition." It is then concluded by these financier philosophers that trade associations and ultimately economic planning—in other words, enforced "cooperation"— are a prime objective for responsible and enlightened modern businessmen.

Such themes of cooperation and rejection of competition are expressed in different ways and with varying degrees of lucidity. Businessmen are not persuasive writers. Their books

---

[306] A very limited audit of the Federal Reserve System was voted by Congress in 1974.

tend to be turgid, superficially self-seeking, and somewhat weightily pedantic. A few such examples will, however, demonstrate how Wall Street corporate socialists made their case.

Bernard Baruch was the outstanding corporate socialist whose ideas we shall examine in the next chapter. After Baruch and the Warburgs, also discussed in the next chapter, the next most prolific writer was influential banker Otto Kahn of Kuhn, Loeb & Co.

Kahn is notable for his support of both the Bolshevik Revolution and Benito Mussolini, support which he concretized in such totalitarian expressions as, "The deadliest foe of democracy is not autocracy but liberty frenzied."[307] On socialism, Otto Kahn stated his sympathy toward its objectives on many occasions. For instance, his address to the socialist League of Industrial Democracy in 1924 included the following:

> Let me point out that such measures as, for instance, the progressive income tax, collective bargaining by employees, the eight-hour day, the governmental supervision and regulation of railroads and of similar natural monopolies or semi-monopolies, are approved by the sense of justice of the business community, provided the application of such measures is kept within the limits of reason, and that they would not be repealed by business if it had the power to repeal them.
>
> What you Radicals and we who hold opposing views differ about, is not so much the end as the means, not so much what should be brought about as how it should and can be brought about, believing as we do, that rushing after the Utopian not only is fruitless and ineffectual, but gets into the way of, and retards, progress toward realizing attainable improvement.
>
> With all due respect, I venture to suggest that Radicalism too often tends to address itself more to theoretical perfection than to concrete amelioration; to phantom grievances, or grievances of the past, which have lost their reality, rather than to actual matters of the day; to slogans, dogmas, professions, rather than to facts.[308]

A number of these financier-philosophers from Wall Street were trustees of the Brookings Institution in Washington D.C., responsible for many of the policy guides to achieve this desired system. Robert S. Brookings, founder of the Brookings Institution, is generally termed an economist, but Brookings himself wrote: "I certainly have no claim to that professional title. I write only as one who, through a long business experience of more than sixty years, has had much to do with manufacturing and distribution... ."[309] In his self-described role of businessman, Brookings published three books: *Industrial Ownership, Economic Democracy,*

---

[307] Otto H. Kahn, Frenzied Liberty: The Myth of a Rich Man's War, Address at University of Wisconsin, Jan. 14, 1918, p. 8.
[308] Otto H. Kahn, Of Many Things, (New York: Boni & Liveright, 1925), p. 175.
[309] R. S. Brookings, Economic Democracy, (New York: Macmillan, 1929), p. xvi.

and *The Way Forward*. In these three books, Brookings argues that classical political economy, as reflected in the work of Adam Smith and his school,

> while logically convincing, was actually incomplete in that it made no allowance for the moral and intellectual development of man and his dependence on nationalism for its expression, so ably presented later by Adam Müller and Frederick List, or for the economic influence of mechanical production upon the relation of capital to labor.[310]

Consequently, but without presenting his evidence, Brookings rejects the free enterprise ideas of Adam Smith and accepts the statist ideas of List—also, by the way, reflected in the Hitlerian corporate state. From rejection of free enterprise Brookings finds it quite easy to deduce a "moral" system rejecting the market place and substituting an approximation to the Marxist labor theory of value. For example, Brookings writes:

> A sound system of economic morality demands therefore that instead of our paying labor merely a market wage, the minimum necessary to secure its services, capital should receive the market wage necessary to secure its services, and the balance should go to labor and the consuming public.[311]

From this quasi-Marxist argument Brookings constructs, rather vaguely and without detailed support, the outlines of proposals needed to combat the "evils" of the prevailing market system. Of these proposals, "The first is the revision of the anti-trust laws in such a way as to permit extensive cooperation."[312] This, argues Brookings, would have two effects: advance research and development and flatten out the business cycle. Just how these objectives follow from "cooperation" is not stated by Brookings, but he cites Herbert Hoover at length to support his argument, and particularly Hoover's article, "If Business Doesn't, Government Will."[313]

Then, like any good socialist, Brookings concludes: "Efficiently managed corporations have nothing to fear from intelligent public supervision designed to protect the public and the trade alike from grasping and intractable minorities."[314] This is necessary because, Brookings argues elsewhere, statistics indicate that most businesses operate inefficiently, "So

---

[310] Ibid., pp. XXI-XXII.
[311] R. S. Brookings, Industrial Ownership (New York: Macmillan, 1925), p. 28.
[312] Ibid., p. 44.
[313] The Nation's Business, June 5, 1924, pp. 7-8.
[314] Brookings, Industrial Ownership, op. cit., p. 56.

we know from sad experience that blind or ignorant competition has failed to make its reasonable contribution through earnings to our national economic needs."[315]

In 1932 Brookings emerged from his shell in *The Way Forward* to become even more outspoken about developments in Soviet Communism:

> The verbal damning of communism now prevalently popular in the United States will get us nowhere. The decision between capitalism and communism hinges on one point. Can capitalism adjust itself to this new age? Can it move out from its old individualism, dominated by the selfish profit motive, and so create a new co-operative epoch with social planning and social control, that it can serve, better than it has, the welfare of all the people? If it can, it can survive. If it cannot, some form of communism will be forced upon our children. Be sure of that![316]

And in the same book Brookings has good words to say about another forced labor system, Italian fascism:

> Although Italy is an autocracy under the dictatorship of the Duce, every economic interest of the country is afforded opportunity for discussion and negotiation so that they may, by mutual agreement, arrive at a fair compromise of their differences. The government will not permit, however, either through lockouts or strikes, any interference with the productivity of the nation, and if, in the last analysis, the groups fail to agree among themselves, the government through its minister or the labor court determines the solution of all problems. In Italy as elsewhere, however, the autocracy of capital seems to exist, and the general feeling among the working classes is that government favors the employers.[317]

What then is preeminent in Brookings' writing is his predilection for any social system, communism, fascism, call it what you will, that reduces individual initiative and effort and substitutes collective experience and operation. What is left unsaid by Brookings and his fellow financier philosophers is the identity of the few running the forced labor collective.

It is implicit in their arguments that the operators of the system will be the corporate socialists themselves.

From the purely theoretical proposals of Brookings we can move to those of George W. Perkins, who combined parallel proposals with some effective, but hardly moral ways of putting them into practice.

---

[315] Brookings, Economic Democracy, op. cit., p. 4.
[316] R. S. Brookings, The Way Forward (New York: Macmillan, 1932), p. 6.
[317] Ibid., p. 8.

George W. Perkins was the forceful, energetic builder of the great New York Life Insurance Company. Perkins was also, along with Kahn and Brookings, an articulate expounder of the evils of competition and the great advantages to be gained from ordered cooperation in business. Perkins preached this collectivist theme as one of a series of lectures by businessmen at Columbia University in December 1907. His speech was hardly a roaring success; biographer John Garraty claims that when it was over:

> ...The President of Columbia, Nicholas Murray Butler, hurried off without a word of congratulations, evidently believing, according to Perkins, that he had unwittingly invited a dangerous radical to Morningside Heights. For Perkins had attacked some of the basic concepts of competition and free enterprise.[318]

Garraty summarizes Perkins' business philosophy:

> The fundamental principle of life is co-operation rather than competition — such was the idea that Perkins developed in his talk. Competition is cruel, wasteful, destructive, outmoded; co-operation, inherent in any theory of a well-ordered Universe, is humane, efficient, inevitable and modern.[319]

Again, as with Brookings, we find proposals for "elimination of waste" and more "planning" for material and human resources and the concept that big business has "responsibilities to society" and is more likely to act fairly toward labor than small business. These high-sounding phrases are, of course, impressive—particularly if New York Life Insurance had lived up to its social do-good sermons. Unfortunately, when we probe further, we find evidence of wrongdoing by New York Life Insurance and investigation of this wrongdoing by the State of New York, which found a decidedly antisocial ring about New York Life's corporate behavior. In 1905-06 the Armstrong Committee (the New York State Legislature Joint Committee on Investigation of Life Insurance) found that New York Life Insurance Company had been a liberal contributor to the Republican National Committee in 1896, 1900, and 1904. Without question, these financial contributions were to advance the interests of the company in political circles. In 1905 John A. McCall, president of New York Life Insurance, was called before the New York investigating committee and proceeded to advance the idea that the defeat of Byran and free silver coinage was for him a *moral* issue. According to McCall, "....I consented to a payment to defeat Free Silver, not to defeat the Democratic party, but to defeat the Free Silver heresy, and thank God that I did it."[320]

---

[318] John A. Garraty, Right Hand Man: The Life of George W. Perkins, (New York: Harper & Row, n.d.), p. 216.
[319] Ibid.
[320] Quoted in Louise Overacker, Money in Elections, (New York: Macmillan, 1932), p. 18.

At the same hearing the vice president of Mutual Life Insurance also advanced the interesting concept that business had a "duty" to "scotch" unwelcome ideas and policies. The history of corporate financing of politics has hardly maintained the principles of the Constitution and a free society. More specifically, there is a gross inconsistency between the social do-good principles of cooperation advanced by Perkins and his fellow businessmen and the contemporary antisocial behavior of his own New York Life Insurance Company.

In brief, the principles of corporate socialism are but a thin veneer for the acquisition of wealth by a few at the expense of the many.

We can now look profitably at the preaching of those financiers more intimately associated with Roosevelt and the New Deal. One such financier-philosopher who expressed his collectivist ideas in writing was Edward Filene (1860-1937) The Filenes were a family of highly innovative businessmen, owners of the large department store William Filene's Sons Co. in Boston. A vice president of Filene's became one of the three musketeers running the National Recovery Administration in 1933; the other two of the triumvirate were Walter Teagle, president of Standard Oil and John Raskob, vice president of Du Pont and General Motors.

From the turn of the century Edward Filene concerned himself with public affairs. He served as chairman of the Metropolitan Planning Commission of Boston, promoter of people's banks, and provided assistance to various cooperative movements. Filene was active in the Red Cross and the U.S. Chamber of Commerce; a founder of the League to Enforce Peace; a founder and later president of the Cooperative League, subsequently renamed the Twentieth Century Fund; and a member of the Foreign Policy Association and the Council on Foreign Relations. In Roosevelt's era Filene was chairman of the Massachusetts State Recovery Board and active in the 1936 campaign for FDR's reelection. Filene wrote several books, of which two, *The Way Out* (1924)[321] and *Successful Living in this Machine Age*, (1932)[322], express his philosophical leanings. In *The Way Out*, Filene emphasizes the theme of reducing waste, and the shortsightedness of competition and stresses the value of cooperation between business and government. Filene summarizes his argument as follows:

> Two things are clear. The first is that the business in order to be good business must itself be conducted as a public service. The second is that the finest possible public service of business men is that rendered in and through the private businesses of the world.[323]

---

[321] Edward A. Filene, The Way Out, (A Forecast of Coming Changes in American Business and Industry) (New York: Doubleday, Page, 1924).
[322] Edward A. Filene, Successful Living in this Machine Age (New York: Simon & Schuster, 1932).
[323] Filene, The Way Out, op. cit., p. 281.

This "public service is private business" theme is expanded in another of his books:

> My own attitude is that business must undertake social planning, but neither for the purpose of snuffing out new theories nor of preserving old ones, but because there has been a social revolution. The old order has gone and by no possibility can we bring it back. We are living in a new world. It is a world in which mass production has related everybody to everybody; and our plans, therefore, must take everybody into consideration.[324]

We also find in Filene "the road to peace is the balance of power" argument—a repeat of a 19th-century formula resurrected by Henry Kissinger in the 1970s and one that has always ultimately led to war rather than peace. Filene phrases his version as follows:

> No wonder there was war. Peace, it was soon discovered, could be maintained only by a balance of power between the larger competitors, and that balance of power was frequently upset. Eventually the whole impossible situation exploded in the greatest war of human history. The World War did not cause the world change which we have lately been noting. It was, rather, one of the phenomena of that change, just as the French Revolution was a phenomenon of the First Industrial Revolution.[325]

This theme of promotion of the public interest as a matter of primary benefit to business itself is also found in Myron C. Taylor, chairman of United States Steel Company. The public interest, Taylor argues, needs cooperation by business for rational production. The blindness of big business is clear when Taylor denies this would also be restraint of trade. Taylor omits to explain how we can adjust production to consumption without compulsion of those who may not want to cooperate. Taylor summarizes his proposals as follows:

> The point, then, is to discover what we as a nation possess and to learn to use it rather than go out in search of the new only because it is new. The primary responsibility is on industry to find ways to promote the public interest and the interests of its own producers, employees, distributors, and customers, by making and carrying out whatever constructive plans may be permissible under the present laws, acting openly and, so far as possible, in cooperation with the Government. I confess I find it extremely hard to believe that constructive, cooperative plans sincerely undertaken by a basic industry for rationally adjusting production to demand in that industry, and which avoid any attempt artificially to fix or control prices, can be fairly regarded as in restraint of trade and commerce. For

---

[324] Filene, Successful Living in This Machine Age, op. cit., p. 269.
[325] Ibid., p. 79.

the sole effect would be to remove vital impairments of production, trade, and commerce, and to promote the public interests.[326]

The Standard Oil contribution to this liturgy is expressed by Walter C. Teagle, president of Standard Oil Company of New Jersey and appointed by President Roosevelt to a top position in his NRA. Teagle phrases his version of corporate socialism as follows:

> The ills of the oil industry are peculiar to that industry and require peculiar remedies. These are modification of anti-trust laws, cooperation among producers, and the exercise of the policing power of the States.[327]

More bluntly than the others, Teagle wants the police power of the State to enforce voluntary cooperation:

> Voluntary cooperation within the industry is not sufficient to remedy its ills. It would not be sufficient even if legal restrictions on cooperation were removed, although tremendous progress would result from the removal of such restrictions.
> To protect the correlative rights of producers and to enforce adequate conservation laws the police power of the State must be employed. This is a matter for State, rather than Federal action, but cooperation among various States and among the operating units of the industry will also be needed if production in the country at large is to be limited to the nation's markets.
> The solution of the problem therefore depends upon voluntary cooperation within the industry, upon exercise of the police power of the State, and upon cooperation among the various States concerned and among unites(sic) of the industry in the different States. To permit this both State and Federal anti-trust laws will need to be revised.[328]

These extracts reflect the basic outlook of our Wall Street financier philosophers. These were not minor figures on the Street. On the contrary, they were the powerful and influential elements and in significant cases associated with Roosevelt and the New Deal. Otto Kahn was a prime mover in the Federal Reserve System. Lamont and Perkins were key figures in the banking and insurance fields. Businessman Brookings gave his name and money to the influential research institute that produced the reports upon which much policy came to be based. Louis Kirstein, a vice president of Filene's firm, and Walter Teagle of Standard Oil

---

[326] From Samuel Crowther, A Basis for Stability, (Boston: Little, Brown, 1932), p. 59.
[327] Ibid., p. 111.
[328] Ibid., p. 113.

became two of the three dominant men who ran the National Recovery Administration under Bernard Baruch's protégé Hugh Johnson.

Bernard Baruch was probably the most prestigious Wall Streeter of all time, perhaps even exceeding in influence both Morgan and Rockefeller. We will examine Baruch and the Warburgs next.

What was the philosophy of the financiers so far described? Certainly anything but laissez-faire competition, which was the last system they envisaged. Socialism, communism, fascism or their variants were acceptable. The ideal for these financiers was "cooperation," forced if necessary. Individualism was out, and competition was immoral. On the other hand, cooperation was consistently advocated as moral and worthy, and nowhere is compulsion rejected as immoral. Why? Because, when the verbiage is stripped away from the high-sounding phrases, compulsory cooperation was their golden road to a legal monopoly. Under the guise of public service, social objectives, and assorted do-goodism it is fundamentally "Let society go to work for Wall Street."

CHAPTER 6

PRELUDE TO THE NEW DEAL

Whichever party gains the day, tyrants or demagogues are most sure to take the offices.
                              Assemblyman Clinton Roosevelt of New York, 1841.

The full story of the construction of corporate socialism in the United States, as envisaged by the financier-philosophers identified in the previous chapter, is beyond the scope of this book, but we can gain greater perspectives through a brief look at a few facets of the historical process: for example, Clinton Roosevelt's system a century before FDR, Bernard Baruch's War Industries Board, and Paul Warburg's Federal Reserve System.

In 1841 FDR's distant cousin, Assemblyman Clinton Roosevelt of New York, proposed a scheme resembling the New Deal for economic planning and control of society by the few. Under President Woodrow Wilson in 1918 Bernard Baruch, corporate socialist *par excellence*, followed the broad outline of the Roosevelt scheme, almost certainly unknowingly and probably attributable to some unconscious parallelism of action, when he established the War Industries Board, the organizational forerunner of the 1933 National Recovery Administration. Some of the 1918 WIB corporate elite appointed by Baruch—Hugh Johnson, for example—found administrative niches in Roosevelt's NRA. In 1922 then-Secretary of Commerce Herbert Hoover an up and coming Wall Streeter Franklin D. Roosevelt joined forces to promote trade associations, implementing Bernard Baruch's postwar economic planning proposals. Shortly thereafter, former socialist editor Benito Mussolini marched on Rome and established—with liberal help from the J.P. Morgan Company—the Italian corporate state whose organizational structure is distinctly reminiscent of Roosevelt's NRA. In the United States glorification of Mussolini and his Italian achievements was promoted by the ever-present financiers Thomas Lamont, Otto Kahn, and others. We will mention only briefly Wall Street involvement with both Bolshevik Russia and Hitler's Germany—both totalitarian states governed by a self-appointed elite—as full treatment of these aspects is covered in other volumes.[329] In brief, construction of FDR's National Recovery Administration was but one facet of a wider historical process—construction of economic systems where the few could profit at the expense of the many, the citizen-taxpayer-in-the-street—and all of course promoted under the guise of the public good, whether it was Stalin's Russia, Mussolini's Italy, Hitler's Germany, or Roosevelt's New Deal.

ASSEMBLYMAN CLINTON ROOSEVELT'S NRA — 1841

New York Assemblyman Clinton Roosevelt was a 19th-century cousin of Franklin Delano Roosevelt and incidentally also related to President Theodore Roosevelt, John Quincy Adams, and President Martin Van Buren. Clinton Roosevelt's only literary effort is contained in a rare booklet dated 1841.[330] In essence this is a Socratic discussion between author Roosevelt and a "Producer" presumably representing the rest of us (i.e., the many). Roosevelt proposes a totalitarian government along the lines of George Orwell's 1984 society, where all individuality is submerged to a collective run by an elitist aristocratic group (i.e., the few) who enact all legislation. Roosevelt demanded ultimate, but not immediate, abandonment of the Constitution

> P. [Producer] But I ask again: Would you at once abandon the old doctrines of the Constitution?
> A. [Author] Not by any means. Not any more than if one were in a leaky vessel he should spring overboard to save himself from drowning. It is a ship put hastily together when we left the British flag, and it was then thought an experiment of very doubtful issue.[331]

This early expression of Rooseveltian family skepticism toward the Constitution brings to mind the Supreme Court rejection in October 1934 (*Schechter Poultry Corp. v. U.S.*) of another Rooseveltian departure, an "unfettered" departure according to the court, from the rules of a constitutional society: the National Recovery Act, itself an uncanny replica of Clinton Roosevelt's 1841 program for a collective economy.

---

[329] For Wall Street and the early Bolsheviks see Sutton, *Bolshevik Revolution*, op. cit. Wall Street involvement with the rise of Hitler and German Nazism is the topic of a forthcoming book.
[330] Clinton Roosevelt, *The Science of Government Founded on Natural Law* (New York: Dean & Trevett, 1841). There are two known copies of this book: one in the Library of Congress, Washington D.C. and another in the Harvard University Library. The existence of the book is not recorded in the latest edition of the Library of Congress catalog, but was recorded in the earlier 1959 edition (page 75). A facsimile edition was published by Emanuel J. Josephson, as part of his *Roosevelt's Communist Manifesto* (New York: Chedney Press, 1955).
[331] Ibid.

The earlier Rooseveltian system depended "First, on the art and science of cooperation. This is to bring the whole to bear for our mutual advantage."[332] It is this cooperation, i.e., the ability to bring the whole to bear for the interest of the few, that is, as we have seen, the encompassing theme of the writings and preachings of Otto Kahn, Robert Brookings, Edward Filene, Myron Taylor, and the other financier-philosophers discussed in Chapter 5. In the Roosevelt schema each man rises through specified grades in the social system and is appointed to that class of work to which he is best suited, choice of occupation being strictly circumscribed. In the words of Clinton Roosevelt:

> P. Whose duty will it be to make appointments to each class?
> A. The Grand Marshal's.
> P. Who will be accountable that the men appointed are the best qualified?
> A. A Court of physiologists, Moral Philosophers, and Farmers and Mechanics, to be chosen by the Grand Marshal and accountable to him.
> P. Would you constrain a citizen to submit to their decisions in the selection of a calling?
> A. No. If any one of good character insisted, he might try until he found the occupation most congenial to his tastes and feelings.[333]

Production in the system had to be equated with consumption, and the handling of "excesses and deficiencies" reflected the ideas pursued in the Swope Plan,[334] the literary base of Roosevelt's NRA. The system is certainly akin to that used in Bernard Baruch's War Industries Board during World War I. This is how Clinton Roosevelt describes the duties of the Marshal of Creation, whose job it is to balance production and consumption:

> P. What is the duty of the Marshal of the Creating or Producing order?
> A. It is to estimate the amount of produce and manufactures necessary to produce a sufficiency in each department below him. When in operation, he shall report excesses and deficiencies to the Grand Marshal.
> P. How shall he discover such excesses and deficiencies?
> A. The various merchants will report to him the demand and supplies in every line of business, as will be seen hereafter.
> P. Under this order are agriculture, manufactures and commerce, as I perceive. What then is the duty of the Marshal of Agriculture?
> A. He should have under him four regions, or if not, foreign commerce must make good the deficiency.
> P. What four regions?

---

[332] Ibid.
[333] Ibid.
[334] See Appendix A.

A. The temperate, the warm, the hot region and the water region.
P. Why divide them thus?
A. Because the products of these different regions require different systems of cultivation, and are properly subject to different minds.[335]

Then there is a Marshal of Manufacturers overseeing the whole system—similar to Baruch's position as economic dictator in 1918 and Hugh Johnson's position as Administrator of the National Recovery Administration in 1933. The Marshal's functions are described by Clinton Roosevelt as follows:

P. What are the duties of the Marshal of Manufacturers?
A. He shall divide men into five general classes, according to the printed diagram.
1st. The manufacturers of all the means of defence against the weather. 2d. All kinds of viands.
3d. Metals and minerals.
4th. Chemicals.
5th. Machinery.
All these have on the printed diagrams, banners, with a glory on one side and an appropriate motto on the reverse, showing the advantage each class is to all others: and by the way, we would remark, this should be universally adopted, to give a just direction to man's love of glory.
By a reference to the chart, and what has been before observed, the duties of the officers under this department will all be obvious.

The industrial categories of 1841 are not of course precisely the categories of 1930, but a generalized similarity can be traced. The 1st division is clothing and fabrics, limited in 1841 to cotton, wool, and linen, but extended today to synthetic materials, including plastics and fibers. The 2nd division is that devoted to foodstuffs. The 3rd division is devoted to raw materials, and the 4th division includes medicines. The 5th is machinery. Today the 5th division comprises the many subdivisions of electronics, mechanical and civil engineering, but the five categories could be utilized to divide a modern economy.

Clinton Roosevelt's society can be summed in his phrase, "The system should rule, and the system should look chiefly to the general good."

BERNARD BARUCH'S WARTIME DICTATORSHIP

---

[335] Clinton Roosevelt, The Science of Government Founded on Natural Law, op. cit.

While the Federal Reserve System and its private legal monopoly of the money supply has been a fount of wealth for its operators, the ultimate goal of making society work for the few as outlined by Frederick Howe and Clinton Roosevelt can be brought about only by planned control of the whole economy, and this requires compulsory adherence of the many smaller entrepreneurs to the dictates of the few deciding the plans to be followed.

The genesis of Roosevelt's NRA, a system that included compulsory adherence by small enterpreneurs to a plan devised by big business, can be traced from Bernard Baruch's U.S. War Industries Board, established and elaborated as an emergency wartime measure. In 1915, before the U.S. entered World War I, Howard E. Coffin, then chairman of General Electric, headed the U.S. Committee on Industrial Preparedness. In company with Bernard Baruch and Daniel Willard of the Baltimore and Ohio Railroad, Coffin was also a member of the Advisory Commission to the Council of National Defense. In 1915 Bernard Baruch was invited by President Woodrow Wilson to design a plan for a defense mobilization committee. This Baruch plan subsequently became the War Industries Board, which absorbed and replaced the old General Munitions Board. Margaret L. Coit, Baruch's biographer, describes the War Industries Board as a concept similar to cooperative trade associations, a device long desired by Wall Street to control the unwanted rigors of competition in the market place:

> Committees of industry, big business and small business, both represented in Washington, and both with Washington representation back home—this could be the backbone of the whole structure.[336]

By March 1918 President Wilson acting without Congressional authority, had endowed Baruch with more power than any other individual had been granted in the history of the United States. The War Industries Board, with Baruch as its chairman, became responsible for building all factories and for the supply of all raw material, all products, and all transportation, and all its final decisions rested with chairman Bernard Baruch. In brief, Baruch became economic dictator of the United States, or "Marshal of Manufacturers" in Clinton Roosevelt's scheme. Yet, as Margaret Coit points out, "... the creation of this office was never specifically authorized by an Act of Congress."[337]

So by the summer of 1918 Baruch, with extraordinary and unconstitutional powers, had, in his own words, "finally developed a scheme of positive 'control' over the major portion

---

[336] Margaret L. Coit, Mr. Baruch (Boston: Houghton, Mifflin, 1957), p. 147.
[337] Ibid., p. 172.

of the industrial fabric... Success bred courage for more success, and trade after trade was taken under control with an increasing willingness on the part of the interests affected."[338]

At the time of the Armistice the W.I.B. comprised Baruch (chairman), Alexander Legge of International Harvester (vice chairman), with E.B. Parker and R.S. Brookings (whose ideas we have already examined) in charge of price fixing. Assistants to the chairman were: Herbert Bayard Swope, brother of Gerard Swope of General Electric; Clarence Dillon of the Wall Street firm Dillon, Read & Co.; Harrison Williams; and Harold T. Clark.[339]

Baruch's final report on W.I.B. activity was much more than a history of its operations; it was also a specific plan and recommendation for economic planning in peacetime.

Baruch was not content merely to summarize the lessons to be learned for planning in war or for industrial preparedness in time of uneasy peace. On the contrary, Baruch's conclusions were directed, in his own words, to the "industrial practices of peace" and to make recommendations "relating to the business practices of normal times." The bulk of the conclusions relate to change-over of a planned wartime economic system to a planned peacetime economic system, and even the suggestions for wartime practice are related to peacetime functions. Baruch suggested that the most important "direct war lessons to be derived" from the operation of the War Industries Board were:

1. The establishment of a peacetime skeleton organization with 50 commodity divisions, meeting to keep abreast of the development of industry and develop information. The thrust of this proposal was that the information needed for peacetime planning should be collected and that the direction of the organization should stem from large-scale or major industry.
2. That the government "should devise some system for protecting and stimulating internal production of certain raw materials used in war," and
3. That war-related industries should be encouraged by the government to maintain skeleton organizations for wartime use.

Apart from these quite elementary suggestions, Baruch is exclusively concerned in the report with peacetime "planning." First we are presented with the canard that, in some

---

[338] Bernard M. Baruch, American Industry in the War: A Report of the War Industries Board (March 1921), with an introduction by Hugh S. Johnson (New York: Prentice-Hall, 1941) (including "a reprint of the report of the War Industries Board of World War I, Mr. Baruch's own program for total mobilization of the nation as presented to the War Policies Commission in 1931, and current material on priorities and price fixing").

[339] For a complete list of W.I.B. personnel see Grosvenor B. Clarkson, Industrial America in the World War (New York: Houghton, Mifflin, 1923), Appendix III. In the light of Chapter 11, below, it is intriguing to note numerous W.I.B. committee members with offices at 120 Broadway including Murry W. Guggenheim, Stephen Birch (Kennecott Copper), Edward W. Brush (American Smelting and Refining), F. Y. Robertson (United States Metals Refining Co.), Harry F. Sinclair (Sinclair Refining Co.), Charles W. Baker, (American Zinc), and Sidney J. Jennings (United States Smelting, Refining and Mining Co.)

unstated way, "the processes of trade" have changed and are now forced to give way before "certain new principles of supervision." This non sequitur is followed by the statement:

> We have been gradually compelled to drift away from the old doctrine of Anglo-American law, that the sphere of Government should be limited to preventing breach of contract, fraud, physical injury and injury to property, and that the Government should exercise protection only over non competent persons.

It is necessary, writes Baruch, for government "to reach out its arm" to protect "competent individuals against the discriminating practices of mass industrial power." While Baruch points to Federal control of the railroads and the merchant fleet, he does not state why the representatives of big business would be the best fitted to exercise this control. In other words, *why* the fox is proposed as the most competent being to run the chicken coop is left unstated. Baruch then slashes at the Sherman and Clayton anti-trust laws on the grounds that these statutes are merely efforts to force industry into the mold of "simpler principles sufficient for the conditions of a bygone day," and lauds the achievement of the War Industries Board because it had constructed hundreds of trade associations controlling prices and methods of distribution and production:

> Many businessmen have experienced during the war, for the first time in their careers, the tremendous advantages, both to themselves and to the general public, of combination, of cooperation and common action with their natural competitors.

If these cooperative attributes are not continued, argues Baruch, then businessmen will be tempted "and many of them will be unable to resist" to conduct "their business for private gain with little reference to general public welfare." On the other hand, trade associations can be of the greatest public benefit to achieve the desired end of cooperation. Baruch concludes:

> The question, then is what kind of Government organization can be devised to safeguard the public interest while these associations are preserved to carry on the good work of which they are capable.

Baruch, like any good socialist, proposes government organizations to develop these principles of cooperation and coordination.

If the reader will shed for a moment the idea of a mutual antagonism between communism and capitalism, he will readily see in the writing of Bernard Baruch the basic objectives of Karl Marx writing in *The Communist Manifesto*. What is different between the two systems are the names of the elitist few running the operation known as state planning; the vanguard of the proletariat in Karl Marx is replaced by the vanguard of big business in Bernard Baruch.

Who would gain from Baruch's proposal? The consumer? Not at all, because consumer interests are *always* protected by free competition in the market place, where goods and services are produced at the least cost, in the most efficient manner, and the consumer is given maximum choice among competing producers. The gainers from Baruch's proposals would be the few who control major industrial sectors—particularly iron and steel, raw materials, electrical goods, that is, those industries already well established and fearful of competition from more enterprising newcomers. In other words, the gainers from his proposal would be Bernard Baruch and the Wall Street coterie that effectively controls big business through its interlocking directorships. The gut issue then is: who benefits from these proposals for trade associations and government coordination of industry? The principal, indeed the only major benefactors—apart from the swarms of academic advisers, bureaucrats, and planners—would be the financial elite in Wall Street.

So here we have, in Baruch's own words and ideas, an implementation of Frederic Howe's injunction to "make society work for you," the monopolist. This is also in the form of a proposal comparable to Clinton Roosevelt's system. There is no evidence that Baruch had heard of Clinton Roosevelt. There was no need for him to have done so; the advantages of restraint of trade and opportunity have always been obvious to the already established enterprise. It will therefore come as no surprise to find Bernard Baruch at the very core of the Roosevelt NRA, which itself parallels many of Baruch's post-war proposals, and who had a $200,000 investment in the election of FDR. It explains why Baruch's World War I personnel turn up in the New Deal. General Hugh Johnson, for example, spent the 1920s studying industrial organization at Baruch's expense and emerged in 1933 as boss of the National Recovery Administration. It also explains why Franklin Delano Roosevelt, a Wall Streeter himself for much of the 1920s, was cofounder with Herbert Hoover—another Wall Streeter in the 1920s—of the first of the trade associations proposed by Baruch, the American Steel Construction Association, discussed in the next chapter.

Parallel to Bernard Baruch's ideas, which came to fruition in the NRA, there is a much more successful contemporary example of corporate socialism in practice: the Federal Reserve System.

PAUL WARBURG AND CREATION OF THE FEDERAL RESERVE SYSTEM

Although many had a hand, or thought they had, in fashioning the Federal Reserve legislation, essentially the system was the brain child of one man: Paul Warburg, brother of Max Warburg, whom we met in Chapter 3. Paul Moritz Warburg (1868-1932) descended from the German banking family of Oppenheim. After early training in the offices of Samuel Montagu & Co. in London and the Banque Russe Pour le Commerce Etranger in Paris, Warburg entered the family banking house of M.M. Warburg & Co. in Hamburg. In 1902 Warburg became a partner in the New York banking house of Kuhn, Loeb & Co. while continuing as a partner in Warburg's of Hamburg. Five years later, in the wake of the financial panic of 1907, Warburg wrote two pamphlets on the U.S. banking system: Defects and Needs of our Banking System and A Plan for a Modified Central Bank.[340]

In the years after 1907, Warburg lost no opportunity to speak and write publicly about the need for banking and currency reform in the United States, and in 1910 he formally proposed a United Reserve Bank of the United States. This plan developed into the Federal Reserve System, and Warburg was appointed by President Woodrow Wilson a member of the first Federal Reserve Board. Major criticism of Warburg erupted during World War I because of brother Max's role in Germany, and he was not reappointed to the Board in 1918. However, from 1921 to 1926, after criticism had abated, Warburg became a member of the Advisory Council of the Federal Reserve Board and served as its president from 1924 to 1926.

After passage of the 1913 Federal Reserve Act, Warburg and his banking associates promptly set about using the legal banking monopoly for their own ends and purposes, as suggested by Frederic Howe. In 1919 Warburg organized the American Acceptance Council and served as chairman of its executive committee in 1919-20 and as its president in 1921-22. Then in 1921 Warburg organized and became chairman of the private International Acceptance Bank, Inc. while still serving on the Advisory Council of the Federal Reserve Board. In 1925 Warburg added two more private acceptance banks: the American and Continental Corp. and the International Acceptance Trust Co. These banks were affiliated with the Warburg-controlled Bank of the Manhattan Company. As an aside it may be noted that Paul Warburg was also a director of the American IG Chemical Corp., the American subsidiary of IG Farben in Germany. I.G. Farben was prominent in bringing Hitler to power in 1933 and manufactured the Zyklon-B gas used in Nazi concentration camps. Warburg was a founding member of the Carl Schurz Memorial Foundation, a propaganda organization established in 1930, a director of the prestigious Council on Foreign Relations, Inc., and a trustee of the Brookings Institution.

But it was through a virtual monopoly of U.S. acceptance banking, achieved by the International Acceptance Bank Inc. and its affiliated units, that Warburg was able to get society to go to work for the Warburgs and their banking friends. Revisionist historian

---

[340] See also Paul Warburg, The Federal Reserve System, Its Origin & Growth; Reflections & Recollections (New York: Macmillan, 1930)

Murray Rothbard has examined the origins of the 1920s inflation that led to the collapse of 1929 and makes this pertinent observation:

> While purchase of U.S. securities has received more publicity, bills bought were at least as important and indeed more important than discounts. Bills bought led the inflationary parade of Reserve credit in 1921 and 1922, were considerably more important than securities in the 1924 inflationary spurt, and equally important in the 1927 spurt. Furthermore, bills bought alone continued the inflationary stimulus in the fatal last half of 1928.[341]

What were these "bills bought" pinpointed by Rothbard as the key culprit of the 1929 depression? Bills bought were acceptances, and almost all were bankers acceptances.

Who created the acceptance market in the United States, largely unknown before 1920? Paul Warburg.

Who gained the lions' share of this acceptance business at artificially low subsidized rates? The International Acceptance Bank, Inc.

Who was the International Acceptance Bank, Inc? Its chairman was Paul Warburg, with Felix Warburg and James Paul Warburg as co-directors. However, a closer look at the make-up of the banks (see below page 95) suggests that it was a vehicle representing the financial élite of Wall Street.

Did the Warburgs and their Wall Street friends know where their financial policy would lead? In other words, did their financial policies of the 1920s have elements of deliberation? There exists a memorandum by Paul Warburg that clearly notes that banks had the capability to prevent inflation:

> If the Government and the banks of the United States were helpless automatons, inflation, no doubt, would have to ensue. But it is insulting our banks to have the impression go out that they should not be capable of cooperating in some common plan of protection such, for instance, as keeping all cash reserves higher than required by the law, if indeed such a step should become advisable for the greater safety of the country.[342]

Consequently, Rothbard quite rightly concludes:

---

[341] Murray N. Rothbard, America's Great Depression (Los Angeles: Nash Publishing Corp. 1972), p. 117.
[342] United States Senate, Hearings, Munitions Industry, Part 25, op. cit., p. 8103.

Surely, Warburg's leading role in the Federal Reserve System was not unconnected with his reaping the lion's share of benefits from its acceptance policy.[343]

In brief, the policy of creating acceptances at subsidized artificial rates was not only inflationary, but was the most important factor, apparently a deliberate banking policy, leading to the inflation of the 1920s and the ultimate collapse in 1929, thus making FDR's New Deal or national economic planning appear necessary. Further, this was, as Rothbard states, "...the grant of special privilege to a small group at the expense of the general public." In other words, Wall Street made American society go to work for a financial oligopoly.

Warburg's revolutionary plan to get American society to go to work for Wall Street was astonishingly simple. Even today, in 1975, academic theoreticians cover their blackboards with meaningless equations, and the general public struggles in bewildered confusion with inflation and the coming credit collapse, while the quite simple explanation of the problem goes un discussed and almost entirely un comprehended. The Federal Reserve System is a legal private monopoly of the money supply operated for the benefit of a few under the guise of protecting and promoting the public interest.

Revolutionary? Yes indeed! But as one of Warburg's admiring biographers commented:

> Paul M. Warburg is probably the mildest-mannered man that ever personally conducted a revolution. It was a bloodless revolution: he did not attempt to rouse the populace to arms. He stepped forth armed simply with an idea. And he conquered. That is the amazing thing. A shy, sensitive man, he imposed his idea on a nation of a hundred million people.[344]

How did this revolution of Warburg's differ from socialist revolution? Only in the fact that under socialism, once the revolution is achieved and the power of the state gathered into the right ideological hands, the accrued personal rewards are not usually as substantial —although the fiefdoms carved out by national socialist Hitler and the modern Soviets may challenge this observation— nor are the results so veiled. The monetary dictatorship of the Soviets is obvious. The monetary dictatorship of the Federal Reserve System is muted and evaded.

We should then take a closer look at the International Acceptance Bank, the vehicle used for this revolutionary exploitive maneuver because it provides valid signals that Wall

---

[343] Murray Rothbard, America's Great Depression, op. cit., p. 119.
[344] Harold Kellock, "Warburg, the Revolutionist," in The Century Magazine, May 1915, p. 79.

Street would also have a real interest in national economic planning and an FDR type of New Deal.

THE INTERNATIONAL ACCEPTANCE BANK, INC.

The bank was founded in 1921 in New York and affiliated with Warburg's Bank of the Manhattan Company. However, the board of directors suggests that the most important elements in Wall Street also had a significant interest and control in and profited from the International Acceptance Bank. Further, we find a striking link-up between its affiliated financial institutions and a general scheme to establish corporate socialism in the United States.

As we have noted, Paul M. Warburg was chairman of the board: his brother Felix, also a partner in Kuhn Loeb & Co., and his son James P. Warburg were co directors. The vice chairman of the board was John Stewart Baker, also president and director of the Bank of Manhattan Trust Co. and International Manhattan Co., as well as chairman of the executive committee and director of the Manhattan Trust Co. Baker was also director of the American Trust Co. and the New York Title and Mortgage Co. F. Abbot Goodhue was president and director of International Acceptance Bank, on the board of the other Warburg banks, and a director of the First National Bank of Boston. Other directors of the International Acceptance Bank were Newcomb Carlton, director of the Rockefeller-controlled Chase National Bank, the Morgan-controlled Metropolitan Life Insurance Co., and other such major companies as the American Express Co., the American Sugar Refining Co., and the American Telegraph and Cable Co. Newcomb Carlton was also a director of American Telegraph and Cable and a director of American International Corporation, a company intimately involved with the Bolshevik Revolution.[345] Another director of International Acceptance Bank who was also a director of American International Corp. was Charles A. Stone, located at 120 Broadway and a director of the Federal Reserve Bank from 1919 to 1932. Bronson Winthrop was also a director of both American International Corp. and International Acceptance Corp. Thus, three directors of International Acceptance Bank had interlocking directorships with American International Corp., the key vehicle in U.S. involvement in the Bolshevik revolution.

Another director of International Acceptance Bank was David Franklin Houston, who was also a director of the Carnegie Corp., the Morgan-controlled Guaranty Trust Co., U.S. Steel, and A.T.& T., as well as president of the Mutual Life Insurance Co. Other directors of I.A.B. included Philip Stockton, president of the First National Bank of Boston, and a director of A.T. & T., General Electric, International Power Securities, and many other companies; William

---

[345] See Sutton, Bolshevik Revolution, op. cit., Chapter 8.

Skinner, director of Irving Trust Co., Equitable Life Assurance, and the Union Square Savings Bank; Charles Bronson Seger, director of Aviation Corp., Guaranty Trust Co., and W.A. Harriman; Otto V. Schrenk, director of Agfa Ansco Corp., Krupp Nirosta, and Mercedes Benz Co.; and Henry Tatnall, director of the Girard Trust Co. Paul Warburg was also a director of Agfa Ansco, Inc., a firm 60 per cent owned by I. G. Farben and a "front" for I.G. in the United States.

In sum, the directors of International Acceptance Bank reflected the most powerful sectors of Wall Street: the Morgans, the Rockefellers, and Harriman, as well as the Boston bankers.

Further, there was a lifelong and intimate Warburg association with the Roosevelts from childhood to the New Deal. This Warburg–Roosevelt association is illustrated by an extract from James P. Warburg's memoirs: "It so happened that I had known the President elect's eldest son, James Roosevelt, for some years, because he had been living in one of the cottages on my Uncle Felix's estate in White Plains."[346]

Later the same James P. Warburg became adviser to President Franklin D. Roosevelt on domestic and international monetary affairs. The Warburg's deep interest in the NRA program is reflected in a 1933 Warburg memorandum to FDR:

> Memorandum for the President: Domestic Currency Problem. The Administration has, in my judgment, never faced a more serious situation than it does today. The entire recovery program, which is the heart of its policy, is jeopardized by uncertainty and doubt in the monetary field. The National Recovery Act cannot possibly function to any useful end if there is fear of currency depreciation of an unknown amount and fear as to monetary experimentation. There has already been a tremendous flight of capital, and this flight will continue at an increasing pace so long as uncertainty prevails.[347]

Then, following the Warburg proclivity for monopoly, James Warburg recommended to FDR that *all* monetary ideas, actions, and decisions be centralized in the Treasury Department and the Federal Reserve Board.

Obviously, this proposal would ensure that all monetary decisions were made by the élitist group associated with the International Acceptance Bank and the Federal Reserve System. The Secretary of the Treasury in July 1933, when James Warburg wrote his memorandum to FDR, was William H. Woodin, who had been director of FRB of New York from 1925 to 1931. We can also cite FDR's own associations with the Federal Reserve

---

[346] James P. Warburg, The Long Road Home: The Autobiography of a Maverick (Garden City: Doubleday, 1964), p. 106.
[347] Franklin D. Roosevelt and Foreign Affairs, Vol. I, p. 325. Memorandum of James P. Warburg to Roosevelt, July 24, 1933

System. His "favorite uncle" Frederic Delano was appointed vice chairman of the Federal Reserve Board by President Woodrow Wilson in 1914, and from 1931 to 1936 Delano served as chairman of the board of the Federal Reserve Bank of Richmond, Virginia. FDR appointed Delano chairman of the National Resources Planning Board in 1934.

In 1933-34 the United States faced the greatest financial crisis in its history. And what did FDR do? He called in as the financial doctors the very operators responsible for the crisis —as sensible a policy as allowing the lunatics to run the asylum.

So we find associations between Franklin D. Roosevelt, the Warburg family, and the Warburg-inspired central banking system ranging from childhood to Warburg's appointment as a key monetary adviser to FDR. We shall see later that it was Warburg who determined the final shape of the National Industrial Recovery Administration. On the other hand, the Warburg family and their Wall Street friends controlled the private monopoly money supply known as the Federal Reserve System and through the International Acceptance Bank exploited that monopoly for their own purposes.

The Founding Fathers demonstrated a profound wisdom and insight into the dangers of a monopoly of paper money issue that is reflected in Article I, Section 9 of the U.S. Constitution: "No State shall...make any Thing but gold and silver Coin a Tender in Payment of Debts...."

A constitutional challenge to the issue of Federal Reserve notes by a private banking monopoly, the Federal Reserve System, is overdue. Hopefully, the value of the dollar will not have to be reduced to zero, as the mark was in post-World War I Germany, before such a challenge is initiated and sustained by the Supreme Court of the United States.

Chapter 7

Roosevelt, Hoover, and the Trade Councils

> *People of the same trade seldom meet together even for merriment and diversion, but the conversation ends in a conspiracy against the public, or on some contrivance to raise prices.*
> Adam Smith, An Inquiry into the Nature and Causes of the Wealth of Nations (London: George Routledge, 1942), p. 102.

The idea of getting society to work for a privileged group within that society originated neither among the corporate socialists in Wall Street, nor in the financial community at large, nor even among the Marxian socialists. In fact, the notion predates our own industrial society, and there is an interesting parallel between the codes of New Deal America (which we shall examine later) and 13th-century trade legislation in England.[348]

A Medieval New Deal

In 1291 the tanners of Norwich, England were brought before the local court charged with organizing and coding their tanning activities to the detriment of local citizens. Two years later in 1293, the cobblers and saddle makers of Norwich were faced with similar charges. By "greasing" the legislators, the political power structure of medieval Norwich was brought around to the view that perhaps the tanners needed protection, after all.

This protection came to incorporate the same basic principles of economic planning that almost 700 years later were put forward in the Roosevelt New Deal. So in 1307 the tanning industry of Norwich was legally coded and wages and conditions of work prescribed, all done under the guise of protecting the consumer, but in practice granting a legal monopoly to the tanners.

---

[348] See Erwin F. Meyer, "English Medieval Industrial Codes" in The American Federationist, January 1934. Meyer draws some fascinating parallels between the medieval guilds and NRA practice under Roosevelt. In medieval times the result, as in the 1930s was to create "an oligarchy of capitalists" in the English economy.

In the decade before the New Deal, during the 1920s Wall Streeter Roosevelt was active on behalf of business to promote these same basic ideas of using the police power of the state to restrain trade, to advance cooperation, and to utilize government regulation to inhibit unwelcome competition from more efficient outsiders. The trade associations of the 1920s were more demure in their proposals than the 13th-century Norwich tanners, but the underlying principle was the same.

Unfortunately, Franklin D. Roosevelt's role in the Wall Street of the 1920s has been ignored by historians. Daniel Fusfield does correctly observe that FDR "took an active part in the trade association movement that was to develop into the N.R.A. of the early New Deal;"[349] on the other hand Fusfield, who offers the only extensive description of FDR's business activities, concludes that his attitude toward business was "a curious mixture." FDR, says Fusfield, was "insistent that mere profits were not a full justification for business activity," that a businessman must also "have the motive of public service." This to Fusfield was inconsistent with participation "in a number of outright speculative and promotional ventures that had little to do with serving the public."[350]

Fusfield and his fellow historians of the Roosevelt era have failed to note that "public service" for a businessman is absolutely consistent with "profit maximization;" in fact, public service is the easiest and certainly the most lucrative road to profit maximization. Further, the riskier and more speculative the business, presumably the greater is the advantage to be gained from public service.

When we take this more realistic view of social do-goodism, then Wall Streeter Roosevelt's attitude toward business is not at all "curious." It is in fact a consistent program of profit maximization.

THE AMERICAN CONSTRUCTION COUNCIL

The American Construction Council (A.C.C.), formed in May 1922, was the first of numerous trade associations created in the 1920s, devices used to raise prices and reduce output. The original proposal and the drive for the council came from Secretary of Commerce Herbert Hoover, and the council operated under the leadership of Franklin D. Roosevelt, then just beginning his Wall Street career following his service as Assistant Secretary of the Navy. The stated public objectives of the A.C.C. were a "code of ethics" (a euphemism for restraint of trade), efficiency, and standardization of production. Most importantly, but less publicized, the A.C.C. was to provide the industry with an opportunity to fix its own price

---

[349] Daniel R. Fusfield, The Economic Thought of Franklin D. Roosevelt and the Origins of the New Deal.
[350] Ibid.

and production levels without fear of antitrust prosecutions by the government. The New York Times reported:

> It is these tremendous possibilities, in dedication to the public service and the elimination of waste, that have fired the imaginations of Mr. Hoover and Mr. Roosevelt and invited them to accept positions of leadership in the movement.[351]

Like the price-fixing committees of Baruch's War Industries Board, the A.C.C. was in effect a primitive industry association, although the high-sounding stated object of the council was:

> ... to place the construction industry on a high plane of integrity and efficiency and to correlate the efforts toward betterment made by existing agencies through an association dedicated to the improvement of the service within the construction industry... ."[352]

and so to stabilize conditions for the benefit of the industry, labor, and the general public. This objective was also Baruch's objective for peacetime trade associations: to regulate industry under government control, while citing the public good. In the American Construction Council the public good was announced as the elimination of the scandals found by the Lockwood Commission investigating the New York building industry.

However, as that scandal dealt in great part with exclusive dealing and similar coercive conditions forced upon contractors and erectors by the United States Steel Corporation and Bethlehem Steel, the announced public good makes little sense. These industry giants were controlled by the Morgan interests on Wall Street who were, as we shall see, also at the root of the A.C.C. proposal. In brief, the alleged antisocial conditions to be solved by a trade association could have been halted much more simply and effectively by a memorandum from J.P. Morgan and his associates; there was no necessity to promote a trade association to halt such abuses. So we must look elsewhere for the reason for trade associations. The real reason, of course, is to protect industry from unwelcome competition and to establish monopoly conditions for those already in the business. As Howe told us, a legal monopoly is the sure road to profit. It was formation of this legal monopoly that induced Roosevelt and Herbert Hoover to join hands against the public interest, although, according to Freidel:

> FDR's friend Elliott Brown, warned him against the "socialistic" tendencies of these associations and of Hoover specifically. Socialistic, because the moment a combination is formed, the Government will assert an interest and will express that interest through the

---

[351] The New York Times, May 15, 1922, p. 19.
[352] Cited in Fusfield, Economic Thought, op. cit., p. 102.

medium of some clerk in the Department of Commerce, who will approve or disapprove many matters affecting the initiative and welfare of all peepul (sic).[353]

FDR's role is not really surprising. He was then attempting to get a business career underway. He had political contacts and was more than willing, indeed eager, to use these. On the other hand, there is an odd dichotomy in the ideas and practices of Herbert Hoover in this area of the relationship between government and business. Herbert Hoover declared his adherence to the principles of free enterprise and individual initiative and his suspicion of government intervention. These assertions were mixed with other contrary statements encouraging, indeed authorizing, government intervention on almost trivial grounds. Unfortunately, Herbert Hoover's Memoirs, the only finally authoritative source, do not resolve these conflicts. The American Construction Council is not mentioned in Hoover's Memoirs, although Volume II, "The Cabinet and the Presidency," underlines the evils of government intervention in the economy, pointing to communism, socialism, and fascism to comment, "This left wing cure for all business evil" now appears as "national planning." Hoover added that business "abuses" were only "marginal" and rather than have government intervention" ... beyond and better than even that was cooperation in the business community to cure its own abuses."[354]

On the other hand, Hoover's private correspondence with Roosevelt on the American Construction Council suggests that Hoover, while in favor of government intervention, was careful to disguise this continuing interest for fear of bringing public opposition down upon his own head and ruining the proposal. A letter from Hoover to Roosevelt dated June 12, 1923 makes this point:

> June 12, 1923
> Franklin D. Roosevelt, Vice Pres.
> Fidelity and Deposit Company of Maryland 120 Broadway
> New York City
> My Dear Roosevelt:
> I am in somewhat of a quandary about your telegram of June 7th. I had hoped that the Construction Council would be solely originated from the industries without pressure from the Administration. Otherwise it will soon take on the same opposition that all Governmental touches to this problem immediately accrue.
> The vast sentiment of the business community against Government interference tends to destroy even a voluntary effort if it is thought to be carried on at Government inspiration.
> Yours faithfully

---

[353] Freidel, The Ordeal, op. cit., p. 152.
[354] The Memoirs of Herbert Hoover. The Cabinet and the Presidency 1920-1933, (London: Hollis and Carter 1952), p. 67.

Herbert Hoover

In any event, the American Construction Council was a cooperative association of business, labor, and government

> formed at Washington on June 19 at the suggestion and under the guidance of Secretary Hoover of the Department of Commerce (who) has taken the first steps toward putting into operation a program of construction effort which, it is hoped, will eliminate many of the evils which have developed in the industry during the past decade.[355]

Thus, it was free enterpriser Herbert Hoover who became the sponsor of the first of the trade associations, the American Construction Council, which was designed to include

> architects, engineers, construction labor, general contractors, sub- contractors, materials and equipment manufacturers, material and equipment dealers, bond, insurance and real estate interests and the construction departments of Federal, State and municipal governments.[356]

The organization meeting of the American Construction Council was held at FDR's house in New York and attended by about 20 persons. This group discussed the concept of the council and particularly whether it

> should be a clearing house for the different national associations, a clerical clearing house, or whether it should be an active, aggressive (sic) militant organization in this service of the public good of the construction industry.[357]

It was unanimously decided that the council should be a militant aggressive organization and not just a clearing house for information. This concept was discussed with Dwight Morrow of the J.P. Morgan firm; with Mr. Dick, secretary to Judge Gary of the U.S. Steel Corporation; with Gano Dunn, president of J.G. White Engineering Corporation; and with Stone & Webster. It is interesting to note that most of these persons and firms are prominent in my previous volume, *Wall Street and the Bolshevik Revolution.*

After the financial establishment had expressed support of A.C.C., the construction industry at large was approached for its reaction. This preliminary work culminated in an organizational meeting at the Hotel Washington, Washington D.C., on Tuesday, June 20,

---

[355] The New York Times, July 9, 1922, VIII 1:3.
[356] The New York Times, May 15, 1922, p. 19, col. 8.
[357] Minutes of the Executive Board of the American Construction Council, June 20, 1922. FDR Files, Group 14: American Construction Council.

1922. Franklin D. Roosevelt was elected president of the council, and John B. Larner, vice president of the American Bankers Association, was elected treasurer. The chairman of the finance committee was Willis H. Booth of Guaranty Trust Company. The committee then established its committees and laid down priorities for its problems.

Roosevelt's interpretation of the causes for the problems of the construction industry were reported by The New York Times: "Muddling through has been the characteristic method employed by the construction industry for the last few years. There has been no system, no cooperation, no intensive national planning."

After pointing out that a railroad man is not laid off because of bad weather, Roosevelt commented:

> In construction work, however, we have that great bugbear in our economic life, the seasonal job. All the work is crowded into the summer months, none of the work is carried on during the winter. The results of this piling on are plain. In the summer we have scarcity of labor and skyrocketing of prices, in the winter unemployment and cutting of incomes. The only thing that lasts throughout the year is the bitterness of men engaged in the work.[358]

How did FDR propose to change all this?

> A large part of the work can be spread over the year. There is no reason in the world why a skilled mechanic living in New York, for instance, should be called down in June to help put up a public building in Georgia. Georgia can build in seasons of the year in which it is impossible for New York to build; so can Louisiana, so can all the Southern States.

Roosevelt's suggestion, an aimless non sequitur, was that the construction industry must "get together on this situation: move construction materials during off season and spread labor around." At an early board of governors' meeting, held at FDR's home in New York on May 16, 1923, FDR called attention to the road the council had followed: "The American Construction Council was organized, but frankly, it has not done one darned thing from that time to this except collect dues from some 115 different organizations, I think."

FDR put the basic choice to the assembled governors: did they want to continue the old way, "Build all we can, paying any old price as long as we get the orders?" Because if that was the case, said FDR, "We might just as well adjourn." On the other hand, he

---

[358] The New York Times, June 4, 1922. One searches in vain for a practicable, workable proposal to solve the alleged problems of the construction industry. The most valid suggestions put forward by Roosevelt and his fellow planners required changing the weather to allow year-round construction or movement of men and materials by "planning." Of course, a market system moves men and materials automatically, a point presumably unknown to FDR.

continued, that did not appear to be the view of the majority, and "We want to go back to the real basic purpose of the Council, which was to prevent this sort of thing." Then followed a series of proposed resolutions, adopted unanimously, that would have the effect of slowing down construction. The council continued to have its problems, summarized in a letter of April 29, 1924 from executive vice president D. Knickerbocker Boyd to Franklin D. Roosevelt, "to call attention to the very serious condition of affairs existing at this time." Boyd reminded FDR that the executive secretary, Dwight L. Hoopingarner, had served "practically" without pay, and that $7000 in back salary was owed to him. Boyd added, "This is not just or right and it should not be allowed to continue. He should not only be paid all back fees promptly but assured of prompt pay in the future—or the work should be stopped." Then Boyd commented that he, too, expected recompense for the time expended on council work, noting that time expended to date amounted to $3168.41, in addition to traveling expenses. Boyd suggested that the council face up squarely to its responsibilities, place itself on an adequate financial footing, or dissolve. The final paragraph of Boyd's letter demonstrates the fundamental objective of those promoting the American Construction Council:

> If the Council should go out of existence it would, in my opinion, be a country-wide calamity—as I doubt whether after this second effort to nationalize the great building industry on human lines, enough people with the enthusiasm, faith and patience could be found to make a third attempt.

Franklin D. Roosevelt, president of American Construction Council, had argued for "economic planning;" now the executive vice president acknowledges an "effort to nationalize" the construction industry. This effort to organize the construction industry under the somnolent eye of the government, statedly for the public good, failed.

Chapter 8

Wall Street Buys The New Deal

> *B.M. [Bernard Baruch] played a more effective role. Headquarters just didn't have any money. Sometimes they couldn't even pay the radio bill for the candidate's speeches. They had practically nothing to carry on the campaign in the critical state of Maine. Every time a crisis came, B.M. either gave the necessary money, or went out and got it.*
>
> Hugh S. Johnson, The Blue Eagle from Egg to Earth
(New York: Doubleday, Doran, 1935), p. 141.
On FDR's campaign in 1932.

The 1928 Presidential campaign matched Governor Alfred E. Smith, a Catholic with backing from Tammany Hall and a collectivist coloring to his politicking, against Herbert Hoover, a Quaker with a professed leaning to traditional American individualism and self- help. Herbert Hoover won by 21,392,000 votes to Smith's 15,016,000.

Where did the Wall Street banker-philosophers place their support and influence in the Smith-Hoover election? On the basis of the accepted interpretation of the philosophy of financiers, their support should have gone to Herbert Hoover. Hoover promoted the dearly beloved trade associations, dearly loved, that is, by the financial and business community. Further, in *American Individualism*[359] Herbert Hoover made it clear that the ideal system for America was, in his own words, "no system of laissez faire" but, on the contrary, a regulated economy. On the other hand, the most vocally political member of the Wall Street financial establishment in 1928 was John J. Raskob, vice president of Du Pont and of General Motors and a director of Bankers Trust Co. and the County Trust Co. At the personal insistence of Governor Al Smith, Raskob became chairman of the Finance Committee of the Democratic Party. Raskob was also the largest single contributor, giving more than $350,000 to the campaign. What were the policy objectives sought by Raskob and his allies that made Al Smith so attractive a candidate?

In 1928 the key elements of what became the National Recovery program were given a public airing by John J. Raskob, Bernard Baruch, and other Wall Streeters. The promotion

---

[359] New York: Doubleday, Page 1922.

of Roosevelt's NRA actually dates from the 1928 Raskob speeches made in the Al Smith Presidential campaign. Although both Al Smith and Herbert Hoover depended heavily on Wall Street's "golden circle" for election funds, as we shall detail later in this chapter, the Du Pont-Raskob-Baruch money was heavily on Al Smith.

Smith, of course, lost the 1928 election for the Democrats, and Herbert Hoover became the Republican President. In spite of luke-warm Wall Street treatment, Hoover appointed many Wall Streeters to his committees and boards. Then in mid-1932, given the blunt choice between a National Recovery program in the form of the Swope Plan or less fascist policies, Hoover declined to institute corporate socialism, identified the Swope Plan for what it was, and brought the wrath of Wall Street down upon his head.

Consequently, we can trace and will trace in this chapter the Baruch proposals for NRA and the financial backing of the two Presidential candidates in each election by Raskob, Baruch, Du Pont, Rockefeller, and others of the financial élite. The main backing in each case went to the Democratic candidate willing to promote corporate socialism. In 1928 this was Al Smith, who was also a director of the Morgan-controlled Metropolitan Life Insurance Company; in 1930 it went to Roosevelt with the early bird pre convention contributions for the 1932 Hoover-Roosevelt contest. This was followed in mid-1932 by withdrawal of a great deal of Wall Street support from Herbert Hoover and the wholesale transfer of influence and money toward the election of Roosevelt.

Subsequently, FDR did not abandon his backers. The National Recovery Act with its built-in ability to coerce small business was promised and in June 1933 became law. Let's look then more closely at these events and the related evidence.

BERNARD BARUCH'S INFLUENCE ON FDR

According to his own statements Hugh Johnson, the Administrator of Roosevelt's NRA, went through a training program in the 1920s under Bernard Baruch's tutelage. Johnson records this experience as follows:

> I doubt if anybody had any more direct or complete access to sources of information than B.M. and he always gave me a free hand in the consultation and use of such scientists and experts as I might need. I was for several years the only Research Staff which he permanently maintained. That and what went before was a great training for service in NRA because these studies covered a considerable segment of the whole of American industry and the experience with government linked the two together.[360]

---

[360] Hugh S. Johnson, The Blue Eagle from Egg to Earth (New York: Doubleday, Doran, 1935), p. 116.

Johnson himself views the Raskob speeches of September and October 1928 in the Al Smith campaign as the start of Roosevelt's NRA: "There was nothing particularly new in the essence or principles developed. We had worked out and expressed precisely the same philosophy in Al Smith's campaign in 1928... ."[361]

Al Smith, the 1928 Democratic Presidential candidate was, as we have noted, a director of Metropolitan Life Insurance, the largest life insurance company in the U.S. and controlled by J.P. Morgan, and the greater part of his campaign funds came from the golden circle in Wall Street. Bernard Baruch outlined the NRA plan itself on May 1, 1930 —an auspicious day for a socialist measure— in a speech at Boston. The content of NRA was all there, the regulation, codes, enforcement, and the carrot of welfare for the workers. It was repeated in Baruch's platform of June 1932—the one that Herbert Hoover refused to adopt. The NRA was presented again by Baruch in testimony before the Senate and in speeches before the Brookings Institution and at Johns Hopkins University. In all, Hugh Johnson counts ten documents and speeches, all presented before the election of Roosevelt in 1932, in which "will be found the development of the economic philosophy of the 1928 campaign and of almost all that happened since. Of a part of this philosophy NRA was a concrete expression."[362]

The following extracts from Baruch's May 1, 1930 speech contain the core of his proposals:

> What business needs is a common forum where problems requiring cooperation can be considered and acted upon with the constructive, non political sanction of government. It may have been sound public policy to forbid by law anything that looked to regulation of production when the world was in fear of famine but it is public lunacy to decree unlimited operation of a system which periodically disgorges indigestible masses of unconsumable products. No repressive, inquisitorial, mediocre bureau will answer—we must have a new concept for this purpose—a tribunal invested like the Supreme Court, with so much prestige and dignity that our greatest business leaders will be glad to divest themselves of all personal interest in business and there serve. Like the Supreme Court also it must be absolutely non-political.
>
> It should have no power to repress or coerce but it should have power to convoke conference, to suggest and to sanction or license such commonsense cooperation among industrial units as will prevent our economic blessings from becoming unbearable burdens. Its sole punitive power should be to prescribe conditions of its licenses and then to revoke those licenses for infringement of such conditions.

---

[361] Ibid., p. 141.
[362] Ibid., p. 157.

Its deliberations should be in the open and should be wholly scientific, briefed like an engineer's report, and published to the world. Such a system would safeguard the public interest and should be substituted for the blind inhibitory blankets of the Sherman and Clayton Acts...

It is not government in business in the sense which is here condemned. It is only a relaxation of the grip government has already taken on business by the Anti-Trust Acts. There is no fallacy in restricting ruinous excess production—a policy which the Federal Government is now vigorously urging on Agriculture. Yet if there is nothing in the change of concept from bureaucratic precedent to that of an open forum where business can practice group self-government, acting on its own motion under sanction of non-political, constructive and helpful tribunal —then the idea is not practicable. But that there is a possibility of such industrial self-government under governmental sanction was clearly demonstrated in 1918. Many difficulties suggest themselves. In the first place anything done in the elation and fervor of war must be accepted as a criterion only with caution.

In the regulation of production price is one consideration. That is a subject which is loaded with dynamite.

There are other obvious reservations. The thought is revived at this critical moment because it seems worthy of consideration as an aid in a threatening economic development 'of unusual extent' and as an alternative to governmental interference and vast extension of political powers in the economic field—an eventuality which, in the absence of constructive action by business itself, is almost as certain as death and taxes.[363]

Baruch wanted by his own words a resurrection of the trade associations, relaxation of anti-trust laws, and control of business leaders and casts the reader back to the War Industries Board of 1918. To be sure, Baruch suggests "no power to coerce" and "open" deliberations, but such protestations of good faith carry small weight in the light of economic history and past furious efforts to establish cartels and combinations in restraint of trade by this same group. It was to further this end that financial support for both Democrats and Republican candidates was forthcoming; the greater part of the financing originated in a relatively small geographical area of New York.

WALL STREET FINANCES THE 1928 PRESIDENTIAL CAMPAIGN

The direction of political support can be measured and identified by related financial support. The origins of the financial contributions to the Smith and Hoover campaigns of 1928 can be identified, and we find, contrary to prevailing beliefs, that it was the Democrats who received the lion's share of funds from Wall Street; as we have seen, it was in the

---

[363] Ibid., pp. 156–7. Italics in original.

Democratic campaign that the outlines of the National Recovery Act were first promulgated by Baruch and Raskob.

After the 1928 Presidential election the Steiwer Committee of the U.S. House of Representatives investigated the sources of campaign funds funneled into the election[364]. The detailed information was published, but the Steiwer Committee did not probe into the corporate origins and affiliations of the contributors: it merely listed names and amounts contributed. Table XIII in the report is entitled "Persons contributing sums of $5,000 and over in behalf of Republican presidential candidate." The Republican Presidential candidate was, of course, Herbert Hoover. This table lists full names and the amounts contributed, but without the affiliation of the contributors. Similarly, Table XIV of the report is entitled "Persons contributing sums of $5,000 and over in behalf of Democratic presidential candidate." Again, full names and amounts are given, but the affiliations of the person are not stated.

These lists were taken and matched by the author to the *Directory of Directors in the City of New York 1929-1930*.[365] Where the contributor as listed by the Steiwer Committee was identified as having an address within a one-mile circle of 120 Broadway in New York, the name and amount contributed were noted. No notation was made of persons not in the directory and most probably resident outside of New York City, but a record was kept of the sums of money contributed by the non New York residents. In other words, two totals were constructed from the Steiwer Committee data: (1) contributions from persons listed as directors of companies headquartered in New York and (2) contributions from all other persons. In addition, a list of names of the New York contributors was compiled. In practice, the research procedure was biased against inclusion of the New York-based directors. For example, in the Democratic Party list Van-Lear Black was listed by the author as a non-New York resident, although Black was chairman of the Fidelity & Casualty Co; the company had offices at 120 Broadway, and Franklin D. Roosevelt was their New York vice president in the early 1920s. However, Black was based in Baltimore and therefore not counted as a New York director. Again Rudolph Spreckels, the sugar millionaire, was listed in the Steiwer Committee report for a $15,000 contribution, but is not listed in the New York total, as he did not base himself in New York. Similarly, James Byrne contributed $6500 to the Smith for President campaign, but is not listed as a New York director — he was a director of the Fulton Savings Bank in Brooklyn and outside the one-mile circle. Jesse Jones, the Texas banker, contributed $20,000, but is not listed as a New York director

---

[364] United States Congress, Senate Special Committee investigating Presidential campaign expenditures, Presidential Campaign Expenditures. Report Pursuant to S. Res. 234, February 25 (Calendar Day, February 28), 1929. 70th Congress, 2nd session. Senate Rept. 2024 (Washington: Government Printing Office, 1929). Cited hereafter as Steiwer Committee Report.
[365] New York: Directory of Directors Co., 1929.

because he was a Texas, not a New York, banker. In other words, the definition of a Wall Street contributor was very tightly and consistently drawn.

Major Wall Street Contributors to the Al Smith For President Campaign — 1928

Name	Contributions 1924 deficit campaign	1928	1928 deficit contribution	Total
John J. Raskob (Du Pont and General Motors)	—	$110,000	$250,000	$360,000
William F. Kenny (W.A. Harriman)	$25,000	$100,000	$150,000	$275,000
Herbert H. Lehman	$10.000	$100.00	$150,000	$260,000
M.J. Meehan (120 Broadway)	—	$50,000	$100,000	$150,000

Source: Adapted from Louise Overacker, Money in Elections (New York: Macmillan, 1932), p. 155.

Under this restricted definition the total amount contributed by Wall Street directors, mostly connected with major banks, to the Al Smith 1928 Presidential campaign was $1,864,339. The total amount contributed by persons not within this golden circle was $500,531, which makes a grand total of $2,364,870. In brief, the percentage of the Al Smith for President campaign funds coming from persons giving more than $5000 and also identified as Wall Street directors was 78.83 per cent. The percentage from donors outside the golden circle was a mere 21.17 per cent. Looking at the total Al Smith contributors another way, the large contributors (over $5000) to the Smith campaign, those in the best position to ask and receive political favors, put up almost four dollars out of five.

The identity of the larger contributors to both the Al Smith campaign and the Democratic National Committee fund is listed in the attached tables.

Contributors of $25,000 or More to Democratic National Committee January to December 1928 (including contributions listed in previous table)

			NOTE
Herbert H. Lehman and Edith A. Lehman	Lehman Brothers, and Studebaker Corp.	$135,000	FDR's chief political adviser
John J. Raskob	Vice president of Du Pont and General Motors	$110,000	NRA administrator
Thomas F. Ryan	President, Bankers Mortgage Co., Houston	$75,000	Chairman, Reconstruction Finance Corp.

Name	Affiliation	Amount	Notes
Harry Payne Whitney	Guaranty Trust	$50,000	See Chap. 10: "The Butler Affair"
Pierre S. Du Pont	Du Pont Company, General Motors	$50,000	See Chap. 10: "The Butler Affair"
Bernard M. Baruch	Financier, 120 Broadway	$37,590	NRA planner
Robert Sterling Clark	Singer Sewing Machine Co.	$35,000	See Chap. 10: "The Butler Affair"
John D. Ryan	National City Bank, Anaconda Copper	$27,000	—
William H. Woodin	General Motors	$25,000	Secretary of Treasury, 1932

Source: Steiwer Committee Report, op. cit.

Contributions to the Democratic Presidential Primary 1928 by Directors* of the County Trust Company.

Name of Director	Contribution to Campaign and Deficit	Other Affiliations
Vincent Astor	$10,000	Great Northern Railway, U.S. Trust Co. Trustee, N.Y. Public Library Metropolitan Opera
Howard S. Cullman	$6,500	Vice President, Cullman Brothers, Inc.
William J. Fitzgerald	$6,000	—
Edward J. Kelly	$6,000	—
William F. Kenny	$275,000 **	President and Director, William F. Kenny Co. Director, The Aviation Corp., Chrysler Corp.
Arthur Lehman	$14,000 ***	Partner, Lehman Brothers. Director, American International Corp., RKO Corp., Underwood-Elliott-Fisher Co.
M.J. Meehan	$150,000**	61 Broadway
Daniel J. Mooney	—	120 Broadway
John J. Raskob	$360,000 **	Director, American International Corp., Bankers Trust Co., Christiania Securities Co. Vice President, E.I. Du Pont de Nemours & Co. and General Motors Corp.
James J. Riordan	$10,000	—
Alfred E. Smith	—	Presidential Candidate Director: Metropolitan Life Insurance Co.
Total	$842,000	

Notes: *The following directors of County Trust Company did not contribute (according to the records): John J. Broderick, Peter J. Carey, John J. Cavanagh, William H. English, James P. Geagan, G. Le Boutillier, Ralph W. Long, John J. Pulleyn, and Parry D. Saylor.
**Includes contributions to the campaign deficit.
***Excludes contributions by other members of the Lehman family to the Democratic Presidential campaign that totalled $168,000.

Looking at the names in these tables, it would be neither unkind nor unfair to say that the Democratic candidate was bought by Wall Street before the election. Moreover, Al Smith was a director of the County Trust Company, and the County Trust Company was the source of an extraordinarily large percentage of Democratic campaign funds.

HERBERT HOOVER'S ELECTION FUNDS

When we turn to Herbert Hoover's 1928 campaign, we also find a dependence on Wall Street financing, originating in the golden mile, but not nearly to the same extent as in Al Smith's campaign. Of a large donations total for Herbert Hoover of $3,521,141, about 51.4 per cent came from within this golden mile in New York and 48.6 per cent from outside the financial district.

Contributions of $25,000 or More to Republican National Committee, January to December 1928

Mellon family	Mellon National Bank		$50,000
Rockefeller family	Standard Oil		$50,000
Guggenheim family	Copper smelting		$75,000
Eugene Meyer	Federal Reserve Bank		$25,000
William Nelson Cromwell	Wall Street attorney		$25,000
Otto Kahn	Equitable Trust Company		$25,000
Mortimer Schiff	Banker		$25,000
		Total	$275,000

Source: Steiwer Committee Report, op. cit.

Herbert Hoover was, of course, elected President; his relationship to the rise of corporate socialism has been misinterpreted in most academic and media sources. The bulk of liberal-oriented literature holds that Herbert Hoover was some kind of unreconstructed laissez faire Neanderthal. But this view is rejected by Hoover's own statements: for example:

Those who contended that during the period of my administration our economic system was one of laissez faire have little knowledge of the extent of government regulation. The economic philosophy of laissez faire, or "dog eat dog," had died in the United States forty years before, when Congress passed the Interstate Commerce Commission and the Sherman Anti-Trust Acts.[366]

Murray Rothbard points out[367] that Herbert Hoover was a prominent supporter of Theodore Roosevelt's Progressive Party and, according to Rothbard, Hoover "challenged in a neo-Marxist manner, the orthodox laissez-faire view that labor is a commodity and that wages are to be governed by laws of supply and demand."[368] As Secretary of Commerce Hoover pushed for government cartelization of business and for trade associations, and his "outstanding" contribution, according to Rothbard," was to impose socialism on the radio industry," while the courts were working on a reasonable system of private property rights in radio frequencies. Rothbard explains these ventures into socialism on the grounds that Hoover "was ... the victim of a terribly inadequate grasp of economics."[369] Indeed, Rothbard argues that Herbert Hoover was the real creator of the Roosevelt New Deal.

Although the evidence presented here suggests that Baruch and Raskob had more to do with FDR's New Deal, there is some validity to Rothbard's argument. Hoover's practical policies were not consistent. There are some pro-free market actions; there are many anti-free market actions. It seems plausible that Hoover was willing to accept a part, possibly a substantial part, of a socialist program, but had a definite limit beyond which he was not willing to go.

During the course of the 1920s, in the years after the formation of the American Construction Council, more than 40 codes of practice compiled by trade associations were adopted. When he became President, and in spite of his early association with the A.C.C., Herbert Hoover promptly ended these industrial codes. He did this on the grounds that they were probably illegal associations to police prices and production and that no government could regulate these in the interest of the public. Then in February 1931 the U.S. Chamber of Commerce formed a group entitled the Committee on Continuity of Business and Employment under Henry I. Harriman. This committee came up with proposals very much like those of the New Deal: that production should be balanced to equal consumption, that the Sherman anti-trust laws should be modified to allow agreements in restraint of trade, that a national economic council should be set up under the auspices of the U.S. Chamber of Commerce, and that provision should be made for shorter hours in industry, for pensions,

---

[366] The Memoirs of Herbert Hoover: The Cabinet and the Presidency 1920-1923 (London: Hollis and Carter, 1952), p. 300.
[367] New Individualist Review, Winter, 1966.
[368] Ibid., p. 5.
[369] Ibid., p.10.

and for unemployment insurance. This was followed by yet another Hoover committee known as the Committee on Work Periods in Industry under P.W. Litchfield, president of Goodyear Tire and Rubber Company. Then still another committee under Standard Oil Company of New Jersey president Walter Teagle recommended sharing work, a proposal endorsed by the Litchfield Committee. Then came the Swope Plan in 1931 (see Appendix A). The plans were forthcoming, but Herbert Hoover did very little about them.

So, under Herbert Hoover, while big business was prolific in publicizing plans designed to modify the Sherman anti-trust act, allow self regulation by industry, and establish codes in restraint of trade. President Herbert Hoover did nothing to encourage these ventures.

In fact, Hoover recognized the Swope Plan as a fascist measure and recorded this in his memoirs, along with the melancholy information that Wall Street gave him a choice of buying the Swope plan—fascist or not—and having their money and influence support the Roosevelt candidacy. This is how Herbert Hoover described the ultimatum from Wall Street under the heading of "Fascism comes to business—with dire consequences":

> Among the early Roosevelt fascist measures was the National Industry Recovery Act (NRA) of June 16, 1933. The origins of this scheme are worth repeating. These ideas were first suggested by Gerard Swope (of the General Electric Company) at a meeting of the electrical industry in the winter of 1932. Following this, they were adopted by the United States Chamber of Commerce. During the campaign of 1932, Henry I. Harriman, president of that body, urged that I agree to support these proposals, informing me that Mr. Roosevelt had agreed to do so. I tried to show him that this stuff was pure fascism; that it was merely a remaking of Mussolini's "corporate state" and refused to agree to any of it. He informed me that in view of my attitude, the business world would support Roosevelt with money and influence. That for the most part, proved true.[370]

WALL STREET BACKS FDR FOR GOVERNOR OF NEW YORK

The chief fund raiser in FDR's 1930 reelection campaign was Howard Cullman, Commissioner of the Port of New York and a director of the County Trust Company. Freidel[371] lists the campaign contributors in 1930 without their corporate affiliations. When we identify the corporate affiliations of these contributors, we find once again that County Trust Company of 97 Eighth Avenue, New York had an extraordinarily large interest in FDR's reelection. Apart from Howard Cullman, the following major contributors to FDR's campaign were also

---

[370] Herbert Hoover, The Memoirs of Herbert Hoover: The Great Depression 1929-1941 (New York: Macmillan, 1952), p. 420.
[371] Freidel, The Ordeal, op. cit, p. 159.

directors of the County Trust Company: Alfred Lehman, Alfred (Al) Smith, Vincent Astor, and John Raskob. Another director was FDR's old friend Dan Riordan, a customer from Fidelity & Deposit days at 120 Broadway, and William F. Kenny, yet another FDR supporter and director of County Trust. To place this list in focus, we must remember that Freidel lists 16 persons as major contributors to this campaign, and of this 16 we can identify no less than five as directors of County Trust and two other unlisted directors as known FDR supporters. Other prominent Wall Streeters financing FDR's 1930 campaign were the Morgenthau family (with the Lehmans, the heaviest contributors); Gordon Rentschler, president of the National City Bank and director of the International Banking Corporation; Cleveland Dodge, director of the National City Bank and the Bank of New York; Caspar Whitney; August Heckscher of the Empire Trust Company (120 Broadway); Nathan S. Jones of Manufacturers Trust Company; William Woodin of Remington Arms Company; Ralph Pulitzer; and the Warburg family. In brief, in the 1930 campaign the bulk of FDR's financial backing came from Wall Street bankers.

Contributors to the Pre Convention Expenses of FDR ($3,500 and Over)

Name	Amount	Affiliation
Edward Flynn	$21,500	Director of Bronx County Safe Deposit Co.
W.H. Woodin	$20,000	Federal Reserve Bank of New York, Remington Arms Co.
Frank C. Walker	$15,000	Boston financier
Joseph Kennedy	$10,000	—
Lawrence A. Steinhardt	$ 8,500	Member of Guggenheim, Untermeyer & Marshall, 120 Broadway
Henry Morgenthau	$ 8,000	Underwood-Elliott-Fisher
F.J. Matchette	$ 6,000	—
Lehman family	$ 6,000	Lehman Brothers, 16 William Street
Dave H. Morris	$ 5,000	Director of several Wall Street firms
Sara Roosevelt	$ 5,000	—
Guy P. Helvering	$ 4,500	
H.M. Warner	$ 4,500	Director, Motion Picture Producers & Distributors of America
James W. Gerard	$ 3,500	Financier, 57 William Street
Total	$117,500	

Shortly after FDR's reelection in 1930, these backers started to raise funds for the 1932 Presidential campaign. These "early bird" pre convention contributions have been described by Flynn: "These contributors, who helped early when the need was great, so thoroughly won Roosevelt's devotion that in most instances they ultimately received substantial returns in public offices and honors."[372]

WALL STREET ELECTS FDR IN 1932

In 1932 Bernard Baruch was the key operator working behind the scenes—and sometimes not so much behind the scenes—to elect FDR, with the money and influence of big business (see epigraph to this chapter). Further, Bernard Baruch and Hugh Johnson collected numerous statistics and materials over the 1920s decade supporting their concept of national economic planning through trade associations. Johnson recounts how this information became available to FDR's speech writers. During the Roosevelt campaign of 1932:

> Ray Moley and Rex Tugwell came up to B.M.'s house and we went over all the material that B.M. and I had collected and summarized in our years of work. They, with Adolph Berle, had long before worked out the subjects of what they thought would be an ideal scheme of economic speeches for a Presidential candidate, but they had few facts. From that moment we joined Ray Moley's forces and we all went to work to find for Franklin Roosevelt the data which he welded into the very remarkable series of simply expressed speeches on homely economics which convinced this country that here was the leader upon whom it could rely.[373]

In rereading the FDR campaign speeches, it becomes obvious that they lack concreteness and specific facts. Presumably the Moley-Tugwell team set out the general theme and Baruch and Johnson introduced supporting statements in such areas as credit expansion, the consequences of speculation, the role of the Federal Reserve system, and so on. It is remarkable, but perhaps not surprising, that these Baruch- influenced speeches took the reader back to World War I, cited the contemporary emergency as greater than that of the war, and then subtly suggested similar Baruchian solutions. For example, at the Jefferson Day Dinner speech of April 18, 1932 Roosevelt said, or was prompted to say:

> Compare this panic stricken policy of delay and improvisation with that devised to meet the emergency of war fifteen years ago. We met specific situations with considered, relevant

---

[372] John T. Flynn, "Whose Child is the NRA?" Harper's Magazine Sept. 1932, pp. 84-5.
[373] Hugh S. Johnson, The Blue Eagle from Egg to Earth, op. cit., pp. 140-1.

measures of constructive value. There were the War Industries Board, the Food and Fuel Administration, the War Trade Board, the Shipping Board and many others.[374]

Then in May 22, 1932 Roosevelt addressed himself to the theme "The Country Needs, the Country Demands, Persistent Experimentation" and called for national economic planning. This speech was followed on July 2, 1932 by the first hint of the New Deal.

Finally, in accepting the nomination for the Presidency at Chicago, FDR said "I pledge you—I pledge myself to a New Deal for the American People."

NOTE: Freidel's list of pre-convention contributors to Franklin Delano Roosevelt's 1932 Presidential campaign.

1932 Reconvention Contributors[375] (over $2,000)	Affiliations
James W. Gerard	Gerard, Bowen & Halpin (see Julian A. Gerard)
Guy Helvering	—
Col. E.M. House, New York	—
Joseph P. Kennedy, 1560 Broadway	Ambassador to Court of St. James New England Fuel & Transportation Co.
Henry Morgenthau, Sr.	Bank of N.Y. & Trust Co. (Asst. Comptroller)
Underwood-Elliott-Fisher 1133 Fifth Avenue	American Savings Bank (Trustee)
Dave Hennen Morris	—
Mrs. Sara Delano Roosevelt, Hyde Park, N.Y.	FDR's mother
Laurence A. Steinhardt 120 Broadway	Guggenheim, Untermeyer & Marshall
Harry M. Warner 321W. 44th St.	Motion Picture Producers & Distributors of America, Inc.
William H. Woodin Secretary of the Treasury	American Car & Foundry; Remington Arms Co.
Edward J. Flynn 529 Courtlandt Ave.	Bronx County Safe Deposit Co.
James A. Farley adds to this list:	
William A. Julian	Director, Central Trust Co.
Jesse I. Straus 1317 Broadway	President, R.H. Macy & Co. N.Y. Life Insurance
Robert W. Bingham	Publisher, Louisville Courier-Journal
Basil O'Connor 120 Broadway	FDR's law partner

---

[374] The Public Papers and Addresses of Franklin D. Roosevelt; Vol. I, The Genesis of the New Deal, 1928-1932 (New York: Random House, 1938), p. 632.
[375] Freidel, The Ordeal, op. cit., p. 172.

CHAPTER 9

FDR AND THE CORPORATE SOCIALISTS

THE SWOPE PLAN

> *I think this is as revolutionary as anything that happened in this country in 1776, or in France in 1789, or in Italy under Mussolini or in Russia under Stalin.*
> Senator Thomas P. Gore in the National Recovery Administration Hearings,
> U.S. Senate Finance Committee, May 22, 1933.

Although the New Deal and its most significant component, the National Recovery Administration (NRA), are generally presented as the progeny of FDR's brain trust, as we have seen the essential principles had been worked out in detail long before FDR and his associates came to power. The FDR group did little more than put the stamp of academic approval to an already prepared plan.

The roots of the Roosevelt NRA are of peculiar importance. As we have seen in Chapter 6, allowing for vast changes in the industrial structure, NRA approximated a schema worked out in 1841 by FDR's ancestor, Assemblyman Clinton Roosevelt of New York.

Then we noted that wartime dictator Bernard Baruch was preparing an NRA-like program in the 1920s and that he and his assistant Hugh Johnson were very much an integral part of the preliminary planning. Further, the Roosevelt NRA was in its details a plan presented by Gerard Swope (1872-1957) long-time president of General Electric Company.

This Swope Plan[376] was in turn comparable to a German plan worked out in World War I by his opposite number Walter Rathenau, head of German General Electric (Allgemeine Elektizitäts Gesellschaft) in Germany, where it was known as the Rathenau Plan. So let's take a closer look at the Swope Plan.

THE SWOPE FAMILY

---

[376] See Appendix A for the full text.

The Swope family was of German origin. In 1857 Isaac Swope, a German immigrant, settled in St. Louis as a manufacturer of watch cases. Two of Swope's sons, Herbert Bayard Swope and Gerard Swope, subsequently rose to the peak of American enterprise. Herbert Bayard Swope was long-time editor of the New York *World*, a racetrack devotee, a close friend of Bernard Baruch, and used by FDR as an unofficial envoy during the New Deal period. Herbert's brother Gerard made his career with General Electric Company. Swope started as a helper on the factory floor in 1893, became a sales representative in 1899, manager of the St. Louis office in 1901, and director of the Western Electric Company in 1913. During World War I Swope was assistant director of purchase, storage, and traffic in the Federal government under General George W. Goethals and planned the U.S. Army procurement program. In 1919 Swope became the first president of the International General Electric Company. Successful promotion of G.E.'s foreign business brought him to the presidency of G.E. in 1922 to succeed Edwin Rice, Jr. Swope remained as G.E.'s president from 1922 until 1939.

General Electric was a Morgan-controlled company and always had one or two Morgan partners on its board, while Swope was also a director of other Wall Street enterprises, including International Power Securities Co. and the National City Bank.

Gerard Swope's political development began in the 1890s. Biographer David Loth reports that, soon after coming to Chicago, Swope was introduced to socialists Jane Addams, Ellen Gates Starr, and their Hull House Settlement. This interest in social affairs developed to culminate in the 1931 Swope plan for stabilization of industry, 90 per cent of which consisted of a scheme for workmen's compensation, life and disability insurance, old-age pensions, and unemployment protection. The Swope plan is an extraordinary document. One short paragraph removes all industry from the anti-trust laws—a long-time industrial goal—while numerous lengthy paragraphs detail proposed social plans. In sum, the Swope Plan was a transparent device to lay the groundwork for the corporate state by defusing potential labor opposition with a massive welfare carrot.

The Swope Plan and Bernard Baruch's earlier and similar proposal became the Roosevelt National Recovery Act. The Wall Street origins of NRA did not go unnoticed when the act was debated by Congress. Witness for example, the indignant, but not altogether accurate, outburst of Senator Huey P. Long:

> I come here now and I complain. I complain in the name of the people of my country, of the sovereign State I represent. I complain in the name of the people wherever else it may be known. I complain if it be true, as I am informed by Senators on this floor, that under this act Mr. Johnson, a former employee of Mr. Baruch, has been put in charge of the

administration of the act, and has already called as his aides the head of the Standard Oil Co., the head of General Motors, and the head of the General Electric Co.

I complain if Mr. Peek, who is an employee of Mr. Baruch, or has been, as I have been informed on the floor of the Senate, has been placed in charge of administering the Farm Act, however good a man he may be and whatever his ideas may be.

I complain if Mr. Brown, who, I am informed on the floor of the Senate, has been made an influential manipulator of the office of the Bureau of the Director of the Budget, has been an employee of Mr. Baruch, and is now given this authority. I complain because, on the 12th day of May 1932, before we went to Chicago to nominate a President of the United States, I stood in this very place on this floor and told the people of this country that we were not going to have the Baruch influence, at that time so potent with Hoover, manipulating the Democratic Party before nomination, after nomination, or after election.[377]

Huey Long was correct to point up the Wall Street dominance of NRA, but his identifications are a little haphazard. Hugh Johnson, long-time associate of Bernard Baruch, was indeed appointed head of NRA. Further, Johnson's principal assistants in NRA were three corporate heads: Walter C. Teagle, president of Standard Oil of New Jersey; Gerard Swope, president of General Electric and author of the Swope Plan; and Louis Kirstein, vice president of William Filene's Sons of Boston. As we have seen Filene was a long-time proponent of corporate socialism. The "head of General Motors" cited by Senator Long was Alfred P. Sloan, not related to NRA, but G.M. vice president John Raskob, who was the big fund raiser in 1928 and 1932 and behind-the-scenes operator promoting the election of Franklin D. Roosevelt in 1932. In other words, key positions in NRA and in the Roosevelt Administration itself were manned by men from Wall Street. The Public relations explanation for business men turned bureaucrats is that businessmen have the experience and should become involved in public service. The intent in practice has been to control industry. It should not, however, surprise us if the corporate socialists go to Washington D.C. after election of their favorite sons to take over the reins of monopoly administration. One would have to be naive to think it would be otherwise after the massive election investments recorded in Chapter 8.

Before President Roosevelt was inaugurated in March 1933, a so-called brain trust was more or less informally put to work on economic plans for the Roosevelt era. This group comprised General Hugh Johnson, Bernard Baruch (see p. 106 for his political contributions), Alexander Sachs of Lehman Brothers (see p. 117 for political contributions), Rexford G. Tugwell, and Raymond Moley. This small group, three from Wall Street and two academics, generated Roosevelt's economic planning.

---

[377] Senator Huey P. Long, Congressional Record, June 8, 1933, p. 5250.

This link between Bernard Baruch and NRA planning has been recorded by Charles Roos in his definitive volume on NRA:

> Early in March 1933 Johnson and Baruch started on a hunting trip and en route stopped in Washington. Moley had dinner with them and proposed that Johnson remain in Washington to draft a plan for industrial recovery... . The idea appealed to Baruch, and he promptly granted Johnson leave of absence from his regular duties. Then Johnson and Moley, after some study of the various proposals believed by the latter to have merit, proceeded to draw up a bill which would organize industry in an attack on the depression.[378]

According to Roos, Johnson's first NRA draft was on two sheets of foolscap paper and provided simply for suspension of the anti-trust laws, together with almost unlimited authority for President Roosevelt to do almost anything he wished with the economy, including licensing and control of industry. According to Roos, "It was, of course, rejected by the Administration, since it would have made the President a dictator, and such power was not desired."

This seemingly incidental rejection of unwanted dictatorial power by the Roosevelt administration may be of some significance. In Chapter 10 we will describe the Butler affair, an attempt by the same Wall Street interests to install Roosevelt as a dictator or replace him with a more pliant figurehead in case of his objection. Johnson's first draft attempts were to set up NRA in a form consistent with Roosevelt as an economic dictator, and its rejection by Roosevelt is consistent with serious charges laid at the feet of Wall Street (p. 141). At this point in the planning, according to Roos, Johnson and Moley were joined by Tugwell and later by Donald R. Richberg, a Chicago labor attorney. The three proceeded to draft a more "comprehensive" bill, whatever that meant.

General Hugh Johnson, was appointed head of the National Recovery Administration created under the title of the N.I.R.A. and believed for a while that he was also to head the Public Works Administration. The plans and diagrams drawn up by General Johnson and Alexander Sachs of Lehman Brothers assumed that the NRA head would also direct the public works program.

Consequently, we can find the roots of the NRA bill and the Public Works Administration in this small Wall Street group. Their effort reflects both the Swope and the Baruch plans for corporate socialism, with an initial attempt to provide for a corporate dictatorship in the United States.

---

[378] Charles F. Ross, NRA Economic Planning (Indianapolis: The Principia Press 1937), p. 37.

Socialist Planners of the 1930s

There were, of course, many other plans in the early 1930s; indeed, economic planning was endemic among the academics, politicians, and businessmen of this era. The weight of informed opinion considered economic planning essential to raise America from the depression. Those who doubted the efficacy and wisdom of economic planning were few and far between. Unfortunately, in the early 1930s no empiric experience existed to demonstrate that economic planning is inefficient, creates more problems than it solves, and leads to loss of individual freedom. To be sure, Ludwig von Mises had written Socialism and made his accurate predictions on the chaos of planning, but von Mises was even then an unknown economic theoretician. There is a mystical lure to economic planning. Its proponents always implicitly visualize themselves as the planners, and the anti capitalist psychology, so well described by von Mises, is the psychological pressure behind the scenes to make the plan come about. Even today in 1975, long after economic planning has been totally discredited, we still have the siren song of prosperity by planning. J. Kenneth Galbraith is one prominently vocal example, no doubt because Galbraith's personal estimate of his abilities and wisdom is greater than that of America at large. Galbraith recognizes that planning offers a means to exercise his assumed abilities to the full. The rest of us are to be coerced into the plan by the police power of the state: a negation of liberal principles perhaps, but logic was never a strong point among the economic engineers.

In any case, in the 1930s economic planning had many more enthusiastic proponents and far fewer critics than today. Almost everyone was a Galbraith, and the basic content of the plans proposed was notably similar to his. The table below lists the more prominent plans and their outstanding attributes. Industry, always anxious to find shelter from competition in the police power of the state, itself proposed three plans. The most important of these industry plans, the Swope plan, had compulsory features for all companies with more than 50 employees, combining continuous regulation with, as we have noted, extraordinarily costly welfare proposals. The Swope plan is reproduced in full as Appendix A; the full text reflects the lack of well thought-out administrative proposals and the preponderance of irresponsible give-away welfare features. The first few paragraphs of the plan give the core of Swope's proposals: trade associations, enforced by the state and with power of enforcement concentrated in the hands of major corporations through a system of industrial votes. While 90 per cent of the proposal text is devoted to give-away pensions for workers, unemployment insurance, life insurance and so on, the core is in the first few paragraphs. In brief, the Swope Plan was a carrot to get what Wall Street so earnestly desired: monopoly trade associations with the ability to use state power to enforce monopoly—Frederic Howe's maxim of "get society to work for you" in practice.

Economic Stabilization Plans: 1933

Name of Plan	Proposal for Industry	Government Regulation	Welfare Proposals
Industry Plans			
Swope Plan (General Electric)	Trade Associations, membership compulsory after three years for companies with 50 or more employees. Rulings mandatory	Continuous regulation by Federal Trade Commission	Life and disability insurance, pensions, and unemployment insurance
U.S. Chamber of Commerce Plan	National Economic Council; power not mandatory	No regulation	Individual corporation plans; public works planning
Associated General Contractors of America Plan	Grant by Congress of greater power to Federal Reserve Board. Bond issues to be authorized for revolving fund for construction; bond for increasing public and semipublic construction. Federal Reserve to guarantee solvency of banks	Financial regulation. Licensing of contractors. Establishment of construction credit bureaus	Stimulation of employment through greater building and construction activity. State bonds for public buildings; development of home loan bank
Labor Plans			
American Federation of Labor Plan	National Economic Council; power not mandatory	No regulation	Spread jobs; maintenance of wages; guarantees of jobs; long range stabilization plans. Five day week and shorter day immediately. Program of public building
Academic and General			
Stuart Chase Plan	Revival of War Industries Board using coercive, mandatory power, confined to 20 or 30 basic industries	Continuous regulation	National employment bureaus; reduction of hours; unemployment insurance; raising of wages; allocation of labor
National Civic Federation Plan	"Business Congress" of industrial organizations. No limitations or restrictions; full and complete power to fix prices or combine	Continuous regulation	Unemployment insurance plan. Raise wages

Beard Plan	National Economic Council," authorized by Congress, to coordinate finance, operation, distribution, and public service enterprises. Each industry governed by subsidiary syndicates	Continuous regulation	Use of unemployed on housing and public project programs

The U.S. Chamber of Commerce plan was similar to the Swope plan, but required only voluntary compliance with the code and did not embody the extensive welfare clauses of the Swope plan. The Chamber of Commerce plan was also based on voluntary compliance, not the coercive government regulation inherent in the Swope proposal.

The third industry plan was put forward by the Associated General Contractors of America. The AGC plan proposed that greater powers be granted the Federal Reserve System to guarantee banks bonds for public construction and, not surprisingly, establishment of special construction credit bureaus financed by the state, coupled with licensing of contractors. In brief, the AGC wanted to keep out competition and tap Federal (taxpayers') funds for promotion of the construction industry.

The American Federation of Labor plan proposed a National Economic Council to spread and guarantee jobs and embark on economic planning for stabilization. The unions did not push for government regulation.

The academic plans were notable in the sense that they supported industry objectives. Stuart Chase, a well-known socialist, came up with something very close to the Wall Street plans: in effect, a revival of Bernard Baruch's 1918 War Industries Board, with coercive power granted to industry, but confined to 20 or 30 basic industries, with continuous regulation. The Chase plan was an approximation of Italian fascism. The Beard plan also proposed syndicates along Italian lines, with continuous regulation and use of the unemployed in public programs á la Marx and The Communist Manifesto. The National Civic Federation advocated the total planning concept: full and complete power to fix prices and combinations, with state regulation and welfare features to appease labor.

Almost no one, except of course Ludwig von Mises, pointed to the roots of the problem to draw the logical conclusion from economic history that the best economic planning is no economic planning.[379]

SOCIALISTS GREET THE SWOPE PLAN

---

[379] Should the reader wish to pursue the explanation for this pervasive inability to see the obvious, he could start in no better place than Ludwig von Mises, The Anti-Capitalistic Mentality (New York; Van Nostrand, 1956).

Orthodox socialists greeted Swope's plan with a curious, if perhaps understandable, restraint. On the one hand, said the socialists, Swope had recognized the evils of unrestrained capitalism. On the other hand the Swope system, complained the socialists, would leave control of industry in the hands of industry itself rather than to the state. As Norman Thomas explained:

> Mr. Swope's scheme of regulation is a probably unconstitutional plan for putting the power of government behind the formation of strong capitalist syndicates which will seek to control the government which regulates them and, failing that, will fight it.[380]

Socialist criticism of General Electric's Swope did not consider whether the Swope system would work or had operational efficiency or how it proposed to work; orthodox socialist criticism was limited to the observation that control would be in the wrong hands if industry took over and not in the right hands of the government planners, that is, the socialists themselves. In sum, the dispute was over who was going to control the economy: Mr. Gerard Swope or Mr. Norman Thomas.

Consequently, the Thomas criticism of Swope has a curious duality, sometimes praiseful:

> Certainly it is significant that at least one of our authentic captains of industry, one of the real rulers of America, has overcome the profound and bewildered reluctance of the high and mighty to go beyond the sorriest platitudes in telling us how to break the depression they did so much to cause and so little to avert. Obviously Mr. Swope's speech had its good points...[381]

At other times Thomas is skeptical and points out that Swope, "... no longer trusts individual initiative, competition and the automatic working of markets," but proposes to gear the system to the benefit of "the stockholding class."

There is no evidence that Gerard Swope and his associates ever trusted individual initiative, competition, and free markets any more than did Norman Thomas. This is an important observation because, once we abandon the myths of all capitalists as entrepreneurs and all liberal planners as saviors of the little man, we see them both for what they are: totalitarians and the opponents of individual liberty. The only difference between them is who is to be the director.

---

[380] "A Socialist Looks at the Swope Plan," The Nation, Oct. 7, 1931, p. 358.
[381] Ibid., p. 357.

The Tree Musketeers of NRA

The National Recovery Administration, most important segment of the New Deal, was then designed, constructed, and promoted by Wall Street. In essence, the NRA originated with Bernard Baruch and his long-time assistant General Johnson. In detail, NRA was the Swope Plan, and its general principles were promoted over the years by numerous prominent Wall Streeters.

There were, of course, planning variants from the socialists and Marxist-influenced planners, but these variants were not the versions that finally became NRA. NRA was essentially fascist in that industry, not central state planners, had the authority to plan, and these industrial planners came from the New York financial establishment. Bernard Baruch's office was at 120 Broadway; the offices of Franklin D. Roosevelt (the New York offices of Fidelity & Deposit and the law offices of Roosevelt & O'Connor) were also at 120 Broadway. Gerard Swope's office and the executive offices of General Electric Company were at the same address. We can therefore say in a limited sense that the Roosevelt NRA was born at 120 Broadway, New York City.

General Hugh Johnson had three principal assistants in NRA, and "these three musketeers were on the job longer and they walked in and out of my office whenever they discovered anything that needed attention."[382] The three assistants were Wall Streeters from major industries who themselves held prominent positions in major firms in these industries: Gerard Swope, president of General Electric, Walter C. Teagle, of Standard Oil of New Jersey, and Louis Kirstein of William Filene's Sons, the retail merchants. Through this trio, a dominant element of big business was in control at the very peak of NRA. This concentration of control explains the thousands of complaints of NRA oppression that came from medium and small businessmen.

Who were these men? As we have noted, Gerard Swope of General Electric had been assistant to General Johnson in the War Industries Board of World War I. While NRA was under discussion, Johnson "suggested his name to Secretary Roper at once." General Electric was in 1930 the largest of the electrical equipment manufacturers, with Westinghouse holding many of the basic patents in the field, as well as a large interest in RCA and many international subsidiaries and affiliates. In the late 1920s G.E. and Westinghouse produced about three quarters of the basic equipment for distributing and generating electric power in the U.S. General Electric, however was the dominant firm in the electrical equipment industry.[383] Under NRA the National Electrical Manufacturers Association (NEMA) was

---

[382] Hugh S. Johnson, The Blue Eagle from Egg to Earth, op. cit., p. 217.
[383] For more information see Harry W. Laidler, Concentration of Control in American Industry (New York: Crowell, 1931), Chapter XV.

designated as the agency for supervising and administering the electrical industry code. NEMA moved promptly and by July 1933 presented the second code of "fair competition" for the President's signature.

Johnson's second musketeer was Walter Teagle, chairman of the board of the Standard Oil of New Jersey. Standard of New Jersey was the biggest integrated oil company in the U.S., and only Royal Dutch challenged it in international sales. Jersey Standard was controlled by the Rockefeller family, whose holdings in the early 1930s have been estimated at between 20 and 25 per cent.[384] One might therefore say that Teagle represented the Rockefeller interests in NRA, whereas Swope represented the Morgan interests. It is interesting to note in passing that the largest Standard competitor was Gulf Oil, controlled by the Mellon interests, and there were persistent efforts early in the Roosevelt administration to prosecute Mellon for tax evasion.

The third of Johnson's three musketeers at NRA was Louis Kirstein, vice president of Filene's of Boston. Edward Filene is notable for his books on the advantages of trade associations, fair competition, and cooperation (see page 81 below).

The peak of the Roosevelt National Recovery Administration consisted of the president of the largest electrical corporation, the chairman of the largest oil company, and the representative of the most prominent financial speculator in the United States.

In brief, the administration of NRA was a reflection of the New York financial establishment and its pecuniary interests. Further, as we have seen, since the plan itself originated in Wall Street, the presence of businessmen in the administration of NRA cannot be explained on the basis of their experience and administrative ability. NRA was a creature of Wall Street implemented by Wall Streeters.

THE OPPRESSION OF SMALL BUSINESS

The proponents of the National Industrial Recovery Act made a great show that NRA would protect the small businessman who, it was alleged, had suffered in the past from unfair application of the anti-trust laws; the suspension of the anti-trust laws would remove their more unwelcome features, while NRA would preserve their welcome antimonopoly provisions. Senator Wagner stated that all industry would formulate the proposed industrial codes, not just big business. Senator Borah, on the contrary, contended that "monopoly" was about to receive a service it had coveted for over 25 years, that is, "the death of the antitrust laws" and that the NRA industrial codes "are going to be combinations or contracts in restraint of trade, or it would not be necessary to suspend the antitrust laws." Senator

---

[384] Ibid., p. 20.

Borah also pointedly accused Senator Wagner of betraying the legitimate businessman for the sake of Wall Street:

> The elder Rockefeller did not need any criminal law to aid him when he was building up his wealth. He destroyed the independents everywhere; he scattered them to the four winds; he concentrated his great power. But the Senator would not only give to the combines all the power to write their code, but would give them the power to indict and prosecute the man who violated the code, although he might be pursuing a perfectly legitimate business. Mr. President, I do not care how much we strengthen, how much we build up, how much we buttress the antitrust law; I object to a suspension in any respect whatever, because I know that when those laws are suspended, we give these 200 non banking corporations, which control the wealth of the United States, a stupendous power, which can never be controlled except through the criminal laws enforced by the courts.[385]

Senator Borah then cited Adam Smith (see p. 99) to effect, pointing out that no definition of fair competition was in the bill and that codes of fair competition would degenerate into the dictates of the major corporations. Similarly, Senator Gore pointed to the possibility that the President could require all members of an industry to be licensed and that this meant that the President could revoke a license at his pleasure, an obvious infringement on due process of law and basic property rights:

> SENATOR GORE. Could the President revoke that license at this pleasure?
> SENATOR WAGNER. Yes, for a violation of the code imposed by the Federal Government.
> SENATOR GORE. On what sort of hearing?
> SENATOR WAGNER. After a hearing. It is provided that a hearing may be had, before a license can be revoked.
> SENATOR GORE. That is something that really affects the life and death of a particular industry or enterprise, if he has the power to revoke the license.
> SENATOR WAGNER. Yes; it is a sanction.
> SENATOR GORE. What I wanted to ask you. Senator, is this: Do you think you could place that power in the hands of an executive officer?
> SENATOR WAGNER. I do, in the case of an emergency.
> SENATOR GORE. To exterminate an industry?
> SENATOR WAGNER. All of these powers, of course, are lodged in one individual, and we have just got to rely upon him to administer it fairly and justly. We had the same sort of power during the war.
> SENATOR GORE. I know that, and Mr. Hoover, if I may use these words, put free-born American citizens out of business without trial by jury.

---

[385] Congressional Record, 1933, p. 5165.

SENATOR WAGNER. The philosophy of this bill is to encourage voluntary action and initiative on the part of industry, and I doubt whether or not these compulsory methods will be used at all except on very rare occasions; but if you are going to lift the standard, you have got to have some sanctions in order to enforce the code that may be adopted.

SENATOR GORE. I understand, but if you are going to carry out this system you have to have power to carry it out. My point is why in a free country a free man ought to be required to take out a license to engage in legitimate industry, and why somebody under our constitutional system should be given the power to destroy the value of his property, which you do when you bring about a situation where he cannot operate. That seems to me approaching the point of taking property without due process of law.[386]

When we examine the results of the N.I.R.A., even a few short months after passage of the bill, we find that these Senatorial fears were fully justified and that President Roosevelt had abandoned the small businessman of the United States to the control of Wall Street. Many industries were dominated by a few major firms, in turn under control of Wall Street investment houses. These major firms were dominant, through the three musketeers, in establishing the NRA codes. They had the most votes and could and did set prices and conditions ruinous to smaller firms.

The iron and steel industry is a good example of the manner in which large firms dominated the NRA code. In the 1930s two leading companies, United States Steel, with 39 per cent, and Bethlehem Steel, with 13.6 per cent, controlled over half of the country's steel ingot capacity. The board of U.S. Steel included J.P. Morgan and Thomas W. Lamont, as well as chairman Myron C. Taylor. The board of Bethlehem included Percy A. Rockefeller and Grayson M-P. Murphy of Guaranty Trust, whom we shall meet again in Chapter 10.

In 1930 the largest stockholders of U.S. Steel were George F. Baker and George F. Baker, Jr., with combined shares of 2000 preferred and 107,000 common; Myron C. Taylor head of the Finance Committee of U.S. Steel owned 27,800 shares of common; J. P. Morgan held 1261 shares; and James A. Farrell had title to 4850 shares of preferred stock. These men were also substantial Presidential campaign contributors. For example, in Hoover's 1928 campaign they contributed

J.P. Morgan	$5,000
J.P. Morgan Company	$42,500
George F. Baker	$27,000
George F. Baker Jr	$20,000

---

[386] United States Senate, National Industrial Recovery, Hearings before Committee on Finance, 73rd Congress, 1st Session, S.17 and H.R. 5755 (Washington: Government Printing Office, 1933), p. 5.

Myron C. Taylor............................$25,000

In the NRA, we find that U.S. Steel and Bethlehem Steel effectively controlled the whole industry by virtue of their votes in the industrial codes; of a total of 1428 votes, these two companies alone were allowed a total of 671 votes, or 47.2 per cent, perilously close to outright control and with undoubted ability to find an ally among the smaller but still significant companies.

NRA-Voting Strength in the Iron and Steel Industry Code

Company[387]	Votes in Code Authority	Percentage of Total
U.S. Steel	511	36.0
Bethlehem Steel	160	11.2
Republic Steel	86	6.0
National Steel	81	5.7
Jones and Laughlin	79	5.5
Youngstown Sheet & Tube	74	5.1
Wheeling Steel	73	5.1
American Rolling Mill	69	4.8
Inland Steel	51	3.6
Crucible Steel	38	2.7
McKeesport Tin Plate	27	1.9
Allegheny Steel	21	1.5
Spang-Chalfant	17	1.2
Sharon Steel Hoop	16	1.1
Continental Steel	16	1.1

Source: NRA Report Operation of the Basing Point System in the Iron and Steel Industry.

Although U.S. Steel and Bethlehem were the major units in the iron and steel industry before passage of the NRA, they were unable to control competition from numerous smaller firms. After the passage of NIRA, these two firms were able, through their dominance of the code system, also to dominate the iron and steel industry.

John D. Rockefeller organized the Standard Oil trust in 1882 but, as a result of court orders under the Sherman Act, the cartel was dissolved into 33 independent companies. In

---

[387] In addition, the following smaller firms had votes: Acme Steel (9), Granite City Steel (8), Babcock and Wilcox (8), Alan Wood (7), Washburn Wire (7), Interlake Iron (7), Follansbee Bros. (6), Ludlum Steel (6), Superior Steel (6), Bliss and Laughlin (6), Laclede Steel (5), Apollo Steel (5), Atlantic Steel (4), Central Iron and Steel (4), A.M. Byers Company (4), Sloss-Sheffield (4), Woodward Iron (3), Firth-Sterling (2), Davison Coke and Iron (2), Soullin Steel (1), Harrisburg Pipe (1), Eastern Rolling Mill (1), Michigan Steel Tube (1), Milton Manufacturing Company (1), and Cranberry Furnace (1).

1933 these companies were still controlled by the Rockefeller family interests; the Sherman Act was more shadow than substance:

Company	Net income (1930) in Million $$
Standard Oil of New Jersey	57
Standard Oil of Indiana	46
Standard Oil of California	46
Standard Oil of New York	16

Offices of the "independent" Standard companies continued to be located at Rockefeller headquarters, at this time at 25 and 26 Broadway. During the 1920s new capital entered, and there was a relative shift in the importance of the various Standard Oil companies.

By the time of the New Deal the largest single unit was Standard Oil of New Jersey, in which the Rockefeller interests held a 20 to 25 per cent interest. The president of New Jersey Standard, Walter S. Teagle, became one of the three musketeers of NRA.

When we look at the auto industry in 1930 we find that two companies, Ford and General Motors, sold about three quarters of the cars produced in the United States. If we include Chrysler, the three companies sold about five sixths of all U.S. automobiles produced:

Ford Motor Co......................................40 percent
General Motors..................................35 percent
Chrysler Corp.......................................8 percent

Under its founder, Henry Ford, the Ford Motor Company had little use for politics, although James Couzens, one of the original Ford stockholders, later became Senator from Michigan. Ford maintained its executive offices in Dearborn, Michigan and only a sales office in New York. Ford was also vehemently anti-NRA and anti-Wall Street, and Henry Ford is notable by reason of his absence from the lists of contributors to Presidential campaigns.

On the other hand, General Motors was a creature of Wall Street. The firm was controlled by the J.P. Morgan firm; the chairman of the board was Pierre S. Du Pont, of the Du Pont Company, which in 1933 had about a 25 per cent interest in General Motors. In 1930 the General Motors board comprised Junius S. Morgan, Jr. and George Whitney of the Morgan firm; directors from the First National Bank and Bankers Trust; seven directors from Du Pont; and Owen D. Young of General Electric.

Another example is the International Harvester Company, in 1930 under its president Alexander Legge the giant of the agricultural equipment industry. Legge was part of the

NRA. The agricultural equipment combination was formed in 1920 by the J.P. Morgan Company and controlled about 85 per cent of the total production of harvesting machines in the United States. In 1930, the firm was still dominant in the industry:

Company	Assets	Percentage of Market
International Harvester (11 Broadway)	$384 millions (1929)	60
Deere & Co.	$107	17
J.I. Case	$55	8
Others	$100	15
Total	$646 millions	100

In 1930 at least 80 large companies were mining bituminous coal in the United States; of these, two—Pittsburgh Coal and Consolidation Coal—were dominant. Pittsburgh Coal was under control of the Pittsburgh banking family, the Mellons. Consolidation Coal was largely owned by J.D. Rockefeller, who owned 72 per cent of the preferred and 28 per cent of the common stock. Both the Mellons and the Rockefellers were heavy political contributors. Similarly, anthracite production was concentrated in the hands of the Reading Railroad, which mined 44 per cent of U.S. hard coal. Reading was controlled by the Baltimore and Ohio Railroad, which held 66 per cent of its stock, and the chairman of B & O was E.T. Stotesbury, a partner in the Morgan firm.

When we look at machine-building firms in the United States in 1930, we find that the largest by far was General Electric—and president Swope of G.E. was intimately connected with NRA.

Major Machine Building Firms (1929)

Firm	Assets in Millions	Profits (1929) in Millions	Sales (1929) in Millions
General Electric, 120 Broadway	$500	$71	$415.3
American Radiator & Standard Sanitary, 40 W. 40th St.	$226	$20	
Westinghouse Electric, 150 Broadway	$225	$27	$216.3
Baldwin Locomotive, 120 Broadway	$100	$3	$40
American Locomotive, 30 Church St.	$106	$7	
American Car & Foundry, 30 Church St.	$120	$2.7	
International Business Machines, 50 Broadway	$40	$6.7	
Otis Elevator, 260 11th Avenue	$57	$8	
Crane Company	$116	$11.5	

As we glance down the list we note that American Car & Foundry (whose president, Woodin, became Secretary of the Treasury under Roosevelt), American Radiator & Standard, and Crane Company were all prominent contributors to FDR.

Given this dominant influence of large firms in the NRA and the Roosevelt administration, it is not surprising that NRA was administered in a manner oppressive to small business. Even in the brief life of NRA, until it was declared unconstitutional, we find evidence of oppression: witness the complaints by small business in the industries we have discussed compared to other industries in small business with many more units:

Industry	Numbers of Complaints of Oppression (January-April 1934)
Major Industry	
Iron and Steel	66
Investment Banking	47
Petroleum	60
Electrical Manufacturing	9
Small Business	
Cleaning and Dyeing	31
Ice	12
Printing	22
Boot and Shoes	10
Laundry	9

Source: Roos, NRA Economic Planning, p. 411, from unpublished NRA data.

CHAPTER 10

FDR, MAN ON THE WHITE HORSE

> *In the last few weeks of the committee's official life it received evidence showing that certain persons had made an attempt to establish a fascist organization in this country. There is no question that these attempts were discussed, were planned, and might have been placed in execution when and if the financial backers deemed it expedient....*
>
> *This committee received evidence from Maj. Gen. Smedley D. Butler (retired), twice decorated by the Congress of the United States ... your committee was able to verify all the pertinent statements made by General Butler....*
>
> John W. McCormack, Chairman, Special Committee on Un-American Activities, House of Representatives, February 15, 1935.

Just before Christmas 1934, news of a bizarre plot to install a dictator in the White House surfaced in Washington and New York, and the story—one of unparalleled significance— was promptly smothered by Congress and the establishment press.[388]

On November 21, 1934 *The New York Times* printed the first portion of the Butler story as told to the House Un-American Activities Committee, giving it front-page treatment and an intriguing lead paragraph:

> A plot of Wall Street interests to overthrow President Roosevelt and establish a fascist dictatorship, backed by a private army of 500,000 ex- soldiers and others, was charged by Major Gen. Smedley D. Butler, retired Marine Corps officer...

---

[388] See Jules Archer, The Plot to Seize the White House (New York: Hawthorn Books, 1973) Archer's book is "the first effort to tell the whole story of the plot in sequence and full detail." Also see George Wolfskill, The Revolt of the Conservatives (Boston: Houghton, Mifflin, 1962), which has extensive material on the plot. The interested reader should also take a look at George Seldes, One Thousand Americans (New York: Honi & Gaer, 1947).

Unfortunately, while these books have kept the event alive—a valiant effort that should by no means be underrated— they do reflect an amteurish confusion of fascism with moderation. Supporters of the Constitution would, of course, absolutely reject the dictatorial efforts described. Some groups, such as the American Conservative Union for instance, have for a decade aimed their attacks at the targets identified by Archer and Seldes. The misinterpretation by the latter authors is accentuated because confusion over the meaning of conservatism also prevented these authors from exploring the possibility that Wall Street had none other than Franklin Delano Roosevelt in mind as "the man on the white horse."

The New York Times report added that General Butler, "... had told friends ... that General Hugh S. Johnson, former NRA administrator, was scheduled for the role of dictator, and J.P. Morgan & Co. as well as Murphy & Co. were behind the plot."

After this promising opening, *The New York Times* reporting gradually faded away and finally disappeared. Fortunately, enough information has since surfaced to demonstrate that the Butler Affair or the Plot to Seize the White House is an integral part of our story of FDR and Wall Street.

GRAYSON M-P. MURPHY COMPANY, 52 BROADWAY

The central figure in the plot was Major General Smedley Darlington Butler, a colorful, popular, widely known Marine Corps officer, twice decorated with the Congressional Medal of Honor and a veteran of 33 years of military service. General Butler testified in 1934 to the McCormack-Dickstein Committee investigating Nazi and Communist activities in the United States that a plan for a White House dictatorship was outlined to him by two members of the American Legion: Gerald C. MacGuire, who worked for Grayson M-P. Murphy & Co., 52 Broadway, New York City, and Bill Doyle, whom Butler identified as an officer of the American Legion. General Butler testified that these men wanted to "unseat the Royal Family in control of the American Legion at the Convention to be held in Chicago, and [were] very anxious to have me take part in it." A scheme was outlined to General Butler: he was to come before the convention as a legion delegate from Honolulu; there would be two or three hundred American Legion members in the audience; and "these planted fellows were to begin to cheer and start a stampede and yell for a speech, then I was to go to the platform and make a speech."

The prepared speech was to be written by Morgan associate John W. Davis. To prove his Wall Street financial backing, MacGuire showed General Butler a bank book listing deposits of $42,000 and $64,000 and mentioned that their source was Grayson M-P. Murphy, director of Guaranty Trust Company and other Morgan-controlled companies. A millionaire banker, Robert S. Clark, with offices in the Stock Exchange Building at 11 Wall Street, was also involved.

Robert Clark was incidentally known to General Butler from his China campaign days. MacGuire and Doyle also offered Butler a substantial sum to make a similar speech before the convention of the Veterans of Foreign Wars at Miami Beach. According to MacGuire, his group had investigated the background of Mussolini and Italian fascism, Hitler's organization in Germany, and the Croix de Feu in France and hinted that it was time to establish a similar organization in the United States. General Butler testified to the Congressional committee about MacGuire's statement in the following words:

He said, "The time has come now to get the soldiers together."
"Yes," I said, "I think so, too." He said, "I went abroad to study the part that the veteran plays in the various set-ups of the governments that they have abroad. I went to Italy for 2 or 3 months and studied the position that the veterans of Italy occupy in the Fascist set-up of Government, and I discovered that they are the background of Mussolini. They keep them on the pay rolls in various ways and keep them contented and happy; and they are his real backbone, the force on which he may depend, in case of trouble, to sustain him. But that set-up would not suit us at all. The soldiers of America would not like that. I then went to Germany to see what Hitler was doing, and his whole strength lies in organizations of soldiers, too. But that would not do. I looked into the Russian business. I found that the use of the soldiers over there would never appeal to our men. Then I went to France, and I found just exactly the organization we are going to have. It is an organization of super soldiers." He gave me the French name for it, but I do not recall what it is. I never could have pronounced it, anyhow. But I do know that it is a super organization of members of all the other soldiers' organizations of France, composed of noncommissioned officers and officers. He told me that they had about 500,000 and that each one was a leader of 10 others, so that it gave them 5,000,000 votes. And he said, "Now, that is our idea here in America—to get up an organization of that kind."[389]

What would be the objective of this super organization? According to the previously cited *New York Times*[390], General Butler is reported to have testified that the affair was an attempted *coup d'etat* to overthrow President Roosevelt and replace him with a fascist dictator. This interpretation is repeated by Archer, Seldes, and other writers. However, this was not the accusation made by General Butler to the committee. Butler's precise statement concerning the projected organization, the use to which it was to be put when established, and the role of President Roosevelt is as follows; General Butler reported on his conversation with MacGuire:

I said, "What do you want to do with it when you get it up?"
"Well," he said, "we want to support the President."
I said, "The President does not need the support of that kind of an organization. Since when did you become a supporter of the President? The last time I talked to you you were against him."
He said, "Well, he is going to go along with us now."
"Is he?"
"Yes."

---

[389] House of Representatives, Investigation of Nazi Propaganda Activities and Investigation of Certain Other Propaganda Activities, Hearings No. 73-D.C.-6, op. cit., p. 17.
[390] The New York Times, Nov. 21, 1934.

"Well, what are you going to do with these men, suppose you get these 500,000 men in America? What are you going to do with them?"

"Well," he said, "they will be the support of the President."

I said, "The President has got the whole American people. Why does he want them?"

He said, "Don't you understand the set-up has got to be changed a bit? Now, we have got him—we have got the President. He has got to have more money. There is not any more money to give him. Eighty percent of the money now is in Government bonds, and he cannot keep this racket up much longer. He has got to do something about it. He has either got to get more money out of us or he has got to change the method of financing the Government, and we are going to see to it that he does not change that method. He will not change it."

I said, "The idea of this great group of soldiers, then, is to sort of frighten him, is it?"

"No, no, no; not to frighten him. This is to sustain him when others assault him."

I said, "Well I do not know about that. How would the President explain it?"

He said: "He will not necessarily have to explain it, because we are going to help him out. Now, did it ever occur to you that the President is overworked? We might have an Assistant President, somebody to take the blame; and if things do not work out, he can drop him."

He went on to say that it did not take any constitutional change to authorize another Cabinet official, somebody to take over the details of the office— take them off the President's shoulders. He mentioned that the position would be a secretary of general affairs—a sort of super secretary.

CHAIRMAN [Congressman McCormack]. A secretary of general affairs?

BUTLER. That is the term used by him—or a secretary of general welfare—I cannot recall which. I came out of the interview with that name in my head. I got that idea from talking to both of them, you see. They had both talked about the same kind of relief that ought to be given the President, and he said: "You know, the American people will swallow that. We have got the newspapers. We will start a campaign that the President's health is failing. Everybody can tell that by looking at him, and the dumb American people will fall for it in a second."

And I could see it. They had that sympathy racket, that they were going to have somebody take the patronage off of his shoulders and take all the worries and details off of his shoulders, and then he will be like the President of France.

I said, "So that is where you got this idea?"

He said: "I have been traveling around looking around. Now, about this super organization—would you be interested in heading it?"

I said, "I am interested in it, but I do not know about heading it. I am very greatly interested in it, because you know. Jerry, my interest is, my one hobby is, maintaining a democracy. If you get these 500,000 soldiers advocating anything smelling of Fascism, I am going to get 500,000 more and lick the hell out of you, and we will have a real war right at home. You know that."

"Oh, no. We do not want that. We want to ease up on the President."

"Yes; and then you will put somebody in there you can run; is that the idea? The President will go around and christen babies and dedicate bridges, and kiss children. Mr. Roosevelt will never agree to that himself."

"Oh yes; he will. He will agree to that."[391]

In other words, the Wall Street plot was not to dispose of President Roosevelt at all, but to kick him upstairs and install an Assistant President with absolute powers. Just why it was necessary to go to the trouble of installing an Assistant President is unclear because the Vice President was in office. In any event, it was planned to run the United States with a Secretary of General Affairs, and the gullible American public would accept this under the guise of necessary protection from a communist take-over.

At this point it is interesting to recall the role of many of these same financiers and financial firms in the Bolshevik Revolution—a role, incidentally, that could not have been known to General Butler[392] —and the use of similar Red scare tactics in the 1922 United Americans organization. Grayson M-P. Murphy was, in the early 1930s, a director of several companies controlled by the J.P. Morgan interests, including the Guaranty Trust Company, prominent in the Bolshevik Revolution, the New York Trust Company, and Bethlehem Steel, and was on the board of Inspiration Copper Company, National Aviation Corporation, Intercontinental Rubber Co., and U.S. & Foreign Securities. John W. Davis, the speech writer for General Butler, was a partner in Davis, Polk, Wardwell, Gardner & Reed of 15 Broad Street. Both Polk and Wardwell of this prestigious law firm, as well as Grayson Murphy, had roles in the Bolshevik Revolution. Further, Davis was also a co-director with Murphy in the Morgan-controlled Guaranty Trust Co. and a co director with Presidential hopeful Al Smith in the Metropolitan Life Insurance Co., as well as director of the Mutual Life Insurance Co., the U.S. Rubber Co., and American Telephone and Telegraph, the controlling unit of the Bell System.

Fortunately for history. General Butler discussed the offer with an impartial newspaper source at a very early point in his talks with MacGuire and Doyle. The McCormack- Dickstein Committee heard testimony under oath from this confidant, Paul Comley French. French confirmed the facts that he was a reporter for *The Philadelphia Record* and the *The New York Evening Post* and that General Butler had told him about the plot in September 1934.

---

[391] House of Representatives, Investigation of Nazi Propaganda Activities and Investigation of Certain Other Propaganda Activities, Hearings No. 73-D.C.-6, op. cit., pp. 17-18.
[392] See Sutton, Bolshevik Revolution, op. cit.

Subsequently, on September 13, 1934 French went to New York and met with MacGuire. The following is part of French's statement to the Committee:

> MR. FRENCH. [I saw] Gerald P. MacGuire in the offices of Grayson M.-P. Murphy & Co., the twelfth floor of 52 Broadway, shortly after 1 o'clock in the afternoon. He has a small private office there and I went into his office. I have here some direct quotes from him. As soon as I left his office I got to a typewriter and made a memorandum of everything that he told me. "We need a Fascist government in this country," he insisted, "to save the Nation from the communists who want to tear it down and wreck all that we have built in America. The only men who have the, patriotism to do it are the soldiers and Smedley Butler is the ideal leader. He could organize a million men over night." During the conversation he told me he had been in Italy and Germany during the summer of 1934 and the spring of 1934 and had made an intensive study of the background of the Nazi and Fascist movements and how the veterans had played a part in them. He said he had obtained enough information on the Fascist and Nazi movements and of the part played by the veterans, to properly set up one in this country.
>
> He emphasized throughout his conversation with me that the whole thing was tremendously patriotic, that it was saving the Nation from communists, and that the men they deal with have that crackbrained idea that the Communists are going to take it apart. He said the only safeguard would be the soldiers. At first he suggested that the General organize this outfit himself and ask a dollar a year dues from everybody. We discussed that, and then he came around to the point of getting outside financial funds, and he said that it would not be any trouble to raise a million dollars.
>
> During the course of the conversation he continually discussed the need of a man on a white horse, as he called it, a dictator who would come galloping in on his white horse. He said that was the only way; either through the threat of armed force or the delegation of power, and the use of a group of organized veterans, to save the capitalistic system.
>
> He warmed up considerably after we got under way and he said, "We might go along with Roosevelt, and then do with him what Mussolini did with the King of Italy." It fits in with what he told the general [Butler], that we would have a Secretary of General Affairs, and if Roosevelt played ball, swell; and if he did not, they would push him out.[393]

ACKSON MARTINDELL, 14 WALL STREET

The sworn testimony of General Smedley Butler and Paul French in the committee hearings has a persistent thread. General Butler rambled from time to time, and some parts of his statement are vague, but there is obviously a lot more to the story than an innocent

---

[393] House of Representatives, Investigation of Nazi Propaganda Activities and Investigation of Certain Other Propaganda Activities, Hearings No. 73-D.C.-6, op. cit., p. 26.

gathering of American Legion members into a super organization. Is there any independent evidence to confirm General Butler and Paul French? Unknown to both Butler and French, Guaranty Trust had been involved in Wall Street maneuverings in the Bolshevik Revolution in 1917, so indicating at least a predisposition to mix financial business with dictatorial politics; two of the persons involved in the plot were directors of Guaranty Trust. Also, before the hearings were abruptly halted, the committee heard evidence from an independent source, which confirmed many details recounted by General Butler and Paul French. In December 1934 Captain Samuel Glazier, Commanding Officer of the CCC Camp at Elkridge, Maryland[394], was called before the committee.

On October 2, 1934, testified Captain Glazier, he had received a letter from A.P. Sullivan, Assistant Adjutant General of the U.S. Army, introducing a Mr. Jackson Martindell, "who will be shown every courtesy by you." This letter was sent to Glazier by command of Major General Malone of the U.S. Army. Who was Jackson Martindell? He was a financial counsel with offices at 14 Wall Street, previously associated with Stone & Webster & Blodget, Inc., investment bankers of 120 Broadway, and with Carter, Martindell & Co., investment bankers at 115 Broadway.[395] Martindell was a man of substance, living according to The New York Times, "... in the centre of a beautiful sixty acre estate" that he had bought from Charles Pfizer[396], and was sufficiently influential for General Malone to arrange a conducted tour of the Elkridge, Maryland Conservation Corps Camp.

Martindell's association with Stone & Webster (120 Broadway) is significant and by itself warrants a follow-up on his associates in the Wall Street area.

Captain Glazier provided Martindell with the requested camp tour and testified to the committee that Martindell posed numerous questions about a similar camp for men to work in industry rather than in forests. A week or so after the visit. Captain Glazier visited Martindell's New Jersey home, learned that he was a personal friend of General Malone, and was informed that Martindell wanted to organize camps similar to the CCC to train 500,000 young men. The overtones of this talk, as reported by Glazier, were anti-semitic and suggested an attempted coup d'etat in the United States; the organization sponsoring this overthrow was called American Vigilantes, whose emblem was a flag with a red eagle on a blue background in lieu of the German swastika. This was in part an independent verification of General Butler's testimony.

---

[394] Ibid., Parts 1-2. Based on Testimony before the McCormack-Dickstein Committee.
[395] 120 Broadway is the topic of a chapter in this book and a previous book, Sutton, Bolshevik Revolution, op. cit. Stone & Webster is also prominent in the earlier book.
[396] The New York Times, Dec. 28, 1934.

GERALD C. MACGUIRE'S TESTIMONY

Gerald MacGuire, one of the accused plotters, was called before the committee and testified at length under oath. He stated that he met General Butler in 1933 and that his reasons for visiting Butler were, (1) to discuss the Committee for a Sound Dollar and (2) that he thought Butler would be a "fine man to be commander of the Legion."

MacGuire admitted that he had told General Butler that he was a member of the distinguished guest committee of the American Legion; he had a "hazy recollection" that millionaire Robert S. Clark had talked to Butler, but "denied emphatically" making arrangements for Clark to meet Butler. MacGuire admitted sending Butler postcards from Europe, that he had had a conversation with the general at the Bellevue-Stratford Hotel, and that he had told Butler that he was going to the convention in Miami. However, when asked whether he had told Butler about the role veterans played in European governments, he replied that he had not, although he stated that he had told Butler that in his opinion "Hitler would not last another year in Germany and that Mussolini was on the skids."[397]

MacGuire's testimony on his meeting with French differed substantially from French's account:

> QUESTION. Now, what did Mr. French call to see you about, Mr. MacGuire?
> ANSWER. He called, according to Mr. French's story, to meet me, and to make my acquaintance, because I had known General Butler, and I was a friend of his, and he wanted to know me, and that was mainly the object of his visit.
> QUESTION. Nothing else discussed?
> ANSWER. A number of things discussed; yes. The position of the bond market, the stock market; what I thought was a good buy right now; what he could buy if he had seven or eight hundred dollars; the position of the country; the prospects for recovery, and various topics that any two men would discuss if they came together.
> QUESTION. Nothing else?
> ANSWER. Nothing else, excepting this, Mr. Chairman: As I said yesterday, I believe, when Mr. French came to me, he said. General Butler is, or has, again been approached by two or three organizations—and I think he mentioned one of them as some Vigilante committee of this country— and he said, "What do you think of it?" and I think I said to him, "Why, I don't think the General ought to get mixed up with any of those affairs in this country. I think these fellows are all trying to use him; to use his name for publicity purposes, and to get membership, and I think he ought to keep away from any of these organizations."

---

[397] House of Representatives, Investigation of Nazi Propaganda Activities and Investigation of Certain Other Propaganda Activities, Hearings No. 73-D.C.-6, op. cit., p. 45.

QUESTION. Nothing else?
ANSWER. Nothing else. That was the gist of the entire conversation.[398]

MacGuire further testified that he worked for Grayson Murphy and that Robert S. Clark had put up $300,000 to form the Committee for a Sound Dollar.

The McCormack-Dickstein Committee was able to confirm the fact that Robert Sterling Clark transmitted money to MacGuire for political purposes:

> He [MacGuire] further testified that this money was given him by Mr. Clark long after the Chicago Convention of the Legion, and that he had also received from Walter E. Frew of the Corn Exchange Bank & Trust Co. the sum of $1,000, which was also placed to the credit of the Sound Money Committee.
>
> MacGuire then testified that he had received from Robert Sterling Clark approximately $7200, for his traveling expenses to, in and from Europe, to which had been added the sum of $2500 on another occasion and $1000 at another time, and he stated under oath, that he had not received anything from anybody else and further testified that he had deposited it in his personal account at the Manufacturers Trust Co., 55 Broad Street.
>
> MacGuire further testified that he had a drawing account of $432 a month right now, to which were added some commissions. Later MacGuire testified that the $2500 and the $1000 were in connection with the organization of the Committee for a Sound Dollar.
>
> Chairman McCormack then directed the following question: "Did Mr. Clark contribute any money in any other way, besides the $30,000. and the other sums that you have enumerated he gave to you personally?" to which MacGuire replied, "No sir, he has been asked several times to contribute to different funds, but he has refused."[399]

In its New York press release the committee noted several discrepancies in MacGuire's testimony on receipt of funds. The section reads as follows:

> Neither could MacGuire remember what the purpose of his trip was to Washington or whether he had given the Central Hanover Bank thirteen one thousand dollar bills or that he had bought one of the letters of credit with a certified check drawn on the account of Mr. Christmas.
>
> In the course of the questioning MacGuire could not remember whether he had ever handled thousand dollar bills, and certainly could not remember producing thirteen of them at one time in the bank. It must be remembered in this connection, that the $13,000 purchase with one thousand dollar bills at the bank, came just six days after Butler claims MacGuire showed him eighteen one thousand dollars bills in Newark.

---

[398] Ibid., p. 45.
[399] Press release. New York City, p. 12.

From the foregoing, it can readily be seen that in addition to the $30,000 which Clark gave MacGuire for the Sound Money Committee that he produced approximately $75,000 more which MacGuire reluctantly admitted on being confronted with the evidence.

This $75,000 is shown in the $26,000 that went into the Manufacturers Trust account, $10,000 in currency at the luncheon, the purchase of letters of credit totaling $30,300, of which Christmas' certified check was represented as $15,000, expenses to Europe close to $8,000. This still stands unexplained. Whether there was more and how much, the Committee does not yet know.[400]

The committee then asked MacGuire an obvious question: whether he knew Jackson Martindell. Unfortunately, an equally obvious error in MacGuire's answer was allowed to pass by unchallenged. The committee transcript reads as follows:

By the Chairman:
QUESTION. Do you know Mr. Martindell, Mr. MacGuire?
ANSWER. Mr. Martin Dell? No, sir; I do not.
THE CHAIRMAN. Is that his name?
MR. DICKSTEIN. I think so.[401]

So, in brief, we have three reliable witnesses—General Butler, Paul French, and Captain Samuel Glazier—testifying under oath about plans of a plot to install a dictatorship in the United States. And we have contradictory testimony from Gerald MacGuire that clearly warrants further investigation. Such investigation was at first the committee's stated intention: "The Committee is awaiting the return to this country of both Mr. Clark and Mr. Christmas. As the evidence stands, it calls for an explanation that the Committee has been unable to obtain from Mr. MacGuire."[402]

But the Committee did not call either Mr. Clark or Mr. Christmas to give evidence. It made no further effort—at least, no further effort appears on the public record—to find an explanation for the inconsistencies and inaccuracies in MacGuire's testimony, testimony that was given to the committee under oath.

SUPPRESSION OF WALL STREET INVOLVEMENT

---

[400] Ibid., p. 13.
[401] House of Representatives, Investigation of Nazi Propaganda Activities and Investigation of Certain Other Propaganda Activities, Hearings No. 73-D.C.-6, op. cit., p. 85.
[402] Press release, New York City, p. 13.

The story of an attempted take-over of executive power in the United States was suppressed, not only by parties directly interested, but also by several institutions usually regarded as protectors of constitutional liberty and freedom of inquiry. Among the groups suppressing information were (1) the Congress of the United States, (2) the press, notably *Time* and *The New York Times*, and (3) the White House itself. It is also notable that no academic inquiry has been conducted into what is surely one of the more ominous events in recent American history. Suppression is even more regrettable in the light of the current trend toward collectivism in the United States and the likelihood of another attempt at a dictatorial takeover using supposed threats from either the left or the right as a pretext.

Suppression by the House Un-American Activities Committee took the form of deleting extensive excerpts relating to Wall Street financiers including Guaranty Trust director Grayson Murphy, J.P. Morgan, the Du Pont interests, Remington Arms, and others allegedly involved in the plot attempt. Even today, in 1975, a full transcript of the hearings cannot be traced.

Some of the deleted portions of the transcript were unearthed by reporter John Spivak.[403] A reference to NRA Administrator Hugh Johnson will show the type of information suppressed; the Committee suppressed the words in italics from the printed testimony; Butler speaks to MacGuire:

> I said, "Is there anything stirring about it yet?"
> "Yes," he says; "you watch; in two or three weeks you will see it come out in the papers. There will be big fellows in it" ... and in about two weeks the American Liberty League appeared, which was just about what he described it to be. *We might have an assistant President, somebody to take the blame; and if things do not work out, he can drop him. He said, "That is what he was building up Hugh Johnson for. Hugh Johnson talked too damn much and got him into a hole, and he is going to fire him in the next three or four weeks."*
> I said, "How do you know all this?"
> "Oh," he said, "we are in with him all the time. We know what is going to happen."[404]

The testimony of Paul French was also censored by the House Committee. Witness the following extract from French's testimony referring to John W. Davis, J.P. Morgan, the Du Pont Company, and others in Wall Street and which strongly corroborates General Butler's testimony:

> At first he [MacGuire] suggested that the General [Butler] organize this outfit himself and ask a dollar a year dues from everybody. We discussed that, and then he came around to

---

[403] See Jules Archer, The Plot to Seize the White House, op. cit.
[404] George Seldes, One Thousand Americans, op. cit, p. 288.

> the point of getting outside financial funds, and he said it would not be any trouble to raise a million dollars. He said he could go to John W. Davis [attorney for J.P. Morgan & Co.] or Perkins of the National City Bank, and any number of persons to get it. Of course, that may or may not mean anything. That is, his reference to John W. Davis and Perkins of the National City Bank. During my conversation with him I did not of course commit the General to anything. I was just feeling him along.
>
> Later, we discussed the question of arms and equipment, and he suggested that they could be obtained from the Remington Arms Co., on credit through the Du Ponts.
>
> I do not think at that time he mentioned the connections of Du Pont with the American Liberty League, but he skirted all around it. That is, I do not think he mentioned the Liberty League, but he skirted all around the idea that that was the back door; one of the Du Ponts is on the board of directors of the American Liberty League and they own a controlling interest in the Remington Arms Co ... He said the General would not have any trouble enlisting 500,000 men.[405]

John L. Spivak, the reporter who unearthed the suppression in the Congressional transcripts, challenged Committee Cochairman Samuel Dickstein of New York with his evidence. Dickstein admitted that:

> the Committee had deleted certain parts of the testimony because they were hearsay."
> "But your published reports are full of hearsay testimony." "They are?" he said.
> "Why wasn't Grayson Murphy called? Your Committee knew that Murphy's men are in the anti-Semitic espionage organization Order of '76?"
> "We didn't have the time. We'd have taken care of the Wall Street groups if we had the time. I would have no hesitation in going after the Morgans."
> "You had Belgrano, Commander of the American Legion, listed to testify. Why wasn't he examined?"
> "I don't know. Maybe you can get Mr. McCormack to explain that. I had nothing to do with it."[406]

The fact remains that the committee did not call Grayson Murphy, Jackson Martindell, or John W. Davis, all directly accused in sworn testimony. Further, the committee deleted all portions of the testimony involving other prominent persons: J.P. Morgan, the Du Ponts, the Rockefeller interests, Hugh Johnson, and Franklin D. Roosevelt. When Congressman Dickstein pleaded his innocence to John Spivak, it was inconsistent with his own letter to President Roosevelt, in which he claims to have placed restrictions even upon public distribution of the committee hearings, as printed, "in order that they might not get into

---

[405] Ibid., pp. 289-290.
[406] John L. Spivak, A Man in his Time (New York: Horizon Press, 1967), pp. 311, 322-25.

other than responsible hands." The final report issued by the committee in February 15, 1935 buried the story even further. John L. Spivak sums up the burial succinctly: "I... studied the Committee's report. It gave six pages to the threat by Nazi agents operating in this country and eleven pages to the threat by communists. It gave one page to the plot to seize the Government and destroy our democratic system."[407]

The role of leading newspapers and journals of opinion in reporting the Butler affair is equally suspect. In fact, their handling of the event has the appearance of outright distortion and censorship. The veracity of some major newspapers has been widely questioned in the last 50 years[408], and in some quarters the media have even been accused of a conspiracy to suppress "everything in opposition to the wishes of the interest served." For example, in 1917 Congressman Callaway inserted in The Congressional Record the following devastating critique of Morgan control of the press:

> MR. CALLAWAY. Mr. Chairman, under unanimous consent, I insert in the Record at this point a statement showing the newspaper combination, which explains their activity in this war matter, just discussed by the gentleman from Pennsylvania (Mr. Moore):
> In March, 1915, the J.P. Morgan interests, the steel, shipbuilding, and powder interests, and their subsidiary organizations, got together 12 men high up in the newspaper world and employed them to select the most influential newspapers in the United States and a sufficient number of them to control generally the policy of the daily press of the United States.
> These 12 men worked the problem out by selecting 179 newspapers, and then began by an elimination process, to retain only those necessary for the purpose of controlling the general policy of the daily press throughout the country. They found it was only necessary to purchase the control of 25 of the greatest papers. The 25 papers were agreed upon; emissaries were sent to purchase the policy, national and international, of these papers; an agreement was reached; the policy of the papers was bought, to be paid for by the month; an editor was furnished for each paper to properly supervise and edit information regarding the questions of preparedness, militarism, financial policies, and other things of national and international nature considered vital to the interests of the purchasers.
> This contract is in existence at the present time, and it accounts for the news columns of the daily press of the country being filled with all sorts of preparedness arguments and misrepresentations as to the present condition of the United States Army and Navy and the possibility and probability of the United States being attacked by foreign foes.
> This policy also included the suppression of everything in opposition to the wishes of the interests served. The effectiveness of this scheme has been conclusively demonstrated by the character of stuff carried in the daily press throughout the country since March 1915. They have resorted to anything necessary to commercialize public sentiment and sandbag the

---

[407] Ibid., p. 331.
[408] See Herman Dinsmore, All the News That Fits, (New Rochelle: Arlington House, 1969).

National Congress into making extravagant and wasteful appropriations for the Army and Navy under the false pretense that it was necessary. Their stock argument is that it is "patriotism." They are playing on every prejudice and passion of the American people.[409]

In the Butler affair the accused interests are also those identified by Congressman Callaway: the J.P. Morgan firm and the steel and powder industries. General Butler accused Grayson Murphy, a director of the Morgan-controlled Guaranty Trust Company; Jackson Martindell, associated with Stone & Webster, allied to the Morgans; the Du Pont Company (the powder industry); and Remington Arms Company, which was controlled by Du Pont and the Morgan-Harriman financial interests. Further, the firms that appear in the suppressed 1934 Congressional testimony are J.P. Morgan, Du Pont, and Remington Arms. In brief, we can verify 1934 Congressional suppression of information that supports the earlier 1917 charges of Congressman Callaway.

Does such suppression extend to major news journals? We can take two prime examples; *The New York Times* and *Time* magazine. If such a combination as Callaway charges did exist, then these two journals would certainly be among "25 of the greatest papers involved in the 1930s." *The New York Times* reporting of the "plot" opens up with a front-page headline article on November 21, 1934: "Gen. Butler Bares 'Fascist Plot' to Seize Government by Force," with the lead paragraph quoted above (p. 143). This *Times* article is a reasonably good job of reporting and includes a forthright statement by Congressman Dickstein: "From present indications Butler has the evidence. He's not going to make any serious charges unless he has something to back them up. We'll have men here with bigger names than his." Then the Times article records that "Mr. Dickstein said that about sixteen persons mentioned by General Butler to the Committee would be subpoenaed, and that a public hearing might be held next Monday." The Times also includes outright and sometimes enraged denials from Hugh Johnson, Thomas W. Lamont, and Grayson M-P. Murphy of Guaranty Trust.

The following morning, November 22, the *Times* made a major switch in reporting the plot. The disclosures were removed to an inside page, although the testimony now concerned Gerald MacGuire, one of the accused plotters. Further, a decided change in the attitude of the committee can be discerned. Congressman McCormack is now reported as saying that "the committee has not decided whether to call any additional witnesses. He said that the most important witness, aside from Mr. MacGuire, was Robert Sterling Clark, a wealthy New Yorker with offices in the Stock Exchange Building."

While the *Times* reporting was consigned to an inside single column, the editorial page, its most influential section, carried a lead editorial that set the tone for subsequent reporting.

---

[409] Congressional Record, Vol. 55, pp. 2947-8 (1917).

Under the head "Credulity Unlimited," it contended that the Butler charge was a "bald and unconvincing narrative. ... The whole story sounds like a gigantic hoax ... it does not merit serious discussion," and so on. In brief, *before* the 16 important witnesses were called, before the evidence was on the record, *before* the charge was investigated. The New York Times decided that it wanted to hear nothing about this story because it was a hoax, not fit to print.

The next day, November 23, the Times changed its reporting still further. The headlines were now about Reds and Red Union Strife and concerned alleged activities by communists in American trade unions, while the Butler testimony and the developing evidence were secreted deep within the reporting of Red activities. The resulting story was, of course, vague and confused, but it effectively buried the Butler evidence.

On November 26, the hearings continued, but the committee itself now had cold feet and issued a statement: "This Committee has had no evidence before it that would in the slightest degree warrant calling before it such men as John W. Davis, General Hugh Johnson, General James G. Harbord, Thomas W. Lamont, Admiral William S. Sims, or Hanford MacNider."

It should be noted that these names had come up in sworn testimony, later to be deleted from the official record. The Times pursued its reporting of this development in abbreviated form on an inside page under the head, "Committee Calm over Butler 'Plot', Has No Evidence to Warrant Calling Johnson and Others." On November 27 the *Times* reporting declined to five column inches on an inside page under the ominous head "Butler Plot Inquiry Not To Be Dropped." The December hearings were reported by the *Times* on a front page (December 28 1934), but the plot was now twisted to "Reds Plot to Kidnap the President, Witness Charges at House Inquiry."

Reviewing the story of the Butler Affair in the *Times* 40 years after the event and comparing its story to the printed official testimony, itself heavily censored, it is obvious that the newspaper, either under its own initiative or under outside pressure, decided that the story was not to be made public. Consistent with this interpretation, we find that The New York Times, the "newspaper of record," omits the Butler testimony from entries in its annual index, depended upon by researchers and scholars. The *Times* Index for 1934 has an entry "BUTLER (Maj Gen), Smedley D," but lists only a few of his speeches and a biographic portrait. The Butler testimony is not listed. There is an entry, "See also: Fascism-U.S.," but under that cross-reference there is listed only: "Maj Gen S.D. Butler charges plot to overthrow present govt; Wall Street interests and G.P. MacGuire implicated at Cong com hearing." The only significant Wall Street name mentioned in the index is that of R.S. Clark, who is reported as "puzzled" by the charges. None of the key Morgan and Du Pont associates cited by General Butler is listed in the *Index*. In other words, there appears to have been a deliberate attempt by this newspaper to mislead historians.

Time magazine's reporting descended to fiction in its attempts to reduce General Butler's evidence to the status of absurdity. If ever a student wants to construct an example of biased reporting, there is a first-rate example in a comparison of the evidence presented to the McCormack-Dickstein Committee by General Butler with the subsequent *Time* reportage. The December 3rd 1934 issue of *Time* ran the story under the head "Plot Without Plotters," but the story bears no resemblance at all to the testimony, not even the censored testimony. The story portrays General Butler leading a half-million men along U. S. Highway 1 with the cry, "Men, Washington is but 30 miles away! Will you follow me?" Butler was then depicted as taking over the U.S. government by force from President Roosevelt. The remainder of the *Time* story is filled with dredges from Butler's past and an assortment of denials from the accused. Nowhere is there any attempt to report the statements made by General Butler, although the denials by J.P. Morgan, Hugh Johnson, Robert Sterling Clark, and Grayson Murphy are cited correctly. Two photographs are included: a genial grandfatherly J.P. Morgan and General Butler in a pose that universally symbolizes lunacy—a finger pointed to his ear. The reporting was trashy, dishonest, and disgraceful journalism at its very worst. Whatever our thoughts may be on Nazi propaganda or Soviet press distortion, neither Goebbels nor *Goslit* ever attained the hypnotic expertise of *Time's* journalists and editors. The fearful problem is that the opinions and mores of millions of Americans and of English speakers around the world have been molded by this school of distorted journalism.

To keep our criticism in perspective, it must be noted that *Time* was apparently impartial in its pursuit of lurid journalism. Even Hugh S. Johnson, administrator of NRA and one of the alleged plotters in the Butler Affair, was a target of *Time's* mischief. As Johnson reports it in his book:

> I stood in the reviewing stand in that parade and there were hundreds of people I knew who waved as they went past. Down below were massed batteries of cameras, and I knew if I raised my hand higher than my shoulders, it would seem and be publicized as a "Fascist salute." So I never did raise it higher. I just stuck my arm out straight and wiggled my hand around. But that didn't help me—Time came out saying I had constantly saluted au Mussolini and even had a photograph to prove it, but it wasn't my arm on that photograph. It wore the taped cuff sleeve of a cut-away coat and a stiff round cuff with an old fashioned cuff button and I never wore either in my whole life. I think it was the arm of Mayor O'Brien who stood beside me which had been faked onto my body.[410]

---

[410] Hugh S. Johnson, The Blue Eagle from Egg to Earth, op. cit., p.267

An assessment of the Butler affair

The most important point to be assessed is the credibility of General Smedley Darlington Butler. Was General Butler lying? Was he telling the truth? Was he exaggerating for the sake of effect?

General Butler was an unusual man and a particularly unusual man to find in the armed forces: decorated twice with the Medal of Honor, an unquestioned leader of men, with undoubted personal bravery, deep loyalty to his fellow men, and a fierce sense of justice. All these are admirable qualities. Certainly, General Butler was hardly the type of man to tell lies or even exaggerate for a petty reason. His flair for the dramatic does leave open a possibility of exaggeration, but deliberate lying is most unlikely.

Does the evidence support or reject Butler? Reporter Paul French of *The Philadelphia Record* wholly supports Butler. Evidence by Captain Glazier, commander of the CCC camp, supports Butler. In these two cases there is no discrepancy in the evidence. The statements of MacGuire made under oath to Congress do not support Butler. We have therefore a conflict of sworn evidence. Further, MacGuire was found at fault on several points by the committee; he used the evasion of "do not recall" on a number of occasions and, in major areas such as the financing by Clark, MacGuire unwillingly supports Butler. There is a hard core of plausibility to the Butler story. There is some possibility of exaggeration, perhaps not untypical for a man of Butler's flamboyant personality, but this is neither proven nor disproven.

Without question, the Congress of the United States did a grave disservice to the cause of freedom in suppressing the Butler story. Let us hope that some Congressmen or some Congressional committee, even at this late date, will pick up the threads and release the full uncensored testimony. We may also hope that the next time around, in some comparably important matter, The New York Times will live up to its claim to be the newspaper of record, a name it justified so admirably four decades later in the Watergate Investigation.

Chapter 11

The Corporate Socialists at 120 Broadway, New York City

> *Already he [FDR] had begun to reappear at the office of the Fidelity and Deposit Company at 120 Broadway. He did not yet visit his law office at 52 Wall Street, because of the high front steps—he could not bear the thought of being carried up them in public. At 120 Broadway he could manage, by himself, the one little step up from the sidewalk.*
>
> Frank Freidel, Franklin D. Roosevelt:
> The Ordeal (Boston; Little, Brown, 1954), p. 119.

As in *Wall Street and the Bolshevik Revolution*, we find many of the leading characters (including FDR) and firms, even a few of the events, described in this book located at a single address, the Equitable Office Building at 120 Broadway, New York City.

Franklin D. Roosevelt's office in the early 1920s when he was vice president of the Fidelity and Deposit Company was at 120 Broadway. Biographer Frank Freidel records above his reentry to the building after his crippling polio attack. At that time, Bernard Baruch's office was also at 120 Broadway and Hugh Johnson, later to be the administrator of NRA, was Bernard Baruch's research assistant at the same address.

The executive offices of General Electric and the offices of Gerard Swope, author of the Swope Plan that became Roosevelt's NRA, were also there. The Bankers Club was on the top floor of this same Equitable Office Building and was the location of a 1926 meeting by the Butler Affair plotters. Obviously, there was a concentration of talent at this particular address deserving greater description.

The Bolshevik Revolution and 120 Broadway

In Wall Street and the Bolshevik Revolution, we noted that revolution related financiers were concentrated at a single address in New York City, the same Equitable Office Building. In 1917 the headquarters of the No. 2 District of the Federal Reserve System, the most important of the Federal Reserve districts, was located at 120 Broadway; of nine directors of the Federal Reserve Bank of New York, four were physically located at 120 Broadway, and two of these directors were simultaneously on the board of American International Corporation. The American International Corporation had been founded in 1915 by the Morgan interests with enthusiastic participation by the Rockefeller and Stillman groups. The general offices of A.I.C. were at 120 Broadway. Its directors were heavily interlocked with other major Wall Street financial and industrial interests, and it was determined that American International Corporation had a significant role in the success and consolidation of the 1917 Bolshevik Revolution. A.I.C. executive secretary William Franklin Sands, asked for his opinion of the Bolshevik Revolution by the State Department within a few weeks of the outbreak in November 1917 (long before even a fraction of Russia came under Soviet control), expressed strong support for the revolution. Sands' letter is reprinted in *Wall Street and the Bolshevik Revolution*. A memorandum to David Lloyd George, Prime Minister of England, from Morgan associate Dwight Morrow also urged support for the Bolshevik revolutionaries and backing for its armies. A director of the FRB of New York, William Boyce Thompson, donated $1 million to the Bolshevik cause and intervened with Lloyd George on behalf of the emerging Soviets.

In brief, we found an identifiable pattern of pro-Bolshevik activity by influential members of Wall Street concentrated in the Federal Reserve Bank of New York and the American International Corporation, both at 120 Broadway. By 1933 the bank had moved to Liberty Street.

THE FEDERAL RESERVE BANK OF NEW YORK AND 120 BROADWAY

The names of individual FRB directors changed between 1917 and the 1930s, but it was determined that, although the FRB had moved, four FRB directors still had offices at this address in the New Deal period, as shown in the following table:

Directors of the Federal Reserve Bank of New York in the New Deal Period

Name	Directorships Held for Companies Located at 120 Broadway
Charles E. Mitchell	Director of the FRB of New York, 1929-1931, and director of Corporation Trust Co. (120 Broadway)
Albert H. Wiggin	Succeeded Charles E. Mitchell as Director, FRB of New York, 1932-34, and Director of American International Corp, and Stone and Webster, Inc. (both 120 Broadway)
Clarence M. Woolley	Director FRB of New York, 1922-1936, and director, General Electric Co. (120 Broadway)
Owen D. Young	Director FRB of New York, 1927-1935, and chairman, General Electric Co. (120 Broadway)

Persons and firms located at:

120 BROADWAY
Franklin Delano Roosevelt
Bernard Baruch
Gerard Swope
Owen D. Young

42 BROADWAY
Herbert Clark Hoover

Others

American International Corp.
The Corporation Trust Co. Empire Trust Co. Inc.
Fidelity Trust Co.
American Smelting & Refining Co.
Armour & Co. (New York Office).
Baldwin Locomotive Works
Federal Mining & Smelting Co.
General Electric Co.
Kennecott Copper Corp.
Metal & Thermit Corp.
National Dairy Products Corp.
Yukon Gold Co.
Stone & Webster & Blodget, Inc.

Grayson M-P Murphy (52 Broadway)
International Acceptance Bank, (52 Cedar St.)
International Acceptance Trust (52 Cedar St.)
International Manhattan Co. Inc. (52 Cedar St.)
Jackson Martindell (14 Wall St.)
John D. Rockefeller, Jr. (26 Broadway)
Percy A. Rockefeller (25 Broadway)
Robert S. Clark (11 Wall St.)

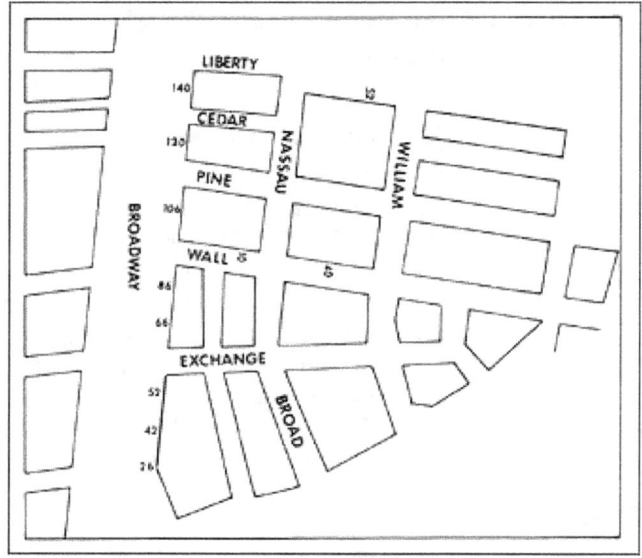

Map of Wall Street Area Showing Office Locations for persons and firms mentioned in this book.

AMERICAN INTERNATIONAL CORPORATION AND 120 BROADWAY

The American International Corporation (AIC) was formed in 1915 by a coalition of Morgan, Stillman and Rockefeller interests; its general offices were at 120 Broadway from 1915 through the 1920s. The great excitement in Wall Street about formation of AIC brought about a concentration of the most powerful financial elements on its board of directors— in effect a monopoly organization for overseas development and exploitation.[411] Of nine directors on the board in 1930, five were on the AIC board in 1917 at the time of the Bolshevik Revolution: Matthew C. Brush, president and chairman of the executive committee of American International Corporation and director of the Empire Trust Company; Pierre S. Du Pont, member of the Du Pont family and a director of the Bankers Trust Company; Percy A. Rockefeller, of the Rockefeller family and director of National City Bank; Albert H. Wiggin, director of the Federal Reserve Bank of New York and the Rockefeller Chase National Bank; and Beekman Winthrop, of the Warburgs' International Banking Corporation and the National City Bank. Several prominent financiers joined the board of AIC during the 1920s, including Frank Altschul and Halstead G. Freeman of the Chase National Bank, Arthur Lehman of Lehman Brothers and the Manufacturers Trust Company, and John J. Raskob, vice president of Du Pont and director of General Motors and the Bankers Trust Company.

---

[411] See Sutton, Bolshevik Revolution, op. cit.

Mathew C. Brush, president, director, and chairman of the executive committee of American International Corporation and president of Allied Machinery, a subsidiary company, was also director and member of the executive committee of International Acceptance Bank (see Chapter 6), director and member of the executive committee of Barnsdall Corporation[412], director of Empire Trust Company (120 Broadway) and Equitable Office Corporation (which owned and operated the building at 120 Broadway), director of Georgian Manganese Company[413], and director and member of the Executive Committee of the Remington Arms Co., identified by General Butler in the last chapter. Matthew C. Brush was indeed in the vanguard of Wall Street.

Brush's political contributions, unlike those of other AIC directors, were apparently limited to $5000 to the campaign of Herbert Hoover in 1928. Brush was director of International Acceptance Bank, which profited from the inflation of the 1920s, as well as a director of Remington Arms (a suppressed name in the Butler Affair) while serving as president of American International, but appears to have been on the fringes of the occurrences explored in this book. On the other hand, four directors of American International have been identified as substantial financial supporters of Franklin D. Roosevelt: Frank Altschul, Pierre S. Du Pont, Arthur Lehman, and John J. Raskob between 1928 and 1932. The Lehman family and John J. Raskob were, as we have seen, at the very heart of Roosevelt's support. It is significant that AIC, the key vehicle for American participation in the Bolshevik Revolution, should also be unearthed, even in an incidental form, in a study of the Roosevelt era.

THE BUTLER AFFAIR AND 120 BROADWAY

Testimony to the House Un-American Activities Committee on the attempt to convert the Roosevelt administration into a dictatorship with Major General Butler in a key role as Secretary of General Affairs had several links to 120 Broadway. There were at least half a dozen persons whom the committee should have subpoenaed to investigate the statements made under oath by General Butler, Captain Glazier, and Paul French; of these, four were located in, or had a significant connection with, 120 Broadway.

According to accused plotter Gerald MacGuire, the original meeting of the alleged participants was held in 1926 at the Bankers Club, 120 Broadway. The following extract

---

[412] Barnsdall Corporation was the company that in 1921 entered the Soviet Union to reopen theCaucasian oil fields for the Soviets and so enabled the Soviet Union to generate the foreign exchange required to develop a Sovietized Russia; see Sutton, Western Technology and Soviet Economic Development, 1917 to 1930 (Stanford: Hoover Institution, 1968), Vol. I.
[413] Ibid.

from the committee hearings, records MacGuire's statement; the questioner was Chairman McCormack:

> QUESTION. How long have you known Clark?
> ANSWER. Well, I believe I said that I have done business with him and known him since 1925 or 1926.
> QUESTION. Did he ever give you that kind of money before to use, as you say—in the way that he wanted you to represent him in these transactions?
> ANSWER. In what transactions?
> QUESTION. In those money transactions, since that time?
> ANSWER. In what money transactions?
> QUESTION. What I mean is this, since 1926, at the time that you met him and after; this was really the first time that you got this money without any receipt or papers or anything at all?
> ANSWER. Yes.
> QUESTION. And this dinner was at the Bankers Club, at 120 Broadway, wasn't it?
> ANSWER. Yes.
> QUESTION. Who was that dinner given to; was it given to anybody specially?
> ANSWER. It was a regular luncheon.
> QUESTION. Who was present at your table?
> ANSWER. Mr. Christmas.
> QUESTION. And yourself?
> ANSWER. Yes.
> QUESTION. And Mr. Clark?
> ANSWER. Yes.[414]

Thus, although the original meeting that brought together Robert S. Clark, his attorney Christmas, and bond salesman Gerald MacGuire was held at 120 Broadway, and Christmas and Clark were linked in numerous ways to MacGuire, neither Christmas nor Clark were called by the committee. Further, Captain Samuel Glazier of the CCC Camp at Elkridge, Maryland reported to the committee that Jackson Martindell had inquired about the training of 500,000 civilian soldiers for political purposes. Martindell was not called by the committee to challenge or confirm the testimony implicating him in the Butler Affair.

The Du Pont Company, cited in the suppressed portion of the testimony, was located at 120 Broadway. Hugh S. Johnson, named by General Butler as a probable participant, had been located at 120 Broadway when working as research assistant to Baruch; Baruch's office

---

[414] House of Representatives, Investigation of Nazi Propaganda Activities and Investigation of Certain Other Propaganda Activities, Hearings No. 73-D.C.-6, op. cit., p. 80. "Mr. Clark" was Robert Sterling Clark and "Mr. Christmas" was Clark's attorney.

was at the same address.[415] Clark, MacGuire, and Grayson M-P. Murphy had offices just down the street from No. 120; Clark at 11 Wall Street and MacGuire and Murphy at 52 Broadway.

It is also significant that names suppressed by the committee were located at 120 Broadway: the Du Pont Company executive office and Du Pont subsidiary Remington Arms. The other named participants, MacGuire, Clark, Christmas, Martindell, Grayson M-P. Murphy (at Rockefeller headquarters, 25 Broadway) were all located within a few blocks of 120 Broadway and within the previously described golden circle.

FRANKLIN D. ROOSEVELT AND 120 BROADWAY

We have noted that FDR's preferred office—he had two in the early 1920s—was the one at 120 Broadway. FDR's Georgia Warm Springs Foundation, Inc. was formed as a Delaware company in July 1926 with offices at 120 Broadway and remained at that address at least through 1936. The 1934 annual report for Georgia Warm Springs Foundation shows that its president was listed as Franklin D. Roosevelt, The White House, Washington D.C., with the head office of the foundation shown at 120 Broadway. The vice president and assistant secretary was Raymond H. Taylor, with secretary- treasurer Basil O'Connor, both shown at the 120 Broadway address.

Basil O'Connor was a close associate and business partner of Franklin D. Roosevelt. Born in 1892, O'Connor received his law degree from Harvard in 1915 and then joined the New York law firm of Cravath and Henderson for one year, leaving to work with Streeter & Holmes in Boston for three years. In 1919 Basil O'Connor established a law practice in New York under his own name. In 1925 the firm of Roosevelt and O'Connor was created, lasting until FDR's inauguration in 1933. After 1934, O'Connor was senior partner in O'Connor & Farber and in 1944 succeeded Norman H. Davis as chairman of the American Red Cross.

O'Connor was a director of several companies: in the 1920s, of New England Fuel Oil Corp., in the 1940s of the American Reserve Insurance Co. and the West Indies Sugar Corp. From 1928 until his death he was responsible for administration of the Georgia Warm Springs Foundation.

The Roosevelt New Deal was a gold mine to some of FDR's associates, including Basil O'Connor. Globe & Rutgers was an insurance company recapitalized with government funds, and the reorganization proved a rich source of fees for attorneys handling the liquidation and reorganization. Of these attorneys President Roosevelt's former firm of O'Connor & Farber demanded the largest single fee until Jesse Jones of the Reconstruction Finance

---

[415] United States Senate, Digest of Data From the Files of a Special Committee to Investigate Lobbying Activities, 74th Congress, Second Session, Part I: List of Contributions, (Washington, 1936), p. 3.

Corporation cut it down. Here is a letter Jesse Jones wrote to Earle Bailie of J. & W. Seligman & Company about these fees:

> October 6, 1933. Dear Mr. Bailie:
> Our board is unwilling to invest in or lend upon stock in an insurance company, if indeed we have the right to do so, that contemplates paying such lawyers' fees, reorganization or otherwise, as is proposed in the case of the Globe & Rutgers, which we understand from information to be
>
> | | |
> |---|---|
> | Basil O'Connor | $200,000 |
> | Root, Clark, Buckner & Ballantine | 165,000 |
> | Sullivan & Cromwell | 95,000 |
> | Prentice & Townsend | 50,000 |
> | Cravath, de Gersdorff, Swaine & Wood | 37,500 |
> | Martin Conboy | 35,000 |
> | Joseph V. McKee | 25,000 |
> | Coudert Brothers | 12,000 |
>
> or a total of $619,500. Even the suggested reduction to a total of $426,000 would be very much more than what would appear to this Corporation to be proper fees to be paid by an insurance company that is being recapitalized with Government funds.
> Yours very truly, JESSE J. JONES

Under court orders Mr. O'Connor's firm was paid $100,000 in 1934 and $35,000 more the following year.[416]

CONCLUSIONS ABOUT 120 BROADWAY

It is virtually impossible to develop an unshakable conclusion about the significance of 120 Broadway; explanations can range from conspiracy to coincidence.

What can we prove with direct, rather than circumstantial, evidence?

First, we know that U.S. assistance to the Bolshevik Revolution originated in the Wall Street golden circle in 1917 and was heavily concentrated at this particular address. Second, when FDR entered the business world in 1921, one of the two FDR offices was at this address, as was his law partnership with Basil O'Connor, and the Georgia Warm Springs Foundation. Third, Bernard Baruch and his assistant Hugh Johnson, later part of the planning and administration of the National Industry Recovery Act, were in the same building. NRA was a logical sequel to the trade associations of the 1920s, and FDR had a prominent role, along with Herbert Hoover, in the implementation of trade association agreements in the

---

[416] Jesse H. Jones, Fifty Billion Dollars pp. 209-210.

1920s. Fourth, there was an association between General Electric and the Bolshevik Revolution, at least in building up the early Soviet Union. Executive offices of G.E. were at this address, as were those of Gerard Swope, the president of G.E. who authored the Swope plan.

Finally, the bizarre Butler affair had a few links with 120 Broadway. For example, this was Du Pont's New York address, although Remington Arms was at Rockefeller headquarters, 25 Broadway. Most of the plotters had other addresses, but still all within the golden circle.

Nothing is proven by a common geographical location. While 120 Broadway was a massive building, it was by no means the largest in New York City. But how does one explain the concentration of so many links to so many important historical events at one address? One could argue that birds of a feather flock together. On the other hand, it is more than plausible that these Wall Streeters were following the maxim laid down by Frederick Howe and found it more convenient, or perhaps more efficient for their purposes, to be at a single address. The point to hold in mind is that no other such geographical concentration exists and, if we ignore the persons and firms at 120 Broadway, there is no case for any relationship between these historical events and Wall Street. Which, incidentally, is also an excellent reason for retaining one's perspective in accepting the fact that we are discussing a small fraction of the banking community, a fraction that has in effect betrayed the financial center of a free economy.

CHAPTER 12

FDR AND THE CORPORATE SOCIALISTS

At the first meeting of the Cabinet after the President took office in 1933, the financier and adviser to Roosevelt, Bernard Baruch, and Baruch's friend General Hugh Johnson, who was to become the head of the National Recovery Administration, came in with a copy of a book by Gentile, the Italian Fascist theoretician, for each member of the Cabinet, and we all read it with great care.
                                               Mrs. Frances Perkins, Secretary of Labor under FDR.

It is worth recalling at this point the epigraph to Chapter 1, that Franklin D. Roosevelt privately believed that the U.S. government was owned by a financial élite. There is, of course, nothing notably original about this observation: it was commonplace in the 19th century. In modern times, it has been averred by such dissimilar writers as Robert Welch and William Domhoff that America is controlled by a financial elite based in New York.

The Soviets, who are not always altogether inaccurate, have used this theme in their propaganda for decades, and it was a Marxist theme before Lenin came along.[417]

It was under Roosevelt that quaint Keynesian notions—the modern versions of John Laws' con game with paper money—were introduced to Washington, and so the seeds of our present economic chaos were laid in the early 1930s under Roosevelt. Contemporary double digit inflation, a bankrupt Social Security system, bumbling state bureaucracy, rising unemployment—all this and more can be traced to Franklin Delano Roosevelt and his legislative whirlwind.

---

[417] It may be superfluous to record this literature, but for the sake of completeness and the benefit of the innocent reader, a few titles may be included: William Domhoff, Who Rules America? (Englewood Cliffs, N.J.: Prentice-Hall, 1967); Ferdinand Lundberg, The Rich and the Super Rich (New York: Lyle Stuart, 1968), and Gary Allen, None Dare Call It Conspiracy (Seal Beach, Calif.: Concord Press, 1972) Certainly, if sheer weight of printed paper has any influence, the power of any financial élite should have collapsed long ago. The establishment does appear to have considerable endurance, but nowhere near as much influence as many believe. The most important leg sustaining the credibility and so the power of the élite is the academic community. This group has, in large part, swapped truth and integrity for a piece of the political power and the financial action. Apparently academics can be bought—and you don't have to pay overly much!

But while we now pay the price for these unsound and irresponsible policies, so pervasive is prevailing misinformation that even the identity of the originators of Roosevelt's New Deal and their reasons have been forgotten. While our economists cover their blackboards with meaningless static equations, a dynamic looting operation of the economy has been in progress by the authentic formulators of the liberal New Deal.

While the bleeding heart social engineers have screamed at capitalism as the cause of the world's misery, they have been blissfully unaware that their own social formulas in part emanated from—and have certainly been quietly subsidized by—these same so-called capitalists. The tunnel vision of our academic world is hard to beat and equalled only by their avarice for a piece of the action.

What we do find is that government intervention into the economy is the root of our present problems; that a Wall Street cotérie has substantive, if subtle, muscle within this government structure to obtain legislation beneficial to itself; and that a prime example of this self-seeking legislation to establish legal monopoly under big business control was FDR's New Deal and, in particular, the National Recovery Administration.

The name Franklin Delano Roosevelt should suggest, but rarely does, a link with Wall Street. Both Delano and Roosevelt are prominent names in the history of American financial institutions.

Who was Franklin Delano Roosevelt?

Roosevelt's pre political career can be described only as that of financier. Both his family and career before 1928 and his election as Governor of New York were in the business world, more specifically the financial world. Between 1921 and 1928 Roosevelt was a director of 11 corporations headquartered in the Wall Street golden circle and president of a major trade association. The American Construction Council.

Furthermore, Roosevelt was not only president of United European Investors, Ltd., formed to take pecuniary advantage of the misery of German hyperinflation, but was one of the organizers of American Investigation Corporation, a high-powered financial syndicate. Roosevelts formed the financial firm Roosevelt & Son in the late 18th century, and Delanos operated in the financial arena from at least the mid 19th century.

Roosevelts and Delanos may not have reaped the great wealth of Morgans and Rockefellers, but they were known and respected names in the halls of international finance. Even in the 1920s we find Uncle Frederic Delano on the Federal Reserve Board, and George Emlen Roosevelt as a director of Guaranty Trust, the bête noire of the Street if there ever was one.

It is also reliably recorded that Theodore Roosevelt's Progressive Party, the first step to the modern welfare-warfare state, was financed by the J.P. Morgan interests; consequently, it should not surprise us to find Wall Street backing Roosevelt in 1928, 1930, and 1932.

In brief, we have shown that Roosevelt was a Wall Streeter, descended from prominent Wall Street families and backed financially by Wall Street. The policies implemented by the Roosevelt régime were precisely those required by the world of international finance. It should not be news to us that international bankers influence policy. What appears to have been neglected in the history of the Roosevelt era is that, not only did FDR reflect their objectives, but was more inclined to do so than the so-called reactionary Herbert Hoover. In fact, Hoover lost in 1932 because, in his own words, he was unwilling to accept the Swope Plan, alias NRA, which he termed, not incorrectly, "a fascist measure."

We cannot say that Wall Streeter Roosevelt was always a highly ethical promoter in his financial flotations. Buyers of his promotions lost money, and substantial money, as the following brief table based on the data presented suggests:

How Investors Fared With FDR at the Helm

Company Associated with FDR	Issue Price of Stock	Subsequent Price History
United European Investors, Ltd	10,000 marks (about $13)	Company wound up, stock-holders offered $7.50
International Germanic Trust Company, Inc.	$170	Went to $257 in 1928, liquidated in 1930 at $19 a share

Loss of stockholders' funds, however, can be an accident or mismanagement. Many honest financiers have stumbled. However, association with persons of known ill repute such as Roberts and Gould in United European Investors, Ltd. was not accidental.

FDR's association with the American Construction Council brings to mind Adam Smith's *obita dicta* that the law "... cannot hinder people of the same trade from sometimes assembling together, but it ought to do nothing to facilitate such assemblies, much less to render them necessary."[418] Why not? Because the American Construction Council was in the interests of the construction industry, not in those of the consumer of construction services.

The New York bonding business was made to order for FDR. As vice president of the Fidelity & Deposit Company of Maryland, FDR knew precisely how to operate in the world of politicized business, where price and product quality in the market place are replaced by "Whom do you know?" and "What are your politics?"

The United European Investors caper was an attempt to take advantage of the misery of German 1921-23 hyperinflation. The firm operated under a Canadian charter, no doubt because Canadian registration requirements were more lenient at that time. The most conspicuous observation concerns FDR's associates at U.E.I., including John von Berenberg

---

[418] Adam Smith, An Inquiry Into the Nature and Causes of the Wealth of Nations (London: George Routledge n.d.), p. 102.

Gossler, a HAPAG co director of German Chancellor Cuno, who was responsible for the inflation! Then there was William Schall, FDR's New York associate, who had only a few years earlier been involved with German espionage in the United States—at 120 Broadway. The Roberts-Gould element in United European Investors was under criminal investigation; FDR knew they were under investigation, but continued his business associations.

Then we found that the background of the New Deal was speckled with prominent financiers. The economic recovery part of the New Deal was a creation of Wall Street— specifically Bernard Baruch and Gerard Swope of General Electric—in the form of the Swope Plan. So in Chapter 5 we expanded upon the idea of the politicization of business and formulated the thesis of corporate socialism: that the political way of running an economy is more attractive to big business because it avoids the rigors and the imposed efficiency of a market system. Further, through business control or influence in regulatory agencies and the police power of the state, the political system is an effective way to gain a monopoly, and a legal monopoly always leads to wealth. Consequently, Wall Street is intensely interested in the political arena and supports those political candidates able to maximize the amount of political decision-making under whatever label and minimize the degree to which economic decisions in society are made in the market place. In brief,

Wall Street has a vested interest in politics because through politics it can make society go to work for Wall Street. It can also thus avoid the penalties and risks of the market place.

We examined an early version of this idea: Clinton Roosevelt's planned society, published in 1841. We then briefly discussed Bernard Baruch's 1917 economic dictatorship and his declared intent to follow the course of a planned economy in peacetime and traced Baruch and his economic assistant Hugh Johnson to the very core of the National Recovery Administration. Some attention was then given to the Federal Reserve System as the most prominent example of private legal monopoly and to the role of the Warburgs through the International Acceptance Bank and the manner in which the bank was able to get society to go to work for Wall Street. In a final look at the years before FDR's New Deal we reviewed the operation of the American Construction Council, a trade association, the concept of which originated with Herbert Hoover, but with FDR as its president. The council had, as its stated objectives, limitation of production and regulation of industry, a euphemism for industry control for maximization of its own profits.

Then we examined the financial contributions of the 1928, 1930, and 1932 elections on the ground that such contributions are a very accurate measure of political inclinations. In 1928, an extraordinary percentage of the larger contributions, those over $25,000, came from Wall Street's golden circle. Such large sums are important because their contributors are more than likely to be identifiable after the election when they ask favors in return for their earlier subsidies. We found that no less than 78.83 per cent of the over $1000 contributions to the Al Smith for President campaign came from a one-mile circle centered on 120 Broadway. Similarly 51.4 per cent, a lesser but still significant figure, of Hoover's contributions came from within this same area. Then we demonstrated that, after his election, Herbert Hoover was given an ultimatum by Wall Street: either accept the Swope Plan (the NRA) or the money and influence of Wall Street would go to FDR who was willing to sponsor that scheme. To his eternal credit, Herbert Hoover refused to introduce such planning on the ground that it was equivalent to Mussolini's fascist state. FDR was not so fussy.

In FDR's 1930 campaign for Governor of New York, we identified a major Wall Street influence. There was an extraordinary flow of funds via the County Trust Company, and John J. Raskob of Du Pont and General Motors emerged as Chairman of the Democratic Campaign Committee and a power behind the scenes in the election of FDR. Seventy- eight per cent of the pre-convention "early-bird" contributions for FDR's 1932 Presidential bid came from Wall Street.

The Swope Plan was a scheme to force American industry into compulsory trade associations and provide exemption from the anti-trust laws. It was baited with a massive welfare carrot to quiet the misgivings of labor and other groups. The administrator of the National Recovery Administration, which developed from the Swope Plan, was Baruch's assistant. General Hugh Johnson. The three musketeers, Johnson's circle of assistants, comprised Gerard Swope of General Electric, Walter Teagle, of Standard Oil of New Jersey, and Louis Kirstein of Filene's of Boston. Adherence to the NRA codes was compulsory for all firms with more than 50 employees. The Swope NRA Plan was greeted favorably by such socialists as Norman Thomas, whose main objection was only that they, the orthodox socialists, were not to run the plan.

Fortunately, NRA failed. Big business attempted to oppress the little man. The codes were riddled with abuses and inconsistencies. It was put out of its misery by the Supreme Court in the Schechter Poultry decision of 1935, although its failure was evident long before the Supreme Court decision. Because of failure of NRA, the so-called 1934 Butler Affair becomes of peculiar interest. According to General Smedley Butler's testimony to Congress, supported by independent witnesses, there was a plan to install a dictator in the White House. President Roosevelt was to be kicked upstairs and a new General Secretary— General Butler was offered the post—was to take over the economy on behalf of Wall Street. Far-fetched as this accusation may seem, we can isolate three major statements of fact:

1. There was independent confirmation of General Butler's statements and in some measure unwilling confirmation by one of the plotters.

2. There existed a motive for Wall Street to initiate such a desperate gamble: the NRA-Swope proposal was foundering.

3. The alleged identity of the men behind the scenes is the same as those identified in the Bolshevik Revolution and in the political promotion of FDR.

Unfortunately, and to its lasting shame. Congress suppressed the core of the Butler testimony. Further, *The New York Times* first reported the story fairly, but then buried and distorted its coverage, even to the extent of incomplete indexing. We are left with the definite possibility that failure of the Baruch-Swope-Johnson NRA plan was to be followed by a more covert, coercive take-over of American industry. This occurrence deserves the fullest attention that unbiased scholars can bring to it. Obviously, the full story has yet to emerge.

Once again, as in the earlier volume, we found a remarkable concentration of persons, firms and events at a single address—120 Broadway, New York City. This was FDR's office address as president of Fidelity & Deposit Company. It was Bernard Baruch's address and the address of Gerard Swope. The three main promoters of the National Recovery Administration—FDR, Baruch, and Swope—were located at the same address through the 1920s. Most disturbing of all, it was found that the original meeting for the Butler Affair was held in 1926 at the Bankers Club, also located at 120 Broadway.

No explanation is yet offered for this remarkable concentration of talent and ideas at a single address. Quite obviously, it is an observation that must be accounted for sooner or later. We also found a concentration of directors of American International Corporation, the vehicle for Wall Street involvement in the Bolshevik revolution, and heavy contributors to the Roosevelt campaign.

Can we look at this story in any wider perspective? The ideas behind the Roosevelt New Deal were not really those of Wall Street; they actually go back to Roman times. From 49 to 44 B.C. Julius Caesar had his new deal public works projects; in 91 A.D. Domitian had his equivalent of the American Construction Council to stop overproduction. The ultimate fall of Rome reflected all the elements we recognize today: extravagant government spending, rapid inflation, and a crushing taxation, all coupled with totalitarian state regulation.[419]

Under Woodrow Wilson Wall Street achieved a central banking monopoly, the Federal Reserve System. The significance of the International Acceptance Bank, controlled by the financial establishment in Wall Street, was that the Federal Reserve banks used the police power of the state to create for themselves a perpetual money-making machine: the ability to create money with a stroke of a pen or the push of a computer key. The Warburgs, key figures in the International Acceptance Bank—an overseas money-making machine—

---

[419] H. J. Haskell, The New Deal in Old Rome: How Government in the Ancient World Tried to Deal with Modern Problems (New York: Knopf, 1947), pp. 239–40.

were advisers to the Roosevelt administration and its monetary policies. Gold was declared a "barbaric relic," opening the way to worthless paper money in the United States. In 1975, as we go to press, the fiat inconvertible dollar is obviously on the way to ultimate depreciation.

Did Wall Street recognize the result of removing gold as backing for currency? Of course it did! Witness Paul Warburg to a Congressional Committee: Abandonment of the gold standard means wildly fluctuating foreign exchanges and, therefore, the destruction of the free inflow of foreign capital and business. Weak countries will repudiate—or, to use the more polite expression, "fund their debts"—but there will be no general demonetization of gold. Gold at the end of the war will not be worth less but more.[420]

The inevitable conclusion forced upon us by the evidence is that there may indeed exist a financial élite, as pointed out by Franklin D. Roosevelt, and that the objective of this élite is monopoly acquisition of wealth. We have termed this élite advocates of corporate socialism. It thrives on the political process, and it would fade away if it were exposed to the activity of a free market. The great paradox is that the influential world socialist movement, which views itself as an enemy of this élite, is in fact the generator of precisely that politicization of economic activity that keeps the monopoly in power and that its great hero, Franklin D. Roosevelt, was its self-admitted instrument.

---

[420] United States Senate, Hearings, Munitions Industry, Part 25, op. cit., p. 8105.

Appendix A

The Swope Plan

1. All industrial and commercial companies (including subsidiaries) with 50 or more employees, and doing an interstate business, may form a trade association which shall be under the supervision of a federal body referred to later.

2. These trade associations may outline trade practices, business ethics, methods of standard accounting and cost practice, standard forms of balance sheet and earnings statement, etc., and may collect and distribute information on volume of business transacted, inventories of merchandise on hand, simplification and standardization of products, stabilization of prices, and all matters which may arise from time to time relating to the growth and development of industry and commerce in order to promote stabilization of employment and give the best service to the public. Much of this sort of exchange of information and data is already being carried on by trade associations now in existence. A great deal more valuable work of this character is possible.

3. The public interest shall be protected by the supervision of companies and trade associations by the Federal Trade Commission or by a bureau of the Department of Commerce or by some federal supervisory body specially constituted.

4. All companies within the scope of this plan shall be required to adopt standard accounting and cost systems and standardized forms of balance sheet and earnings statement. These systems and forms may differ for the different industries, but will follow a uniform plan for each industry as adopted by the trade association and approved by the federal supervisory body.

5. All companies with participants or stockholders numbering 25 or more, and living in more than one state, shall send to its participants or stockholders and to the supervisory body at least once each quarter a statement of their business and earnings in the prescribed form. At least once each year they shall send to the participants or stockholders and to the supervisory body a complete balance sheet and earnings statement in the prescribed form. In this way the owners will be kept informed of the conditions of the business in such detail that there may be no criticism of irregularity or infrequency of statements or methods of presentation.

6. The federal supervisory body shall cooperate with the Internal Revenue Department and the trade associations in developing for each industry standardized forms of balance sheet and income statement, depending upon the character of the business, for the purpose of reconciling

methods of reporting assets and income with the basis of values and income calculated for federal tax purposes.

7. All of the companies of the character described herein may immediately adopt the provisions of this plan but shall be required to do so within 3 years unless the time is extended by the federal supervisory body. Similar companies formed after the plan becomes effective may come in at once but shall be required to come in before the expiration of 3 years from the date of their organization unless the time is extended by the federal supervisory body.

8. For the protection of employees, the following plans shall be adopted by all of these companies:

> A. **A WORKMEN'S COMPENSATION ACT**, which is part of the legislation necessary under this plan, shall, after careful study, be modeled after the best features of the laws which have been enacted by the several states.
>
> B. **LIFE AND DISABILITY INSURANCE.** All employees of companies included in this plan may, after two years' service with such companies, and shall, before the expiration of five years of service, be covered by life and disability insurance.

1) The form of policy shall be determined by the association of which the Company is a member and approved by the federal supervisory body. The policy will belong to the employee and may be retained by him and kept in full force when he changes his employment or otherwise discontinues particular service as outlined later.

2) The face value of a policy shall be for an amount approximately equal to one year's pay, but not more than $5,000, with the exception that the employee may, if he desires, increase at his own cost the amount of insurance carried, subject to the approval of the Board of Administrators, later defined.

3) The cost of this life and disability insurance shall be paid one half by the employee and one-half by the company for which he works, with the following exception: the company's cost shall be determined on the basis of premiums at actual age of employees less than 35 years old and on the basis of 35 years of age for all employees 35 or over and shall be a face value of approximately one-half a year's pay but limited to a maximum premium for $2,500 of insurance. An employee taking out insurance at age 35 or over will pay the excess premium over the amount based upon age 35. This will remove the necessity for restriction against engaging employees or transferring them from one company to another because of advanced age, as it will place no undue burden of high premiums upon the company.

4) The life and disability insurance may be carried by a life insurance company selected by the trade association and approved by the federal supervisory body or may be carried by a company organized by the trade association and approved by the federal supervisory body, or a single company may be formed to serve all associations.

5) The administration of the insurance plan for each company shall be under the direction of a Board of Administrators consisting of representatives, one-half elected by the employee members. The powers and duties of the Board for each company will be to formulate general

rules relating to eligibility of employees, etc., but such rules shall be in consonance with the general plan laid down by the General Board of Administration of the trade association of which the company is a member, and approved by the federal supervisory body.

6) Provision for the continuation of a policy after an employee leaves one company and goes to another in the same association, or goes to a company in another trade association; continuance of the policy after retirement on pension; provisions with regard to beneficiaries; total or partial disability; method of payment of premiums by payroll deductions or otherwise, weekly, monthly or annually, shall be embodied in the plan formulated by the trade association, with the approval of the federal supervisory body.

7) If an employee leaves a company to go with one which is not a member of the trade association; if he engages in business for himself; or if he withdraws from industrial or commercial occupation, he may elect to retain the portion of the policy for which he has paid, in whole, or in part, by the continued payment of the proportional full premium costs, or he may receive a paid up policy, or be paid the cash surrender value for the part for which he has been paying the premiums. The cash surrender value of that portion of the policy paid for by the company will be paid to the company which paid the premiums.

C. PENSIONS. All employees of companies included in this plan shall be covered by old age pension plans which will be adopted by the trade associations and approved by the federal supervisory body. The principal provisions will be as follows:

1) All employees may, after two years of service with a company coming within the scope of this plan, and shall, before the expiration of five years of service, be covered by the old age pension plan.

2) All employees after two years' service may, and after five years' service shall be required to, put aside a minimum of one per cent of earnings, but not more than $50 per year, for the pension fund. The employee may, if he desires, put aside a larger amount, subject to the approval of the Board of Administrators.

3) The Company shall be required to put aside an amount equal to the minimum stated above, namely one per cent of earnings of employees, but not more than $50 per year per employee.

4) The above minimum percentage shall be the same for all employees who are less than 35 years of age when payments begin and the minimum percentage for these employees shall remain the same thereafter. The percentage to be set aside by employees coming into the pension plan at 35 years of age or over shall be so determined that it will provide a retiring allowance at age 70 the same as though they had begun one per cent payments at the age of 35. These provisions enable employees to go from one company to another in the same association or to different associations at any age with provision for retiring allowances which will be not less than the minimum rate of an employee who entered the pension plan at age 35.

5) The amounts set aside by the employee and the company with interest compounded semiannually at five per cent until retirement at age 70, for a typical average employee, would provide an annuity of approximately one-half pay.

6) The administration of the pension plan for each company shall be under the direction of a Board of Administrators, consisting of representatives, one-half appointed by the management and one half elected by the employee members. The powers and duties of the Board for each company will be to formulate general rules relating to eligibility of employees, conditions of retirement, etc., but such rules shall be in consonance with the general plan laid down by the General Board of Administration of the trade association of which the company is a member, and approved by the federal supervisory body.

7) The amounts collected from the employees and the companies shall be placed with the pension trust organized by the association, the management of which shall be under the direction of the General Board of Administration referred to hereafter. In no case shall such funds be left under the control of an individual company.

8) The Pension trust shall invest all funds and place them to the credit of the individual employees, including the income earned by the trust. If an employee goes from one company to another in the same association, the funds accumulated to his credit shall be continued to his credit with proper record of transfer. If an employee goes to a company in another association, the funds accumulated to his credit shall be transferred to his credit in the pension trust of the association to which he goes. If an employee goes to a company which does not come under these provisions or which is not a member of a trade association; goes into business for himself; or withdraws from an industrial or commercial occupation, the amount of his payments plus the interest at the average rate earned by the funds shall be given to him. If an employee dies before reaching retirement age, his beneficiary will receive the amount of his payments plus interest at the average rate earned by the funds. When an employee reaches retirement age, the entire amount accumulated to his credit, including his own payments and those of the company, plus accumulated interest, will be given to him in the form of an annuity. If an employee goes to a company which does not come under these provisions or which is not a member of a trade association; goes into business for himself; or withdraws from industrial or commercial occupation, he may elect to let the amount to his credit (namely, his own payments plus those of the company and the accumulated interest) remain with the pension trust for transfer, if he should return to the employ of any company coming within the provisions of this plan. If he does not return to the employ of a company coming under these provisions, he may at any time thereafter withdraw the amount of his own payments plus interest at the average rate earned by the funds up to that time. Company contributions and accumulated interest credited to employees who die, or for reasons indicated above, receive or withdraw their own contributions and interest, shall be returned to the employer or employers who made the contributions.

9) The rules governing the payments of pensions on retirement and all other rules governing its continuance shall be made by the trade association, approved by the federal supervisory

body, and observed by the General Board of Administration and the Boards of Administration of the member companies.

D. **UNEMPLOYMENT INSURANCE.** All employees on piece work, hourly work daily, weekly, or monthly work, with normal pay of $5,000 per year or less (approximately $96.15 per week) shall be covered by unemployment insurance.

1) All such employees may, after two years of service with a company coming within the provisions of this plan, and shall, after five years of service, be each required to put aside a minimum of one per cent of earnings, but not more than $50 per year for an unemployment insurance fund.

2) The company shall be required to put aside an amount equal to that put aside by the employees, as set forth above, namely one per cent of the earnings of each employee, but not more than $50 per year for each such employee.

3) If a company regularizes and guarantees employment for at least 50 per cent of the normal wage paid each year to such employees, the company assessment for employees covered by such guarantee need not be made, but the employees will pay in a minimum of one per cent of earnings, but not more than $50 per year, into a special fund for their own benefit.

If such an employee leaves the company, dies or retires on pension, the amount to his credit in the special fund plus interest at the average rate earned by the special fund, shall be given to him or to his beneficiaries or added to his pension.

4) If a company so plans its work that it is able to reduce unemployment, when the amount of such company's credit in the normal unemployment fund is equal to but not less than 5 per cent of the normal annual earnings of the employees covered, the company may cease making payment to the fund. Employees' payments will continue.

The company will resume payments when its credit in the normal unemployment fund falls below 5 per cent of normal annual earnings of the employees covered.

5) When the weekly payments made from the fund for unemployment benefits amount to 2 per cent or more of the average weekly earnings of participating employees, the company shall declare an unemployment emergency, and normal payments by the employees and the company shall cease. Thereafter all employees of the company (including the highest officers) receiving 50 per cent or more of their average full-time earnings shall pay 1 per cent of their current earnings to the unemployment fund. A similar amount shall be paid into the fund by the company. The unemployment emergency shall continue until normal conditions are restored, which shall be determined by the Board of Administrators of each company. Thereupon normal payments will be resumed.

6) The main provisions for the distribution of the funds shall follow along these lines, unless modified by the Board of Administrators as set forth in Section D, paragraph 7 hereof. A certain small percentage of the normal payments of the employees and the company may be considered as available for helping participating employees in need. A larger percentage of such normal payments may be considered as available for loans to participating employees in amounts not

exceeding $200 each, with or without interest as may be determined by the Board. The balance of the funds shall be available for unemployment payments. Unemployment payments shall begin after the first two weeks of unemployment and shall amount to approximately 50 per cent of the participating employee's average weekly or monthly earnings for full time, but in no case more than $20 per week. Such payments to individual employees shall continue for no longer than ten weeks in any twelve consecutive months unless extended by the Board. When a participating employee is working part-time because of lack of work and receiving less than 50 per cent of his average weekly or monthly earnings for full time, he shall be eligible for payments to be made from the fund, amounting to the difference between the amount he is receiving as wages from the company and the maximum he may be entitled to as outlined above.

7) The custody and investment of funds and administration of the unemployment insurance plan for each company shall be under the direction of a Board of Administrators consisting of representatives, one-half appointed by the management and one-half elected by the employee members. The powers and duties of the Board shall be to formulate general rules relating to eligibility of employees, the waiting period before benefits are paid, amounts of benefits and how long they shall continue in any year, whether loans shall be made in time of unemployment or need, whether a portion of the funds shall be placed at the disposal of the Board for relief from need arising from causes other than unemployment, etc., but such rules shall be in consonance with the general plan laid down by the General Board of Administration of the trade association of which the company is a member, and approved by the federal supervisory body.

8) If an employee leaves the company and goes to work for another company coming within the provisions of this plan, the proportionate amount remaining of his normal contributions, plus interest at the average rate earned by the funds, shall be transferred to such company and to his credit. If he leaves for other reasons, dies or retires on pension, the proportionate amount remaining of his normal payment, plus interest at the average rate earned by the funds, shall be given to him, or to his beneficiary, or added to his pension. When such employee's credit is transferred to another company, or paid to the employee or to his beneficiary under this provision, an equal amount shall be paid to the cooperating company.

GENERAL ADMINISTRATION. Each trade association will form a General Board of Administration which shall consist of nine members, three to be elected or appointed by the association, three to be elected by the employees of the member companies, and three, representing the public, to be appointed by the federal supervisory body. The members of the General Board, except employee representatives, shall serve without compensation. The employee representatives shall be paid their regular rates of pay for time devoted to Board work, and all members shall be paid traveling expenses, all of which shall be borne by the trade association. The powers and duties of this General Board shall be to interpret the life and disability insurance, pension and unemployment insurance plans adopted by the trade association and approved by the federal supervisory body, supervise the individual company Boards of Administration, form and direct a pension trust for the custody, investment, and disbursements of the pension funds, and in general supervise and direct all activities connected with life and disability insurance, pension and unemployment insurance plans.

APPENDIX B

SPONSORS OF PLANS PRESENTED FOR ECONOMIC PLANNING IN THE UNITED STATES AT APRIL 1932.[421]

American Engineering Council, New York.
American Federation of Labor, Washington.
Associated General Contractors, Washington.
Charles A. Beard, New Milford, Conn.
Ralph Borsodi, author and economist. New York.
Chamber of Commerce of the United States, Washington.
Stuart Chase, author and economist. Labor Bureau, New York.
Wallace B. Donham, Dean, Harvard School of Business.
Fraternal Order of Eagles (Ludlow bill).
Jay Franklin, author, The Forum.
Guy Greer, economist, The Outlook.
Otto Kahn, banker. New York.
Senator Robert M. La Follette, U.S. Senate.
Lewis L. Lorwin, economist, Brookings Institute, Washington.
Paul M. Mazur, investment banker. New York.
McGraw-Hill Publishing Co., New York.
New England Council, Boston.
Progressive Conference (La Follette bill).
P. Redmond, economist, Schenectady, N.Y.
Sumner Slichter, economist and author, Madison Wis.
George Soule, editor, The New Republic.
C. R. Stevenson, of Stevenson, Jordan, and Harrison, New York.
Gerard Swope, president, General Electric Co.
Wisconsin Regional Plan, State Legislature, Madison, Wis.
National Civic Federation, New York.

---

[421] List Compiled by U.S. Dept. of Commerce.

SELECTED BIBLIOGRAPHY

UNPUBLISHED SOURCES

Franklin D. Roosevelt's archives at Hyde Park, New York

PUBLISHED SOURCES

Archer, Jules. *The Plot to Seize the White House*, (New York: Hawthorn Books, 1973)

Baruch, Bernard M., Baruch, *The Public Years*, (New York: Holt, Rinehart and Winston, 1960)

Bennett, Edward W., *Germany and the Diplomacy of the Financial Crisis*, 1931, (Cambridge: Harvard University Press, 1962)

Bremer, Howard, *Franklin Delano Roosevelt*, 1882-1945, (New York; Oceana Publications, Inc., 1971),

Burton, David H., *Theodore Roosevelt*, (New York: Twayne Publishers, Inc., 1972)

Davis, Kenneth S., *FDR, The Beckoning of Destiny 1882-1928, A History*, (New York: G. P. Putnam's Sons, 1971)

Dilling, Elizabeth, *The Roosevelt Red Record and Its Background*, (Illinois: by the Author, 1936)

Farley, James A., *Behind the Ballots, The Personal History of a Politician*, (New York; Harcourt, Brace and Company, 1938)

Filene, Edward A., *Successful Living in this Machine Age*, (New York: Simon and Schuster, 1932)

Filene, Edward A., The Way Out, A Forecast of Coming Changes in American Business and Industry, (New York: Doubleday, Page & Company, 1924)

Flynn, John T., *The Roosevelt Myth*, (New York: The Devin-Adair Company, 1948)

Freedman, Max, *Roosevelt and Frankfurter*, Their Correspondence— 1928–1945, (Boston, Toronto: Little, Brown and Company, 1967)

Freidel, Frank, *Franklin D. Roosevelt, The Ordeal*, (Boston: Little, Brown and Company, 1952)

Hanfstaengl, Ernst, *Unheard Witness*, (New York: J.B. Lippincott Company, 1957)

Haskell, H.J., The New Deal in Old Rome, How Government in the Ancient World Tried to Deal with Modern Problems (New York: Alfred A. Knopf, 1947.)

Hoover, Herbert C., *Memoirs. The Great Depression, 1929–1941*, (New York: Macmillan Company, 1952), Vol. 3.

Howe, Frederic C., *The Confessions of a Monopolist*, (Chicago; The Public Publishing Company, 1906)

Hughes, T.W., *Forty Years of Roosevelt*, (1944...T.W. Hughes)

Ickes, Harold L., Administrator, *National Planning Board Federal Emergency Administration of Public Works*, (Washington, D.C. Government Printing Office, 1934). Final Report 1933–34.

Johnson, Hugh S., *The Blue Eagle from Egg to Earth*, (New York: Doubleday, Doran & Company, Inc., 1935)

Josephson, Emanuel M., *Roosevelt's Communist Manifesto*. Incorporating a reprint of *Science of Government Founded on Natural Law*, by Clinton Roosevelt, (New York: Chedney Press, 1955)

Kahn, Otto H., *Of Many Things*, (New York: Boni & Liveright, 1926)

Kolko, Gabriel, The Triumph of Conservatism, A Reinterpretation of American History, (London: Collier-Macmillan Limited, 1963)

Kuczynski, Robert P., *Bankers' Profits from German Loans*, (Washington, D.C.: The Brookings Institution, 1932)

Laidler, Harry W., *Concentration of Control in American Industry*, (New York: Thomas Y. Crowell Company, 1931)

Lane, Rose Wilder, *The Making of Herbert Hoover*, (New York: The Century Co., 1920)

Leuchtenburg, William E., *Franklin D. Roosevelt and the New Deal 1932–1940*, (New York, Evanston, and London: Harper & Row, 1963)

Moley, Raymond, *The First New Deal* (New York: Harcourt Brace & World, Inc., n.d.)

Nixon, Edgar B., Editor, *Franklin D. Roosevelt and Foreign Affairs*, (Cambridge: The Belknap Press of Harvard University Press, 1969), Volume I: January 1933-February 1934. Franklin D. Roosevelt Library. Hyde Park, New York.

Overacker, Louise, *Money in Elections*, (New York: The Macmillan Company, 1932)

Pecora, Ferdinand, *Wall Street Under Oath, The Story of our Modern Money Changers*, (New York: Augustus M. Kelley Publishers, 1968)

Peel, Roy V., and Donnelly, Thomas C., *The 1928 Campaign An Analysis*, (New York: Richard R. Smith, Inc., 1931)

Roos, Charles Frederick, *NRA Economic Planning*, (Bloomington, Indiana: The Principia Press, Inc., 1937)

Roosevelt, Elliott and Brough, James, *An Untold Story, The Roosevelts of Hyde Park*, (New York: G.P. Putnam's Sons, 1973)

Roosevelt, Franklin D., *The Public Papers and Addresses of Franklin D. Roosevelt*, (New York: Random House, 1938), Volume One.

Roosevelt, Franklin D., *The Public Papers and Addresses of Franklin D. Roosevelt*, (New York: Random House, 1938), Vol. 4.

Schlesinger, Arthur M., Jr., *The Age of Roosevelt, The Crisis of the Old Order 1919– 1933*, (Boston: Houghton Mifflin Company, 1957)

Seldes, George, *One Thousand Americans*, (New York: Boni & Gaer, 1947).

Spivak, John L. *A Man in His Time*, (New York: Horizon Press, 1967)

Stiles, Leia, *The Man Behind Roosevelt, The Story of Louis McHenry Howe*, (New York: The World Publishing Company, 1954)

United States Congress, House of Representatives. Special Committee on Un-American Activities. *Investigation of Nazi Propaganda Activities and Investigation of Certain Other Propaganda Activities*. Dec 29, 1934. (73rd Congress, 2nd session. Hearings No. 73-D. C.-6). (Washington, Government Printing Office; 1935)

United States Congress, Senate. Special committee to investigate lobbying activities. *List of contributions.* Report pursuant to S. Res. 165 and S. Res. 184. (74th Congress, 2d session). Washington, Government Printing Office, 1936)

United States Congress. Senate. Hearings before a subcommittee of the committee on military affairs. *Scientific and Technical Mobilization.* March 30, 1943. (78th Congress, 1st session. S. 702). Part I. (Washington, Government Printing Office, 1943)

United States Congress. House of Representatives. Special Committee on Un-American activities (1934) *Investigation of Nazi and other propaganda,* (74th Congress, 1st session. Report No. 153) (Washington, Government Printing Office)

United States Congress. Senate, Hearings before the Committee on Finance. *National Industrial Recovery.* S. 1712 and H.R. 5755, May 22, 26, 29, 31, and June 1, 1933. (73rd Congress, 1st session) (Washington, Government Printing Office, 1933)

United States Congress. Senate. Special committee investigating presidential campaign expenditures. *Presidential campaign expenditures.* Report pursuant to S. Res. 234, Feb 25 (calendar day, February 28), 1929. (70th Congress, 2nd session. Senate Rept. 2024). (Washington, Government Printing Office, 1929)

Warren, Harris, Gaylord, *Herbert Hoover and the Great Depression,* (New York: Oxford University Press, 1959)

Wolfskill, George, The Revolt of the Conservatives, A History of The American Liberty League 1934-1940, (Boston: Houghton Mifflin Company, 1962)

WALL STREET AND THE RISE OF HITLER

Dedicated to the memory of Floyd Paxton — entrepreneur, inventor, writer, and American, who believed in and worked for individual rights in a free society under the Constitution.

Preface

This is the third and final volume of a trilogy describing the role of the American corporate socialists, otherwise known as the Wall Street financial elite or the Eastern Liberal Establishment, in three significant twentieth-century historical events: the 1917 Lenin-Trotsky Revolution in Russia, the 1933 election of Franklin D. Roosevelt in the United States, and the 1933 seizure of power by Adolf Hitler in Germany.

Each of these events introduced some variant of socialism into a major country — *i.e.,* Bolshevik socialism in Russia, New Deal socialism in the United States, and National socialism in Germany.

Contemporary academic histories, with perhaps the sole exception of Carroll Quigley's *Tragedy And Hope,* ignore this evidence. On the other hand, it is understandable that universities and research organizations, dependent on financial aid from foundations that are controlled by this same New York financial elite, would hardly want to support and to publish research on these aspects of international politics. The bravest of trustees is unlikely to bite the hand that feeds his organization.

It is also eminently clear from the evidence in this trilogy that "public-spirited businessmen" do not journey to Washington as lobbyists and administrators in order to serve the United States. They are in Washington to serve their own profit-maximizing interests. Their purpose is not to further a competitive, free-market economy, but to manipulate a politicized regime, call it what you will, to their own advantage.

It is business manipulation of Hitler's accession to power in March 1933 that is the topic of *Wall Street and the Rise of Hitler.*

July, 1976
Antony C. Sutton

Antony C. Sutton

Introduction

Unexplored Facets of Naziism

Since the early 1920s unsubstantiated reports have circulated to the effect that not only German industrialists, but also Wall Street financiers, had some role — possibly a substantial role — in the rise of Hitler and Naziism. This book presents previously unpublished evidence, a great deal from files of the Nuremburg Military Tribunals, to support this hypothesis. However, the full impact and suggestiveness of the evidence cannot be found from reading this volume alone. Two previous books in this series, *Wall Street and the Bolshevik Revolution*[422] and *Wall Street and FDR*[423], described the roles of the same firms, and often the same individuals and their fellow directors, hard at work manipulating and assisting the Bolshevik revolution in Russia in 1917, backing Franklin D. Roosevelt for President in the United States in 1933, as well as aiding the rise of Hitler in pre-war Germany. in brief, this book is part of a more extensive study of the rise of modern socialism and the corporate socialists.

This politically active Wall Street group is more or less the same elitist circle known generally among Conservatives as the "Liberal Establishment," by liberals (for instance G. William Domhoff) as "the ruling class,"[424] and by conspiratorial theorists Gary Allen[425] and Dan Smoot[426] as the "Insiders." But whatever we call this self-perpetuating elitist group, it is apparently fundamentally significant in the determination of world affairs, at a level far behind and above that of the elected politicians.

The influence and work of this same group in the rise of Hitler and Nazi Germany is the topic of this book. This is an area of historical research almost totally unexplored by the academic world. It is an historical minefield for the unwary and the careless not aware of the intricacies of research procedures. The Soviets have long accused Wall Street bankers of backing international fascism, but their own record of historical accuracy hardly lends

---

[422] (New York: Arlington House Publishers, 1974)
[423] (New York: Arlington House Publishers, 1975)
[424] *The Higher Circles: The Governing Class in America*, (New York: Vintage, 1970)
[425] *None Dare Call It Conspiracy*, (Rossmoor: Concord Press, 1971). For another view based on "inside" documents, see Carroll Quigley, *Tragedy and Hope*, (New York: The Macmillan Company, 1966)
[426] *The Invisible Government*, (Boston: Western Islands, 1962)

their accusations much credence in the West, and they do not of course criticize support of their own brand of fascism.

This author falls into a different camp. Previously accused of being overly critical of Sovietism and domestic socialism, while ignoring Wall Street and the rise of Hitler, this book hopefully will redress an assumed and quite inaccurate philosophical imbalance and emphasize the real point at issue: Whatever you call the collectivist system — Soviet socialism, New Deal socialism, corporate socialism, or National socialism — it is the average citizen, the guy in the street, that ultimately loses out to the boys running the operation at the top. Each system in its own way is a system of plunder, an organizational device to get everyone living (or attempting to live) at the expense of everyone else, while the elitist leaders, the rulers and the politicians, scalp the cream off the top.

The role of this American power elite in the rise of Hitler should also be viewed in conjunction with a little-known aspect of Hitlerism only now being explored: the mystical origins of Naziism, and its relations with the Thule Society and with other conspiratorial groups. This author is no expert on occultism or conspiracy, but it is obvious that the mystical origins, the neo-pagan historical roots of Naziism, the Bavarian Illuminati and the Thule Society, are relatively unknown areas yet to be explored by technically competent researchers. Some research is already recorded in French; probably the best introduction in English is a translation of *Hitler et la Tradition Cathare* by Jean Michel Angebert.[427]

Angebert reveals the 1933 crusade of *Schutzstaffel* member Otto Rahn in search of the Holy Grail, which was supposedly located in the Cathar stronghold in Southern France. The early Nazi hierarchy (Hitler and Himmler, as well as Rudolph Hess and Rosenberg) was steeped in a neo-pagan theology, in part associated with the Thule Society, whose ideals were close to those of the Bavarian Illuminati. This was a submerged driving force behind Naziism, with a powerful mystical hold over the hard-core S.S. faithful. Our contemporary establishment historians barely mention, let alone explore, these occult origins; consequently, they miss an element equally as important as the financial origins of National Socialism.

In 1950 James Stewart Martin published a very readable book, *All Honorable Men*[428] describing his experiences as Chief of the Economic Warfare Section of the Department of Justice investigating the structure of Nazi industry. Martin asserts that American and British businessmen got themselves appointed to key positions in this post-war investigation to divert, stifle and muffle investigation of Nazi industrialists and so keep hidden their own involvement. One British officer was sentenced by court martial to two years in jail for

---

[427] Published in English as *The Occult and the Third Reich*, (The mystical origins of Naziism and the search for the Holy Grail), (New York: The Macmillan Company, 1974). See also Reginald H. Phelps, " 'Before Hitler Came:' Thule Society and Germanen Orden" in the *Journal of Modern History*, September 1968, No. 3.
[428] (Boston: Little Brown and Company, 1950)

protecting a Nazi, and several American officials were removed from their positions. Why would American and British businessmen want to protect Nazi businessmen? In public they argued that these were merely German businessmen who had nothing to do with the Nazi regime and were innocent of complicity in Nazi conspiracies. Martin does not explore this explanation in depth, but he is obviously unhappy and skeptical about it. The evidence suggests there was a concerted effort not only to protect Nazi businessmen, but also to protect the collaborating elements from American and British business.

The German businessmen could have disclosed a lot of uncomfortable facts: In return for protection, they told very little. It is undoubtedly *not* coincidental that the Hitler industrialists on trial at Nuremburg received less than a slap on the wrist. We raise the question of whether the Nuremburg trials should not have been held in Washington — with a few prominent U.S. businessmen as well as Nazi businessmen in the dock!

Two extracts from contemporary sources will introduce and suggest the theme to be expanded. The first extract is from Roosevelt's own files. The U.S. Ambassador in Germany, William Dodd, wrote FDR from Berlin on October 19, 1936 (three years after Hitler came to power), concerning American industrialists and their aid to the Nazis:

> Much as I believe in peace as our best policy, I cannot avoid the fears which Wilson emphasized more than once in conversations with me, August 15, 1915 and later: the breakdown of democracy in all Europe will be a disaster to the people. But what can you do? At the present moment more than a hundred American corporations have subsidiaries here or cooperative understandings.
>
> The DuPonts have three allies in Germany that are aiding in the armament business. Their chief ally is the I. G. Farben Company, a part of the Government which gives 200,000 marks a year to one propaganda organization operating on American opinion. Standard Oil Company (New York sub-company) sent $2,000,000 here in December 1933 and has made $500,000 a year helping Germans make Ersatz gas for war purposes; but Standard Oil cannot take any of its earnings out of the country except in goods. They do little of this, report their earnings at home, but do not explain the facts. The International Harvester Company president told me their business here rose 33% a year (arms manufacture, I believe), but they could take nothing out. Even our airplanes people have secret arrangement with Krupps. General Motor Company and Ford do enormous businesses/sic] here through their subsidiaries and take no profits out. I mention these facts because they complicate things and add to war dangers.[429]

---

[429] Edgar B. Nixon, ed., *Franklin D. Roosevelt and Foreign Affairs*, Volume III: September 1935-January 1937, (Cambridge: Belknap Press, 1969), p. 456.

Second, a quote from the diary of the same U.S. Ambassador in Germany. The reader should bear in mind that a representative of the cited Vacuum Oil Company — as well as representatives of other Nazi, supporting American firms — was appointed to the post-war Control Commission to de-Nazify the Nazis:

> *January 25. Thursday. Our Commercial Attache brought Dr. Engelbrecht, chairman of the Vacuum Oil Company in Hamburg, to see me. Engelbrecht repeated what he had said a year ago: "The Standard Oil Company of New York, the parent company of the Vacuum, has spent 10,000,000 marks in Germany trying to find oil resources and building a great refinery near the Hamburg harbor." Engelbrecht is still boring wells and finding a good deal of crude oil in the Hanover region, but he had no hope of great deposits. He hopes Dr. Schacht will subsidize his company as he does some German companies that have found no crude oil. The Vacuum spends all its earnings here, employs 1,000 men and never sends any of its money home. I could give him no encouragement.*[430]

And further:

> *These men were hardly out of the building before the lawyer came in again to report his difficulties. I could not do anything. I asked him, however: Why did the Standard Oil Company of New York send $1,000,000 over here in December, 1933, to aid the Germans in making gasoline from soft coal for war emergencies? Why do the International Harvester people continue to manufacture in Germany when their company gets nothing out of the country and when it has failed to collect its war losses? He saw my point and agreed that it looked foolish and that it only means greater losses if another war breaks loose.*[431]

The alliance between Nazi political power and American "Big Business" may well have looked foolish to Ambassador Dodd and the American attorney he questioned. In practice, of course, "Big Business" is anything but foolish when it comes to promoting its own self-interest. Investment in Nazi Germany (along with similar investments in the Soviet Union) was a reflection of higher policies, with much more than immediate profit at stake, even though profits could not be repatriated. To trace these "higher policies" one has to penetrate the financial control of multinational corporations, because those who control the flow of finance ultimately control the day-to-day policies.

Carroll Quigley[432] has shown that the apex of this international financial control system before World War II was the Bank for International Settlements, with representatives from

---

[430] Edited by William E. Dodd Jr. and Martha Dodd, *Ambassador Dodd's Diary*, 1933-1938, (New York: Harcourt Brace and Company, 1941), p. 303.
[431] Ibid, p. 358.
[432] Quigley, op. cit.

the international banking firms of Europe and the United States, in an arrangement that continued throughout World War II. During the Nazi period, Germany's representative at the Bank for International Settlements was Hitler's financial genius and president of the Reichsbank, Hjalmar Horace Greeley Schacht.

HJALMAR HORACE GREELEY SCHACHT

Wall Street involvement with Hitler's Germany highlights two Germans with Wall Street connections — Hjalmar Schacht and "Putzi" Hanfstaengl. The latter was a friend of Hitler and Roosevelt who played a suspiciously prominent role in the incident that brought Hitler to the peak of dictatorial power — the Reichstag fire of 1933.[433]

The early history of Hjalmar Schacht, and in particular his role in the Soviet Union after the Bolshevik Revolution of 1917, was described in my earlier book, *Wall Street and the Bolshevik Revolution*. The elder Schacht had worked at the Berlin office of the Equitable Trust Company of New York in the early twentieth century. Hjalmar was born in Germany rather than New York only by the accident of his mother's illness, which required the family to return to Germany. Brother William Schacht was an American-born citizen. To record his American origins, Hjalmar's middle names were designated "Horace Greeley" after the well-know Democrat politician. Consequently, Hjalmar spoke fluent English and the post-war interrogation of Schacht in Project Dustbin was conducted in both German and English. The point to be made is that the Schacht family had its origins in New York, worked for the prominent Wall Street financial house of Equitable Trust (which was controlled by the Morgan firm), and throughout his life Hjalmar retained these Wall Street connections.[434] Newspapers and contemporary sources record repeated visits with Owen Young of General Electric; Farish, chairman of Standard Oil of New Jersey; and their banking counterparts. In brief, Schacht was a member of the international financial elite that wields its power behind the scenes through the political apparatus of a nation. He is a key link between the Wall Street elite and Hitler's inner circle.

This book is divided into two major parts. Part One records the buildup of German cartels through the Dawes and Young Plans in the 1920s. These cartels were the major supporters of Hitler and Naziism and were directly responsible for bringing the Nazis to power in 1933. The roles of American I. G. Farben, General Electric, Standard Oil of New Jersey, Ford, and other U.S. firms is outlined. Part Two presents the known documentary evidence on the financing of Hitler, complete with photographic reproduction of the bank

---

[433] For more information about "Putzi" Hanfstaengl, see Chapter Nine.
[434] See Sutton, *Wall Street and the Bolshevik Revolution*, op. cit., for Sehacht's relations with Soviets and Wall Street, and his directorship of a Soviet bank.

transfer slips used to transfer funds from Farben, General Electric, and other firms to Hitler, through Hjalmar Horace Greeley Schacht.

Chapter One

Wall Street Paves the Way for Hitler

> *The Dawes Plan, adopted in August 1924, fitted perfectly into the plans of the German General Staffs military economists.* (Testimony before United States Senate, Committee on Military Affairs, 1946.)

The post-World War II Kilgore Committee of the United States Senate heard detailed evidence from government officials to the effect that,

> *...when the Nazis came to power in 1933, they found that long strides had been made since 1918 in preparing Germany for war from an economic and industrial point of view.*[435]

This build-up for European war both before and after 1933 was in great part due to Wall Street financial assistance in the 1920s to create the German cartel system, and to technical assistance from well-known American firms which will be identified later, to build the German Wehrmacht. Whereas this financial and technical assistance is referred to as "accidental" or due to the "short-sightedness" of American businessmen, the evidence presented below strongly suggests some degree of premeditation on the part of these American financiers. Similar and unacceptable pleas of "accident" were made on behalf of American financiers and industrialists in the parallel example of building the military power of the Soviet Union from 1917 onwards. Yet these American capitalists were willing to finance and subsidize the Soviet Union while the Vietnam war was underway, knowing that the Soviets were supplying the other side.

The contribution made by American capitalism to German war preparations before 1940 can only be described as phenomenal. It was certainly crucial to German military capabilities.

For instance, in 1934 Germany produced domestically only 300,000 tons of natural petroleum products and less than 800,000 tons of synthetic gasoline; the balance was imported. Yet, ten years later in World War II, after transfer of the Standard Oil of New

---

[435] United States Congress. Senate. Hearings before a Subcommittee of the Committee on Military Affairs. Elimination of German Resources for War. Report pursuant to S. Res. 107 and 146, July 2, 1945, Part 7, (78th Congress and 79th Congress), (Washington: Government Printing Office, 1945), hereafter cited as Elimination of German Resources.

Jersey hydrogenation patents and technology to I. G. Farben (used to produce synthetic gasoline from coal), Germany produced about 6 1/2 million tons of oil — of which 85 percent (5 1/2 million tons) was synthetic oil using the Standard Oil hydrogenation process. Moreover, the control of synthetic oil output in Germany was held by the I. G. Farben subsidiary, Braunkohle-Benzin A. G., and this Farben cartel itself was created in 1926 with Wall Street financial assistance.

On the other hand, the general impression left with the reader by modern historians is that this American technical assistance was accidental and that American industrialists were innocent of wrongdoing. For example, the Kilgore Committee stated:

> *The United States accidentally played an important role in the technical arming of Germany. Although the German military planners had ordered and persuaded manufacturing corporations to install modern equipment for mass production, neither the military economists nor the corporations seem to have realized to the full extent what that meant. Their eyes were opened when two of the chief American automobile companies built plants in Germany in order to sell in the European market, without the handicap of ocean freight charges and high German tariffs. Germans were brought to Detroit to learn the techniques of specialized production of components, and of straight-line assembly. What they saw caused further reorganization and refitting of other key German war plants. The techniques learned in Detroit were eventually used to construct the dive-bombing Stukas .... At a later period I. G. Farben representatives in this country enabled a stream of German engineers to visit not only plane plants but others of military importance, in which they learned a great deal that was eventually used against the United States.[436]*

Following these observations, which emphasize the "accidental" nature of the assistance, it has been concluded by such academic writers as Gabriel Kolko, who is not usually a supporter of big business, that:

> *It is almost superfluous to point out that the motives of the American firms bound to contracts with German concerns Were not pro. Nazi, whatever else they may have been.[437]*

Yet, Kolko to the contrary, analyses of the contemporary American business press confirm that business journals and newspapers were fully aware of the Nazi threat and its nature, while warning their business readers of German war preparations. And even Kolko admits that:

---

[436] Elimination of German Resources, p. 174.
[437] Gabriel Kolko, "American Business and Germany, 1930-1941", *The Western Political Quarterly*, Volume XV, 1962.

> The business press [in the United States] was aware, from 1935 on, that German prosperity was based on war preparations. More important, it was conscious of the fact that German industry was under the control of the Nazis and was being directed to serve Germany's rearmament, and the firm mentioned most frequently in this context was the giant chemical empire, I. G. Farben.[438]

Further, the evidence presented below suggests that not only was an influential sector of American business aware of the nature of Naziism, but for its own purposes aided Naziism wherever possible (and profitable) —*with full knowledge that the probable outcome would be war involving Europe and the United States.* As we shall see, the pleas of innocence do not accord with the facts.

1924: THE DAWES PLAN

The Treaty of Versailles after World War I imposed a heavy reparations burden on defeated Germany. This financial burden — a real cause of the German discontent that led to acceptance of Hitlerism — was utilized by the international bankers for their own benefit.

The opportunity to float profitable loans for German cartels in the United States was presented by the Dawes Plan and later the Young Plan. Both plans were engineered by these central bankers, who manned the committees for their own pecuniary advantages, and although technically the committees were not appointed by the U.S. Government, the plans were in fact approved and sponsored by the Government.

Post-war haggling by financiers and politicians fixed German reparations at an annual fee of 132 billion gold marks. This was about one quarter of Germany's total 1921 exports. When Germany was unable to make these crushing payments, France and Belgium occupied the Ruhr to take by force what could not be obtained voluntarily. In 1924 the Allies appointed a committee of bankers (headed by American banker Charles G. Dawes) to develop a program of reparations payments. The resulting Dawes Plan was, according to Georgetown University Professor of International Relations Carroll Quigley, "largely a J.P. Morgan production."[439] The Dawes Plan arranged a series of foreign loans totaling $800 million with their proceeds flowing to Germany. These loans are important for our story because the proceeds, raised for the greater part in the United States from dollar investors, were utilized in the mid-1920s to create and consolidate the gigantic chemical and steel combinations of I. G. Farben and Vereinigte Stahlwerke, respectively. These cartels not only helped Hitler to

---

[438] Ibid, p. 715.
[439] Carroll Quigley, op. cit.

power in 1933; they also produced the bulk of key German war materials used in World War II.

Between 1924 and 1931, under the Dawes Plan and the Young Plan, Germany paid out to the Allies about 86 billion marks in reparations. At the same time Germany borrowed abroad, mainly in the U.S., about 138 billion marks — thus making a net German payment of only three billion marks for reparations. Consequently, the burden of German monetary reparations to the Allies was actually carried by foreign subscribers to German bonds issued by Wall Street financial houses — at significant profits for themselves, of course. And, let it be noted, these firms were owned by the same financiers who periodically took off their banker hats and donned new ones to become "statesmen." As "statesmen" they formulated the Dawes and Young Plans to "solve" the "problem" of reparations. As bankers, they floated the loans. As Carroll Quigley points out,

> *It is worthy of note that this system was set up by the inter. national bankers and that the subsequent lending of other people's money to Germany was very profitable to these bankers.*[440]

Who were the New York international bankers who formed these reparations commissions?

The 1924 Dawes Plan experts from the United States were banker Charles Dawes and Morgan representative Owen Young, who was president of the General Electric Company. Dawes was chairman of the Allied Committee of Experts in 1924. In 1929 Owen Young became chairman of the Committee of Experts, supported by J.P. Morgan himself, with alternates T. W. Lamont, a Morgan partner, and T. N. Perkins, a banker with Morgan associations. In other words, the U.S. delegations were purely and simply, as Quigley has pointed out, J. P. Morgan delegations using the authority and seal of the United States to promote financial plans for their own pecuniary advantage. As a result, as Quigley puts it, the "international bankers sat in heaven, under a rain of fees and commissions."[441]

The German members of the Committee of Experts were equally interesting. In 1924 Hjalmar Schacht was president of the Reichsbank and had taken a prominent role in organization work for the Dawes Plan; so did German banker Carl Melchior. One of the 1928 German delegates was A. Voegler of the German steel cartel Stahlwerke Vereinigte. In brief, the two significant countries involved — the United States and Germany —were represented by the Morgan bankers on one side and Schacht and Voegler on the other, both

---

[440] Ibid, p. 308.
[441] Carroll Quigley, op. cit., p. 309.

of whom were key characters in the rise of Hitler's Germany and subsequent German rearmament.

Finally, the members and advisors of the Dawes and Young Commissions were not only associated with New York financial houses but, as we shall later see, were directors of firms within the German cartels which aided Hitler to power.

1928: THE YOUNG PLAN

According to Hitler's financial genie, Hjalmar Horace Greeley Schacht, and Nazi industrialist Fritz Thyssen, it was the 1928 Young Plan (the successor to the Dawes Plan), formulated by Morgan agent Owen D. Young, that brought Hitler to power in 1933. Fritz Thyssen claims that,

> *I turned to the National Socialist Party only after I became convinced that the fight against the Young Plan was unavoidable if complete collapse of Germany was to be prevented.*[442]

The difference between the Young Plan and the Dawes Plan was that, while the Young Plan required payments in goods produced in Germany financed by foreign loans, the Young Plan required monetary payments and "In my judgment [wrote Thyssen] the financial debt thus created was bound to disrupt the entire economy of the Reich."

The Young Plan was assertedly a device to occupy Germany with American capital and pledge German real assets for a gigantic mortgage held in the United States. It is noteworthy that German firms with U.S. affiliations evaded the Plan by the device of temporary foreign ownership. For instance, A.E.G. (German General Electric), affiliated with General Electric in the U.S., was sold to a Franco-Belgian holding company and evaded the conditions of the Young Plan. It should be noted in passing that Owen Young was the major financial backer for Franklin D. Roosevelt in the United European venture when FDR, as a budding Wall Street financier, endeavoured to take advantage of Germany's 1925 hyperinflation. The United European venture was a vehicle to speculate and to profit upon the imposition of the Dawes Plan, and is clear evidence of private financiers (including Franklin D. Roosevelt) using the power of the state to advance their own interests by manipulating foreign policy.

---

[442] Fritz Thyssen, *I Paid Hitler*, (New York: Farrar & Rinehart, Inc., n.d.), p. 88.

Schacht's parallel charge that Owen Young was responsible for the rise of Hitler, while obviously self-serving, is recorded in a U.S. Government Intelligence report relating the interrogation of Dr. Fritz Thyssen in September, 1945:

> *The acceptance of the Young Plan and its financial principles increased unemployment more and more, until about one million were unemployed.*
> *People were desperate. Hitler said he would do away with unemployment. The government in power at that time was very bad, and the situation of the people was getting worse. That really was the reason of the enormous success Hitler had in the election. When the last election came, he got about 40%.*[443]

However, it was Schacht, not Owen Young, who conceived the idea which later became the Bank for International Settlements. The actual details were worked out at a conference presided over by Jackson Reynolds, "one of the leading New York bankers," together with Melvin Traylor of the First National Bank of Chicago, Sir Charles Addis, formerly of the Hong Kong and Shanghai Banking Corporation, and various French and German bankers.[444] The B.I.S. was essential under the Young Plan as a means to afford a ready instrument for promoting international financial relations. According to his own statements, Schacht also gave Owen Young the idea that later became the post-World War II International Bank for Reconstruction and Development:

> *"A bank of this kind will demand financial co-operation be, tween vanquished and victors that will lead to community of interests which in turn will give rise to mutual confidence and understanding and thus promote and ensure peace."*
> *I can still vividly recall the setting in which this conversation took place. Owen Young was seated in his armchair puffing away at his pipe, his legs outstretched, his keen eyes fixed unswervingly on me. As is my habit when propounding such arguments I was doing a quiet steady "quarter-deck" up and down the room. When I had finished there was a brief pause. Then his whole face lighted up and his resolve found utterance in the words:*
> *"Dr. Schacht, you gave me a wonderful idea and I am going to sell it to the world."*[445]

B.I.S. — THE APEX OF CONTROL

---

[443] U.S. Group Control Council (Germany), Office of the Director of Intelligence, Intelligence Report No. EF/ME/1, 4 September 1945. Also see Hjalmar Schacht, *Confessions of "the old Wizard"*, (Boston: Houghton Mifflin, 1956)
[444] Hjalmar Schacht, op cit., p. 18. Fritz Thyssen adds, "Even at the time Mr. Dillon, a New York Banker of Jewish origin whom I much admire told me 'In your place I would not sign the plan.'"
[445] Ibid, p. 282.

This interplay of ideas and cooperation between Hjalmar Sehacht in Germany and, through Owen Young, the J.P. Morgan interests in New York, was only one facet of a vast and ambitious system of cooperation and international alliance for world control. As described by Carroll Quigley, this system was "... nothing less than to create a world system of financial control, in private hands, able to dominate the political system of each country and the economy of the world as a whole.[446]

This feudal system worked in the 1920s, as it works today, through the medium of the private central bankers in each country who control the national money supply of individual economies. In the 1920s and 1930s, the New York Federal Reserve System, the Bank of England, the Reichs-bank in Germany, and the Banque de France also more or less influenced the political apparatus of their respective countries indirectly through control of the money supply and creation of the monetary environment. More direct influence was realized by supplying political funds to, or withdrawing support from, politicians and political parties. In the United States, for example, President Herbert Hoover blamed his 1932 defeat on withdrawal of support by Wall Street and the switch of Wall Street finance and influence to Franklin D. Roosevelt.

Politicians amenable to the objectives of financial capitalism, and academies prolific with ideas for world control useful to the international bankers, are kept in line with a system of rewards and penalties. In the early 1930s the guiding vehicle for this international system of financial and political control, called by Quigley the "apex of the system," was the Bank for International Settlements in Basle, Switzerland. The B.I.S. apex continued its work during World War II as the medium through which the bankers — who apparently were not at war with each other — continued a mutually beneficial exchange of ideas, information, and planning for the post-war world. As one writer has observed, war made no difference to the international bankers:

> *The fact that the Bank possessed a truly international staff did, of course, present a highly anomalous situation in time of war. An American President was transacting the daily business of the Bank through a French General Manager, who had a German Assistant General Manager, while the Secretary-General was an Italian subject. Other nationals occupied other posts. These men were, of course, in daily personal contact with each other.*
>
> *Except for Mr. McKittrick [see infra] theft were of course situated permanently in Switzerland during this period and were not supposed to be subject to orders of their government at any time. However, the directors of the Bank remained, of course, in their respective countries and had no direct contact with the personnel of the Bank. It is alleged,*

---

[446] Carroll Quigley, op. cit., p. 324.

however, that H. Schacht, president of the Reichsbank, kept a personal representative in Basle during most of this time.[447]

It was such secret meetings, "... meetings more secret than any **ever** held by Royal Ark Masons or by any Rosicrucian Order..."[448] between the central bankers at the "apex" of control that so intrigued contemporary journalists, although they only rarely and briefly penetrated behind the mask of secrecy.

BUILDING THE GERMAN CARTELS

A practical example of international finance operating behind the scenes to build and manipulate politico-economic systems is found in the German cartel system. The three largest loans handled by the Wall Street international bankers for German borrowers in the 1920s under the Dawes Plan were for the benefit of three German cartels which a few years later aided Hitler and the Nazis to power. American financiers were directly represented on the boards of two of these three German cartels. This American assistance to German cartels has been described by James Martin as follows: "These loans for reconstruction became a vehicle for arrangements that did more to promote World War II than to establish peace after World War I.[449]

The three dominant cartels, the amounts borrowed and the Wall Street floating syndicate were as follows:

German Cartel	Wall Street Syndicate	Amount Issued
Elektrizitats-Gesellschaft (A.E.G.) (German General Electric)	National City Co.	$35,000,000
Vereinigte Stahlwerke (United Steelworks)	Dillon, Read & Co.	$70,225,000
American I.G. Chemical (I.G. Farben)	National City Co.	$30,000,000

Looking at all the loans issued[450], it appears that only a handful of New York financial houses handled the German reparations financing. Three houses — Dillon, Read Co.; Harris, Forbes & Co.; and National City Company — issued almost three-quarters of the total face amount of the loans and reaped most of the profits:

---

[447] Henry H. Schloss, *The Bank for International Settlements* (Amsterdam,: North Holland Publishing Company, 1958)
[448] John Hargrave, *Montagu Norman*, (New York: The Greystone Press, n.d.). p. 108.
[449] James Stewart Martin, op. cit., p. 70.
[450] See Chapter Seven for more details of Wall Street loans to German industry.

Wall Street Syndicate Manager	Participation in German industrial issues in U.S. capital market	Profits on German loans*	Percent of total
Dillon, Read & Co.	$241,325,000	$2.7 million	29.2
Harris, Forbes & Co.	186,500,000	1.4 million	22.6
National City Co.	173,000,000	5.0 million	20.9
Speyer & Co.	59,500,000	0.6 million	7.2
Lee, Higginson & Co.	53,000,000	n.a.	6.4
Guaranty Co. of N.Y.	41,575,000	0.2 million	5.0
Kuhn, Loeb & Co.	37,500,000	0.2 million	4.5
Equitable Trust Co.	34,000,000	0.3 million	4.1
TOTAL	$826,400,000	$10.4 million	99.9

Source: See Appendix A
*Robert R. Kuczynski, Bankers Profits from German Loans (Washington, D.C.: Brookings Institution, 1932), p. 127.

After the mid-1920s the two major German combines of I.G. Farben and Vereinigte Stahlwerke dominated the chemical and steel cartel system created by these loans.

Although these firms. had a voting majority in the cartels for only two or three basic products, they were able — through control of these basics — to enforce their will throughout the cartel. I.G. Farben was the main producer of basic chemicals used by other combines making chemicals, so its economic power position cannot be measured only by its capacity to produce a few basic chemicals. Similarly, Vereinigte Stahlwerke, with a pig-iron capacity greater than that of all other German iron and steel producers combined, was able to exercise far more influence in the semi-finished iron and steel products cartel than its capacity for pig-iron production suggests. Even so the percentage output of these cartels for all products was significant:

Vereinigte Stahlwerke products	Percent of German total production in 1938
Pig iron	50.8
Pipes and tubes	45.5
Heavy plate	36.0
Explosives	35.0
Coal tar	33.3
Bar steel	37.1
I.G. Farben	Percent of German total production in 1937
Synthetic methanol	100.0
Magnesium	100.0

Chemical nitrogen	70.0
Explosives	60.0
Synthetic gasoline (high octane)	46.0 (1945)
Brown coal	20.0

Among the products that brought I.G. Farben and Vereinigte Stahlwerke into mutual collaboration were coal tar and chemical nitrogen, both of prime importance for the manufacture of explosives. I. G. Farben had a cartel position that assured dominance in the manufacture and sale of chemical nitrogen, but had only about one percent of the coking capacity of Germany. Hence an agreement was made under which Farben explosives subsidiaries obtained their benzol, toluol, and other primary coal-tar products on terms dictated by Vereinigte Stahlwerke, while Vereinigte Stahlwerke's explosives subsidiary was dependent for its nitrates on terms set by Farben. Under this system of mutual collaboration and inter-dependence, the two cartels, I.G. Farben and Vereinigte Stahlwerke, produced 95 percent of German .explosives in 1957-8 on the eve of World War II. *This production was from capacity built by American loans and to some extent by American technology.*

The I. G. Farben-Standard Oil cooperation for production of synthetic oil from coal gave the I. G. Farben cartel a monopoly of German gasoline production during World War II. Just under one half of German high octane gasoline in 1945 was produced directly by I. G. Farben and most of the balance by its affiliated companies.

In brief, in synthetic gasoline and explosives (two of the very basic elements of modern warfare), the control of German World War II output was in the hands of two German combines created by Wall Street loans under the Dawes Plan.

Moreover, American assistance to Nazi war efforts extended into other areas.[451] The two largest tank producers in Hitler's Germany were Opel, a wholly owned subsidiary of General Motors (controlled by the J.P. Morgan firm), and the Ford A. G. subsidiary of the Ford Motor Company of Detroit. The Nazis granted tax-exempt status to Opel in 1936, to enable General Motors to expand its production facilities. General Motors obligingly reinvested the resulting profits into German industry. Henry Ford was decorated by the Nazis for *his* services to Naziism. (See p. 93.) Alcoa and Dow Chemical worked closely with Nazi industry with numerous transfers of their domestic

U.S. technology. Bendix Aviation, in which the J.P. Morgan-controlled General Motors firm had a major stock interest, supplied Siemens & Halske A. G. in Germany with data on automatic pilots and aircraft instruments. As late as 1940, in the "unofficial war," Bendix Aviation supplied complete technical data to Robert Bosch for aircraft and diesel engine starters and received royalty payments in return.

---

[451] See Gabriel Kolko, op. cit., for numerous examples.

In brief, American companies associated with the Morgan-Rockefeller international investment bankers — not, it should be noted, the vast bulk of independent American industrialists — were intimately related to the growth of Nazi industry. It is important to note as we develop our story that General Motors, Ford, General Electric, DuPont and the handful of U.S. companies intimately involved with the development of Nazi Germany were — except for the Ford Motor Company — controlled by the Wall Street elite — the J.P. Morgan firm, the Rockefeller Chase Bank and to a lesser extent the Warburg Manhattan bank.[452] This book is not an indictment of *all* American industry and finance. It is an indictment of the "apex" — those firms controlled through the handful of financial houses, the Federal Reserve Bank system, the Bank for International Settlements, and their continuing international cooperative arrangements and cartels which attempt to control the course of world politics and economics.

---

[452] In 1956 the Chase and Manhattan banks merged to become Chase Manhattan.

Chapter Two

The Empire of I.G. Farben

Farben was Hitler and Hitler was Farben.
 (Senator Homer T. Bone to Senate Committee on Military Affairs, June 4, 1943.)

On the eve of World War II the German chemical complex of I.G. Farben was the largest chemical manufacturing enterprise in the world, with extraordinary political and economic power and influence within the Hitlerian Nazi state. I. G. has been aptly described as "a state within a state."

The Farben cartel dated from 1925, when organizing genius Hermann Schmitz (with Wall Street financial assistance) created the super-giant chemical enterprise out of six already giant German chemical companies — Badische Anilin, Bayer, Agfa, Hoechst, Weiler-ter-Meer, and Griesheim-Elektron. These companies were merged to become Inter-nationale Gesellschaft Farbenindustrie A.G. — or I.G. Farben for short. Twenty years later the same Hermann Schmitz was put on trial at Nuremburg for war crimes committed by the I. G. cartel. Other I. G. Farben directors were placed on trial but the American affiliates of I. G. Farben and the American directors of I. G. itself were quietly forgotten; the truth was buried in the archives.

It is these U.S. connections in Wall Street that concern us. Without the capital supplied by Wall Street, there would have been no I. G. Farben in the first place and almost certainly no Adolf Hitler and World War II.

German bankers on the Farben *Aufsichsrat* (the supervisory Board of Directors)[453] in the late 1920s included the Hamburg banker Max War-burg, whose brother Paul Warburg was a founder of the Federal Reserve System in the United States. Not coincidentally, Paul Warburg was also on the board of American I. G., Farben's wholly owned U.S. subsidiary. In addition to Max Warburg and Hermann Schmitz, the guiding hand in the creation of the Farben empire, the early Farben *Vorstand* included Carl Bosch, Fritz ter Meer, Kurt Oppenheim

---

[453] German firms have a two-tier board of directors. The *Aufsichsrat* concerns itself with overall supervision, including financial policy, while the *Vorstand* is concerned with day-to-day management.

and George von Schnitzler.[454] All except Max Warburg were charged as "war criminals" after World War II.

In 1928 the American holdings of I. G. Farben *(i.e.,* the Bayer Company, General Aniline Works, Agfa Ansco, and Winthrop Chemical Company) were organized into a Swiss holding company, I.G. Chemic (Inter-nationale Gesellschaft fur Chemisehe Unternehmungen A. G.), controlled by I. G. Farben in Germany. In the following year these American firms merged to become American I. G. Chemical Corporation, later renamed General Aniline & Film. Hermann Schmitz, the organizer of I. G. Farben in 1925, became a prominent early Nazi and supporter of Hitler, as well as chairman of the Swiss I. G. Chemic and president of American I. G. The Farben complex both in Germany and the United States then developed into an integral part of the formation and operation of the Nazi state machine, the Wehrmacht and the S.S.

I. G. Farben is of peculiar interest in the formation of the Nazi state because Farben directors materially helped. Hitler and the Nazis to power in 1933. We have photographic evidence (see page 60) that I.G. Farben contributed 400,000 RM to Hitler's political "slush fund." It was this secret fund which financed the Nazi seizure of control in March 1933. Many years earlier Farben had obtained Wall Street funds for the 1925 cartelization and expansion in Germany and $30 million for American I. G. in 1929, and had Wall Street directors on the Farben board. It has to be noted that these funds were raised and directors appointed years before Hitler was promoted as the German dictator.

THE ECONOMIC POWER OF I. G. FARBEN

Qualified observers have argued that Germany could not have gone to war in 1939 without I. G. Farben. Between 1927 and the beginning of World War II, I.G. Farben doubled in size, an expansion made possible in great part by American technical assistance and by American bond issues, such as the one for $30 million offered by National City Bank. By 1939 I. G. acquired a participation and managerial influence in some 380 other German firms and over 500 foreign firms. The Farben empire owned its own coal mines, its own electric power plants, iron and steel units, banks, research units, and numerous commercial enterprises. There were over 2,000 cartel agreements between I. G. and foreign firms — including Standard Oil of New Jersey, DuPont, Alcoa, Dow Chemical, and others in the United States, The full story of I,G, Farben and its world-wide ae-tivities before World War II can

---

[454] Taken from *Der Farben-Konzern* 1928, (Hoppenstedt, Berlin: 1928), pp. 4-5.

never be known, as key German records were destroyed in 1945 in anticipation of Allied victory. However, one post-war investigation by the U.S, War Department concluded that:

> Without I. G.'s immense productive facilities, its intense re. search, and vast international affiliations, Germany's prosecution of the war would have been unthinkable and impossible; Farben not only directed its energies toward arming Germany, but concentrated on weakening her intended victims, and this double-barreled attempt to expand the German industrial potential for war and to restrict that of the rest of the world was not conceived and executed "in the normal course of business." The proof is overwhelming that I. G. Farben officials had full prior knowledge of Germany's plan for world conquest and of each specific aggressive act later undertaken.[455]

Directors of Farben firms *(i.e.,* the "I. G. Farben officials" referred to in the investigation) included not only Germans but also prominent American financiers. This 1945 U.S. War Department report concluded that I.G.'s assignment from Hitler in the prewar period was to make Germany self-sufficient in rubber, gasoline, lubricating oils, magnesium, fibers, tanning agents, fats, and explosives. To fulfill this critical assignment, vast sums were spent by I.G. on processes to extract these war materials from indigenous German raw materials - in particular the plentiful German coal resources. Where these processes could not be developed in Germany ,they were acquired from abroad under cartel arrangements. For example, the process for iso-octane, essential for aviation fuels, was obtained from the United States,

> ... in fact entirely [from] the Americans and has become known to us in detail in its separate stages through our agreements with them [Standard Oil of New Jersey] and is being used very extensively by us.[456]

The process for manufacturing tetra-ethyl lead? essential for aviation gasoline, was obtained by I. G. Farben from the United States, and in 1939 I.G. was sold $20 million of high-grade aviation gasoline by Standard Oil of New Jersey. Even before Germany manufactured tetra-ethyl lead by the American process it was able to "borrow" 500 tons from the Ethyl Corporation. This loan of vital tetra-ethyl lead was not repaid and I.G. forfeited the $1 million security. Further, I.G. purchased large stocks of magnesium from Dow Chemical for incendiary bombs and stockpiled explosives, stabilizers, phosphorus, and cyanides from the outside world.

---

[455] *Elimination of German Resources,* p. 943.
[456] Ibid, p. 945.

In 1939, out of 43 major products manufactured by I.G., 28 were of "primary concern" to the German armed forces. Farben's ultimate control of the German war economy, acquired during the 1920s and 1930s with Wall Street assistance, can best be assessed by examining the percentage of German war material output produced by Farben plants in 1945. Farben at that time produced 100 percent of German synthetic rubber, 95 percent of German poison gas (including all the Zyklon B gas used in the concentration camps), 90 percent of German plastics, 88 percent of German magnesium, 84 percent of German explosives, 70 percent of German gunpowder, 46 percent of German high octane (aviation) gasoline, and 33 percent of German synthetic gasoline.[457] (See Chart 2-1 and Table 2-1.)

Table 2-1: German Army (Wehrmacht) Dependence on I.G. Farben Production (1943):

Product	Total German Production	Percent Produced by I.G. Farben
Synthetic Rubber	118,600 tons	100
Methanol	251,000 tons	100
Lubricating Oil	60,000 tons	100
Dyestuffs	31,670 tons	98
Poison Gas	—	95
Nickel	2,000 tons	95
Plastics	57,000 tons	90
Magnesium	27,400 tons	88
Explosives	221,000 tons	84
Gunpowder	210,000 tons	70
High Octane (Aviation) Gasoline	650,000 tons	46
Sulfuric Acid	707,000 tons	35

Dr. von Schnitzler, of the I.G. Farben *Aufsichsrat*, made the following pertinent statement in 1943:

---

[457] *New York Times*, October 21, 1945, Section 1, pp. 1, 12.

It is no exaggeration to say that without the services of German chemistry performed under the Four Year Plan the prosecution of modern war would have been unthinkable.[458]

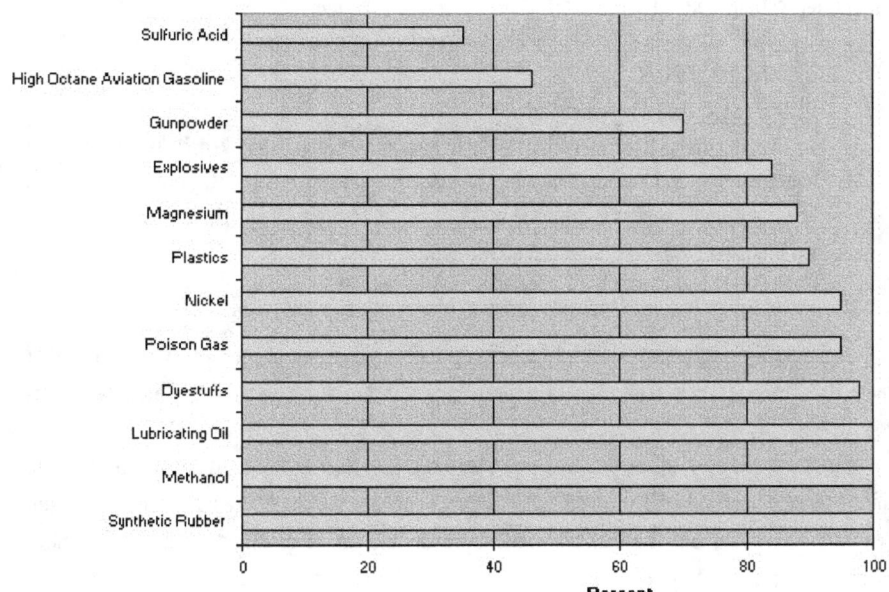

Chart 2-1: German Army (Wehrmacht) Dependence on I.G. Farben Production (1943):

Unfortunately, when we probe the technical origins of the more important of these military materials — quite apart from financial Support for Hitler — we find links to American industry and to American businessmen. There were numerous Farben arrangements with American firms, including cartel marketing arrangements, patent agreements, and technical exchanges as exemplified in the Standard Oil-Ethyl technology transfers mentioned above. These arrangements were used by I.G. to advance Nazi policy abroad, to collect strategic information, and to consolidate a world-wide chemical cartel.

One of the more horrifying aspects of I.G. Farben's cartel was the invention, production, and distribution of the Zyklon B gas, used in Nazi concentration camps. Zyklon B was pure Prussic acid, a lethal poison produced by I.G. Farben Leverkusen and sold from the Bayer sales office through Degesch, an independent license holder. Sales of Zyklon B amounted to almost three-quarters of Degesch business; enough gas to kill 200 million humans was produced and sold by I.G. Farben. The Kilgore Committee report of 1942 makes it clear that the I.G. Farben directors had precise knowledge of the Nazi concentration camps and

---

[458] Ibid, p. 947.

the use of I.G. chemicals. This prior knowledge becomes significant when we later consider the role of the American directors in I.G.'s American subsidiary. The 1945 interrogation of I.G. Farben director yon Schnitzler reads:
Q. What did you do when they told you that I.G. chemicals was [sic] being used to kill, to murder people held in concentration camps?

> A. I was horrified.
> Q. Did you do anything about it?
> A. I kept it for me [to myself] because it was too terrible .... I asked Muller-Cunradi is it known to you and Ambros and other directors in Auschwitz that the gases and chemicals are being used to murder people.
> Q. What did he say?
> A. Yes: it is known to all I.G. directors in Auschwitz.[459]

There was no attempt by I.G. Farben to halt production of the gases — a rather ineffective way for von Schnitzler to express any concern for human life, "because it was too terrible."

The Berlin N.W. 7 office of I.G. Farben was the key Nazi overseas espionage center. The unit operated under Farben director Max Ilgner, nephew of I.G. Farben president Hermann Schmitz. Max Ilgner and Hermann Schmitz were on the board of American I.G., with fellow directors Henry Ford of Ford Motor Company, Paul Warburg of Bank of Manhattan, and Charles E. Mitchell of the Federal Reserve Bank of New York.

At the outbreak of war in 1939 VOWI employees were ordered into the Wehrmacht but in fact continued to perform the same work as when nominally under I.G. Farben. One of the more prominent of these Farben intelligence workers in N.W. 7 was Prince Bernhard of the Netherlands, who joined Farben in the early 1930s after completion of an 18-month period of service in the black-uniformed S.S.[460]

The U.S. arm of the VOWI intelligence network was Chemnyco, Inc. According to the War Department,

---

[459] *Elimination of German Resources.*

[460] Bernhard is today better known for his role as chairman of the secretive, so-called Bilderberger meetings. See U.S. Congress, House of Representatives, Special Committee on Un-American Activities, *Investigation of Nazi Propaganda Activities and Investigation of Certain other Propaganda Activities.* 73rd Congress, 2nd Session, Hearings No. 73-DC-4. (Washington: Government Printing Office, 1934), Volume VIII, p. 7525.

> *Utilizing normal business contacts Chemnyco was able to transmit to Germany tremendous amounts of material ranging from photographs and blueprints to detailed descriptions of whole industrial plants.*[461]

Chemnyco's vice president in New York was Rudolph Ilgner, an American citizen and brother of American I, G. Farben director Max Ilgner. In brief, Farben operated VOWI, the Nazi foreign intelligence operation, before World War II and the VOWI operation was associated with prominent members of the Wall Street Establishment through American I.G. and Chemnyco.

The U.S. War Department also accused I.G. Farben and its American associates of spearheading Nazi psychological and economic warfare programs through dissemination of propaganda via Farben agents abroad, and of providing foreign exchange for this Nazi propaganda. Farben's cartel arrangements promoted Nazi economic warfare — the outstanding example being the voluntary Standard Oil of New Jersey restriction on development of synthetic rubber in the United States at the behest of I. G. Farben. As the War Department report puts it:

> *The story in short is that because of Standard Oil's determination to maintain an absolute monopoly of synthetic rubber developments in the United States, it fully accomplished I.G.'s purpose of preventing United States production by dissuading American rubber companies from undertaking independent research in developing synthetic rubber processes.*[462]

In 1945 Dr. Oskar Loehr, deputy head of the I.G. "Tea Buro," confirmed that I. G. Farben and Standard Oil of New Jersey operated a "preconceived plan" to suppress development of the synthetic rubber industry in the United States, to the advantage of the German Wehrmacht and to the disadvantage of the United States in World War II.

Dr. Loehr's testimony reads (in part) as follows:

> Q. Is it true that while the delay in divulging the buna [synthetic rubber] processes to American rubber companies was taking place, Chemnyco and Jasco were in the meantime keeping I.G. well informed in regard to synthetic rubber development in the U.S.?
> A. Yes.
> Q. So that at all times I.G. was fully aware of the state of the development of the American synthetic rubber industry?
> A. Yes.

---

[461] Ibid p. 949.
[462] Ibid p. 952.

Q. Were you present at the Hague meeting when Mr. Howard [of Standard Oil] went there in 1939?
A. No.
Q. Who was present?
A. Mr. Ringer, who was accompanied by Dr. Brown of Ludwigshafen. Did they tell you about the negotiations?
A. Yes, as far as they were on the buna part of it.
Q. Is it true that Mr. Howard told I.G. at this meeting that the developments in the U.S. had reached such a stage that it would no longer be possible for him to keep the information in regard to the buna processes from the American companies?
A. Mr. Ringer reported it.
Q. Was it at that meeting that for the first time Mr. Howard told I.G. the American rubber companies might have to be informed of the processes and he assured I.G. that Standard Oil would control the synthetic rubber industry in the U.S.? Is that right?
A. That is right. That is the knowledge I got through Mr. Ringer.
Q. So that in all these arrangements since the beginning of the development of the synthetic rubber industry the suppression of the synthetic rubber industry in the U.S. was part of a preconceived plan between I.G. on the one hand and Mr. Howard of Standard Oil on the other?
A. That is a conclusion that must be drawn from the previous facts.[463]

I.G. Farben was pre-war Germany's largest earner of foreign exchange, and this foreign exchange enabled Germany to purchase strategic raw materials, military equipment, and technical processes, and to finance its overseas programs of espionage, propaganda, and varied military and political activities preceding World War II. Acting on behalf of the Nazi state, Farben broadened its own horizon to a world scale which maintained close relations with the Nazi regime and the Wehrmaeht. A liaison office, the *Vermittlungsstelle W,* was established to maintain communications between I.G. Farben and the German Ministry of War:

> The aim of this work is the building up o.[a tight organ izatton for armament in the I.G. which could be inserted without difficulty in the existing organization of the I.G. and the individual plants. In the case of war, I.G. will be treated by the authorities concerned with armament questions as one big plant which, in its task for the armament, as far as it is possible to do so from the technical point of view, will regulate itself without any organizational influence from outside (the work in this direction was in principle agreed upon with the Ministry of War Wehrwirtschaftsant) and from this office with the Ministry of Economy. To the field of the work of the Vermittlungsstelle W belongs, besides the

---

[463] Ibid p. 1293.

organizational set-up and long-range planning, the continuous collaboration with regard to the armament and technical questions with the authorities of the Reich and with the plants of the I.G.[464]

Unfortunately the files of the *Vermittlungsstelle* offices were destroyed prior to the end of the war, although it is known from other sources that from 1934 onwards a complex network of transactions evolved between I.G. and the Wehrmacht. In 1934 I. G. Farben began to mobilize for war, and each I.G. plant prepared its war production plans and submitted the plans to the Ministries of War and Economics. By 1935-6 war games were being held at I.G. Farben plants and wartime technical procedures rehearsed.[465] These war games were described by Dr. Struss, head of the Secretariat of I.G.'s Technical Committee:

> *It is true that since 1934 or 1935, soon after the establishment of the Vermittlungsstelle W in the different works, theoretical war plant games had been arranged to examine how the effect of bombing on certain factories would materialize. It was particularly taken into consideration what would happen if 100- or 500-kilogram bombs would fall on a certain factory and what would be the result of it. It is also right that the word Kriegsspiele was used for it.*
>
> *The Kriegsspiele were prepared by Mr. Ritter and Dr. Eckell, later on partly by Dr. yon Brunning by personal order on Dr. Krauch's own initiative or by order of the Air Force, it is not known to me. The tasks were partly given by the Vermittlung-sstelle W and partly by officers of the Air Force. A number of officers of all groups of the Wehrmacht (Navy, Air Force, and Army) participated in these Kriegsspiele.*
>
> *The places which were hit by bombs were marked in a map of the plant so that it could be ascertained which parts of the plant were damaged, for example a gas meter or an important pipe line. As soon as the raid finished, the management of the plant ascertained the damages and reported which part of the plant had to stop working; they further reported what time would be required in order to repair the damages. In a following meeting the consequences of the Kriegsspiele were described and it was ascertained that in the case of Leuna [plant] the damages involved were considerably high; especially it was found out that alterations of the pipe lines were to be made at considerable cost.*[466]

Consequently, throughout the 1930s I. G. Farben did more than just comply with orders from the Nazi regime. Farben was an initiator and operator for the Nazi plans for world conquest. Farben acted as a research and intelligence organization for the German Army and voluntarily initiated Wehrmacht projects. In fact the Army only rarely had to approach

---

[464] Ibid p. 954.
[465] Ibid p. 954.
[466] Ibid, pp. 954-5.

Farben; it is estimated that about 40 to 50 percent of Farben projects for the Army were initiated by Farben itself. In brief, in the words of Dr, von Schnitzler:

> Thus, in acting as it had done, I.G. contracted a great responsibility and constituted a substantial aid in the chemical domain and decisive help to Hitler's foreign policy, which led to war and to the ruin of Germany. Thus, I must conclude that I.G. is largely responsible for Hitler's policy.

POLISHING I. G. FARBEN'S PUBLIC IMAGE

This miserable picture of pre-war military preparation was known abroad and had to be sold — or disguised — to the American public in order to facilitate Wall Street fund-raising and technical assistance on behalf of I. G. Farben in the United States. A prominent New York public relations firm was chosen for the job of selling the I.G. Farben combine to America. The most notable public relations firm in the late 1920s and 1930s was Ivy Lee & T.J. Ross of New York. Ivy Lee had previously undertaken a public relations campaign for the Rockefellers, to spruce up the Rockefeller name among the American public. The firm had also produced a syncophantic book entitled *USSR*, undertaking the same clean-up task for the Soviet Union — even while Soviet labor camps were in full blast in the late 20s and early 30s.

From 1929 onwards Ivy Lee became public relations counsel for I. G. Farben in the United States. In 1934 Ivy Lee presented testimony to the House Un-American Activities Committee on this work for Farben.[467] Lee testified that I.G. Farben was affiliated with the American Farben firm and "The American I.G. is a holding company with directors such people as Edsel Ford, Walter Teagle, one of the officers of the City Bank .... " Lee explained that he was paid $25,000 per year under a contract made with Max Ilgner of I.G. Farben. His job was to counter criticism levelled at I.G. Farben within the United States. The advice given by Ivy Lee to Farben on this problem was acceptable enough:

> In the first place, I have told them that they could never in the world get the American people reconciled to their treatment of the Jews: that that was just foreign to the American mentality and could never be justified in the American public opinion, and there was no use trying.

---

[467] U.S. Congress. House of Representatives, Special Committee on Un-American Activities, *Investigation of Nazi Propaganda Activities* and *Investigation of Certain Other Propaganda Activities*, op. cit.

> *In the second place, anything that savored of Nazi propaganda in this country was a mistake and ought not to be under. taken. Our people regard it as meddling with American affairs, and it was bad business.*[468]

The initial payment of $4,500 to Ivy Lee under this contract was made by Hermann Schmitz, chairman of I.G. Farben in Germany. It was deposited in the New York Trust Company under the name of I. G. Chemic (or the "Swiss I.G.," as Ivy Lee termed it).

However, the second and major payment of $14,450 was made by William von Rath of the American I.G. and also deposited by Ivy Lee in New York Trust Company, for the credit of his personal account. (The firm account was at the Chase Bank.) This point about the origin of the funds is important when we consider the identity of directors of American I.G., because payment by American I.G. meant that the bulk of the Nazi propaganda funds were not of German origin. *They were American funds earned in the U.S. and under control of American directors, although used for Nazi propaganda in the United States.*

In other words, most of the Nazi propaganda funds handled by Ivy Lee were *not* imported from Germany.

The use to which these American funds were put was brought out under questioning by the House Un-American Activities Committee:

> Mr. DICKSTEIN. As I understand you, you testified that you received no propaganda at all, and that you had nothing to do with the distribution of propaganda in this country?
> Mr. LEE. I did not testify I received none Mr. Dickstein.
> Mr. DICKSTEIN. I will eliminate that part of the question, then.
> Mr. LEE. I testified that I disseminated none whatever.
> Mr. DICKSTEIN. Have you received or has your firm received any propaganda literature from Germany at any time?
> Mr. LEE. Yes, sir.
> Mr. DICKSTEIN. And when was that?
> Mr. LEE. Oh, we have received — it is a question of what you call propaganda. We have received an immense amount of literature.
> Mr. DICKSTEIN. You do not know what that literature was and what it contained?
> Mr. LEE. We have received books and pamphlets and newspaper clippings and documents, world without end.
> Mr. DICKSTEIN. I assume someone in your office would go over them and see what they were?
> Mr. LEE. Yes, sir.

---

[468] Ibid, p. 178.

Mr. DICKSTEIN. And then after you found out what they were, I assume you kept copies of them?

Mr. LEE. In some cases, yes: and in some, no. A great many of them, of course, were in German, and I had what my son sent me. He said they were interesting and significant, and those I had translated or excerpts of them made.[469]

Finally, Ivy Lee employed Burnham Carter to study American new paper reports on Germany and prepare suitable pro-Nazi replies. It should be noted that this German literature was not Farben literature, it was official Hitler literature:

Mr. DICKSTEIN. In other words, you receive this material that deals with German conditions today: You examine it and you advise them. It has nothing to do with the German Government, although the material, the literature, is official literature of the Hitler regime. That is correct, is it not?

Mr. LEE. Well, a good deal of the literature was not official.

Mr. DICKSTEIN. It was not I.G. literature, was it?

Mr. LEE. No; I.G. sent it to me.

Mr. DICKSTEIN. Can you show us one scrap of paper that came in here that had anything to do with the I.G.?

Mr. LEE. Oh, yes. They issue a good deal of literature. But I do not want to beg the question. There is no question whatever that under their authority I have received an immense amount of material that came from official and unofficial sources.

Mr. DICKSTEIN. Exactly. In other words, the material that was sent here by the I.G. was material spread — we would call it propaganda t by authority of the German Government. But the distinction that you make in your statement is, as I take it, that the German Government did not send it to you directly; that it was sent to you by the I.G.

Mr. LEE. Right.

Mr. DICKSTEIN. And it had nothing to do with their business relations just now.

Mr. LEE. That is correct.

THE AMERICAN I.G. FARBEN

Who were the prominent Wall Street establishment financiers who directed the activities of American I.G., the I.G. Farben affiliate in the United States promoting Nazi propaganda?

American I.G. Farben directors included some of the more prominent members of Wall Street. German interests re-entered the United States after World War I, and successfully overcame barriers designed to keep I.G. out of the American market. Neither seizure of

---

[469] Ibid, p. 183.

German patents, establishment of the Chemical Foundation, nor high tariff walls were a major problem.

By 1925, General Dyestuff Corporation was established as the exclusive selling agent for products manufactured by Gasselli Dyestuff (renamed General Aniline Works, Inc., in 1929) and imported from Germany. The stock of General Aniline Works was transferred in 1929 to American I.G. Chemical Corporation and later in 1939 to General Aniline & Film Corporation, into which American I.G. and General Aniline Works were merged. American I.G. and its successor, General Aniline & Film, is the unit through which control of I.G.'s enterprises in the U.S. was maintained. The stock authorization of American I.G. was 3,000,000 common A shares and 3,000,000 common B shares. In return for stock interests in General Aniline Works and Agfa-Ansco Corporation, I.G. Farben in Germany received all the B shares and 400,000 A shares. Thirty million dollars of convertible bonds were sold to the American public and guaranteed as to principal and interest by the German I.G. Farben, which received an option to purchase an additional 1,000,000 A shares.

Table 2-2: The Directors of American I.G. at 1930: American I.G.

American I.G. Director	Citizenship	Other Major Associations
Carl BOSCH	German	FORD MOTOR CO. A-G
Edsel B. FORD	U.S.	FORD MOTOR CO. DETROIT
Max ILGNER	German	Directed I.G. FARBEN N.W.7 (INTELLIGENCE) office. Guilty at Nuremberg War Crimes Trials.
F. Ter MEER	German	Guilty at Nuremberg War Crimes Trials
H.A. METZ	U.S.	Director of I.G. Farben Germany and BANK OF MANHATTAN (U.S.)
C.E. MITCHELL	U.S.	Director of FEDERAL RESERVE BANK OF N.Y. and NATIONAL CITY BANK
Herman SCHMITZ	German	On boards of I.G. Farben (President) (Germany) Deutsche Bank (Germany) and BANK FOR INTERNATIONAL SETTLEMENTS. Guilty at Nuremberg War Crimes Trials.
Walter TEAGLE	U.S.	Director FEDERAL RESERVE BANK OF NEW YORK and STANDARD OIL OF NEW JERSEY
W.H. von RATH	Naturalized	Director of GERMAN GENERAL U.S. ELECTRIC (A.E.G.)
Paul M. WARBURG	U.S.	First member of the FEDERAL RESERVE BANK OF NEW YORK and BANK OF MANHATTAN
W.E. WEISS	U.S.	Sterling Products

Source: Moody's Manual of Investments; 1930, p. 2149.
Note: Walter DUISBERG (U.S.), W. GRIEF (U.S.), and Adolf KUTTROFF (U.S.) were also Directors of American I.G. Farben at this period.

The management of American I.G. (later General Aniline) was dominated by I.G. or former I.G. officials. (See Table 9..9..) Hermann Schmitz served as president from 1929 to 1936 and was then succeeded by his brother, Dietrich A. Schmitz, a naturalized American citizen, until 1941. Hermann Schmitz, who was also a director of the bank for International Settlements, the "apex" of the international financial control system. He remained as chairman of the board of directors from 1936 to 1939.

The original board of directors included nine members who were, or had been, members o[the board of I.G. Farben in Germany (Hermann Schmitz, carl Bosch, Max Ilgner, Fritz ter Meer, and Wilfred Grief), or had been previously employed by I.G. Farben in Germany (Walter Duisberg, Adolph Kuttroff, W.H. yon Rath, Herman A. Metz). Herman A. Metz was an American citizen, a staunch Democrat in politics and a former comptroller of the City of New York. A tenth, W.E. Weiss, had been under contract to I.G.

Directors of American I.G. were not only prominent in Wall Street and American industry but more significantly were drawn from a few highly influential institutions:

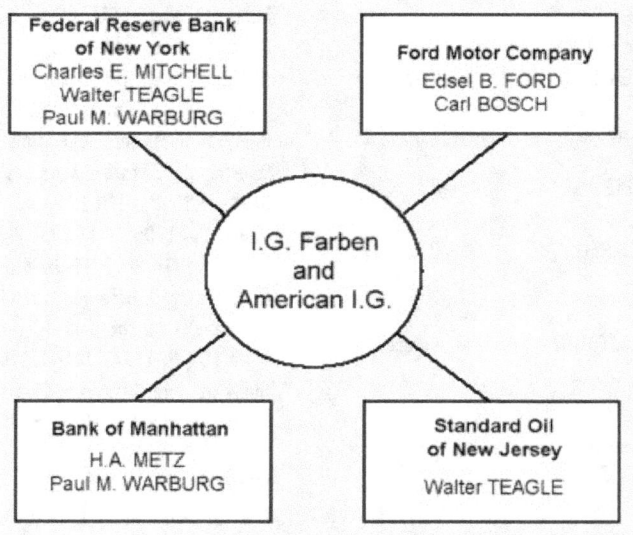

The remaining four members of the American I.G. board were prominent American citizens and members of the Wall Street financial elite: C.E. Mitchell, chairman of National City Bank and the Federal Reserve Bank of New York; Edsel B. Ford, president of Ford

Motor Company; W.C. Teagle, another director of Standard Oil of New Jersey; and, Paul Warburg, first member of the Federal Reserve Bank of New York and chairman of the Bank of Manhattan Company.

Directors of American I.G. were not only prominent in Wall Street and American industry but more significantly were drawn from a few highly influential institutions. (See chart above.)

Between 1929 and 1939 there were changes in the make-up of the board of American I.G. The number of directors varied from time to time, although a majority always had I.G. backgrounds or connections, and the board never had less than four American directors. In 1939 — presumably looking ahead to World War II — an effort was made to give the board a more American complexion, but despite the resignation of Hermann Schmitz, Carl Bosch, and Walter Duisberg, and the appointment of seven new directors, seven members still belonged to the I.G. group. This I.G. predominance increased during 1940 and 1941 as American directors, including Edsel Ford, realized the political unhealthiness of I.G. and resigned.

Several basic observations can be made from this evidence. First, the board of American I.G. had three directors from the Federal Reserve Bank of New York, the most influential of the various Federal Reserve Banks. American I.G. also had interlocks with Standard Oil of New Jersey, Ford Motor Company, Bank of Manhattan (later to become the Chase Manhattan), and A.E.G. (German General Electric). Second, three members of the board of this American I.G. were found guilty at Nuremburg War Crimes Trials. These were the German, not the American, members. Among these Germans was Max Ilgner, director of the I.G. Farben N.W. 7 office in Berlin, *i.e.,* the Nazi pre-war intelligence office. If the directors of a corporation are collectively responsible for the activities of the corporation, then the American directors should also have been placed on trial at Nuremburg, along with the German directors — that is, if the purpose of the trials was to determine war guilt. Of course, if the purpose of the trials had been to divert attention away from the U.S. involvement in Hitler's rise to power, they succeeded very well in such an objective.

Chapter Three

General Electric Funds Hitler

> *Among the early Roosevelt fascist measures was the National Industry Recovery Act (NRA) of June 16, 1933. The origins of this scheme are worth repeating. These ideas were first suggested by Gerard Swope of the General Electric Company ... following this they were adopted by the United States Chamber of Commerce...*
> (Herbert Hoover, The Memoirs of Herbert Hoover: The Great Depression, 1929-1941, New York: The Macmillan Company, 1952, p. 420)

The multi-national giant General Electric has an unparalleled role in twentieth-century history. The General Electric Company electrified the Soviet Union in the 1920s and 1930s, and fulfilled for the Soviets Lenin's dictum that "Socialism = electrification."[470] The Swope Plan, created by General Electric's one-time president Gerard Swope, became Franklin D. Roosevelt's New Deal, by a process deplored by one-time President Herbert Hoover and described in *Wall Street and FDR*.[471] There was a long-lasting, intimate relationship between Swope and Young of General Electric Company and the Roosevelt family, as there was between General Electric and the Soviet Union. In 1936 Senator James A. Reed of Missouri, an early Roosevelt supporter, became aware of Roosevelt's betrayal of liberal ideas and attacked the Roosevelt New Deal program as a "tyrannical" measure "leading to despotism, [and] sought by its sponsors under the communistic cry of 'Social Justice.'" Senator Reed further charged on the floor of the Senate that Franklin D. Roosevelt was a "hired man for the economic royalists" in Wall Street and that the Roosevelt family "is one of the largest stockholders in the General Electric Company."[472]

As we probe into behind-the-scenes German interwar history and the story of Hitler and Naziism, we find both Owen D. Young and Gerard Swope of General Electric tied to the rise of Hitlerism and the suppression of German democracy. That General Electric directors are

---

[470] For the technical details see the three-volume study, Antony C. Sutton, *Western Technology and Soviet Economic Development*, (Stanford, California: Hoover Institution Press, 1968, 1971), 1973), hereafter cited as *Western Technology Series*.
[471] (New York: Arlington House Publishers, 1975)
[472] *New York Times*, October 6, 1936. See also Antony C. Sutton, *Wall Street and FDR*, op. cit.

to be found in each of these three distinct historical categories — i.e., the development of the Soviet Union, the creation of Roosevelt's New Deal, and the rise of Hitlerism — suggests how elements of Big Business are keenly interested in the socialization of the world, for their own purposes and objectives, rather than the maintenance of the impartial market place in a free society.[473] General Electric profited handsomely from Bolshevism, from Roosevelt's New Deal socialism, and, as we shall see below, from national socialism in Hitler's Germany.

GENERAL ELECTRIC IN WEIMAR GERMANY

Walter Rathenau was, until his assassination in 1922, managing director of Allgemeine Elekrizitats Gesellschaft (A.E.G,), or German General Electric, and like Owen Young and Gerard Swope, his counterparts in the U.S., he was a prominent advocate of corporate socialism. Walter Rathenau spoke out publicly against competition and free enterprise, Why? Because both Rathanau and Swope wanted the protection and cooperation of the state for their own corporate objectives and profit. (But not of course for anybody else's objectives and profits.) Rathanau expressed their plea in *The New Political Economy:*

> The new economy will, as we have seen, be no state or governmental economy but a private economy committed to a civic power of resolution which certainly will require state cooperation for organic consolidation to overcome inner friction and increase production and endurance.[474]

When we disentangle the turgid Rathenau prose, this means that the power of the State was to be made available to private firms for their own corporate purposes, *i.e.,* what is popularly known as national socialism. Rathenau spoke out publicly against competition and free enterprise. inheritance."[475] Not their *own* wealth, so far as can be determined, but the wealth of others who lacked political pull in the State apparatus.

Owen D. Young of General Electric was one of the three U.S. delegates to the 1923 Dawes Plan meeting which established the German reparations program. And in the Dawes and Young Plans we can see how some private firms were able to benefit from the power of the State. The largest single loans from Wall Street to Germany during the 1920s were

---

[473] Of course, socialist pleading by businessmen is still with us. Witness the injured cries when President Ford proposed deregulation of airlines and trucking. See for example *Wall Street Journal,* November 25, 1975.
[474] Mimeographed Translation in Hoover Institution Library, p. 67. Also see Walter Rathenau, *In Days to Come,* (London: Allen & Unwin, n.d.)
[475] Ibid, p. 249.

reparations loans; it was ultimately the U.S. investor who paid for German reparations. The cartelization of the German electrical industry under A.E.G. (as well as the steel and chemical industries discussed in Chapters One and Two) was made possible with these Wall Street loans:

Date of Offering	Borrower	Managing Bank in the U.S.	Face Amount of Issue
Jan. 26, 1925	Allgemeine Elektrizitats-Gesellschaft (A. E, G.)	National City Co.	$10,000,000
Dec. 9, 1925	Allgemeine Elektrizitats-Gesellschaft (A. E.G.)	National City Co.	10,000,000
May 22, 1928	Allgemeine Elektrizitats-Gesellschaft (A.E.G.)	National City Co.	10,000,000
June 7, 1928	Allgemeine Elektrizitats-Gesellschaft (A. E.G.)	National City Co.	5,000,000

In 1928, at the Young Plan reparations meetings, we find General Electric president Owen D. Young in the chair as the chief U.S. delegate, appointed by the U.S. government to use U.S. government power and prestige to decide international financial matters enhancing Wall Street and General Electric profits. In 1930 Owen D. Young, after whom the Young Plan for German reparations was named, became chairman of the Board of General Electric Company in New York City. Young was also chairman of the Executive Committee of Radio Corporation of America and a director of both German General Electric (A.E.G.) and Osram in Germany. Young also served on the boards of other major U.S. corporations, including General Motors, NBC, and RKO; he was a councilor of the National Industrial Conference Board, a director of the International Chamber of Commerce, and deputy chairman of the board of the Federal Reserve Bank of New York.

Gerard Swope was president and director of General Electric Company as well as French and German associated companies, including A.E.G. and Osram in Germany. Swope was also a director of RCA, NBC, and the National City Bank of New York. Other directors of International General Electric at this time reflect Morgan control of the company, and both Young and Swope were generally known as the Morgan representatives on the G.E. board, which included Thomas Cochran, another partner in the J.P. Morgan firm. General Electric director Clark Haynes Minor was president of International General Electric in the 1920s. Another director was Victor M. Cutter of the First National Bank of Boston and a figure in the *"Banana* Revolutions" in Central America.

In the late 1920s Young, Swope, and Minor of International General Electric moved into the German electrical industry and gained, if not control as some have reported, then at least a substantial say in the internal affairs of both A.E.G. and Osram. In July 1929 an agreement was reached between General Electric and three German firms — A.E.G., Siemens & Halske, and Koppel and Company — which between them owned all the shares in Osram, the electric bulb manufacturer. General Electric purchased 16% percent of Osram stock and reached a joint agreement for international control of electric bulbs production and marketing. Clark Minor and Gerard Swope became directors of Osram.[476]

In July 1929 great interest was shown in rumors circulating in German financial circles that General Electric was also buying into A.E.G. and that talks to this end were in progress between A.E.G. and G.E.[477] In August it was confirmed that 14 million marks of common A.E.G. stock were to be issued to General Electric. These shares, added to shares bought on the open market, gave General Electric a 25-percent interest in A.E.G. A closer working agreement was signed between the two companies, providing the German company U.S. technology and patents. It was emphasized in the news reports that A.E.G. would not have participation in G.E., but that on the other hand G.E. would finance expansion of A.E.G. in Germany.[478] The German financial press also noted that there was no A.E.G. representation on the board of G.E. in the United States but that five Americans were now on the board of A.E.G. The *Vossische Zeitung* recorded,

> *The American electrical industry has conquered the worM, and only a few of the remaining opposing bastions have been able to withstand the onslaught...*[479]

By 1930, unknown to the German financial press, General Electric had similarly gained an effective technical monopoly of the Soviet electrical industry and was soon to penetrate even the remaining bastions in Germany, particularly the Siemens group. In January 1930 three G.E. men were elected to the board of A.E.G. — Clark H. Minor, Gerard Swope, and E. H. Baldwin — and International General Electric (I.G.E.) continued its moves to merge the world electrical industry into a giant cartel under Wall Street control.

In February General Electric focused on the remaining German electrical giant, Siemens & Halske, and while able to obtain a large block of debentures issued on behalf of the German firm by Dillon, Read of New York, G.E. was not able to gain participation or directors on the Siemens board. While the German press recognized even this limited control as" an historical economic event of the first order and an important step toward a future

---

[476] *New York Times*, July 2, 1929.
[477] Ibid, July 28, 1929.
[478] Ibid, August 2, 1929 and August 4, 1929.
[479] Ibid, August 6, 1929.

world electric trust,"[480] Siemens retained its independence from General Electric — and this independence is important for our story. The *New York Times* reported,

> *The entire press emphasizes the fact that Siemens, contrary to A.E.G., maintains its independence for the future and points out that no General Electric representative will sit on Stemen's board of directors.*[481]

There is no evidence that Siemens, either through Siemens & Halske or Siemens-Schukert, participated directly in the financing of Hitler. Siemens contributed to Hitler only slightly and indirectly through a share participation in Osram. On the other hand, both A.E.G. and Osram directly financed Hitler through the Nationale Treuhand in substantial ways. Siemens retained its independence in the early 1930s while both A.E.G. and Osram were under American dominance and with American directors. *There is no evidence that Siemens, without American directors, financed Hitler. On the other hand, we have irrefutable documentary evidence (see page 56) that both German General Electric and Osram, both with American directors, financed Hitler.*

In the months following the attempted Wall Street take over of Siemens, the pattern of a developing world trust in the electrical industry clarified; there was an end to international patent fights and the G.E. interest in A.E.G. increased to nearly 30 percent.[482]

Consequently, in the early 1930s, as Hitler prepared to grab dictatorial power in Germany — backed by some, but by no means all, German and American industrialists — the German General Electric (A.E.G.) was owned by International General Electric (about 30 percent), the Gesellschaft für Electrische Unternemungen (25 percent), and Ludwig Lowe (25 percent). International General Electric also had an interest of about 16 2/3rds percent in Osram, and an additional indirect influence in Companies Linked to German General Electric through Common Electric Directors:

---

[480] Ibid, February 2, 1930.
[481] Ibid, February 2, 1930.
[482] Ibid, May 11, 1930. For the prewar machinations of General Electric, Osram, and the Dutch company N.V. Philips Gloeilampenfabrieken of Eindhoven Holland, see Chapter 11, *"Electric Eels,"* in James Stewart Martin, *op cit.* Martin was Chief of the Economic Warfare Division of the U.S. Department of Justice and comments that "The A.E.G. of Germany was largely controlled by the American company, General Electric." The assumption by this author is that the G.E. influence was somewhat less than controlling although substantial enough. Because of Martin's official position and access to official documents, not known to the author, his statement that A.E.G. was "largely controlled" by U.S. General Electric cannot be lightly dismissed. However, if we accept that G.E. "largely controlled" A.E.G., then the most serious questions arise which clamor for investigation. A.E.G. was a prime financier of Hitler and "control" would more deeply implicate the U.S. parent company than is suggested by the evidence presented here.

Companies Linked to German General Electric through Common Electric Directors	Directors of German General Electric (A.E.G.)	Relationship of Linked Firm with Financing of Hitler
Accumulatoran-Fabrik	Quandt	Direct Finance
	Pfeffer	
Osram	Mamroth	Direct Finance
	Peierls	
Deutschen Babcock-Wilcox	Landau	Not known
	Wolff	
Vereinigte Stahlwerke	Nathan	Direct Finance
	Kirdorf	
	Goldschmidt	
Krupp	Nathan	Direct Finance
	Klotzbach	
	Bucher	
I.G. Farben	Flechtheim	Direct Finance
	von Rath	
Allianz u. Stuttgarten Verein	von Rath	Reported, but not substantiated
	Wolff	
Phoenix	Fahrenhorst	Direct Finance
Thyssen	Fahrenhorst	Direct Finance
Demag	Fahrenhorst	Direct Finance
	Flick	
Dynamit Gelsenkirchener	Flechtheim	Through I.G. Farben
	Kirdorf	
Bergwerks	Flechtheim	Direct Finance
	Young	
International General Electric	Swope	Through A.E.G.
	Minor	
	Baldwin	
American I.G. Farben	von Rath	Through I.G. Farben
International Bank (Amsterdam)	H. Furstenberg	Not known
	Goldschmidt	

Osram through A.E.G. directors. On the board of A.E.G., apart from the four American directors (Young, Swope, Minor, and Baldwin), we find Pferdmenges of Oppenheim & Co. (another Hitler financier), and Quandt, who owned 75 percent of Accumlatoren-Fabrik, a major direct financier of Hitler. In other words, among the German board members of A.E.G. we find representatives from several of the German firms that financed Hitler in the 1920s and 1930s.

GENERAL ELECTRIC AND THE FINANCING OF HITLER

The tap root of modern corporate socialism runs deep into the management of two affiliated multi-national corporations: General Electric Company in the United States and its foreign associates, including German General Electric (A.E.G.), and Osram in Germany. We have noted that Gerard Swope, second president and chairman of General Electric, and Walter Rathanau of A.E.G. promoted radical ideas for control of the State by private business interests.

From 1915 onwards International General Electric (I.G.E.), located at 120 Broadway in New York City, acted as the foreign investment, manufacturing, and selling organization for the General Electric Company. I.G.E. held interests in overseas manufacturing companies including a 25 to 30-percent holding in German General Electric (A.E.G.), plus holdings in Osram G.m.b.H. Kommanditgesellschaft, also in Berlin. These holdings gave International General Electric four directors on the board of A.E.G., and another director at Osram, and significant influence in the internal domestic policies of these German companies. The significance of this General Electric ownership is that A.E.G. and Osram were prominent suppliers of funds for Hitler in his rise to power in Germany in 1933. A bank transfer slip dated March 2, 1933 from A.E.G. to Delbruck Schickler & Co. in Berlin requests that 60,000 Reichsmark be deposited in the "Nationale Treuhand" (National Trusteeship) account for Hitler's use. This slip is reproduced on page 56.

I.G. Farben was the most important of the domestic financial backers of Hitler, and (as noted elsewhere) I.G. Farben controlled American I.G. Moreover, several directors of A.E.G. were also on the board of I.G. Farben — i.e., Hermann Bucher, chairman of A.E.G. was on the I.G. Farben board; so were A.E.G. directors Julius Flechtheim and Walter von Rath. I.G. Farben contributed 30 percent of the 1933 Hitler National Trusteeship (or takeover) fund.

Walter Fahrenhorst of A.E.G. was also on the board of Phoenix A-G, Thyssen A-G and Demag A-G — and all were contributors to Hitler's fund. Demag A-G contributed 50,000 RM to Hitler's fund and had a director with A.E.G.— the notorious Friedrich Flick, and early Hitler supporter, who was later convicted at the Nuremberg Trials. Accumulatoren Fabrik A-G was a Hitler contributor (25,000 RM, see page 60) with two directors on the A.E.G. board, August Pfeffer and Gunther Quandt. Quandt personally owned 75 percent of Accumulatoren Fabrik.

Osram Gesellschaft, in which International General Electric had a 16 2/3rds direct interest, also had two directors on the A.E.G. board: Paul Mamroth and Heinrich Pferls. Osram contributed 40,000 RM directly to the Hitler fund. The Otto Wolff concern, Vereinigte Stahlwerke A-G, recipient of substantial New York loans in the 1920s, had three directors on the A.E.G. board: Otto Wolff, Henry Nathan and Jakob Goldschmidt. Alfred Krupp yon Bohlen, sole owner of the Krupp organization and an early supporter of Hitler, was a member of the Aufsichsrat of A.E.G. Robert Pferdmenges, a member of Himmler's Circle of Friends, was also a director of A, E.G.

In other words, almost all of the German directors of German General Electric were financial supporters of Hitler and associated not only with A.E.G. but with other companies financing Hitler.

Walter Rathenau[483] became a director of A,E.G. in 1899 and by the early twentieth century was a director of more than 100 corporations. Rathenau was also author of the" Rathenau Plan," which bears a remarkable resemblance to the "Swope Plan" — i.e., FDR's New Deal but written by Swope of G.E. *In other words, we have the extraordinay coincidence that the authors of New Deal-tike plans in the U.S. and Germany were also prime backers of their implementers: Hitler in Germany and Roosevelt in the U.S.*

Swope was chairman of the board of General Electric Company and International General Electric. In 1932 the American directors of A.E.G, were prominently connected with American banking and political circles as follows:

GERARD SWOPE	Chairman of International General Electric and president of General Electric Company, director of National City Bank (and other companies), director of A.E.G. and Osram in Germany. Author of FDR's New Deal and member of numerous Roosevelt organizations.
Owen D. Young	Chairman of board of General Electric, and deputy chairman, Federal Reserve Bank of New York. Author, with J. P, Morgan, of the Young Plan which superseded the Dawes Plan in 1929. (See Chapter One.)
CLARK H. Minor	President and director of International General Electric, director of British Thomson Houston, Compania Generale di Electtricita (Italy), and Japan Electric Bond & Share Company (Japan).

In brief, we have hard evidence of unquestioned authenticity (see p, 56) to show that German General Electric contributed substantial sums to Hitler's political fund. There were four American directors of A.E.G. (Baldwin, Swope, Minor, and Clark), which was 80 percent owned by International General Electric. Further, I.G.E. and the four American directors were the largest single interest and consequently had the greatest single influence in A.E.G. actions and policies. Even further, almost all other directors of A.E.G. were connected with firms (I. G. Farben, Accumulatoren Fabrik, *etc.)* which contributed directly — as firms — to Hitler's political fund. However, only the German directors of A.E.G were placed on trial in Nuremburg in 1945.

---

[483] Son of Emil Rathenau, founder of A.E.G., born in 1867 and assassinated in 1922.

Technical Cooperation with Krupp

Quite apart from financial assistance to Hitler, General Electric extended its assistance to cartel schemes with other Hitler backers for their mutual benefit and the benefit of the Nazi state. Cemented tungsten carbide is one example of this G.E.-Nazi cooperation. Prior to November 1928, American industries had several sources for both tungsten carbide and tools and dies containing this hard-metal composition. Among these sources were the Krupp Company of Essen, Germany, and two American firms to which Krupp was then shipping and selling, the Union Wire Die Corporation and Thomas Prosser & Son. In 1928 Krupp obligated itself to grant licenses under United States patents which it owned to the Firth-Sterling Steel Company and to the Ludlum Steel Company. Before 1928, this tungsten carbide for use in tools and dies sold in the United states for about $50 a pound.

The United States patents which Krupp claimed to own were assigned from Osram Kommanditgesellschaft, and had been previously assigned by the Osram Company of Germany to General Electric. However, General Electric had also developed its own patents, principally the Hoyt and Gilson patents, covering competing processes for cemented tungsten carbide. General Electric believed that it could utilize these patents independently without infringing on or competing with Krupp patents. But instead of using the G.E. patents independently in competition with Krupp, or testing out its rights under the patent laws, General Electric worked out a cartel agreement with Krupp to pool the patents of both parties and to give General Electric a monopoly control of tungsten carbide in the United States.

The first step in this cartel arrangement was taken by Carboloy Company, Inc., a General Electric subsidiary, incorporated for the purpose of exploiting tungsten carbide. The 1920s price of around $50 a pound was raised by Carboloy to $458 a pound. Obviously, no firm could sell any great amounts of tungsten carbide in this price range, but the price would maximize profits for G.E. In 1934 General Electric and Carboloy were also able to obtain, by purchase, the license granted by Krupp to the Ludlum Steel Company, thereby eliminating one competitor. In 1936, Krupp was induced to refrain from further imports into the United States. Part of the price paid for the elimination from the American market of tungsten carbide manufactured abroad was a reciprocal undertaking that General Electric and Carboloy would not export from the U.S. Thus these American companies tied their own hands by contract, or permitted Krupp to tie their hands, and denied foreign markets to American industry. Carboloy Company then acquired the business of Thomas Prosser & Son, and in 1937, for nearly $1 million, Carboloy acquired the competing business of the Union Wire Die Corporation. By refusing to sell, Krupp cooperated with General Electric and Carboloy to persuade Union Wire Die Corporation to sell out.

Licenses to manufacture tungsten carbide were then refused. A request for license by the Crucible Steel Company was refused in 1936. A request by the Chrysler Corporation for a license was refused in 1938. A license by the Triplett Electrical Instrument Company was refused on April 25, 1940. A license was also refused to the General Cable Company. The Ford Motor Company for several years expressed strong opposition to the high-price policy followed by the Carboloy Company, and at one point made a request for the right to manufacture for its own use. This was refused. As a result of these tactics, General Electric and its subsidiary Carboloy emerged in 1936 or 1937 with virtually a complete monopoly of tungsten carbide in the United States.

In brief, General Electric — with the cooperation of another Hitler supporter, Krupp — jointly obtained for G,E. a monopoly in the U.S. for tungsten carbide. So when World War II began, General Electric had a monopoly at an established price of $450 a pound — almost ten times more than the 1928 price — and use in the U.S. had been correspondingly restricted, A.E.G. Avoids the Bombs in World War II

By 1939 the German electrical industry had become closely affiliated with two U.S. firms: International General Electric and International Telephone and Telegraph. The largest firms in German electrical production and their affiliations listed in order of importance were:

Firm and Type of Production	Percent of German 1939 production	U.S. Affiliated Firm
Heavy Current Industry		
General Electric (A.E.G.)	40 percent	International General Electric
Siemens Schukert A.G	40 percent	None
Brown Boveri et Cie	17 percent	None
Telephone and Telegraph		
Siemens und Halske	60 percent	None
Lorenz A.G.	85 percent	I.T.T.
Radio		
Telefunken (A.E.G. after 1941)	60 percent	International General Electric
Lorenz	35 percent	I.T.T.
Wire and Cable		
Felton & Guilleaume A.G.	20 percent	I.T.T.
Siemens	20 percent	None
A.E.G.	20 percent	International General Electric

In other words, in 1939 the German electrical equipment industry was concentrated into a few major corporations linked in an international cartel and by stock ownership to two .major U.S. corporations. This industrial complex was never a prime target for bombing in World War II. The A.E.G. and I.T.T. plants were hit only incidentally in area raids and then but rarely. The electrical equipment plants bombed as targets were not those affiliated with U.S. firms. It was Brown Boveri at Mannheim and Siemensstadt in Berlin — which were *not* connected with the U.S. — who were bombed. As a result, German production of electrical war equipment rose steadily throughout World War II, peaking as late as 1944. According to the U.S. Strategic Bombing Survey reports, "In the opinion of Speers' assistants and plant officials, the war effort in Germany was never hindered in any important manner by any shortage of electrical equipment."[484]

One example of the non-bombing policy for German General Electric was the A. E.G. plant at 185 Muggenhofer Strasse, Nuremburg. Study of this plant's output in World War II is of interest because it illustrates the extent to which purely peacetime production was converted to war work. The pre-war plant manufactured household equipment, such as hot plates, electric ranges, electric irons, toasters, industrial baking ovens, radiators, water heaters, kitchen ovens, and industrial heaters. In 1939, 1940 and 1941, most of the Nuremburg plant's production facilities were used for the manufacture of peacetime products. In 1942 the plant's production was shifted to manufacture of war equipment. Metal parts for communications equipment and munitions such as bombs and mines were made. Other war production consisted of parts for searchlights and amplifiers. The following tabulation very strikingly shows the conversion to war work:

Year	Total sales in 1000 RM	Percent for war	Percent ordinary production
1939	12,469	5	95
1940	11,754	15	85
1941	21,194	40	60
1942	20,689	61	39
1948	31,455	67	33
1944	31,205	69	31

---

[484] The United States Strategic Bombing Survey, *German Electrical Equipment Industry/Report,* (Equipment Division, January 1947), p. 4.

The actual physical damage by bombing to this plant was insignificant. No serious damage occurred until the raids of February 20 and 21, 1945, near the end of the war, and then protection had been fairly well developed. Raids during which bombs struck in the plant area and the trifling damage done are listed as follows:

Date of raid	Bombs striking plant	Damage done
March 8, 1943	30 stick type I.B.	Trifling, but 3 storehouses outside the main plant destroyed.
Sept. 9, 1944	None (blast damage)	Trifling, glass and blackout curtain damage.
Nov. 26, 1944	14000 lb. HE in open space in plant grounds	Wood shop destroyed, water main broken.
Feb. 20, 1945	2 HE	3 buildings damaged.
Feb. 21, 1945	5 HE, many I.B.'s	Administration bldg. destroyed & enameling works damaged by HE.

Another example of a German General Electric plant not bombed is the A.E.G. plant at Koppelsdorf producing radar sets and bomber antennae. Other A.E.G. plants which were not bombed[485] and their war equipment production were:

LIST OF A.E.G. FACTORIES NOT BOMBED IN WORLD WAR II

Name of Branch	Location	Product
1. Werk Reiehmannsdoff mit Unterabteilungen in Wallendorf und Unterweissbach	Kries Saalfeld	Measuring Instruments
2. Werk Marktschorgast	Bayreuth	Starters
3. Werk F18ha	Sachsen	Short Wave Sending Sets
4. Werk Reichenbach	Vogtland	Dry Cell Batteries
5. Werk Burglengefeld	Sachsen/S.E. Chemnitz	Heavy Starters
6. Werk Nuremburg	Belringersdorf/Nuremburg	Small Components
7. Werk Zirndorf	Nuremburg	Heavy Starters
8. Werk Mattinghofen	Oberdonau	1 KW Senders 250 Meters & long wave for torpedo boats & U-boats
9. Unterwerk Neustadt	Coburg	Radar Equipment

That the A.E.G. plants in Germany were not bombed in World War II was confirmed by the United States Strategic Bombing Survey, officered by such academics as John K.

---

[485] U.S. Strategic Bombing Survey, Plant Report of A.E.G. (Allgemeine Elektrizitats Gesellschaft), Nuremburg, Germany: June 1945), p. 6.

Galbraith and such Wall Streeters as George W. Ball and Paul H. Nitze. Their "German Electrical Equipment Industry Report" dated January 1947 concludes:

> *The industry has never been attacked as a basic target system, but a few plants, i.e. Brown Boveri at Mannheim, Bosch at Stuutgart and Siemenstadt in Berlin, have been subjected to precision raids; many others were hit in area raids.*[486]

At the end of World War II an Allied investigation team known as FIAT was sent to examine bomb damage to German electrical industry plants. The team for the electrical industry consisted of Alexander G.P.E. Sanders of International Telephone and Telegraph of New York, Whit-worth Ferguson of Ferguson Electric Company, New York, and Erich J. Borgman of Westinghouse Electric. Although the stated objective of these teams was to examine the effects on Allied bombing of German targets, the objective of this particular team was to get the German electrical equipment industry back into production as soon as possible. Whirworth Ferguson wrote a report dated March 31, 1945 on the A.E.G. Ostlandwerke and concluded, "this plant is immediately available for production of fine metal parts and assemblies."[487]

To conclude, we find that both Rathenau of A.E.G. and Swope of General Electric in the U.S. had similar ideas of putting the State to work for their own corporate ends. General Electric was prominent in financing Hitler, it profited handsomely from war production — and yet it managed to evade bombing in World War II. Obviously the story briefly surveyed here deserves a much more thorough — and official — investigation.

---

[486] p. 3. Consequently, "production during the war was adequate until November 1944" and "in the opinion of Speer assistants and plant officials the war effort in Germany was never hindered in any important manner by any shortage of electrical equipment." Difficulties arose only at the very end of the war when the whole economy was threatened with collapse. The report concluded, "All important needs for electrical equipment in 1944 may therefore be said to have been met, since plans were always optimistic."

[487] U.S. Strategic Bombing Survey, AEG-Ostlandwerke GmbH, by Whitworth Ferguson, 31 May 1945.

Chapter Four

Standard Oil Fuels World War II

In two gears Germany will be manufacturing oil and gas enough out of soft coal for a long war. The Standard Oil of New York is furnishing millions of dollars to help.
(Report from the Commercial Attaché, U.S. Embassy in Berlin, Germany, January 1933, to State Department in Washington, D.C,)

The Standard Oil group of companies, in which the Rockefeller family owned a one-quarter (and controlling) interest[488], was of critical assistance in helping Nazi Germany prepare for World War II. This assistance in military preparation came about because Germany's relatively insignificant supplies of crude petroleum were quite insufficient for modern mechanized warfare; in 1934 for instance about 85 percent of German finished petroleum products were imported. The solution adopted by Nazi Germany was to manufacture synthetic gasoline from its plentiful domestic coal supplies. It was the hydrogenation process of producing synthetic gasoline and iso-octane properties in gasoline that enabled Germany to go to war in 1940 — and this hydrogenation process was developed and financed by the Standard Oil laboratories in the United States in partnership with I.G. Farben.

Evidence presented to the Truman, Bone, and Kilgore Committees after World War II confirmed that Standard Oil had at the same time "seriously imperiled the war preparations of the United States."[489] Documentary evidence was presented to all three Congressional committees that before World War II Standard Oil had agreed with I.G. Farben, in the so-called Jasco agreement, that synthetic rubber was within Farben's sphere of influence, while Standard Oil was to have an absolute monopoly in the U.S. *only if and when* Farben allowed development of synthetic rubber to take place in the U.S.:

---

[488] In 1935, John D. Rockefeller, Jr. owned stock valued at $245 million in Standard Oil of New Jersey, Standard Oil of California, and Socony-Vacuun Company, *New York Times,* January 10, 1935.
[489] *Elimination of German Resources,* op cit., p. 1085.

> *Accordingly [concluded the Kilgore Committee] Standard fully accomplished I.G.'s purpose of preventing United States production by dissuading American rubber companies from undertaking independent research in developing synthetic rubber processes.*[490]

Regrettably, the Congressional committees did not explore an even more ominous aspect of this Standard Oil — I.G. Farben collusion: that at this time directors of Standard Oil of New Jersey had not only strategic warfare affiliations to I.G. Farben, but had other links with Hitler's Germany — even to the extent of contributing, through German subsidiary companies, to Heinrich Himmler's personal fund and with membership in Himmler's Circle of Friends as late as 1944.

During World War II Standard Oil of New Jersey was accused of treason for this pre-war alliance with Farben, even while its continuing wartime activities within Himmler's Circle of Friends were unknown. The accusations of treason were vehemently denied by Standard Oil. One of the more prominent of these defenses was published by R.T. Haslam, a director of Standard Oil of New Jersey, in *The Petroleum Times* (December 25, 1943), and entitled "Secrets Turned into Mighty War Weapons Through I.G. Farben Agreement."[491] This was an attempt to turn the tables and present the pre-war collusion as advantageous to the United States.

Whatever may have been Standard Oil's wartime recollections and hasty defense, the 1929 negotiations and contracts between Standard and I.G. Farben were recorded in the contemporary press and describe the agreements between Standard Oil of New Jersey and I.G. Farben and their intent. In April 1929 Walter C. Teagle, president of Standard Oil of New Jersey, became a director of the newly organized American I.G. Farben. Not because Teagle was interested in the chemical industry but because,

> *It has for some years past enjoyed a very close relationship with certain branches of the research work of the I.G. Farbenin-dustrie which bear closely upon the oil industry.*[492]

It was announced by Teagle that joint research work on production of oil from coal had been carried on for some time and that a research laboratory for this work was to be established *in the United States.*[493] In November 1929 this jointly owned Standard — Farben research company was established *under the management of the Standard Oil Company of New Jersey,* and all research and patents relating to production of oil from coal held by both I.G. and Standard were pooled. Previously, during the period 1926-1929, the two

---

[490] Ibid.
[491] *NMT,* I.G. Farben case, p. 1304.
[492] *New York Times,* April 28, 1929.
[493] Ibid.

companies had cooperated in development of the hydrogenation process, and experimental plants had been placed in operation in both the U.S. and Germany. It was now proposed to erect new plants in the U.S. at Bayway, New Jersey and Baytown, Texas, in addition to expansion of the earlier experimental plant at Baton Rouge. Standard announced:

> ... the importance of the new contract as applied to this country lay in the fact that it made certain that the hydrogenation process would be developed commercially in this country under the guidance of American oil interests.[494]

In December 1929 the new company, Standard I.G. Company, was organized. F.A. Howard was named president, and its German and American directors were announced as follows: E.M. Clark, Walter Duisberg, Peter Hurll, R.A. Reidemann, H.G. Seidel, Otto von Schenck, and Guy Wellman.

The majority of the stock in the research company was owned by Standard Oil. The technical work, the process development work, and the construction of three new oil-from-coal plants in the United States was placed in the hands of the Standard Oil Development Company, the Standard Oil technical subsidiary. It is clear from these contemporary reports that the development work on oil from coal was undertaken by Standard Oil of New Jersey within the United States, in Standard Oil plants and with majority financing and control by Standard. The results of this research were made available to I.G. Farben and became the basis for the development of Hitler's oil from-coal-program which made World War II possible.

The Haslam article, written by a former Professor of Chemical Engineering at M.I.T. (then vice president of Standard Oil of New Jersey) argued — contrary to these recorded facts — that Standard Oil was able, through its Farben agreements, to obtain *German* technology for the United States. Haslam cited the manufacture of toluol and paratone (Op-panol), used to stabilize viscosity of oil, an essential material for desert and Russian winter tank operations, and buna rubber. However, this article, with its erroneous self-serving claims, found its way to wartime Germany and became the subject of a "Secret" I.G. Farben memorandum dated June 6, 1944 from Nuremburg defendent and then-Farben official von Knieriem to fellow Farben management officials. This von Knieriem "Secret" memo set out those facts Haslam avoided in his *Petroleum Times* article. The memo was in fact a summary of what Standard was unwilling to reveal to the American public — i.e., the major contribution made by Standard Oil of New Jersey to the Nazi war machine. The Farben

---

[494] Ibid, November 24, 1929.

memorandum states that the Standard Oil agreements were *absolutely essential* for I.G. Farben:

> The closing of an agreement with Standard was necessary for technical, commercial, and financial reasons:technically, because the specialized experience which was available only in a big oil company was necessary to the further development of our process, and no such industry existed in Germany; commercially, because in the absence of state economic control in Germany at that time, IG had to avoid a competitive struggle with the great oil powers, who always sold the best gasoline at the lowest price in contested markets; financially, because IG, which had already spent extraordinarily large sums for the development of the process, had to seek financial relief in order to be able to continue development in other new technical fields, such as buna.[495]

The Farben memorandum then answered the key question: What did I.G. Farben acquire from Standard Oil that was "vital for the conduct of war?" The memo examines those products cited by Haslam — i.e., iso-octane, tuluol, Oppanol-Paratone, and buna — and demonstrates that contrary to Standard Oil's public claim, their technology came to a great extent from the U.S., not from Germany.

On iso-octane the Farben memorandum reads, in part,

> By reason of their decades of work on motor fuels, the Americans were ahead of us in their knowledge of the quality requirements that are called for by the different uses of motor fuels. In particular they had developed, at great expense, a large number of methods of testing gasoline for different uses. On the basis of their experiments they had recognized the good anti, knock quality of iso-octane long before they had any knowledge of our hydrogenation process. This is proved by the single fact that in America fuels are graded in octane numbers, and iso-octane was entered as the best fuel with the number 100. All this knowledge naturally became ours as a result of the agreement, which saved us much effort and protected us against many errors.

I.G. Farben adds that Haslam's claim that the production of iso-octane became known in America only through the Farben hydrogenation process was not correct:

> Especially in the case of iso-octane, it is shown that we owe much to the Americans because in our own work we could draw widely on American information on the behavior of fuels in motors. Moreover, we were also kept currently informed by the Americans on the progress of their production process and its further development.

---

[495] NMT, I.G. Farben case, Volumes VII and VIII, pp. 1304-1311.

> Shortly before the war, a new method for the production of iso-octane was found in America — alkylation with isomerization as a preliminary step. This process, which Mr. Haslain does not mention at all, originates in fact entirely with the Americans and has become known to us in detail in its separate stages through our agreements with them, and is being used very extensively by us.

On toluol, I.G. Farben points to a factual inaccuracy in the Haslam article: toluol was *not* produced by hydrogenation in the U.S. is claimed by Professor Haslam. In the case of Oppanol, the I.G. memo calls Haslam's information "incomplete" and so far as buna rubber is concerned, *"we* never gave technical information to the Americans, nor did technical cooperation in the buna field take place." Most importantly, the Farben memo goes on to describe some products not cited by Haslam in his article:

> As a consequence of our contracts with the Americans, we received from them, above and beyond the agreement, many very valuable contributions for the synthesis and improvement of motor fuels and lubricating oils, which Just now during the war are most useful to us; and we also received other advantages from them. Primarily, the following may be mentioned:
> 1)Above all, improvement of fuels through the addition of tetraethyl-lead and the manufacture of this product. It need not be especially mentioned that without tetraethl-lead the present methods of warfare would be impossible. The fact that since the beginning of the war we could produce tetraethyl-lead is entirely due to the circumstances that, shortly before, the Americans had presented us with the production plans, complete with their know-how. It was, moreover, the first time that the Americans decided to give a license on this process in a foreign country (besides communication of unprotected secrets) and this only on our urgent requests to Standard Oil to fulfill our wish. Contractually we could not demand it, and we found out later that the War Department in Washington gave its permission only after long deliberation.
> 2)Conversion of low-molecular unsaturates into usable gasoline (polymerization). Much work in this field has been done here as well as in America. But the Americans were the first to carry the process through on a large scale, which suggested to us also to develop the process on a large technical scale. But above and beyond that, plants built according to American processes are functioning in Germany.
> 3)In the field of lubricating oils as well, Germany through the contract with America, learned of experience which is extraordinarily important for present day warfare.
> In this connection, we obtained not only the experience of Standard, but, through Standard, the experiences of General Motors and other large American motor companies as well.
> 4)As a further remarkable example of advantageous effect for us of the contract between IG and Standard Oil, the following should be mentioned: in the years 1934 / 1935 our

government had the greatest interest in gathering from abroad a stock of especially valuable mineral oil products (in particular, aviation gasoline and aviation lubricating oil), and holding it in reserve to an amount approximately equal to 20 million dollars at market value. The German Government asked IG if it were not possible, on the basis o fits friendly relations with Standard Oil, to buy this amount in Farben's name; actually, however, as trustee of the German Government. The fact that we actually succeeded by means of the most difficult negotiations in buying the quantity desired by our government from the American Standard Oil Company and the Dutch — English Royal — Dutch — Shell group and in transporting it to Germany, was made possible only through the aid of the Standard Oil Co.

ETHYL LEAD FOR THE WEHRMACHT

Another prominent example of Standard Oil assistance to Nazi Germany — in cooperation with General Motors — was in supplying ethyl lead. Ethyl fluid is an anti-knock compound used in both aviation and automobile fuels to eliminate knocking, and so improve engine efficiency; without such anti-knocking compounds modern mobile warfare would be impractical.

In 1924 the Ethyl Gasoline Corporation was formed in New York City, jointly owned by the Standard Oil Company of New Jersey and General Motors Corporation, to control and utilize U.S. patents for the manufacture and distribution of tetraethyl lead and ethyl fluid in the U.S. and abroad. Up to 1935 manufacture of these products was undertaken *only* in the United States. In 1935 Ethyl Gasoline Corporation transferred its know-how to Germany for use in the Nazi rearmament program. This transfer was undertaken over the protests of the U.S. Government[496].

Ethyl's intention to transfer its anti-knock technology to Nazi Germany came to the attention of the Army Air Corps in Washington, D.C. On December 15, 1934 E. W. Webb, president of Ethyl Gasoline, was advised that Washington had learned of the intention of "forming a German company with the I.G. to manufacture ethyl lead in that country." The War Department indicated that there was considerable criticism of this technological transfer, which might "have the gravest repercussions" for the U.S.; that the commercial demand for ethyl lead in Germany was too small to be of interest; and,

---

[496] See letter from U.S. War Department reproduced as Appendix D.

> ... it has been claimed that Germany is secretly arming [and] ethyl lead would doubtless be a valuable aid to military aeroplanes.[497]

The Ethyl Company was then advised by the Army Air Corps that "under no conditions should you or the Board of Directors of the Ethyl Gasoline Corporation disclose any secrets or 'know-how' in connection with the manufacture of tetraethyl lead to Germany.[498]

On January 12, 1935 Webb mailed to the Chief of the Army Air Corps a "Statement of Facts," which was in effect a denial that any such technical knowledge would be transmitted; he offered to insert such a clause in the contract to guard against any such transfer. However, contrary to its pledge to the Army Air Corps, Ethyl subsequently signed a joint production agreement with I.G. Farben in Germany to form Ethyl G.m.b.H. and with Montecatini in fascist Italy for the same purpose.

It is worth noting the directors of Ethyl Gasoline Corporation at the time of this transfer[499]: E.W. Webb, president and director; C.F. Kettering; R.P. Russell; W.C. Teagle, Standard Oil of New Jersey and trustee of FDR's Georgia Warm Springs Foundation; F. A. Howard; E. M. Clark, Standard Oil of New Jersey; A. P. Sloan, Jr.; D. Brown; J. T. Smith; and W.S. Parish of Standard Oil of New Jersey.

The I.G. Farben files captured at the end of the war confirm the importance of this particular technical transfer for the German Wehrmacht:

> Since the beginning of the war we have been in a position. to produce lead tetraethyl solely because, a short time before the outbreak of the war, the Americans had established plants for us ready for production and supplied us with all available experience. In this manner we did not need to perform the difficult work of development because we could start production right away on the basis of all the experience that the Americans had had for years.[500]

In 1938, just before the outbreak of war in Europe, the German Luftwaffe had an urgent requirement for 500 tons of tetraethyl lead. Ethyl was advised by an official of DuPont that such quantities of ethyl would be used by Germany for military purposes.[501] This 500 tons was loaned by the Ethyl Export Corporation of New York to Ethyl G.m.b.H. of Germany, in a transaction arranged by the Reich Air Ministry with I.G. Farben director

---

[497] United States Congress. Senate. Hearings before a subcommittee of the Committee on Military Affairs. *Scientific and Technical Mobilization*, (78th Congress, 1st session, S. 702), Part 16, (Washington: Government Printing Office, 1944), p. 939. Hereafter cited as *Scientific and Technical Mobilization*.
[498] Ibid.
[499] *Oil and Petroleum Yearbook, 1938*, p. 89.
[500] *New York Times*, October 19, 1945, p. 9.
[501] George W. Stocking & Myron W. Watkins, *Cartels in Action*, (New York: The Twentieth Century Fund, 1946), p. 9.

Mueller-Cunradi. The collateral security was arranged in a letter dated September 21, 1938[502] through Brown Brothers, Harriman & Co. of New York.

STANDARD OIL OF NEW JERSEY AND SYNTHETIC RUBBER

The transfer of ethyl technology for the Nazi war machine was repeated in the case of synthetic rubber. There is no question that the ability of the German Wehrmacht to fight World War II depended on synthetic rubber — as well as on synthetic petroleum — because Germany has no natural rubber, and war would have been impossible without Farben's synthetic rubber production. Farben had a virtual monopoly of this field and the program to produce the large quantities necessary was financed by the Reich:

> *The volume of planned production in this field was far beyond the needs of peacetime economy. The huge costs involved were consistent only with military considerations in which the need for self-sufficiency without regard to cost was decisive.*[503]

As in the ethyl technology transfers, Standard Oil of New Jersey was intimately associated with I.G. Farben's synthetic rubber. A series of joint cartel agreements were made in the late 1920s aimed at a joint world monopoly of synthetic rubber. Hitler's Four Year Plan went into effect in 1937 and in 1938 Standard provided I.G. Farben with its new butyl rubber process. On the other hand Standard kept the German buna process secret within the United States and it was not until June 1940 that Firestone and U.S. Rubber were allowed to participate in testing butyl and granted the buna manufacturing licenses. Even then Standard tried to get the U.S. Government to finance a large-scale buna program — reserving its own funds for the more promising butyl process.[504]

Consequently, Standard assistance in Nazi Germany was not limited to oil from coal, although this was the most important transfer. Not only was the process for tetraethyl transferred to I.G. Farben and a plant built in Germany owned jointly by I.G., General Motors, and Standard subsidiaries; but as late as 1939 Standard's German subsidiary designed a German plant for aviation gas. Tetraethyl was shipped on an emergency basis for the Wehrmacht and major assistance was given in production of butyl rubber, while holding secret in the U.S. the Farben process for buna. In other words, Standard Oil of New Jersey (first under president W.C. Teagle and then under W..S. Farish) consistently aided the Nazi war machine while refusing to aid the United States.

---

[502] For original documents see *NMT*, I.G. Farben case, Volume VIII, pp. 1189-94.
[503] *NMT*, I.G. Farben case, Volume VIII, p. 1264-5.
[504] *Scientific and Technical Mobilization*, p. 543.

This sequence of events was not an accident. President W.S. Farish argued that not to have granted such technical assistance to the Wehrmacht "... would have been unwarranted."[505] The assistance was knowledgeable, ranged over more than a decade, and was so substantive that without it the Wehrmacht could not have gone to war in 1939.

THE DEUTSCHE-AMERIKANISCHE PETROLEUM A.G. (DAPAG)

The Standard Oil subsidiary in Germany, Deutsche-Amerikanische Petroleum A.G. (DAPAG), was 94-percent owned by Standard Oil of New Jersey. DAPAG had branches throughout Germany, a refinery at Bremen, and a head office in Hamburg. Through DAPAG, Standard Oil of New Jersey was represented in the inner circles of Naziism — the Keppler Circle and Himmler's Circle of Friends. A director of DAPAG was Karl Lindemann, also chairman of the International Chamber of Commerce in Germany, as well as director of several banks, including the Dresdner Bank, the Deutsche Reichsbank, and the private Nazi-oriented bank of C. Melchior & Company, and numerous corporations including the HAPAG (Hamburg-Amerika Line). Lindemann was a member of Keppler's Circle of Friends as late as 1944 and so gave Standard Oil of New Jersey a representative at the very core of Naziism. Another member of the board of DAPAG was Emil Helfrich, who was an original member of the Keppler Circle.

In sum, Standard Oil of New Jersey had two members of the Keppler Circle as directors of its German wholly owned subsidiary. Payments to the Circle from the Standard Oil subsidiary company, and from Lindemann and Helffrich as individual directors, continued until 1944, the year before the end of World War II.[506]

---

[505] Robert Engler, *The Politics of Oil*, (New York: The MacMillan Company, 1961), p. 102.
[506] See Chapter Nine for details.

CHAPTER FIVE

I.T.T. WORKS BOTH SIDES OF THE WAR

> *Thus while I.T.T. Focke-Wolfe planes were bombing Allied ships, and I. T. T. lines were passing information to German submarines, I.T.T. direction .finders were saving other ships from torpedoes.*
>
> (Anthony Sampson, The Sovereign State of I.T.T., New York: Stein & Day, 1973, p. 40.)

The multi-national giant International Telephone and Telegraph (I.T.T.)[507] was founded in 1920 by Virgin Islands-born entrepreneur Sosthenes Behn. During his lifetime Behn was the epitome of the politicized businessman, earning his profits and building the I.T.T. empire through political maneuverings rather than in the competitive market place. In 1923, through political adroitness, Behn acquired the Spanish telephone monopoly, Compania Telefonica de Espana. In 1924 I.T.T., now backed by the J.P. Morgan firm, bought what later became the International Standard Electric group of manufacturing plants around the world.

The parent board of I.T.T. reflected the J.P. Morgan interests, with Morgan partners Arthur M. Anderson and Russell Leffingwell. The Establishment law firm of Davis, Polk, Wardwell, Gardiner & Reed was represented by the two junior partners, Gardiner & Reed.

---

[507] For an excellent review of I.T.T.'s worldwide activities, see Anthony Sampson, *The Sovereign State of I.T.T.*, (New York: Stein & Day, 1973).

DIRECTORS OF I.T.T. IN 1933:

Directors	Affiliation with other Wall Street firms
Arthur M. ANDERSON	Partner, J.P. MORGAN and New York Trust Company
Hernand BEHN	Bank of America
Sosthenes BEHN	NATIONAL CITY BANK
F. Wilder BELLAMY	Partner in Dominick & Dominicik
John W. CUTLER	GRACE NATIONAL BANK, Lee Higginson
George H. GARDINER	Partner in Davis, Polk, Wardwell, Gardiner & Reed
Allen G. HOYT	NATIONAL CITY BANK
Russell C. LEFFINGWELL	Partner J.P. MORGAN and CARNEGIE CORP.
Bradley W. PALMER	Chairman, Executive Committee, UNITED FRUIT
Lansing P. REED	Partner in Davis, Polk Wardwell, Gardiner & Reed

The National City Bank (NCB) in the Morgan group was represented by two directors, Sosthenes Behn and Allen G. Hoyt. In brief, I.T.T. was a Morgan-controlled company; and we have previously noted the interest of Morgan-controlled companies in war and revolution abroad and political maneuvering in the United States.[508]

In 1930 Behn acquired the German holding company of Standard Elekrizitäts A.G., controlled by I.T.T. (62.0 percent of the voting stock), A.E.G. (81.1 percent of the voting stock) and Felton & Guilleaume (six percent of the voting stock). In this deal Standard acquired two German manufacturing plants and a majority stock interest in Telefonfabrik Berliner A.G.I.T.T. also obtained the Standard subsidiaries in Germany, Ferdinand Schuchardt Berliner Fernsprech-und Telegraphenwerk A,G., as well as Mix & Genest in Berlin, and Suddeutsche Apparate Fabrik G,m.b.H. in Nuremburg.

It is interesting to note in passing that while Sosthenes Behn's I.T.T. controlled telephone companies and manufacturing plants in Germany, the cable traffic between the U.S. and Germany was under the control of Deutsch-Atlantische Telegraphengesellschaft (the German Atlantic Cable Company). This firm, together with the Commercial Cable Company and Western Union Telegraph Company, had a monopoly in transatlantic U.S.-German cable communications. W.A. Harriman & Company took over a block of 625,000 shares in Deutsch-Atlantische in 1925, and the firm's board of directors included an unusual array of characters, many of whom we have met elsewhere. It included, for example, H. F. Albert, the German espionage agent in the United States in World War I; Franklin D. Roosevelt's former business associate yon Berenberg-Gossler; and Dr. Cuno, a former German chancellor of the 1923

---

[508] See also Sutton, *Wall Street and the Bolshevik Revolution, op. cit.*

inflationary era. I.T.T. in the United States was represented on the board by yon Guilleaume and Max Warburg of the Warburg banking family.

BARON KURT VON SCHRODER AND THE I.T.T.

There is no record that I.T.T. made direct payments to Hitler before the Nazi grab for power in 1933. On the other hand, numerous payments were made to Heinrich Himmler in the late 1930s and in World War II itself through I.T.T. German subsidiaries. The first meeting between Hitler and I.T.T. officials — so far as we know — was reported in August 1933[509], when Sosthenes Behn and I.T.T. German representative Henry Manne met with Hitler in Berchesgaden. Subsequently, Behn made contact with the Keppler circle (see Chapter Nine) and, through Keppler's influence, Nazi Baron Kurt von Schröder became the guardian of I.T.T. interests in Germany. Schröder acted as the conduit for I.T.T. money funneled to Heinrich Himmler's S.S. organization in 1944, *while World War II was in progress, and the United states was at war with Germany.*[510]

Through Kurt Schröder, Behn and his I.T.T. gained access to the profitable German armaments industry and bought substantial interest in German armaments firms, including Focke-Wolfe aircraft. These armaments operations made handsome profits, which could have been repatriated to the United States parent company. But they were reinvested in German rearmament. This reinvestment of profits in German armament firms suggests that Wall Street claims it was innocent of wrongdoing in German rearmament — and indeed did not even know of Hitler's intentions — are fraudulent. Specifically, I.T.T. purchase of a substantial interest in Focke-Wolfe meant, as Anthony Sampson has pointed out, that I.T.T. was producing German planes used to kill Americans and their allies — and it made excellent profits out of the enterprise.

In Kurt von Schröder, I.T.T. had access to the very heart of the Nazi power elite. Who was Schröder? Baron Kurt von Schröder was born in Hamburg in 1889 into an old, established German banking family. An earlier member of the Schröder family moved to London, changed his name to Schroder (without the dierisis) and organized the banking firm of J. Henry Schroder in London and J. Henry Schroder Banking Corporation in New York. Kurt von Schröder also became a partner in the private Cologne Bankhaus, J. H. Stein & Company, founded in the late eighteenth century. Both Schröder and Stein had been promoters, in company with French financiers, of the 1919 German separatist movement which attempted to split the rich Rhineland away from Germany and its troubles. In this escapade prominent

---

[509] *New York Times*, August 4, 1933.
[510] See also Chapter Nine for documentary proof of these I.T.T. payments to the S.S.

Rhineland industrialists met at J. H. Stein's house on January 7, 1919 and a few months later organized a meeting, with Stein as chairman, to develop public support for the separatist movement. The 1919 action failed. The group tried again in 1923 and spearheaded another movement to break the Rhineland away from Germany to come under the protection of France. This attempt also failed. Kurt yon Schrader then linked up with Hitler and the early Nazis, and as in the 1919 and 1923 Rhineland separatist movements, Schröder represented and worked for German industrialists and armaments manufacturers.

In exchange for financial and industrial support arranged by yon Schrader, he later gained political prestige. Immediately after the Nazis gained power in 1933 Schrader became the German representative at the Bank for International Settlements, which Quigley calls the apex of the international control system, as well as head of the private bankers group advising the German Reichsbank. Heinrich Himmler appointed Sehroder an S.S. Senior Group Leader, and in turn Himmler became a prominent member of Keppler's Circle. (See Chapter Nine.)

In 1938 the Schroder Bank in London became the German financial agent in Great Britain, represented at financial meetings by its Managing Director (and a director of the Bank of England), F.C. Tiarks. By World War II Baron Schrader had in this manner acquired an impressive list of political and banking connections reflecting a widespread influence; it was even reported to the U.S. Kilgore Committee that Schrader was influential enough in 1940 to bring Pierre Laval to power in France. As listed by the Kilgore Committee, Sehroder's political acquisitions in the early 1940s were as follows:

SS Senior Group Leader.	Trade Group for Wholesale and Foreign Trade — Manager.
Iron Cross of First and Second Class.	Akademie fur Deutsches Recht (Academy of Germany Law) — Member
Swedish Consul General.	City of Cologne — Councilor.
International Chamber of Commerce — Member of administrative committee.	University of Cologne — Member of board of trustees.
Council of Reich Post Office — Member of advisory board.	Kaiser Wilhelm Foundation — Senator.
German Industrial and Commerce Assembly — Presiding member.	Advisory Council of German-Albanians.
Reich Board of Economic Affairs Member.	Goods Clearing Bureau — Member.
Deutsche Reichsbahn — President of administrative board.	Working Committee of Reich Group for Industry and Commerce — Deputy chairman[511]

---

[511] *Elimination of German Resources*, p. 871.

Schröder's banking connections were equally impressive and his business connections (not listed here) would take up two pages:

Bank for International Settlement — Member of the directorate.

J.H. Stein & Co, Cologne — Partner (Banque Worms was French cortespondent).

Deutsche Reichsbank, Berlin. Adviser to board of directors.

Deutsche Verkehrs-Kredit-Bank, A.G., Berlin (Controlled by Deutsche Reichsbank) — Chairman of board of directors.

Deutsche Ueberseeische Bank (Controlled by Deutsche Bank, Berlin) — Director[512]

Wirtschaftsgruppe Private Bankegewerbe — Leader.

This was the Schröder who, after 1933, represented Sosthenes Behn of I.T.T. and I.T.T. interests in Nazi Germany. Precisely because Schröder had these excellent political connections with Hitler and the Nazi State, Behn appointed Schröder to the boards of all the I.T.T. German companies: Standard Electrizitatswerke A.G. in Berlin, C. Lorenz A.G. of Berlin, and Mix & Genest A.G. (in which Standard had a 94-percent participation).

In the mid-1930s another link was forged between Wall Street and Schröder, this time through the Rockefellers. In 1936 the underwriting and general securities business handled by J. Henry Schroder Banking Corporation in New York was merged into a new investment banking firm — Schroder, Rockefeller & Company, Inc. at 48 Wall Street. Carlton P. Fuller of Schroder Banking Corporation became president and Avery Rockefeller, son of Percy Rockefeller (brother of John D. Rockefeller) became vice president and director of the new firm. Previously, Avery Rockefeller had been associated behind the scenes with J. Henry Schroder Banking Corporation; the new firm brought him out into the open.[513]

WESTRICK, TEXACO, AND I.T.T.

I.T.T. had yet another conduit to Nazi Germany, through German attorney Dr. Gerhard Westrick. Westrick was one of a select group of Germans who had conducted espionage in the United States during World War I. The group included not only Kurt von Schröder and Westrick but also Franz yon Papen — whom we shall meet in company with James Paul Warburg of the Bank of Manhattan in Chapter Ten — and Dr. Heinrich Albert. Albert, supposedly German commercial attache in the U.S. in World War I, was actually in charge of financing yon Papen's espionage program. After World War I Westrick and Albert formed the law firm of Albert & Westrick which specialized in, and profited heavily from, the Wall Street reparations loans. The Albert & Westrick firm handled the German end of the J Henry

---

[512] Ibid.
[513] *New York Times,* July 20, 1936.

Schroder Banking loans, while the John Foster Dulles firm of Sullivan and Cromwell in New York handled the U.S. end of the Schroder loans.

Just prior to World War II the Albert-Papen-Westrick espionage operation in the United States began to repeat itself, only this time around the American authorities were more alert. Westrick came to the U.S. in 1940, supposedly as a commercial attache but in fact as Ribbentrop's personal representative. A stream of visitors to the influential Westrick in-eluded prominent directors of U.S. petroleum and industrial firms, and this brought Westrick to the attention of the FBI.

Westrick at this time became a director of all I.T.T. operations in Germany, in order to protect I.T.T. interests during the expected U.S. involvement in the European war.[514] Among his other enterprises Westrick attempted to persuade Henry Ford to cut off supplies to Britain, and the favored treatment given by the Nazis to Ford interests in France suggests that Westrick was partially successful in neutralizing U.S. aid to Britain.

Although Westrick's most important wartime business connection in the United States was with International Telephone and Telegraph, he also represented other U.S. firms, including Underwood Elliott Fisher, owner of the German company Mercedes Buromaschinen A.G.; Eastman Kodak, which had a Kodak subsidiary in Germany; and the International Milk Corporation, with a Hamburg subsidiary. Among Westrick's deals (and the one which received the most publicity) was a contract for Texaco to supply oil to the German Navy, which he arranged with Torkild Rieber, chairman of the board of Texaco Company.

In 1940 Rieber discussed an oil deal with Hermann Goering, and Westrick in the United States worked for Texas Oil Company. His automobile was bought with Texaco funds, and Westrick's driver's license application gave Texaco as his business address. These activities were publicized on August 12, 1940. Rieber subsequently resigned from Texaco and Westrick returned to Germany. Two years later Rieber was chairman of South Carolina Shipbuilding and Dry Docks, supervising construction of more than $10 million of U.S. Navy ships, and a director of the Guggenheim family's Barber Asphalt Corporation and Seaboard Oil Company of Ohio.[515]

I.T.T. IN WARTIME GERMANY

---

[514] Anthony Sampson reports a meeting between I.T.T. vice president Kenneth Stockton and Westrick in which the preservation of I.T.T. properties was planned. See Anthony Sampson, op. cit., p. 39.

[515] There is no substance to reports that Rieber received $20,000 from the Nazis. These reports were investigated by the F.B.I. with no proof forthcoming. See United States Senate, Subcommittee to Investigate the Administration of the. Internal Security Act, Committee on the Judiciary, *Morgenthau Diary (Germany)*, Volume I, 90th Congress, 1st Session, November 20, 1967, (Washington: U.S. Government Printing Office, 1967), pp. 316-8. On Rieber see also *Appendix to the Congressional Record*, August 20, 1942, p, A 1501-2, Remarks of Hon. John M. Coffee.

In 1939 I.T.T. in the United States controlled Standard Elektrizitats in Germany, and in turn Standard Elektrizitats controlled 94 percent of Mix & Genest. On the board of Standard Elektrizitats was Baron Kurt yon Schrader, a Nazi banker at the core of Naziism, and Emil Heinrich Meyer, brother-in-law of Secretary of State Keppler (founder of the Keppler Circle) and a director of German General Electric. Schrader and Meyer were also directors of Mix & Genest and the other I.T.T. subsidiary, C. Lorenz Company; both of these I.T.T. subsidiaries were monetary contributors to Himmler's Circle of Friends — *i.e.,* the Nazi S.S. slush fund. As late as 1944, Mix & Genest contributed 5,000 RM to Himmler and Lorenz contributed 20,000 RM. In short, during World War II International Telephone and Telegraph was making cash payments to S.S. leader Heinrich Himmler. These payments enabled I.T.T. to protect its investment in Focke-Wolfe, an aircraft manufacturing firm producing fighter aircraft used against the United States.

The interrogation of Kurt von Schröder on November 19, 1945 points up the deliberate nature of the close and profitable relationship between Colonel Sosthenes Behn of I.T.T., Westrick, Schröder, and the Nazi war machine during World War II, and that *this was a deliberate and knowledgeable relationship:*

> Q. You have [told] us in your earlier testimony, a number of companies in Germany in which the International Telephone and Telegraph Company or the Standard Electric Company had a participation. Did either International Telephone and Telegraph Company or the Standard Electric Company have a participation in any other company in Germany?
> A. Yes. The Lorenz Company, shortly before the war, took a participation of about 25 percent in Focke-Wolfe A.G. in Bremen. Focke-Wolfe was making airplanes for the German Air Ministry. I believe that later as Focke-Wolfe expanded and took in more capital that the interest of Lorenz Company dropped a little below this 25 percent.
> Q. So this participation in Focke-Wolfe by Lorenz Company began after Lorenz Company was nearly 100-percent owned and controlled by Colonel Behn through the International Telephone and Telegraph Company?
> A. Yes.
> Q. Did Colonel Behen *[sic]* approve of this investment by the Lorenz Company in Focke-Wolfe?
> A. I am confident that Colonel Behn approved before his representatives who were in close touch with him formally approved the transaction.
> Q. What year was it that the Lorenz Company made the investment which gave it this 25 percent participation in Foeke-Wolfe?
> A. I remember it was shortly before the outbreak of war, that is, shortly before the invasion of Poland. [Ed: 1939]
> Q Would Westrick know all about the details of the participations of Lorenz Company in Foeke-Wolfe, A.G. of Bremen?

A. Yes. Better than I would.

Q. What was the size of the investment that Lorenz Company made in the Focke-Wolfe A.G., of Bremen, which gave them the initial 25 percent participation?

A. 250,000 thousand RM initially, and this was substantially increased, but I don't recall the extent of the additional investments that Lorenz Company made to this Focke-Wolfe A.G. of Bremen.

Q. From 1055, until the outbreak of the European War, was Colonel Behn in a position to transfer the profits from investments of his companies in Germany to his companies in the United States?

A. Yes. While it would have required that his companies take a little less than the full dividends because of the difficulty of securing foreign exchange, the great bulk of the profits could have been transferred to the company of Colonel Behn in the United States. However, Colonel Behn did not elect to do this and at no time did he ask me if I could accomplish this for him. Instead, he appeared to be perfectly content to have all the profits of the companies in Germany, which he and his interests controlled, reinvesting these profits in new buildings and machinery and any other enterprises engaged in producing armaments. Another one of these enterprises, Huth and Company, G.m.b.H., of Berlin, which made radio and radar parts, many of which were used in equipment going to the German Armed Forces. The Lorenz Company as I recall it [had] a 50-percent participation in Huth and Company. The Lorenz Company also had a small subsidiary which acted as a sales agency for the Lorenz Company to private customers.

Q. You were a member of the board of Lorenz Company's board of director, from about 1935 up to the present time. During this time, Lorenz Company and some of the other companies, such as Foeke-Wolfe with which it had large participations, were engaged in the manufacture of equipment for armaments and war production. Did you know or did you hear of any protest made by Colonel Behn or his representatives against these companies engaged in these activities preparing Germany for war?

A. No.

Q. Are you positive that there was no other occasion in which you were asked by either Westrick, Mann [sic], Colonel Behn or any other person connected with the International Telephone and Telegraphic Company interests in Germany, to intervene on behalf of the company with the German authorities.

A. Yes. I don't remember any request for my intervention in any matter of importance to the Lorenz Company or any other International Telephone and Telegraph interests in Germany.

I have read the record of this interrogation and I swear that the answers I have given to the question of Messrs. Adams and Pajus are true to the best of knowledge and belief. s/Kurt yon Schröder

It was this story of I.T.T.-Nazi cooperation during World War II and I.T.T. association with Nazi Kurt von Schröder that I.T.T. *wanted* to conceal — and almost was successful in concealing. James Stewart Martin recounts how during the planning meetings of the Finance Division of the Control Commission he was assigned to work with Captain Norbert A. Bogdan, who out of uniform was vice president of the J. Henry Schroder Banking Corporation of New York. Martin relates that "Captain Bogdan had argued vigorously against investigation of the Stein Bank on the grounds that it was 'small potatoes.'"[516] Shortly after blocking this maneuver, two permanent members of Bogdan's staff applied for permission to investigate the Stein Bank — although Cologne had not yet fallen to U.S. forces. Martin recalls that "The Intelligence Division blocked that one," and so some information on the Stein-Schröder Bank-I.T.T. operation survived.

---

[516] James Stewart Martin, op. cit., p. 52.

Chapter Six

Henry Ford and the Nazis

I would like to outline the importance attached by high [Nazi] officials to respect the desire and maintain the good will of "Ford," and by "Ford" I mean your father, yourself, and the Ford Motor Company, Dearborn.
(Josiah E. Dubois, Jr, Generals in Grey Suits, London: The Bodley Head, 1953, p. 250.)

Henry Ford is often seen to be something of an enigma among the Wall Street elite. For many years in the 20s and 30s Ford was popularly known as an enemy of the financial establishment. Ford accused Morgan and others of using war and revolution as a road to profit and their influence in social systems as a means of personal advancement. By 1938 Henry Ford, in his public statements, had divided financiers into two classes: those who profited from war and used their influence to bring about war for profit, and the "constructive" financiers. Among the latter group he now included the House of Morgan. During a 1938 *New York Times* interview[517] Ford averred that:

> Somebody once said that sixty families have directed the destinies of the nation. It might well be said that if somebody would focus the spotlight on twenty-five persons who handle the nation's finances, the world's real warmakers would be brought into bold relief.

The *Times* reporter asked Ford how he equated this assessment with his long-standing criticism of the House of Morgan, to which Ford replied:

> There is a constructive and a destructive Wall Street. The House of Morgan represents the constructive. I have known Mr. Morgan for many years. He backed and supported Thomas Edison, who was also my good friend...

---

[517] June 4, 1938, 2:2.

After expounding on the evils of limited agricultural production — allegedly brought about by Wall Street — Ford continued,

> ... if these financiers had their way we'd be in a war now. They want war because they make money out of such conflict — out of the human misery that wars bring.

On the other hand, when we probe behind these public statements we find that Henry Ford and son Edsel Ford have been in the forefront of American businessmen who try to walk both sides of every ideological fence in search of profit. Using Ford's own criteria, the Fords are among the "destructive" elements.

It was Henry Ford who in the 1930s built the Soviet Union's first modern automobile plant (located at Gorki) and which in the 50s and 60s produced the trucks used by the North Vietnamese to carry weapons and munitions for use against Americans.[518] At about the same time, Henry Ford was also the most famous of Hitler's foreign backers, and he was rewarded in the 1930s for this long-lasting support with the highest Nazi decoration for foreigners.

This Nazi favor aroused a storm of controversy in the United States and ultimately degenerated into an exchange of diplomatic notes between the German Government and the State Department. While Ford publicly protested that he did not like totalitarian governments, we find in practice that Ford knowingly profited from both sides of World War II — from French and German plants producing vehicles at a profit for the Wehrmacht, and from U.S. plants building vehicles at a profit for the U.S. Army.

Henry Ford's protestations of innocence suggest, as we shall see in this chapter, that he did not approve of Jewish financiers profiting from war (as some have), but if anti-Semitic Morgan[519] and Ford profited from war that was acceptable, moral and "constructive."

HENRY FORD: HITLER'S FIRST FOREIGN BACKER

On December 20, 1922 the *New York Times* reported[520] that automobile manufacturer Henry Ford was financing Adolph Hitler's nationalist and anti-Semitic movements in Munich.

Simultaneously, the Berlin newspaper *Berliner Tageblatt* appealed to the American Ambassador in Berlin to investigate and halt Henry Ford's intervention into German domestic affairs. It was reported that Hitler's foreign backers had furnished a "spacious headquarters"

---

[518] A list of these Gorki vehicles and their model numbers is in Antony G. Sutton, *National Suicide: Military Aid to the Soviet Union*, (New York: Arlington House Publishers, 1973), Table 7-2, p. 125.
[519] The House of Morgan was known for its anti-Semitic views.
[520] Page 2, Column 8.

with a "host of highly paid lieutenants and officials." Henry Ford's portrait was prominently displayed on the walls of Hitler's personal office:

> The wall behind his desk in Hitler's private office is decorated with a large picture of Henry Ford. In the antechamber there is a large table covered with books, nearly all of which are a translation of a book written and published by Henry Ford.[521]

The same *New York Times* report commented that the previous Sunday Hitler had reviewed,

> The so-called Storming Battalion.., 1,000 young men in brand new uniforms and armed with revolvers and blackjacks, while Hitler and his henchmen drove around in two powerful brand-new autos.

The *Times* made a clear distinction between the German monarchist parties and Hitler's anti-Semitic fascist party. Henry Ford, it was noted, ignored the Hohenzollern monarchists and put his money into the Hitlerite revolutionary movement.

These Ford funds were used by Hitler to foment the Bavarian rebellion. The rebellion failed, and Hitler was captured and subsequently brought to trial. In February 1923 at the trial, vice president Auer of the Bavarian Diet testified:

> The Bavarian Diet has long had the information that the Hitler movement was partly financed by an American anti-Semitic chief, who is Henry Ford. Mr. Ford's interest in the Bavarian anti-Semitic movement began a year ago when one of Mr. Ford's agents, seeking to sell tractors, came in contact with Diedrich Eichart, the notorious Pan-German. Shortly after, Herr Eichart asked Mr. Ford's agent for financial aid. The agent returned to America and immediately Mr. Ford's money began coming to Munich.
>
> Herr Hitler openly boasts of Mr. Ford's support and praises Mr. Ford as a great individualist and a great anti-Semite. A photograph of Mr. Ford hangs in Herr Hitler's quarters, which is the center of monarchist movement.[522]

Hitler received a mild and comfortable prison sentence for his Bavarian revolutionary activities. The rest from more active pursuits enabled him to write *Mein Kampf.* Henry Ford's

---

[521] Ibid.

[522] Jonathan Leonard, *The Tragedy of Henry Ford,* (New York: G.P. Putnam's Sons, 1932), p. 208. Also see U.S. State Department Decimal File, National Archives Microcopy M 336, Roll 80, Document 862.00S/6, "Money sources of Hitler," a report from the U.S. Embassy in Berlin.

book, *The International Jew,* earlier circulated by the Nazis, was translated by them into a dozen languages, and Hitler utilized sections of the book verbatim in writing *Mein Kampf.*[523]

We shall see later that Hitler's backing in the late 20s and early 30s came from the chemical, steel, and electrical industry cartels, rather than directly from individual industrialists. In 1928 Henry Ford merged his German assets with those of the I.G. Farben chemical cartel. A substantial holding, 40 percent of Ford Motor A.G. of Germany, was transferred to I.G. Farben; Carl Bosch of I.G. Farben became head of Ford A.G. Motor in Germany.

Simultaneously, in the United States Edsel Ford joined the board of American I.G. Farben. (See Chapter Two.)

HENRY FORD RECEIVES A NAZI MEDAL

A decade later, in August 1938 — after Hitler had achieved power with the aid of the cartels — Henry Ford received the Grand Cross of the German Eagle, a Nazi decoration for distinguished foreigners. The *New York Times* reported it was the first time the Grand Cross had been awarded in the United States and was to celebrate Henry Ford's 75th birthday.[524]

The decoration raised a storm of criticism within Zionist circles in the U.S. Ford backed off to the extent of publicly meeting with Rabbi Leo Franklin of Detroit to express his sympathy for the plight of German Jews:

> My acceptance of a medal from the German people [said Ford] does not, as some people seem to think, involve any sympathy on my part with naziism. Those who have known me for many years realize that anything that breeds hate is repulsive to me.[525]

The Nazi medal issue was picked up in a Cleveland speech by Secretary of Interior Harold Ickes. Ickes criticized both Henry Ford and Colonel Charles A. Lindbergh for accepting Nazi medals. The curious part of the Ickes speech, made at a Cleveland Zionist Society banquet, was his criticism of "wealthy Jews" and *their* acquisition and use of wealth:

---

[523] On this see Keith Sward, *The Legend of Henry Ford,* (New York: Rinehart & Co, 1948), p. 139.
[524] *New York Times,* August 1, 1938.
[525] Ibid., December 1, 1938, 12:2.

> *A mistake made by a non-Jewish millionaire reflects upon him alone, but a false step made by a Jewish man of wealth reflects upon his whole race. This is harsh and unjust, but it is a fact that must be faced.*[526]

Perhaps Ickes was tangentially referring to the roles of the Warburgs in the I.G. Farben cartel: Warburgs were on the board of I.G. Farben in the U.S. and Germany. In 1938 the Warburgs were being ejected by the Nazis from Germany. Other German Jews, such as the Oppenheim bankers, made their peace with the Nazis and were granted "honorary Aryan status."

FORD MOTOR COMPANY ASSISTS THE GERMAN WAR EFFORT

A post-war Congressional subcommittee investigating American support for the Nazi military effort described the manner in which the Nazis succeeded in obtaining U.S. technical and financial assistance as "quite fantastic."[527] Among other evidence the Committee was shown a memorandum prepared in the offices of Ford-Werke A.G. on November 25, 1941, written by Dr. H. F. Albert to R. H. Schmidt, then president of the board of Ford-Werke A.G. The memo cited the advantages of having a majority of the German firm held by Ford Motor Company in Detroit. German Ford had been able to exchange Ford parts for rubber and critical war materials needed in 1938 and 1939 "and they would not have been able to do that if Ford had not been owned by the United States." Further, with a majority American interest German Ford would "more easily be able to step in and dominate the Ford holdings throughout Europe." It was even reported to the Committee that two top German Ford officials had been in a bitter personal feud about who was to control Ford of England, such "that one of them finally got up and left the room in disgust."

According to evidence presented to the Committee, Ford-Werke A.G. was technically transformed in the late 1930s into a German company. All vehicles and their parts were produced in Germany, by German workers using German materials under German direction and exported to European and overseas territories of the United States and Great Britain.

Any needed foreign raw materials, rubber and nonferrous metals, were obtained through the American Ford Company. American influence had been more or less converted into a supporting position *(Hilfsstellung)* for the German Ford plants.

At the outbreak of the war Ford-Werke placed itself at the disposal of the Wehrmacht for armament production. It was assumed by the Nazis that as long as Ford-Werke A.G. had an American majority, it would be possible to bring the remaining European Ford

---

[526] Ibid., December 19, 1938, 5:3.
[527] *Elimination of German Resources,* p. 656.

companies under German influence — i.e., that of Ford-Werke A.G. — and so execute Nazi "Greater European" policies in the Ford plants in Amsterdam, Antwerp, Paris, Budapest, Bucharest, and Copenhagen:

> *A majority, even if only a small one, of Americans is essential for the transmittal of the newest American models, as well as American production and sales methods. With the abolition of the American majority, this advantage, as well as the intervention of the Ford Motor Company to obtain raw materials and exports, would be lost, and the German plant would practically only be worth its machine capacity.*[528]

And, of course, this kind of strict neutrality, taking an international rather than a national viewpoint, had earlier paid off for Ford Motor Company in the Soviet Union, where Ford was held in high regard as the ultimate of technical and economic efficiency to be achieved by the Stak-hanovites.

In July 1942 word filtered back to Washington from Ford of France about Ford's activities on behalf of the German war effort in Europe. The incriminating information was promptly buried and even today only part of the known documentation can be traced in Washington.

We do know, however, that the U.S. Consul General in Algeria had possession of a letter from Maurice Dollfuss of French Ford — who claimed to be the first Frenchman to go to Berlin after the fall of France — to Edsel Ford about a plan by which Ford Motor could contribute to the Nazi war effort. French Ford was able to produce 20 trucks a day for the Wehrmacht, which [wrote Dollfuss] is better than,

> *... our less fortunate French competitors are doing. The reason is that our trucks are in very large demand by the German authorities and I believe that as long as the war goes on and at least for some period of time, all that we shall produce will be taken by the German authorities .... I will satisfy myself by telling you that... the attitude you have taken, together with your father, of strict neutrality, has been an invaluable asset for the production of your companies in Europe.*[529]

Dollfuss disclosed that profits from this German business were already 1.6 million francs, and net profits for 1941 were no less than 58,000,000 francs — because the Germans paid promptly for Ford's output. On receipt of this news Edsel Ford cabled:

---

[528] *Elimination of German Resources*, pp. 657-8.
[529] Josiah E. Dubois, Jr., *Generals in Grey Suits*, (London: The Bodley Head, 1958), p. 248.

> *Delighted to hear you are making progress. Your letters most interesting. Fully realize great handicap you are working under. Hope you and family well.*
>
> *Regards.*
>
> s/ Edsel Ford[530]

Although there is evidence that European plants owned by Wall Street interests were not bombed by the U.S. Air Force in World War II, this restriction apparently did not reach the British Bombing Command. In March 1942 the Royal Air Force bombed the Ford plant at Poissy, France. A subsequent letter from Edsel Ford to Ford General Manager Sorenson about this RAF raid commented, *"Photographs* of the plant on fire were published in American newspapers but fortunately no reference was made to the Ford Motor Company.[531] In any event, the Vichy government paid Ford Motor Company 38 million francs as compensation for damage done to the Poissy plant. This was not reported in the U.S. press and would hardly be appreciated by those Americans at war with Naziism. Dubois asserts that these *private* messages from Ford in Europe were passed to Edsel Ford by Assistant Secretary of State Breckenridge Long. This was the same Secretary Long who one year later suppressed *private* messages through the State Department concerning the extermination of Jews in Europe. 16 Disclosure of those messages conceivably could have been used to assist those desperate people.

A U.S. Air Force bombing intelligence report written in 1943 noted that,

> *Principal wartime activities [of the Ford plant] are probably manufacture of light trucks and of spare parts for all the Ford trucks and cars in service in Axis Europe (including captured Russian Molotovs).[532]*

The Russian Molotovs were of course manufactured by the Ford-built works at Gorki, Russia. In France during the war, passenger automobile production was entirely replaced by military vehicles and for this purpose three large additional buildings were added to the Poissy factory. The main building contained about 500 machine tools, "all imported from the United States and including a fair sprinkling of the more complex types, such as Gleason gear cutters, Bullard automatics and Ingersoll borers.[533]

Ford also extended its wartime activities into North Africa. In December 1941 a new Ford Company, Ford-Afrique, was registered in France and granted all the rights of the former Ford Motor Company, Ltd. of England in Algeria, Tunisia, French Morocco, French

---

[530] Ibid., p. 249.
[531] Ibid., p. 251.
[532] Ibid.
[533] U.S. Army Air Force, *Aiming point report No I.E.2,* May 29, 1943.

Equatorial, and French West Africa. North Africa was not accessible to British Ford so this new Ford Company — registered in German-occupied France — was organized to fill the gap. The directors were pro-Nazi and included Maurice Dollfuss (Edsel Ford's correspondent) and Roger Messis (described by the U.S. Algiers Consul General as "known to this office by repute as unscrupulous, is stated to be a 100 percent pro-German")[534]

The U.S. Consul General also reported that propaganda was common in Algiers about

> ... the collaboration of French-German-American capital and the questionable sincerity of the American war effort, [there] is already pointing an accusing finger at a transaction Which has been for long a subject of discussion in commercial circles.[535]

In brief, there is documentary evidence that Ford Motor Company worked on both sides of World War II. If the Nazi industrialists brought to trial at Nuremburg were guilty of crimes against mankind, then so must be their fellow collaborators in the Ford family, Henry and Edsel Ford. However, the Ford story was concealed by Washington — apparently like almost everything else that could touch upon the name and sustenance of the Wall Street financial elite.

---

[534] U.S. State Department Decimal File, 800/610.1.
[535] Ibid.

CHAPTER SEVEN

WHO FINANCED ADOLF HITLER?

The funding of Hitler and the Nazi movement has yet to be explored in exhaustive depth. The only published examination of Hitler's personal finances is an article by Oron James Hale, "Adolph Hitler: Taxpayer,"[536] which records Adolph's brushes with the German tax authorities before he became *Reichskanzler*, In the 1920s Hitler presented himself to the German tax man as merely an impoverished writer living on bank loans, with an automobile bought on credit. Unfortunately, the original records used by Hale do not yield the source of Hitler's income, loans, or credit, and German law "did not require self-employed or professional persons to disclose in detail the sources of income or the nature of services rendered."[537] Obviously the funds for the automobiles, private secretary Rudolf Hess, another assistant, a chauffeur, and expenses incurred by political activity, came from somewhere.

But, like Leon Trotsky's 1917 stay in New York, it is hard to reconcile Hitler's known expenditures with the precise source of his income.

SOME EARLY HITLER BACKERS

We do know that prominent European and American industrialists were sponsoring all manner of totalitarian political groups at that time, including Communists and various Nazi groups. The U.S. Kilgore Committee records that:

> By 1919 Krupp was already giving financial aid to one of the reactionary political groups which sowed the seed of the present Nazi ideology. Hugo Stinnes was an early contributor to the Nazi Party (National Socialistische Deutsche Arbeiter Partei). By 1924 other prominent industrialists and financiers, among them Fritz Thyssen, Albert Voegler, Adolph [sic] Kirdorf, and Kurt von Schroder, were secretly giving substantial sums to the Nazis. In 1931 members of the coalowners' association which Kirdorf headed pledged

---

[536] *The American Historical Review*, Volume LC, NO. 4, July. 1955. p, 830.
[537] Ibid, fn. (2).

themselves to pay 50 pfennigs for each ton of coal sold, the money to go to the organization which Hitler was building.[538]

Hitler's 1924 Munich trial yielded evidence that the Nazi Party received $20,000 from Nuremburg industrialists. The most interesting name from this period is that of Emil Kirdorf, who had earlier acted as conduit for financing German involvement in the Bolshevik Revolution.[539] Kirdorfs role in financing Hitler was, in his own words:

> *In 1923 I came into contact for the first time with the National-Socialist movement .... I first heard the Fuehrer in the Essen Exhibition Hall. His clear exposition completely convinced and overwhelmed me. In 1927 I first met the Fuehrer personally. I travelled to Munich and there had a conversation with the Fuehrer in the Bruckmann home. During four and a half hours Adolf Hitler explained to me his programme in de tail. I then begged the Fuehrer to put together the lecture he had given me in the form of a pamphlet. I then distributed this pamphlet in my name in business and manufacturing circles.*
>
> *Since then I have placed myself completely at the disposition of his movement, Shortly after our Munich conversation, and as a result of the pamphlet which the Fuehrer composed and I distributed, a number of meetings took place between the Fuehrer and leading personalities in the field of indus. try. For the last time before the taking over of power, the leaders of industry met in my house together with Adolf Hitler, Rudolf Hess, Hermann Goering and other leading personalities of the party.[540]*

In 1925 the Hugo Stinnes family contributed funds to convert the Nazi weekly *Volkischer Beobachter* to a daily publication. Putzi Hanf-staengl, Franklin D. Roosevelt's friend and protegé, provided the remaining funds. Table 7-1 summarizes presently known financial contributions and the business associations of contributors from the United States. Putzi is not listed in Table 7-1 as he was neither industrialist nor financier.

In the early 1930s financial assistance to Hitler began to flow more readily. There took place in Germany a series of meetings, irrefutably documented in several sources, between German industrialists, Hitler himself, and more often Hitler's representatives Hjalmar Sehaeht and Rudolf Hess. The critical point is that the German industrialists financing Hitler were predominantly directors of cartels with American associations, ownership, participation, or some form of subsidiary connection. The Hitler backers were not, by and large, firms of purely German origin, or representative of German family business. Except for Thyssen and

---

[538] *Elimination of German Resources*, p. 648. The Albert Voegler mentioned in the Kilgore Committee list of early Hitler supporters was the German representative on the Dawes Plan Commission. Owen Young of General Electric (see Chapter Three) was a U.S. representative for the Dawes Plan and formulated its successor, the Young Plan.
[539] Antony C. Sutton, *Wall Street and the Bolshevik Revolution*, op. cit.
[540] *Preussiche Zettung*, January 3, 1937.

Kirdoff, in most cases they were the German multi-national firms — *i.e., I.G.* Farben, A.E.G., DAPAG, *etc.* These multi-nationals had been built up by American loans in the 1920s, and in the early 1930s had American directors and heavy American financial participation.

One flow of foreign political funds not considered here is that reported from the European-based Royal Dutch Shell, Standard Oil's great competitor in the 20s and 30s, and the giant brainchild of Anglo-Dutch businessman Sir Henri Deterding. It has been widely asserted that Henri Deterding personally financed Hitler. This argument is made, for instance, by biographer Glyn Roberts in *The Most Powerful Man in the World*. Roberts notes that Deterding was impressed with Hitler as early as 1921:

> ...and the Dutch press reported that, through the agent Georg Bell, he [Deterding] had placed at Hitler's disposal, while the party was "still in long clothes," no less than four million guilders.[541]

It was reported (by Roberts) that in 1931 Georg Bell, Deterding's agent, attended meetings of Ukrainian Patriots in Paris "as joint delegate of Hitler and Deterding."[542] Roberts also reports:

> Deterding was accused, as Edgar Ansell Mowrer testifies in his Germany Puts the Clock Back, of putting up a large sum of money for the Nazis on the understanding that success would give him a more favored position in the German oil market. On other occasions, figures as high as £55,000,000 were mentioned.[543]

Biographer Roberts really found Deterding's strong anti-Bolshevism distasteful, and rather than present hard evidence of funding he is inclined to assume rather than prove that Deterding was pro-Hitler. But pro-Hitlerism is not a necessary consequence of anti-Bolshevism; in any event Roberts offers no proof of finance, and hard evidence of Deterding's involvement was not found by this author.

Mowrer's book contains neither index nor footnotes as to the source of his information and Roberts has no specific evidence for his accusations. There is circumstantial evidence that Deterding was pro-Nazi. He later went to live in Hitler's Germany and increased his share of the German petroleum market. So there may have been some contributions, but these have not been proven.

---

[541] Glyn Roberts, *The Most Powerful Man in the World*, (New York: Covicl, Friede, 1938), p. 305.
[542] Ibid., p. 313.
[543] Ibid., p. 322.

Similarly, in France (on January 11, 1932), Paul Faure, a member of the *Chambre des Députés*, accused the French industrial firm of Schneider-Creuzot of financing Hitler — and incidentally implicated Wall Street in other financing channels.[544]

The Schneider group is a famous firm of French armaments manufacturers. After recalling the Schneider influence in establishment of Fascism in Hungary and its extensive international armaments operations, Paul Fauré turns to Hitler, and quotes from the French paper *LeJournal*, "that Hitler had received 300,000 Swiss gold francs" from subscriptions opened in Holland under the case of a university professor named von Bissing. The Skoda plant at Pilsen, stated Paul Fauré, was controlled by the French Schneider family, and it was the Skoda directors von Duschnitz and von Arthaber who made the subscriptions to Hitler. Fauré concluded:

> ... I am disturbed to see the directors of Skoda, controlled by Schneider, subsidizing the electoral campaign of M. Hitler; I am disturbed to see your firms, your financiers, your industrial cartels unite themselves with the most nationalistic of Germans...

Again, no hard evidence was found for this alleged flow of Hitler funds.

FRITZ THYSSEN AND W.A. HARRIMAN COMPANY OF NEW YORK

Another elusive case of reported financing of Hitler is that of Fritz Thyssen, the German steel magnate who associated himself with the Nazi movement in the early 20s. When interrogated in 1945 under Project Dustbin,[545] Thyssen recalled that he was approached in 1923 by General Ludendorf at the time of French evacuation of the Ruhr. Shortly after this meeting Thyssen was introduced to Hitler and provided funds for the Nazis through General Ludendorf. In 1930-1931 Emil Kirdorf approached Thyssen and subsequently sent Rudolf Hess to negotiate further funding for the Nazi Party. This time Thyssen arranged a credit of 250,000 marks at the Bank Voor Handel en Scheepvaart N.V. at 18 Zuidblaak in Rotterdam, Holland, founded in 1918 with H.J. Kouwenhoven and D.C. Schutte as managing partners.[546] This bank was a subsidiary of the August Thyssen Bank of Germany (formerly von der Heydt's Bank A.G.). It was Thyssen's personal banking operation, and it was affiliated

---

[544] See *Chambre des Deputes — Debats*, February 11, 1932, pp. 496-500.

[545] U.S. Group Control Council (Germany0 Office of the Director of Intelligence, Field Information Agency, Technical). Intelligence Report No. EF/ME/1,4 September 1945. "Examination of Dr. Fritz Thyssen," p, 13, Hereafter cited as Examination of Dr. Fritz Thyssen.

[546] The Bank was known in Germany as *Bank fur Handel und Schiff*.

with the W. A. Harriman financial interests in New York. Thyssen reported to his Project Dustbin interrogators that:

> *I chose a Dutch bank because I did not want to be mixed up with German banks in my position, and because I thought it was better to do business with a Dutch bank, and I thought I would have the Nazis a little more in my hands.*[547]

Thyssen's book *I Paid Hitler*, published in 1941, was purported to be written by Fritz Thyssen himself, although Thyssen denies authorship. The book claims that funds for Hitler — about one million marks — came mainly from Thyssen himself. *I Paid Hitler* has other unsupported assertions, for example that Hitler was actually descended from an illegitimate child of the Rothschild family. Supposedly Hitler's grandmother, Frau Schickelgruber, had been a servant in the Rothschild household and while there became pregnant:

> *... an inquiry once ordered by the late Austrian chancellor, Engelbert Dollfuss, yielded some interesting results, owing to the fact that the dossiers of the police department of the Austro-Hungarian monarch were remarkably complete.*[548]

This assertion concerning Hitler's illegitimacy is refuted entirely in a more solidly based book by Eugene Davidson, which implicates the Frankenberger family, not the Rothschild family.

In any event, and more relevant from our viewpoint, the August Thyssen front bank in Holland — *i.e.*, the Bank voor Handel en Scheepvaart N.V. — controlled the Union Banking Corporation in New York. The Harrimans had a financial interest in, and E. Roland Harriman (Averell's brother) was a director of, this Union Banking Corporation. The Union Banking Corporation of New York City was a joint Thyssen-Harriman operation with the following directors in 1932[549]:

E. Roland HARRIMAN	Vice president of W. A. Harriman & Co., New York
H.J. KOUWENHOVEN	Nazi banker, managing partner of August Thyssen Bank and Bank voor Handel Scheepvaart N.V. (the transfer bank for Thyssen's funds)
J. G. GROENINGEN	Vereinigte Stahlwerke (the steel cartel which also funded Hitler)
C. LIEVENSE	President, Union Banking Corp., New York City
E. S. JAMES	Partner Brown Brothers, later Brown Brothers, Harriman & Co.

---

[547] Examination of Dr. Fritz Thyssen.
[548] Fritz Thyssen, *I Paid Hitler*, (New York: Farrar & Rinehart, Inc., 1941). p. 159.
[549] Taken from *Bankers Directory*, 1932 edition, p, 2557 and Poors, *Directory of Directors*. J.L. Guinter and Knight Woolley were also directors.

In winding up these Russian deals in 1929, Averell Harriman received a windfall profit of $1 million from the usually hard-headed Soviets, who have a reputation of giving nothing away without some present or later *quid pro quo*. Concurrently with these successful moves in international finance, Averell Harriman has always been attracted by so-called "public" service. In 1913 Harriman's "public" service began with an appointment to the Palisades Park Commission. In 1933 Harriman was appointed chairman of the New York State Committee of Employment, and in 1934 became Administrative Officer of Roosevelt's NRA — the Mussolini-like brainchild of General Electric's Gerard Swope.[550] There followed a stream of "public" offices, first the Lend Lease program, then as Ambassador to the Soviet Union, later as Secretary of Commerce.

In winding up these Russian deals in 1929, Averell Harriman received a windfall profit of $1 million from the usually hard-headed Soviets, who have a reputation of giving nothing away without some present or later *quid pro quo*. Concurrently with these successful moves in international finance, Averell Harriman has always been attracted by so-called "public" service. In 1913 Harriman's "public" service began with an appointment to the Palisades Park Commission. In 1933 Harriman was appointed chairman of the New York State Committee of Employment, and in 1934 became Administrative Officer of Roosevelt's NRA — the Mussolini-like brainchild of General Electric's Gerard Swope.[551] There followed a stream of "public" offices, first the Lend Lease program, then as Ambassador to the Soviet Union, later as Secretary of Commerce.

---

[550] See Antony C. Sutton, *Wall Street and FDR*. Chapter Nine, "Swope's Plan," *op. cit*.
[551] See Antony C. Sutton, *Wall Street and FDR*. Chapter Nine, "Swope's Plan," *op. cit*.

TABLE 7-1: FINANCIAL LINKS BETWEEN U.S. INDUSTRIALISTS AND ADOLF HITLER

Date	American Bankers and Industrialists	U.S. Affiliated Firm	German Source		Intermediary for Funds/Agent
1923	Henry FORD	FORD MOTOR COMPANY	—		—
1931	E.R. HARRIMAN	UNION BANKING CORP	Fritz THYSSEN	250,000 RM	Bank voor Handel en Scheepvaart N.V. (Subsidiary of August Thyssen Bank)
1932		Flick (a director of AEG)	Friedrich FLICK	150,000 RM	Direct to NSDAP
		NONE	Emil KIRDORF	600,000 RM	"Nationale Treuhand" a/c at Delbrück Schickler Bank
February-March 1933	Edsel B. FORD C.E. MITCHELL	AMERICAN I.G.	I.G. FARBEN	400,000 RM	"Nationale Treuhand"
February-March 1933	Walter TEAGLE Paul M. WARBURG	NONE	Reichsverband der Automobilindustrie	100,000 RM	"Nationale Treuhand"
February-March 1933	Gerard SWOPE Owen D. YOUNG C.H. MINOR	INTERNATIONAL GENERAL ELECTRIC	A.E.G.	60,000 RM	"Nationale Treuhand"
February-March 1933	E. Arthur BALDWIN	NONE	DEMAG	50,000 RM	
February-March 1933	Owen D. YOUNG	INTERNATIONAL GENERAL ELECTRIC	OSRAM G.m.b.H.	40,000 RM	"Nationale Treuhand"

Date	Name	Company	Amount	Notes
February-March 1933	Sosthenes BEHN	I.T.T.	Telefunken	35,000 RM	"Nationale Treuhand"
February-March 1933		NONE	Karl Herrman	300,000 RM	"Nationale Treuhand"
February-March 1933		NONE	A. Steinke (Director of BYBUAG)	200,000 RM	"Nationale Treuhand"
February-March 1933		NONE	Karl Lange (Machine industry)	50,000 RM	"Nationale Treuhand"
February-March 1933		NONE	F. Springorum (Hoesch A.G.)	36,000 RM	"Nationale Treuhand"
February-March 1933	Edsel B. FORD	Ford Motor Co.	Carl BOSCH (I.G. Farben & Ford Motor A.G.)		
1932-1944	Walter TEAGLE J.A. MOFFETT W.S. FARISH	Standard Oil of N.J.	Emil HELFFRICH (German-American Petroleum Co)		Heinrich Himmler S.S. via Keppler's Circle
1932-1944	Sosthenes BEHN	I.T.T.	Kurt von SCHRÖDER Mix & Genest Lorenz		Heinrich Himmler S.S. via Keppler's Circle

By contrast, E. Roland Harriman confined his activities to private business in international finance without venturing, as did brother Averell, into "public" service. In 1922 Roland and Averell formed W. A. Harriman & Company. Still later Roland became chairman of the board of Union Pacific Railroad and a director of *Newsweek* magazine, Mutual Life Insurance Company of New York, a member of the board of governors of the American Red Cross, and a member of the American Museum of Natural History.

Nazi financier Hendrik Jozef Kouwenhoven, Roland Harriman's fellow-director at Union Banking Corporation in New York, was managing director of the Bank voor Handel en Scheepvaart N.V. (BHS) of Rotterdam. In 1940 the BHS held approximately $2.2 million assets in the Union Banking Corporation, which in turn did most of its business with BHS.[552] In the 1930s Kouwenhoven was also a director of the Vereinigte Stahlwerke A.G., the steel cartel founded with Wall Street funds in the mid-1920s. Like Baron Schroder, he was a prominent Hitler supporter.

Another director of the New York Union Banking Corporation was Johann Groeninger, a German subject with numerous industrial and financial affiliations involving Vereinigte Stahlwerke, the August Thyssen group, and a directorship of August Thyssen Hutte A.G.[553]

This affiliation and mutual business interest between Harriman and the Thyssen interests does not suggest that the Harrimans directly financed Hitler. On the other hand, it does show that the Harrimans were intimately connected with prominent Nazis Kouwenhoven and Groeninger and a Nazi front bank, the Bank voor Handel en Scheepvaart. There is every reason to believe that the Harrimans knew of Thyssen's support for the Nazis. In the case of the Harrimans, it is important to bear in mind their long-lasting and intimate relationship with the Soviet Union and the Harriman's position at the center of Roosevelt's New Deal and the Democratic Party. The evidence suggests that some members of the Wall Street elite are connected with, and certainly have influence with, *all* significant political groupings in the contemporary world socialist spectrum — Soviet socialism, Hitler's national socialism, and Roosevelt's New Deal socialism.

FINANCING HITLER IN THE MARCH 1933 GENERAL ELECTION

Putting the Georg Bell-Deterding and the Thyssen-Harriman cases to one side, we now examine the core of Hitler's backing. In May 1932 the so-called "Kaiserhof Meeting" took place between Schmitz of I.G. Farben, Max Ilgner of American I.G. Farben, Kiep of Hamburg-America Line, and Diem of the German Potash Trust. More than 500,000 marks was raised

---

[552] See *Elimination of German Resources*, pp. 728-30.
[553] For yet other connections between the Union Banking Corp, and German enterprises, see Ibid., pp. 728-30.

at this meeting and deposited to the credit of Rudolf Hess in the Deutsche Bank. It is noteworthy, in light of the "Warburg myth" described in Chapter Ten that Max Ilgner of the American I.G. Farben contributed 100,000 RM, or one-fifth of the total. The "Sidney Warburg" book claims Warburg involvement in the funding of Hitler, and Paul Warburg was a director of American I.G. Farben[554] while Max Warburg was a director of I.G. Farben.

There exists irrefutable documentary evidence of a further role of. international bankers and industrialists in the financing of the Nazi Party and the *Volkspartie* for the March 1933 German election. A total of three million Reichmarks was subscribed by prominent firms and businessmen, suitably "washed" through an account at the Delbruck Schickler Bank, and then passed into the hands of Rudolf Hess for use by Hitler and the NSDAP. This transfer of funds was followed by the Reichstag fire, abrogation of constitutional rights, and consolidation of Nazi power. Access to the Reichstag by the arsonists was obtained through a tunnel from a house where Putzi Hanfstaengel was staying; the Reichstag fire itself was used by Hitler as a pretext to abolish constitutional rights. In brief, within a few weeks of the major funding of Hitler there was a linked sequence of major events: the financial contribution from prominent bankers and industrialists to the 1933 election, burning of the Reichstag, abrogation of constitutional rights, and subsequent seizure of power by the Nazi Party.

The fund-raising meeting was held February 20, 1933 in the home of Goering, who was then president of the Reichstag, with Hjalmar Horace Greeley Schacht acting as host. Among those present, according to I.G. Farben's von Schnitzler, were:

> *Krupp von Bohlen, who, in the beginning of 1933, was president of the Reichsverband der Deutschen Industrie Reich Association of German Industry; Dr. Albert Voegler, the leading man of the Vereinigte Stahlwerke; Von Loewenfeld; Dr, Stein, head of the Gewerkschaft Auguste-Victoria, a mine which belongs to the IG.*[555]

Hitler expounded his political views to the assembled businessmen in a lengthy two-and-one-half hour speech, using the threat of Communism and a Communist take-over to great effect:

> *It is not enough to say we do not want Communism in our economy. If we continue on our old political course, then we shall perish .... It is the noblest task of the leader to find ideals that are stronger than the factors that pull the people together. I recognized even while in the hospital that one had to search for new ideals conducive to reconstruction.*

---

[554] See Chapter Ten.
[555] *NMT*, Volume VII, p. 555.

> *I found them in nationalism, in the value of personality, and in the denial of reconciliation between nations...*
>
> *Now we stand before the last election. Regardless of the outcome, there will be no retreat, even if the coming election does not bring about decision, one way or another. If the election does not decide, the decision must be brought about by other means. I have intervened in order to give the people once more the chance to decide their fate by themselves ....*
>
> *There are only two possibilities, either to crowd back the opponent on constitutional grounds, and for this purpose once more this election; or a struggle will be conducted with other weapons, which may demand greater sacrifices. I hope the German people thus recognize the greatness of the hour.*[556]

After Hitler had spoken, Krupp von Bohlen expressed the support of the assembled industrialists and bankers in the concrete form of a three-million-mark political fund. It turned out to be more than enough to acquire power, because 600,000 marks remained unexpended after the election.

Hjalmar Schacht organized this historic meeting. We have previously described Schacht's links with the United States: his father was cashier for the Berlin Branch of Equitable Assurance, and Hjalmar was intimately involved almost on a monthly basis with Wall Street.

The largest contributor to the fund was I.G. Farben, which comomitted itself for 80 percent (or 500,000 marks) of the total. Director A. Steinke, of BUBIAG (Braunkohlen-u. Brikett-Industrie A.G.), an I.G. Farben subsidiary, personally contributed another 200,000 marks. In brief, 45 percent of the funds for the 1933 election came from I.G. Farben. If we look at the directors of American I.G. Farben — the U.S. subsidiary of I.G. Farben — we get close to the roots of Wall Street involvement with Hitler. The board of American I.G. Farben at this time contained some of the most prestigious names among American industrialists: Edsel B. Ford of the Ford Motor Company, C.E. Mitchell of the Federal Reserve Bank of New York, and Walter Teagle, director of the Federal Reserve Bank of New York, the Standard Oil Company of New Jersey, and President Franklin D. Roosevelt's Georgia Warm Springs Foundation.

Paul M. Warburg, first director of the Federal Reserve Bank of New York and chairman of the Bank of Manhattan, was a Farben director and in Germany his brother Max Warburg was also a director of I.G. Farben. H. A. Metz of I.G. Farben was also a director of the Warburg's Bank of Manhattan. Finally, Carl Bosch of American I.G. Farben was also a director of Ford Motor Company A-G in Germany.

---

[556] Josiah E. Dubois, Jr., *Generals in Grey Suits op. cit.*, p. 323.

Three board members of American I.G. Farben were found guilty at the Nuremburg War Crimes Trials: Max Ilgner, F. Ter Meer, and Hermann Schmitz. As we have noted, the American board members — Edsel Ford, C. E. Mitchell, Walter Teagle, and Paul Warburg — were not placed on trial at Nuremburg, and so far as the records are concerned, it appears that they were not even questioned about their knowledge of the 1933 Hitler fund.

THE 1933 POLITICAL CONTRIBUTIONS

Who were the industrialists and bankers who placed election funds at the disposal of the Nazi Party in 1933? The list of contributors and the amount of their contribution is as follows:

FINANCIAL CONTRIBUTIONS TO HITLER: Feb. 23-Mar. 13, 1933:
(The Hjalmar Schacht account at Delbruck, Schickler Bank)

Political Contributions by Firms (with selected affiliated directors)	Amount Pledged	Percent of Firm Total
Verein fuer die Bergbaulichen Interessen (Kitdorf)	$600,000	45.8
I.G. Farbenindustrie (Edsel Ford, C.E. Mitchell, Walter Teagle, Paul Warburg)	400,000	30.5
Automobile Exhibition, Berlin (Reichsverbund der Automobilindustrie S.V.)	100,000	7.6
A.E.G., German General Electric (Gerard Swope, Owen Young, C.H. Minor, Arthur Baldwin)	60,000	4.6
Demag	50,000	3.8
Osram G.m.b.H. (Owen Young)	40,000	3.0
Telefunken Gesellsehaft ruer drahtlose Telegraphic	85,000	2.7
Accumulatoren-Fabrik A.G. (Quandt of A.E.G.)	25,000	1.9
Total from industry	1,310,000	99.9

Plus Political Contributions by Individual Businessmen:

    Karl Hermann   300,000

    Director A. Steinke (BUBIAG- Braunkohlen—u. Brikett —   200,000
    Industrie A.G.)

    Dir. Karl Lange (Geschaftsfuhrendes Vostandsmitglied des Vereins 50,000
    Deutsches Maschinenbau—Anstalten)

    Dr. F. Springorum (Chairman: Eisen-und Stahlwerke Hoesch A.G.) 36,000

Source: See Appendix for translation of original document.

How can we prove that these political payments actually took place? The payments to Hitler in this final step on the road to dictatorial Naziism were made through the private bank of Delbruck Sehickler. The Delbruck Schickler Bank was a subsidiary of Metallgesellschaft A.G. ("Metall"), an industrial giant, the largest non-ferrous metal company in Germany, and the dominant influence in the world's nonferrous metal 'trading. The principal shareholders of *"Metall"* were I.G. Farben and the British Metal Corporation. We might note incidentally that the British directors on the" Metall" *Aufsichsrat* were Walter Gardner (Amalgamated Metal Corporation) and Captain Oliver Lyttelton (also on the board of Amalgamated Metal and paradoxically later in World War II to become the British Minister of Production).

There exists among the Nuremburg Trial papers the original transfer slips from the banking division of I.G. Farben and other firms listed on page 110 to the Delbruck Schickler Bank in Berlin, informing the bank of the transfer of funds from Dresdner Bank, and other banks, to their *Nationale Treuhand* (National Trusteeship) account. This account was disbursed by Rudolf Hess for Nazi Party expenses during the election. Translation of the I.G. Farben transfer slip, selected as a sample, is as follows:

Translation of I.G, Farben letter of February 27, 1933, advising of transfer of 400,000 Reichsmarks to National Trusteeship account:
I.G. FARBENINDUSTRIE AKTIENGESELLSCHAFT
Bank Department

    Firm: Delbruck Schickler & Co., BERLIN W.8
    Mauerstrasse 63/65, Frankfurt (Main) 20
    Our Ref: (Mention in Reply)
    27 February 1933 B./Goe.

We are informing you herewith that we have authorized the Dresdner Bank in Frankfurt/M., to pay you tomorrow forenoon: RM 400,000 which you will use in favor of the account "NATIONALE TREUHAND" (National Trusteeship).
Respectfully,
I.G. Farbenindustrie Aktiengesellschaft by Order:
(Signed) SELCK (Signed) BANGERT
By special delivery.[557]

At this juncture we should take note of the efforts that have been made to direct our attention away from American financiers (and German financiers connected with American-affiliated companies) who were, involved with the funding of Hitler. Usually the blame for financing Hitler has been exclusively placed upon Fritz Thyssen or Emil Kirdorf. In the case of Thyssen this blame was widely circulated in a book allegedly authored by Thyssen in the middle of World War II but later repudiated by him.[558] Why Thyssen would want to admit such actions before the defeat of Naziism is unexplained.

Emil Kirdorf, who died in 1937, was always proud of his association with the rise of Naziism. The attempt to limit Hitler financing to Thyssen and Kirdorf extended into the Nuremburg trials in 1946, and was challenged only by the Soviet delegate. Even the Soviet delegate was unwilling to produce evidence of American associations; this is not surprising because the Soviet Union depends on the goodwill of these same financiers to transfer much needed advanced Western technology to the U.S.S.R.

At Nuremburg, statements were made and allowed to go unchallenged which were directly contrary to the known direct evidence presented above. For example, Buecher, Director General of German General Electric, was absolved from sympathy for Hitler:

> *Thyssen has confessed his error like a man and has courageously paid a heavy penalty for it. On the other side stand men like Reusch of the Gutehoffnungshuette, Karl Bosch, the late chairman of the I.G. Farben Aufsichtsrat, who would very likely have come to a sad end, had he not died in time. Their feelings were shared by the deputy chairman of the Aufsichtsrat of Kalle. The Siemens and AEG companies which, next to I.G. Farben, were the most powerful German concerns, and they were determined opponents of national socialism.*
>
> *I know that this unfriendly attitude on the part of the Siemens concern to the Nazis resulted in the firm receiving rather rough treatment. The Director General of the AEG (Allgemeine Elektrizitats Gesellschaft), Geheimrat Buecher, whom I knew from my stay in*

---

[557] *NMT*, Volume VII, p. 565.
[558] Fritz Thyssen, *I Paid Hitler*, (New York: Toronto: Farrat & Rinehart, Inc., 1941).

the colonies, was anything but a Nazi. I can assure General Taylor that it is certainly wrong to assert that the leading industrialists as such favored Hitler before his seizure of power.[559]

Yet on page 56 of this book we reproduce a document originating with General Electric, transferring General Electric funds to the National Trusteeship account controlled by Rudolf Hess on behalf of Hitler and used in the 1933 elections.

Similarly, von Schnitzler, who was present at the February 1933 meeting on behalf of I.G. Farben, denied I.G. Farben's contributions to the 1933 Nationale Treuhand:

> *I never heard again of the whole matter [that of financing Hitler], but I believe that either the buro of Goering or Schacht or the Reichsverband der Deutschen Industrie had asked the of fice of Bosch or Schmitz for payment of IG's share in the elec tion fund. As I did not take the matter up again I not even at that time knew whether and which amount had been paid by the IG. According to the volume of the IG, I should estimate IG's share being something like 10 percent of the election fund, but as far as I know there is no evidence that I.G. Farben participated in the payments.*[560]

As we have seen, the evidence is incontrovertible regarding political cash contributions to Hitler at the crucial point of the takeover of power in Germany — and Hitler's earlier speech to the industrialists clearly revealed that a coercive takeover was the premeditated intent.

We know exactly who contributed, how much, and through what channels. It is notable that the largest contributors — I.G. Farben, German General Electric (and its affiliated company Osram), and Thyssen — were affiliated with Wall Street financiers. These Wall Street financiers were at the heart of the financial elite and they were prominent in contemporary American politics. Gerard Swope of General Electric was author of Roosevelt's New Deal, Teagle was one of NRA's top administrators, Paul Warburg and his associates at American

I.G. Farben were Roosevelt advisors. It is perhaps not an extraordinary coincidence that Roosevelt's New Deal — called a "fascist measure" by Herbert Hoover — should have so closely resembled Hitler's program for Germany, and that both Hitler and Roosevelt took power in the same month of the same year — March 1933.

---

[559] *NMT*, Volume VI, pp. 1169-1170.
[560] *NMT*, Volume VII, p. 565.

Chapter Eight

Putzi: Friend of Hitler and Roosevelt

Ernst Sedgewiek Hanfstaengl (or Hanfy or Putzi, as he was more usually called), like Hjalmar Horaee Greeley Sehacht, was another German-American at the core of the rise of Hitlerism. Hanfstaengl was born into a well-known New England family; he was a cousin of Civil War General John Sedgewiek and a grandson of another Civil War General, William Heine. Introduced to Hitler in the early 1920s by Captain Truman-Smith, the U.S. Military Attaehe in Berlin, Putzi became an ardent Hitler supporter, on occasion financed the Nazis and, according to Ambassador William Dodd, "... is said to have saved Hitler's life in 1923."[561]

By coincidence, S.S. leader Heinrich Himmler's father was also Putni's form master at the Royal Bavarian Wilhelms gymnasium. Putzi's student day friends at Harvard University were "such outstanding future figures" as Walter Lippman, John Reed (who figures prominently in *Wall Street and the Bolshevik Revolution),* and Franklin D. Roosevelt. After a few years at Harvard, Putzi established the family art business in New York; it was a delightful combination of business and pleasure, for as he says, "the famous names who visited me were legion, Pierpont Morgan, Toscanini, Henry Ford, Caruso, Santos-Dumont, Charlie Chaplin, Paderewski, and a daughter of President Wilson."[562] It was also at Harvard that Putzi made friends with the future President Franklin Delano Roosevelt:

> *I took most of my meals at the Harvard Club, where I made friends with the young Franklin D. Roosevelt, at that time a rising New York State Senator. Also I received several invitations to visit his distant cousin Teddy, the former President, who had retired to his estate at Sagamore Hill.*[563]

From these varied friendships (or perhaps after reading this book and its predecessors, *Wall Street and FDR* and *Wall Street and the Bolshevik Revolution,* the reader may consider Putzi's friendship to have been confined to a peculiarly elitist circle), Putzi became not only

---

[561] William E. Dodd, *Ambassador Dodd's Diary, 1933-1938,* (New York: Harcourt, Brace & Co., 1941), p. 360.
[562] Ernst Hanfstaengl, *Unheard Witness,* (New York: J.B. Lippincott, 1957), p. 28.
[563] Ibid.

an early friend, backer and financier of Hitler, but among those early Hitler supporters he was, ",, . almost the only person who crossed the lines of his (Hitler's) groups of acquaintances."[564]

In brief, Putzi was an American citizen at the heart of the Hitler entourage from the early 1920s to the late 1930s. In 1943, after falling out of favor with the Nazis and interned by the Allies, Putzi was bailed out of the miseries of a Canadian prisoner of war camp by his friend and protector President Franklin D. Roosevelt. When FDR's actions threatened to become an internal political problem in the United States, Putzi was re-interned in England. As if it is not surprising enough to find both Heinrich Himmler and Franklin D. Roosevelt prominent in Putzi's life, we also discover that the Nazi Stormtrooper marching songs were composed by Hanfstaengl, "including the one that was played by the brownshirt columns as they marched through the Brandenburger Tor on the day Hitler took over power.[565] To top this eye-opener, Putzi averred that the genesis of the Nazi chant "Sieg Heil, Sieg Heil," used in the Nazi mass rallies, was none other than "Harvard, Harvard, Harvard, rah, rah, rah."[566]

Putzi certainly helped finance the first Nazi daily press, the *Volkische Beobachter*. Whether he saved Hitler's life from the Communists is less verifiable, and while kept out of the actual writing process of *Mein Kampf* — much to his disgust — Putzi did have the honor to finance its publication, "and the fact that Hitler found a functioning staff when he was released from jail was entirely due to our efforts."[567]

When Hitler came to power in March 1933, simultaneously with Franklin Delano Roosevelt in Washington, a private "emissary" was sent from Roosevelt in Washington, D.C. to Hanfstaengl in Berlin, with a message to the effect that as it appeared Hitler would soon achieve power in Germany, Roosevelt hoped, in view of their long acquaintance, that Putzi would do his best to prevent any rashness and hot-headedness. "Think of your piano playing and try and use the soft pedal if things get too loud," was FDR's message. *"If things start getting awkward please get in touch with our ambassador at once.*[568]

Hanfstaengl kept in close touch with the American Ambassador in Berlin, William E. Dodd — apparently much to his disgust, because Putzi's recorded comments on Dodd are distinctly unflattering:

> *In many ways, he [Dodd] was an unsatisfactory representative. He was a modest little Southern history professor, who ran his embassy on a shoestring and was probably trying*

---

[564] Ibid., p. 52.
[565] Ibid., p. 53.
[566] Ibid., p. 59.
[567] Ibid., p. 122.
[568] Ibid., pp. 197-8.

to save money out of his pay. At a time when it needed a robust millionaire to compete with the flamboyance of the Nazis, he teetered around self-effacingly as if he were still on his college campus. His mind and his prejudices were small.[569]

In point of fact Ambassador Dodd pointedly tried to decline Roosevelt's Ambassadorial appointment. Dodd had no inheritance and preferred to live on his State Department pay rather than political spoils; unlike the politician Dodd was particular from whom he received money. In any event, Dodd commented equally harshly on Putzi, "... he gave money to Hitler in 1923, helped him write *Mein Kampf,* and was in every way familiar with Hitler's motives ...."

Was Hanfstaengl an agent for the Liberal Establishment in the U.S.? We can probably rule out this possibility because, according to Ladislas Farago, it was Putzi who blew the whistle on top-level British penetration of the Hitler command. Farago reports that Baron William S. de Ropp had penetrated the highest Nazi echelons in pre-World War II days and Hitler used de Ropp "... as his confidental consultant about British affairs.[570] De Ropp was suspected as being a double agent only by Putzi. According to Farago:

> The only person... who ever suspected him of such duplicity and cautioned the Fuehrer about him was the erratic Putzt Hanfstaengl, the Harvard educated chief of Hitler's office dealing with the foreign press.

As Farago notes, "Bill de Ropp was playing the game In both camps — a double agent at the very top."[571] Putzi was equally diligent in warning his friends, the Hermann Goerings, about potential spies in *their* camp. Witness the following extract from Putzi's memoirs, in which he points the accusing finger of espionage at the Goerings' gardener...

> "Herman," I said one day, "I will bet any money that fellow Greinz is a police spy." "Now really, Putzi," Karin [Mrs. Herman Goertng] broke in, "he's such a nice fellow and he's a wonderful gardener." "He's doing exactly what a spy ought to do," I told her, "he has made himself indispensable."[572]

By 1941 Putzi was out of favor with Hitler and the Nazis, fled Germany, and was interned in a Canadian prisoner of war camp. With Germany and the United States now at war Putzi re-calculated the odds and concluded, *"Now* I knew for certain that Germany

---

[569] Ibid., p. 214.
[570] Ladislas Farago, *The Game of the Foxes,* (New York: Bantam, 1973), p. 97.
[571] Ibid., p. 106.
[572] Ernst Hanfstaengl, *Unheard Witness, op.* cit., p. 76.

would be defeated."[573] Putzi's release from the POW camp came with the personal intervention of old friend President Roosevelt:

> One day a correspondent of the Hearst press named Kehoe obtained permission to visit Fort Hens. I managed to have a few words with him in a corner. "I know your boss well," I told him. "Will you do me a small service?" Fortunately he recognized my name.
> I gave him a letter, which he slipped into his pocket. It was addressed to the American Secretary of State, Cordell Hull. A few days later it was on the desk of my Harvard Club friend, Franklin Delano Roosevelt. In it I offered to act as a political and psychological warfare adviser in the war against Germany.[574]

The response and offer to "work" for the American side was accepted. Putzi was installed in comfortable surroundings with his son, U.S. Army Sergeant Egon Hanfstaengl, also there as a personal aide. In 1944, under pressure of a Republican threat to blow the whistle on Roosevelt's favoritism for a former Nazi, Egon was shipped out to New Guinea and Putzi hustled off to England, where the British promptly interned him for the duration of the war, Roosevelt or no Roosevelt,

PUTZI'S ROLE IN THE REICHSTAG FIRE

Putzi's friendships and political manipulations may or may not be of any great consequence, but his role in the Reichstag fire is significant. The firing of the Reichstag on February 27, 1933 is one of the key events of modern times. The fire was used by Adolf Hitler to claim imminent Communist revolution, suspend constitutional rights, and seize totalitarian power. From that point on there was no turning back for Germany; the world was set upon the course to World War II.

At the time the firing of the Reichstag was blamed on the Communists, but there is little question in historical perspective that the fire was deliberately set by the Nazis to provide an excuse to seize political power. Fritz Thyssen commented in the post-war Dustbin interrogations:

> When the Reichstag was burned, everyone was sure it had been done by the communists. I later learned in Switzerland that it was all a lie.[575]

---

[573] Ibid.
[574] Ibid., pp. 310-11.
[575] *Dustbin* report EF/Me/1. Interview of Thyssen, p. 13.

Schacht states quite emphatically:

> Nowadays it would be quite clear that this action could not be fastened on the Communist Party. To what extent individual National Socialists co-operated in the planning and execution of the deed will be difficult to establish, but in view of all that has been revealed in the meantime, the fact must be accepted that Goebbels and Goering each played a leading part, the one in planning, the other in carrying out the plan.[576]

The Reichstag fire was deliberately set, probably utilizing a flammable liquid, by a group of experts. This is where Putzi Hanfstaengl comes into the picture. The key question is how did this group, bent on arson, gain access to the Reichstag to do the job? After 8 p.m. only one door in the main building was unlocked and this door was guarded. Just before 9 p.m. a tour of the building by watchmen indicated all was well; no flammable liquids were noticed and nothing was out of the ordinary in the Sessions Chamber where the fire started. Apparently no one could have gained access to the Reichstag building after 9 p.m., and no one was seen to enter or leave between 9 p.m. and the start of the fire.

There was only one way a group with flammable materials could have entered the Reichstag — through a tunnel that ran between the Reichstag and the Palace of the Reichstag President. Hermann Goering was president of the Reichstag and lived in the Palace, and numerous S.A. and S.S. men were known to be in the Palace. In the words of one author:

> The use of the underground passage, with all its complications, was possible only to National-Socialists, the advance and escape of the incendiary gang was feasible only with the connivance of highly-placed employees of the Reichstag. Every clue, every probability points damningly in one direction, to the conclusion that the burning of the Reichstag was the work of National-Socialists.[577]

How does Putzi Hanfstaengl fit into this picture of arson and political intrigue? Putzi — by his own admission — was in the Palace room at the other end of the tunnel leading to the Reichstag. And according to *The Reichstag Fire Trial*, Putzi Hanfstaengl was actually in the Palace itself during the fire:

> propaganda apparatus stood ready, and the leaders of the Storm Troopers were in their places. With the official bulletins planned in advance, the orders of arrest prepared,

---

[576] Hjalmar Horace Greeley Schacht, *Confessions of" The Old Wizard,"* (Boston: Houghton Mifflin, 1956), p. 276.
[577] George Dimitrov, *The Reichstag Fire Trial,* (London: The Bodley Head, 1934), p. 309.

Karwahne, Frey and Kroyer waiting patiently in their cafe, the preparations were complete, the scheme almost perfect.[578]

Dimitrov also asserts that:

> *The National-Socialist leaders, Hitler, Goering and Goebbels, together with the high National-Socialist officials, Daluege, Hanfstaengl and Albrecht, happened to be present in Berlin on the day of the fire, despite that the election campaign was at its highest pitch throughout Germany, six days before the poll. Goering and Goebbels, under oath, furnished contradictory explanations for their "fortuitous" presence in Berlin with Hitler on that day. The National-Socialist Hanfstaengl, as Goering's "guest," was present in the Palace of the Reichstag President, immediately adjacent to the Reichstag, at the time when the fire broke out, although his "host" was not there at that time.*[579]

According to Nazi Kurt Ludecke, there once existed a document signed by S.A. Leader Karl Ernst — who supposedly set the fire and was later murdered by fellow Nazis — which implicated Goering, Goebbels, and Hanfstaengl in the conspiracy.

ROOSEVELT'S NEW DEAL AND HITLER'S NEW ORDER

Hjalmar Schacht challenged his post-war Nuremburg interrogators with the observation that Hitler's New Order program was the same as Roosevelt's New Deal program in the United States. The interrogators understandably snorted and rejected the observation. However, a little research suggests that not only are the two programs quite similar in content, but that Germans had no trouble in observing the similarities. There is in the Roosevelt Library a small book presented to FDR by Dr. Helmut Magers in December 1933.[580] On the flyleaf of this presentation copy is written the inscription,

> *To the President of the United States, Franklin D. Roosevelt, in profound admiration of his conception of a new economic order and with devotion for his personality. The author, Baden, Germany, November 9, 1933.*

---

[578] Ibid., p. 310.
[579] Ibid., p. 311.
[580] Helmut Magers, *Ein Revolutionar Aus Common Sense*, (Leipzig: R. Kittler Verlag, 1934).

FDR's reply to this admiration for his new economic order was as follows[581]:

> *(Washington) December 19, 1933*
> *My dear Dr. Magers: I want to send you my thanks for the copy of your little book about me and the "New Deal." Though, as you know, I went to school in Germany and could speak German with considerable fluency at one time, I am reading your book not only with great interest but because it will help my German.*
> *Very sincerely yours,*

The New Deal or the "new economic order" was not a creature of classical liberalism. It was a creature of corporate socialism. Big business as reflected in Wall Street strived for a state order in which they could control industry and eliminate competition, and this was the heart of FDR's New Deal. General Electric, for example, is prominent in both Nazi Germany and the New Deal. German General Electric was a prominent financier of Hitler and the Nazi Party, and A.E.G. also financed Hitler both directly and indirectly through Osram.

International General Electric in New York was a major participant in the ownership and direction of both A.E.G. and Osram. Gerard Swope, Owen Young, and A. Baldwin of General Electric in the United States were directors of A.E.G. However, the story does not stop at General Electric and financing of Hitler in 1933.

In a previous book, *Wall Street and the Bolshevik Revolution*, the author identified the role of General Electric in the Bolshevik Revolution and the geographic location of American participants as at 120 Broadway, New York City; the executive offices of General Electric were also at 120 Broadway. When Franklin Delano Roosevelt was working in Wall Street, his address was also 120 Broadway. In fact, Georgia Warm Springs Foundation, the FDR Foundation, was located at 120 Broadway. The prominent financial backer of an early Roosevelt Wall Street venture from 120 Broadway was Gerard Swope of General Electric. And it was "Swope's Plan" that became Roosevelt's New Deal — the fascist plan that Herbert Hoover was unwilling to foist on the United States. In brief, both Hitler's New Order and Roosevelt's New Deal were backed by the same industrialists and in content were quite similar — *i.e.*, they were both plans for a corporate state.

There were then both corporate and individual bridges between FDR's America and Hitler's Germany. The first bridge was the American I.G. Farben, American affiliate of I.G. Farben, the largest German corporation. On the board of American I.G. sat Paul Warburg, of the Bank of Manhattan and the Federal Reserve Bank of New York. The second bridge

---

[581] Nixon, Edgar B., Editor, *Franklin D. Roosevelt and Foreign Affairs*, (Cambridge: The Belknap Press of Harvard University Press, 1969), Volume I: January 1933-February 1934. Franklin D. Roosevelt Library. Hyde Park, New York.

was between International General' Electric, a wholly owned subsidiary of General Electric Company and its partly owned affiliate in Germany, A.E.G. Gerard Swope, who formulated FDR's New Deal, was chairman of I.G.E. and on the board of A.E.G. The third "bridge" was between Standard Oil of New Jersey and Vacuum Oil and its wholly owned German subsidiary, Deutsche-Amerikanisehe Gesellschaft. The chairman of Standard Oil of New Jersey was Walter Teagle, of the Federal Reserve Bank of New York. He was a trustee of Franklin Delano Roosevelt's Georgia Warm Springs Foundation and appointed by FDR to a key administrative post in the National Recovery Administration.

These corporations were deeply involved in both the promotion of Roosevelt's New Deal and the construction of the military power of Nazi Germany. Putzi Hanfstaengl's role in the early days, up to the mid-1930s anyway, was an informal link between the Nazi elite and the White House. After the mid-1930s, when the world was set on the course for war, Putzis importance declined — while American Big Business continued to be represented through such intermediaries as Baron Kurt von Schroder attorney Westrick, and membership in Himmler's Circle of Friends.

Chapter Nine

Wall Street and the Nazi Inner Circle

> *During the entire period of our business contacts we had no inkling of Farben's conniving part in Hitler's brutal policies. We offer any help we can give to see that complete truth is brought to light and that rigid justice is done.*
> (F. W. Abrams, Chairman of the Board, Standard Oil of New Jersey, 1946.)

Adolf Hitler, Hermann Goering, Josef Goebbels, and Heinrich Himmler, the inner group of Naziism, were at the same time heads of minor fiefdoms within the Nazi State. Power groups or political cliques were centered around these Nazi leaders, more importantly after the late 1930s around Adolf Hitler and Heinrich Himmler, Reich-Leader of the S.S. (the dreaded *Schutzstaffel*). The most important of these Nazi inner circles was created by order of the Fuehrer; it was known first as the Keppler Circle and later as Himmler's Circle of Friends.

The Keppler Circle originated as a group of German businessmen supporting Hitler's rise to power before and during 1933. In the mid-1930s the Keppler Circle came under the influence and protection of S.S. chief Himmler and the organizational control of Cologne banker and prominent Nazi businessman Kurt von Schroder. Schroder, it will be recalled, was head of the J.H. Stein Bank in Germany and affiliated with the L. Henry Schroder Banking Corporation of New York. It is within this innermost of the inner circles, the very core of Naziism, that we find Wall Street, including Standard Oil of New Jersey and I.T.T., represented from 1933 to as late as 1944.

Wilhelm Keppler, founder of the original Circle of Friends, typifies the well-known phenomenon of a politicized businessman — *i.e., a* businessman who cultivates the political arena rather than the impartial market place for his profits. Such businessmen have been interested In promoting socialist causes, because a planned socialist society provides a most lucrative opportunity for contracts through political influence.

Scenting such profitable opportunities, Keppler joined the national socialists and was close to Hitler before 1933. The Circle of Friends grew out of a meeting between Adolf

Hitler and Wilhelm Keppler in December 1931. During the course of their conversation — this was several years before Hitler became dictator — the future Fuehrer expressed a wish to have reliable German businessmen available for economic advice when the Nazis took power. *"Try* to get a few economic leaders — they need not be Party members — who will be at our disposal when we come into power."[582] This Keppler undertook to do.

In March 1933 Keppler was elected to the Reichstag and became Hitler's financial expert. This lasted only briefly. Keppler was replaced by the infinitely more capable Hjalmar Schacht, and sent to Austria where in 1938 he became Reichs Commissioner, but still able to use his position to acquire considerable power in the Nazi State. Within a few years he captured a string of lucrative directorships in German firms, including chairman of the board of two I.G. Farben subsidiaries: Braunkohle-Benzin A.G. and Kontinental Oil A.G. Braunkohle-Benzin was the German exploiter of the Standard Oil of New Jersey technology for production of gasoline from coal. (See Chapter Four.)

In brief, Keppler war the chairman of the very firm that utilized American technology for the indispensible synthetic gasoline which enabled the Wehrmacht to go to war in 1939. This is significant because, when linked with other evidence presented in this chapter, it suggests that the profits and control of these fundamentally important technologies for German military ends were retained by a small group of international firms and businessmen operating across national borders.

Keppler's nephew, Fritz Kranefuss, under his uncle's protection, also gained prominence both as Adjutant to S.S. Chief Heinrich Himmler and as a businessman and political operator. It was Kranefuss' link with Himmler which led to the Keppler circle gradually drawing away from Hitler in the 1930s to come within Himmler's orbit, where in exchange for annual donations to Himmler's pet S.S. projects Circle members received political favors and not inconsiderable protection from the S.S.

Baron Kurt von Schroder was, as we have noted, the I.T.T. representative in Nazi Germany and an early member of the Keppler Circle. The original Keppler Circle consisted of:

---

[582] From the affidavit of Wilhem Keppler, *NMT,* Volume VI, p. 285.

THE ORIGINAL (PRE-1932) MEMBERS OF THE KEPPLER CIRCLE

Circle Member	Main Associations
Wilhelm KEPPLER	Chairman of I.G. Farben subsidiary Braunkohle-Benzin A.G. (exploited Standard Oil of N.J. oil from coal technology)
Fritz KRANEFUSS	Keppler's nephew and Adjutant to Heinrich Himmler. On Vorstand of BRABAG
Kurt von SCHRODER	On board of all International Telephone & Telegraph subsidiaries in Germany
Karl Vincenz KROGMANN	Lord Mayor of Hamburg
August ROSTERG	General Director of WINTERSHALL
Otto STEINBRINCK	Vice president of VEREINIGTE STAHLWERKE (steel cartel founded with Wall Street loans in 1926)
Hjalmar SCHACHT	President of the REICHSBANK
Emil HELFFRICH	Board chairman of GERMAN-AMERICAN PETROLEUM CO. (94-percent owned by Standard Oil of New Jersey) (See above under Wilhelm Keppler)
Friedrich REINHARDT	Board chairman COMMERZBANK
Ewald HECKER	Board chairman of ILSEDER HUTTE
Graf von BISMARCK	Government president of STETTIN

THE S.S. CIRCLE OF FRIENDS

The original Circle of Friends met with Hitler in May 1932 and heard a statement of Nazi objectives. Heinrich Himmler then became a frequent participant in the meetings, and through Himmler, various S.S. officers as well as other businessmen joined the group. This expanded group in time became Himmler's Circle of Friends, with Himmler acting as protector and expediter for its members.

Consequently, banking and Industrial interest — were heavily represented in the inner circle of Naziism, and their pre-1933 financial contributions to Hitlerism which we have earlier enumerated were amply repaid. Of the "Big Five" German banks, the Dresdner Bank had the closest connections with the Nazi Party: at least a dozen members of Dresdner Bank's board of directors had high Nazi rank and no fewer than seven Dresdner Bank directors were among Keppler's expanded Circle of Friends, which never exceeded 40.

When we examine the names comprising both the original pre-1933 Keppler Circle and the post-1933 expanded Keppler and Himmler's Circle, we find the Wall Street multi-nationals heavily represented — more so than any other institutional group. Let us take each Wall Street multinational or its German associate in turn — those identified in Chapter Seven as linked to financing Hitler — and examine their links to Keppler and Heinrich Himmler.

I.G. Farben and the Keppler Circle

I.G. Farben was heavily represented within the Keppler Circle: no fewer than eight out of the peak circle membership of 40 were directors of I.G. Farben or a Farben subsidiary. These eight members included the previously described Wilhelm Keppler and his nephew Kranefuss, in addition to Baron Kurt von Schroder. The Farben presence was emphasized by member Hermann Schmitz, chairman of I.G. Farben and a director of Vereinigte Stahlwerke, both cartels built and consolidated by the Wall Street loans of the 1920s. A U.S. Congressional report described Hermann Schmitz as follows:

> Hermann Schmitz, one of the most important persons in Germany, has achieved outstanding success simultaneously in the three separate fields, industry, finance, and government, and has served with zeal and devotion every government in power. He symbolizes the German citizen who out of the devastation of the First World War made possible the Second.
> Ironically, his may be said to be the greater guilt in that in 1919 he was a member of the Reich's peace delegation, and in the 1930's was in a position to teach the Nazis much that theft had to know concerning economic penetration, cartel uses, synthetic materials for war.[583]

Another Keppler Circle member on the I.G. Farben board was Friedrich Flick, creator of the steel cartel Vereinigte Stahlwerke and a director of Allianz Versicherungs A.G. and German General Electric (A.E.G.).

Heinrich Schmidt, a director of Dresdner Bank and chairman of the board of I.G. Farben subsidiary Braunkohle-Benzin A.G., was in the circle; so was Karl Rasehe, another director of the Dresdner Bank and a director of Metallgesellschaft (parent of the Delbruck Schickler Bank) and Accumulatoren-Fabriken A.G. Heinrich Buetefisch was also a director of I.G. Farben and a member of the Keppler Circle. In brief, the I.G. Farben contribution to Rudolf Hess' Nationale Treuhand — the political slush fund — was confirmed after the 1933 takeover by heavy representation in the Nazi inner circle.

How many of these Keppler Circle members in the I.G. Farben complex were affiliated with Wall Street?

---

[583] *Elimination of German Resources*, p. 869.

MEMBERS OF THE ORIGINAL KEPPLER CIRCLE ASSOCIATED WITH U.S. MULTI-NATIONALS

Member of Keppler Circle	I.G. Farben	I.T.T.	Standard Oil of New Jersey	General Electric
Wilhelm KEPPLER	Chairman of Farben subsidiary BRABAG		—	
Fritz KRANEFUSS	On Aufsichrat of BRABAG		—	
Emil Heinrich MEYER		On board of all I.T.T. German subsidiaries: Standard/Mix & Genest/Lorenz	—	Board of A.E.G.
Emil HELFFRICH			Chairman of DAPAG (94-percent owned by Standard of New Jersey	
Friedrich FLICK	I.G. Farben	—	—	Board of A.E.G.
Kurt von SCHRODER		On board of all I.T.T. subsidiaries in Germany		

Similarly, we can identify other Wall Street institutions represented in the early Keppler's Circle of Friends, confirming their monetary contributions to the National Trusteeship Fund operated by Rudolf Hess on behalf of Adolf Hitler. These representatives were Emil Heinrich Meyer and banker Kurt von Schroder on the boards of all the I.T.T. subsidiaries in Germany, and Emil Helffrich, the board chairman of DAPAG, 94-percent owned by Standard Oil of New Jersey.

WALL STREET IN THE S.S. CIRCLE

Major U.S. multi-nationals were also very well represented in the later Heinrich Himmler Circle and made cash contributions to the S.S. (the Sonder Konto S) up to 1944 — while World War II was in progress.

Almost a quarter of the 1944 Sonder Konto S contributions came from subsidiaries of International Telephone and Telegraph, represented by Kurt von Schröder. The 1943 payments from I.T.T. subsidiaries to the Special Account were as follows:

Mix & Genest A.G.	5,000 RM
C. Lorenz AG	20,000 RM
Felten & Guilleaume	25,000 RM
Kurt von Schroder	16,000 RM

And the 1944 payments were:

Mix & Genest A.G	5,000 RM
C. Lorenz AG	20,000 RM
Felten & Guilleaume	20,000 RM
Kurt von Schroder	16,000 RM

Sosthenes Behn of International Telephone and Telegraph transferred wartime control of Mix & Genest, C. Lorenz, and the other Standard Telephone interests in Germany to Kurt von Schroder — who was a founding member of the Keppler Circle and organizer and treasurer of Himmler's Circle of Friends. Emil H. Meyer, S.S. Untersturmfuehrer, member of the Vorstand of the Dresdner Bank, A.E.G., and a director of all the I.T.T. subsidiaries in Germany, was also a member of the Himmler Circle of Friends — giving I.T.T. two powerful representatives at the heart of the S.S.

A letter to fellow member Emil Meyer from Baron von Schroder dated February 25, 1936 describes the purposes and requirements of the Himmler Circle and the long-standing nature of the Special Account 'S' with funds at Schroder's own bank — the J,H. Stein Bank of Cologne:

> To Prof. Dr. Emil H. Meyer
> Berlin, 25 February 1936 (Illegible handwriting)
> S.S. (Untersturmfuchrer) (second lieutenant) Member of the Managing Board (Vorstand) of the Dresdner Bank
> Berlin W. 56, Behrenstr. 38
> Personal!
> To the Circle of Friends of the Reich Leader SS
> At the end of the 2 day's inspection tour of Munich to which the Reich Leader SS had invited us last January, the Circle of Friends agreed to put — each one according to his means — at the Reich Leader's disposal into "Special Account S" (Sonder Konto S), to be established at the banking firm J.H. Stein in Cologne, funds which are to be used for certain tasks outside of the budget.
> This should enable the Reich Leader to rely on all his friends. In Munich it was decided that the undersigned would make themselves available for setting up and handling this account. In the meantime the account was set up and we want every participant to know that in case he wants to make contributions to the Reich Leader for the aforementioned tasks — either on behalf of his firm or the Circle of Friends — payments may be made

to the banking firm J.H. Stein, Cologne (Clearing Account of the Reich Bank, Postal Checking Account No.1392) to the Special Account S.
Heil Hitler!
(Signed) Kurt Baron von Sehroder (Signed) Steinbrinck[584]

This letter also explains why U.S. Army Colonel Bogdan, formerly of the Schroder Banking Corporation in New York, was anxious to divert the attention of post-war U.S. Army investigators away from the J. H. Stein Bank in Cologne to the *"bigger* banks" of Nazi Germany. It was the Stein Bank that held the secrets of the associations of American subsidiaries with Nazi authorities while World War II was in progress. The New York financial interests could not know the precise nature of these transactions (and particularly the nature of any records that may have been kept by their German associates), but they knew that *some* record could well exist of their war-time dealings — enough to embarrass them with the American public. It was this possibility that Colonel Bogdan tried unsuccessfully to head off.

German General Electric profited greatly from its association with Himmler and other leading Nazis. Several members of the Schroder clique were directors of A.E.G., the most prominent being Robert Pferdmenges, who was not only a member of the Keppler or Himmler Circles but was a partner in the aryanized banking house Pferdmenges & Company, the successor to the former Jewish banking house Sal Oppenheim of Cologne. Waldemar von Oppenheim achieved the dubious distinction (for a German Jew) of *"honorary* Aryan" and was able to continue his old established banking house under Hitler in partnership with Pferdmenges.

---

[584] *NMT,* Volume VII, p. 238. "Translation of Document NI-10103, Prosecution Exhibit 788." Letter from von Schroder and Defendant Steinbrinck to Dr. Meyer, Dresdner Bank official, 25 February 1936, noting that the Circle of Friends would put funds at Himmler's disposal "For Certain Tasks outside of the Budget" and had established a "Special Account for this purpose."

MEMBERS OF THE HIMMLER CIRCLE OF FRIENDS WHO WERE ALSO DIRECTORS OF AMERICAN-AFFILIATED FIRMS:

	I.G. Farben	I.T.T.	A.E.G.	Standard Oil of New Jersey
KRANEFUSS, Fritz	X			
KEPPLER, Wilhelm	X			
SCHRODER, Kurt	X			
Von BUETEFISCH, Heinrich		X		
RASCHE, Dr. Karl	X			
FLICK, Friedrich	X		X	
LINDEMANN, Karl				X
SCHMIDT, Heinrich	X			
ROEHNERT, Kellmuth			X	
SCHMIDT, Kurt			X	
MEYER, Dr. Emil		X		
SCHMITZ, Hermann	X			

Pferdmenges was also a director of A.E.G. and used his Nazi influence to good advantage.[585]

Two other directors of German General Electric were members of Himmler's Circle of Friends and made 1943 and 1944 monetary contributions to the Sonder Konto S. These were:

| Friedrich Flick | 100,000 RM |
| Otto Steinbrinck (a Flick associate) | 100,000 RM |

Kurt Schmitt was chairman of the board of directors of A.E.G. and a member of the Himmler Circle of Friends, but Schmitt's name is not recorded in the list of payments for 1943 or 1944.

Standard Oil of New Jersey also made a significant contribution to Himmler's Special Account through its wholly owned (94 percent) German subsidiary, Deutsche-Amerikanische Gesellschaft (DAG). In 1943 and 1944 DAG contributed as follows:

Staatsrat Helfferich of Deutsch-Amerikanische Petroleum A.G.	10,000 RM
Staatsrat Lindemann of Deutsch-Amerikanische Petroleum A.G	10,000 RM
and personally	4,000 RM

---

[585] *Elimination of German Resources*, p. 857.

It is important to note that Staatsrat Lindemann contributed 4,000 RM *personally*, thus making a clear distinction between the corporate contribution of 10,000 RM from Standard Oil of New Jersey's wholly owned subsidiary and the personal contribution from director Linde-mann. In the case of Staatsrat Hellfrich, the only contribution was the Standard Oil contribution of 10,000 RM; there is no recorded personal donation.

I.G. Farben, parent company of American I.G. (see Chapter Two), was another significant contributor to Heinrich Himmler's Sonder Konto S. There were four I.G. Farben directors within the inner circle: Karl Rasche, Fritz Kranefuss, Heinrich Schmidt, and Heinrich Buetefisch. Karl Rasche was a member of the management committee of the Dresdner Bank and a specialist in international law and banking. Under Hitler Karl Rasche became a prominent director of many German corporations, including Accumulatoren-Fabrik A.G. in Berlin, which financed Hitler; the Metallgesellschaft; and Felten & Guilleame, an I.T.T. company. Fritz Kranefuss was a member of the board of directors of Dresdner Bank and a director of several corporations besides I.G. Farben. Kranefuss, nephew of Wilhelm Keppler, was a lawyer and prominent in many Nazi public organizations. Heinrich Schmidt, a director of I.G. Farben and several other German companies, was also a director of the Dresdner Bank.

It is important to note that all three of the above — Rasche, Kranefuss, and Schmidt — were directors of an I.G. Farben subsidiary, Braunkohle-Benzin A.G. — the manufacturer of German synthetic gasoline using Standard Oil technology, a result of the I.G. Farben-Standard Oil agreements of the early 1930s.

In brief, the Wall Street financial elite was well represented in both the early Keppler Circle and the later Himmler Circle.[586]

---

[586] The significant nature of this representation is reflected in Chart 8-1, "Wall Street representation in the Keppler and Himmler Circles, 1933 and 1944."

Chapter Ten

The Myth of "Sidney Warburg"

A vital question, only partly resolved, is the extent to which Hitler's accession to power in 1933 was aided *directly* by Wall Street financiers. We have shown with original documentary evidence that there was *indirect* American participation and support through German affiliated firms, and (as for example in the case of I.T.T.) there was a knowledgeable and deliberate effort to benefit from the support of the Nazi regime. Was this indirect financing extended to direct financing?

After Hitler gained power, U.S. firms and individuals worked on behalf of Naziism and certainly profited from the Nazi state. We know from the diaries of William Dodd, the American Ambassador to Germany, that in 1933 a stream of Wall Street bankers and industrialists filed through the U.S. Embassy in Berlin, expressing their admiration for Adolf Hitler — and anxious to find ways to do business with the new totalitarian regime. For example, on September 1, 1933 Dodd recorded that Henry Mann of the National City Bank and Winthrop W. Aldrich of the Chase Bank both met with Hitler and "these bankers feel they can work with him."[587] Ivy Lee, the Rockefeller public relations agent, according to Dodd "showed himself at once a capitalist and an advocate of Fascism."[588]

So at least we can identify a sympathetic response to the new Nazi dictatorship, reminiscent of the manner in which Wall Street international bankers greeted the new Russia of Lenin and Trotsky in 1917.

Who Was "Sidney Warburg"?

The question posed in this chapter is the accusation that some Wall Street financiers (the Rockefellers and Warburgs specifically have been accused) directly planned and financed Hitler's takeover in 1933, and that they did this from Wall Street. On this question the so-

---

[587] William E. Dodd, *Ambassador Dodd's Diary,* op. cit., p. 31.
[588] Ibid., p. 74.

called myth of "Sidney Warburg" is relevant. Prominent Nazi Franz von Papen has stated in his *Memoirs*[589]:

> ... the most documented account of the National Socialists' sudden acquisition of funds was contained in a book published in Holland in 1933, by the old established Amsterdam publishing house of Van Holkema & Warendorf, called *De Geldbronnen van Het Nationaal-Socialisme (Drie Gesprekken Met Hitler)* under the name "Sidney Warburg."

A book with this title in Dutch by "Sidney Warburg" was indeed published in 1933, but remained on the book stalls in Holland only for a matter of days. The book was purged.[590] One of three surviving original copies was translated into English. The translation was at one time deposited in the British Museum, but is now withdrawn from public circulation and is unavailable for research. Nothing is now known of the original Dutch copy upon which this English translation was based.

The second Dutch copy was owned by Chancellor Schussnigg in Austria, and nothing is known of its present whereabouts. The third Dutch copy found its way to Switzerland and was translated into German. The German translation has survived down to the present day in the Schweizerischen Sozialarchiv in Zurich, Switzerland. A certified copy of the authenticated German translation of this Swiss survivor was purchased by the author in 1971 and translated into English. It is upon this English translation of the German translation that the text in this chapter is based.

Publication of the *"Sidney* Warburg" book was duly reported in the *New York Times* (November 24, 1933) under the title "Hoax on Nazis Feared." A brief article noted that a "Sidney Warburg" pamphlet has appeared in Holland, and the author is not the son of Felix Warburg. The translator is J. G. Shoup, a Belgian newspaperman living in Holland. The publishers and Shoup "are wondering if they have not been the victims of a hoax." The *Times* account adds:

---

[589] Franz von Papen, *Memoirs,* (New York: E.P. Dutton & Co., 1953), p. 229.

[590] The English text for this chapter is translated from an authenticated surviving German translation of a copy of the Dutch edition of *De Geldbronnen van Het Nationaal-Socialisme (Drie Gesprekken Met Hitler)*, or *The Financial Sources of National Socialism (Three conversations with Hitler.* The original Dutch author is given as "Door Sidney Warburg, vertaald door I.G. Shoup" (By Sidney Warburg, as told by I.G. Shoup).

The copy used here was translated from the Dutch by Dr. Walter Nelz, Wilhelm Peter, and Rene Sonderegger in Zurich, February 11, 1947, and the German translation bears an affidavit to the effect that: "The undersigned three witnesses do verify that the accompanying document is none other than a true and literal translation from Dutch into German of the book by Sidney Warburg, a copy of which was constantly at their disposal during the complete process of translation. They testify that they held this original in their hands, and that to the best of their ability they read it sentence by sentence, translating it into German, comparing then the content of the accompanying translation to the original conscientiously until complete agreement was reached."

> *The pamphlet repeats an old story to the effect that leading Americans, including John D. Rockefeller, financed Hitler from 1929 to 1932 to the extent of $32,000,000, their motive being "to liberate Germany from the financial grip of France by bringing about a revolution" Many readers of the pamphlet have pointed out that it contains many inaccuracies.*

Why was the Dutch original withdrawn from circulation in 1933? Because "Sidney Warburg" did not exist and a "Sidney Warburg" was claimed as the author. Since 1933 the "Sidney Warburg" book has been promoted by various parties both as a forgery and as a genuine document. The Warburg family itself has gone to some pains to substantiate its falsity.

What does the book report? What does the book claim happened in Germany in the early 1930s? And do these events have any resemblance to facts we know to be true from other evidence?

From the viewpoint of research methodology it is much more preferable to assume that the "Sidney Warburg" book *is* a forgery, unless we can prove the contrary. This is the procedure we shall adopt. The reader may well ask — then why bother to look closely at a possible forgery? There are at least two good reasons, apart from academic curiosity.

First, the Warburg claim that the book is a forgery has a curious and vital flaw. The Warburgs deny as false a book they admit not to have read it nor even seen. The Warburg denial is limited specifically to non-authorship by a Warburg. This denial is acceptable; but it does not deny or reject the validity of the *contents*. The denial merely repudiates authorship.

Second, we have already identified I.G. Farben as a key financier and backer of Hitler. We have provided photographic evidence (page 64) of the bank transfer slip for 400,000 marks from I.G. Farben to Hitler's *"Nationale* Treuhand" political slush fund account administered by Rudolf Hess. Now it is probable, almost certain, that "Sidney Warburg" did not exist. On the other hand, it *is* a matter of public record that the Warburgs were closely connected with I.G. Farben in Germany and the United States. In Germany Max Warburg was a director of I.G. Farben and in the United States brother Paul Warburg (father of James Paul Warburg) was a director of American I.G. Farben. In brief, we have incontrovertible evidence that *some* Warburgs, including the father of James Paul, the denouncer of the "Sidney Warburg" book, *were* directors of I.G. Farben. And I.G. Farben is known to have financed Hitler. *"Sidney* Warburg" was a myth, but I.G. Farben directors Max Warburg and Paul Warburg were not myths. This is reason enough to push further.

Let us first summarize the book which James Paul Warburg claims is a forgery.

Antony C. Sutton

A Synopsis of the Suppressed "Sidney Warburg" Book

The Financial Sources of National Socialism opens with an alleged conversation between "Sidney Warburg" and joint author/translator I. G. Shoup. "Warburg" relates why he was handing Shoup an English language manuscript for translation into Dutch and publication in Holland In the words of the mythical "Sidney Warburg":

> *There are moments when I want to turn away from a world of such intrigue, trickery, swindling and tampering with the stock exchange... Do you know what I can never understand? How it is possible that people of good and honest character — for which I have ample proof — participate in swindling and fraud, knowing full well that it will affect thousands.*

Shoup then describes "Sidney Warburg" as "son of one of the largest bankers in the United States, member of the banking firm Kuhn, Loeb & Co., New York." "Sidney Warburg" then tells Shoup that he ("Warburg") wants to record for history how national socialism was financed by New York financiers.

The first section of the book is entitled simply *"1929."* It relates that in 1929 Wall Street had enormous credits outstanding in Germany and Austria, and that these claims had, for the most part, been frozen. While France was economically weak and feared Germany, France was also getting the "lion's share" of reparations funds which were actually financed from the United States. In June 1929, a meeting took place between the members of the Federal Reserve Bank and leading American bankers to decide what to do about France, and particularly to cheek her call on German reparations. This meeting was attended (according to the "Warburg" book) by the directors of Guaranty Trust Company, the "Presidents" of the Federal Reserve Banks, in addition to five independent bankers, "young Rockefeller," and Glean from Royal Dutch Shell. Carter and Rockefeller according to the text "dominated the proceedings. The others listened and nodded their heads."

The general consensus at the bankers' meeting was that the only way to free Germany from French financial clutches was by revolution, either Communist or German Nationalist. At an earlier meeting it had previously been agreed to contact Hitler to "try to find out if he were amenable to American financial support." Now Rockefeller reportedly had more recently seen a German-American leaflet about the Hitler national socialist movement and the purpose of this second meeting was to determine if "Sidney Warburg" was prepared to go to Germany as a courier to make personal contact with Hitler.

In return for proferred financial support, Hitler would be expected to conduct an "aggressive foreign policy and stir up the idea of revenge against France." This policy, it was anticipated, would result in a French appeal to the United States and England for assistance in "international questions involving the eventual German aggression." Hitler was not to know about the purpose of Wall Street's assistance. It would be left 'to his reason and resourcefulness to discover the motives behind the proposal." "Warburg" accepted the proposed mission and left New York for Cherbourg on the *Ile de France,* "with a diplomatic passport and letters of recommendation from Carter, Tommy Walker, Rockefeller, Glean and Herbert Hoover."

Apparently, "Sidney Warburg" had some difficulty in meeting Hitler. The American Consul in Munich did not succeed in making contact with the Nazis, and finally Warburg went directly to Mayor Deutzberg of Munich, "with a recommendation from the American Consul," and a plea to guide Warburg to Hitler. Shoup then presents extracts from Hitler's statements at this initial meeting. These extracts include the usual Hitlerian anti-Semitic rantings, and it should be noted that all the anti, Semitic parts in the "Sidney Warburg" book are spoken by Hitler. (This is important because James Paul Warburg claims the Shoup book is totally anti-Semitic.) Funding of the Nazis was discussed at this meeting and Hitler is reported to insist that funds could not be deposited in a German bank but only in a foreign bank at his disposal. Hitler asked for 100 million marks and suggested that "Sidney Warburg" report on the Wall Street reaction through von Heydt at Lutzowufer, 18 Berlin.[591]

After reporting back to Wall Street, Warburg learned that $24 million was too much for the American bankers; they offered $10 million. Warburg contacted von Heydt and a further meeting was arranged, this time with an *"undistinguished* looking man, introduced to me under the name Frey." Instructions were given to make $10 million available at the Mendelsohn & Co. Bank in Amsterdam, Holland. Warburg was to ask the Mendelsohn Bank to make out checks in marks payable to named Nazis in ten German cities.

Subsequently, Warburg travelled to Amsterdam, completed his mission with Mendelsohn & Co., then went to Southampton, England and took the *Olympia* back to New York where he reported to Carter at Guaranty Trust Company. Two days later Warburg gave his report to the entire Wall Street group, but "this time an English representative was there sitting next to Glean from Royal Dutch, a man named Angell, one of the heads of the Asiatic Petroleum Co." Warburg was questioned about Hitler, and "Rockefeller showed unusual interest in Hitler's statements about the Communists."

A few weeks after Warburg's return from Europe the Hearst newspapers showed "unusual interest" in the new German Nazi Party and even the *New York Times* carried regular short reports of Hitler's speeches. Previously these newspapers had not shown too much interest,

---

[591] Note that "von Heydt" was the original name for the Dutch Bank voor Handel en Seheepvaart N.V., a subsidiary of the Thyssen interests and now known to have been used as a funnel for Nazi funds. See *Elimination of German Resources.*

but that now changed.[592] Also, in December 1929 a long study of the German National Socialist movement appeared *"in* a monthly publication at Harvard University."

Part II of the suppressed "Financial Sources of National Socialism" is entitled "1931" and opens with a discussion of French influence on international politics. It avers that Herbert Hoover promised Pierre Laval of France not to resolve the debt question without first consulting the French government and [writes Shoup]:

> *When Wall Street found out about this Hoover lost the respect of this circle at one blow. Even the subsequent elections were affected — many believed that Hoover's failure to get reelected can be traced back to the issue.*[593]

In October 1931, Warburg received a letter from Hitler which he passed on to Carter at Guaranty Trust Company, and subsequently another bankers' meeting was called at the Guaranty Trust Company of-rices. Opinions at this meeting were divided. "Sidney Warburg" reported that Rockefeller, Carter, and McBean were for Hitler, while the other financiers were uncertain. Montague Norman of the Bank of England and Glean of Royal Dutch Shell argued that the $10 million already spent on Hitler was too much, that Hitler would never act. The meeting finally agreed in principle to assist Hitler further, and Warburg again undertook a courier assignment and went back to Germany.

On this trip Warburg reportedly discussed German affairs with "a Jewish banker" in Hamburg, with an industrial magnate, and other Hitler supporters. One meeting was with banker von Heydt and a "Luetgebrunn." The latter stated that the Nazi storm troopers were incompletely equipped and the S.S. badly needed machine guns, revolvers, and carbines.

In the next Warburg-Hitler meeting, Hitler argued that "the Soviets cannot miss our industrial products yet. We will give credit, and if I am not able to deflate France myself, then the Soviets will help me." Hitler said he had two plans for takeover in Germany: (a) the revolution plan, and (b), the legal takeover plan. The first plan would be a matter of three months, the second plan a matter of three years. Hitler was quoted as saying, "revolution costs five hundred million marks, legal takeover costs two hundred million marks

---

[592] Examination of the Index for the *New York Times* confirms the accuracy of the latter part of this statement. See for example the sudden rush of interest by the *New York Times,* September 15, 1930 and the feature article on "Hitler, Driving Force in Germany's Fascism" in the September 21, 1930 issue of the *New York Times.* In 1929 the *New York Times* listed only one brief item on Adolf Hitler. In 1931 it ran a score of substantial entries, in-eluding no fewer than three "Portraits."

[593] Hoover said he lost the support of Wall Street in 1931 because he would not go along with its plan for a New Deal: see Antony C. Sutton, *Wall Street and FDR, op. cit.*

— what will your bankers decide?" After five days a cable from Guaranty Trust arrived for Warburg and is cited in the book as follows:

> *Suggested amounts are out of the question. We don't want to and cannot. Explain to man that such a transfer to Europe will shatter financial market. Absolutely unknown on international territory. Expect long report, before decision is made. Stay there. Continue investigation. Persuade man of impossible demands. Don't forget to include in report own opinion of possibilities for future of man.*

Warburg cabled his report back to New York and three days later received a second cablegram reading:

> *Report received. Prepare to deliver ten, maximum fifteen million dollars. Advise man necessity of aggression against foreign danger.*

The $15 million was accepted for the legal takeover road, not for the revolutionary plan. The money was transferred from Wall Street to Hitler via Warburg as follows — $5 million to be paid at Mendelsohn & Company, Amsterdam; $5 million at the Rotterdamsehe Bankvereinigung in Rotterdam; and $5 million at "Banca Italiana."

Warburg travelled to each of these banks, where he reportedly met Heydt, Strasser and Hermann Goering. The groups arranged for cheeks to be made out to different names in various towns in Germany. In other words, the funds were "laundered" in the modern tradition to disguise their Wall Street origins. In Italy the payment group was reportedly received at the main building of the bank by its president and while waiting in his office two Italian fascists, Rossi and Balbo, were introduced to Warburg, Heydt, Strasser, and Goering. Three days after payment, Warburg returned to New York from Genoa on the *Savoya*.

Again, he reported to Carter, Rockefeller, and the other bankers.

The third section of "Financial Sources of National Socialism" is entitled simply "1933." The section records "Sidney Warburg's" third and last meeting with Hitler — on the night the Reichstag was burned. (We noted in Chapter Eight the presence of Roosevelt's friend Putzi Hanfstaengl in the Reichstag.) At this meeting Hitler informed Warburg of Nazi progress towards legal takeover. Since 1931 the Nationalist Socialist party had tripled in size. Massive deposits of weapons had been made near the German border in Belgium, Holland, and Austria — but these weapons required cash payments before delivery. Hitler asked for a minimum of 100 million marks to take care of the final step in the takeover program. Guaranty Trust wired Warburg offering $7 million at most, to be paid as follows — $2 million to the Renania Joint Stock Company in Dusseldorf (the German branch of Royal

Dutch), and $5 million to other banks. Warburg reported this offer to Hitler, who requested the $5 million should be sent to the Banca Italiana in Rome and (although the report does not say so) presumably the other $2 million was paid to Dusseldorf. The book concludes with the following statement from Warburg:

> *I carried out my assignment strictly down to the last detail. Hitler is dictator of the largest European country. The world has now observed him at work for several months. My opinion of him means nothing now. His actions will prove if he is bad, which I believe he is. For the sake of the German people I hope in my heart that I am wrong. The world continues to suffer under a system that has to bow to a Hitler to keep itself on its feet. Poor world, poor humanity.*

This is a synopsis of "Sidney Warburg's" suppressed book on the financial origins of national socialism in Germany. Some of the information in the book is now common knowledge — although only part was generally known in the early 1930s. It is extraordinary to note that the unknown author had access to information that only surfaced many years later — for example, the identity of the von Heydt bank as a Hitler financial conduit. Why was the book taken off the bookstands and suppressed? The stated reason for withdrawal was that "Sidney Warburg" did not exist, that the book was a forgery, and that the Warburg family claimed it contained anti-Semitic and libelous statements.

The information in the book was resurrected after World War II and published in other books in an anti-Semitic context which does not exist in the original 1933 book. Two of these post-war books were Rene Sonderegger's *Spanischer Sommer* and Werner Zimmerman's *Liebet Eure Feinde*.

Most importantly James P. Warburg of New York signed an affidavit in 1949, which was published as an appendix in von Papen's *Memoirs*. This Warburg affidavit emphatically denied the authenticity of the "Sidney Warburg" book and claimed it was a hoax, Unfortunately, James P. Warburg focuses on the 1947 Sonderegger anti-Semitic book *Spanischer Sommer*, not the original suppressed "Sidney Warburg" book published in 1933 — where the only anti-Semitism stems from Hitler's alleged statements.

In other words, the Warburg affidavit raised far more questions than it resolved. We should therefore look at Warburg's 1949 affidavit denying the authenticity of *Financial Sources of National Socialism*.

JAMES PAUL WARBURG'S AFFIDAVIT

In 1953 Nazi Franz von Papen published his *Memoirs*.[594] This was the same Franz von Papen who had been active in the United States on behalf of German espionage in World War I. In his *Memoirs*, Franz von Papen discusses the question of financing Hitler and places the blame squarely on industrialist Fritz Thyssen and banker Kurt von Sehroder. Papen denies that he (Papen) financed Hitler, and indeed no credible evidence has been forthcoming to link von Papen with Hitler's funds (although Zimmerman in *Liebert Eure Feinde* accuses Papen of donating 14 million marks). In this context von Papen mentions "Sidney Warburg's" *The Financial Sources of National Socialism*, together with the two more recent post-World War II books by Werner Zimmerman and Rene Sonderegger (alias Severin Reinhardt).[595] Papen adds that:

> James P. Warburg is able to refute the whole falsification in his affidavit... For my own part I am most grateful to Mr. Warburg for disposing once and for all of this malicious libel. It is almost impossible to refute accusations of this sort by simple negation, and his authoritative denial has enabled me to give body to my own protestations.[596]

There are two sections to Appendix II of Papen's book. First is a statement by James P. Warburg; second is the affidavit, dated July 15, 1949.

The opening paragraph of the statement records that in 1933 the Dutch publishing house of Holkema and Warendorf published *De Geldbronnen van Het Nationaal-Socialisme. Drie Gesprekken Met Hitler*, and adds that,

> This book was allegedly written by "Sidney Warburg." A partner in the Amsterdam firm of Warburg & Co. informed James P. Warburg of the book and Holkema and Warendorf were informed that no such person as "Sidney Warburg" existed. They thereupon withdrew the book from circulation.

James Warburg then makes two sequential and seemingly contradictory statements:

> ... the book contained a mass of libelous material against various members of my family and against a number of prominent banking houses and individuals in New York· I have never to this day seen a copy of the book. Apparently only a handful of copies escaped the publisher's withdrawal.

---

[594] Franz von Papen, *Memoirs*, (New York: E.P. Dutton & Co., Inc., 1958). Translated by Brian Connell.
[595] Werner Zimmerman, *Liebet Eure Feinde*, (Frankhauser Verlag: Thielle-Neuchatel, 1948), which contains a chapter, "Hitler's geheime Geldgeber" (Hitler's secret financial supporters) and Rene Sonderegger, *Spanischer Sommer*, (Afroltern, Switzerland: Aehren Verlag, 1948).
[596] Franz von Papen, *Memoirs*, op. cit., p. 23.

Now on the one hand Warburg claims he has never seen a copy of the "Sidney Warburg" book, and on the other hand says it is *"libelous"* and proceeds to construct a detailed affidavit on a sentence by sentence basis to refute the information supposedly in a book he claims not to have seen! It is very difficult to accept the validity of Warburg's claim he has "never to this day seen a copy of the book." Or if indeed he had not, then the affidavit is worthless.

James Warburg adds that the "Sidney Warburg" book is "obvious anti-Semitism," and the thrust of Warburg's statement is that the *"Sidney* Warburg" story is pure anti-Semitic propaganda. In fact (and Warburg would have discovered this fact if he had read the book), the *only* anti-Semitic statements in the 1933 book are those attributed to Adolf Hitler, whose anti-Semitic feelings are hardly any great discovery. Apart from Hitler's ravings there is nothing in the original "Sidney Warburg" book remotely connected with anti-Semitism, unless we classify Rockefeller, Glean, Carter, McBean, *etc.* as Jewish. *In fact, it is notable that not a single Jewish banker is named in the book — except for the mythical "Sidney Warburg" who is a courier, not one of the alleged money givers.* Yet we know from an authentic source (Ambassador Dodd) that the Jewish banker Eberhard von Oppenheim did indeed give 200,000 marks to Hitler[597], and it is unlikely "Sidney Warburg" would have missed this observation if he was deliberately purveying false anti-Semitic propaganda.

The first page of James Warburg's statement concerns the 1933 book. After the first page James Warburg introduces Rene Sonderegger and another book written in 1947. Careful analysis of Warburg's statement and affidavit point up that his denials and assertions essentially refer to Sonderegger and *not* to Sidney Warburg. Now Sonderegger was anti-Semitic and probably was part of a neo-Nazi movement after World War II, but this claim of anti-Semitism cannot be laid to the 1933 book — and that is the crux of the question at issue. In brief, James Paul Warburg starts out by claiming to discuss a book he has never seen but knows to be libelous and anti-Semitic, then without warning shifts the accusation to another book which was certainly anti-Semitic but was published a decade later. Thus, the Warburg affidavit so thoroughly confuses the two books that the reader is lead to condemn the mythical" Sidney Warburg" along with Sonderegger.[598] Let us look at some of J.P. Warburg's statements:

| James P. Warburg's Sworn Affidavit New York City, July 15, 1949 | Author's Comments on James P. Warburg Affidavit |

---

[597] William E. Dodd, Ambassador Dodd,s Diary, op. cit. pp, 593-602.
[598] The reader should examine the complete Warburg statement and affidavit; see Franz von Papen, *Memoirs, op. cit.* pp. 593-602.

1. Concerning the wholly false and malicious allegations made by Rene Sonderegger of Zurich, Switzerland, *et al.*, as set forth in the foregoing part of this statement, I, James Paul Warburg, of Greenwich, Connecticut, U.S.A., depose as follows:

Note that the affidavit concerns Rene Sonderegger, not the book published by J.G. Shoup in 1933.

2. No such person as "Sidney Warburg" existed in New York City in 1933, nor elsewhere, as far as I know, then or at any other time.

We can assume that the name "Sidney Warburg" is a pseudonym, or used falsely.

3. I never gave any manuscript, diary, notes, cables, or any other documents to any person for translation and publication in Holland, and, specifically, I never gave any such documents to the alleged J.G. Shoup of Antwerp. To the best of my knowledge and recollection I never at any time met any such person.

The affidavit confines itself to grant of materials "for translation and publication in Holland."

4. The telephone conversation between Roger Baldwin and myself, reported by Sonderegger, never took place at all and is pure invention.

Reported by Sonderegger, not "Sidney Warburg."

5. I did not go to Germany at the request of the President of the Guaranty Trust Company in 1929, or at any other time.

But Warburg did go to Germany in 1929 and 1930 for the International Acceptance Bank, Inc.

6. I did go to Germany on business for my own bank, The International Acceptance Bank Inc., of New York, in both 1929 and 1930. On neither of these occasions did I have anything to do with investigating the possible prevention of a Communist revolution in Germany by the promotion of a Nazi counterrevolution. As a matter of recorded fact, my opinion at the time was that there was relatively little danger of a Communist revolution in Germany and a considerable danger of a Nazi seizure of power, I am in a position to prove that, on my return from Germany after the Reichstag elections of 1930, I warned my associates that Hitler would very likely come to power in Germany and that the result would be either a Nazi-dominated Europe or a second world war — perhaps both. This can be corroborated as well as the fact that, as a consequence of my warning, my bank proceeded to reduce its German commitments as rapidly as possible.

Note that Warburg, by his own statement, told his banking associates that Hitler would come to power. This claim was made in 1930 — and the Warburgs continued as directors with I.G. Farben and other pro-Nazi firms.

7. I had no discussions anywhere, at any time, with Hitler, with any Nazi officials, or with anyone else about providing funds for the Nazi Party. Specifically, I had no dealing of this sort with Mendelssohn & Co., or the Rotterdamsche Bankvereiniging or the Banca Italiana. (The latter is probably meant to read Banca d'Italia, with which I likewise had no such dealings.)

There is no evidence to contradict this statement. So far as can be traced Warburgs were not connected with these banking firms except that the Italian correspondent of Warburg's Bank of Manhattan was "Banca Commerciale Italiana" — which is close to "Banca Italiana."

8. In February 1933 (see pages 191 and 192 of Spanischer Sommer) when I am alleged to have brought Hitler the last installment of American funds and to have been received by Goering and Goebbels as well as by Hitler himself, I can prove that I was not in Germany at all. I never set foot in Germany after the Nazis had come to power in January 1933. In January and February I was in New York and Washington, working both with my bank and with President-elect Roosevelt on the then-acute banking crisis. After Mr. Roosevelt's inauguration, on March 3, 1933, I was working with him continuously helping to prepare the agenda for the World Economic Conference, to which I was sent as Financial Adviser in early June. This is a matter of public record.

There is no evidence to contradict these statements. "Sidney Warburg" provides no supporting evidence for his claims.
See *Wall Street and FDR*, for details of FDR's German associations.

9. The foregoing statements should suffice to demonstrate that the whole "Sidney Warburg" myth and the subsequent spurious identification of myself with the non-existent" Sidney" are fabrications of malicious falsehood without the slightest foundation in truth.

No. James P. Warburg states he has never seen the original "Sidney Warburg" book published in Holland in 1933. Therefore his affidavit only applies to the Sonderegger book which is inaccurate. Sidney Warburg may well be a myth, but the association of Max Warburg and Paul Warburg with I.G. Farben and Hitler is not a myth.

DOES JAMES WARBURG INTEND TO MISLEAD?

It is true that" Sidney Warburg" may well have been an invention, in the sense that" Sidney Warburg" never existed. We *assume* the name is a fake; but *someone* wrote the book. Zimmerman and Sonderegger may or may not have committed libel to the Warburg name, but unfortunately when we examine James P. Warburg's affidavit as published in von Papen's *Memoirs* we are left as much in the dark as ever. There are three important and unanswered questions: (1) why would James P. Warburg claim as a forgery a book he has not read; (2) why does Warburg's affidavit avoid the key question and divert discussion away from "Sidney Warburg" to the anti-Semitic Sonderegger book published in 1947; and (3) why would James P. Warburg be so insensitive to Jewish suffering in World War II to publish his affidavit in the *Memoirs* of Franz von Papen, who was a prominent Nazi at the heart of the Hitler movement since the early days of 1933?

Not only were the German Warburgs persecuted by Hitler in 1938, but millions of Jews lost their lives to Nazi barbarism. It seems elementary that anyone who has suffered and was sensitive to the past sufferings of German Jews would avoid Nazis, Naziism, and neo-Nazi books like the plague. Yet here we have Nazi von Papen acting as a genial literary host to self-described anti-Nazi James P. Warburg, who apparently welcomes the opportunity. Moreover, the Warburgs had ample opportunity to release such an affidavit with wide publicity without utilizing neo-Nazi channels.

The reader will profit from pondering this situation. The only logical explanation is that some of the facts in the "Sidney Warburg" book are either true, come close to the truth, or are embarrassing to James P. Warburg. One cannot say that Warburg *intends* to mislead (although this might seem an obvious conclusion), because businessmen are notoriously illogical writers and reasoners, and there is certainly nothing to exempt Warburg from this categorization.

Some Conclusions from the "Sidney Warburg" Story.

"Sidney Warburg" never existed; in this sense the original 1933 book is a work of fiction. However, many of the then-little-known facts recorded in the book are curate; and the James Warburg affidavit is not aimed at the original boo but rather at an anti-Semitic book circulated over a decade later.

Paul Warburg was a director of American I.G. Farben and thus connected with the financing of Hitler. Max Warburg, a director of German I.G. Farben, signed — along with Hitler himself — the document which appointed Hjalmar Schacht to the Reichsbank. These verifiable connections between the Warburgs and Hitler suggest the "Sidney Warburg" story cannot be abandoned as a total forgery without close examination.

Who wrote the 1933 book, and why? I.G. Shoup says the notes were written by a Warburg in England and given to him to translate. The War-burg motive was alleged to be genuine remorse at the amoral behavior of Warburgs and their Wall Street associates. Does this sound like a plausible motive? It has not gone unnoticed that those same Wall Streeters who plot war and revolution are often in their private lives genuinely decent citizens; it is not beyond the realm of reason that one of them had a change of heart or a heavy conscience. But this is not proven.

If the book was a forgery, then by whom was it written? James War-burg admits he does not know the answer, and he writes: "The original purpose of the forgery remains somewhat obscure even today."[599]

Would any government forge the document? Certainly not the British or U.S. governments, which are both indirectly implicated by the book. Certainly not the Nazi government in Germany, although James Warburg appears to suggest this unlikely possibility. Could it be France, or the Soviet Union, or perhaps Austria? France, possibly because France feared the rise of Nazi Germany. Austria is a similar possibility. The Soviet Union is a possibility because the Soviets also had much to fear from Hitler. So it is plausible that France, Austria, or the Soviet Union had some hand in the preparation of the book.

Any private citizen who forged such a book without inside government materials would have to be remarkably well informed. Guaranty Trust is not a particularly well-known bank outside New York, yet there is an extraordinary degree of plausibility about the involvement of Guaranty Trust, because it was the Morgan vehicle used for financing and infiltrating the Bolshevik revolution.[600] Whoever named Guaranty Trust as the vehicle for funding Hitler either knew a great deal more than the man in the street, or had authentic government information. What would be the motive behind such a book?

The only motive that seems acceptable is that the unknown author had knowledge a war was in preparation and hoped for a public reaction against the Wall Street fanatics and their industrialist friends in Germany — before it was too late. Clearly, *whoever* wrote the book, his motive almost certainly was to warn against Hitlerian aggression and to point to its Wall Street source, because the technical assistance of American companies controlled by Wall Street was still needed to build Hitler's war machine. The Standard Oil hydrogenation patents and financing for the oil from coal

plants, the bomb sights, and the other necessary technology had not been fully transferred when the "Sidney Warburg" book was written. Consequently, this could have been a book designed to break the back of Hitler's supporters abroad, to inhibit the planned transfer of U.S. war-making potential, and to eliminate financial and diplomatic support of the Nazi state. If this was the goal, it is regrettable that the book failed to achieve any of these purposes.

---

[599] Franz von Papen, *Memoirs, op.* cit., p. 594.
[600] See Antony C. Sutton, *Wall Street and the Bolshevik Revolution*, op. cit.

CHAPTER ELEVEN

WALL STREET-NAZI COLLABORATION IN WORLD WAR II

Behind the battle fronts in World War II, through intermediaries in Switzerland and North Africa, the New York financial elite collaborated with the Nazi regime, Captured files after the war yielded a mass of evidence demonstrating that for some elements of Big Business, the period 1941-5 was "business as usual." For instance, correspondence between U.S. firms and their French subsidiaries reveals the aid given to the Axis military machine — while the United States was at war with Germany and Italy. Letters between Ford of France and Ford of the U.S. between 1940 and July 1942 were analyzed by the Foreign Funds Control section of the Treasury Department. Their initial report concluded that until mid-1942:

> *(1) the business of the Ford subsidiaries in France substantially increased; (2) their production was solely for the benefit of the Germans and the countries under its occupation; (3) the Germans have "shown clearly their wish to protect the Ford interests" because of the attitude of strict neutrality maintained by Henry Ford and the late Edsel Ford; and (4) the increased activity of the French Ford subsidiaries on behalf of the Germans received the commendation of the Ford family in America.*[601]

Similarly, the Rockefeller Chase Bank was accused of collaborating with the Nazis in World War II France, while Nelson Rockefeller had a soft job in Washington D.C.:

> *Substantially the same pattern of behavior was pursued by the Paris office of the Chase Bank during German occupation, An examination of the correspondence between Chase, New York, and Chase, France, from the date of the fall of France to May, 1942 discloses that: (1) the manager of the Paris office appeased and collaborated with the Germans to place the Chase banks in a "privileged position;" (2) the Germans held the Chase Bank in a very special esteem — owing to the international activities of our (Chase) head office and the pleasant relations which the Paris branch has been maintaining with many of their (German) banks and their (German) local organizations and higher officers; (3)the Paris manager was "very vigorous in enforcing restrictions against Jewish property, even going so far as to*

---

[601] *Morgenthau Diary (Germany).*

refuse to release funds belonging to Jews in anticipation that a decree with retroactive provisions prohibiting such release might be published in the near future by the occupying authorities;" (4)the New York office despite the above information took no direct steps to remove the undesirable manager from the Paris office since it "might react against our (Chase) interests as we are dealing, not with a theory but with a situation."[602]

An official report to then-Secretary of the Treasury Morgenthau concluded that:

These two situations [i.e., Ford and Chase Bank] convince us that it is imperative to investigate immediately on the spot the activities of subsidiaries of at least some of the larger American firms which were operating in France during German occupation.[603]

Treasury officials urged that an investigation be started with the French subsidiaries of several American banks — that is, Chase, Morgan, National City, Guaranty, Bankers Trust, and American Express. Although Chase and Morgan were the only two banks to maintain French offices throughout the Nazi occupation, in September 1944 all the major New York banks were pressing the U.S. Government for permission to re-open pre-war branches.

Subsequent Treasury investigation produced documentary evidence of collaboration between both Chase Bank and J.P. Morgan with the Nazis in World War II. The recommendation for a full investigation is cited in full as follows:

TREASURY DEPARTMENT INTER-OFFICE COMMUNICATION

Date: December 20, 1944

To: Secretary Morgenthau From: Mr. Saxon

Examination of the records of the Chase Bank, Paris, and of Morgan and Company, France, have progressed only far enough to permit tentative conclusions and the revelation of a few interesting facts:

CHASE BANK, PARIS

a. Niederman, of Swiss nationality, manager of Chase, Paris, was unquestionably a collaborator;

b. The Chase Head Office in New York was informed of Nieder-man's collaborationist policy but took no steps to remove him. Indeed there is ample evidence to show that the Head Office in New York viewed Niederman's good relations with the Germans as an excellent means of preserving, unimpaired, the position of the Chase Bank in France;

c. The German authorities were anxious to keep the Chase open and indeed took exceptional measures to provide sources of revenue;

---

[602] *Ibid.*
[603] *Ibid.*

d. The German authorities desired *"to* be friends" with the important American banks because they expected that these banks would be useful after the war as an instrument of German policy in the United States;

e. The Chase, Paris showed itself most anxious to please the German authorities in every possible way. For example, the Chase zealously maintained the account of the German Embassy in Paris, "as every little thing helps" (to maintain the excellent relations between Chase and the German authorities);

f. The whole objective of the Chase policy and operation was to maintain the position of the bank at any cost.

MORGAN AND COMPANY, FRANCE

a. Morgan and Company regarded itself as a French bank, and therefore obligated to observe French banking laws and regulations, whether Nazi-inspired or not; and did actually do so;

b. Morgan and Company was most anxious to preserve the continuity of its house in France, and, in order to achieve this security, worked out a modus vivendi with the German authorities;

c. Morgan and Company had tremendous prestige with the German authorities, and the Germans boasted of the splendid cooperation of Morgan and Company;

d. Morgan continued its prewar relations with the great French industrial and commercial concerns which were working for Germany, including the Renault Works, since confiscated by the French Government, Peugeot [sic], Citroen, and many others.

e. The power of Morgan and Company in France bears no relation to the small financial resources of the firm, and the enquiry now in progress will be of real value in allowing us for the first time to study the Morgan pattern in Europe and the manner in which Morgan has used its great power;

f. Morgan and Company constantly sought its ends by playing one government against another in the coldest and most unscrupulous manner.

Mr. Jefferson Caffery, U.S. Ambassador to France, has been kept informed of the progress of this investigation and at all times gave me full support and encouragement, in principle and in fact. Indeed, Mr. Caffery himself who asked me how the Ford and General Motors subsidiaries in France had acted during the occupation, and expressed the desire that we should look into these companies after the bank investigation was completed.

RECOMMENDATION

I recommend that this investigation, which, for unavoidable reasons, has progressed slowly up to this time, should now be pressed urgently and that additional needed personnel be sent to Paris as soon as possible.[604]

The full investigation was never undertaken, and no investigation has been made of this presumably treasonable activity down to the present day.

---

[604] *Ibid., pp. 800-2.*

American I.G. in World War II

Collaboration between American businessmen and Nazis in Axis Europe was paralleled by protection of Nazi interests in the United States. In 1939 American I.G. was renamed General Aniline & Film, with General Dyestuffs acting as its exclusive sales agent in the U.S. These names effectively disguised the fact that American I.G. (or General Aniline & Film) was an important producer of major war materials, including atabrine, magnesium, and synthetic rubber. Restrictive agreements with its German parent I.G. Farben reduced American supplies of these military products during World War II.

An American citizen, Halbach, became president of General Dyestuffs in 1930 and acquired majority control in 1939 from Dietrich A. Schmitz, a director of American I.G. and brother of Hermann Schmitz, director of I.G. Farben in Germany and chairman of the board of American I.G. until the outbreak of war in 1939. After Pearl Harbor, the U.S. Treasury blocked Halbach's bank accounts. In June 1942 the Alien Property Custodian seized Halbach's stock in General Dyestuffs and took over the firm as an enemy corporation under the Trading with the Enemy Act. Subsequently, the Alien Property Custodian appointed a new board of directors to act as trustee for the duration of the war. These actions were reasonable and usual practice, but when we probe under the surface another and quite abnormal story emerges.

Between 1942 and 1945 Halbach was nominally a consultant to General Dyestuffs. In fact Halbach ran the company, at $82,000 per year, Louis Johnson, former Assistant Secretary of War, was appointed president of General Dyestuffs by the 'U.S. Government, for which he received $75,000 a year. Louis Johnson attempted to bring pressure to bear on the U.S. Treasury to unblock Halbach's blocked funds and allow Halbach to develop policies contrary to the interests of the U.S., then at war with Germany. The argument used to get Halbach's bank accounts unblocked was that Halbach was running the company and that the Government-appointed board of directors "would have been lost without Mr. Halbach's knowledge."

During the war Halbach filed suit against the Alien Property Custodian, through the Establishment law firm of Sullivan and Cromwell, to oust the U.S. Government from its control of I.G. Farben companies. These suits were unsuccessful, but Halbach was successful in keeping the Farben cartel agreements intact throughout World War II; the Alien Property Custodian never did go into court during World War II on the pending anti-trust suits. Why not? Leo T. Crowley, head of the Alien Property Custodian's office, had John Foster Dulles as his advisor, and John Foster Dulles was a partner in the above-mentioned Sullivan and Cromwell firm, which was acting on behalf of Halbach in its suit against the Alien Property Custodian.

There were other conflict of interest situations we should note. Leo T. Crowley, the Alien Property Custodian, appointed Victor Emanuel to the boards of both General Aniline & Film and General Dyestuffs. Before the war Victor Emanuel was director of the J. Schroder Banking Corporation. Schroder, as we have already seen, was a prominent financier of Hitler and the Nazi party — *and at that very time was a member of Himmler's Circle of Friends, making substantial contributions to S.S. organizations in Germany.*

In turn Victor Emanuel appointed Leo Crowley head of Standard Gas & Electric (controlled by Emanuel) at $75,000 per annum. This sum was in addition to Crowley's salary from the Alien Property Custodian and $10,000 a year as head of the U.S. Government Federal Deposit Insurance Corporation. By 1945 James E. Markham had replaced Crowley as A.P.C. and was also appointed by Emanuel as a director of Standard Gas at $4,850 per year, in addition to the $10,000 he drew as Alien Property Custodian.

The wartime influence of General Dyestuffs and this cozy government-business coterie on behalf of I.G. Farben is exemplified in the ease of American Cyanamid. Before the war I.G. Farben controlled the drug, chemical, and dyestuffs industries in Mexico. During World War II it was proposed to Washington that American Cyanamid take over this Mexican industry and develop an "independent" chemical industry with the old I.G. Farben firms seized by the Mexican Alien Property Custodian.

As hired hands of Schroder banker Victor Emanuel, Crowley and Markham, who were also employees of the U.S. Government, attempted to deal with the question of these I.G. Farben interests in the United States and Mexico. On April 13, 1943 James Markham sent a letter to Secretary of State Cordell Hull objecting to the proposed Cyanamid deal on the grounds it was contrary to the Atlantic Charter and would interfere with the aim of establishing independent firms in Latin America. The Markham position was supported by Henry A. Wallace and Attorney General Francis Biddle.

The forces aligned against the Cyanamid deal were Sterling Drug, Inc. and Winthrop. Both Sterling and Winthrop stood to lose their drug market in Mexico if the Cyanamid deal went through. Also hostile to the Cyanamid deal of course was I.G. Farben's General Aniline and General Dyestuffs, dominated by Victor Emanuel, banker Sehroder's former associate.

On the other hand, the State Department and the Office of the Coordinator of Inter-American affairs — which happened to be Nelson Rockefeller's wartime baby — *supported* the proposed Cyanamid deal. The Rockefellers are, of course, also interested in the drug and chemical industries in Latin America. In brief, an American monopoly under influence of Rockefeller would have replaced a Nazi I.G. Farben monopoly.

I.G. Farben won this round in Washington, but more ominous questions are raised when we look at the bombing of Germany in wartime by the U.S.A.A.F. It has long been rumored, but never proven, that Farben received favored treatment — i.e., that it was not bombed.

James Stewart Martin comments as follows on favored treatment received by I.G. Farben in the bombing of Germany:

> Shortly after the armies reached the Rhine at Cologne, we were driving along the west bank within sight of the undamaged I.G. Farben plant at Leverkusen across the river. Without knowing anything about me or my business he (the jeep driver) began to give me a lecture about I.G. Farben and to point at the con. trast between the bombed-out city of Cologne and the trio of untouched plants on the fringe: the Ford works and the United Rayon works on the west bank, and the Farben works on the east bank..[605]

While this accusation is very much of an open question, requiring a great deal of skilled research into the U.S.A.A.F. bombing records, other aspects of favoritism for the Nazis are well recorded.

At the end of World War II, Wall Street moved into Germany through the Control Council to protect their old cartel friends and limit the extent to which the denazification fervor would damage old business relationships. General Lucius Clay, the deputy military governor for Germany, appointed businessmen who opposed denazification to positions of control over the denazification proceeds. *William H. Draper of Dill. on, Read, the firm which financed the German cartels back in the 1920s, became General Clay's deputy.*

Banker William Draper, as Brigadier General William Draper, put his control team together from businessmen who had represented American business in pre-war Germany. The General Motors representation in-eluded Louis Douglas, a former director of G.M., and Edward S. Zdunke, a pre-war head of General Motors in Antwerp, appointed to supervise the Engineering Section of the Control Council. Peter Hoglund, an expert on German auto industry, was given leave from General Motors. The personnel selection for the Council was undertaken by Colonel Graeme K. Howard — former G,M. representative in Germany and author of a book which "praises totalitarian practices [and] justifies German aggression..."[606]

Treasury Secretary Morgenthau was deeply disturbed at the implications of this Wall Street monopoly of the fate of Nazi Germany and prepared a memorandum to present to President Roosevelt. The complete Morgenthau memorandum, dated May 29, 1945, reads as follows:

MEMORANDUM

May 29, 1945

---

[605] *James Stewart Martin, All Honorable Men, op. cit., p. 75.*
[606] *Morgenthau Diary (Germany), p. 1543. Colonel Graeme K. Howard's book was entitled, America and a New World Order, (New York: Scribners, 1940).*

Lieutenant-General Lucius D. Clay, as Deputy to General Eisenhower, actively runs the American element of the Control Council for Germany. General Clay's three principal advisers on the Control Council staff are.

1. Ambassador Robert D. Murphy, who is in charge of the Political Division.

2. Louis Douglas, whom General Clay describes as my personal adviser on economical, financial and governmental matters." Douglas resigned as Director of the Budget in 1934; and for the following eight years he attacked the government's fiscal policies. Since 1940, Douglas has been president of the Mutual Life Insurance Company, and since December 1944, *he has been a director of the General Motors Corporation.*

3. Brigadier-General William Draper, who is the director of the Economics Division of the Control Council. General Draper is a partner of the banking firm of Dillon, Read and Company, Sunday's *New York Times* contained the announcement of key personnel who have been appointed by General Clay and General Draper to the Economic Division of the Control Council. The appointments include the following:

1. R.J. Wysor is to be in charge of the metallurgical matters. Wysor was president of the Republic Steel Corporation from 1937 until a recent date, and prior thereto, he was associated with the Bethlehem Steel, Jones and Laughlin Steel Corporation and the Republic Steel Corporation.

2. Edward X. Zdunke is to supervise the engineering section. Prior to the war, Mr. Zdunke was head of General Motors at Antwerp.

3. Philip Gaethke is to be in charge of mining operations. Gaethke was formerly connected with Anaconda Copper and was manager of its smelters and mines in Upper Silesia before the war.

4. Philip P. Clover is to be in charge of handling oil matters. He was formerly a representative of the Socony Vacuum Oil Company in Germany.

5. Peter Hoglund is to deal with industrial production problems. Hoglund is on leave from General Motors and is said to be an expert on German production.

6. Calvin B. Hoover is to be in charge of the Intelligence Group on the Control Council and is also to be a special advisor to General Draper. In a letter to the Editor of the *New York Times* on October 9, 1944, Hoover wrote as follows:

> *The publication of Secretary Morgenthau's plan for dealing with Germany has disturbed me deeply ... such a Carthaginian peace would leave a legacy of hate to poison international relations for generations to come... the void in the economy of Europe which would exist through the destruction of all German industry is something which is difficult to contemplate.*

7. Laird Bell is to be Chief Counsel of the Economic Division. He is a well-known Chicago lawyer and in May 1944, was elected the president of the *Chicago Daily News*, after the death of Frank Knox.

One of the men who helped General Draper in the selection of personnel for the Economics Division was Colonel Graeme Howard, a vice-president of General Motors, who was in charge of their overseas business and who was a leading representative of General Motors in Germany prior to the war. Howard is the author of a book in which he praises totalitarian practices, justifies German aggression and the Munich policy of appeasement, and blames Roosevelt for precipitating the war.

So when we examine the Control Council for Germany under General Lucius D. Clay we find that the head of the finance division was Louis Douglas, director of the Morgan-controlled General Motors and president of Mutual Life Insurance. (Opel, the General Motors German subsidiary, had been Hitler's biggest tank producer.) The head of the Control Council's Economics Division was William Draper, a partner in the Dillon, Read firm that had so much to do with building Nazi Germany in the first place. All three men were, not surprisingly in the light of more recent findings, members of the Council on Foreign Relations.

WERE AMERICAN INDUSTRIALISTS AND FINANCIERS GUILTY OF WAR CRIMES?

The Nuremburg War Crimes Trials proposed to select those responsible for World War II preparations and atrocities and place them on trial. Whether. such a procedure is morally justifiable is a debatable matter; there is some justification for holding that Nuremburg was a political farce far removed from legal principle.[607] However, if we assume that there *is* such legal and moral justification, then surely any such trial should apply to *all*, irrespective of nationality. What for example should exempt Franklin D. Roosevelt and Winston Churchill, but not exempt Adolf Hitler and Goering? If the offense is preparation for war, and not blind vengeance, then justice should be impartial.

The directives prepared by the U.S. Control Council in Germany for the arrest and detention of war criminals refers to "Nazis" and "Nazi sympathizers," not "Germans." The relevant extracts are as follows:

> a. You will search out, arrest, and hold, pending receipt by you of further instructions as to their disposition, Adolph Hitler, his chief Nazi associates, other war criminals and all persons who have participated in planning or carrying out Nazi enterprises involving or resulting in atrocities or war crimes.

---

[607] The reader should examine the essay, "The Return to War Crimes," in James J. Martin, *Revisionist Viewpoints*, (Colorado: Ralph Mules, 1971).

Then follows a list of the categories of persons to be arrested, including:

> *(8) Nazis and Nazi sympathizers holding important and key positions in (a) National and Gau Civic and economic organizations; (b) corporations and other organizations in which the government has a major financial interest; (c) industry, commerce, agriculture, and finance; (d) education; (e) the judicial; and (f) the press, publishing houses and other agencies disseminating news and propaganda.*

Top American industrialists and financiers named in this book are covered by the categories listed above. Henry Ford and Edsel Ford respectively contributed money to Hitler and profited from German wartime production. Standard Oil of New Jersey, General Electric, General Motors, and I.T.T. certainly made financial or technical contributions which comprise *prima facie* evidence of "participating in planning or carrying out Nazi enterprises."

There is, in brief, evidence which suggests:

(a) cooperation with the Wehrmacht (Ford Motor Company, Chase Bank, Morgan Bank);
(b) aid to the Nazi Four Year Plan and economic mobilization for war (Standard Oil of New Jersey);
(c) creating and equipping the Nazi war machine (I.T.T.);
(d) stockpiling critical materials for the Nazis (Ethyl Corporation);
(e) weakening the Nazis' potential enemies (American I.G. Farben); and,
(f) carrying on of propaganda, intelligence, and espionage (American I.G. Farben and Rockefeller public-relations man Ivy Lee).

At the very least there is sufficient evidence to demand a thorough and impartial investigation. However, as we have noted previously, these same firms and financiers were prominent in the 1933 election of Roosevelt and consequently had sufficient political pull to squelch threats of investigation. Extracts from the Morgenthau diary demonstrate that Wall Street political power was sufficient even to control the appointment of officers responsible for the denazification and eventual government of post-war Germany.

Did these American firms know of their assistance to Hitler's military machine? According to the firms themselves, emphatically not. They claim innocence of any intent to aid Hitler's Germany. Witness a telegram sent by the chairman of the board of Standard Oil of New Jersey to Secretary of War Patterson after World War II, when preliminary investigation of Wall Street assistance was under way:

> *During the entire period of our business contacts, we had no inkling of Farben's conniving part in Hitler's brutal politics, We offer any help we can give to see that complete truth is brought to light, and that rigid justice is done.*
>
> F.W. Abrams, Chairman of Board

Unfortunately, the evidence presented is contrary to Abrams' telegraphed assertions. Standard Oil of New Jersey not only aided Hitler's war machine, but had knowledge of this assistance. Emil Helfferich, the board chairman of a Standard of New Jersey subsidiary, was a member of the Keppler Circle *before* Hitler came to power; he continued to give financial contributions to Himmler's Circle as late as 1944.

Accordingly, it is not at all difficult to visualize why Nazi industrialists were puzzled by *"investigation"* and assumed at the end of the war that their Wall Street friends would bail them out and protect them from the wrath of those who had suffered. These attitudes were presented to the Kilgore Committee in 1946:

> You might also be interested in knowing, Mr. Chairman, that the top I.G. Farben people and others, when we questioned them about these activities, were inclined at times to be very in. dignant. Their general attitude and expectation was that the war was over and we ought now to be assisting them in helping to get I.G. Farben and German industry back on its feet. Some of them have outwardly said that this questioning and investigation was, in their estimation, only a phenomenon of short duration, because as soon as things got a little settled they would expect their friends in the United States and in England to be coming over. Their friends, so they said, would put a stop to activities such as these investigations and would see that they got the treatment which they regarded as proper and that assistance would be given to them to help reestablish their industry.[608]

---

[608] *Elimination of German Resources*, p. 652.

Chapter Twelve

Conclusions

We have demonstrated with documentary evidence a number of critical associations between Wall Street international bankers and the rise of Hitler and Naziism in Germany.

First: that Wall Street financed the German cartels in the mid-1920s which in turn proceeded to bring Hitler to power.

Second: that the financing for Hitler and his S.S. street thugs came in part from affiliates or subsidiaries of U.S. firms, including Henry Ford in 1922, payments by I.G. Farben and General Electric in 1933, followed by the Standard Oil of New Jersey and I.T.T. subsidiary payments to Heinrich Himmler up to 1944.

Third: that U.S. multi-nationals under the control of Wall Street profited handsomely from Hitler's military construction program in the 1930s and at least until 1942.

Fourth: that these same international bankers used political influence in the U.S. to cover up their wartime collaboration and to do this infiltrated the U.S. Control Commission for Germany.

Our evidence for these four major assertions can be summarized as follows:

In Chapter One we presented evidence that the Dawes and Young Plans for German reparations were formulated by Wall Streeters, temporarily wearing the hats of statesmen, and these loans generated a rain of profits for these international bankers. Owen Young of General Electric, Hjalmar Schacht, A. Voegler, and others intimately connected with Hitler's accession to power had earlier been the negotiators for the U.S. and German sides, respectively. Three Wall Street houses — Dillon, Read; Harris, Forbes; and, National City Company — handled three-quarters of the reparations loans used to create the German cartel system, including the dominant I.G. Farben and Vereinigte Stahlwerke, which together produced 95 percent of the explosives for the Nazi side in World War II.

The central role of I.G. Farben in Hitler's *coup d' état* was reviewed in Chapter Two. The directors of American I.G. (Farben) were identified as prominent American businessmen: Walter Teagle, a dose Roosevelt associate and backer and an NRA administrator; banker Paul Warburg (his brother Max Warburg was on the board of I.G. Farben in Germany); and Edsel Ford. Farben contributed 400,000 RM directly to Schacht and Hess for use in the crucial 1933 elections and Farben was subsequently in the forefront of military development in Nazi Germany.

A donation of 60,000 RM was made to Hitler by German General Electric (A.E.G.), which had four directors and a 25-30 percent interest held by the U.S. General Electric parent company. This role was described in Chapter Three, and we found that Gerard Swope, an originator of Roosevelt's New Deal (its National Recovery Administration segment), together with Owen Young of the Federal Reserve Bank of New York and Clark Minor of International General Electric, were the dominant Wall Streeters in A.E.G. and the most significant single influence.

We also found no evidence to indict the German electrical firm Siemens, which was *not* under Wall Street control. In contrast, there is documentary evidence that both A.E.G. and Osram, the other units of the German electrical industry — both of which had U.S. participation and control — *did* finance Hitler. In fact, almost all directors of German General Electric were Hitler backers, either directly through A.E.G. or indirectly through other German firms, G.E. rounded out its Hitler support by technical cooperation with Krupp, aimed at restricting U.S. development of tungsten carbide, which worked to the detriment of the U.S. in World War II. We concluded that A.E.G. plants in Germany managed, by a yet unknown maneuver, to avoid bombing by the Allies.

An examination of the role of Standard Oil of New Jersey (which was and is controlled by the Rockefeller interests) was undertaken in Chapter Four. Standard Oil apparently did not finance Hitler's accession to power in 1933 (that part of the "myth of Sidney Warburg" is not proven). On the other hand, payments were made up to 1944 by Standard Oil of New Jersey, to develop synthetic gasoline for war purposes on behalf of the Nazis and, through its wholly owned subsidiary, to Heinrich Himmler's S.S. Circle of Friends for political purposes. Standard Oil's role was technical aid to Nazi development of synthetic rubber and gasoline through a U.S. research company under the management control of Standard Oil. The Ethyl Gasoline Company, jointly owned by Standard Oil of New Jersey and General Motors, was instrumental in supplying vital ethyl lead to Nazi Germany — over the written protests of the U.S. War Department — with the clear knowledge that the ethyl lead was for Nazi military purposes.

In Chapter Five we demonstrated that International Telephone and Telegraph Company, one of the more notorious multi-nationals, worked both sides of World War II through Baron Kurt von Schroder, of the Schroder banking group. I.T.T. also held a 28-percent interest in Focke-Wolfe aircraft, which manufactured excellent German fighter planes. We also found that Texaco (Texas Oil Company) was involved in Nazi endeavors through German attorney Westrick, but dropped its chairman of the board Rieber when these endeavors were publicized.

Henry Ford was an early (1922) Hitler backer and Edsel Ford continued the family tradition in 1942 by encouraging French Ford to profit from arming the German Wehrmacht, Subsequently, these Ford-produced vehicles were used against American soldiers as they landed in France in 1944. For his early recognition of, and timely assistance to, the Nazis, Henry Ford received a Nazi medal in 1938. The records of French Ford suggest Ford Motor received kid glove treatment from the Nazis after 1940.

The provable threads of Hitler financing are drawn together in Chapter Seven and answer with precise names and figures the question, who financed Adolf Hitler? This chapter indicts Wall Street and, incidentally, no one else of consequence in the United States except the Ford family. The Ford family is not normally associated with Wall Street but is certainly a part of the "power elite."

In earlier chapters we cited several Roosevelt associates, including Teagle of Standard Oil, the Warburg family, and Gerard Swope. In Chapter Eight the role of Putzi Hanfstaengl, another Roosevelt friend and a participant in the Reichstag fire, is traced. The composition of the Nazi inner circle during World War II, and the financial contributions of Standard Oil of New Jersey and I.T.T. subsidiaries, are traced in Chapter Nine. Documentary proof of these monetary contributions is presented. Kurt von Schrader is identified as the key intermediary in this S.S. "slush fund."

Finally, in Chapter Ten we reviewed a book suppressed in 1934 and the "myth of 'Sidney Warburg.'" The suppressed book accused the Rockefellers, the Warburgs, and the major oil companies of financing Hitler. While the name "Sidney Warburg" was no doubt an invention, the extraordinary fact remains that the argument in the suppressed "Sidney Warburg" book is remarkably close to the evidence presented now. It also remains a puzzle why James Paul Warburg, fifteen years later, would want to attempt, in a rather transparently slipshod manner, to refute the contents of the "Warburg" book, a book he claims not to have seen. It is perhaps even more of a puzzle why Warburg would choose Nazi von Papen's *Memoirs* as the vehicle to present his refutation.

Finally, in Chapter Eleven we examined the roles of the Morgan and Chase Banks in World War II, specifically their collaboration with the Nazis in France while a major war was raging.

In other words, as in our two previous examinations of the links between New York international bankers and major historical events, we find a provable pattern of subsidy and political manipulation.

THE PERVASIVE INFLUENCE OF INTERNATIONAL BANKERS

Looking at the broad array of facts presented in the three volumes of the Wall Street series, we find persistent recurrence of the same names: Owen Young, Gerard Swope, Hjalmar Schacht, Bernard Baruch, *etc.;* the same international banks: J.P. Morgan, Guaranty Trust, Chase Bank; and the same location in New York: usually 120 Broadway.

This group of international bankers backed the Bolshevik Revolution and subsequently profited from the establishment of a Soviet Russia. This group backed Roosevelt and profited from New Deal socialism. This group also backed Hitler and certainly profited from German armament in the 1930s. When Big Business should have been running its business operations at Ford Motor, Standard of New Jersey, and so on, we find it actively and deeply involved in political upheavals, war, and revolutions in three major countries.

The version of history presented here is that the financial elite knowingly and with premeditation assisted the Bolshevik Revolution of 1917 in concert with German bankers. After profiting handsomely from the German hyper-inflationary distress of 1923, and planning to place the German reparations burden onto the backs of American investors, Wall Street found it had brought about the 1929 financial crisis.

Two men were then backed as leaders for major Western countries: Franklin D. Roosevelt in the United States and Adolf Hitler in Germany. The Roosevelt New Deal and Hitler's Four Year Plan had great similarities. The Roosevelt and Hitler plans were plans for fascist takeovers of their respective countries. While Roosevelt's NRA failed, due to then-operating constitutional constraints, Hitler's Plan succeeded.

Why did the Wall Street elite, the international bankers, want Roosevelt and Hitler in power? This is an aspect we have not explored. According to the "myth of 'Sidney Warburg,'" Wall Street wanted a policy of revenge; that is, it wanted war in Europe between France and Germany. We know even from Establishment history that both Hitler and Roosevelt acted out policies leading to war.

The link-ups between persons and events in this three-book series would require another book. But a single example will perhaps indicate the remarkable concentration of power within a relatively few organizations, and the use of this power.

On May 1st, 1918, when the Bolsheviks controlled only a small fraction of Russia (and were to come near to losing even that fraction in the summer of 1918), the American League to Aid and Cooperate with Russia was organized in Washington, D.C. to support the Bolsheviks. This was not a "Hands off Russia" type of committee formed by the Communist Party U.S.A. or its allies. It was a committee *created by Wall Street* with George P. Whalen of Vacuum Oil Company as Treasurer and Coffin and Oudin of General Electric, along with Thompson of the Federal Reserve System, Willard of the Baltimore & Ohio Railroad, and assorted socialists.

When we look at the rise of Hitler and Naziism we find Vacuum Oil and General Electric well represented. Ambassador Dodd in Germany was struck by the monetary and technical contribution by the Rockefeller-controlled Vacuum Oil Company in building up military gasoline facilities for the Nazis. The Ambassador tried to warn Roosevelt. Dodd believed, in his apparent naiveté of world affairs, that Roosevelt would intervene, but Roosevelt himself was backed by these same oil interests and Walter Teagle of Standard Oil of New Jersey and the NRA was on the board of Roosevelt's Warm Springs Foundation. So, in but one of many examples, we find the Rockefeller-controlled Vacuum Oil Company prominently assisting in the creation of Bolshevik Russia, the military build-up of Nazi Germany, and backing Roosevelt's New Deal.

Is the United States Ruled by a Dictatorial Elite?

Within the last decade or so, certainly since the 1960s, a steady flow of literature has presented a thesis that the United States is ruled by a self-perpetuating and unelected power elite. Even further, most of these books aver that this elite controls, or at the least heavily influences, all foreign and domestic policy decisions, and that no idea becomes respectable or is published in the United States without the tacit approval, or perhaps lack of disapproval, of this elitist circle.

Obviously the very flow of anti-establishment literature by itself testifies that the United States cannot be wholly under the thumb of any single group or elite. On the other hand, anti-establishment literature is not fully recognized or reasonably discussed in academic or media circles. More often than not it consists of a limited edition, privately produced, almost hand-to-hand circulated. There are *some* exceptions, true; but not enough to dispute the observation that anti-establishment critics do not easily enter normal information/distribution channels.

Whereas in the early and mid-1960s, any concept of rule by a conspiratorial elite, or indeed any kind of elite, was reason enough to dismiss the proponent out of hand as a "nut case," the atmosphere for such concepts has changed radically. The Watergate affair probably added the final touches to a long-developing environment of skepticism and doubt. We are almost at the point where anyone who accepts, for example, the Warren Commission report, or believes that that the decline and fall of Mr. Nixon did not have some conspiratorial aspects, is suspect. In brief, no one any longer really believes the Establishment information process. And there is a wide variety of alternative presentations of events now available for the curious.

Several hundred books, from the full range of the political and philosophical spectrum, add bits and pieces of evidence, more hypotheses, and more accusations. What was not too long ago a kooky idea, talked about at midnight behind closed doors, in hushed and almost conspiratorial whispers, is now openly debated — not, to be sure, in Establishment newspapers but certainly on non-network radio talk shows, the underground press, and even from time to time in books from respectable Establishment publishing houses.

So let us ask the question again: Is there an unelected power elite behind the U.S. Government?

A substantive and often-cited source of information is Carroll Quigley, Professor of International Relations at Georgetown University, who in 1966 had published a monumental modern history entitled *Tragedy and Hope*.[609] Quigley's book is apart from others in this revisionist vein, by virtue of the fact that it was based on a two-year study of the internal documents of one of the power centers. Quigley traces the history of the power elite:

> ... the powers of financial capitalism had another far reaching aim, nothing less than to create a world system of financial control in private hands able to dominate the political system of each country and the economy of the world as a whole.

Quigley also demonstrates that the Council on Foreign Relations, the National Planning Association, and other groups are "semi-secret" policy-making bodies under the control of this power elite.

In the following tabular presentation we have listed five such revisionist books, including Quigley's. Their essential theses and compatibility with the three volumes of the "Wall Street" series are summarized. It is surprising that in the three major historical events noted, Carroll Quigley is not at all consistent with the "Wall Street" series evidence. Quigley goes a long way to provide evidence for the *existence* of the power elite, but does not penetrate the *operations* of the elite.

Possibly, the papers used by Quigley had been vetted, and did not include documentation on elitist manipulation of such events as the Bolshevik Revolution, Hitler's accession to power, and the election of Roosevelt in 1933. More likely, these political manipulations may not be recorded at all in the files of the power groups. They may have been unrecorded actions by a small *ad hoc* segment of the elite. It is noteworthy that the documents used by this author came from government sources, recording the day-to-day actions of Trotsky, Lenin, Roosevelt, Hitler, J.P. Morgan and the various firms and banks involved.

On the other hand, such authors as Jules Archer, Gary Allen, Helen P. Lasell, and William Domhoff, writing from widely different political standpoints[610] *are* consistent with the "Wall

---

[609] Carroll Quigley, *Tragedy and Hope, op. cit.*
[610] There are many others; the author selected more or less at random two conservatives (Allen and Lasell) and two liberals (Archer and Domhoff).

Street" evidence. These writers present a hypothesis of a power elite manipulating the U.S. Government. The "Wall Street" series demonstrates how this hypothesized "power elite" has manipulated specific historical events.

Obviously any such exercise of unconstrained and supra-legal power is unconstitutional, even though wrapped in the fabric of law-abiding actions. We can therefore legitimately raise the question of the existence of a subversive force operating to remove constitutionally guaranteed rights.

THE NEW YORK ELITE AS A SUBVERSIVE FORCE

Twentieth-century history, as recorded in Establishment textbooks and journals, is inaccurate. It is a history which is based solely upon those official documents which various Administrations have seen fit to release for public consumption.

Table: IS THE EVIDENCE IN THE "WALL STREET" SERIES CONSISTENT WITH RELATED REVISIONIST ARGUMENTS PRESENTED ELSEWHERE?
(1) New York: MacMillan, 1966.
(2) New York: Hawthorn, 1973.
(3) Seal Beach: Concord Press, 1971.
(4) New York: Liberty, 1963.
(5) New Jersey: Prentice Hall, 1967.

Author and Title:	Essential Thesis:	Is the Thesis Consistent with: (1) Wall Street and the Bolshevik Revolution	(2) Wall Street and FDR	(3) Wall Street and the Rise of Hitler
Carroll QUIGLEY: Tragedy and Hope (1) "Semi-secret" Eastern Establishment	"Semi-secret" Eastern Establishment and interlocks have dominant role in planning and policy in U.S.	Quigley does not include evidence of Wall Street in the Bolshevik Revolution (pp. 385-9)	No: Quigley's argument is totally inconsistent with above (see p. 533)	Quigley's account of the rise of Hitler (pp. 529-33) does not include evidence of Establishment involvement.
Jules ARCHER: Plot to Seize the White House (2)	In 1933-4 there was a Wall Street conspiracy to remove FDR and install a fascist dictatorship in the United States.	Not relevant, but Wall Street elements cited by Archer were involved in the Bolshevik Revolution.	Yes: in general Archer's evidence is consistent, except that the role of FDR is interpreted differently.	Those parts in Archer bearing on Hitler and Nazism are consistent with the above.
Gary ALLEN: None Dare Call It Conspiracy (3)	There exists a secret conspiracy (the Council on Foreign Relations) to install a dictatorship in the U.S. and ultimately to control the world.	Yes, except for minor variances on financing.	Not included in Allen but is consistent.	Not included in Allen but is consistent.
Helen P. LASELL: Power Behind the Government Today (4)	The Council on Foreign Relations is a secret subversive organization dedicated to the overthrow of Constitutional government in the U.S.	Lasell's evidence is consistent with above.	Lasell's evidence is consistent with above.	Lasell's evidence is consistent with above
William DOMHOFF: Who Rules America? (5)	There is a "power elite" which controls all major banks, corporations, foundations, the executive branch, and the regulatory agencies of the U.S. government.	Above series extends Domhoffs argument to foreign policy.	Above series extends Domhoff's argument to Presidential elections.	Above series extends Domhoffs argument to foreign policy.

But an accurate history cannot be based on a selective release of documentary archives. Accuracy requires access to all documents. In practice, as previously classified documents in the U.S. State Department files, the British Foreign Office, and the German Foreign Ministry archives and other depositories are acquired, a new version of history has emerged; the prevailing Establishment version is seen to be, not only inaccurate, but designed to hide a pervasive fabric of deceit and immoral conduct.

The center of political power, as authorized by the U.S. Constitution, is with an elected Congress and an elected President, working within the framework and under the constraints of a Constitution, as interpreted by an unbiased Supreme Court. We have in the past *assumed* that political power is consequently carefully exercised by the Executive and legislative branch, after due deliberation and assessment of the wishes of the electorate. In fact, nothing could be further from this assumption. The electorate has long suspected, but now knows, that political promises are worth nothing. Lies are the order of the day for policy implementors. Wars are started (and stopped) with no shred of coherent explanation. Political words have never matched political deeds. Why not? Apparently because the center of political power has been elsewhere than with elected and presumably responsive representatives in Washington, and this power elite has its own objectives, which are inconsistent with those of the public at large.

In this three-volume series we have identified for three historical events the seat of political power in the United States — the power behind the scenes, the hidden influence on Washington — as that of the financial establishment in New York: the private international bankers, more specifically the financial houses of J.P. Morgan, the Rockefeller-controlled Chase Manhattan Bank, and in earlier days (before amalgamation of their Manhattan Bank with the former Chase Bank), the Warburgs.

The United States has, in spite of the Constitution and its supposed constraints, become a quasi-totalitarian state. While we do not (yet) have. the overt trappings of dictatorship, the concentration camps and the knock on the door at midnight, we most certainly do have threats and actions aimed at the survival of non-Establishment critics, use of the Internal Revenue Service to bring dissidents in line, and manipulation of the Constitution by a court system that is politically subservient to the Establishment.

It is in the pecuniary interests of the international bankers to centralize political power — and this centralization can best be achieved within a collectivist society, such as socialist Russia, national socialist Germany, or a Fabian socialist United States.

There can be no full understanding and appreciation of twentieth-century American politics and foreign policy without the realization that this financial elite effectively monopolizes Washington policy.

In case after case, newly released documentation implicates this elite and confirms this hypothesis. The revisionist versions of the entry of the United States into World Wars I and II, Korea, and Vietnam reveal the influence and objectives of this elite.

For most of the twentieth century the Federal Reserve System, particularly the Federal Reserve Bank of New York (which is outside the control of Congress, unaudited and uncontrolled, with the power to print money and create credit at will), has exercised a virtual monopoly over the direction of the American economy. In foreign affairs the Council on Foreign Relations, superficially an innocent forum for academics, businessmen, and politicians, contains within its shell, perhaps unknown to many of its members, a power center that unilaterally determines U.S. foreign policy. The major objective of this submerged — and obviously subversive — foreign. policy is the acquisition of markets and economic power *(profits,* if you will), for a small group of giant multi-nationals under the virtual control of a few banking investment houses and controlling families.

Through foundations controlled by this elite, research by compliant and spineless academics, "conservatives" as well as "liberals," has been directed into channels useful for the objectives of the elite essentially to maintain this subversive and unconstitutional power apparatus.

Through publishing houses controlled by this same financial elite unwelcome books have been squashed and useful books promoted; fortunately publishing has few barriers to entry and is almost atomistically competitive. Through control of a dozen or so major newspapers, run by editors who think alike, public information can be almost orchestrated at will. Yesterday, the space program; today, an energy crisis or a campaign for ecology; tomorrow, a war in the Middle East or some other manufactured "crisis."

The total result of this manipulation of society by the Establishment elite has been four major wars in sixty years, a crippling national debt, abandonment of the Constitution, suppression of freedom and opportunity, and creation of a vast credibility gulf between the man in the street and Washington, D.C. While the transparent device of two major parties trumpeting artificial differences, circus-like conventions, and the cliche of "bipartisan foreign policy" no longer carries credibility, and the financial elite itself recognizes that its policies lack public acceptance, it is obviously prepared to go it alone without even nominal public support.

In brief, we now have to consider and debate whether this New York-based elitist Establishment is a subversive force operating with deliberation and knowledge to suppress the Constitution and a free society. That will be the task ahead in the next decade.

THE SLOWLY EMERGING REVISIONIST TRUTH

The arena for this debate and the basis for our charges of subversion is the evidence provided by the revisionist historian. Slowly, over decades, book by book, almost line by line, the truth of recent history has emerged as documents are released, probed, analyzed, and set within a more valid historical framework.

Let us consider a few examples. American entry into World War II was supposedly precipitated, according to the Establishment version, by the Japanese attack on Pearl Harbor. Revisionists have established that Franklin D. Roosevelt and General Marshall *knew* of the impending Japanese attack and did nothing to warn the Pearl Harbor military authorities.

The Establishment wanted war with Japan. Subsequently, the Establishment made certain that Congressional investigation of Pearl Harbor would fit the Roosevelt whitewash. In the words of Percy Greaves, chief research expert for the Republican minority on the Joint Congressional Committee investigating Pearl Harbor:

> *The complete facts will never be known. Most of the so-called investigations have been attempts to suppress, mislead, or confuse those who seek the truth. From the beginning to the end, facts and files have been withheld so as to reveal only those items of information which benefit the administration under investigation. Those seeking the truth are told that other facts or documents cannot be revealed because they are intermingled in personal diaries, pertain to our relations with foreign countries, or are sworn to contain no information of value.*[611]

But this was not the first attempt to bring the United States into war, or the last. The Morgan interests, in concert with Winston Churchill, tried to bring the U.S. into World War I as early as 1915 and succeeded in doing so in 1917. Colin Thompson's *Lusitania* implicates President Woodrow Wilson in the sinking of the *Lusitania* — a horror device to generate a public backlash to draw the United States into war with Germany. Thompson demonstrates that Woodrow Wilson knew *four days beforehand* that the *Lusitania* was carrying six-million rounds of ammunition plus explosives, and therefore, "passengers who proposed to sail on that vessel were sailing in violation of statute of this country."[612]

The British Board of Inquiry under Lord Mersey was *instructed* by the British Government "that it is considered politically expedient that Captain Turner, the master of the *Lusitania*, be most prominently blamed for the disaster."

In retrospect, given Colin Thompson's evidence, the blame is more fairly to be attributed to President Wilson, "Colonel" House, J.P. Morgan, and Winston Churchill; this conspiratorial

---

[611] Percy L. Greaves, Jr., "The Pearl Harbor Investigation," in Harry Elmer Harnes, *Perpetual War for Perpetual Peace*, (Caldwell: Caxton Printers, 1953), p. 13-20.
[612] Colin Simpson, *Lusitania*, (London: Longman, 1972), p. 252.

elite should have been brought to trial for willful negligence, if not treason. It is to Lord Mersey's eternal credit that after performing his "duty" under instructions from His Majesty's government, and placing the blame on Captain Turner, he resigned, rejected his fee, and from that date on refused to handle British government commissions. To his friends Lord Mersey would only say about the *Lusitania* case that it was a "dirty business."

Then in 1933-4 came the attempt by the Morgan firm to install a fascist dictatorship in the United States. In the words of Jules Archer, it was planned to be a Fascist *putsch* to take over the government and *"run* it under a dictator on behalf of America's bankers and industrialists."[613] Again, a single courageous individual emerged — General Smedley Darlington Butler, who blew the whistle on the Wall Street conspiracy. And once again Congress stands out, particularly Congressmen Dickstein and MacCormack, by its gutless refusal to do no more than conduct a token whitewash investigation.

Since World War II we have seen the Korean War and the Vietnamese War — meaningless, meandering no-win wars costly in dollars and lives, with no other major purpose but to generate multibillion-dollar armaments contracts. Certainly these wars were not fought to restrain communism, because for fifty years the Establishment has been nurturing and subsidizing the Soviet Union which supplied armaments to the other sides in both wars — Korea and Vietnam. So our revisionist history will show that the United States directly or indirectly armed both sides in at least Korea and Vietnam.

In the assassination of President Kennedy, to take a domestic example, it is difficult to find anyone who today accepts the findings of the Warren Commission — except perhaps the members of that Commission. Yet key evidence is still hidden from public eyes for 50 to 75 years. The Watergate affair demonstrated even to the man in the street that the White House can be a vicious nest of intrigue and deception.

Of all recent history the story of Operation Keelhaul[614] is perhaps the most disgusting. Operation Keelhaul was the forced repatriation of millions of Russians at the orders of President (then General) Dwight D. Eisenhower, in direct violation of the Geneva Convention of 1929 and the long-standing American tradition of political refuge. Operation Keelhaul, which contravenes all our ideas of elementary decency and individual freedom, was undertaken at the direct orders of General Eisenhower and, we may now presume, was a part of a long-range program of nurturing collectivism, whether it be Soviet communism' Hitler's Naziism, or FDR's New Deal. Yet until recent publication of documentary evidence

---

[613] Jules Archer, *The Plot to Seize the White House*, (New York: Hawthorn Book, 1973), p. 202.
[614] See Julius Epstein, *Operation Keelhaul*, (Old Greenwich: Devin Adair, 1973).

by Julius Epstein, anyone who dared to suggest Eisenhower would betray millions of innocent individuals for political purposes was viciously and mercilessly attacked.[615]

What this revisionist history really teaches us is that our willingness as individual citizens to surrender political power to an elite has cost the world approximately two-hundred-million persons killed from 1820 to 1975. Add to that untold misery the concentration camps, the political prisoners, the suppression and oppression of those who try to bring the truth to light.

When will it all stop? It will not stop until we act upon one simple axiom: that the power system continues only so long as *individuals* want it to continue, and it will continue only so long as *individuals* try to get something for nothing. The day when a majority of individuals declares or acts as if it wants nothing from government, declares it will look after its own welfare and interests, then on *that* day power elites are doomed. The attraction to *"go* along" with power elites is the attraction of something for nothing. That is the bait. The Establishment always offers something for nothing; but the something is taken from someone else, as taxes or plunder, and awarded elsewhere in exchange for political support.

Periodic crises and wars are used to whip up support for other plunder-reward cycles which in effect tighten the noose around our individual liberties. And of course we have hordes of academic sponges, amoral businessmen, and just plain hangers-on, to act as non-productive recipients for the plunder.

Stop the circle of plunder and immoral reward and elitist structures collapse. But not until a majority finds the moral courage and the internal fortitude to reject the something-for-nothing con game and replace it by voluntary associations, voluntary communes, or local rule and decentralized societies, will the killing and the plunder cease.

---

[615] See for example Robert Welch, *The Politician*, (Belmont, Mass.: Belmont Publishing Co., 1963).

Appendix A

Program of the National Socialist German Workers Party

Note: This program is important because it demonstrates that the nature of Naziism was known publicly as early as 1920.

THE PROGRAM

The program of the German Workers' Party is limited as to period. The leaders have no intention, once the aims announced in it have been achieved, of setting up fresh ones, merely in order to increase the discontent of the masses artificially, and so ensure the continued existence of the Party.

1. We demand the union of all Germans to form a Great Germany on the basis of the right of the self-determination enjoyed by nations.
2. We demand equality of rights for the German People in its dealings with other nations, and abolition of the Peace Treaties of Versailles and St. Germain.
3. We demand land and territory (colonies) for the nourishment of our people and for settling our superfluous population.
4. None but members of the nation may be citizens of the State. None but those of German blood, whatever their creed, may be members of the nation. No Jew, therefore, may be a member of the nation.
5. Any one who is not a citizen of the State may live in Germany only as a guest and must be regarded as being subject to foreign laws.
6. The right of voting on the State's government and legislation is to be enjoyed by the citizen of the State alone. We demand therefore that all official appointments, of whatever kind, whether in the Reich, in the country, or in the smaller localities, shall be granted to citizens of the State alone.
7. We oppose the corrupting custom of Parliament of filling posts merely with a view to party considerations, and without reference to character or capability.

8. We demand that the State shall make it its first duty to promote the industry and livelihood of citizens of the State. If it is not possible to nourish the entire population of the State, foreign nationals (non-citizens of the State) must be excluded from the Reich.
All non-German immigration must be prevented. We demand that all non-Germans, who entered Germany subsequent to August 2nd, 1914, shall be required forthwith to depart from the Reich.
9. All citizens of the State shall be equal as regards rights and duties.
10. It must be the first duty of each citizen of the State to work with his mind or with his body. The activities of the individual may not clash with the interests of the whole, but must proceed within the frame of the community and be for the general good.
We demand therefore:
11. Abolition of incomes unearned by work.

ABOLITION OF THE THRALDOM OF INTEREST

12. In view of the enormous sacrifice of life and property demanded of a nation by every war, personal enrichment due to a war must be regarded as a crime against the nation. We demand therefore ruthless confiscation of all war gains,
13. We demand nationalisation of all businesses which have been up to the present formed into companies (Trusts).
14. We demand that the profits from wholesale trade shall be shared out.
15. We demand extensive development of provision for old age.
16. We demand creation and maintenance of a healthy middle class, immediate communalisation of wholesale business premises, and their lease at a cheap rate to small traders, and that extreme consideration shall be shown to all small purveyors to the State, district authorities and smaller localities.
17. We demand land-reform suitable to our national requirements, passing of a law for confiscation without compensation of land for communal purposes; abolition of interest on land loans, and prevention of all speculation in land.
18. We demand ruthless prosecution of those whose activities are injurious to the common interest. Sordid criminals against the nation, usurers, profiteers, etc. must be punished with death, whatever their creed or race.
19. We demand that the Roman Law, which serves the materialistic world order, shall be replaced by a legal system for all Germany.
20. With the aim of opening to every capable and industrious German the possibility of higher education and of thus obtaining advancement, the State must consider a thorough re-construction of our national system of education. The curriculum of all educational establishments must be brought into line with the requirements of practical life. Comprehension of the State idea (State sociology) must be the school objective, beginning with the first dawn of intelligence in the pupil. We demand development of the gifted children of poor parents, whatever their class or occupation, at the expense of the State.
21. The State must see to raising the standard of health in the nation by protecting mothers and infants, prohibiting child labour, increasing bodily efficiency by obligatory gymnastics and sports

laid down by law, and by extensive support of clubs engaged in the bodily development of the young.

22. We demand abolition of a paid army and formation of a national army.

23. We demand legal warfare against conscious political lying and its dissemination in the Press. In order to facilitate creation of a German national Press we demand:

(a) that all editors of newspapers and their assistants, employing the German language, must be members of the nation;

(b) that special permission from the State shall be necessary before non-German newspapers may appear. These are not necessarily printed in the German language;

(c) that non-Germans shall be prohibited by law from participating financially in or influencing German newspapers, and that the penalty for contravention of the law shall be suppression of any such newspaper, and immediate deportation of the non-German concerned in it.

It must be forbidden to publish papers which do not conduce to the national welfare. We demand legal prosecution of all tendencies in art and literature of a kind likely to disintegrate our life as a nation, and the suppression of institutions which militate against the requirements above-mentioned.

24. We demand liberty for all religious denominations in the State, so far as they are not a danger to it and do not militate against the moral feelings of the German race.

The Party, as such, stands for positive Christianity, but does not bind itself in the matter of creed to any particular confession. It combats the Jewish-materialist spirit within us and without us, and is convinced that our nation can only achieve permanent health from within on the principle:

THE COMMON INTEREST BEFORE SELF

25. That all the foregoing may be realised we demand the creation of a strong central power of the State. Unquestioned authority of the politically centralised Parliament over the entire Reich and its organisation; and formation of Chambers for classes and occupations for the purpose of carrying out the general laws promulgated by the Reich in the various States of the confederation. The leaders of the Party swear to go straight forward — if necessary to sacrifice their lives — in securing fulfillment of the foregoing Points. Munich, February 24th, 1920.

Source: Official English translation by E. Dugdale, reprinted from Kurt G, W. Ludecke, *I Knew Hitler* (New York: Charles Scribner's Sons, 1937),

Appendix B

Affidavit of Hjalmar Schacht

I, Dr. Hjalmar Schacht, after having been warned that I will be liable to punishment for making false statements, state herewith under oath, of my own free will and without coercion, the following:

The amounts contributed by the participants in the meeting of 20 February 1933 at Goering's house were paid by them to the bankers, Delbruck, Schickler & Co., Berlin, to the credit of an account "Nationale Treuhand" (which may be translated as National Trusteeship). It was arranged that I was entitled to dispose of this account, which I administered as a trustee, and that in case of my death, or that in case the trusteeship should be terminated in any other way, Rudolf Hess should be entitled to dispose of the account.

I disposed of the amounts of this account by writing out checks to Mr. Hess. I do not know what Mr. Hess actually did with the money.

On 4 April 1933, I closed the account with Delbruck, Schickler & Co. and had the balance transferred to the "Account Ic" with the Reichsbank which read in my name. Later on I was ordered directly by Hitler, who was authorized by the assembly of 20 February 1933 to dispose of the amounts collected, or through Hess, his deputy, to pay the balance of about 600,000 marks to Ribbentrop.

I have carefully read this affidavit (one page) and have signed it. I have made the necessary corrections in my own handwriting and initialed each correction in the margin of the page. I declare herewith under oath that I have stated the full truth to the best of my knowledge and belief.

(Signed) Dr. Hjalmar Schacht
12 August 1947

In a subsequent affidavit of 18 August 1947 (NI-9764, Pros. Ex 54), Schacht declared the following with regard to the above interrogation: "I made all of the statements appearing in this interrogation to Clifford Hyanning, a financial investigator of the American Forces of my own free will and without coercion. I have reread this interrogation today and can state that all of the facts contained therein are true to my best knowledge and belief. I declare herewith under oath and I have stated the full truth to the best of my knowledge and belief."

Source: Copy of Document Prosecution Exhibit 55. *Trials of War Criminals before the Nuremburg Military Tribunals under Control Council Law No. 10*, Nuremburg, October 1946-April 1949, Volume VII, I.G. Farben, (Washington: U.S. Government Printing Office, 1952).

APPENDIX C

ENTRIES IN THE "NATIONAL TRUSTEESHIP" ACCOUNT FOUND IN THE FILES OF THE DELBRUCK, SCHICKLER CO. BANK

NATIONAL TRUSTEESHIP
REICHSBANK PRESIDENT DR. HJALMAR SCHACHT,
BERLIN-ZEHLENDORF

Date	Description	Amount	Date	Amount
Feb. 23	Debibk (Deutsche Bank Diskonto-Gesellschaft) Verein fuer die bergbaulichen Interessen, Essen		Feb. 23	200,000.00
24	Transfer to account Rudolf Hess, at present in Berlin	100,000.00	24	
24	Karl Herrmann		25	150,000.00
	Automobile Exhibition, Berlin		25	100,000.00
25	Director A. Steinke		27	200,000.00
25	Demag A.G., Duisberg		27	50,000.00
27	Telefunken Gesellschaft ruer draht lose Telegraphie Berlin		28	85,000.00
	Osram G.m.b.H., Berlin		28	40,000.00
27	Bayerische Hypotheken-und Wech selbank, branch office Munich, Kauflingerstr. In favor of Verlag Franz Eher Nachf, Munich	100,000.00	28	
27	Transfer to account Rudolf Hess, Berlin	100,000.00	27	
28	I.G. Farbenindustrie A.G. Frankfurt/M		Mar. 1	400,000.00
28	Telegraph expenses for transfer to Munich	8.00	Feb. 28	
Mar. 1	Your Payment		Mar. 2	125,000.00
2	Telegr. transfer to Bayerische Hypotheken-und Wechselbank, Munich branch office, Bayerstr.			

	for account Josef Jung	400,000.00	2	
	Telegr. transfer expenses	23.00	2	
	Account transfer Rudolf Hess	300,000.00		
2	Reimbursement from Director Karl Lange, Berlin		3	30,000.00
3	Reimbursement from Dir. Karl Lange, 'Maschinen-industrie' Account		4	20,000.00
	Reimbursement from Verein ruer die bergbaulichen Interessen, Essen		4	100,000.00
	Reimbursement from Karl Herrmann, Berlin, Dessauerstr. 28/9		4	150,000.00
	Reimbursement from Allgemeine Elektrizitaetsgesellschaft, Berlin		4	60,000.00
7	Reimbursement from General-direktor Dr. F. Springorum, Dortmund		8	36,000.00
8	Reichsbank transfer: Bayerische Hypotheken-und Wechselbank,			
	branch office Kauffingerstr.	100,000.00	8	
		1,100,031.00		1,696,000.00
		1,100,031.00	Mar.8	1,696,000.00
Mar. 8	Bayerische Hypotheken-und Wechselbank, Munich, branch office Bayerstr.	100,000.00	8	
	Transfer to account Rudolf Hess	250,000.00	7	
10	Accumulatoren-Fabrik A.G. Berlin		11	25,000.00
13	Verein f.d. bergbaulichen Interessen, Essen		14	300,000.00
14	Reimbursement Rudolf Hess	200,000.00	14	

29	Reimbursement Rudolf Hess	200,000.00	29	
April 4	Commerz-und Privatbank Dep. Kasse N. Berlin W.9 Potsdamerstr. 1 f. Special Account S 29	99,000.00	Apr. 4	
5	Interests according to list 1 percent		5	404.50
	Phone bills	1.00	5	
	Postage	2.50	5	
	Balance	72,370.00	5	
	Balance carried over	2,021,404.50		2,021,404.50
			Apr. 5	72,370.00

APPENDIX D

LETTER FROM U.S. WAR DEPARTMENT TO ETHYL CORPORATION

Exhibit No, 144
(Handwritten) Mr, Webb sent copies for other Directors
Copy to: Mr. Alfred P. Sloan, Jr., General Motors Corp,, New York City, Mr. Donaldson Brown, General Motors Corp., New York City.
December 15, 1934.
Mr. E. W. Webb,
President Ethyl Gasoline Corporation, 185 E, 42nd Street, New York City. Dear Mr. Webb: I learned through our Organic Chemicals Division today that the Ethyl Gasoline Corporation has in mind forming a German company with the I.G. to manufacture Ethyl lead in that country.
I have just had two weeks in Washington, no inconsiderable part of which was devoted to criticising the interchanging with foreign companies of chemical knowledge which might have a military value. Such giving of information by an industrial company might have the gravest repercussions on it. The Ethyl Gasoline Corporation would be no exception, in fact, would probably be singled out for special attack because of the ownership of its stock.
It should seem. on the face of it, that the quantity of Ethyl lead used for commercial purposes in Germany would be too small to go after. It has been claimed that Germany is secretly arming. Ethyl lead would doubtless be a valuable aid to military aeroplanes.
I am writing you this to say that in my opinion under no conditions should you or the Board of Directors of the Ethyl Gasoline Corporation disclose any secrets or 'know how' in connection with the manufacture of tetraethyl lead to Germany.
I am informed that you will be advised through the Dyestuffs Division of the necessity of disclosing the information which you have received from Germany to appropriate War Department officials.
Yours very truly,

Source: United States Senate, Hearings before a Subcommittee of the Committee on Military Affairs, *Scientific and Technical Mobilization,* 78th Congress, Second Session, Part 16, (Washington D.C.: Government Printing Office, 1944), p. 939.

APPENDIX E

EXTRACT FROM MORGENTHAU DIARY (GERMANY) REGARDING SOSTHENES BEHN OF I.T.T.

March 16, 1945
11:30 a.m.

GROUP MEETING
Bretton Woods — I.T. & T. — Reparations

Present:
Mr. White
Mr. Fussell
Mr. Feltus
Mr. Coe
Mr. DuBois
Mrs. Klotz

H.M., Jr.: Frank, can you boil *down* this business on I.T.&T.?

Mr. Coe: Yes, sir. I.T. &T. by the way did transfer or did get $15 million yesterday or a few days ago of their debts in dollars paid to them by the Spanish Government and that they are allowed to do under our general license, so that's all right. However, it is in part in their representation to us, part of a deal for the sale of the company in Spain, so they are trying thereby to force our hand. Now, the proposition which they have had up over some years in different forms now takes this form. They can get their receivables paid off in dollars, which they say they have not been able to do hitherto — either $15 million now and $10 million or $11 million later. They will sell the company to Spain and take in return $30 million worth of bonds — Spanish Government bonds — which are to be amortized over a number of years and roughly at the rate of $2 million per annum, and they are to receive 90% of those exports in order to amortize bonds faster, if they are to export it to the United States.

H. M. Jr.: Like the match dealer I mentioned in my speech.

Mr. Coe: That's right. The Spanish Government. They are willing, they say — they are able to get from the Spanish Government assurances, that these will not be, that the shares which the Spanish Government intends to resell will not go to anybody on the black list, and so forth. In some negotiations we have had with them over the last few weeks, they have been willing to come further on that. Our hesitation on the matter relates to two things; First, that you can't trust Franco, and that if they are able — if Franco is able to sell $50 million worth of shares Of this company in Spain in the next period of time, he may very well sell it to pro-German interests. It seems doubtful that he would be able to dispose of it to the Spaniards, so that is the first thing. The second thing we can't document too well, but I think it is more pronounced in my mind than in the minds of the Foreign Funds and legal people. I don't think we can really trust Behn either.

Mr. White: I'm sure you can't.

Mr. Coe: We have records here of interviews, going far back, that some of your men had with Behn — Klaus was one — in which Behn said that he had had conversations with Goering with the proposition that Goering was to hold I.T. &T.'s property in Germany, and as you recall, I.T. &T. here did try to purchase General Aniline and make it an American company thereby and that was part of the deal which Behn told State and our lawyers very frankly he had discussed. He thought it was perfectly all right protecting property: That was before we entered the war,

H. M., Jr.: I don't remember that,

Mr. Coe: The man in charge of their properties now is Westrick who you recall came over here and was mixed up with Texaco. They tried in every way to cook up deals earlier to escape. They are tied up with top German group and etc. On the other hand, Colonel Behn has been used several times as an emissary by the State Department, and I believe he is personally on very good terms with Stettinius. We have heard from State on this letter saying they have no objections. We proposed to you earlier — the letter which I sent in to you suggesting that you ask State, if in view of our safe haven objectives, they still said yes. I am confident from talking with them on the phone the last day or two, they will write back and say yes, they still think it is a good deal.

H. M., Jr.: This is the position I am in. As you gentlemen know I am overextended now and I can't go into this thing personally, and I think that we are just going to have to throw the thing in the lap of the State Department, and if they want to clear it, all right. I just haven't got the time or the energy to fight them on that basis.

Mr. Coe: Then we ought to license it now.

Mr. White: First you ought to get a letter. I agree with the Secretary on this point of view that this fellow Behn is not to be trusted around the corner. There is something about this deal that looks suspicious and has been for the last couple of years we have been dealing with him. However, it is one thing to believe that and another thing to defend that before the pressure that will be brought in here that they are trying to deprive this company of the business deal, but I think that what we might do is get the State Department on record that in view of a safe haven project they don't think that there is any danger that any of these assets — I would cite some of them, spell the letter out. Get them down on record and even make them a little frightened and hold out or they will at least have had the record and you will have called their attention to these dangers. This fellow Behn hates our guts anyway. We have been standing between him and deals for 4 years, at least.

H. M., Jr.: Follow what White said. Something along that line. "Dear Mr, Stettinius; I am bothered about these things due to the following facts, and I would like you to advise me whether we should or should not .... "

Mr. White: "In view of the danger that German assets may be cloaked here, the future —" and let him come back and say, "No," and we'll watch him.

Mr. Coe: We said we wanted to give Acheson something Monday.

H. M., Jr.: And if you get that ready for me by tomorrow morning, I'll sign it. *Mr. Coe:* O.K.

Source: United States Senate, Subcommittee to Investigate the Administration of the Internal Security Act. Committee on the Judiciary, *Morgenthau Diarty (Germany),* Volume I, 90th Congress, 1st Session, November 20, 1967, (Washington D.C.: U.S. Government Printing Office, 1967), p. 320 of Book 828. (Page 976 of U,S. Senate print.)

Note: "*Mr.* White" is Harry Dexter White. "Dr. Dubois" is Josiah E. Dubois, Jr., author of the book, *Generals in Grey Suits* (London: The Bodley Head, 1953). "H.M., Jr." is Henry Morgenthau, Jr., Secretary of the Treasury.

This memorandum is important because it accuses Sosthenes Behn of attempting to make behind-the-scenes deals in Nazi Germany "for 4 years, at least" — *i.e.* while the rest of the U.S. was at war, Behn and his friends were still doing business as usual with Germany. This memorandum supports the evidence presented in Chapters Five and Nine concerning the influence of I.T.T. in the Himmler inner circle and adds Herman Goering to the list of I. T. T. contacts.

Selected Bibliography

Allen, Gary. *None Dare Call It Conspiray.* Seal Beach, California: Concord Press, 1971.

Ambruster, Howard Watson. *Treason's Peace.* New York: The Beechhurst Press, 1947.

Angebert, Michel. *The Occult and the Third Reich.* New York: The Macmillan Company, 1974.

Archer, Jules. *The Plot to Seize the White House.* New York: Hawthorn Books, 1973.

Baker, Philip Noel. *Hawkers of Death.* The Labour Party, England, 1984.

Barnes, Harry Elmer. *Perpetual War for Perpetual Peace.* Caldwell, Idaho: Caxton Printers, 1958.

Bennett, Edward W. *Germany and the Diplomacy of the Financial Crisis, 1931.* Cambridge: Harvard University Press, 1962.

Der Farben-Konzern 1928. Hoppenstedt, Berlin, 1928.

Dimitrov, George, *The Reichstag Fire Trial.* London: The Bodley Head, 1984.

Dodd, William E. Jr., and Dodd, Martha. *Ambassador Dodd's Diary, 1933-1938.* New York: Harcourt Brace and Company, 1941.

Domhoff, G. William. *The Higher Circles: The Governing Class in America.* New York: Vintage, 1970.

Dubois, Josiah E., Jr. *Generals in Grey Suits.* London: The Bodley Head, 1958.

Engelbrecht, H.C. *Merchants of Death.* New York: Dodd, Mead & Company, 1984.

Engler, Robert. *The Politics of Oil.* New York: The Macmillan Company, 1961.

Epstein, Julius. *Operation Keelhaul.* Old Greenwich: Devin Adair, 1978.

Farago, Ladislas. *The Game of the Foxes.* New York: Bantam, 1978.

Flynn, John T. *As We Go Marching,* New York: Doubleday, Doran and Co., Inc., 1944.

Guerin, Daniel. *Fascisme et grand capital.* Paris: Francois Maspero, 1965.

Hanfstaengl, Ernst. *Unheard Witness.* New York: J. B. Lippincott, 1957.

Hargrave, John. *Montagu Norman.* New York: The Greystone Press, n.d.

Harris, C.R.S. *Germany's Foreign Indebtedness.* London: Oxford University Press, 1985.

Helfferich, Dr. Karl. *Germany's Economic Progress and National Wealth, 1888.1913.* New York: Germanistic Society of America, 1914.

Hexner, Ervin. *International Cartels.* Chapel Hill: The University of North Carolina Press, 1945.

Howard, Colonel Graeme K. *America and a New Worm Order.* New York: Scribners, 1940.

Kolko, Gabriel. "American Business and Germany, 1930-1941," *The Western Political Quarterly,* Volume XV, 1962.

Kuezynski, Robert R. *Bankers' Profits from German Loans,* Washington, D.C.: The Brookings Institution, 1982.

Leonard, Jonathan. *The Tragedy of Henry Ford.* New York: G.P. Putnam's Sons, 1932.

Ludecke, Kurt G.W. *I Knew Hitler.* New York: Charles Scribner's Sons, 1937.

Magers, Helmut. *Ein Revolutionar Aus Common Sense.* Leipzig: R. Kittler Verlag, 1934.

Martin, James J, *Revisionist Viewpoints.* Colorado: Ralph Mules, 1971.

Martin, James Stewart. *All Honorable Men,* Boston: Little Brown and Company, 1950.

Muhlen, Norbert. *Schacht: Hitler's Magician.* New York: Longmans, Green and Co., 1939.

Nixon, Edgar B. *Franklin D. Roosevelt and Foreign Affairs.* Cambridge: Belknap Press, 1969.

Oil and Petroleum Yearbook, 1938.

Papen, Franz yon. *Memoirs.* New York: E.P. Dutton & Co., 1953.

Peterson, Edward Norman. *Hjalmar Schacht.* Boston: The Christopher Publishing House, 1954.

Phelps, Reginald H. *"Before Hitler Came": Thule Society and Germanen Orden,* in the *Journal of Modern History,* September, 1963.

Quigley, Carroll, *Tragedy and Hope.* New York: The Macmillan Company, 1966.

Ravenscroft, Trevor, *The Spear of Destiny.* New York: G.P. Putnam's Sons, 1973.

Rathenau, Walter. *In Days to Come.* London: Allen & Unwin, n.d.

Roberts, Glyn. *The Most Powerful Man in the World.* New York: Covici, Friede, 1938.

Sampson, Anthony. *The Sovereign State of* I.T.T. New York: Stein & Day, 1975.

Schacht, Hjalmar. *Confessions of "The Old Wizard."* Boxton: Houghton Mifflin, 1956.

Schloss, Henry H. *The Bank for International Settlements.* Amsterdam: North Holland Publishing Company, 1958.

Seldes, George. *Iron, Blood and Profits.* New York and London: Harper & Brothers Publishers, 1934.

Simpson, Colin. *Lusitania.* London; Longman, 1972.

Smoot, Dan. *The Invisible Government.* Boston: Western .Islands, 1962, Strasser, Otto. *Hitler and I.* London: Jonathan Cape, n.d.

Sonderegger, Rene. *Spanischer Sommer.* Affoltern, Switzerland: Aehren Verlag, 1948.

Stocking, George W, and Watkins, Myron W. *Cartels in Action.* New York: The Twentieth Century Fund, 1946.

Sutton, Antony C. *National Suicide: Military Aid to the Soviet Union.* New York: Arlington House Publishers, 1978.
    Wall Street and the Bolshevik Revolution. New York: Arlington House Publishers, 1974.
    Wall Street and FDR. New York: Arlington House Publishers, 1975.
    Western Technology and Soviet Economic Development, 1917-1930. Stanford, California: Hoover Institution Press, 1968.
    Western Technology and Soviet Economic Development, 1980-1945. Stanford, California: Hoover Institution Press, 1971.
    Western Technology and Soviet Economic Development, 1945-1965. Stanford, California: Hoover Institution Press, 1973.

Sward, Keith. *The Legend of Henry Ford.* New York: Rinehart & Co., 1948.

Thyssen, Fritz. *I Paid Hitler.* New York: Farrar & Rinehart, Inc., n.d. "Trials of War Criminals Before the Nuremburg Military Tribunals Under Control Council Law No. 10," Volume VIII, I.G. Farben case, Nuremburg, October 1946-April 1949. Washington: Government Printing Of-flee, 1953. United States Army Air Force, Aiming point report No. I.E.2 of May 29, 1943.

United States Senate, Hearings before the Committee on Finance. *Sale of Foreign Bonds or Securities in the United States.* 72nd Congress, 1st Session, S. Res. 19, Part I, December 18, 19, and 21, 1931. Washington: Government Printing Office, 1931.

United States Senate, Hearings before a Subcommittee of the Committee on Military Affairs. *Scientific and Technical Mobilization.* 78th Congress, 2nd Session, S. Res. 107, Part 16, August 29 and September 7, 8, 12, and 13, 1944. Washington: Government Printing Office, 1944.
United States Congress. House of Representatives. *Special Committee on Un-American Activities and Investigation of Certain Other Propaganda Activities.* 73rd Congress, 2nd Session, Hearings No. 73-DC-4. Washington: Government Printing Office, 1934.

United States Congress. House of Representatives. Special Committee on Un-American Activities (1934). *Investigation of Nazi and other Propaganda Activities.* 74th Congress, 1st Session, Report No. 153. Washington: Government Printing Office, 1934.

United States Congress. Senate. Hearings before a Subcomittee of the Committee on Military Affairs. *Elimination of German Resources for War.* Report pursuant to S. Res. 107 and 146, July 2, 1945, Part 7. 78th Congress and 79th Congress. Washington: Government Printing Office, 1945.

United States Congress. Senate. Hearings before a Subcomittee of the Committee on Military Affairs. *Scientific and Technical Mobilization.* 78th Congress, 1st session, S. 702, Part 16, Washington: Government Printing Office, 1944.

United States Group Control Council (Germany), Office of the Director of Intelligence, Field Information Agency. Technical Intelligence Report No. EF/ME/1. September 4, 1945.

United States Sente. Subcommittee to Investigate the Administration of the Internal Security Act, Committee on the Judiciary. *Morgenthau Diary (Germany).* Volume 1, 90th Congress, 1st Session, November 20, 1967. Washington: U.S. Government Printing Office, 1967.

United States State Department Decimal File.

United States Strategic Bombing Survey. *AEG-Ostlandwerke GmbH,* by Whitworth Ferguson. 81 May 1945.

United States Strategic Bombing Survey. *German Electrical Equipment Industry Report.* Equipment Division, January 1947.

United States Strategic Bombing Survey, *Plant Report of A.E.G.* (Allgemeine Elektrizitats Gesellschaft). Nuremburg, Germany: June 1945.

Zimmerman, Werner. *Liebet Eure Feinde.* Frankhauser Verlag: Thielle-Neuchatel, 1948.

Other Publications

Ezra's interest in money as a phenomenon, in contrast to the usual attitude toward money as something to get, is a legitimate one.

Omnia Veritas Ltd presents:

Ezra Pound
This Difficult Individual

by

Eustace Mullins

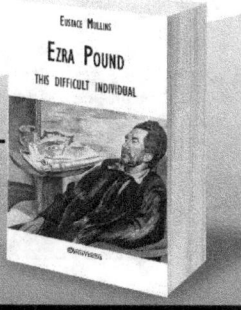

An illustration for his own monetary theories...

The Story of the Medical Conspiracy Against America

Omnia Veritas Ltd presents:

Murder by Injection

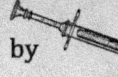

by

Eustace Mullins

The cynicism and malice of these conspirators is something beyond the imagination of most Americans.

Christ did not wish to be followed by robots and sleepwalkers, He desired man to awaken, and to attain the full use of his earthly powers.

Omnia Veritas Ltd presents:

My Life in Christ

by

Eustace Mullins

THIS is the story of my life in Christ

 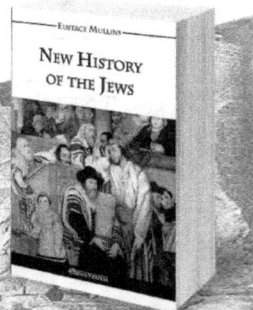

New History of the Jews

by Eustace Mullins

Throughout the history of civilization, one particular problem of mankind has remained constant.

Only one people has irritated its host nations in every part of the civilized world

The Curse of Canaan
A demonology of history

by Eustace Mullins

Liberalism, more popularly known as secular humanism, can be traced in an unbroken line all the way back to the Biblical "Curse of Canaan."

Humanism is the logical result of the demonology of history

 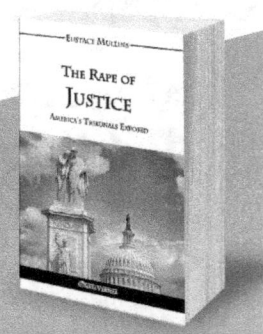

The Rape of Justice

by Eustace Mullins

America's Tribunals Exposed

American should know just what is going on in our courts

OMNIA VERITAS

Omnia Veritas Ltd presents:

THE SECRETS OF THE FEDERAL RESERVE

by

EUSTACE MULLINS

HERE ARE THE SIMPLE FACTS OF THE GREAT BETRAYAL

Will we continue to be enslaved by the Babylonian debt money system?

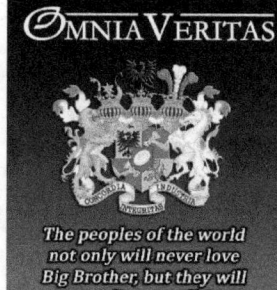

OMNIA VERITAS

Omnia Veritas Ltd presents:

THE WORLD ORDER

OUR SECRET RULERS

A Study in the Hegemony of Parasitism

by

EUSTACE MULLINS

The peoples of the world not only will never love Big Brother, but they will soon dispose of him forever.

The program of the World Order remains the same; Divide and Conquer

OMNIA VERITAS

Omnia Veritas Ltd presents:

Confessions of a British Spy

by

HEMPHER

"The biggest enemies of Islam are the **Jews** and **mushriks**."

The hidden origin of Whahhabism finally revealed!

Discover the most cunning British foreign policy ever!

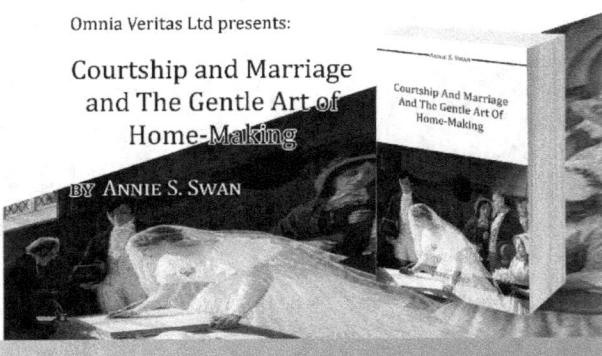

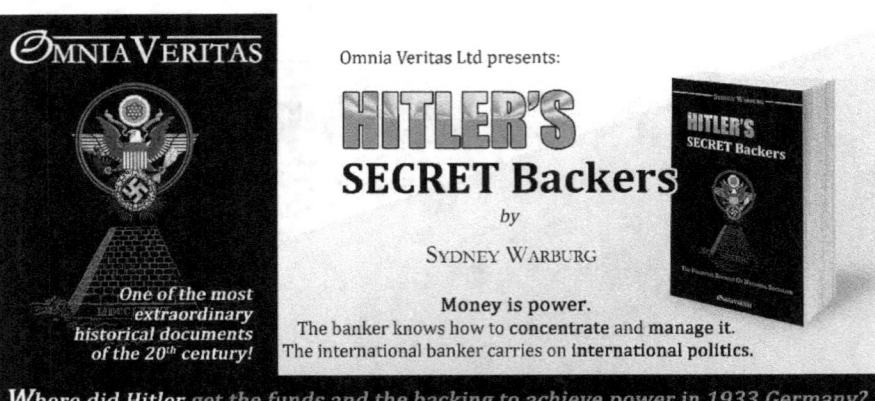

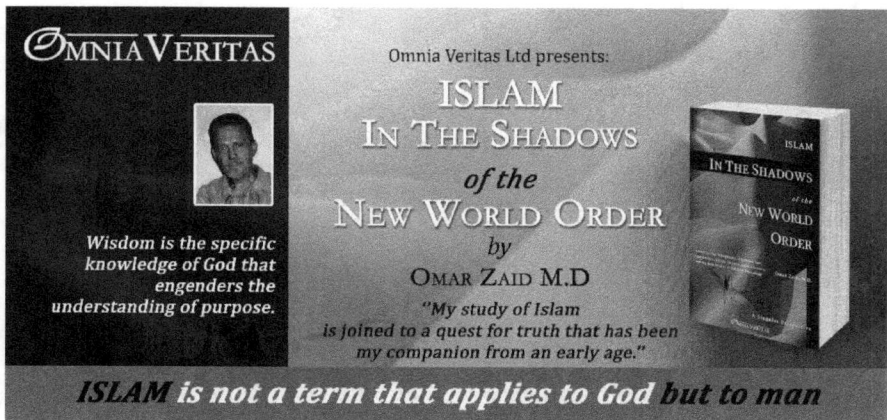

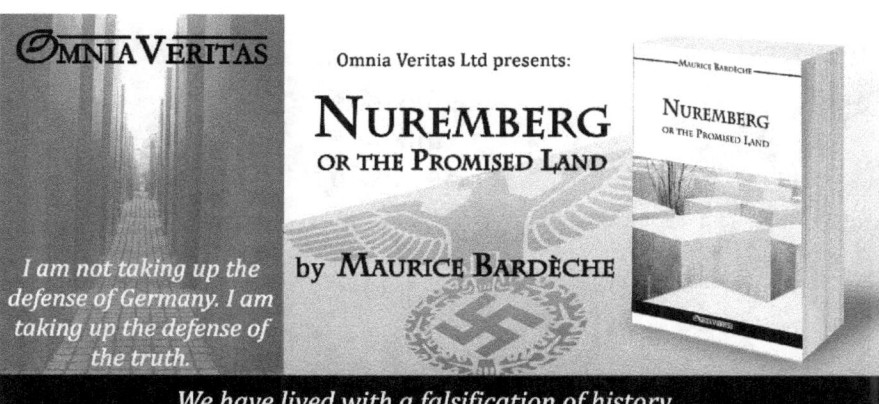

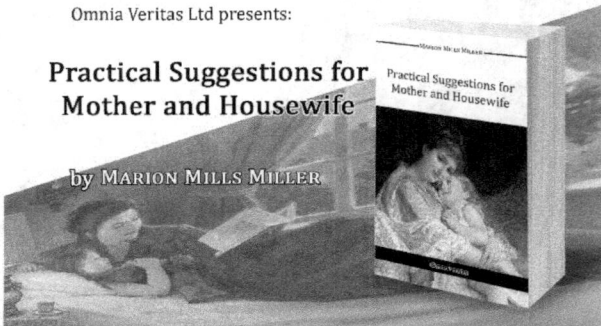

Omnia Veritas Ltd presents:

Practical Suggestions for Mother and Housewife

by MARION MILLS MILLER

The **mother** or matron was named from the most **tender** and **sacred** of human functions

What tender associations halo the names of wife, mother, sister and daughter!

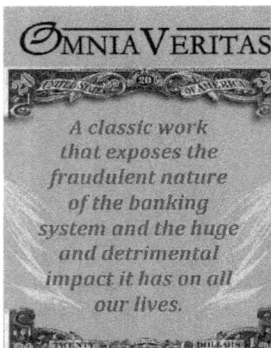

Omnia Veritas Ltd presents:

PROMISE to PAY

by ROBERT MCNAIR WILSON

An inquiry into The Modern Magic called "HIGH FINANCE"

A classic work that exposes the fraudulent nature of the banking system and the huge and detrimental impact it has on all our lives.

The creation of money should be in the hands of the State or Head of Government and not in the hands of private banking.

Omnia Veritas Ltd presents:

Sane Sex Life and Sane Sex Living

by H. W. LONG

The time has come for a **book** like this to command the attention of **medical** men...

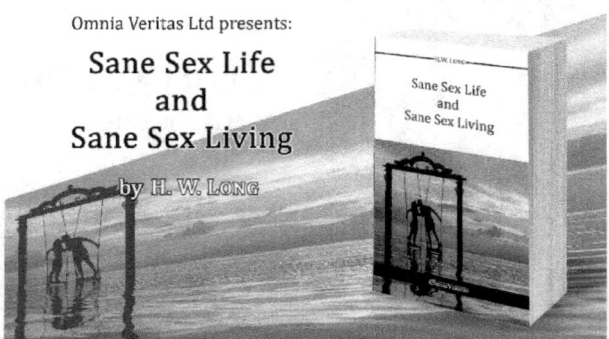

... they never learned sex. They never realized its fundamentals...

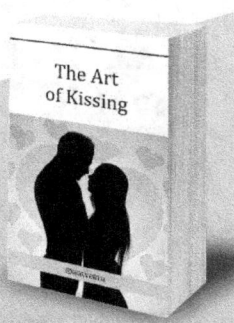

Omnia Veritas Ltd presents:

The Gentlemen's Book of Etiquette, and Manual of Politeness

A complete guide for a gentleman's conduct in all his relations towards society

BY

CECIL B. HARTLEY

To make your **politeness** part of yourself, inseparable from every action, is the height of **gentlemanly** elegance and finish of **manner**.

As you treat the world, so the world will treat you

Omnia Veritas Ltd presents:

THE HIGH COST OF VENGEANCE

BY FREDA UTLEY

France and Britain refused to listen to the statesmen who said that you can have peace or vengeance, not both...

The victors refused even to discuss the terms of peace with the vanquished

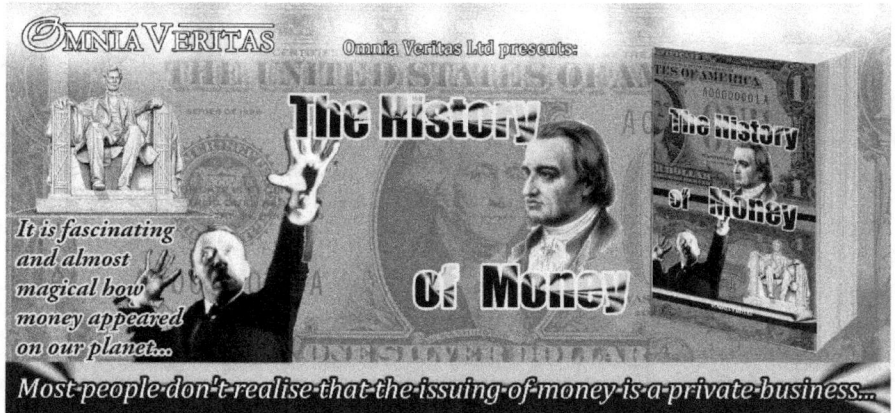

Omnia Veritas Ltd presents:

The History of Money

It is fascinating and almost magical how money appeared on our planet...

Most people don't realise that the issuing of money is a private business...

Omnia Veritas Ltd presents:

The Ladies' Book of Etiquette, and Manual of Politeness

A complete hand book for the use of the lady in polite society

BY

FLORENCE HARTLEY

... to be truly a **lady**, one must carry the **principles** into every circumstance of life

Politeness is goodness of heart put into daily practice

Omnia Veritas Ltd presents:

THE LEGALIZED CRIME OF BANKING

by

SILAS WALTER ADAMS

A free press is the guardian genius of a just, honest, and humane democracy, as Lincoln put it:

"To sin by silence when they know they should protest, makes cowards of men."

"There is a great deal of difference between a **moral wrong** and a **legal right**"

A liberating and much acclaimed book on the Federal Reserve system!

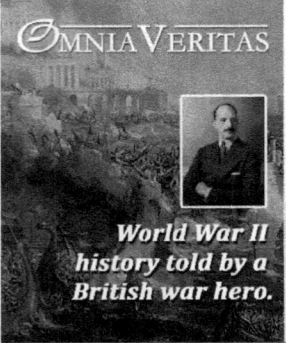

Omnia Veritas Ltd presents :

THE NAMELESS WAR

World War II history told by a British war hero.

A first hand testimony of WWII; after reading this book, you'll never look at history the same way again...

An astonishing account of *forbidden history* !

Omnia Veritas Ltd presents:

The plot against the Church

by MAURICE PINAY

It can be stated without fear of exaggeration that no book in the present century has been the object of so many commentaries in the world press...

A magnificent and imposing compilation of documents and sources of undeniable importance and authenticity

Omnia Veritas Ltd presents:

THE RIDDLE OF THE JEW'S SUCCESS

by THEODOR FRITSCH

the Jews, however, in spite of their dispersion amongst the nations...

... still feel that they are a special people and a special race

Omnia Veritas Ltd presents:

The Servile State

by HILAIRE BELLOC

"If we do not restore the Institution of Property we cannot escape restoring the Institution of Slavery; there is no third course."

Surprisingly compelling and enlightening, an **indispensable** of any **serious economic study**

Hilaire Belloc's classic in a new edition!

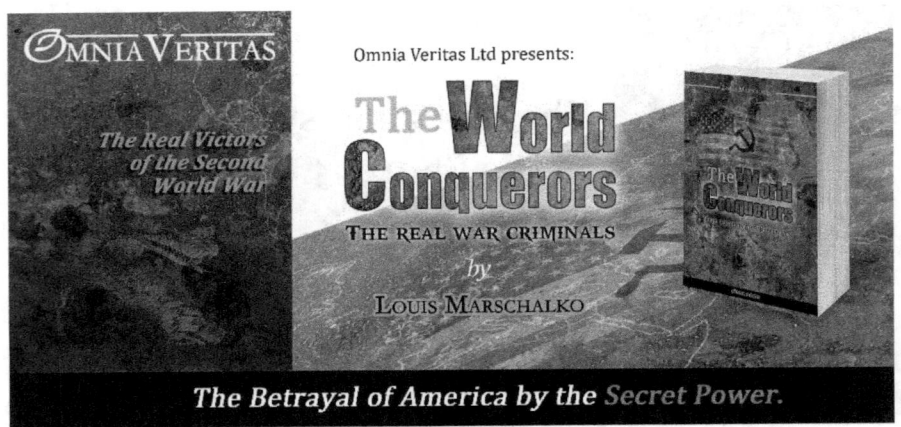

The Betrayal of America by the Secret Power.

Omnia Veritas Ltd presents:

THE ZIONISTS

by

GEO. W. ARMSTRONG

The fundamental ideology or philosophy of Zionism is that the Jews are the "chosen people"

and that God promised them that they should possess and rule the world...

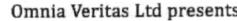

Omnia Veritas Ltd presents:

TRIFFLES FOR A MASSACRE

by

LOUIS-FERDINAND CÉLINE

«... this splendid book, is the first sign of the "revolt of the natives."»

There's a book you won't hear a word about

Omnia Veritas Ltd presents:

USURY,
A Scriptural, Ethical and Economic View

BY **CALVIN ELLIOT**

The **moral** nature of an act does not depend on the enacted statutes of human **legislators**, and the laws of economics are **eternal**.

The word usury was very odious to the Christian mind and conscience

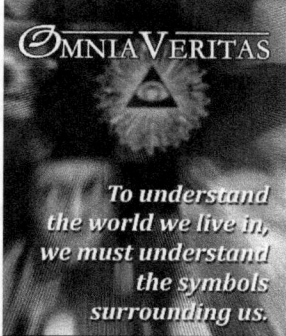

Omnia Veritas Ltd presents:

The VigilantCitizen
"Symbols Rule The World, Not Words Nor Laws"

ARTICLES COMPILATION

The occult symbolism in movies & music

To understand the world we live in, we must understand the symbols surrounding us.

The occult references of the entertainment industry !

Omnia Veritas Ltd presents:

Woman, her Sex and Love Life

by **WILLIAM J. ROBINSON M.D.**

Yes, **love** is a **woman's** whole life. Some **modern women** might object to this...

they will tell you if you enjoy their confidence that they are unhappy...

www.omnia-veritas.com

www.ingramcontent.com/pod-product-compliance
Lightning Source LLC
Chambersburg PA
CBHW050828230426
43667CB00012B/1916